Power and Civilization

David Cooperman
UNIVERSITY OF MINNESOTA

E. V. Walter
BRANDEIS UNIVERSITY

POWER AND CIVILIZATION

Political Thought in the Twentieth Century

Thomas Y. Crowell Company, New York   Established 1834

First Printing, March, 1962
Second Printing, June, 1964

Designed by Mina Baylis

Manufactured in the United States of America
by Vail-Ballou Press, Inc., Binghamton, N.Y.

To our fathers Henry Cooperman

and Abraham Walter

Preface

AMONG ITS SEVERAL HAZARDS, the twentieth century harbors perils of interpretation. Few eras have produced such violent change—social, economic, and political—as our own. So elusive are patterns of thought and action in such a time, so swiftly may the realities and possibilities men create today be destroyed tomorrow, that the student of political thought is hard put to sort out the ideas that will have enduring significance. Few eras, moreover, have produced such noise in the realm of ideas. "Anyone desiring a quiet life," wrote Trotsky, "has done badly to be born in the twentieth century." The clamor adds to the confusion, because so bewildering is the cacophony of voices condemning and advocating that one may mistake the loudest assertions in the political din for the most significant. We have in this volume tried to orchestrate the voices so that the most important themes may be clearly heard and understood.

Our method has been to assemble readings that represent the major themes in current political and social thought, and to link those themes in our own interpretive essays, combining the reading selections and the chapters of original interpretation with introductory notes on the life and work of the authors of the selections. The readings are drawn from the widest range of authorship, bringing together the work of social scientists, philosophers, men of letters, publicists, and political leaders. It was never our intention for the collection of readings to be a museum of ideas or an inventory; nor would it be accurate to call it an anthology. The book from beginning to end is an interpretation, conveyed not only in our own writing but also in our criteria for selecting the readings and in their very organization—their arrangement into thematic categories, and the ways in which we relate them to one another. This form deals with contemporary ideas in a way that is decisive, yet not dogmatic. In the same volume the reader has before him both our argument and much of the evidence on which it is based. Our conclusions he will weigh for himself; we invite him to dispute our judgments, and we urge him to search the material for patterns beyond those we have revealed.

As Albert Camus contended, our political and philosophical beliefs have led us into a blind alley so that now we must call everything into question.* With him and many other observers, we hold that political thinking is becoming unhinged from political events and that it is growing less adequate to comprehend the realities of the world today. The old arsenal of concepts and abstractions is turning into a museum of antiquities; the old political positions—radicalism, liberalism, and conservatism—once active movements of attack or defense, now show signs of freezing into ineffectual postures on an unfamiliar battleground. In this book we discuss how political ideas in the twentieth century have changed—through their own inner logic as well as through their responses to political events and social transformations—to arrive at their present condition. Our argument also reveals why well-worn assumptions and conceptions ought to be reexamined for their relevance to the facts of twentieth-century life.

Yet this book is not another jeremiad about the "decline" of political theory, for we think the obsolescence of conceptions describes not the destiny of political thought but only its present situation. We believe that the necessary concepts will emerge. Some thinkers are returning to the classics for insight into meeting the needs of the present. Others are analyzing contemporary data with new techniques. If as a result of these efforts new abstractions and principles do appear, the present age will take on a different aspect—as a time not only of great unrest but also of earnest search and preparation.

* *Actuelles II: Chroniques 1948–53* (Paris: Librairie Gallimard, 1953), p. 41.

We have included the readings we consider most significant for our purposes in this volume. The amount of material we first gathered for inclusion but decided to omit would make up at least two more volumes of the present size. We hope the documentation and extensive bibliographic footnotes will lead the reader to many sources beyond the reading selections.

The readings have been reproduced with footnotes omitted and with obvious misspellings and printer's errors corrected. Where the context recommends it, we have changed titles and subtitles.

We have received encouragement, advice, and help with the manuscript from many friends. They are not responsible, of course, for deficiencies in it or for our opinions. We want to express thanks for suggestions and encouragement to Jack Gallagher, Ned Polsky, Mulford Q. Sibley, Benjamin N. Nelson, Maurice R. Stein, Philip Siegelman, David Kettler, Kurt H. Wolff, Morris Watnick, Neil Friedman, Joseph S. Murphy, and Stanley Diamond. Fred H. Blum has helpfully checked the translation from Carl Schmitt's "The Concept of the Political." Brandeis University has given financial assistance in meeting some of the typing expenses. We are grateful for Julanne Lynn's excellent editorial ability and patience. In the years of preparation, many students and assistants were generous with enthusiasm and skill, helping to assemble, test, criticize, type, and proofread portions of the manuscript. We cannot name them all but we want especially to mention Urban Plain, Jr., Eugene Weinstein, Jean George, Betty Kornhauser, Judith McCombs Benjamin, Ernst Benjamin, Laurel Weinstein, Ellen Levine, Maryellen Hurwitz, Judith Wittner, Edward Friedman, Harvey Glasser, Bruce Litwer, Howard Schuman, Madeline Geltman, Linda Heller, Martha Case Moore, Ruth Talley, Jean Haskell and Lacey C. Walter.

Were there a place for a second dedication, we should inscribe our devotion and gratitude to our wives, Suzanne E. Cooperman and Ruth Christine Ice. They were our constant partners in this labor, and we are especially grateful for their keen literary judgment and warm encouragement.

D.C.
E.V.W.

January, 1962

Contents

The faith in effort   Political responses to economic issues   The concentration of economic power   The redefinition of liberalism   Socialism   The attack on liberalism   New theological perspectives   Conservatism and aristocratic discontent   Integral nationalism: the supremacy of power

Power and Civilization

Part One

THE
TWILIGHT OF
MODERNISM
1918-1939

THE RELATION BETWEEN CIVILIZATION and the political system is one of the most persistent questions in the history of social thought. For each age the question is restated, framed in new concepts, and expressed in a new vocabulary. Aristotle and Polybius sought the connection between constitutional cycles and cultural change; medieval churchmen searched for the mysterious empire concealed in the "ages of the world" from Babylon to Rome; Montesquieu hunted for the political secret of Roman "grandeur and decadence"; Marx investigated the link between the forces and the relations of production.

Late in the nineteenth century, the Swiss historian Jacob Burckhardt examined civilizations by tracing out the interrelationship of three institutional configurations—religious, cultural, and political. He decided that wherever political institutions predominated, they debilitated the other orders of society. The coming age—the twentieth century—would see power systems expand until they absorbed the artistic, religious, and other previously autonomous regions of human life. Whatever the wisdom of his conclusion or the accuracy of his prophecies, his attention was directed, we believe, to one of the most important problems of our time: the relation between power and civilization. Because we believe it is the crucial issue of contemporary political and social thought, we have chosen it as the central theme of this book.

In the past, politics has been significant in determining public destinies and private fortunes, but the political system usually was part of an order in which other forms of organization—the family, clan, church, economic unit, to mention a few—influenced or even balanced the controls exercised by the state. We recognize that the influence of these social organizations has far from disappeared, but their impact has diminished in degree and changed in kind. Contemporary civilization is directed by the political order, and it is difficult to express the relationship between power and other institutions in the ethical and legal categories of traditional political theory. Power seems to have grown beyond the reach of immemorial restraints. The old writers lived in another world. With an optimism now archaic, they numbered the extrinsic limitations on power: the reason and conscience of mankind; the plural countervailing pressures of rival social formations; human dignity; the spontaneous impulse to freedom. These have faded like lost saints, cherished but invoked in vain. The old way of stating the problem—power *and* society; politics *and* law, *and* custom, *and* morals—is unreal, for power is reluctant, if not absolutely unwilling, to enter into partnerships.

When we refer to systems of *power,* we mean not merely who gets what, when, and how, nor simply the relation between individuals in which one controls the behavior of the other for his own ends. Instead we think of the organized network of control and subordination in which some men—by tradition, by force, or by mandate—direct the energies of all, according to certain values and by specific techniques. This direction of energies may be unlimited in principle, as in totalitarian systems, or it may restrict itself to only a portion of life space, as in pluralist societies. However, in every society today the political system has a greater impact on the life chances of more individuals than any other social organization; it shapes the framework in which lives are lived, and influences the destiny of all.

Our use of the word *civilization* bears an inescapable double meaning. The older meaning, given by classical antiquity and accepted by the Enlightenment, signified a social order in which minds were cultivated and spirits refined. It was a form of life that revered ethical and aesthetic ideals, cherished patterns of humane conduct, admired nobility of spirit, and respected standards of conscience which were often violated but seldom unrecognized. According to the newer meaning, the term is used simply in a descriptive sense to refer to an integrated system of custom, values, and organization. This meaning is also subtly changing and, responding to intellectual, political, and social changes discussed in this book, becoming more political. According to the most extreme formulation of this meaning, the world is divided into Occidental, Slavic, Oriental, and African "civilizations," each of which is or will ultimately become a power complex with lesser political systems arranged in orbits around the major power.

At present, politics does not dominate civilizations entirely, and many other factors contribute to directing their course, but the collision of giant power systems has shaken the foundations of civilized life. The politicization of social and personal existence in Nazi Germany, Fascist Italy, Soviet Russia, and China has tended to dissolve the idea of civilization and to raise one of the most important questions of our time: is the totalitarian system in its pure form or "ideal type" another *kind* of civilization, or is it the destructive negation of civilization itself? Or, to put the question another way, has the older meaning of the term *civilization* become entirely irrelevant in the analysis of totalitarianism? These queries raise still another question: are the nontotalitarian societies generating forces that will drive them in similar directions?

Totalitarian systems have emerged and expanded with shocking speed. Their impact on the world wrought changes in the very states that opposed them and in neutral nations as well. The patterns of thought and action in our time, therefore, cannot be sufficiently understood without the careful study of totalitarianism. For this reason, the sections on totalitarianism in this volume deal with historical events in greater detail to provide the reader with as much concreteness as possible within the limits of our work. In these sections, we have tried to weave together events, some description of institutions, official statements of doctrine, and what we consider to be significant interpretations of these events, institutions, and doctrines. With less emphasis on historical description, a similar pattern of presentation will be found in the rest of the book as well. We have not limited ourselves to selections from technical writing, and have included readings like Sherwood Anderson's "Loom Dance" to convey the emotional impact of certain experiences and to reveal the political importance they have by the immediacy of their images.

Our focus is on the period we shall call *postmodern,* the meaning of which is explained in Part Two. The readings in Part One represent the literature of what we term the *interbellum,* the period from 1918 to 1939, which we think of as the twilight of modernism. When we refer to the *modern* era itself, we divide it into two stages: early and late. By *early-modern* thought we mean the ideas expressed in the literature of the post-medieval but preindustrial age, that is, from the Renaissance through the eighteenth century. By *late-modern* thought we mean the ideas of 1815–1914, the century between the end of the Napoleonic period and the outbreak of World War I.

"Political thought" is used as a generic term in this volume to include utterances that may be classified as political myth and ideology as well as political theory. Myth and ideology are less rational than theory. When we refer to *myth,* we accept the definition used by many anthropologists and philosophers: a configuration of images and ideas giving durative significance to experience, moving men to action, encouraging solidarity, and purporting to justify events, but responding directly to needs and emotions and usually not passing the rational tests of consistency and verifiability.

By *ideology* we mean a system of ideas (often a mixture of myths and theories) repetitively invoked to rationalize and defend a regime or a social movement. When Marx used the term, he defined it as a set of political illusions produced by the social experiences and the interests of a class—often the blind reaction of a dying class to its precarious political situation. Ideology was a false picture of reality, screening the members of the class from a clear vision of historical laws and economic forces. Karl Mannheim extended the term to mean almost any systematic rationalization for an established order. In this volume, the word refers to a system of ideas and emotionally charged symbols defending and justifying an established order, a reform movement, or a revolutionary movement—legitimating power or violence, exhorting the faithful, and purportedly explaining events and prophesying the future. By an "official ideology" we mean the set of ideas and symbols propagated and sanctioned by the central authority of an organized group as "correct" which the members of the group can be counted on to iterate and respond to unreflectively.

In contrast to myth and ideology, a *theory* is a rational explanation of political phenomena, conforming to standards of precision, consistency, and verifiability. Yet, despite such rational criteria, the reader should keep in mind that the term "political theory" is used in several ways and covers quite different logical operations and a variety of purposes.

Paradoxically, in our time, as politics becomes more dominant in the lives of men, political theory in the classic tradition has given way to other kinds of explanation. Social-scientific generalizations as well as the logical and semantic analysis of political terms and statements are replacing many of the interpretive functions once performed by political theory in the grand style. These newer modes of thought are often more careful and precise. Whether they are sufficient to explain the large-scale predicaments of power and civilization is doubtful; they are not even meant to do so. We do not know what modes of understanding the future will bring. But we can begin to grasp the work of extrication and liberation that must come first, and we can begin reordering our perceptions to gain fresh insights into a changing political reality. The readings in this volume and our interpretations do not resolve the crucial problems or eliminate the perplexities; but power and civilization confront one another dramatically. We hope that in the reader's mind it will be a creative encounter.

Let us begin by considering the intellectual revolution that ushered in the present age.

I

Passage from modernism

ONE MAY SAY THAT the twentieth century was born in 1918, for World War I destroyed an old order. The war, it is clear, unsettled social institutions, rending the subtle fabric of actions, habits, traditions, symbols, beliefs, and attitudes. In the universe of social and political thought, the war contributed to an intellectual revolution which put an end to the domination of ideas that we shall designate as characteristically modern.

THE INTELLECTUAL REVOLUTION

Political thought in the decade preceding World War I was predominantly a mixture of ideas from the Enlightenment seasoned in half a century of historicism and theories of evolution. In his book *A Generation of Materialism: 1871–1900,* Carlton J. H. Hayes has described the turn of the century as "the climax of the Enlightenment." If the turn of the century was its climax, then World War I, we would add, was its denouement and catastrophe.

At the core of late-modern political thought (1815–1914) one finds a trinity of conceptions which may be briefly identified as *reason, liberty,* and *progress.* These three conceptions were related to another nuclear idea— that of *civilization.* To understand the transformations of political thought in the twentieth century, one must trace the destiny of this set of ideas, examining their development and mutual relations and how they fit into an intellectual system.

By *intellectual system* we mean a configuration of ideas so related to one another that a change in one involves a change in all, and the destruction of even one major element results in the destruction of the entire system. Such a system is an architectonic arrangement of general beliefs and con- victions supported by a number of metaphysical assumptions and cemented by mental habits and attitudes. If a system is *dominant,* then it regulates the concerns, visions, thoughts, and actions of a large number of persons, usually without reflection or effort on their part. The point at which a previously dominant system of ideas is superseded by a new spirit is often thought of as an intellectual revolution.

Not all writers in the nineteenth century associated themselves with the dominant system of ideas. But even the "traditionalists," who dissociated themselves from it, did not deny that the ideas represented the spirit of the age. They criticized the ideas, hated their time, and attacked "modern" forms of thinking, despising the meanings given to reason, liberty, and progress. Joseph de Maistre, his colleagues of the counter-Enlightenment, and Feodor Dostoevsky are examples of traditionalist writers drawn from different intellectual traditions.

THE OLYMPIANS

The writers associated with the dominant intellectual system, inspired by its sanguine mood and expressing its cheerful spirit, we shall call the *olympians.* However, the nineteenth century was also the home of writers whom we shall identify as the *titans,* who grew out of the olympian system but whose work was destined to help dethrone it.

Our metaphoric distinction is taken from Greek mythology. When the ancient Greeks tried to explain conflicting elements in human nature— good versus evil, civilized versus primitive—they resorted to the story of the war between the two families of gods, the Titans and their descendants and ultimate conquerors, the Olympians. In this chapter we describe how the olympians expired and the titans prevailed. The children of the twentieth century, like mankind in the Orphic myth, are fashioned from both olympian and titan elements. The struggle is over, but we are its heirs.

We are aware that in our usage we are reversing the traditional titan-olympian order of descent. Our license has good precedent. Percy Bysshe Shelley assures us in the Preface to *Prometheus Unbound*, a lyric drama about a friend of mankind descended from the Titans, that the Greeks themselves employed "a certain arbitrary discretion. They by no means conceived themselves bound to adhere to the common interpretation or to imitate in story as in title their rivals and predecessors."

To be sure, the writers in each category exhibited some characteristics of the other from time to time. The olympian figures, who ranged on high, had moments of sublime bitterness as they looked down. "Viewed from the heights of reason," Goethe wrote, "all life looks like some malignant disease and the world like a madhouse." [1] Nevertheless, his ultimate vision, like that of his fellow olympians, was of "A land like the Paradise here, round about." The titans, on the other hand, characteristically remained "true to the earth," revealed how "The World is deep," and gazed from the abyss, believing with Zarathustra that "Out of the deepest must the highest come to its height." [2] The difference in their vision was crucial. The titans saw destructive forces latent in Western civilization. The olympians saw increasing harmony and improvement, and shared common assumptions about rationality, freedom, progress, and civilization; their outlook was sanguine, reasonable, lofty, and confident. The intellectual revolution of the twentieth century not only upset assumptions and ideas, but also extinguished the olympian radiance.

We have pointed out that the titans, in the first place, had been nourished in the olympian world and grew out of it. In the case of transitional minds, olympian ideals remained prominent at the same time that titan conceptions were developing. In the early part of this chapter we discuss Karl Marx with the olympians, but later we deal with him as a titan, for his ideals and prophetic vision remained olympian but his analysis of the latent processes in Western civilization was to be absorbed in the titan style of thought. The case of Freud is not the same, but similar: some of his ideals were olympian; his analysis belongs to the titans.

[1] Quoted in Thomas Mann, *Essays*, trans. H. T. Lowe-Porter (New York: Vintage Books, 1957), p. 53.
[2] Friedrich Nietzsche, "Thus Spake Zarathustra," trans. Thomas Common, in *The Philosophy of Nietzsche* (New York: The Modern Library, 1927), p. 169.

REASON, LIBERTY, AND PROGRESS

Reason and liberty have always carried political meanings and have usually appeared together, justifying each other. We assume that the reader is familiar enough with the history of political thought to excuse us from engaging in a discussion of how these terms have been used and abused in systems of political theory. We hope it will be enough to point out that the writers of the Enlightenment drew on the treasures of antiquity for many political conceptions, and that few discussions of reason and liberty in early-modern political thought would have been incomprehensible to Plato, Aristotle, and Cicero.

In the nineteenth century, writers transformed modern political thought by enlarging the domain of political conceptions, shifting attention from state to society and from government to social controls, just as many historians were shifting their focus from political to social history. This transformation implied a different way of defining and understanding the common life.

The distinction between state and society was not new to the nineteenth century. Writers like John Locke and Thomas Paine previously had conceived of society as an ultimate source of authority that judged the legitimacy of governmental actions. The newer conception, however, viewed society as the ultimate source of power, and an integral whole which was in some way primary, from which political organization was derivative and subordinate. Some writers identified the term *society* with economic organization and material culture, others with the spirit of the people. The beginnings of the conception may be seen in the work of Giovanni Battista Vico (1668–1744) and Baron de Montesquieu (1689–1755). They brought forth the notion of society as a unity embracing the totality of human relationships, but the conception as we know it did not fully develop until political theorists had understood the industrial revolution and had lived in industrial society.

The Scottish moralists Adam Smith and Adam Ferguson, living in the midst of the Scottish Enlightenment and stirred by the effects of the industrial revolution on tradition and social structure, had perceived that the development of "civil society" was related to the division of labor. Ferguson suggested in his *Essay on the History of Civil Society* (1767) that the division of labor and its widespread effects distinguished "the rude nations of mankind" from "the civilized, polished and commercial nations." Later, in the nineteenth century, most social theorists simply assumed without question that division of labor was "progressive."

Eventually, new concepts and a new vocabulary emerged. Coexisting with the classical political typology of monarchy, tyranny, aristocracy, oligarchy, and democracy, there were other classifications—savagery, barbarism, feudalism, capitalism, industrialism, socialism, communism. The new names represented underlying principles of social organization and tended to have two meanings: the economic organization of society and a type of mentality. Political theorists believed, moreover, that "underneath" all forms there was a substance called society, and that society followed a natural course of growth from savagery to civilization, culminating in industrial society which, like Homo sapiens, was the superior and final product of the evolutionary process. They dropped the age-old distinction between pure and degenerate constitutions and instead contrasted progressive and backward societies.

The ancients were not troubled about the problem of social change, for the drama of political change occupied their attention, and social change was so slow in their world as to be inconspicuous. This does not mean, however, that the ancients were not interested in what political scientists today call "political culture," for they understood that forms of government were intimately related to the individual personality and every kind of collective behavior. The underlying principle of each political form was reflected, they believed, in the depths of personality, in cultural ideals, and in customs. In a democracy, Plato argued, even the dogs, horses, and donkeys caught the principle of behavior from their masters. But the prime mover in social change was political. A state was defined by its political organization, meaning the distribution of power, Aristotle said. The constitution was the active, formal element, initiating change and defining the common life; people and customs were the passive, material elements. Thus the ancients had believed in the primacy of politics, for political action, broadly conceived, produced the cycle of constitutions which in turn affected personality, society, and culture.

Following their ancient models, most early-modern theorists believed in cyclical theories of growth and decline, but the cyclical theory of civilization receded until its reappearance in the twilight of modernism. The single-track theory of social evolution was destined to become the dominant idea of civilization in the nineteenth century. Immanuel Kant had written in 1784: "Men work themselves gradually out of barbarity if only intentional artifices are not made to hold them in it." Voltaire had thought that social progress was unilinear, and that all societies were moving toward the same civilization. Except for the romantic movement in Germany, there were few notions in the Enlightenment of what anthropologists today would call multilinear evolution. The idea of society could not be conceived apart from the notion of a stage of civilization.

As *society* tended to displace *government* as the domain of political theory, the conceptions of reason and liberty took on additional meanings. Higher forms of civilization were considered to be more rational and more free. Thought and action were being liberated by the process of social evolution; any number of late-modern thinkers could have declared, "Mankind was born in chains but evolution is setting it free."

Primitive mentality was considered irrational and mythical, inferior to civilized thought which was rational and scientific, and writers assumed without much question that the primitive mind was *structurally* different from the modern mind. Not until the twilight of modernism did anthropological writers such as Bronislaw Malinowski, Paul Radin, and A. R. Radcliffe-Brown bring forth arguments that routed the Victorian conceptions of primitivism associated with Sir James George Frazer and Lucien Lévy-Bruhl.

Moreover, the idea of reason in society was fused with the notion of *rationalization* in the economic sense, meaning division of labor, the progressive improvement of the factory system of production, and the logic of efficiency. Thus industrial civilization was considered to be more rational than previous social forms.

At the same time the concept of liberty was changing to mean not only freedom from governmental or ecclesiastic coercion but also liberation from more encompassing social controls. The difference may be seen by comparing the political thought of John Milton with that of John Stuart Mill. In his *Free Commonwealth* (1659), Milton's conception of civil liberty was confined entirely to the sphere of state and government.[3] In contrast, Mill's celebrated essay *On Liberty* published in 1859, exactly two centuries later, addressed itself to "Civil, or Social Liberty: the nature and limits of the power which can be legitimately exercised by society over the individual." Mill explained:

Society can and does execute its own mandates: and if it issues wrong mandates instead of right, or any mandates at all in things with which it ought not to meddle, it practices a social tyranny more formidable than many kinds of po-

[3] *The Works of John Milton* (New York: Columbia University Press, 1932), VI, 141.

litical oppression, since, though not usually upheld by such extreme penalties, it leaves fewer means of escape, penetrating more deeply into the details of life, and enslaving the soul itself. Protection, therefore, against the tyranny of the magistrate is not enough: there needs protection also against the tyranny of the prevailing opinion and feeling; against the tendency of society to impose, by other means than civil penalties, its own ideas and practices as rules of conduct on those who dissent from them. . . . There is a limit to the legitimate interference of collective opinion with individual independence: and to find that limit, and maintain it against encroachment, is as indispensable to a good condition of human affairs, as protection against political despotism.[4]

Mill was influenced deeply by the social philosophy of Auguste Comte (1798–1857), although he disapproved of its many collectivist implications and believed that Comte's excessive emphasis on the requirements of the social whole tended to ignore the concrete needs of living individuals. Comte's ideas depended heavily on the work of Henri de Saint-Simon (1760–1825), who accepted a theory of primitivism typical of early-modern social thought and similar in many respects to the state-of-nature theory of Thomas Hobbes and Jean Jacques Rousseau.[5] This doctrine held that in savagery and barbarism, the conditions antecedent and contrary to civilization, division of labor was rudimentary and society was loosely knit, weak, and relatively unorganized. Civilization, in contrast, was distinguished by its strong bonds of social cooperation. The history of humanity blindly but inexorably moved toward more powerful association and more efficient exploitation of nature through social organization. In short, the historical movement of society, according to Saint-Simonian doctrine, was from individualism to collectivism.[6]

Based on different anthropological assumptions, a contradictory idea emerged in late-modern social thought. Civilization, many nineteenth-century olympians were convinced, moved from collectivism to individualism; civilization had liberated men from the "cake of custom" and despotic social controls of the collectivity so that actions were determined no longer by family, tribe, or village but by the autonomous will of the individual man. As Sir Henry Maine put it in his influential book *Ancient Law* (1861):

[4] *On Liberty,* ed. R. B. McCallum (Oxford: Basil Blackwell & Mott, Ltd., 1946), p. 4.
[5] Students of early-modern political theory usually concentrate on the differences between Hobbes's and Rousseau's conception of the state of nature. The similarities should not be overlooked.
[6] For Mill's acceptance of these Saint-Simonian and Comtean ideas, see his essay "Civilization" in *Dissertations and Discussions* (3 vols.; Boston: Spencer Press, Inc., 1865), I, 186 ff.

Starting, as from one terminus of history, from a condition of society in which all the relations of Persons are summed up in the relations of Family, we seem to have steadily moved towards a phase of social order in which all these relations arise from the free agreement of Individuals.

. . . we may say that the movement of the progressive societies has hitherto been a movement *from Status to Contract*.[7]

Maine's argument was extremely complex, and he was certainly not an "individualist," but the social Darwinists drew from Maine's work rather stark individualistic conclusions.

In part of the idealist philosophy on the Continent and in the left-Hegelian movement, freedom meant the unimpeded exercise of autonomous will and the power to shape the conditions of life. Karl Marx and Friedrich Engels tried to synthesize Saint-Simonian ideals of inevitable collectivism with the values of individual freedom. Only when mankind achieved the collective control of nature, they argued, would individual men be free to determine their own destinies. Comparing civilized man's economic relation to nature with that of the savage, Marx wrote:

The freedom in this field cannot consist of anything else but of the fact that socialized man, the associated producers, regulate their interchange with nature rationally, bring it under their common control, instead of being ruled by it as by some blind power . . . .[8]

Ultimately, Engels added in *Anti-Dühring*, in the free society of the future,

Men's own social organisation which has hitherto stood in opposition to them as if arbitrarily decreed by nature and history, will then become the voluntary act of men themselves. The objective, external forces which have hitherto dominated history will then pass under the controls of men themselves. It is only from this point that men, with full consciousness, will fashion their own history. . . . It is humanity's leap from the realm of necessity into the realm of freedom.[9]

Similar convictions about social progress and civilization were shared by writers with diverse political persuasions. Conservative writers believed that the status quo, the highest product of social evolution, was to be

[7] H. S. Maine, *Ancient Law* (Everyman's Library; London: J. M. Dent & Sons, Ltd., 1954), pp. 99–100.
[8] Karl Marx, *Capital*, trans. E. Untermann (Chicago: C. H. Kerr and Company, 1909), III, 954.
[9] Friedrich Engels, *Anti-Dühring*, in Emile Burns, ed., *A Handbook of Marxism* (New York: International Publishers, 1935), p. 299.

guarded and cherished, and that governmental tampering or revolutionary action might upset the forces of nature and cause degeneration or reversion to a lower stage. Radical writers, including apocalyptic socialists such as Marx in 1848 and Lenin in 1917, considered bourgeois society higher and more rational than its predecessors, preparing the way for the civilization of the future.

Karl Marx and Herbert Spencer (1820–1903) held several underlying assumptions in common despite profound political differences. Both argued that societies which came later in time were *therefore* better than those which had gone before. Each contended that his system provided *the* scientific premises for moral action. Spencer wrote: "My ultimate purpose, lying behind all proximate purposes, has been that of finding for the principles of right and wrong, in conduct at large, a scientific basis." [10] Marx would not have denied this purpose in his own work. In addition, both thinkers identified what they thought were descriptive laws of society with their prescriptions for politics. Spencer's laws were derived from "nature," Marx's from "history." Both insisted that the processes they described were inevitable. Finally, both had a "scientific faith" that evolution, or history, would grind on until that day when such artifices as politics would drop away, leaving man standing in happiness and innocence at the end of time. Marx could have stated some of his own views in the words written by Spencer in 1862: "Evolution can end only in the establishment of the greatest perfection and the most complete happiness." [11]

Olympian confidence in progress and civilization and pride in the triumph of reason and freedom, despite a few warning voices to the contrary, dominated social and political thought until the eve of the war. As late as 1913, J. B. Bury, the distinguished historian, wrote:

> The struggle of reason against authority has ended in what appears now to be a decisive and permanent victory for liberty. In the most civilized and progressive countries, freedom of discussion is recognized as a fundamental principle.[12]

---

[10] Herbert Spencer, *The Data of Ethics* (New York: Burt, 1879), p. iii, cited in Richard Hofstadter, *Social Darwinism in American Thought: 1860–1915* (Philadelphia: University of Pennsylvania Press, 1945), p. 26.

[11] Herbert Spencer, *First Principles* (4th ed., reprinted; New York: De Witt Revolving Fund, 1958), p. 511. It is interesting that this expression of unqualified optimism, the concluding line of Chapter XXII, appeared in this book as late as the fourth edition (1880), but was omitted from the sixth edition (1900).

[12] J. B. Bury, *A History of Freedom of Thought* (London: Oxford University Press, 1913), p. 246.

Bury announced that this "victory is permanent; that intellectual freedom is now assured to mankind as a possession for ever." He considered the possibility that "a revolutionary social movement . . . led by men inspired by faith in formulas (like the men of the French Revolution)" might reverse the trend and "turn back the clock," but this chance was dismissed simply by the thought that the long conquest which had been necessary to establish freedom and reason had made men consciously realize their value. "Perhaps," he concluded, "this conviction will be strong enough to resist all conspiracies against liberty." [13]

THE TITANS

The nineteenth century, as we have already observed, produced another race of thinkers, sprung from olympian stock and educated by olympian books and teachers; but their vocation in philosophy and in social science led them to rise up and utter prophetic thunder against their world and to write books exposing the fatal contradictions in Western institutions. We shall limit our very brief discussion to six of the titans: Søren Kierkegaard, Danish philosopher (1813–1855); Friedrich Nietzsche, German philosopher (1844–1900); Sigmund Freud, Austrian neurologist and founder of psychoanalysis (1856–1939); Karl Marx, German philosopher, social theorist, and political revolutionary (1818–1883); Émile Durkheim, French sociologist (1858–1917); and Max Weber, German social theorist (1864–1920).

These titans probed the interior of the soul, society, and European culture, drawing attention away from the manifest and to the latent. In their own lifetime, their work ruffled but did not perturb their olympian contemporaries; they were not taken seriously until the olympian world had been shattered and the subterranean realm exposed. As writers of our own time turn against the nineteenth century with a sense of reproach and a feeling of betrayal, the work of the titans is being reexamined, and they are being canonized as patrons of new orthodoxies—an ironic fate, for many of them despised disciples.

A number of the titans may be identified with what was known in the first half of the nineteenth century as the "Younger Generation," which means that their first commitments were to philosophic Idealism, that is, the dominant systems of Hegel and then Schelling. They reacted violently

[13] *Ibid.*

against Idealism to take revolutionary positions in philosophy and in social thought. In the winter of 1841 at the University of Berlin, among the students who listened to Schelling's lectures and turned away in disappointment were Søren Kierkegaard, Mikhail Bakunin, and Friedrich Engels. The revulsion sped Kierkegaard to his formulation of existentialism in philosophy and religion; Engels soon began his partnership with Marx; and Bakunin eventually became the founder of apocalyptic anarchism.

Karl Jaspers has discussed the importance of Kierkegaard, Nietzsche, and Marx for our own age, pointing out that these three thinkers, though belonging to the nineteenth century, have only come into their own in the twentieth:

They foresaw and gave utterance to what was to come because they saw the germs of it in their own age. . . .
When we study these three thinkers it is as if we were being initiated into the depths of our own age. Without them we remain as if asleep. They unlock the modern consciousness. They throw their light and growing shadow on to our age, whereas their own age refused their influence. . . . [They] form the intellectual threshold of our epoch. The break in the continuity of the European spirit which had already been under way for a long time unconsciously now took place in the form of a high intellectual impulse. The crossing of the threshold which they brought to light may be a catastrophe or the beginning of a new creation, evil and disastrous or the prelude to new authentic human life. But anyone who, after these three have lived, evades the threshold, rejects it without having experienced its essential nature, must inevitably remain unclear in his own spirit, fall victim to something he does not but could know at first hand and be defenceless against the inroads of modernity. . . .
Their thought not only lays bare a disaster that has already taken place. It is in itself a still continuing process of destruction. Certainly they arouse us into consciousness of new potentialities, but at the same time they immediately overlay this consciousness with ideas which have for many an irresistible fascination. Their insight seems to lead only to destruction or new dogmatisms. . . .
To reach down to the original truth in the work of these thinkers, one has to work one's way through a thick undergrowth of misunderstanding. Their true themes, criteria and motives have been obscured in a bewildering variety of new orthodoxies and every new reader passes through the experience of succumbing to temptations in his own study of their works, of having constantly to separate the truth from all the incipient aberrations. . . .[14]

Politically these writers had nothing in common; the opinions of Kierkegaard, for example, who felt strong affection for the monarchy, con-

[14] Karl Jaspers, "The Importance of Nietzsche, Marx, and Kierkegaard in the History of Philosophy," *The Hibbert Journal*, XLIX (1950–1951), 226–34.

tain nothing but bitter enmity for anything like the revolutionary socialism of Marx. Yet in retrospect the works of these titans, along with those of Freud, Durkheim, and Weber, have converged despite all obvious diversity and mutual antipathy to play a role in the destructive movement against the late-modern system of thought with its reliance on reason, freedom, progress, and civilization.

To understand this destructive role, one may list the cultural values that the olympians esteemed most highly:

1) Their religion: the doctrines and practices of rational religion which, they felt, justified their sense of superiority over the heathen rest of the world.

2) Their lofty morality: the characteristic, in popular usage, most closely identified with Victorianism.

3) Intellectual progress: science, high cultural attainments, rationality in thought and action, the intellectualization of actions formerly based on habit and tradition, the permanent establishment of civilized mentality.

4) Economic progress: industrial production, worldwide trade, and the impressive material benefits of industrial civilization.

5) Individuation: the process of liberation from the collectivity and the social controls of "backward" or "stationary" societies.

6) Administrative order, social predictability, and what today we would call "rationalization."

Kierkegaard devoted his prodigious authorship to revealing the illusions of his time. In the name of religious authenticity, he exposed the "forgeries" of official religion, attacking "established Christendom, which might rather be called the caricature of true Christianity." Furthermore, in the name of seriousness, he attacked the temper of his age, which "leaves everything standing but cunningly empties it of significance." [15] In the twentieth century, Kierkegaard's work has been used as a foundation for existentialist philosophy and for the battle against liberal theology.

Nietzsche, recognizing that "The Europeans now imagine themselves as representing, in the main, the highest types of men on earth," deflated the olympian pride by a thrust into one of its most sensitive areas. His open "campaign against morality" exposed the most cherished values of his age and proclaimed that conventional morality was based on selfishness, fear, weakness, and the instincts of the herd.

Freud's theory of the unconscious upset the olympian assumption that

[15] Søren Kierkegaard, *The Present Age*, trans. Alexander Dru (London: Oxford University Press, 1940), p. 15. Italics removed.

reason lay at the heart of enlightened humanity. Joseph Conrad and other writers were coming to similar conclusions, expressed in books such as *The Heart of Darkness*. Freud knew that his work had effects similar to the Copernican and Darwinian revolutions, two previous blows to human self-esteem. He explained:

> . . . man's craving for grandiosity is now suffering the third and most bitter blow from the present-day psychological research which is endeavouring to prove to the "ego" of each one of us that he is not even master in his own house but that he must remain content with the veriest scraps of information about what is going on unconsciously in his own mind.[16]

Freud's demonstration that the civilized mind coexists with an ineradicable component of primitive and infantile mentality also eliminated the distance between modern and savage, with important consequences for the conception of civilization.

We have spoken of Marx above as an olympian. Indeed, he shared the olympian notions of civilization; yet other aspects of his work belong with the titans. Probing for the life and death principle of capitalist civilization, he threw a cloud over the notion of economic progress. Countless rebuttals of his work have been written, trying to demonstrate why his prophecies were bound to be false. Nevertheless, his theory of Western society with the argument that in its bowels capitalism carries the seeds of its own destruction is still a source of anxiety to those who concern themselves with economic progress.

Durkheim and Weber, because they are later writers than the other four, do not share some of the characteristics of those titans. Nevertheless, their work revealed that two of the tendencies the olympians had extolled were also negative forces. Durkheim showed that the process of individuation, which the olympians had identified with freedom, contained seeds of destruction. As men were liberated from the collectivity and lost the sense of community that insured the subordination of individual desires to traditional social controls, they were filled with a spirit of unrest and discontent, which Durkheim called *anomie* (anomy). In its effects, "Anomy, in fact, begets a state of exasperation and irritated weariness which may turn against the person himself or another according to circumstances; in the first case, we have suicide, in the second, homicide." [17]

[16] Sigmund Freud. *A General Introduction to Psychoanalysis,* trans. J. Rivière (New York: Liveright Publishing Corp., 1935), p. 252.
[17] *Suicide,* trans. J. A. Spaulding and G. Simpson (Glencoe: The Free Press, 1951), p. 357.

Similarly, in part of his immense work Weber showed the dehumanizing effects of rationalization and bureaucratization, forces shaping modern civilization. In contrast to many of the olympians, who had admired these factors, he pointed out sadly: "The fate of our times is characterized by rationalization and intellectualization and, above all, by the 'disenchantment of the world.' " [18]

THE IMPACT OF THE WAR

Why a system of ideas collapses is a complex problem that we cannot discuss here; but we believe that in order to endure, a system must provide emotional compensation for privations and offer a satisfactory explanation of reality. The impact of World War I and fundamental changes in Western society rendered the olympian world view unreal and mocked its most cherished values.

The concepts of progress, reason, liberty, and civilization were intimately tied to the notion that advanced societies were to become progressively more peaceful. This idea had appeared plausible in the world of the mid-Victorians, who had lived through a half-century of peace; there was no major conflict between the defeat of Napoleon and the Franco-Prussian War. When Henry Thomas Buckle, the exemplar of olympian historians, wrote his *History of Civilization in England* in 1855, the Crimean War, which had just broken out, did not ruffle his equanimity. The long peace had merely been broken, he claimed, by "the encroachments of the uncivilized Russians on the still more uncivilized Turks." Buckle was certain that only "a people whose intellect is not cultivated" would willingly engage in warfare, and announced: "That this barbarous pursuit is, in the progress of society, steadily declining, must be evident, even to the most hasty reader of European history." [19] Buckle and his fellow olympians considered war to be an atavism of darker ages, destined to disappear with mental progress, with science and technology, and with the industrialization of society. Today it seems to us that there is no necessary connection between technological advance and peace—indeed, some thinkers in our midst assume the opposite and consider technological progress to be the bearer of doom to the Western world—but to the Enlightenment and to

[18] "Science as a Vocation," in H. H. Gerth and C. Wright Mills, eds., *From Max Weber: Essays in Sociology* (New York: Oxford University Press, Inc., 1946), p. 155.
[19] Henry Thomas Buckle, *History of Civilization in England* (3 vols., rev. ed.; London: Longmans, Green & Co., Inc., 1885), I, 190.

the olympians, the connection between progress and peace was built into the very concept of society.

This connection may be seen clearly in the work of Herbert Spencer, who virtually dominated Victorian social thought. Society, as defined by Spencer, had evolved from savagery through barbarism to its culmination in the industrial form. Early societies were militant; advanced societies, peaceful. Raymond Aron has explained in *The Century of Total War:*

The contrast between industrial and military societies seemed an obvious fact to many sociologists of the last century. From Saint-Simon to Spencer it was accepted that societies based on peaceful labor and exchange represented a type in marked contrast with societies dominated by the military caste and motivated by ambition for conquest. Europe knows today that industry, far from preventing war, gives it a limitless scope. Consciously or not, contemporary philosophers of history have made this fact central in their thought.[20]

[20] Raymond Aron, *The Century of Total War* (Boston: Beacon Press, 1955), p. 56.

II

The sense of crisis

DECLINE OR PROGRESS?

WHEN WAR BROKE OUT, as we said, it gave the lie to the olympian equation of progress with peace, and the bitter contradiction helped shatter the entire system of thought. Furthermore, the war stimulated men to reexamine their assumptions about progress and civilization. The first three readings in this volume open with this problem. Valéry declared that the decline of civilization was related to a crisis of modernism and wrote that Europeans had learned with a shock that "a civilization is as fragile as a life." Freud admitted that the war had provoked a cultural crisis, and yet asserted that the crisis could *not* be construed as a decline of civilization. Dewey attempted to salvage the olympian system, but argued that the conception of progress had to be redefined.

Anxiety about civilization and its direction or fate was in the air. The best-known book dealing with the subject, Oswald Spengler's *Decline of the West,* appeared in 1918 and captured the imagination of the postwar generation. Those who would not accept Spengler's thesis or his sweeping, strained, and uneven scholarship nevertheless were compelled to come to grips with his idea.

According to Spengler, civilizations were like living organisms which are born, thrive, grow old, and decay. Western civilization, he argued, inexorably had entered its period of decline. The war, he claimed, ". . . was no longer a momentary constellation of casual facts . . . but the type of *a historical change of phase* occurring within a great historical organism of definable compass at the point preordained for it hundreds of years ago." [1]

However, other writers took different views of the crisis. In 1919, George Bernard Shaw wrote in the Preface to his play *Heartbreak House:*

I have said that men assumed that war had reversed the order of nature, and that all was lost unless we did the exact opposite of everything we had found necessary and beneficial in peace. But the truth was worse than that. The war did not change men's minds in any such impossible way. What really happened was that the impact of physical death and destruction, the one reality that every fool can understand, tore off the masks of education, art, science and religion from our ignorance and barbarism, and left us glorying grotesquely in the licence suddenly accorded to our vilest passions and most abject terrors. Ever since Thucydides wrote his history, it has been on record that when the angel of death sounds his trumpet the pretences of civilization are blown from men's heads into the mud like hats in a gust of wind.[2]

In 1915, Sigmund Freud had written his essay "Thoughts for the Times on War and Death" in a similar vein. He argued that Western civilization was not doomed but merely passing through a time of stress, and observed that in tranquil periods all civilizations live beyond their psychological means. Primitive hostility is not eradicated by civilization but only held in check, and in wartime, conditions permit it to escape from below the surface and manifest itself as "barbaric" behavior. When the normal controls are restored, Freud argued, one may expect dramatic changes and a return to "civilized" behavior.

Cyclical theories of civilization and culture returned to challenge the previously dominant idea of inevitable progress. The notion of progress was condemned as a myth and, necessarily, fated to be cast out or revised. While some writers rejected it, liberals like John Dewey began the work of revision. We had a shallow faith in progress before the war, Dewey said, and we mistakenly assumed that any change was a form of progress; we have

---

[1] Oswald Spengler, *The Decline of the West,* trans. C. F. Atkinson (New York: Alfred A. Knopf, Inc., 1934), I, 47.
[2] *Heartbreak House, Great Catherine, and Playlets of the War* (London: Constable & Co., Ltd., 1919), p. xxi.

learned our lesson, and now must see that change in the conditions of life is not progress but merely "an *opportunity* for progress."

Liberalism redefined concepts that had been part of the olympian system, thereby strengthening itself and remaining the most important ideology of the interbellum, although it did not satisfy demands or answer questions called forth by the war. Yet liberalism was a midwife to political thinking between the wars, bringing forth movements of opposition. For its own reasons, each intellectual path in the twentieth century has condemned liberalism: socialists, dialectical theologians, conservatives, nationalists, and totalitarians, have in common a negative reaction to liberalism.

THE SEQUENCE OF DISASTERS

The sense of crisis was continually renewed by international events between 1918 and 1939 and intensified by social change. Some writers expected to return to the old ways after the war, but others recognized that the quality of life was different, that the world had changed irreversibly, and that the old Continental convictions and the whole Victorian way of seeing, believing, and acting were no longer possible. Russia, Italy, and Germany were destined for violent, revolutionary change. The other societies were also transformed, more subtly and less radically. Political writers adjusted to an apocalyptic mood, formulating their ideas while enduring or expecting war, fearing economic disaster, and dreading the power of their own states. At the turn of the century, utopia had been at hand; by midcentury, multitudes expected the end of the world.

For a brief period after World War I, from 1924 to 1930, men hoped that another catastrophe could be averted through the League of Nations and the effort to restore a balance of power in Europe. But the war had dislocated the European economic system, and the depression shattered hopes that the West could return to a "normal" life. As E. H. Carr observed, ". . . the winter of 1930–31 shattered the last defenses of optimism; and serious people began to talk of the impending collapse of civilization."

The Revolution and then the consolidation of the Stalin regime made Russia loom as the enemy on the flank of Europe. The inflation in Europe, the great depression and unemployment, and the fear of bolshevism created a turmoil out of which two more totalitarian systems emerged. In Raymond Aron's description,

Europe, tormented by three ideologies as well as by the traditional rivalries of the powers, slid rapidly into disaster. The war, beginning in 1939 with the Russo-German alliance and the partition of Poland, this time spread throughout the world, reviving and extending the war which had been raging in China since the early thirties. When, at the end of six years, the conflagration died down, the earth had been scorched from Europe to Asia.

Across the world the two solitary survivors girded their loins for the final contest while the crash of the first atomic bomb was still reverberating.[3]

IDEOLOGY AND POLITICS

Some writers continued to explain the torment and dislocation of the age as a crisis of mind and spirit. A typical Platonic interpretation held the ultimate cause to be the secularization of values. For example, W. R. Inge, the "gloomy dean" of St. Paul's Cathedral, wrote an essay published in *The Spectator* in 1924 entitled "How Civilizations Die" in which he argued that when men lose transcendental spiritual convictions they turn to materialism and sensuality, with disastrous effects. This argument is still with us. In *Ideas Have Consequences* (1948), Richard M. Weaver likewise argues that when the transcendental values associated in Western civilization with the ideas of Plato, Aristotle, and St. Thomas were routed by the philosophical victory of nominalism in the fourteenth century, it changed "the whole orientation of culture," leading ultimately to "the dissolution of the West."

A similar argument with a different *political* turn may be found in an influential book, *The Treason of the Intellectuals,* written by Julien Benda in 1928. According to Benda, writers in the present age had become apologists for power—spokesmen for "practical" solutions, insisting on political "realism." The modern "directors of conscience"—the "clerks" or intellectuals—were so absorbed in nationalism and the power of nations, he argued, they had abdicated the true vocation of the clerk, namely, the ancient, respected role of the disinterested and unpractical man who held aloft universal ideals by which men might measure their practice. In the past, Benda observed, national egotism and passions had been opposed by the clerks, for intellectuals and men of learning had upheld the universal values of humanism against the warfare of particular differences.

Now intellectuals had become "realists," meaning to Benda defenders

---

[3] Raymond Aron, *The Century of Total War* (Boston: Beacon Press, 1955), p. 95.

of nationalism and of national wars. This realism was an act of treason and at the same time an abdication from a high vocation:

As soon as the "clerk" claims that he does not disregard the interests of the nation or of the established classes, he is inevitably beaten. . . . The grandeur of his teaching lies precisely in [the] absence of practical value, and . . . the right morality for the prosperity of the kingdoms which are of this world, is not his, but Caesar's.

In the past, when nations and men fell from humanist ideals, their lapse had not been defended by the apologetics which "realistic" men of the present age have been so eager to turn out. The logical end of this realism, Benda believed, "is the organized slaughter of nations or classes." He accused the intellectuals of having betrayed civilization, and sadly wondered whether civilization, which he understood as "moral supremacy conferred on the cult of the spiritual and on the feeling of the universal," might turn out to have been nothing more than "a lucky accident in man's development." [4]

Despite their agreement that ideology was a crucial political problem, writers differed in their conceptions of its nature. Those who claimed that the loss of transcendental, rational convictions led to cultural and political disaster contrasted sharply with those who argued, as had Edmund Burke at the time of the French Revolution, that abstract reason should be kept out of politics. In this vein, the well-known Spanish philosopher José Ortega y Gasset distinguished between abstract reason and historical reason. What made ideology dangerous, he believed, was not that it embraced "realism" but rather that it ignored "reality." In their fervor, men take on a strange disdain for realities: they turn their backs to the latter and become the "impassioned slaves of ideas as such." Idea and reality tend to become divorced in politics, and in every revolutionary period, "intelligence, in the pursuit of its normal development, reaches a stage at which it discovers its power of constructing, with means exclusively its own, theoretical edifices on a large scale and perfect in form." Utopias embodying ideas of abstract perfection are fashioned, but a utopia is not compatible with politics and its plan inevitably fails. The failure of utopia begets counterutopia, until finally their mutual failure brings about fatigue, disillusionment, and indifference. Thus political life fluctuates between

---

[4] Julien Benda, *The Great Betrayal*, trans. Richard Aldington (London: Routledge & Kegan Paul, 1928), pp. 152–56.

enthusiasm for radical utopias and inert patterns of tradition and habit. But the rationalist mind expects too much from politics, wrecking the social order by expecting to mold it to concepts framed by pure reason.[5]

In contrast to Ortega y Gasset, who feared an excess of abstract reason in politics, others were afraid that the age suffered from a profound underlying antiintellectualism and irrationalism. Such an atmosphere, they believed, had a direct destructive effect on liberal and democratic institutions. Liberalism and democracy, explained Sir Ernest Barker, an eminent British political theorist, were sustained by a balance of political institutions—party, electorate, parliament, and cabinet; and the balance depended on a habit of approaching collective problems by debate and rational discussion, not by ideology and emotion.[6]

The flight from reason had philosophic sources according to R. G. Collingwood, a distinguished Oxford philosopher and archaeologist. The distrust of reason, he wrote, began in philosophy and could only end in the destruction of deliberative institutions and the manipulation of mass emotions. Civilizations were destroyed from within, Collingwood declared; the "irrationalist epidemic" would sap the structure of politics and society, and "if it ran through Europe unchecked would in a relatively short time destroy everything that goes by the name of European civilization."[7]

THE POLITICS OF MASS BEHAVIOR

Among the disturbing notions circulated by the war, by the anxiety about cultural decline, and by the discussion of ideology and irrationalism, the idea of barbarism turned attention to mass behavior and to the new role of the masses in political life. Ortega y Gasset's book *The Revolt of the Masses* attracted attention, yet there was still a great deal of "faith in the people."

In politics two notions struggled for dominance. There were still populist movements on the Continent: in Russian thought, a folk *mystique, Narodnichestvo,* glorified the common people as the font of goodness and wisdom, and similar elements may be found in the *Volk* romanticism of German

[5] José Ortega y Gasset, *The Modern Theme,* trans. James Clough (New York: W. W. Norton & Company, Inc., 1933), pp. 115–20.
[6] Ernest Barker, *The Citizen's Choice* (Cambridge: Cambridge University Press, 1937), pp. 25–41; *Reflections on Government* (London: Oxford University Press, 1942), Parts I, II.
[7] R. G. Collingwood, *An Essay on Metaphysics* (London: Oxford University Press, 1940), pp. 133 ff.

thought. In America, the progressive movement injected populist enthusiasm into thought and literature, elevating "the people" as the source of wisdom and improvement, proclaiming the age as the century of the common man. The New Deal owed much of its emotional vitality to progressivist populism.

At the same time, reviving some old aristocratic concepts, the contrary notion of the revolt of the masses emerged with vigor and persistence. Some writers argued that the masses were a danger to liberty and order, a chaotic force to be controlled by a political and intellectual elite. In the mass, they wrote, men behave qualitatively differently from the way they act as individuals because the mass is a social condition that permits them to regress mentally to a primitive state—to the primitive horde or to the infantile ego.

The nineteenth century had known genres of mass psychology and crowd sociology, and twentieth-century writers used no conceptions that were not already familiar. Indeed, since the French Revolution, mass behavior had been a lively matter for discussion by students of social change.

Some writers thought that the historical development of Western society might in the future bring more political importance to masses. Preceding Ortega y Gasset by seventy years, John Stuart Mill had suggested:

The most remarkable of those consequences of advancing civilization, which the state of the world is now forcing upon the attention of thinking minds, is this, —that power passes more and more from individuals, and small knots of individuals, to masses; that the importance of masses becomes constantly greater, that of individuals less.[8]

Most nineteenth-century writers had considered the crowd or the mass to be a spontaneous and ephemeral social entity. In his *Group Psychology and the Analysis of the Ego* (1921), Sigmund Freud provided a new point of departure for modern works on the social-psychology of leadership and examined permanent organizations such as the church and the army, but not until the rise of totalitarian movements in the twenties and thirties did writers, among them Emil Lederer, turn their attention to the *politics* of mass behavior. In this period the totalitarian state emerged as something new: totalitarian leaders swept themselves into power by channeling mass anxiety.

Many discussions of mass society deal with the masses as a remote entity; no one, of course, would think of identifying himself as a mass man. For this reason, to add a subjective dimension to the problem of mass be-

[8] John Stuart Mill, *Dissertations and Discussions* (Boston: Spencer Press, Inc., 1865), I, 189.

havior, we are including in the readings a very brief selection from Hans Fallada's book *Little Man, What Now?* This fragment conveys dramatically what it means to *be* a mass man, and we hope that the reader will keep it in mind later when he reads the section on bureaucracy as well.

CHANGES IN ECONOMY AND SOCIETY

The emergence of the masses and the idea of a mass society accompanied the metamorphoses in technology and economic systems, which were rapid and dramatic after the war, accelerating transformations that had been working, less obviously, for over seventy years. As the writers we discussed above diagnosed the crisis of the age as an affliction of mind and spirit, others offered interpretations that stressed economic and technological changes. They grew more sensitive to the problems of work and life in advanced industrial civilization and discussed how economic problems were also problems of power.

Persistently, they raised the old fear of the mechanization of man. The rationalization of the productive process had increased machine work and had impressed standards of machinelike efficiency on the work left to men, making new demands on the lives of workers, imposing new forms of discipline. Two currents of thought responded to this dilemma. On the one hand, optimists like the writers in the technocracy movement predicted a utopian future in which automatic machines would do all the work, leaving humanity blessed with leisure in a society benevolently administered by engineers and technicians. On the other hand, a number of writers prophesied the enslavement of mankind by the very instruments it had created. Both thoughts were familiar. Edward Bellamy's political novel *Looking Backward* (1888) had helped set the pattern for the former; the latter, the pessimistic current, had haunted Western literature since the industrial revolution—remember Mary Shelley's *Frankenstein* (1818)—and appeared poignantly in Karel Capek's *R.U.R.* (1923), a play in which humans vanish from the earth and the robots they created acquire souls and prevail. This kind of thinking in the 1920's, fearful of the power of the machine and of the "efficiency experts" who applied the Taylor (time-and-motion study) system, appears below in Sherwood Anderson's "Loom Dance." This selection carries the same immediate impact as does the extract from Fallada's writing. The excerpt from Daniel Bell's book, *Work and Its Discontents,* shows how the logic of rationalization, explained technically by the economist Joseph Schumpeter and illustrated dramatically in Anderson's "Loom Dance," has made its way into the present. Finally, the concluding pages of Max Weber's classic, *The Protestant Ethic and the Spirit of Capitalism,* point to the passing of the spirit of ascetic Puritanism, which, according to Weber, had originally given birth to capitalist institutions.

BUREAUCRACY AND LEADERSHIP

The second selection from Max Weber's work describes the crucial role of bureaucracy in contemporary civilization and in modern systems of power. Hans Gerth and C. Wright Mills, sociologists who have studied bureaucracy and who are also extremely familiar with Max Weber's work, have explained:

There is a tendency to interpret modern history, and particularly the twentieth century, in terms of an increasing bureaucratization. In whatever domain of thought the question has arisen there have been able presentations of the facts of the centralization of industrial and administrative organization. But it is not only in statistical curves that such phenomena receive notice. They make up the stuff of several philosophies of history.

It is no accident that Max Weber is more and more frequently quoted for his thesis that the historical drift may be seen as a bureaucratization of industrial societies, irrespective of their constitutional governments. It is this *form* of organization which is taken to be the substance of history, the more so as it is identified with a growing rationality of modern society.[9]

This conception of bureaucracy and its transformation of contemporary society has persuaded some theorists that old categories such as capitalism and socialism are obsolete. According to Karl Mannheim, the crisis of our time must be understood as the passage from a laissez-faire to a planned society. James Burnham went so far as to argue, in the midst of sharp controversy, that the critical events of the century are the result of a "managerial revolution." [10] R. A. Dahl and C. E. Lindblom in a more recent book contended that the old isms are unreal, and that the proper way to examine political and economic problems is to understand the "ra-

[9] H. H. Gerth and C. Wright Mills, "A Marx for the Managers," *Ethics,* LII (1941–1942), 200.

[10] James Burnham, "The Theory of the Managerial Revolution," *Partisan Review,* VIII (1941), 181–97; *The Managerial Revolution* (New York: John Day Company, Inc., 1941). He revised his views somewhat in *The Machiavellians, Defenders of Freedom* (New York: John Day Company, Inc., 1943).

tional social techniques" by which behavior is calculated and controlled in all societies and the processes by which social goals are achieved.[11]

A weakness of both liberalism and traditional socialism in their conceptions of power was exposed by a disillusioned socialist, Robert Michels. After a thorough study of the German Social-Democratic party, Michels argued that socialism would not exorcise the spell of oligarchy; on the contrary, socialist parties themselves were controlled by elites. The principle that Max Weber had called "the advantage of the small number" Michels saw ruling every form of organized life, and oligarchy was not the product of feudalism or of capitalism but inherent in the very nature of political organization. Because "the mass *per se* is amorphous, and therefore needs division of labour, specialization, and guidance," oligarchy is inevitable. "The principle cause of oligarchy," he claimed, "is to be found in the technical indispensability of leadership."

The iron law of oligarchy, however, did not lead Michels to prefer it. On the contrary, his sympathies remained with the democratic impulse. One should not conclude from "the outright existence of oligarchical tendencies in every form of democracy" that democratic movements were futile, for throughout history they have profoundly influenced and even destroyed established oligarchies. Political systems are continually formed by the conflict between oligarchic and democratic tendencies, and even if Michels considered the attempt to limit oligarchic controls as a "desperate enterprise," he also expressed the conviction that it would be an error to reject this attempt and to abandon the endeavor "to discover a social order which will render possible the complete realization of the idea of popular sovereignty."

[11] R. A. Dahl and C. E. Lindblom, *Politics, Economics, and Welfare* (New York: Harper & Brothers, 1953).

Decline or Progress?

PAUL VALÉRY
1871-1945

PAUL VALÉRY WAS ONE of those remarkable Europeans who
sought to express his philosophy in poetry and his poetry in philosophy. No aspect of human concern was alien to him as he explored the
possibilities of civilized self-realization. Although he is primarily known as
a postsymbolist poet, his verse was but one form of an attempt to represent all
the subtleties of consciousness. Valéry's essays on science and history and his
critical literary pieces reveal his subjectivist passion for discovering and depict-
ing what is essentially human.

Valéry attributed his inclination to "sense" ideas to his childhood in a
small Mediterranean coastal town where he was devoted "to the deities: sea,
sky, and sun." He spurned his law studies and began to cultivate an interest
in aesthetics and poetry. Early in his career he was influenced by Mallarmé,
Rimbaud, and Poe, among others, and was apparently headed for a successful
literary career when he underwent an emotional and intellectual crisis. He became preoccupied with the "singular drama" that was taking place within himself, and there began a period of twenty years during which he published little
but studied and developed his ideas. Among the works published during this
time was one foretelling the rise of totalitarianism in Germany, Japan, and
Russia (*Une Conquête Méthodique*). A few years before World War I, he began to write poetry for publication; his major poem, *La Jeune Parque*, appeared
in 1917.

Valéry's speculations on politics, like his works on science, were infused with an artistic sensibility that throws on these subjects a novel, delicate light. The essay *La Crise de l'Esprit*, translated below, is the first of some forty commentaries on politics written during his lifetime.

Despite his forebodings of disaster in postwar civilization, he committed himself to its defense and became President of the League of Nations Committee for Intellectual Co-operation in 1936. He was elected to the French Academy in 1925, and occupied the chair of poetry at the Collège de France from 1937 until a year before his death.

Like other poets of his time he was concerned with the rise of mass society and dictatorship and the decline of spiritual freedom. Writing shortly before World War II he said, ". . . dictatorship merely completes the system of pressures and bonds of which modern men, in those countries which are politically most free, are the more or less conscious victims."

[1]   The Crisis of the Mind

We later civilizations . . . we too now know that we are mortal.

We had long heard tell of whole worlds that had vanished, of empires sunk without a trace, gone down with all their men and all their machines into the unexplorable depths of the centuries, with their gods and their laws, their academies and their sciences pure and applied, their grammars and their dictionaries, their Classics, their Romantics, and their Symbolists, their critics and the critics of their critics . . . We were aware that the visible earth is made of ashes, and that ashes signify something. Through the obscurity of history we could make out the phantoms of great ships laden with riches and intellect; we could not count them. But the disasters that had sent them down were, after all, none of our affair.

Elam, Nineveh, Babylon were but beautiful vague names, and the total ruin of those worlds had as little significance for us as their very existence. But France, England, Russia . . . these too would be beautiful names. *Lusitania,* too, is a beautiful name. And we see now that the abyss of history is deep enough to hold us all. We are aware that a civilisation has the same fragility as a life. The circumstances that could send the works of

From Paul Valéry, *History and Politics,* Vol. X in Jackson Mathews, ed., *The Collected Works of Paul Valéry,* Bollingen Series XLV (New York: Pantheon Books, Inc., 1962). Reprinted by permission.

Keats and Baudelaire to join the works of Menander are no longer inconceivable; they are in the newspapers.

* * *

That is not all. The searing lesson is more complete still. It was not enough for our generation to learn from its own experience how the most beautiful things and the most ancient, the most formidable and the best ordered, can perish by *accident;* in the realm of thought, feeling, and common sense, we witnessed extraordinary phenomena: paradox suddenly become fact, and obvious fact brutally belied.

I shall cite but one example: the great virtues of the German peoples have begotten more evils, than vices were ever bred by idleness. With our own eyes, we have seen conscientious labor, the most solid learning, the most serious discipline and application adapted to appalling ends.

So many horrors could not have been possible without so many virtues. Doubtless, much science was needed to kill so many, to waste so much property, annihilate so many cities in so short a time; but *moral qualities* in like number were also needed. Are Knowledge and Duty, then, suspect?

* * *

So the Persepolis of the spirit is no less ravaged than the Susa of material fact. Everything has not been lost, but everything has sensed that it might perish.

An extraordinary shudder ran through the marrow of Europe. She felt in every nucleus of her mind that she could no longer recognize herself, that she was ceasing to be herself, that she was about to lose consciousness, a consciousness acquired through centuries of bearable calamities, by thousands of men of the first rank, from innumerable geographical, ethnic, and historical coincidences.

So—as though in desperate defense of her own physiological being and resources—all her memory confusedly returned. Her great men and her great books came back pell-mell. Never has so much been read, nor with such passion, as during the war: ask the booksellers. . . . Never have people prayed so much and so deeply; ask the priests. All the saviors, founders, protectors, martyrs, heroes, all the fathers of their country, the sacred heroines, the national poets were invoked. . . .

And in the same disorder of mind, at the summons of the same anguish, all cultivated Europe underwent the rapid revival of her innumerable ways of thought: dogmas, philosophies, heterogeneous ideals; the three ways of explaining the World, the thousand and one versions of Christianity, the two dozen kinds of positivism; the whole spectrum of intellectual light spread out its incompatible colors, illuminating with a strange and contradictory gleam the death agony of the European soul. While inventors were feverishly searching their imaginations and the annals of former wars for the means of doing away with barbed wire, of outwitting submarines, or paralyzing the flight of airplanes, her soul was intoning at the same time all the incantations it ever knew, and giving serious consideration to the most bizarre prophecies; she sought refuge, guidance, consolation throughout the whole register of her memories, past acts, and ancestral attitudes. Such are the known effects of anxiety, the disordered behavior of a mind fleeing from reality to nightmare and from nightmare back to reality, terrified, like a rat caught in a trap.

The military crisis may be over. The economic crisis is still with us in all its force. But the intellectual crisis, being more subtle and, by its nature, assuming the most deceptive appearances (since it takes place in the very realm of dissimulation) . . . this crisis will hardly allow us to grasp its true extent, its *phase*.

No one can say what will be dead or alive tomorrow, in literature, philosophy, esthetics; no one yet knows what ideas and modes of expression will be inscribed on the casualty list, what novelties will be proclaimed.

Hope, of course, remains—singing in an undertone:

Et cum vorandi vicerit libidinem
Late triumphet imperator spiritus.

But hope is only man's mistrust of the clear foresight of his mind. Hope suggests that any conclusion unfavorable to us *must be* an error of the mind. And yet the facts are clear and pitiless: thousands of young writers and young artists have died; the illusion of a European culture has been lost, and knowledge has been proved impotent to save anything whatever; science is mortally wounded in its moral ambitions and, as it were, put to shame by the cruelty of its applications; idealism is barely surviving, deeply stricken, and called to account for its dreams; realism is hopeless, beaten, routed by its own crimes and errors; greed and abstinence are equally flouted; faiths are confused in their aim—cross against cross, crescent against crescent; and even the skeptics, confounded by the sudden, violent, and moving events that play with our minds as a cat with a mouse . . .

even the skeptics lose their doubts, recover, and lose them again, no longer master of the motions of their thought.

The swaying of the ship has been so violent that the best-hung lamps have finally overturned.

* * *

What gives this critical condition of the mind its depth and gravity is the patient's condition when she was overcome.

I have neither the time nor the power to define the intellectual situation in Europe in 1914. And who could pretend to draw a picture of that situation? The subject is immense, requiring every order of knowledge, and endless information. Besides, when such a complex whole is in question, the difficulty of reconstructing the past, even the recent past, is altogether comparable to that of constructing the future, even the near future; or rather, they are the same difficulty. The prophet is in the same boat as the historian. Let us leave them there.

For all I need is a vague general recollection of what was being thought just before the war, the kinds of intellectual pursuit then in progress, the works being published.

So if I disregard all detail and confine myself to a quick impression, to that *natural whole* given by a moment's perception, I see . . . *nothing!* Nothing . . . and yet an infinitely potential nothing.

The physicists tell us that if the eye could survive in an oven fired to the point of incandescence, it would see . . . nothing. There would be no unequal intensities of light left to mark off points in space. That formidable contained energy would produce invisibility, indistinct equality. Now, equality of that kind is nothing else than a perfect state of *disorder*.

And what made that disorder in the mind of Europe? The free coexistence, in all her cultivated minds, of the most dissimilar ideas, the most contradictory principles of life and learning. That is the characteristic of a *modern* epoch.

I am not averse to generalizing the notion of "modern" to name a certain way of life, rather than making it purely a synonym of *contemporary*. There are moments and places in history to which *we moderns* could return without too greatly disturbing the harmony of those times, without seeming objects infinitely curious and conspicuous . . . creatures, shocking, dissonant, and unassimilable. Wherever our entrance would create the least possible sensation, that is where we should feel almost at home. It is clear that Rome in the time of Trajan, or Alexandria under

the Ptolemies, would take us in more easily than many places less remote
in time but more specialized in a single type of manners and entirely given
over to a single race, a single culture, and a single system of life.

Well then! Europe in 1914 had perhaps reached the limit of modernism
in this sense. Every mind of any scope was a crossroads for all shades of
opinion; every thinker was an international exposition of thought. There
were works of the mind in which the wealth of contrasts and contradictory
tendencies was like the insane displays of light in the capitals of those
days: eyes were fatigued, scorched. . . . How much material wealth, how
much labor and planning it took, how many centuries were ransacked,
how many heterogeneous lives were combined, to make possible such a
carnival, and to set it up as the supreme wisdom and the triumph of
humanity?

*   *   *

In a book of that era—and not one of the most mediocre—we should
have no trouble in finding: the influence of the Russian ballet, a touch of
Pascal's gloom, numerous impressions of the Goncourt type, something of
Nietzsche, something of Rimbaud, certain effects due to a familiarity with
painters, and sometimes the tone of a scientific publication . . . the whole
flavored with an indefinably British quality difficult to assess! . . . Let us
notice, by the way, that within each of the components of this mixture other
bodies could well be found. It would be useless to point them out: it would
be merely to repeat what I have just said about modernism, and to give
the whole history of the European mind.

*   *   *

Standing, now, on an immense sort of terrace of Elsinore that stretches
from Basle to Cologne, bordered by the sands of Nieuport, the marshes of
the Somme, the limestone of Champagne, the granites of Alsace . . . our
Hamlet of Europe is watching millions of ghosts.

But he is an intellectual Hamlet, meditating on the life and death of
truths; for ghosts, he has all the subjects of our controversies; for remorse,
all the titles of our fame. He is bowed under the weight of all the discoveries
and varieties of knowledge, incapable of resuming this endless activity; he
broods on the tedium of rehearsing the past and the folly of always trying
to innovate. He staggers between two abysses—for two dangers never
cease threatening the world: order and disorder.

Every skull he picks up is an illustrious skull. *Whose was it?** This one

* [Hamlet's words are in English in the French text. Ed. Note.]

was *Leonardo*. He invented the flying man, but the flying man has not exactly served his inventor's purposes. We know that, mounted on his great swan (*il grande uccello sopra del dosso del suo magnio cecero*) he has other tasks in our day than fetching snow from the mountain peaks during the hot season to scatter it on the streets of towns. And that other skull was *Leibnitz,* who dreamed of universal peace. And this one was *Kant* . . . Kant, who begat Hegel, who begat Marx, who begat. . . .

Hamlet hardly knows what to make of so many skulls. But suppose he forgets them! Will he still be himself? . . . His terribly lucid mind contemplates the passage from war to peace: darker, more dangerous than the passage from peace to war; all peoples are troubled by it. . . . "What about Me," he says, "what is to become of Me, the European intellect? . . . And what is peace? . . . *Peace is perhaps that state of things in which the natural hostility between men is manifested in creation rather than destruction as in war.* Peace is a time of creative rivalry and the battle of production; but am I not tired of producing? . . . Have I not exhausted my desire for radical experiment, indulged too much in cunning compounds? . . . Should I not perhaps lay aside my hard duties and transcendent ambitions? . . . Perhaps follow the trend and do like Polonius who is now director of a great newspaper; like Laertes, who is something in aviation; like Rosenkrantz, who is doing God knows what under a Russian name?

"Farewell, ghosts! The world no longer needs you—or me. By giving the name of progress to its own tendency to a fatal precision, the world is seeking to add to the benefits of life the advantages of death. A certain confusion still reigns; but in a little while all will be made clear, and we shall witness at last the miracle of an animal society, the perfect and ultimate anthill."

SIGMUND FREUD
1856-1939

THE VERY IDEA OF CIVILIZATION was changed by Freud. He indicated both how fragile its foundations can be and also how it can provide men with the strength for greatness and nobility. His own life was a tribute to the possibilities of personal courage in an age of collective action. After World War I, in the face of the willful refusal of many people to recognize that deep psychic tremors plague civilizations, Freud wrote, "We dwell upon the evil in human beings with the greater emphasis only because others deny it, thereby making the mental life of mankind not indeed better, but incomprehensible." Of all twentieth-century thinkers, he, more than any other, illumined aspects of human conduct that had long been hidden by the optimistic façade of the nineteenth century.

At the beginning of a promising career of neurological research, Freud became interested in the psychological aspects of mental illness. He studied with Charcot in France in 1885–1886, and then returned to Vienna where he began his work of unlocking the recesses of living memory and exploring the foundations of personality. These efforts were aided by his reading in literature and philosophy, full of intimations of the underground origins of behavior. Gradually, through painstaking and painful analysis of patients and of himself, he evolved the techniques and theories of psychoanalysis: free association; the theories of repression, unconscious processes, resistance analysis, and sexual development; and the general theory of character formation. In 1900, he published the epic work *The Interpretation of Dreams,* which in retrospect seems to signal not the beginning of a new century but of a new age.

Freud applied his findings to the study of culture and civilization in such works as *Totem and Taboo* (1912–1913), *Group Psychology and the Analysis of the Ego* (1921), *The Future of an Illusion* (1927), and *Civilization and Its Discontents* (1930). While these and other writings contain much that is probably undemonstrable, his brilliant speculations nonetheless provided the starting point for subsequent examinations of the impact of society on personality.

Two important lines of thought concerning politics and civilization stem from a few assertions in *Civilization and Its Discontents*. One is the suggestion, which at first resembles Rousseau's theories, that the "substitution of the power of a united number for the power of a single man is the decisive step towards civilization. The essence of it lies in the circumstance that the members of the community have restricted their possibilities of gratification, whereas the individual recognized no such restrictions." This view links politics with civilization in an eternally tragic way: it consigns man to be grateful to the polity for providing the conditions of civility, but at the same time condemns him to be forever resentful for having to renounce immediate instinctual gratification. The second assertion states: "That which began in relation to the father ends in relation to the community." It refers authority to conscience and carries further Plato's reflections on social organization and character structure.

In his last years, Freud fled from the kind of collective madness which he knew could easily overwhelm humanity and which, in its individual forms, he as a physician tried to bring under the control of reason.

[2]   Thoughts for the Times on War and Death

I. THE DISILLUSIONMENT OF THE WAR

Swept as we are into the vortex of this war-time, our information one-sided, ourselves too near to focus the mighty transformations which have already taken place or are beginning to take place, and without a glimmering of the inchoate future, we are incapable of apprehending the significance of the thronging impressions, and know not what value to attach to the judgments we form. We are constrained to believe that never has any event been destructive of so much that is valuable in the common wealth of humanity, nor so misleading to many of the clearest intelligences, nor so debasing to the highest that we know. Science herself has lost her passionless impartiality; in their deep embitterment her servants seek for weapons from her with which to contribute towards the defeat of the enemy. The anthropologist is driven to declare the opponent inferior and degenerate; the psychiatrist to publish his diagnosis of the enemy's disease of mind or spirit. But probably our sense of these immediate evils is disproportionately

From Sigmund Freud, *Collected Papers* (London: The Hogarth Press, Ltd., 1956), IV, 288–304, 316–17. Reprinted by permission.

strong, and we are not entitled to compare them with the evils of other times of which we have not undergone the experience.

The individual who is not himself a combatant—and so a wheel in the gigantic machinery of war—feels conscious of disorientation, and of an inhibition in his powers and activities. I believe that he will welcome any indication, however slight, which may enable him to find out what is wrong with himself at least. I propose to distinguish two among the most potent factors in the mental distress felt by non-combatants, against which it is such a heavy task to struggle, and to treat of them here: the disillusionment which this war has evoked; and the altered attitude towards death which this—like every other war—imposes on us.

When I speak of disillusionment, everyone at once knows what I mean. One need not be a sentimentalist; one may perceive the biological and psychological necessity of suffering in the economics of human life, and yet condemn war both in its means and in its aims, and devoutly look forward to the cessation of all wars. True, we have told ourselves that wars can never cease so long as nations live under such widely differing conditions, so long as the value of individual life is in each nation so variously computed, and so long as the animosities which divide them represent such powerful instinctual forces in the mind. And we are prepared to find that wars between the primitive and the civilized peoples, between those races whom a colour-line divides, nay, wars with and among the undeveloped nationalities of Europe or those whose culture has perished—that for a considerable period such wars would occupy mankind. But we permitted ourselves to have other hopes. We had expected the great ruling powers among the white nations upon whom the leadership of the human species has fallen, who were known to have cultivated world-wide interests, to whose creative powers were due our technical advances in the direction of dominating nature, as well as the artistic and scientific acquisitions of the mind—peoples such as these we had expected to succeed in discovering another way of settling misunderstandings and conflicts of interest. Within each of these nations there prevailed high standards of accepted custom for the individual, to which his manner of life was bound to conform if he desired a share in communal privileges. These ordinances, frequently too stringent, exacted a great deal from him, much self-restraint, much renunciation of instinctual gratification. He was especially forbidden to make use of the immense advantages to be gained by the practice of lying and deception in the competition with his fellow-men. The civilized state regarded these accepted standards as the basis of its existence; stern were its proceedings when an impious hand was laid upon them; frequent the pronouncement that to subject them even to examination by a critical intelligence was entirely impracticable. It could be assumed, therefore, that the state itself would respect them, nor would contemplate undertaking any infringement of what it acknowledged as the basis of its own existence. To be sure, it was evident that within these civilized states were mingled remnants of certain other races who were universally unpopular and had therefore been only reluctantly, and even so not to the fullest extent, admitted to participation in the common task of civilization, for which they had shown themselves suitable enough. But the great nations themselves, it might have been supposed, had acquired so much comprehension of their common interests, and enough tolerance for the differences that existed between them, that "foreigner" and "enemy" could no longer, as still in antiquity, be regarded as synonymous.

Relying on this union among the civilized races, countless people have exchanged their native home for a foreign dwelling-place, and made their existence dependent on the conditions of intercourse between friendly nations. But he who was not by stress of circumstances confined to one spot, could also confer upon himself, through all the advantages and attractions of these civilized countries, a new, a wider fatherland, wherein he moved unhindered and unsuspected. In this way he enjoyed the blue sea, and the grey; the beauty of the snow-clad mountains and of the green pasture-lands; the magic of the northern forests and the splendour of the southern vegetation; the emotion inspired by landscapes that recall great historical events, and the silence of nature in her inviolate places. This new fatherland was for him a museum also, filled with all the treasures which the artists among civilized communities had in the successive centuries created and left behind. As he wandered from one gallery to another in this museum, he could appreciate impartially the varied types of perfection that miscegenation, the course of historical events, and the special characteristics of their mother-earth had produced among his more remote compatriots. Here he would find a cool inflexible energy developed to this highest point; there, the gracious art of beautifying existence; elsewhere, the sense of order and fixed law—in short, any and all of the qualities which have made mankind the lords of the earth.

Nor must we forget that each of these citizens of culture had created for himself a personal "Parnassus" and "School of Athens." From among the great thinkers and artists of all nations he had chosen those to whom he conceived himself most deeply indebted for what he had achieved in enjoyment and comprehension of life, and in his veneration had associated them with the immortals of old as well as with the more familiar masters of his own tongue. None of these great figures had seemed to him alien because he had spoken another language—not the incomparable investigator of the passions of mankind, nor the intoxicated worshipper of beauty, nor the vehement and threatening prophet, nor the subtle mocking satirist; and never did he on this account rebuke himself as a renegade towards his own nation and his beloved mother-tongue.

The enjoyment of this fellowship in civilization was from time to time disturbed by warning voices, which declared that as a result of long-prevailing differences wars were unavoidable, even among the members of a fellowship such as this. We refused to believe it; but if such a war indeed must be, what was our imaginary picture of it? We saw it as an opportunity for demonstrating the progress of mankind in communal feeling since the era when the Greek Amphictyones had proclaimed that no city of the league might be demolished, nor its olive-groves hewn down, nor its water cut off. As a chivalrous crusade, which would limit itself to establishing the superiority of one side in the contest, with the least possible infliction of dire sufferings that could contribute nothing to the decision, and with complete immunity for the wounded who must of necessity withdraw from the contest, as well as for the physicians and nurses who devoted themselves to the task of healing. And of course with the utmost precautions for the non-combatant classes of the population—for women who are debarred from war-work, and for the childern who, grown older, should be enemies no longer but friends and co-operators. And again, with preservation of all the international undertakings and institutions in which the mutual civilization of peace-time had been embodied.

Even a war like this would have been productive of horrors and sufferings enough; but it would not have interrupted the development of ethical relations between the greater units of mankind, between the peoples and the states.

Then the war in which we had refused to believe broke out, and brought —disillusionment. Not only is it more sanguinary and more destructive than any war of other days, because of the enormously increased perfection of weapons of attack and defence; but it is at least as cruel, as embittered, as implacable as any that has preceded it. It sets at naught all those restrictions known as International Law, which in peace-time the states had bound themselves to observe; it ignores the prerogatives of the wounded and the medical service, the distinction between civil and military sections of the population, the claims of private property. It tramples in blind fury on all that comes in its way, as though there were to be no future and no good-will among men after it has passed. It rends all bonds of fellowship between the contending peoples, and threatens to leave such a legacy of embitterment as will make any renewal of such bonds impossible for a long time to come.

Moreover, it has brought to light the almost unbelievable phenomenon of a mutual comprehension between the civilized nations so slight that the one can turn with hate and loathing upon the other. Nay, more—that one of the great civilized nations is so universally unpopular that the attempt can actually be made to exclude it from the civilized community as "barbaric," although it long has proved its fitness by the most magnificent co-operation in the work of civilization. We live in the hope that the impartial decision of history will furnish the proof that precisely this nation, this in whose tongue we now write, this for whose victory our dear ones are fighting, was the one which least transgressed the laws of civilization—but at such a time who shall dare present himself as the judge of his own cause?

Nations are in a measure represented by the states which they have formed; these states, by the governments which administer them. The individual in any given nation has in this war a terrible opportunity to convince himself of what would occasionally strike him in peace-time—that the state has forbidden to the individual the practice of wrong-doing, not because it desired to abolish it, but because it desires to monopolize it, like salt and tobacco. The warring state permits itself every such misdeed, every such act of violence, as would disgrace the individual man. It practises not only the accepted stratagems, but also deliberate lying and deception against the enemy; and this, too, in a measure which appears to surpass the usage of former wars. The state exacts the utmost degree of obedience and sacrifice from its citizens, but at the same time treats them as children by maintaining an excess of secrecy, and a censorship of news and expressions of opinion that renders the spirits of those thus intellectually oppressed defenceless against every unfavorable turn of events and every sinister rumour. It absolves itself from the guarantees and contracts it had formed with other states, and makes unabashed confession of its rapacity and lust for power, which the private individual is then called upon to sanction in the name of patriotism.

Nor may it be objected that the state cannot refrain from wrong-doing, since that would place it at a disadvantage. It is no less disadvantageous, as a general rule, for the individual man to conform to the customs of morality and refrain from brutal and arbitrary conduct; and the state but seldom proves able to indemnify him for the sacrifices it exacts. It cannot be a matter for astonishment, therefore, that this relaxation of all the moral ties between the greater units of mankind should have had a seducing influence on the morality of individuals; for our conscience is not the inflexible judge that ethical teachers are wont to declare it, but in its origin is "dread of the community" and nothing else. When the community has no rebuke to make, there is an end of all suppression of the baser passions, and men perpetrate deeds of cruelty, fraud, treachery and barbarity so imcompatible with their civilization that one would have held them to be impossible.

Well may that civilized cosmopolitan, therefore, of whom I spoke, stand helpless in a world grown strange to him—his all-embracing patrimony disintegrated, the common estates in it laid waste, the fellow-citizens embroiled and debased!

In criticism of his disillusionment, nevertheless, certain things must be said. Strictly speaking, it is not justified, for it consists in the destruction of —an illusion! We welcome illusions because they spare us emotional distress, and enable us instead to indulge in gratification. We must not then complain if now and again they come into conflict with some portion of reality, and are shattered against it.

Two things in this war have evoked our sense of disillusionment: the destitution shown in moral relations externally by the states which in their interior relations pose as the guardians of accepted moral usage, and the brutality in behaviour shown by individuals, whom, as partakers in the highest form of human civilization, one would not have credited with such a thing.

Let us begin with the second point and endeavour to formulate, as succinctly as may be, the point of view which it is proposed to criticize. How do we imagine the process by which an individual attains to a higher plane of morality? The first answer is sure to be: He is good and noble from his very birth, his very earliest beginnings. We need not consider this any further. A second answer will suggest that we are concerned with a developmental process, and will probably assume that this development consists in eradicating from him the evil human tendencies and, under the influence of education and a civilized environment, replacing them by good ones. From that standpoint it is certainly astonishing that evil should show itself to have such power in those who have been thus nurtured.

But this answer implies the thesis from which we propose to dissent. In reality, there is no such thing as "eradicating" evil tendencies. Psychological—more strictly speaking, psycho-analytic—investigation shows instead that the inmost essence of human nature consists of elemental instincts, which are common to all men and aim at the satisfaction of certain primal needs. These instincts in themselves are neither good nor evil. We but classify them and their manifestations in that fashion, according as they meet the needs and demands of the human community. It is admitted that all those instincts which society condemns as evil—let us take as representatives the selfish and the cruel—are of this primitive type.

These primitive instincts undergo a lengthy process of development before they are allowed to become active in the adult being. They are inhibited, directed towards other aims and departments, become commingled, alter their objects, and are to some extent turned back upon their possessor. Reaction-formations against certain instincts take the deceptive form of a change in content, as though egoism had changed into altruism, or cruelty into pity. These reaction-formations are facilitated by the circumstance that many instincts are manifested almost from the first in pairs of opposites, a very remarkable phenomenon—and one strange to the lay public—which is termed the "ambivalence of feeling." The most easily observable and comprehensible instance of this is the fact that intense love and intense hatred are so often to be found together in the same person. Psycho-analysis adds that the conflicting feelings not infrequently have the same person for their object.

It is not until all these "vicissitudes to which instincts are subject" have been surmounted that what we call the character of a human being is formed, and this, we know, can only very inadequately be classified as "good" or "bad." A human being is seldom altogether good or bad; he is usually "good" in one relation and "bad" in another, or "good" in certain external circumstances and in others decidedly "bad." It is interesting to learn that the existence of strong "bad" impulses in infancy is often the actual condition for an unmistakable inclination towards "good" in the adult person. Those who as children have been the most pronounced egoists may well become the most helpful and self-sacrificing members of the community; most of our sentimentalists, friends of humanity, champions of animals, have been evolved from little sadists and animal-tormentors.

The transformation of "bad" instincts is brought about by two co-operating factors, an internal and an external. The internal factor consists in an influence on the bad—say, the egoistic—instincts exercised by erotism, that is, by the human need for love, taken in its widest sense. By the admixture of *erotic* components the egoistic instincts are transmuted into *social*

ones. We learn to value being loved as an advantage for which we are willing to sacrifice other advantages. The external factor is the force exercised
by up-bringing, which advocates the claims of our cultural environment,
and this is furthered later by the direct pressure of that civilization by
which we are surrounded. Civilization is the fruit of renunciation of instinctual satisfaction, and from each new-comer in turn it exacts the same
renunciation. Throughout the life of the individual there is a constant replacement of the external compulsion by the internal. The influences of
civilization cause an ever-increasing transmutation of egoistic trends into
altruistic and social ones, and this by an admixture of erotic elements. In
the last resort it may be said that every internal compulsion which has been
of service in the development of human beings was originally, that is, in the
evolution of the human race, nothing but an external one. Those who are
born today bring with them as an inherited constitution some degree of a
tendency (disposition) towards transmutation of egoistic into social instincts, and this disposition is easily stimulated to achieve that effect. A
further measure of this transformation must be accomplished during the
life of the individual himself. And so the human being is subject not only to
the pressure of his immediate environment, but also to the influence of the
cultural development attained by his forefathers.

If we give the name of *cultural adaptability* to a man's personal capacity
for transformation of the egoistic impulses under the influence of the erotic,
we may further affirm that this adaptability is made up of two parts, one
innate and the other acquired through experience, and that the relation of
the two to each other and to that portion of the instinctual life which remains untransformed is a very variable one.

Generally speaking, we are apt to attach too much importance to the
innate part, and in addition to this we run the risk of overestimating the
general adaptability to civilization in comparison with those instincts which
have remained in their primitive state—by which I mean that in this way we
are led to regard human nature as "better" than it actually is. For there is,
besides, another factor which obscures our judgment and falsifies the issue
in too favourable a sense.

The impulses of another person are naturally hidden from our observation. We deduce them from his actions and behaviour, which we trace to
motives born of his instinctual life. Such a conclusion is bound to be, in
many cases, erroneous. This or that action which is "good" from the civilized point of view may in one instance be born of a "noble" motive, in another not so. Ethical theorists class as "good" actions only those which are

the outcome of good impulses; to the others they refuse their recognition. But society, which is practical in its aims, is little troubled on the whole by this distinction; it is content if a man regulates his behaviour and actions by the precepts of civilization, and is little concerned with his motives.

We have seen that the external compulsion exercised on a human being by his up-bringing and environment produces a further transformation towards good in his instinctual life—a turning from egoism towards altruism. But this is not the regular or necessary effect of the external compulsion. Education and environment offer benefits not only in the way of love, but also employ another kind of premium system, namely, reward and punishment. In this way their effect may turn out to be that he who is subjected to their influence will choose to "behave well" in the civilized sense of the phrase, although no ennoblement of instinct, no transformation of egoistic into altruistic inclinations, has taken place within. The result will, roughly speaking, be the same; only a particular concatenation of circumstances will reveal that one man always acts rightly because his instinctual inclination compels him so to do, and the other is "good" only in so far and for so long as such civilized behaviour is advantageous for his own egoistic purposes. But superficial acquaintance with an individual will not enable us to distinguish between the two cases, and we are certainly misled by our optimism into grossly exaggerating the number of human beings who have been transformed in a civilized sense.

Civilized society, which exacts good conduct and does not trouble itself about the impulses underlying it, has thus won over to obedience a great many people who are not thereby following the dictates of their own natures. Encouraged by this success, society has suffered itself to be led into straining the moral standard to the highest possible point, and thus it has forced its members into a yet greater estrangement from their instinctual dispositions. They are consequently subjected to an unceasing suppression of instinct, the resulting strain of which betrays itself in the most remarkable phenomena of reaction and compensation formations. In the domain of sexuality, where such suppression is most difficult to enforce, the result is seen in the reaction-phenomena of neurotic disorders. Elsewhere the pressure of civilization brings in its train no pathological results, but is shown in malformations of character, and in the perpetual readiness of the inhibited instincts to break through to gratification at any suitable opportunity. Anyone thus compelled to act continually in the sense of precepts which are not the expression of instinctual inclinations, is living, psychologically speaking, beyond his means, and might objectively be designated a hypocrite, whether this difference be clearly known to him or not. It is undeniable that our contemporary civilization is extraordinarily favourable to the production of this form of hypocrisy. One might venture to say that it is based upon such hypocrisy, and that it would have to submit to far-reaching modifications if people were to undertake to live in accordance with the psychological truth. Thus there are very many more hypocrites than truly civilized persons—indeed, it is a debatable point whether a certain degree of civilized hyprocrisy be not indispensable for the maintenance of civilization, because the cultural adaptability so far attained by those living to-day would perhaps not prove adequate to the task. On the other hand, the maintenance of civilization even on so questionable a basis offers the prospect of each new generation achieving a farther-reaching transmutation of instinct, and becoming the pioneer of a higher form of civilization.

From the foregoing observations we may already derive this consolation—that our mortification and our grievous disillusionment regarding the uncivilized behaviour of our world-compatriots in this war are shown to be unjustified. They were based on an illusion to which we had abandoned ourselves. In reality our fellow-citizens have not sunk so low as we feared, because they had never risen so high as we believed. That the greater units of humanity, the peoples and states, have mutually abrogated their moral restraints naturally prompted these individuals to permit themselves relief for awhile from the heavy pressure of civilization and to grant a passing satisfaction to the instincts it holds in check. This probably caused no breach in the relative morality within their respective national frontiers.

We may, however, obtain insight deeper than this into the change brought about by the war in our former compatriots, and at the same time receive a warning against doing them an injustice. For the evolution of the mind shows a peculiarity which is present in no other process of development. When a village grows into a town, a child into a man, the village and the child become submerged in the town and the man. Memory alone can trace the earlier features in the new image; in reality the old materials or forms have been superseded and replaced by new ones. It is otherwise with the development of the mind. Here one can describe the state of affairs, which is a quite peculiar one, only by saying that in this case every earlier stage of development persists alongside the later stage which has developed from it; the successive stages condition a co-existence, although it is in reference to the same materials that the whole series of transformations has been fashioned. The earlier mental state may not have manifested itself for years, but none the less it is so far present that it may at any time again become the mode of expression of the forces in the mind, and that exclusively, as though all later developments had been annulled, undone. This extraordinary plasticity of the evolution that takes place in the mind is not unlimited in its scope; it might be described as a special capacity for retroversion— for regression—since it may well happen that a later and higher stage of evolution, once abandoned, cannot be reached again. But the primitive stages can always be reestablished; the primitive mind is, in the fullest meaning of the word, imperishable.

What are called mental diseases inevitably impress the layman with the idea of destruction of the life of mind and soul. In reality, the destruction relates only to later accretions and developments. The essence of mental disease lies in a return to earlier conditions of affective life and functioning. An excellent example of the plasticity of mental life is afforded by the state of sleep, which every night we desire. Since we have learnt to interpret even absurd and chaotic dreams, we know that whenever we sleep we cast off our hard-won morality like a garment, only to put it on again next morning. This divestiture is naturally unattended by any danger because we are paralyzed, condemned to inactivity, by the state of sleep. Only through a dream can we learn of the regression of our emotional life to one of the earliest stages of development. For instance, it is noteworthy that all our dreams are governed by purely egoistic motives. One of my English friends put forward this proposition at a scientific meeting in America, whereupon a lady who was present remarked that that might be the case in Austria, but she could maintain for herself and her friends that *they* were altruistic in their dreams. My friend, although himself of English race, was obliged to contradict the lady emphatically on the ground of his personal experience in dream-analysis, and to declare that in their dreams highminded American ladies were quite as egoistical as the Austrians.

Thus the transformations of instinct on which our cultural adaptability is based, may also be permanently or temporarily undone by the experiences of life. Undoubtedly the influences of war are among the forces that can bring about such regression; therefore we need not deny adaptability for culture to all who are at the present time displaying uncivilized behaviour, and we may anticipate that the refinement of their instincts will be restored in times of peace.

There is, however, another symptom in our world-compatriots which has perhaps astonished and shocked us no less than the descent from their ethical nobility which has so greatly distressed us. I mean the narrowmindedness shown by the best intellects, their obduracy, their inaccessibility to the most forcible arguments, their uncritical credulity for the most disputable assertions. This indeed presents a lamentable picture, and I wish to say emphatically that in this I am by no means a blind partisan who finds all the intellectual shortcomings on one side. But this phenomenon is much easier to account for and much less disquieting than that which we have just considered. Students of human nature and philosophers have long taught us that we are mistaken in regarding our intelligence as an independent force and in overlooking its dependence upon the emotional life. Our intelligence, they teach us, can function reliably only when it is removed from the influences of strong emotional impulses; otherwise it behaves merely as an instrument of the will and delivers the inference which the will requires. Thus, in their view, logical arguments are impotent against affective interests, and that is why reasons, which in Falstaff's phrase are "as plenty as blackberries," produce so few victories in the conflict with interests. Psycho-analytic experience has, if possible, further confirmed this statement. It daily shows that the shrewdest persons will all of a sudden behave like imbeciles as soon as the needful insight is confronted by an emotional resistance, but will completely regain their wonted acuity once that resistance has been overcome. The logical infatuations into which this war has deluded our fellow-citizens, many of them the best of their kind, are therefore a secondary phenomenon, a consequence of emotional excitement, and are destined, we may hope, to disappear with it.

Having in this way come to understand once more our fellow-citizens who are now so greatly alienated from us, we shall the more easily endure the disillusionment which the nations, those greater units of the human race, have caused us, for we shall perceive that the demands we make upon them ought to be far more modest. Perhaps they are reproducing the course of individual evolution, and still to-day represent very primitive phases in the organization and formation of higher unities. It is in agreement with this that the educative factor of an external compulsion towards morality, which we found to be so effective for the individual, is barely discernible in them. True, we had hoped that the extensive community of interests established by commerce and production would constitute the germ of such a compulsion, but it would seem that nations still obey their immediate passions far more readily than their interests. Their interests serve them, at most, as rationalizations for their passions; they parade their interests as their justification for satisfying their passions. Actually why the national units should disdain, detest, abhor one another, and that even when they are at peace, is indeed a mystery. I cannot tell why it is. It is just as though when it becomes a question of a number of people, not to say millions, all individual moral acquirements were obliterated, and only the most primitive, the oldest, the crudest mental attitudes were left. Possibly only future stages in development will be able in any way to alter this regrettable state of affairs. But a little more truthfulness and upright dealing on all sides, both in the personal relations of men to one another and between them and those who govern them, should also do something towards smoothing the way for this transformation.

* * *

II. WAR AND OUR ATTITUDE TOWARDS DEATH

Our unconscious is just as inaccessible to the idea of our own death, as murderously minded towards the stranger, as divided or ambivalent towards the loved, as was man in earliest antiquity. But how far we have moved from this primitive state in our conventionally civilized attitude towards death!

It is easy to see the effect of the impact of the war on this duality. It strips us of the later accretions of civilization, and lays bare the primal man in each of us. It constrains us once more to be heroes who cannot believe in their own death; it stamps the alien as the enemy, whose death is to be brought about or desired; it counsels us to rise above the death of those we love. But war is not to be abolished; so long as the conditions of existence among the nations are so varied, and the repulsions between peoples so intense, there will be, must be, wars. The question then arises: Is it not we who must give in, who must adapt ourselves to them? Is it not for us to confess that in our civilized attitude towards death we are once more living psychologically beyond our means, and must reform and give truth its due? Would it not be better to give death the place in actuality and in our thoughts which properly belongs to it, and to yield a little more prominence to that unconscious attitude towards death which we have hitherto so carefully suppressed? This hardly seems indeed a greater achievement, but rather a backward step in more than one direction, a regression, but it has the merit of taking somewhat more into account the true state of affairs, and of making life again more endurable for us. To endure life remains, when all is said, the first duty of all living beings. Illusion can have no value if it makes this more difficult for us.

We remember the old saying: *Si vis pacem, para bellum*. If you desire peace, prepare for war.

It would be timely thus to paraphrase it: *Si vis vitam, para mortem*. If you would endure life, be prepared for death.

JOHN DEWEY
1859-1952

JOHN DEWEY DEVOTED HIS TALENTS not only to philosophy but also to public persuasion, and his long career left its mark in many areas of contemporary life. While his writing covered almost every field of philosophical investigation, he had also a great share in constructing the intellectual foundations of contemporary liberalism and progressive education. He was born in Vermont, educated at the University of Vermont and at Johns Hopkins, became a village schoolteacher, and then taught at several universities until he retired from Columbia in 1930.

His philosophy was practical, intended to solve the most simple and the most complex problems of men, and also highly systematic, integrating logic, psychology, education, moral and political ideals, religion, science, and art. In all his work, he trusted that life could be improved by the application of intelligence; and he also believed that there was no necessary conflict between individual and society, for he assumed that men grew more individual and more free by sharing experience.

Dewey's political thought reflected his general philosophical point of view. He considered the formal idea of the state inadequate to designate the concrete actions needed for the construction of a democratic community. His conception of democracy resembled Whitman's poetic vision. Democracy, he wrote, "is a name for a life of free and enriching communion." In *The Public and Its Problems* (1927), he echoed the fears of many writers that industrialization had unraveled the fabric of public life, shattering the kind of communication necessary for a viable democracy. In this book and in other works such as *Liberalism and Social Action* (1935) and *Freedom and Culture* (1939) he described the techniques of social action and the forms of organization required in contemporary society to create the great democratic community.

The subtleties of Dewey's work are often obscured by his unabashed idealism and what now seems to be a facile optimism. In recent years, moreover, his name has been the object of a wide variety of criticism, for it has come to represent many facets of American thought and institutions of the 1930's. The criticism may be more valid as an index of the contemporary state of mind than as a measure of Dewey's thought. His work will have to be assessed again in the next generation—when there is more historical distance between Dewey and his critics. Of lasting interest will be his systematic joining of liberal and democratic values in a fashion consistent with the main currents of American thought and action.

[3]   Progress

Some persons will see only irony in a discussion of progress at the present time. Never was pessimism easier. Others will recognize in it a fine exhibition of courage and faith, and find the manifestation heartening. There is indeed every cause for discouragement. But discouragement affords just the occasion for a more intelligent courage. If our optimism was too complacent, it is because it was too thoughtless, too sentimental. Never was there a time when it was more necessary to search for the conditions upon which progress depends, until we can reaffirm our faith in its possibility upon grounds better than those upon which we have too blindly relied.

If we have been living in a fools' paradise, in a dream of automatic uninterrupted progress, it is well to be awakened. If we have been putting our trust in false gods, it is a good thing to have our confidence shaken, even rudely. We may be moved to find truer gods. If the reeds upon which we relied have broken, it is well for us to have discovered their frailty. If we have been looking in the wrong direction, we now have a sufficiently strong stimulus to direct our attention elsewhere. We can hardly welcome the war merely because it has made us think, and has made us realize how many of the things we called thoughts were asylums for laziness. But since the war has come, we may welcome whatever revelations of our stupidity and carelessness it brings with it; and set about the institution of a more manly and more responsible faith in progress than that in which we have indulged in the past.

For there can be no blinking the fact that much of that faith was childish and irresponsible. We confused rapidity of change with advance, and we

From *International Journal of Ethics,* XXVI (1916), 311–22. Reprinted by permission of Mrs. John Dewey and The University of Chicago Press.

took certain gains in our own comfort and ease as signs that cosmic forces were working inevitably to improve the whole state of human affairs. Having reaped where we had not sown, our undisciplined imaginations installed in the heart of history forces which were to carry on progress whether or no, and whose advantages we were progressively to enjoy. It is easy to understand why our minds were taken captive by the spectacle of change, and why we should have confused progress with change. It is not necessary to rehearse an account of the barriers which for thousands of years kept human society static. Nor is it necessary to do more than allude to the various inventions which by facilitating migration and travel, communication and circulation of ideas and reciprocal criticism, and the production and distribution of goods in a world-wide market, have broken down those barriers. The release of energies has gone on for a century and a half to a degree which we are still impotent to realize. Persons and things have been endlessly redistributed and mingled. The fixed has given way to the mobile; the settled to the free. It was doubtless inevitable that, in its contrast with static conditions and ideals, this mobility and freedom should be taken for progress. Such it doubtless is in some respects. But the present crisis is in vain, so far as our intelligence is concerned, if it does not make us see that in the main this rapid change of conditions affords an *opportunity* for progress, but is not itself progress.

We have confused, I repeat, rapidity of change with progress. We have confused the breaking down of barriers by which advance is made possible with advance itself. Except with respect to the conservatives who have continuously bemoaned all change as destructive, these statements seem to me to sum up fairly well the intellectual history of the epoch that is closing. The economic situation, the problem of poverty by the side of great wealth, of ignorance and absence of a fair chance in life by the side of culture and unlimited opportunity, have, indeed, always served to remind us that after all we were dealing with an opportunity for progress rather than with an accomplished fact. It reminded us that the forces which were revolutionizing society might be turned in two ways: that they actually were employed for two diverse and opposed ends. But the display was not dramatic enough, not sensational enough, to force the lesson home. The war stages the lesson in a sufficiently striking way.

We had been told that the development of industry and commerce had brought about such an interdependence of peoples that war was henceforth out of the question—at least upon a vast scale. There are men now fighting who had written and lectured to that effect. But it is now clear that commerce also creates jealousies and rivalries and suspicions which are potent for war. We were told that nations could not long finance a war under modern conditions: economists had demonstrated that to the satisfaction of themselves and others. We see now that they had underrated both the production of wealth and the extent to which it could be mobilized for destructive purposes. We were told that the advance of science had made war practically impossible. We now know that science has not only rendered the enginery of war more deadly, but has also increased the powers of resistance and endurance when war comes. If all this does not demonstrate that the forces which have brought about complicated and extensive changes in the fabric of society do not of themselves generate progress I do not know what a demonstration would be. Has man subjugated physical nature only to release forces beyond his control?

Two things are apparent. First, progress depends not on the existence of social change but on the direction which human beings deliberately give that change. Secondly, ease of social change is a condition of progress. Side by side with the fact that the mere substitution of a dynamic or readily changing social structure for a static society does not accomplish progress, stands the fact that this substitution furnishes the opportunity for progress. We cannot too much insist upon the fact that until men got control of natural forces civilization was a local accident. It depended upon the ability of a small number of men to command, with assurance, the labor and services of other men. Any civilization based mainly upon ability to exploit the energies of men is precarious; it is at the mercy of internal revolt and external overflow. By exploring the heaps of rubbish scattered over the face of the earth, we are just beginning to learn how many civilizations have arisen in the past only to sink into rubbish heaps. The dominion of man over the labor of other men is a shaky basis for civilization. And civilization never attained stability upon such a basis. The scientific conquest of nature has at least given us another basis. We have now a sure method. Wholesale permanent decays of civilization are impossible. As long as there exists a group of men who understand the methods of physical science and are expert in their use, recovery, under the worst of circumstances, of the material basis of culture is sure and relatively speedy. While the modern man was deceived about the amount of progress he had made, and especially deceived about the automatic certainty of progress, he was right in thinking that for the first time in history mankind is in command of the possibility of progress. The rest is for us to say.

I might almost as well stop here. For it seems to me that about all which

I can say about the future of progress at the present time is that it depends upon man to say whether he wants it or not. If we want it, we can have it —if we are willing to pay the price in effort of intelligence. The conditions are at hand. We do not of course wholly control the energies of nature; we shall never wholly do so. But we are in possession of a method which enables us to forecast desirable physical changes and to set about securing them. So much is the secure result of the scientific revolution of the last three hundred years. We also know that it is not possible to bring about these physical changes without effecting at the same time vast social changes. The men who invented the stationary and locomotive steam engine, and the men who have since then harnessed both steam and electricity to all sorts of ends, have produced social changes by the side of which those produced by Alexander, Caesar and Napoleon are insignificant. And the same process is going on as long as applied science goes on, whatever we may think about its worth. But, I repeat, while social change, thus brought about, represents an indispensable condition of progress, it does not present a guarantee for progress. The latter depends upon deliberate human foresight and socially constructive work. Hence we have first of all to change our attitude. Instead of congratulating ourselves upon its presence and certainty as a gift of the gods, as we have been wont to do, we have to recognize that it is a human and intentional product—as much so in principle as a telephone or irrigation or a self-binding reaper, and as much more so in fact as the factors upon which it depends are more complex and more elusive.

The doctrine of evolution has been popularly used to give a kind of cosmic sanction to the notion of an automatic and wholesale progress in human affairs. Our part, the human part, was simply to enjoy the usufruct. Evolution inherited all the goods of Divine Providence and had the advantage of being in fashion. Even a great and devastating war is not too great a price to pay for an awakening from such an infantile and selfish dream. Progress is not automatic; it depends upon human intent and aim and upon acceptance of responsibility for its production. It is not a wholesale matter, but a retail job, to be contracted for and executed in sections. I doubt if the whole history of mankind shows any more vicious and demoralizing ethic than the recent widespread belief that each of us, as individuals and as classes, might safely and complacently devote ourselves to increasing our own possessions, material, intellectual, and artistic, because progress was inevitable anyhow.

In dwelling upon the need of conceiving progress as a responsibility and

not as an endowment, I put primary emphasis upon responsibility for intelligence, for the power which foresees, plans and constructs in advance.
We are so overweighted by nature with impulse, sentiment and emotion,
that we are always tempted to rely unduly upon the efficacy of these things.
Especially do we like to entrust our destiny to them when they go by
eulogistic names—like altruism, kindliness, peaceful feelings. But [in] spite
of the dogma which measures progress by increase in these sentiments,
there is no reason that I know of to suppose that the basic fund of these
emotions has increased appreciably in thousands and thousands of years.
Man is equipped with these feelings at birth as well as with emotions of
fear, anger, emulation and resentment. What appears to be an increase in
one set and a decrease in the other set is, in reality, a change in their social
occasions and social channels. Civilized man has not a better endowment of
ear and eye than savage man; but his social surroundings give him more
important things to see and hear than the savage has, and he has the wit
to devise instruments to reinforce his eye and ear—the telegraph and telephone, the microscope and telescope. But there is no reason for thinking
that he has less natural aggressiveness or more natural altruism—or ever
will have—than the barbarian. But he may live in social conditions that
create a relatively greater demand for the display of kindliness and which
turn his aggressive instincts into less destructive channels. There is at any
time a sufficient amount of kindly impulses possessed by man to enable
him to live in amicable peace with all his fellows; and there is at any time a
sufficient equipment of bellicose impulses to keep him in trouble with his
fellows. An intensification of the exhibition of one may accompany an intensification of the display of the other, the only difference being that social
arrangements cause the kindly feelings to be displayed toward one set of
fellows and the hostile impulses toward another set. Thus, as everybody
knows, the hatred toward the foreigner characterizing peoples now at war
is attended by an unusual manifestation of mutual affection and love within
each warring group. So characteristic is this fact that that man was a good
psychologist who said that he wished that this planet might get into war
with another planet, as that was the only effective way he saw of developing a world-wide community of interest in this globe's population.

I am not saying this to intimate that all impulses are equally good or
that no effective control of any of them is possible. My purpose is, in lesser
part, to suggest the futility of trying to secure progress by immediate or
direct appeal to even the best feelings in our makeup. In the main, there
is an adequate fund of such feelings. What is lacking is adequate social

stimulation for their exercise as compared with the social occasions which evoke less desirable emotions. In greater part, my purpose is to indicate that since the variable factor, the factor which may be altered indefinitely, is the social conditions which call out and direct the impulses and sentiments, the positive means of progress lie in the application of intelligence to the construction of proper social devices. Theoretically, it is possible to have social arrangements which will favor the friendly tendencies of human nature at the expense of the bellicose and predatory ones, and which will direct the latter into channels where they will do the least harm or even become means of good. Practically this is a matter of the persistent use of reflection in the study of social conditions and the devising of social contrivances.

I have already said that the indispensable preliminary condition of progress has been supplied by the conversion of scientific discoveries into inventions which turn physical energy, the energy of sun, coal and iron, to account. Neither the discoveries nor the inventions were the product of unconscious physical nature. They were the product of human devotion and application, of human desire, patience, ingenuity and mother wit. The problem which now confronts us, the problem of progress, is the same in kind, differing in subject-matter. It is a problem of discovering the needs and capacities of collective human nature as we find it aggregated in racial or national groups on the surface of the globe, and of inventing the social machinery which will set available powers operating for the satisfaction of those needs.

This is a large order. But it is not, with reasonable limits, one hopeless to undertake. It is much more within the bounds of legitimate imagination than would have been, five centuries ago, the subjugation of physical nature which has since been achieved. The chief difficulty lies in the primary step: it consists in getting a sufficiently large number of persons to believe in its desirability and practicability. In spite of its discipline by the achievements of physical science our imagination is cowardly and irresponsible. We do not believe that study, foresight and planning will do for the human relations of human beings what they have done for our relationship to physical nature.

We are living still under the dominion of a laissez-faire philosophy. I do *not* mean by this an individualistic as against a socialistic philosophy. I mean by it a philosophy which trusts the direction of human affairs to nature, or Providence, or evolution, or manifest destiny—that is to say, to accident—rather than to a contriving and constructive intelligence. To put our faith in the collective state instead of in individual activity is quite as laissez-faire a proceeding as to put it in the results of voluntary enterprise. The only genuine opposite to a go-as-you-please let-alone philosophy is a philosophy which studies specific social needs and evils with a view to constructing the special machinery for which they call.

So far I have avoided any contrast of the so-called progressive attitude with the so-called conservative attitude. I cannot maintain that reserve any longer. While in general, the opposite of the progressive attitude is not so much conservatism as it is disbelief in the possibility of constructive social engineering, the conservative mind is a large factor in propagating this disbelief. The hard and fast conservative is the man who cannot conceive that existing institutions, constitutions, and social arrangements are mechanisms for achieving social results. To him, *they* are the results; they are final. If he could once cure himself of this illusion, he would be willing to admit that they grew up at haphazard and cross purposes, and mainly at periods quite unlike the present. Admitting this, he would be ready to conceive the possibility that they are as poor mechanisms for accomplishing needed social results as were the physical tools which preceded the mastery of nature by mind. He would then be free: Not freed just to get emotionally excited about something called progress in general, but to consider what improved social mechanisms or contrivances are demanded at the present day. . . .

I hope these remarks at least illustrate what is meant by the dependence of progress upon a foreseeing and contriving intelligence as well as what is meant by saying that it is a retail job. I can only point out the need, so far as they coincide in the further interests of peace with the interest of progress, of an international commerce commission; of an international tariff board; of an international board for colonies and one for the supervision of relations with those backward races which have not as yet been benevolently, or otherwise, assimilated by the economically advanced peoples. Such things are not counsels of perfection. They are practical possibilities as soon as it is genuinely recognized that the guarantee of progress lies in the perfecting of social mechanisms corresponding to specific needs.

EMIL LEDERER
1882-1939

EMIL LEDERER RECEIVED his early education in Vienna. Specializing in law and economics, he earned a doctorate in jurisprudence at Vienna and another in political science at Munich. He taught at the Universities of Heidelberg and Berlin, and became editor of the *Archiv für Sozialwissenschaft* after having worked as managing editor under the supervision of Max Weber and Werner Sombart. He made important contributions to modern German economic theory, and was the first to call attention to the white-collar worker and his significance in the modern economy.

He was professor of economics at the University of Berlin when Hitler came to power in 1933, and in November of that year was one of the 117 professors dismissed from the University. He continued his work in the United States, and became the first dean of the Graduate Faculty of Political and Social Science in the New School for Social Research. He contributed to the Encyclopedia of Social Sciences and wrote several books and articles on economics, sociology, and political science. His work in social psychology and revolutionary movements interested theorists of totalitarianism, and many of his ideas have been absorbed in later writing on the politics of mass society.

[4]   Modern Masses

. . . the crowd is amorphous; it is purely emotional; reason will fail to impress it; it is ready to act. In all these respects the crowd is different from the social group, which at least potentially may be led by arguments and be ready to respond to arguments, though it may follow only those corresponding to the purposes for which the group was formed. These differences between the crowd and a social group, however small the crowd and however large the group may be, lie in the fact that the crowd is amorphous, while the group, at least in one respect, is homogeneous and thus partial. Every group coexists with other groups. Every crowd is, psychologically, a whole, apart from or beyond which no other social being exists or has a right to exist. It feels, so to speak, totalitarian. We shall see the importance of this psychological fact for our modern world. This difference between groups and crowds does not preclude the possibility that a group might act as a crowd. But as soon as the group does so act it tends to become amorphous, as in riots and strikes. . . .

The crowd is not a phenomenon identical wherever and whenever it appears, and should therefore be conceived of as an historical phenomenon showing the features of the period during which it originated. The existence and activity of the crowd presupposes a common cultural basis in the broadest sense of the word. The masses must have something in common: evaluations, common historical experiences which are important for everybody (such as defeat or victory in wars), religious feelings or race-consciousness. Beyond that they must be able to speak, and in modern times to read, the same language. If we think of masses apart from their common experiences or evaluations and their common language, then nothing remains but a "herd," from which modern masses are clearly distinguished. The emotions, and especially the substance of the emotions, change, and also the manner of expression. With a modern feeling or phenomenon like patriotism, for instance, the political importance of crowds is on the increase. The attenuation of religious feelings accounts for another change, which, perhaps, may not be permanent. Changes in technique lead to new ways of

Reprinted from *State of the Masses* by Emil Lederer (New York: W. W. Norton & Company, Inc., 1940), pp. 34, 36–46. By permission of W. W. Norton & Company, Inc. Copyright 1940 by W. W. Norton & Company, Inc.

utilizing crowds. The types of leaders popular with different peoples must also be considered.

Thus crowds are to be taken as social phenomena, changing as every social phenomenon does with changing conditions, and modern civilization favors the formation of crowds.

MASS-ACTION AND LEADERSHIP

So far we have dealt with crowds in general, amorphous masses living emotionally. But the phenomenon is not sufficiently described unless we mention two other elements: the action and the leader. Masses tend to be active. I would not say that they are dynamic. This word, too frequently used nowadays, should be restricted in sociology to a phenomenon, such as a group or institution, which by its very nature is driven into action pointing toward universal changes. Such social phenomena tend to become something which as yet they are not: there is a *Zielstrebigkeit,* a consciousness of purpose; they are, so to speak, alive. Thus a fraternity, a club or a trade union may be called dynamic when it wants to expand or to extend its activities. The crowd, on the other hand, is more likely than such a dynamic institution to burst into sudden action, but it tends to spend its energies: its activity is comparable rather to an explosion than to an action. From this follows the function of crowds in history: in revolutions, as a pressure on the political structure, and recently as the motive power of fascist dictatorships.

The crowd is amorphous and therefore cannot act unless it is integrated. Though some irregular action may follow upon a sudden shock to the crowd—for instance, if it becomes known in a revolutionary situation that some of the revolutionary protagonists have been imprisoned, as in the riots in Vienna in July 1927—usually the crowd will act only if there is a leader. If everything is ripe for action, the situation will suggest to people who are apt to become leaders that they accept the challenge. There are always potential leaders within the crowd, and as it is one of the characteristic features of a leader to realize and take advantage of a situation which "calls for a leader," it seems as if the situation would create a leader. When a group is suddenly faced by a dangerous situation, such as a fire or a snowstorm in the mountains, the appeal is to the daring, cool, considerate man, who will respond and become "the leader" at once. In similar fashion, when a multitude merges into a crowd, creating a psychological unity, an opportunity is offered to another type of "leader"—the emotional, passionate man, who feels what is in the air more strongly than the crowd. This leader, by giving expression to his feeling, can "tune up" the crowd. Hidden qualities which may be entirely unknown in normal circumstances are suddenly of the greatest importance and make for a new grouping in which the failure of yesterday may acquire power.

The qualities of successful leaders give another clue to the psychological condition of the crowd. They must not only feel the emotions through which the crowd comes into existence, but they must be able to express them, to find words which make the crowd feel that it is their emotions which are expressed. The real leader of a crowd will be a man with charisma. Charisma, originally a religious or theological concept, means that the man endowed with it is the tool, the mouthpiece of God, the man through whom the will of God is expressed and realized. The man with charisma acts according to the will of God. He represents God's will to such a degree that he may even argue with God, may even disagree—which indicates that he is of the same substance as God, though originally sent by God. The crowd feels this quality in the leader. It feels, rightly or wrongly, that the leader has other sources of wisdom than science or experience; it thinks that for him logical reasoning is not necessary. Its confidence will be without limit; it will give him full power. The leader makes no mistakes, and even if he should his mistakes will contribute to the ultimate success.

The relation between the masses and the leader is therefore of the same type as that between a people and the founder of a religion. We call this power of the leader magic. This quality of exerting a magic influence is not very rare, and can be found on a very high and on a very low level. The magic can be a dark and sinister force, playing upon violent and barbaric emotions. It is alarmingly true that the personality of the leader makes the crowd and will direct its actions. There is a great range within which he can lead. Inasmuch as crowds are historical forces, the requirements for leadership are subject to change. In our time crowds are called upon more frequently than in former epochs, and the personal element has therefore gained importance to a degree unknown in the past. The emotions which the leader utilizes will always be directed toward the realization of a special goal which must be emphasized and defended against other positions; enemies will be attacked, the merits of the crowd's own aims will be praised. The oratory of the leader cannot be restricted to a lyrical expression of feelings, but will necessarily be dramatic in its fight against other ideas and ideals.

This fight is propaganda. The mere expression of emotions, even the mere appeal to emotions, by music or flags or floodlights or any means whatever, may also be called propaganda. But most decisive is the utilization of arguments which are adapted to the special purpose rather than to the finding of truth. As far as propaganda aims at the unleashing of crowds, a special technique is necessary because of the psychological conditions in which the mind of the crowd works. This technique has been developed into perfection within the last decades, when "the age of the masses" has dawned in Europe.

A multitude whose attention is directed toward a certain purpose becomes a crowd or mass. It will tend to be active, and its activity may reach into any field: religion, race-struggle, politics in general. Revolutionary masses are usually thought of in this connection.

We have distinguished these masses strictly from social groups, which are homogeneous in at least one respect. Many writers, for instance Le Bon, Ortega y Gasset and many sociologists, speak of masses wherever many people are assembled. Five thousand workers in a trade union meeting they would call "masses." I think this terminology is misleading: such meetings of social groups may lead to violent action, the members may behave emotionally, but still they will be restricted in their activities to the special purposes for which they were formed. They will have to reckon with the existence of other groups; their activity therefore will point in a certain direction. Mass-actions on the other hand will frequently be uncertain as to their next and ultimate goals. Masses can be psychologically unbalanced, ready to act, but without knowing any definite purpose. They may simply parade or storm a prison, or kill the head of the state, or overthrow the government, or demand and obtain the dissolution of the parliament. The general direction in which they will move may be fairly certain, but the way in which their urge toward action will materialize is uncertain. Even if the goal is certain, for instance the overthrow of an unpopular government, it is frequently quite uncertain in what way this goal will be obtained and where this action may ultimately lead. Hence the great chance for a leader to utilize the power of active masses, be they religious, racial or political, directing their outbursts toward ends which are in line with the general mass-feelings, but not at all distinctly formulated or planned.

"ABSTRACT" MASSES

Up to the last decades we could speak of masses only when people were gathered in great numbers. Throughout history the masses are "the street." The street, i.e., the appearance in the street of great numbers united by the same purpose, was the power frequently dreaded, frequently appealed to. The masses were sometimes "called out"—which presupposes that they had been in some rough way previously organized. They had met in smaller groups on street corners, in beer halls; the living word of innumerable people had given expression to their feelings. As tension increased, the impulse to congregate grew stronger, and at a given moment the masses appeared on the street, ready to act.

Nowadays it is not only the voice of the orator which forms the masses. There is the press, which speaks the language of the man of the street; it coins slogans which make their way, and it forms the mind. It addresses the average man as he is addressed in a crowd, and thus he feels as if he were in the crowd; and it uses the same means as are used in the crowd—propaganda of every variety. Crowd-feeling is pre-formed and may materialize at any time, when the situation is ripe; this accounts for riotous outbreaks as well as for the consolidation of the whole population in time of a national crisis, such as war.

Everyone has been surprised by the influence of the radio. The radio makes it possible to address vast masses with almost no costs and almost no exertion on the part of the public, for whom in many countries reading is hard labor. In spite of the fact that the listener is alone, usually sitting in his home perhaps with his family or a few friends, he can be affected as if he were in a crowd. This may either be explained by the fact that he knows what it means to be in a crowd, and that his awareness of other hundreds of thousands tuned in on the same program disposes him to listen as if he were in the crowd; or it may be attributed to certain qualities of voice and wording, of which we do not yet know enough. But just as the average man within the crowd is carried away by the speaker's eyes, gestures, voice, so can he be influenced by the radio—especially if he is in the mood to be influenced, which depends on circumstances of the general situation.

Thus an "abstract crowd" may be formed. But only in a democracy—by the vote—could it exert power. Paradoxically, therefore, the democratic system offers the opportunity to sweep men into power by the democratic action of crowds which no leader would dare call out because he would fear the risks of a revolution.

THE TOTALITARIAN STATE: THE MASS-STATE

In the course of history masses frequently have played a great role. In revolutions, in coups d'état and also in the ordinary current of events (when popular demands were backed by mass-demonstrations), masses have frequently swayed the decisions. But in these cases the masses were called up for certain purposes, and after they had functioned they relapsed again into obscurity; only in revolutionary periods are they more frequently appealed to. But modern political leaders, prospective dictators, have made them the basis of a movement which aims not only at permanence but at the domination, the swallowing up, of the state; they have institutionalized the masses, making them a political and social steam roller, crushing social groups of every kind. In this epoch masses are the permanent basis of a political system, the nature of which is determined by this fact.

The totalitarian state is the state of the masses; it is different from any state which is based on, and accepts the existence of, social groups. It is bound to change everything. It has built up a spirit in accordance with the mass-movement: it destroys any potential source of political opposition, and it establishes a center of power which is above and beyond any attack. There is no state in history which can be compared to this totalitarian state, and it is easy now to see why: there has never been a state which destroyed the social structure to such an extent, and there has never been a time which offered the technical opportunities of today to transform the whole people into masses and to keep them in this state.

HANS FALLADA
1893-1947

HANS FALLADA, THE PSEUDONYM of Rudolph Ditzen, was a German author who wrote several novels some of which received serious attention from literary critics as well as international popular acclaim. Following many years of struggle and desperation, the success of *Little Man, What Now?* (1933) surprised him. After Hitler came to power, Ditzen preferred to remain in Germany, "to write books and live in the country," and accommodated himself to the Nazi regime. This accommodation, however, fell short of success, for in 1943 the Nazis pronounced his books "undesirable." He died soon after the war in a Berlin hospital at the age of fifty-three, reading the proofs of his last book, *Every Man Dies Alone*.

[5] Little Man, What Now?

Here comes the little man Pinneberg; he wants a hundred marks—or perhaps it will be a hundred and twenty, he has no idea what will remain after the hospital charges are deducted. He walks into a vast, resplendent edifice. He looks small and shabby in the mammoth hall. Pinneberg, my poor fellow, a hundred marks—? Here we deal in millions. The hundred marks are important to you? To us they are quite unimportant, well, no, that is not wholly true, as you will see later on. This building was in fact constructed out of your contributions, and those of people as small as you, but you are not to think of that now. We use your contributions exactly as we are permitted to do by law.

It was a consolation to Pinneberg to observe that behind the railing were seated employees, in some sense colleagues of his own. Otherwise he might have been completely overwhelmed by all these sumptuous woods and marbles.

Pinneberg looked sharply about him; there was the right counter, letter P. No formidable bars or grating—just a young man sitting on the other side of the counter.

"Pinneberg, Johannes. Number 606,867. My wife has had a baby and I wrote to you about the benefit due."

The young man, busy over a card-index, did not look up. He reached out a hand: "Membership card."

"Here it is. I wrote to you."

"Birth-certificate."

Pinneberg said quietly: "But I wrote to you, and sent you all the papers I got from the hospital."

The young man looked up. "Well, what do you want then?"

"I want to ask if the matter has been settled. Whether the money has been sent. I need it."

"We all do."

Pinneberg asked still more quietly: "Has it been sent?"

"I don't know," said the young man. "If you applied for it in writing, your claim will have been dealt with by letter."

"Could you find out if it's been fixed up?"

"Everything here is dealt with promptly."

"But it ought to have reached me yesterday."

"Why yesterday? How do you know?"

"I reckoned up the time."

"Reckoned up the time? How can you know how matters are disposed of here? There are several departments."

Pinneberg said very quietly and firmly: "Would you mind finding out whether it's been settled or not?"

The young man looked at Pinneberg, Pinneberg looked at the young man. They were both very neatly dressed—Pinneberg had to be on account of his profession—they were both well washed and shaved, both had clean nails, both were employees.

But they were enemies, deadly enemies, for one of them sat behind the railing and the other stood in front of it.

"Nothing but useless bother," growled the young man. But he felt Pinneberg's eyes upon him, and disappeared into the background. In the background was a door, and through it the young man disappeared. Pinneberg watched him go. There was a notice above the door, and Pinneberg's sight was not good enough to read the inscription on it, but the longer he looked at it the more convinced he was that it read: "Men."

Inwardly he raged.

After quite a while, indeed after a very long while, the young man appeared through the same door.

Pinneberg looked at him anxiously, but the other would not raise his eyes. He sat down, picked up Pinneberg's membership card, laid it on the counter: "Your claim has been dealt with."

"Has the money been sent? Yesterday or today?"

"It has been dealt with in writing, I tell you."

"When, please?"

"Yesterday."

Pinneberg looked at the young man once more. He felt uneasy, he was sure that door led to the lavatories. "If I don't find that money at home, I tell you—!" he said threateningly.

But the young man noticed him no more. He was talking to his neighbor about "crazy people."

Changes in Economy and Society

JOSEPH A. SCHUMPETER
1883-1950

AN ECONOMIC THEORIST and political economist, Joseph A. Schumpeter was concerned with the relation between cultural values and economic systems.

Schumpeter was born in Triesch, Moravia, and spent his boyhood in Vienna. He took his law degree at the University of Vienna and studied economics with Karl Menger and Eugen Böhm-Bawerk. When he was barely twenty-five, he published *Das Wesen und der Hauptinhalt der theoretischen Nationalökonomie,* which established him as one of the ablest young European economists. His work *The Theory of Economic Development* (1912) extended his reputation further. He was Minister of Finance in Austria in a brief and turbulent period following World War I. After teaching economics at the University of Bonn, Germany, in the mid-1920's, he was a visiting professor at Harvard University, and in 1932 he went there to stay until his death.

Besides *Capitalism, Socialism, and Democracy* (1942), he published the monumental two-volume work *Business Cycles* in 1939. An enormous output of articles in many journals attests to his boundless energy. He is still remembered at Harvard for his generous expenditure of time with students.

Schumpeter believed that the rise of capitalism and the introduction of innovations was the work of business elites—of a type that would gradually die out because of the changing nature of democratic-capitalistic nations. He predicted that forces within these systems would lead to the decline of capitalism in ways different from those which Marx had forecast. He disapproved of many of these changes, but looked forward to them with stoic curiosity.

[6]   Rationalization and Capitalism

Now the rational attitude presumably forced itself on the human mind primarily from economic necessity; it is the everyday economic task to which we as a race owe our elementary training in rational thought and behavior—I have no hesitation in saying that all logic is derived from the pattern of the economic decision or, to use a pet phrase of mine, that the economic pattern is the matrix of logic. This seems plausible for the following reason. Suppose that some "primitive" man uses that most elementary of all machines, already appreciated by our gorilla cousins, a stick, and that this stick breaks in his hand. If he tries to remedy the damage by reciting a magic formula—he might for instance murmur Supply and Demand or Planning and Control in the expectation that if he repeats this exactly nine times the two fragments will unite again—then he is within the precincts of pre-rational thought. If he gropes for the best way to join the fragments or to procure another stick, he is being rational in our sense. Both attitudes are possible of course. But it stands to reason that in this and most other economic actions the failure of a magic formula to work will be much more obvious than could be any failure of a formula that was to make our man victorious in combat or lucky in love or to lift a load of guilt from his conscience. This is due to the inexorable definiteness and, in most cases, the quantitative character that distinguish the economic from other spheres of human action, perhaps also to the unemotional drabness of the unending rhythm of economic wants and satisfactions. Once hammered in, the rational habit spreads under the pedagogic influence of favorable experiences to the other spheres and there also opens eyes for that amazing thing, the Fact.

This process is independent of any particular garb, hence also of the capitalistic garb, of economic activity. So is the profit motive and self-

From Joseph A. Schumpeter, *Capitalism, Socialism, and Democracy* (New York: Harper & Brothers, 1950), pp. 122–24. Copyright 1942, 1947 by Joseph A. Schumpeter. Copyright 1950 by Harper & Brothers.

interest. Pre-capitalist man is in fact no less "grabbing" than capitalist man. Peasant serfs for instance or warrior lords assert their self-interest with a brutal energy all their own. But capitalism develops rationality and adds a new edge to it in two interconnected ways.

First it exalts the monetary unit—not itself a creation of capitalism— into a unit of account. That is to say, capitalist practice turns the unit of money into a tool of rational cost-profit calculations, of which the towering monument is double-entry bookkeeping. Without going into this, we will notice that, primarily a product of the evolution of economic rationality, the cost-profit calculus in turn reacts upon that rationality; by crystallizing and defining numerically, it powerfully propels the logic of enterprise. And thus defined and quantified for the economic sector, this type of logic or attitude or method then starts upon its conqueror's career subjugating—rationalizing —man's tools and philosophies, his medical practice, his picture of the cosmos, his outlook on life, everything in fact including his concepts of beauty and justice and his spiritual ambitions.

SHERWOOD ANDERSON
1876-1941

SHERWOOD ANDERSON, BORN in Camden, Ohio, the son of a poor harness maker, spent his early adult years in drift and search. From peaceful patrol duty in the Spanish-American War, he turned to advertising in Chicago. After some success there, he became disenchanted and moved to Cleveland and then to Elyria, Ohio, where he was the manager of a paint factory in 1907. He began to compose his experiences, and the more he wrote the more estranged he became from his business and family life. In 1912, he left his factory office and wandered to Chicago where he spent his time writing advertising copy and developing a realistic literary style for his novels.

Anderson took part in the brief "literary renaissance" in Chicago, publishing *Winesburg, Ohio* in 1919. This work along with Sinclair Lewis's *Main Street* introduced a new realism into American literature. *Winesburg, Ohio* was drawn from Anderson's early life and evoked haunting national memories of a passing existence. Beneath its realistic style there is a blending of judgment, lament, and nostalgia for the loss of love, community, and native artisanship. These themes were continued in *Poor White* (1920), and appear in subsequent works such as *Many Marriages* (1922–1923) and *Dark Laughter* (1925). Although he was a prolific writer, his novels and stories did not move far from the refrains and echoes of his past.

In the late 1920's and early 1930's he became interested in the lot of the Southern mill worker, and during the depression he identified himself politically with the radical left.

Alfred Kazin wrote of Anderson, ". . . the significance of his whole career is that though he could catch, as no one else could, the inexpressible grandeur of those special moments in experience, he was himself caught between them."

[7]   Loom Dance

They had brought a "minute-man" into one of the Southern cotton-mill towns. A doctor told me this story. The minute-men come from the North. They are efficiency experts. The North, as everyone knows, is the old home of efficiency. The minute-man comes into a mill with a watch in his hand. He stands about. He is one of the fathers of "stretch-out" system. The idea is like this:

There is a woman here who works at the looms. She is a weaver. She is taking care, let us say, of 30 looms. The question is—is she doing all she can?

It is put up to her. "If you can take care of more looms you can make more money." The workers are all paid by the piece-work system.

"I will stand here with this watch in my hand. You go ahead and work. Be natural. Work as you always did.

"I will watch every movement you make. I will coordinate your movements.

"Now, you see you have stopped to gossip with another woman, another weaver.

"That time you talked for four minutes.

"Time is money, my dear.

From *The New Republic,* LXII (April 30, 1930), 292–94. Copyright © 1930 by *The New Republic.* Reprinted by permission.

"And you have gone to the toilet. You stayed in there seven minutes. Was that necessary? Could you not have done everything necessary in three minutes?

"Three minutes here, four minutes there. Minutes, you see, make hours and hours make cloth."

I said it was put up to her, the weaver. Well, you know how such things are put up to the employees in any factory. "I am going to try this," he says, "do you approve?"

"Sure."

What else is to be said?

There are plenty of people out of work, God knows.

You don't want to lose your job, do you?

(The boss speaking.)

"Well, I asked them about it. They all approved.

"Why I had several of them into my office. 'Is everything all right?' I asked. 'Are you perfectly satisfied about everything?'

" 'Sure,' they all said."

It should be understood, if you do not understand, that the weaver in the modern cotton mill does not run his loom. He does not pull levers. The loom runs on and on. It is so arranged that if one of the threads among many thousand threads breaks, the loom automatically stops.

It is the weaver's job to spring forward. The broken thread must be found. Down inside the loom there are little steel fingers that grasp the threads. The ends of the broken thread must be found and passed through the finger that is to hold just that thread. The weaver's knot must be tied. It is a swiftly made, hard little knot. It will not show in the finished cloth. The loom may run for a long time and no thread break, and then, in a minute, threads may break in several looms.

The looms in the weaving-rooms are arranged in long rows. The weaver passes up and down. Nowadays, in modern mills, she does not have to change the bobbins. The bobbins are automatically fed into the loom. When a bobbin has become empty it falls out and a new one takes its place. A full cylinder of bobbins is up there, atop the loom. The full bobbins fall into their places as loaded cartridges fall into place when a revolver is fired.

So there is the weaver. All she, or he, has to do is to walk up and down. Let us say that 20 or 30 looms are to be watched. The looms are of about the breadth of an ordinary writing desk or the chest of drawers standing in your bedroom.

You walk past 20 or 30 of them, keeping your eyes open. They are all in rapid motion, dancing. You must be on the alert. You are like a school teacher watching a group of children.

But these looms, these children of the weaver, do not stand still. They dance in their places. There is a play of light from the factory windows and from the white cloth against the dark frames of the looms.

Belts are flying. Wheels are turning.

The threads—often hundreds to the inch—lie closely in the loom, a little steel finger holding each thread. The bobbin flies across, putting in the cross threads. It flies so rapidly the eye cannot see it.

That is a dance, too.

The loom itself seems to jump off the floor. There is a quick jerky movement, a clatter. The loom is setting each cross thread firmly in place, making firm, smooth cloth.

The dance of the looms is a crazy dance. It is jerky, abrupt, mechanical. It would be interesting to see some dancer do a loom dance on the stage. A new kind of music would have to be found for it.

There are 15 looms dancing, 20, 30, 40. Lights are dancing over the looms. There is always, day in, day out, this strange jerky movement, infinitely complex. The noise in the room is terrific.

The job of the minute-man is to watch the operator. This woman makes too many false movements. "Do it like this."

The thing is to study the movements, not only of the weavers but of the machines. The thing is to more perfectly co-ordinate the two.

It is called by the weavers the "stretch-out."

It is possible by careful study, by watching an operator (a weaver) hour after hour, standing with watch in hand, following the weaver up and down, to increase the efficiency by as much as 100 percent. It has been done.

Instead of 36 looms, let us say 72. Something gained, eh? Every other operator replaced.

Let us say a woman weaver makes twelve dollars a week. Let her make 16. That will be better for her.

You still have $8 gained.

What about the operator replaced? What of her?

But you cannot think too much of that if you are to follow modern industry. To every factory new machines are coming. They all throw workmen out of work. That is the whole point. The best brains in America are engaged in that. They are making more and more complex, strange and wonderful machines that throw people out of work.

They don't do it for that reason. The mill owner doesn't buy for that reason. To think of mill owners as brutes is just nonsense. They have about as much chance to stop what is going on as you have.

What is going on is the most exciting thing in modern life. Modern industry is a river in flood, it is a flow of refined power.

It is a dance.

The minute-man the doctor told me about made a mistake. He was holding his watch on the wrong woman.

She had been compelled to go to the toilet and he followed her to the door and stood there, watch in hand.

It happened that the woman had a husband, also a weaver, working in the same room.

He stood watching the man who was holding the watch on his wife in there. His looms were dancing—the loom dance.

And then suddenly he began to dance. He hopped up and down in an absurd, jerky way. Cries, queer, seemingly meaningless cries, came from his throat.

He danced for a moment like that and then he sprang forward. He knocked the minute-man down. Other weavers, men and women, came running. Now they were all dancing up and down. Cries were coming from many throats.

The weaver who was the husband of the woman back of the door had knocked the minute-man down, and now was dancing upon his body. He kept making queer sounds. He may have been trying to make the music for the new loom dance.

The minute-man from the North was not a large man. He was slender and had blue eyes and light, curly hair and wore glasses.

The glasses had fallen on the floor.

His watch had fallen on the floor.

All the looms in the room kept running.

Lights danced in the room.

The looms kept dancing.

A weaver was dancing on a minute-man's watch.

A weaver was dancing on a minute-man's glasses.

Other weavers kept coming.

They came running. Men and women came from the spinning-room.

There were more cries.

There was music in the mill.

And really you must get into your picture the woman—in there.

We can't leave her out.

She would be trying, nervously, to arrange her clothes. She would have heard her husband's cries.

She would be dancing, grotesquely, in a confined place.

In all the mills, the women and girls hate more than anything else being watched when they go to the toilet.

They speak of that among themselves. They hate it more than they hate long hours and low wages.

There is a kind of deep human humiliation in that.

There is this secret part of me, this secret function, the waste of my body being eliminated. We do not speak of that. It is done secretly.

We must all do it and all know we must all do it. Rightly seen it is but a part of our relations with nature.

But we civilized people are no longer a part of nature. We live in houses. We go into factories.

These may be part of nature, too. We are trying to adjust ourselves. Give us time.

You—do not stand outside of this door to this little room, holding a watch in your hand, when I go in here.

There are some things in this world, even in our modern mass-production world, not permitted.

There are things that will make a weaver dance the crazy dance of the looms.

There was a minute-man who wanted to co-ordinate the movements of weavers to the movements of machines.

He did it.

The legs of weavers became hard and stiff like legs of looms. There was an intense up and down movement. Cries arose from many throats. They blended strangely with the clatter of looms.

As for the minute-man, some other men, foremen, superintendents and the like, got him out of there. They dragged him out at a side door and into a mill yard. The yard became filled with dancing, shouting men, women and girls. They got him into another machine, an automobile, and hurried him away. They patched him up. The doctor who patched him up told me the story.

He had some ribs broken and was badly bruised, but he lived all right. He did not go back into the mill.

The "stretch-out" system was dropped in that mill in the South. The loom dance of the weavers stopped it that time.

DANIEL BELL
1919-

DANIEL BELL TEACHES SOCIOLOGY at Columbia University, but he
has also made a career as a magazine editor and writer, having
worked as managing editor of *The New Leader* and as labor editor of *Fortune*
magazine. Industrial and political sociology are his major fields of interest. He
has written *Work and Its Discontents* (1956) and *The End of Ideology* (1960),
and edited *The New American Right* (1955).

[8]   *Technology and the Worker's Life*

The contemporary enterprise was set up to obey three peculiar tech-
nologics: the logic of size, the logic of "metric" time and the logic of
hierarchy. Each of the three, the product of engineering rationality, has
imposed on the worker a set of constraints with which he is forced to
wrestle every day. These condition the daily facts of his existence.

For the man whose working day is from eight in the morning to five in
the afternoon, the morning begins long before the time he is to arrive at
his place of work. After a hasty wash and a quick breakfast, he is off in his
car or on the streetcar, bus or subway; often he may have to spend an hour
or more in getting to the plant. (There seems to be a law, as Bertrand
Russell has noted, that improvements in transportation do not cut down

From Daniel Bell, *Work and Its Discontents* (Boston: Beacon Press, Inc., 1956),
pp. 3–5, 9–10, 45–47, 49–54. Reprinted by permission of The Free Press of Glencoe,
Illinois.

traveling time but merely increase the area over which people have to travel.)

Although this is the most obvious fact about modern work, few writers have concerned themselves with it, or with the underlying assumption: that large masses of human labor should be brought to a common place of work. The engineer believes that concentration is technologically efficient: under one roof there can be brought together the source of power, the raw materials, the parts and the assembly lines. So we find such huge megaliths as Willow Run, now used by General Motors, a sprawling shed spanning an area two-thirds of a mile long and a quarter of a mile wide; or such roofed-over, mile-long pavements as the Boeing plant in Wichita, Kansas.

This belief in the efficacy of size was conditioned by the type of energy first used—the limited amount of power available through the use of steam. Since steam dissipates quickly, the engineer tended to crowd as many productive units as possible along the same shaft, or within the range of steam pressure that could be carried by pipes without losses due to excessive condensation. These considerations led, too, to the bunching of workers in the layout of work, since the machines had to be located along a straight-line shafting.

The introduction of electric power and electric motors opened the way to greater flexibility; and within the plant these opportunities were taken. Newer work-flow designs have avoided the antiquated straight-line shafts and aisles of the older factory. Yet the outward size of the factory remained unchallenged. Why? In part because the engineer conceives of efficiency in technological terms alone; and he is able to do so because a major cost— the travel time of the worker—can be discounted. But the question can be posed: should large masses of persons be brought to a common place of work? Which is cheaper to transport: working men twice daily, or materials and mechanical parts, let us say, twice a week? As Percival and Paul Goodman so pertinently note in their book, *Communitas:* "The time of life of a piece of metal is not consumed while it waits for its truck; a piece of metal does not mind being compressed like a sardine." What the Goodmans propose is production in "bits and pieces" rather than integrated assembly. If the plants were located near workers' communities, the men would not have to travel; the processed materials would be brought to several places for manufacture, and the parts would then be collected for assembly. Yet the question is rarely considered, for few industries pay directly for their workers' travel time. Calculations in terms of market costs alone do not force the enterprise to take into account such factors as the time used in going to and from work, or the costs of roads and other transport to the factory site, which are paid for by the employee or by the community as a whole out of taxes.

In his travel to and from work the worker is chained by time. Time rules the work economy, its very rhythms and motions. (After consulting Gulliver on the functions of his watch, the Lilliputians came to the belief that it was his God.)

* * *

The logic of hierarchy, the third of the logics created by modern industry, is, thus, not merely the sociological fact of increased supervision which every complex enterprise demands, but a peculiarly technological imperative. In a simple division of labor, for example, the worker had a large measure of control over his own working conditions, i.e., the set-up and make-ready, the cleaning and repairing of machines, obtaining his own materials, and so on. Under a complex division of labor, these tasks pass out of his control and he must rely on management to see that they are properly done. This dependence extends along the entire process of production. As a result, modern industry has had to devise an entire new managerial superstructure which organizes and directs production. This superstructure draws in all possible brain work away from the shop; everything is centered in the planning and schedule and design departments. And in this new hierarchy there stands a figure known neither to the handicrafts nor to industry in its infancy—the technical employee. With him, the separation of functions becomes complete. The worker at the bottom, attending only to a detail, is divorced from any decision or modification about the product he is working on.

These three logics of size, time and hierarchy converge in that great achievement of industrial technology, the assembly line: the long parallel lines require huge shed space; the detailed breakdown of work imposes a set of mechanically paced and specified motions; the degree of coordination creates new technical, as well as social, hierarchies.

* * *

ARCADIA AND UTOPIA

. . . While the assembly line brought the work to the workers, tending to grip them bodily to the rhythm of the line, the vast development of automatic controls and the continuous flow creates the possibility of eliminating

the workers from production completely. On its present scale and complexity, the continuous-flow innovation dates back only to 1939, when
Standard Oil of New Jersey and M. W. Kellogg Company erected the first
of the oil industry's great fluid-catalytic crackers. In these new plants, the
raw material, fluid or gas, flows continuously in at one end, passes through
intricate processing stages and debouches in a 24-hour stream of products
at the other. The whole plant is run from central control rooms by a few
men at the control panels, while mobile maintenance crews take care of
any breakdowns. The new Ford engine plant in Cleveland, opened in 1952,
provides almost a continuous operation from the original pouring of sand
and the casting of molds to the flow of molten iron and the shaking out of
fully cast engine blocks, with few human hands involved in the operation
other than to speed the flow of work by checking empty gauges, and to
operate the high overhead cranes which lift the mass of metals. Thus
foundry work, the grimiest of human denigration, has given way to the
machine.

This new industrial revolution is symbolized in the word "automation."
The term itself was coined in 1948 by the engineering division of the Ford
Motor Company to describe the operations of some new "transfer machines"
which mechanically unload the stampings from the body presses and position them before machine tools that automatically drill and bore the holes
for other parts to be inserted. The purists among the engineers dismiss the
Ford process as "advanced mechanization," or grudgingly call it "Detroit
automation." For them the term "automation" is reserved for processes in
which high-speed, self-correcting (i.e. feedback) instruments control the
operations of other machines. Automatic devices, they point out, are quite
ancient. The Romans had an hydraulic float valve to regulate the water
level in their storage tanks. The Dutch used such devices to keep windmills facing into the wind. James Watt devised a "flyball governor" to keep
his steam engine clacking at constant speed. Quite ingeniously, the old
Yankee flour mills of 150 years ago operated with true "automation" principles: the grain from wagons was unloaded into a hopper where, after being mechanically weighed, it was carried by a screw-type conveyor and
bucket elevator to the top floor; there, by force of gravity, the grain flowed
into hoppers which regulated the amounts fed to the millstones; the ground
grain, now flour, was sifted mechanically through screens into barrels, and
conveyed away by barge or wagon.

Whatever the claims of the ancients, what is new today is the simultaneous introduction of so many different processes whereby direct human

labor has been eliminated and mechanical or electronic devices regulate the flow of work.

* * *

Americans, with their tendency to exaggerate new innovations, have conjured up wild fears about changes that automation may bring. Norbert Wiener, whose book on "cybernetics" was responsible in part for the vogue of "communication theory," has pictured a dismal world of unattended factories turning out mountains of goods which a jobless population will be unable to buy. Such projections are silly. Even if automatic controls were suddenly introduced, regardless of cost considerations, into all the factories that could use them, only about 8 per cent of the labor force would be directly affected.

It is evident that automation will produce disruptions; and many workers, particularly older ones, may find it difficult ever again to find suitable jobs. It is also likely that small geographical pockets of the United States may find themselves becoming "depressed areas" as old industries fade or are moved away. But it is unlikely that the economic effects of automation may be any greater, say, than the social disruptions which follow shifts in taste, or substitution of products, or changes in mores. The rise of a functional style in architecture, for example, has meant a decrease in the ranks of brick masons, plasterers, painters and molders. The substitution of oil for coal has cut in half the required number of miners. The fact that young people now marry at an earlier age has produced a sharp slump in the textile and clothing industries, for marrying earlier means that one dresses up less, dresses more casually and spends more of the family budget for house and furniture.

Whether the nation can absorb all such disruptions depends on the general level of economic activity, and this itself is a function of the productive growth of the economy. Over the last decade and a half Americans have learned, through a flexible tax and fiscal policy, how to regulate the economy and stimulate its growth. The government, as gyroscope, can offset overproduction and underconsumption. The question is largely one of politics rather than economics, of the willingness of the government to act, when necessary.

Automation, however, will have enormous social effects. Just as factory work impressed its rhythms on society, so the rhythms of automation will give a new character to work, living and leisure.

Automation will change the basic composition of the labor force, cre-

ating a new *salariat* instead of a *proletariat,* as automatic processes reduce
the number of industrial workers required in production. In the chemical
industry, for example, output rose, from 1947 to 1954, over 50 per cent,
while the number of "blue-collar" workers increased only 1.3 per cent. At
the same time, the number of non-production workers, that is, professional,
supervisory, clerical, and sales personnel, increased by 50 per cent. In 1947,
the ratio of production workers to non-production workers was 3:1. In
1954, in a seven-year period, the ratio had dropped to 2:1.

In its most important consequence, the advent of automation means
that a corporation no longer has to worry about a large labor supply. This
means that new plants can be located away from major cities, and closer to
markets or to sources of raw materials and fuels. Sylvania, for example,
which has forty-three plants, has built its most recent ones in such out-of-
the-way places as Nelsonville, Ohio; Burlington, Iowa; and Shawnee, Oklahoma. The company has also insisted that its plants be smaller, and it
placed a limit of 700 persons to be employed in a plant. In this way, the
corporation can exercise new social controls. The works manager can know
all the men personally, and the social divisions of the small town will
recapitulate the social gradations in the plant. Under these conditions a new
manorial society may be in the making.

The decentralization of industry may equally revolutionize the social
topography of the United States as a whole. As new plants are built on the
outskirts of towns and workers live along the radial fringes of the spreading
city, the distinction of the urban and the surburban becomes increasingly
obliterated. In its place may appear one scenery, standard for town, suburb,
countryside and wild. And environment, as William James has noted, is an
extension of ego. In the new topography we may arrive at what the editors
of the British *Architectural Review* have called "Subutopia."

But more than topographical changes are involved. The very matutinal
patterns will change as well. The major economic fact is that, under automation, depreciation rather than labor becomes the major cost. And when
labor is relatively cheap, it becomes uneconomical to keep an enormously
expensive machine idle. To write off the high capital investment, more and
more of the automated plants may expand shift operations in order to keep
the plant running twenty-four hours a day. And so more and more workers
may find themselves working "out of hours." In such work communities, the
rhythms of sleeping, eating, social and sexual life become skewed. A man
on the regular eight-to-four shift follows a cycle of *work, recreation* and
sleep, while during the same day the fellow on the four-to-twelve shift is on
a cycle of *recreation, work* and *sleep,* while the night man goes through his

twenty-four hours in *sleep, recreation* and *work*. Where this occurs, friendship patterns may change abruptly. When the wife and children follow a "normal" routine while the man sleeps through the day, home and sex life become disjointed.

This break-up of the work day—and why should men work while the sun is shining; it is a relic of rustic days—is accentuated by a different aspect of the changing economic pattern of the country. As incomes rise and hours are reduced, more and more families begin to spend increasing amounts of money on recreation and travel. This rising demand for entertainment and services, for hotels, motels, vacation resorts, garages, theatres, restaurants, television, requires more individuals to work "out-of-hours"— evenings and week-ends—in catering to these desires. In the next decade perhaps a fourth or more of the labor force will be working special hours. The multiplication of such special work groups, with their own internal life and modes of recreation, is one of the features of a consumer-oriented culture.

For the individual worker, automation may bring a new concept of self. For in automation men finally lose the "feel" of work. Whatever the derogating effects, the men who use power-driven tools sense these instruments, almost as in driving an automobile, as an extension and enlargement of their own bodies, their machines responding, almost organically, to their commands and adding new dexterity and power to their own muscle skills. As a machine tender, a man now stands outside work, and whatever control once existed by "setting a bogey" (i.e., restricting output) is finally shattered. As one steelworker said, "You can't slow down the continuous annealer in order to get some respite." With the new dial-sets, too, muscular fatigue is replaced by mental tension, the interminable watching, the endless concentration. (In the puritan morality, the devil could always find work for "idle hands," and the factory kept a man's hands busy. But that morality ignored the existence of the fantasy life, and its effects. Now, with machine watching, there will be idle hands, but no "idle minds." An advance in morality?)

Yet there is a gain for the worker in these new processes. Automation requires workers who can think of the plant as a whole. If there is less craft, less specialization, there is the need to know more than one job, to link boiler and turbine, to know the press and the borer and to relate their jobs to each other.

Most important, perhaps, there may be an end, too, to the measurement of work. Modern industry began not with the factory but with the measurement of work. When the worth of the product was defined in production units, the worth of the worker was similarly gauged. Under the unit concept, the time-study engineers calculated that a worker would produce more units for more money. This was the assumption of the wage-incentive schemes (which actually are output-incentive schemes), and the engineering morality of a "fair day's pay for a fair day's work."

But under automation, with continuous flow, a worker's worth can no longer be evaluated in production units. Hence output-incentive plans, with their involved measurement techniques, may vanish. In their place, as Adam Abruzzi foretells, may arise a new work morality. Worth will be defined not in terms of a "one best way," not by the slide rule and stop watch, not in terms of fractioned time or units of production, but on the basis of planning and organizing and the continuously smooth functioning of the operation. Here the team, not the individual worker, will assume a new importance; and the social engineer will come into his own. And work itself?

MAX WEBER
1864-1920

MAX WEBER'S WORK has become an ideal for modern social scientists. The passionate devotion with which he pursued his calling was worthy of the Puritan saints he studied so well. Yet, his style largely concealed the feeling which he gave to the task of probing the recesses of social history in search of the patterns that would make it meaningful.

From 1882, when he attended the University of Heidelberg, through his years at the universities of Berlin and Göttingen, he was undistinguishable from other law students and young graduates. But his Ph.D. and higher-law degree dissertations, written in 1889 and 1891, demonstrated remarkable scholarly talents. From 1892 to 1897 he took on a huge amount of work as governmental consultant, research worker, and professor of economics at Freiburg University and then at Heidelberg. After his father's death in 1897, his burdens overwhelmed him and he suffered from severe depressions and anxieties. Not until 1902 was he able to resume his teaching and scholarly pursuits.

In 1904 Weber visited the United States, and his sharp observations enriched his works on Protestantism and capitalism and on bureaucracy and democracy. The years until his death were taken up with intensive study and writing, punctuated by such duties as consultant to a government commission drafting the Weimar Constitution.

In politics Weber combined a dutiful commitment to the fate of Germany with severe criticism of many of his country's leaders, parties, classes, and institutions. His philosophy of life was stoic, his outlook on the future—tragic.

So many concerns of the contemporary social scientist were stimulated by Weber: capitalism and Protestantism, bureaucracy, the sociology of religions, a typology of authority, the subtle interdependencies of legal, political, and economic institutions. Much of his writing on these subjects appeared in his famous two-volume *Wirtschaft und Gesellschaft*. In these studies he abstracted a wealth of historical data by using ideal-type concepts to define his terms clearly and by linking them systematically in general theories.

Weber addressed himself as well to problems of methodology in the social sciences and to questions of ethics in science and politics. One of his major themes was that of the increasing rationalization of Western civilization. In his typical style, Weber both admired its value and shuddered at its possibilities.

[9]   The Changing Spirit of Capitalism

The Puritan wanted to work in a calling; we are forced to do so. For when asceticism was carried out of monastic cells into everyday life, and began to dominate worldly morality, it did its part in building the tremendous cosmos of the modern economic order. This order is now bound to the technical and economic conditions of machine production which to-day determine the lives of all the individuals who are born into this mechanism, not only those directly concerned with economic acquisition, with irresistible force. Perhaps it will so determine them until the last ton of fossilized coal is burnt.* In Baxter's view the care for external goods should only lie on the shoulders of the "saint like a light cloak, which can be thrown aside at any moment." † But fate decreed that the cloak should become an iron cage.

* [Or until the last particle of matter is turned into energy! Ed. Note.]
† [Richard Baxter (1615–1691) was one of the prominent English Puritan writers who Weber believed exemplified the Protestant-capitalist man. Ed. Note.]

From Max Weber, *The Protestant Ethic and the Spirit of Capitalism*, trans. Talcott Parsons (New York: Charles Scribner's Sons, 1958), pp. 181–82. Reprinted by permission of Charles Scribner's Sons and George Allen & Unwin Ltd.

Since asceticism undertook to remodel the world and to work out its ideals in the world, material goods have gained an increasing and finally an inexorable power over the lives of men as at no previous period in history. To-day the spirit of religious asceticism—whether finally, who knows?—has escaped from the cage. But victorious capitalism, since it rests on mechanical foundations, needs its support no longer. The rosy blush of its laughing heir, the Enlightenment, seems also to be irretrievably fading, and the idea of duty in one's calling prowls about in our lives like the ghost of dead religious beliefs. Where the fulfilment of the calling cannot directly be related to the highest spiritual and cultural values, or when, on the other hand, it need not be felt simply as economic compulsion, the individual generally abandons the attempt to justify it at all. In the field of its highest development, in the United States, the pursuit of wealth, stripped of its religious and ethical meaning, tends to become associated with purely mundane passions, which often actually give it the character of sport.

No one knows who will live in this cage in the future, or whether at the end of this tremendous development entirely new prophets will arise, or there will be a great rebirth of old ideas and ideals, or, if neither, mechanized petrification, embellished with a sort of convulsive self-importance. For of the last stage of this cultural development, it might well be truly said: "Specialists without spirit, sensualists without heart; this nullity imagines that it has attained a level of civilization never before achieved."

Bureaucracy and Leadership

MAX WEBER *
1864-1920

[10] Bureaucracy

TECHNICAL ADVANTAGES
OF BUREAUCRATIC ORGANIZATION

The decisive reason for the advance of bureaucratic organization has always been its purely technical superiority over any other form of organization. The fully developed bureaucratic mechanism compares with other organizations exactly as does the machine with the non-mechanical modes of production.

Precision, speed, unambiguity, knowledge of the files, continuity, discretion, unity, strict subordination, reduction of friction and of material and personal costs—these are raised to the optimum point in the strictly bu-

* For a biographical sketch of Weber, see pages 84–85.

From *From Max Weber: Essays in Sociology,* translated and edited by H. H. Gerth and C. Wright Mills (New York: Oxford University Press, Inc., 1946), pp. 214, 215–16, 228–29, 232–33. Copyright 1946 by Oxford University Press, Inc. Reprinted by permission.

reaucratic administration, and especially in its monocratic form. As compared with all collegiate, honorific, and avocational forms of administration, trained bureaucracy is superior on all these points. And as far as complicated tasks are concerned, paid bureaucratic work is not only more precise but, in the last analysis, it is often cheaper than even formally unremunerated honorific service.

* * *

Today, it is primarily the capitalist market economy which demands that the official business of the administration be discharged precisely, unambiguously, continuously, and with as much speed as possible. Normally, the very large, modern capitalist enterprises are themselves unequalled models of strict bureaucratic organization. Business management throughout rests on increasing precision, steadiness, and, above all, the speed of operations. This, in turn, is determined by the peculiar nature of the modern means of communication, including, among other things, the news service of the press. The extraordinary increase in the speed by which public announcements, as well as economic and political facts, are transmitted exerts a steady and sharp pressure in the direction of speeding up the tempo of administrative reaction towards various situations. The optimum of such reaction time is normally attained only by a strictly bureaucratic organization.

Bureaucratization offers above all the optimum possibility for carrying through the principle of specializing administrative functions according to purely objective considerations. Individual performances are allocated to functionaries who have specialized training and who by constant practice learn more and more. The 'objective' discharge of business primarily means a discharge of business according to *calculable rules* and 'without regard for persons.'

'Without regard for persons' is also the watchword of the 'market' and, in general, of all pursuits of naked economic interests. A consistent execution of bureaucratic domination means the leveling of status 'honor.' Hence, if the principle of the free-market is not at the same time restricted, it means the universal domination of the 'class situation.' That this consequence of bureaucratic domination has not set in everywhere, parallel to the extent of bureaucratization, is due to the differences among possible principles by which politics may meet their demands.

The second element mentioned, 'calculable rules,' also is of paramount importance for modern bureaucracy. The peculiarity of modern culture, and specifically of its technical and economic basis, demands this very 'calculability' of results. When fully developed, bureaucracy also stands, in a specific sense, under the principle of *sine ira ac studio.* Its specific nature, which is welcomed by capitalism, develops the more perfectly the more the bureaucracy is 'dehumanized,' the more completely it succeeds in eliminating from official business love, hatred, and all purely personal, irrational, and emotional elements which escape calculation. This is the specific nature of bureaucracy and it is appraised as its special virtue.

The more complicated and specialized modern culture becomes, the more its external supporting apparatus demands the personally detached and strictly 'objective' *expert,* in lieu of the master of older social structures, who was moved by personal sympathy and favor, by grace and gratitude. Bureaucracy offers the attitudes demanded by the external apparatus of modern culture in the most favorable combination.

*   *   *

BUREAUCRACY AND DEMOCRACY

The progress of bureaucratization in the state administration itself is a parallel phenomenon of democracy, as is quite obvious in France, North America, and now in England. Of course one must always remember that the term 'democratization' can be misleading. The *demos* itself, in the sense of an inarticulate mass, never 'governs' larger associations; rather, it is governed, and its existence only changes the way in which the executive leaders are selected and the measure of influence which the *demos,* or better, which social circles from its midst are able to exert upon the content and the direction of administrative activities by supplementing what is called 'public opinion.' 'Democratization,' in the sense here intended, does not necessarily mean an increasingly active share of the governed in the authority of the social structure. This may be a result of democratization, but it is not necessarily the case.

We must expressly recall at this point that the political concept of democracy, deduced from the 'equal rights' of the governed, includes these postulates: (1) prevention of the development of a closed status group of officials in the interest of a universal accessibility of office, and (2) minimization of the authority of officialdom in the interest of expanding the sphere of influence of 'public opinion' as far as practicable. Hence, wherever possible, political democracy strives to shorten the term of office by election and recall and by not binding the candidate to a special expertness. Thereby democracy inevitably comes into conflict with the bureaucratic tendencies which, by its fight against notable rule, democracy has produced. The generally loose term 'democratization' cannot be used here, in so far as it is understood to mean the minimization of the civil servants' ruling power in favor of the greatest possible 'direct' rule of the *demos,* which in practice means the respective party leaders of the *demos.* The most decisive thing here—indeed it is rather exclusively so—is the *leveling of the governed* in opposition to the ruling and bureaucratically articulated group, which in its turn may occupy a quite autocratic position, both in fact and in form.

* * *

THE PERMANENT CHARACTER
OF THE BUREAUCRATIC MACHINE

Once it is fully established, bureaucracy is among those social structures which are the hardest to destroy. Bureaucracy is *the* means of carrying 'community action' over into rationally ordered 'societal action.' Therefore, as an instrument for 'societalizing' relations of power, bureaucracy has been and is a power instrument of the first order—for the one who controls the bureaucratic apparatus.

Under otherwise equal conditions, a 'societal action,' which is methodically ordered and led, is superior to every resistance of 'mass' or even of 'communal action.' And where the bureaucratization of administration has been completely carried through, a form of power relation is established that is practically unshatterable.

The individual bureaucrat cannot squirm out of the apparatus in which he is harnessed. In contrast to the honorific or avocational 'notable,' the professional bureaucrat is chained to his activity by his entire material and ideal existence. In the great majority of cases, he is only a single cog in an ever-moving mechanism which prescribes to him an essentially fixed route of march. The official is entrusted with specialized tasks and normally the mechanism cannot be put into motion or arrested by him, but only from the very top. The individual bureaucrat is thus forged to the community of all the functionaries who are integrated into the mechanism. They have a common interest in seeing that the mechanism continues its functions and that the societally exercised authority carries on.

The ruled, for their part, cannot dispense with or replace the bureaucratic apparatus of authority once it exists. For this bureaucracy rests upon expert training, a functional specialization of work, and an attitude set for habitual and virtuoso-like mastery of single yet methodically integrated functions. If the official stops working, or if his work is forcefully interrupted, chaos results, and it is difficult to improvise replacements from among the governed who are fit to master such chaos. This holds for public administration as well as for private economic management. More and more the material fate of the masses depends upon the steady and correct functioning of the increasingly bureaucratic organizations of private capitalism. The idea of eliminating these organizations becomes more and more utopian.

*   *   *

The objective indispensability of the once-existing apparatus, with its peculiar, 'impersonal' character, means that the mechanism—in contrast to feudal orders based upon personal piety—is easily made to work for anybody who knows how to gain control over it. A rationally ordered system of officials continues to function smoothly after the enemy has occupied the area; he merely needs to change the top officials. This body of officials continues to operate because it is to the vital interest of everyone concerned, including above all the enemy.

*   *   *

THE POWER POSITION OF BUREAUCRACY

Everywhere the modern state is undergoing bureaucratization. But whether the *power* of bureaucracy within the polity is universally increasing must here remain an open question.

The fact that bureaucratic organization is technically the most highly developed means of power in the hands of the man who controls it does not determine the weight that bureaucracy as such is capable of having in a particular social structure. The ever-increasing 'indispensability' of the officialdom, swollen to millions, is no more decisive for this question than is the view of some representatives of the proletarian movement that the economic indispensability of the proletarians is decisive for the measure of their social and political power position. If 'indispensability' were decisive, then where slave labor prevailed and where freemen usually abhor work as a dishonor, the 'indispensable' slaves ought to have held the positions of power, for they were at least as indispensable as officials and proletarians are today. Whether the power of bureaucracy as such increases cannot be decided *a priori* from such reasons. The drawing in of economic interest groups or other non-official experts, or the drawing in of non-expert lay representatives, the establishment of local, inter-local, or central parliamentary or other representative bodies, or of occupational associations— these *seem* to run directly against the bureaucratic tendency. How far this appearance is the truth must be discussed in another chapter rather than in this purely formal and typological discussion. In general, only the following can be said here:

Under normal conditions, the power position of a fully developed bureaucracy is always overtowering. The 'political master' finds himself in the position of the 'dilettante' who stands opposite the 'expert,' facing the trained official who stands within the management of administration. This holds whether the 'master' whom the bureaucracy serves is a 'people,' equipped with the weapons of 'legislative initiative,' the 'referendum,' and the right to remove officials, or a parliament, elected on a more aristocratic or more 'democratic' basis and equipped with the right to vote a lack of confidence, or with the actual authority to vote it. It holds whether the master is an aristocratic, collegiate body, legally or actually based on self-recruitment, or whether he is a popularly elected president, a hereditary and 'absolute' or a 'constitutional' monarch.

ROBERT MICHELS
1876-1936

POLITICAL SCIENTIST, SOCIOLOGIST, AND ECONOMIST, Robert Michels thought of himself as an intellectual intermediary between the cultures of Germany and Italy. He brought German sociology to Italy, editing and translating the work of Georg Simmel and Max Weber, and carried Italian social science to Germany, applying to the study of German political institutions the principles of Gaetano Mosca and Vilfredo Pareto. The relationship between Michels and Pareto, however, was complex and stormy. Michels said that whenever he borrowed an idea from Pareto, he expressed his gratitude by citing the source, but the courtesy, he charged, was not returned.

Michels was born in Cologne, Germany, of a wealthy family which had produced manufacturers and generals. He traveled extensively as a young man, at an early age became an admirer of Italian culture, and studied in several European cities, attending the universities of Paris, Munich, Leipzig, Halle, and Turin. His political activity began in the syndicalist and radical left wing of the German Social-Democratic party. He was an intimate friend of Georges Sorel and Arturo Labriola, well-known syndicalist and socialist theorists and revolutionaries, and his radical political activity before World War I provided the experience for later writing about political parties, the labor movement, and the political role of intellectuals.

Michels grew disillusioned with the Social-Democratic party—with its tendency to compromise and to desert ideals, the absence of democratic control in its own internal organization, and its bureaucratic stagnation. But the failures of the party, he concluded, were implicit in the very structure of organized life and caused the defeat of democracy and equality in all social organizations. He moved away from socialism and democratic egalitarianism to an aristocratic liberalism, but insisted that democratic principles must be retained as critical and regulative ideals.

Since his early radical opinions had made it impossible for Michels to have an academic career in Germany, he began teaching in Italy at the University of Turin in 1906. In 1914 he moved to the University of Basel in Switzerland

and thereafter lectured occasionally at other places, including the University of Chicago in 1927. He was called to the University of Perugia by Mussolini in 1928, where he spent the rest of his life teaching. He remained aloof from the Fascist regime, however, and, like Gaetano Mosca and Benedetto Croce often confronted Mussolini with defiance. Just before his death he was engaged in a study of the restratification of European societies after World War I, employing the principle of recurrent elites.

[11]   The Trend to Oligarchy

Leadership is a necessary phenomenon in every form of social life. Consequently it is not the task of science to inquire whether this phenomenon is good or evil, or predominantly one or the other. But there is great scientific value in the demonstration that every system of leadership is incompatible with the most essential postulates of democracy. We are now aware that the law of the historic necessity of oligarchy is primarily based upon a series of facts of experience. Like all other scientific laws, sociological laws are derived from empirical observation. In order, however, to deprive our axiom of its purely descriptive character, and to confer upon it that status of analytical explanation which can alone transform a formula into a law, it does not suffice to contemplate from a unitary outlook those phenomena which may be empirically established; we must also study the determining causes of these phenomena. Such has been our task.

Now, if we leave out of consideration the tendency of the leaders to organize themselves and to consolidate their interests, and if we leave also out of consideration the gratitude of the led towards the leaders, and the general immobility and passivity of the masses, we are led to conclude that the principal cause of oligarchy in the democratic parties is to be found in the technical indispensability of leadership.

The process which has begun in consequence of the differentiation of functions in the party is completed by a complex of qualities which the leaders acquire through their detachment from the mass. At the outset, leaders arise SPONTANEOUSLY; their functions are ACCESSORY and GRATUITOUS. Soon, however, they become PROFESSIONAL leaders, and in this second stage of development they are STABLE and IRREMOVABLE.

From Robert Michels, *Political Parties* (Glencoe, Ill.: The Free Press, 1949), pp. 417–22. Reprinted by permission.

It follows that the explanation of the oligarchical phenomenon which thus results is partly PSYCHOLOGICAL; oligarchy derives, that is to say, from the psychical transformations which the leading personalities in the parties undergo in the course of their lives. But also, and still more, oligarchy depends upon what we may term the PSYCHOLOGY OF ORGANIZATION ITSELF, that is to say, upon the tactical and technical necessities which result from the consolidation of every disciplined political aggregate. Reduced to its most concise expression, the fundamental sociological law of political parties (the term "political" being here used in its most comprehensive significance) may be formulated in the following terms: "It is organization which gives birth to the dominion of the elected over the electors, of the mandataries over the mandators, of the delegates over the delegators. Who says organization, says oligarchy."

Every party organization represents an oligarchical power grounded upon a democratic basis. We find everywhere electors and elected. Also we find everywhere that the power of the elected leaders over the electing masses is almost unlimited. The oligarchical structure of the building suffocates the basic democratic principle. That which IS oppresses THAT WHICH OUGHT TO BE. For the masses, this essential difference between the reality and the ideal remains a mystery. Socialists often cherish a sincere belief that a new *élite* of politicians will keep faith better than did the old. The notion of the representation of popular interests, a notion to which the great majority of democrats, and in especial the working-class masses of the German-speaking lands, cleave with so much tenacity and confidence, is an illusion engendered by a false illumination, is an effect of mirage. In one of the most delightful pages of his analysis of modern Don Quixotism, Alphonse Daudet shows us how the "brav' commandant" Bravida, who has never quitted Tarascon, gradually comes to persuade himself, influenced by the burning southern sun, that he has been to Shanghai and has had all kinds of heroic adventures. Similarly the modern proletariat, enduringly influenced by glib-tongued persons intellectually superior to the mass, ends by believing that by flocking to the poll and entrusting its social and economic cause to a delegate, its direct participation in power will be assured.

The formation of oligarchies within the various forms of democracy is the outcome of organic necessity, and consequently affects every organization, be it socialist or even anarchist. Haller * long ago noted that in every

* [Karl Ludwig von Haller, 1768–1854. The Swiss political theorist was known during the period of reaction to the French Revolution for his conservative social philosophy. Ed. Note.]

form of social life relationships of dominion and of dependence are created by Nature herself. The supremacy of the leaders in the democratic
and revolutionary parties has to be taken into account in every historic
situation present and to come, even though only a few and exceptional
minds will be fully conscious of its existence. The mass will never rule except *in abstracto*. Consequently the question we have to discuss is not
whether ideal democracy is realizable, but rather to what point and in what
degree democracy is desirable, possible, and realizable at a given moment.
In the problem as thus stated we recognize the fundamental problem of
politics as a science. Whoever fails to perceive this must, as Sombart * says,
either be so blind and fanatical as not to see that the democratic current
daily makes undeniable advance, or else must be so inexperienced and
devoid of critical faculty as to be unable to understand that all order and
all civilization must exhibit aristocratic features. The great error of socialists, an error committed in consequence of their lack of adequate psychological knowledge, is to be found in their combination of pessimism regarding the present, with rosy optimism and immeasurable confidence
regarding the future. A realistic view of the mental condition of the masses
shows beyond question that even if we admit the possibility of moral improvement in mankind, the human materials with whose use politicians and
philosophers cannot dispense in their plans of social reconstruction are not
of a character to justify excessive optimism. Within the limits of time for
which human provision is possible, optimism will remain the exclusive
privilege of utopian thinkers.

The socialist parties, like the trade unions, are living forms of social
life. As such they react with the utmost energy against any attempt to
analyse their structure or their nature, as if it were a method of vivisection.
When science attains to results which conflict with their apriorist ideology,
they revolt with all their power. Yet their defence is extremely feeble. Those
among the representatives of such organizations whose scientific earnestness
and personal good faith make it impossible for them to deny outright the
existence of oligarchical tendencies in every form of democracy, endeavour
to explain these tendencies as the outcome of a kind of atavism in the mentality of the masses, characteristic of the youth of the movement. The
masses, they assure us, are still infected by the oligarchic virus simply because they have been oppressed during long centuries of slavery, and have
never yet enjoyed an autonomous existence. The socialist regime, however,
will soon restore them to health, and will furnish them with all the capac-

* [Werner Sombart, who is discussed in Chapter III. Ed. Note.]

ity necessary for self-government. Nothing could be more anti-scientific than the supposition that as soon as socialists have gained possession of governmental power it will suffice for the masses to exercise a little control over their leaders to secure that the interests of these leaders shall coincide perfectly with the interests of the led. This idea may be compared with the view of Jules Guesde, no less anti-scientific than anti-Marxist (though Guesde proclaims himself a Marxist), that whereas Christianity has made God into a man, socialism will make man into a god.

The objective immaturity of the mass is not a mere transitory phenomenon which will disappear with the progress of democratization *au lendemain du socialisme.* On the contrary, it derives from the very nature of the mass as mass, for this, even when organized, suffers from an incurable incompetence for the solution of the diverse problems which present themselves for solution—because the mass *per se* is amorphous, and therefore needs division of labour, specialization, and guidance. "L'espèce humaine veut être gouvernée; elle le sera. J'ai honte de mon espèce," wrote Proudhon from his prison in 1850. Man as individual is by nature predestined to be guided, and to be guided all the more in proportion as the functions of life undergo division and subdivision. To an enormously greater degree is guidance necessary for the social group.

From this chain of reasoning and from these scientific convictions it would be erroneous to conclude that we should renounce all endeavours to ascertain the limits which may be imposed upon the powers exercised over the individual by oligarchies (state, dominant class, party, etc.). It would be an error to abandon the desperate enterprise of endeavouring to discover a social order which will render possible the complete realization of the idea of popular sovereignty. . . .

III

Political responses

DURING THE INTERBELLUM, the twilight of modernism, men responded to the sense of crisis in several ways. Those who accepted the notion of a crisis of civilization did not exhibit, as a rule, the apathy and despair that seem to accompany the idea in postmodern days, but instead sounded the alarm and called for action to meet the danger, to stem the tide. Others, who believed that not civilization but specific institutions—economic, political, or social—were in danger, also called for action. The rest, who rejected the notion of crisis altogether and instead saw in events nothing more than rapid changes and temporary dislocations, remained optimistic and active. Pragmatism with its political strategy of "social engineering" was the dominant philosophy.

The twenties and thirties were a period of intense political interest and activity. Old creeds revived and new theoretical alignments were drawn up. Political reflection and discussion thrived in a climate of experimentalism. Politics won not only popular enthusiasm but also the attention of philosophers, scientists, and men of letters, who entered the arena of public debate without reluctance.

In this period men responded to particular ideas for a new reason: olympians and titans had subscribed to a concept because it was *true,* the pragmatic men of the interbellum because it was *useful*. These men rejected formalistic and rationalistic definitions of truth; they cared more about the consequences of their ideas. The title of Max Lerner's book, *Ideas Are Weapons,* captures the prevailing attitude. No social theory drew attention unless it was also a strategy. Inexorable laws of nature and of history had lost their charm. Instead, men preferred to concentrate on programs to be accomplished by human effort and applied intelligence. It is as if the engine of the olympian express had failed, but the passengers believed they could still reach the utopian destination if they were to get out and push.

THE FAITH IN EFFORT

The philosophic foundations of pragmatism, on which new patterns of social and political thought in the interbellum were often based, were established in the previous generation by C. S. Peirce (1840–1914) and William James (1842–1910). In the interbellum, pragmatism and instrumentalism were elaborated further by John Dewey in the United States, F. C. S. Schiller in England, and Hans Vaihinger in Germany. The new society demanded social reform. Pragmatism was the ideal philosophy for that moment in history, for it made skepticism a virtue and gave men a theoretical ground for social action.

William James said in his *Essays on Pragmatism* that "theories . . . become instruments" and tell us "the ways in which existing realities may be *changed.*" Out of each idea must be extracted its "practical cash value," for the function of thought is to help us control the world.

Knowledge rests on useful fictions, Hans Vaihinger (1852–1933) argued similarly in *The Philosophy of As-If,* and neither theory nor practice can get along without fictions. "What we call *truth* is really only the most expedient form of error." There is no absolute or objective standard of truth, and "The higher aspects of life are based upon noble delusions." Acting "as if" ideas were true makes them true.

Besides a philosophic base, the reform movement also required a theory of society more congenial to calculated change and social welfare than the laissez-faire conceptions of Herbert Spencer and his American counterpart, William Graham Sumner (1840–1910). Spencer's theories of social evolution gave way to the sociology of Lester Frank Ward (1841–1913), which respected human planning and effort. Human evolution is different from animal evolution, Ward argued in his books *Pure Sociology* and *Applied Sociology,* for "the environment transforms the animal, while man transforms the environment." Every time man has touched "matter . . . with the wand of reason it has responded by satisfying a want." Against Spencer and Sumner, Ward declared that civilization was improved by rational intervention, and that no human institution was outside the realm of the spirit of improvement: "Government is one of [the] artificial products of man's devising, and his right to change it is the same as his right to create it. That he has greatly improved it there is no doubt; that he will still further perfect it there is every promise." [1]

Ward's theories were welcomed by the writers of the interbellum, for he had developed a theory of society that allowed planning to cooperate with evolution, that demolished laissez-faire sociology, and that argued powerfully for *meliorism*—the activity that the later writers called "social engineering."

With such a conception of society and with pragmatism as a philosophic foundation, men were armed for the task of reform, and the battleground on which ideologies realigned and closed ranks was the field of political economy.

POLITICAL RESPONSES TO ECONOMIC ISSUES

The question of economic planning and the nature of the good society had been stimulated by the fate of the economy during the war. Indeed, governments had intervened in economic activity before 1914—consider the history of imperialism, protective tariffs, and welfare legislation—but World War I had permitted extraordinary controls, establishing the precedent, however fumbling and hesitant, of a planned economy. For the first time in the modern world, material resources, economic wealth, and productive energy were organized under governmental control. Even moral sentiments came into its sphere of dominion to satisfy the political demand for patriotism and loyalty.

After the war, a "return to normalcy" was officially proclaimed, but economic life was never the same again, and by the time of the Great Depression the question of what to do about the economy was the major topic of political deliberation. In the range of political thought responding to the changes in economic life, five major positions answered the question

[1] Lester F. Ward, *The Psychic Factors of Civilization* (2nd ed.; Boston: Ginn & Company, 1906), p. 287.

of how much government control was required in the economic system.

At the extreme left, anarchists and syndicalists argued that a good society would be without a state. Economic activity, they declared, was natural and spontaneous as compared to the artificial and coercive nature of political activity. The free society would have an economy but no political system. At the extreme right, totalitarian theorists argued that war is merely an extension of politics, and since politics controls and directs all of life within the state, it follows that the economy should be subordinated to political and military necessities. In the minds of most totalitarian theorists and in the reality of the totalitarian systems, power emerged as total control, pressing its claim over every area of life.

Between these two extremes stood three more moderate positions. The old political and economic theory associated with the Austrian and Manchester schools of economics, sometimes called laissez-faire liberalism and usually identified today as a conservative position, persevered, condemning the changes in modern society and arguing that a free society existed only when political and economic spheres were kept separate. Political activity was to be restricted to keeping order and to performing a limited number of traditional functions.

The measures taken by governments to cope with the depression of the thirties stimulated a theory of welfare capitalism and the notion of a mixed economy. This position recommended broad social legislation for the benefit of low-income groups, government spending to control the business cycle, progressive taxation, and subsidies for ailing industries. Today this position is usually identified as liberal in its politics.

Finally, democratic socialism and industrial democracy were the positions of men who argued that no society could be free so long as economic life—especially the process of production—was dominated by private groups. Socialists claimed that the forces of production belonged to the community as a whole, that the public should control the instruments of production, that economic policy should be made by democratic methods, and that the managers of economic institutions should be held responsible to the people.

THE CONCENTRATION OF ECONOMIC POWER

The economic systems of all the industrial societies, whether capitalist democracy, Fascist command economy, or Soviet state economy, had similar characteristics. Each developed forms of scientific management, labor discipline, and economic concentration.

Although Lenin had previously condemned scientific management, in 1919 he reversed himself and proclaimed: "We should try out every scientific and progressive suggestion of the Taylor system. . . ." [2] The Soviet economy was constrained to adopt forms of industrial organization and discipline very similar to those of the capitalist systems. Moreover, Lenin urged:

Our gains, our decrees, our laws, our plans, must be secured by the solid forms of everyday labor discipline. This is the most difficult, but also the most promising, problem, for only its solution will give us socialism. We must learn to combine the stormy, energetic breaking of all restraint on the part of the toiling masses with iron discipline during work, with absolute submission to the will of one person, the Soviet director, during work. [3]

Within the capitalist societies, as the rationalization of economic processes and the advance of technology brought the workers' behavior under more efficient control, the structure and social function of the economic enterprise was changing. Manufacturing and financial corporations grew to giant size, absorbing smaller units or forcing them out of existence. Continental economies were dominated by interlocking cartels. In the United States, A. A. Berle and G. C. Means in their well-known study *The Modern Corporation and Private Property* (1932) described the gigantic growth of the corporation as the dominant form of economic organization. Internally, the corporation drifted toward managerial oligarchy; externally, it assumed political functions, informally absorbing powers that had belonged exclusively to the state.

Liberals and socialists as well as some conservatives deplored the trend toward monopolies and the growing concentration of economic power and wealth. Cartels and large corporations attracted the attention of critics of the economy who observed that these very large economic units were in fact controlled by a small circle of managers. The stark fact of economic oligarchy with its influence on the political apparatus was a stumbling block

[2] The Taylor System of scientific management is named after Frederick Winslow Taylor (1856–1915), an American machinist who became an early efficiency expert or consulting engineer in management. The system is a method of time-and-motion study used in industries to increase productive efficiency.

[3] Quoted in John R. Commons, ed., *Trade Unionism and Labor Problems,* 2d Series (Boston: Ginn and Company, 1921), p. 197.

to the democratic aspirations of the classical liberal-democratic political theory which had grown up with capitalist economics. In most of its forms liberal-democratic theory argued for a balanced society with an open class structure and a representative political system dominated by no class or faction. The idea that a balance of power depended on a balance of economic institutions was at least as old as James Harrington's seventeenth-century *Oceana* and remained in the main stream of classical liberalism.

The facts of oligopoly, monopolistic competition and economic concentration were met in different ways. Some liberals simply considered the conditions to be the result of conspiracy by evil businessmen who might be restrained by law. Others denied the signs and argued that the economy was still largely regulated by the price mechanism and the free competition of small producers. Still other approaches accepted the evidence of economic concentration but claimed that it followed inevitably from the inefficiency of small-scale production and from the increasing rationalization and growth of technology. But political writers inclined toward Manchester liberalism or the Austrian school objected to this principle of inevitability and asserted that economic concentration and monopoly were the bitter fruits of governmental interference, subsidies, and tariffs that nourished some firms to giant strength and crushed others. Finally, some writers accepted the evidence without equivocation and abandoned the liberal camp for a "conservative" position, defending oligarchical controls with the claim that power goes naturally to the superior few and that the subordinate multitude was indeed by nature equipped only to serve or perish.

Socialist critics on the other hand took hold of the evidence of concentration as a weapon in their arsenal. It was an old story to socialists that political life was dominated by ruling classes which controlled the instruments of production. Democratic socialists argued that the concentration of wealth and power was appropriate to the highest stage of capitalism, but that history and inexorable economic laws were at last making it possible for the workers to organize their own political party, to expropriate the ruling class by peaceful means, and to control the economy. Economic life would be under public rather than private control, and the natural consequence would be a democratic political organization.

The issue of the scope of governmental power in economic life raised other questions—the nature of society, the effect of rational intervention in social and economic processes, the lines between public and private spheres—and provided a rallying point for postures and programs of action.

The issue also stimulated the expression of attitudes toward reform and reconstruction, brought forth attempts to formulate more precise positions on social change, and encouraged debate about the meaning of liberalism.

THE REDEFINITION OF LIBERALISM

Liberalism at this time was a loose term that referred not to a clear position but to a sanguine and comfortable attitude toward reform. Practical problems roused theoretical discussions and efforts to redefine liberalism as a political formula, to give it intellectual organization and political direction, but without avail; as an intellectual and political system, liberalism remained ambiguous. Yet had it not existed, its enemies could not have invented it; nor could they have defined themselves, for its principles and mentality helped give identity to the movements that appeared in opposition. Liberalism served as midwife to the styles of political thought that emerged in this period, but its own image varied with the character of each opponent. Socialists saw it as the ideology of the bourgeoisie, aristocratic conservatives and the new nationalists as the mentality of an age, theologians as the spirit of pride, and totalitarians as the expression of a corrupt and dying world.

The struggle of its adherents to define liberalism were particularly important in America, for here especially the collection of ideas associated with classical liberalism, containing many ambiguities and political alternatives, could be used equally by the left and the right: by men interested in reform and fundamental change and by those opposed to all kinds of change. On the one hand, liberalism was identified with rugged individualism, laissez-faire, and the defense of capitalism; on the other hand, it had also come to stand for progressivism, social reform, reconstruction, planning, and the criticism of capitalist institutions.

In the readings from Wilson, Lippmann, and Dewey, one may find three typical "liberal" attitudes toward economic policy, social change, and the question of reform.

The Moral Necessity for Reform

One need not argue whether Woodrow Wilson was really a liberal or a conservative—his Calvinist disposition and the circumstances of his time made him an interesting mixture of both.

Wilson knew very well that the old order had changed and that the

economic system was losing its resemblance to nineteenth-century capitalism. The new capitalism, dominated by large corporations, was inexorable
and mechanical, soulless in its operation, Wilson argued, and created human misery even though good men without evil intentions ran these organizations. Wilson had faith, however, that efforts of will and moral intention could change the operation of the system and bring it under human
control.

In his thought one finds remnants of the social-gospel approach to
political problems; the belief that the source of true reform is moral and
spiritual and that institutions may be perfected by pure motives; and a
strong sense of the need for stability and the preservation of order—internal and external.

In the essay below, Wilson expressed his conviction that "the salvation of civilization" depended on making the world safe from irrational
revolution, and this stability in turn depended on the reform of capitalism.
The causes of world unrest, Wilson said, were spiritual, resulting from the
systematic denial of natural rights; it was unjust to deprive the masses of
men of their due, and revolutions basically were struggles for justice. A
civilization could not survive materially unless it were redeemed spiritually;
nor would capitalism survive if privation provoked men to rage. Some men
declared that capitalism was "indispensable to the industrial support and
development of modern civilization," but capitalism could be justified,
Wilson said, only if it fulfilled human needs and rights. The solution to social
and political problems, however, lay not in the external reconstruction of
institutions but in the hearts of men. He felt confident that fundamental
solutions could be found within the given economic and social system
through the conversion of men to the spirit of good will.

Liberalism in a Conservative Role

In his definition of liberalism, Walter Lippmann made it clear that he
was not opposed to reform, nor was he against all government intervention.
Liberalism was not the same as laissez-faire, he declared. Reforms were
necessary, and the liberal approved them, Lippmann argued, but he was
irrevocably opposed to harmonious schemes of social reconstruction, for
"the Good Society has no architectural design." The liberal temper protested against attempts to mold life according to a blueprint.

Lippmann assumed that society was made up of a multitude of spontaneous transactions and voluntary relationships, and that since "huge masses
of men have become dependent upon one another through the division of

labor in countless, infinitely complex transactions, their activities cannot be planned and directed by public officials." Lippmann called economic planners unrealistic because they sought to regulate the economy as if it were a system, and he identified the administration of a comprehensive plan with arbitrary power. Liberalism, he argued, resisted arbitrary power and sought to bring it under control, for the freedom of a voluntary society depended on the restraints imposed by the law. "The liberal state is to be conceived as the protector of equal rights by dispensing justice among individuals. It seeks to protect men against arbitrariness, not arbitrarily to direct them." The violence of conflict and competition in the economy was not to be met by economic regulation but should be controlled by the courts and the rule of law.

Attempts to direct the economy, Lippmann claimed, would lead inevitably to despotism under a few politicians and administrators. Rather than accept the judgment of a few, liberalism "relies upon the development of the latent faculties of all men, shaped by their free transactions with one another," and leaves the destiny of civilization not to politicians but to the whole genius of mankind.

Progressivism

Against the kind of argument presented by Lippmann, another position, which also styled itself as liberal, contended that to leave the economy unregulated and unplanned was to assent to the arbitrary domination of the few who actually controlled it. Transactions and economic relationships were not free as Lippmann assumed, it was argued, but really are manipulated by those fortunate enough to be in positions of economic and social power. John Dewey pointed out, "It is absurd to conceive liberty as that of the business entrepreneur and ignore the immense regimentation to which workers are subjected, intellectual as well as manual workers." Freedom, Dewey claimed, meant the opportunity to share in the cultural resources of civilization, and in the time he was writing, he said, only a few were fortunate enough to have this opportunity. Where Lippmann opposed calculated and intended social change because it would represent merely the will of a few administrators and politicians, Dewey suggested that such change would be desirable and that it could be in the interest of the entire community. According to Dewey, liberalism stood for the application of intelligence to social problems and the satisfaction of as many claims and needs as possible.

JOHN DEWEY'S SOCIAL PHILOSOPHY   Although the high days of the progressive movement were in the period before World War I, the movement found its philosophy most cogently expressed in the voluminous writing of John Dewey, most of which appeared in the twenties and thirties. Dewey's social philosophy inspired many of the writers and political leaders who saw in the New Deal an instrument of political transformation and social reconstruction.

The basic elements of Dewey's social thought, appearing in most of his writing on political issues, were his pragmatism, instrumentalism, progressivism, and democratic populism. As a pragmatist he believed (as did the philosopher William James, the sociologist Lester Frank Ward, and the legal theorist Roscoe Pound) that all human claims, wants, needs, or interests were equally valid, and the function of the good society was to arrange human wants and needs in a casuistic scale and order things so that as many persons as possible might benefit from the social resources available at the time.

As an instrumentalist, he believed that ideas proceeded from practical experience, and that intelligence—not tradition, habit, or emotion—was man's best tool to solve problems, although he wisely recognized that authority and inertia and not intelligence were the most potent influences on human minds. The proper function of philosophy, he believed, was not abstract speculation but social engineering, and in this task its model was the method of science. As a progressive Dewey was sanguine about the future, dedicated to cultivating change and growth.

Finally, his democratic populism committed him to the idea of creating moral community and encouraging democratic participation in culture, for he was repelled by passive consumption and apathy. When the masses of men were submerged, he felt, the entire social body was deprived of their potential resources. "The mass usually become unaware that they have a claim to the development of their own powers. Their experience is so restricted that they are not conscious of restriction." Democracy as a way of life recognized "the necessity for the participation of every mature human being in formation of the values that regulate the living of men together: which is necessary from the standpoint of both the general social welfare and the full development of human beings as individuals." The justification of democracy was experience, for

. . . democratic political forms are simply the best means that human wit has devised up to a special time in history. But they rest back upon the idea that no man or limited set of men is wise enough or good enough to rule others without their consent; the positive meaning of this statement is that all those who are affected by social institutions must have a share in producing and managing them.

The keystones of Dewey's liberalism were development and freedom, and he insisted that the fundamental freedom was freedom of mind—the released intelligence.

SOCIALISM

Democratic socialists would have argued against Dewey that the application of intelligence to social problems was not enough to release men from brutalized lives and to make a better civilization. To carry out the principle of democratic participation in culture and to allow more people to share in the fruits of civilization, the men whose labor supported the economy should gain control of the economy and thereby take their destinies in their own hands. Liberal defenders of capitalism argued that socialism would mean regimentation, but Harold Laski replied that in the present system most lives were already regimented and dismal:

The true goods of life, in fact, security, knowledge, the enjoyment of beauty, only a few in the present social order can hope to know. The rest will live a life of unending routine, uncertain of the morrow, and on the threshold of a great spiritual heritage from entrance to which they are debarred.

Laski contended that the good society was one in which men controlled their own lives—an ideal condition of freedom and power possible under socialism but impossible under capitalism. Laski concluded that freedom required socialization of the essential means of production and the modification of inheritance laws, so that no one could claim a reward from the resources of the community without some proportionate service: "The Socialist does not dogmatise as to the forms such social ownership should take. All that he insists is that until they are effectively the possession of the community, they cannot be fully administered in the interest of the community."

By what methods could such a state be brought about? The revolutionary socialists—Lenin, Trotsky, and Stalin—gave answers to be discussed later in this volume. Democratic socialists offered another alternative, one which, they argued, would not lead to an authoritarian system. In his essay below, Karl Kautsky outlined his idea of the way socialists could come to power by democratic means and transform society for the welfare of all.

THE ATTACK ON LIBERALISM

Socialists generally held that spiritual values would thrive once social institutions were rectified; their outlook was largely secular, rationalistic, and utilitarian. Christian socialists tended to think of religion as a source of inspiration for social reform. In England the piety of the free churches inspired the labor movement and the development of the Labour party in the same way that the social gospel stimulated reform movements in America. The socialist temper, to all intents and purposes, was one of correction and amplification, but was still an heir of liberalism in its most inclusive sense.

The shock of the war and the discontent with liberalism as a world view, as a social philosophy, and as a program for action stimulated many critical currents of political and social thought, of which the essay by Santayana below is one example. There were many other caustic judgments and reevaluations of nineteenth-century premises that the post-Victorian, prewar world took for granted. The attack came from many quarters: theological circles condemned secularism, naturalistic philosophies, liberalism, and the idea of progress; conservatives of various kinds waged a campaign not only against liberalism but against the ideas of democracy and equality as well; at the same time, right-wing nationalists heaped scorn on the organization and policies of the modern state.

NEW THEOLOGICAL PERSPECTIVES

The most novel and one of the most vital currents in the political thought of the twenties and thirties, destined to penetrate the decades that followed as well, was stirred by the reentry of theology into the domain of social thought. The nineteenth century had seemed to accept Auguste Comte's judgment that theology was a backward mode of thought, inferior to scientific ways of thinking, and from around 1850 to 1914 the major writers were philosophic naturalists who excluded theology. The work of theologians, with the exception of the Roman Catholics, had little effect on social theory. Moreover, with the exception again of Catholicism and of certain intransigent strains of Continental Protestantism, theologians had tended to favor the liberal climate and defend Christianity as a system of ethics or stress the ultility of religion. Writers like Adolf von Harnack, Ernst Troeltsch, and Max Weber had made important contributions in the pre-war period to the understanding of the vital role played by religion in social movements, and their work seemed to support the more superficial tendency to reduce religion to social utility. Roman Catholic theology, of course, had persisted in condemning liberalism in most of its forms as the heresy of Modernism.

After 1910 the ecumenical movement helped draw together the strands of Protestant theology. Into Continental theology was injected a measure of Anglo-American optimism, while Anglo-American theology received some of Europe's pessimism. After World War I, the sense of crisis was much more acute in Europe than in the United States, but irresistibly, during the interbellum, it crossed the Atlantic. New religious styles of thought—neo-orthodoxy, religious existentialism, and dialectical theology—were important vehicles in this passage; they helped to give the sense of crisis a form that would fit into a changing American intellectual environment and furnished concepts and language through which it could be understood and expressed. Because of their part in bringing the sense of crisis to America, we must examine in some detail the work of Reinhold Niebuhr and Paul Tillich.

The Protestant Neoorthodox Movement

In 1930 Reinhold Niebuhr, a young American pastor, was profoundly impressed by his experience at an international conference. In an article called "Europe's Religious Pessimism" published in the magazine *Christian Century,* he reported:

The Germans are strongly influenced by the new dialectic theology, called Barthianism in America. They reveal a very profound piety and defend their positions with great dialectic skill. Explicitly and implicitly they accuse the Anglo-Saxon world of not yet being emancipated from the age of enlightenment. They have left the enlightenment behind and have returned to the Reformation. . . . They want faith, revelation and redemption to be something quite different from anything in moral and social experience. They consciously deepen the religious life by narrowing it. This is not the unreflective orthodoxy of our own country. It is a highly intellectual attack upon all forms of intellectualism in religion. The Dutch representatives are in pretty thorough agreement with the Germans.

The English and Americans are, from the perspective of the continentals, similar in their emphasis. They believe in the kingdom of God, which is to say that they believe religion can be made socially and ethically useful. That is regarded as a mistake for various reasons, but chiefly because it betrays them into an optimistic view of history and beguiles them with illusions that any next step in political and social programs is a vestibule to the kingdom of God on earth. . . .

The orthodoxy which impressed Niebuhr was an intellectual position "which has run down every pathway of rationalism and intellectualism until it found that it led nowhere and has come back therefore to give life meaning by an adventure of faith." In contrast, Niebuhr felt little sympathy for

. . . liberal American clergymen with their facile optimism and their blind assumption that they are helping to save the world, while the brutal inevitabilities of international life, high tariffs, international debts, worldwide unemployment, and so forth, unfold themselves without being changed by a hair's breadth for all our Christian idealism.

He concluded that

. . . while pessimism is more dangerous than optimism it is also in many respects more realistic and more spiritual. It does not, at least, lead to the hypocrisy of sanctifying the brutalities of history in the name of a tepid idealism which changes little and pretends much.[4]

In the reading selection below, Niebuhr discussed his pilgrimage from liberalism to neoorthodoxy and the intellectual and moral foundations of his position.

The attack on religious liberalism extended to political liberalism as well. Niebuhr wrote that the liberal mind was "pedestrian and uninspired," had an unreal doctrine of man, and, when confronted with realities, retreated "baffled and confused." In his book *Reflections on the End of an Era,* he observed that when faced with men filled with passion and fury, the liberal soul "can only deprecate their fanaticism and regret their ignorance of the principles of sociology." [5]

World War I, Niebuhr argued, was a reflection of the internal anarchy of Western civilization. Positions like the one expressed by Woodrow Wilson in the reading in this book represented a too-simple moralism that prevented

---

[4] *Christian Century,* XLVII (1930), 1031–33.
[5] Reinhold Niebuhr, *Reflections on the End of an Era* (New York: Charles Scribner's Sons, 1934), p. 262.

the middle classes from seeing the full depth of the problem of man; it left them unable to recognize or understand evil. Niebuhr claimed that he was converted to orthodoxy because the simple moral homilies of liberalism were not relevant to the brutal facts of life.

In contrast to the tepid liberal world, W. M. Horton observed in *Contemporary Continental Theology,* the neoorthodox world was

. . . full of terror as well as glory, demons as well as angels, and only to be known through suffering; yet so fascinating and compelling to those who have known it that they would never again be content in our plumber's paradise, nor exchange their apocalyptic torment for an eternity of our bourgeois bliss.[6]

Besides offering a world view that criticized the inadequate assumptions of the nineteenth century, demolishing the idea of progress, the new theology also discussed at length the irrational springs of human action, and gave an old explanation of why things had gone so terribly wrong with the modern world—original sin. Establishing itself as a major position in modern political thought, neoorthodoxy restored to political discourse the vocabulary of theology, giving that vocabulary some of the significance it had held for the political theory of the sixteenth and seventeenth centuries.

In the first volume of his *Systematic Theology,* Paul Tillich wrote:

It is not an exaggeration to say that today man experiences his present situation in terms of disruption, conflict, self-destruction, meaninglessness, and despair in all realms of life. This experience is expressed in the arts and in literature, conceptualized in existential philosophy, actualized in political cleavages of all kinds, and analyzed in the psychology of the unconscious. It has given theology a new understanding of the demonic-tragic structures of individual and social life.[7]

The new theology was reinforced philosophically by the dialectic genius of the Danish philosopher Søren Kierkegaard (1813–1855), by existentialist comment on his work that came a century later, and also by the renaissance of Russian Orthodox theology. The diaspora of Russian émigré philosophers and theologians—especially Nikolai Berdyaev—who settled in Paris and London had a profound effect on European and American thought. One of the most distinguished theologians of the neoorthodox

___

[6] W. M. Horton, *Contemporary Continental Theology* (New York: Harper & Brothers, 1938), p. xxi.
[7] Paul Tillich, *Systematic Theology* (Chicago: The University of Chicago Press, 1951), I, 49.

movement, whose work has made an important impression on both Europe and America, is Paul Tillich, and the reading selection in Part Two of this volume illustrates the way in which he has engaged political questions.

Political life is complex, Tillich and Niebuhr realized, but the most significant events and characteristic action, they implied, might be interpreted in terms of sin and demonism—the clues to history and to the crisis of modern society. Their conceptions of sin and of evil were in the Pauline and Augustinian traditions. As St. Paul cried out in Romans 7:

> For the good that I would I do not: but the evil which I would not, that I do. Now if I do that I would not, it is no more I that do it, but sin that dwelleth in me. I find then a law, that, when I would do good, evil is present with me. For I delight in the law of God after the inward man: But I see another law in my members, warring against the law of my mind, and bringing me into captivity to the law of sin which is in my members.

Evil was explained to be not the consequence of ignorance or bad conditions but a radical element in the nature of man; man did evil not because he did not know the good, but in spite of his knowledge of the good.

Sin also resulted from the dread or anxiety that came from man's tension between finitude and freedom, between his existence as part of nature and at the same time apart from nature. Man could not tolerate this tension, and in his freedom tended to reject his finitude and to make himself God. The presumption of making oneself the false center of existence was the sin of pride and, in Biblical language, had been the crime of Satan, which, after the fall of man, was transmitted to the core of human personality.

In *Faith and History,* Niebuhr wrote:

> . . . the world is not self-derived. It points beyond itself to its Creator. The failure to recognize this fact is not the fault of the mind but of the person who usurps the central position in the scheme of things and thereby brings confusion into his own life and into the whole order of history. . . . The fact that it is a corruption which has a universal dominion over all men, though it is not by nature but in freedom that men sin, is the "mystery" of "original sin," which will always be an offense to rationalists. But it has the merit of being true to the facts of human existence. . . . The failure to recognize this obvious fact in modern culture accounts for most of its errors in estimating the actual trends of history.[8]

[8] Reinhold Niebuhr, *Faith and History* (New York: Charles Scribner's Sons, 1949), pp. 122–23.

A scientific age seeks and finds specific reasons and causes for particular evils, but misses the point that evil as such is an ineradicable part of human existence. The possibility of evil, Niebuhr suggested, will continue to exist as long as there is human freedom.

Men try to solve their problems by institutional arrangements, which are indeed necessary, but which are distorted by being inflated from their true position of relative value into absolute values. For example, as Niebuhr put it in *Christianity and Power Politics:*

> Modern technical society is desperately in need of the socialization of economic power in order that it may minimize the injustices which result inevitably from endowing the anarchic ego with unlimited power over other life. That the proponents of this necessary social change should confuse the issues by falsely claiming to be the instruments of a perfect society and of a universal culture is itself one of those manifestations of the fateful human tendency to confuse the immediate and the ultimate.[9]

Transforming relative or partial truths into absolute truths is called demonism, a theory which explains a great deal about history and political life. It has reflected itself in what Niebuhr has styled the disjunction between "moral man and immoral society." Man is capable of making choices between good and evil, but groups tend to lose this discrimination. The "collective egotism" of nations has made them presume to be God. Collectives have been morally obtuse, and the "more the moral problem is shifted from the relations of individuals to the relations of groups and collectives, the more the preponderance of the egoistic impulses over the social ones is established." [10]

Niebuhr's historical pessimism, which he has claimed to balance by a religious, metahistorical or transcendental optimism, has fulfilled an important need for thoughtful persons who have discarded the formulas of liberalism, but it has made others in his audience uncomfortable as well. He has approached the arena of political action with tough-mindedness, recommending that it is necessary to combine the realism of the moral cynics (the "children of darkness") with the good will of the idealists (the "children of light"). The only solutions will be "proximate" solutions, often achieved by "ethically directed force."

Though Niebuhr had accepted an orthodox theology, he could not be content with the traditional quietism of orthodoxy. Regarding specific polit-

[9] Reinhold Niebuhr, *Christianity and Power Politics* (New York: Charles Scribner's Sons, 1940), p. 158.
[10] Reinhold Niebuhr, *Moral Man and Immoral Society* (New York: Charles Scribner's Sons, 1948), p. 262.

ical methods, he has confessed he is a pragmatist and that he believes in a "great amount of tactical freedom." His political thought is an interesting synthesis that reminds one of John Adams and some of the Federalists: a theological conviction of human sinfulness combined with the classical liberal conception of a balance of power as a check upon destructive egoistic impulses.

CONSERVATISM AND ARISTOCRATIC DISCONTENT

The novelty and the significance of neoorthodoxy for the development of Anglo-American political thought in this period should not eclipse other positions that also attacked liberalism and made pessimistic arguments about human nature and the political crisis. Aristocratic conservatism, suspicious of the masses, condemning liberalism and democracy, commenting mordantly on the level of mass culture, continued to have its articulate spokesmen.

George Santayana exposed the contradiction between liberalism's esteem for freedom and its tendency to use power to insure conformity to its version of happiness. "The liberal system," he concluded, "which sought to raise the individual, has degraded the masses. . . . Liberal legislation, which was to have reduced government to the minimum of police control, now has undertaken public education, social reform and even the management of industry." Paradoxically, he claimed, liberalism finds itself using tyrannical techniques to free the people from the consequences of freedom.

H. L. Mencken, probably America's most acid critic of political and religious institutions, also considered the mission to extend liberty to the masses a foolish contradiction. One cannot have liberty without virtue, which in turn was possessed only by naturally superior men who have the courage to stand alone. This capacity for courage and isolation was foreign to the herd, which was always in search of security and protection; politicians made their living by manipulating the fear and weakness of the masses. Democracy, therefore, was ridiculous—a "self-devouring" system. Yet other systems had their own weaknesses as well, Mencken recognized. His scorn for democracy was implicit in his contempt for most men; indeed, he believed, "In the long run, it may turn out . . . that civilization, at bottom, is nothing but a colossal swindle." [11]

[11] H. L. Mencken, *Notes on Democracy* (New York: Alfred A. Knopf, Inc., 1926), p. 212.

In a more serious vein, with less frolicsome disdain but as much criticism, Irving Babbitt and Paul Elmer More spoke as representatives of the "classic revival." Today the "new conservatives" give Babbitt and More an important place in the conservative canon. Both assessed the effect of materialism and democracy on the level of culture and civilization. Commercialization, Babbitt wrote, had so dominated social life that "whatever democracy may be theoretically, one is sometimes tempted to define it practically as standardized and commercialized melodrama." Babbitt inherited the theoretical ground of his criticism of democracy from Plato and Aristotle, and also based his assumptions about civilization on classical ideas. The best government, he assumed, would be aristocratic, and in American civilization an aristocracy was certainly necessary to resist the impact of standardized mediocrity. Babbitt's picture of the ideal aristocrat seemed to be a composite of the Victorian Christian gentleman and the guardians in Plato's *Republic*. Babbitt rejected any suggestion of an aristocracy of science, of art, or of power, nor did he think we should "evolve under the guidance of Mr. H. L. Mencken into second-rate Nietzscheans." The "saving remnant" that he contrasted to the "divine average" (the mass) would be composed of earnest, disciplined, moral men whose higher faculties controlled the lower instincts and who would speak truth, dispel confusion, and refuse to mislead the people. Thus, his natural aristocracy would not even be permitted Plato's device of the noble lie.[12]

Babbitt insisted that moral integrity and intellectual seriousness ineluctably led one to traditional doctrines because of the honesty with which such doctrines faced the fact of evil. The survival of civilization, moreover, depended not on innovations but on conventions and traditions, since they grew out of life experience and had the power to bring order out of chaotic impulses and base appetites. In politics, he believed, the Platonic and Aristotelian insights were still the most profound, demonstrating that power must be subordinated to justice or inner proportion, that in the realm of power there is no substitute for the just man, and that problems of power ultimately become problems of character.

Paul Elmer More's aristocratic conservatism was also in the Platonic-Christian political tradition. Political leadership depended on character, which in turn depended on discipline, meaning the control of appetite by the intellect and will. Both Babbitt and More continued the argument of Edmund Burke, who equated political evil with unrestrained passions and

[12] Irving Babbitt, *Democracy and Leadership* (Boston: Houghton Mifflin Company, 1924), pp. 239–314.

abstract ideas. However, More believed that democracy could be improved
—he did not argue for its replacement—by a natural aristocracy. Ultimately, he thought, the fate of civilization depended on whether power was
used "to raise the material welfare of the masses, or to create advantages
for the upward striving of the exceptional." The latter path was the path of
justice, in the sense of proportion, and was the only true path, for: "In
the end the happiness of the people also, in the wider sense, depends on the
common recognition of the law of just subordination." [13]

INTEGRAL NATIONALISM: THE SUPREMACY OF POWER

The style of conservative nationalism expressed in the nineteenth century by writers like Heinrich von Treitschke, Charles Maurras, and Thomas
Carlyle persisted in the 1920's and 1930's, but tended to be absorbed by
ultraright-wing political movements and by the totalitarian systems. Though
they were used by the totalitarians, men like Werner Sombart and Carl
Schmitt remained distinct in their theories, and they should not be considered as official Nazi theorists but rather as fellow travelers. In the case
of Sombart, the Nazi movement appealed to his intense German nationalism and his romantic, organic conception of community.

Like many romantic writers, Sombart hoped that Europe would emerge
from the "desert" of the economic age, which he thought was dominated by
utility, rationalization, secularism, and liberalism that left little room for
the more generous emotions, the Spartan virtues, and the deeper bonds of
community. He interpreted Germany's economic crisis as the end of the
economic era and the beginning of a new epoch. National socialism, to his
mind, was more revolutionary than proletarian socialism, for the latter, he
thought, was an inverted form of capitalism, and national socialism, in contrast, was anticapitalistic. It appears from his writing, however, that what he
opposed was not merely capitalism but, more fundamentally, modern
economics.

Sombart conceived of society as a battleground on which specific social-
psychological types (warriors, priests, traders, and so on), each possessing
a given "spirit," struggled for dominance. The spirit of a particular age or
era, therefore, was little more than the reflection of the dominant spiritual
type. Modern society, which had reached its crisis, was dominated by the

[13] Paul Elmer More, *Aristocracy and Justice* (Boston: Houghton Mifflin Company, 1915), pp. 22–33.

trader and merchant, and he hoped that in Germany national socialism would produce an anticommercial, more "spiritual" culture.

Although his writing was absorbed by the Nazi propaganda machinery, Sombart himself was no mere propagandist, and his writing shows that the intensity of his political thinking and his desire to be treated kindly by the Third Reich did not entirely obscure the world of political reality. His understanding of the alternatives that faced Germany was even prophetic. In 1934 he wrote:

The internal development of society in Germany will surely take on a form different from the present, depending upon whether we become a Russian province or are reduced by the once more victorious western Powers into our component elements; whether we attain the leadership of a "Mid-European Empire" or, in common with France and Italy, build up a pan-European State; whether, in consequence of a victorious war, we are able essentially to enlarge our national body or, finally, whether our frontiers remain as they are. . . . Moreover, I have also left out of consideration the contingency, by no means remote, that Germany in the next ten years might become the camping ground of enemy troops.[14]

Like Sombart, Carl Schmitt was caught up in the political disputation that had begun in Germany a century and a half previously and continued unabated in the Weimar Republic. Schmitt was an admirer of Friedrich Meinecke and, ultimately, of Hobbes, placing himself in the rationalist-realist tradition rather than in the mystical *Volk* romanticism camp. He joined in heaping scorn on parliamentarianism and liberalism, but with a rationale different from that of the romantics. In *The Concept of the Political,* which first appeared in 1927, Schmitt developed an argument which is a terrible simplification of politics, but which ironically reveals the political condition of twentieth-century man. While he lamented the neutralization and depoliticization of the state in the last hundred years, events were actually moving toward an apotheosis of the political in ways that Schmitt had not anticipated but to which he nevertheless assented.

Schmitt's earliest published work had established him as a gifted legal-political scholar. *The Concept of the Political* has little in common with Nazi pseudotheory. It is a work that a theorist can confront and oppose, not merely shun. In its content it may be seen as a bridge between some orthodox *étatiste* positions and totalitarian thought. Although Schmitt's position in this work is authoritarian rather than totalitarian, he nonethe-

[14] Werner Sombart, *A New Social Philosophy,* trans. Karl F. Geiser (Princeton: Princeton University Press, 1937), p. xi.

less elevates political action above all other forms of social conduct (including economic, juridical, aesthetic, or religious) and argues that politics is the core of civilization. Without much effort, his doctrine was stretched to accommodate the political barbarians.

When Hitler came to power, Schmitt hailed the regime as a pure political order. Indeed, he provided much of the jurisprudential defense for the regime during its stabilization-of-power period. His book *Staat, Bewegung, Volk* was the closest thing to a rational political theory Nazism had. He argued that each of the three "members" of the system—the State, the Movement, and the People—was an essential part of the whole and played an essential role in the operation of the regime. He claimed, moreover: "The strength of the National Socialistic State lies in this; that it is ruled and pervaded by the thought of the Fuehrerdom, from top to bottom and in every atom of its existence." [15] Only such a regime, wrote Schmitt, was politicized enough to perform its proper existential function, namely, to destroy its Foe in the Friend-Foe struggle.

In Schmitt's work during the Nazi years one found less of the irrationalism evident in the writing of such Nazi jurists as Helmut Nicolai, who asserted: ". . . no National Socialist science [of law] is possible outside of the racial-legal thought"; [16] and Hans Frank, who declared: "All that is useful to the *Volk* is law; all that harms it, is wrong." [17] On the other hand, his writings did become antisemitic and openly racist in the late thirties.

Still, Schmitt's theories were too rational for the Nazi regime. Apparently he had invested the state with too much political authority. The *Volk* alone, embodied in the Führer, could provide the motive force for politics, wrote Ernst Huber. Consequently, Schmitt lost favor.

Schmitt understood very well that the development of total state power implied total war, and the interpretation of politics as Friend-Foe struggle recognized a perennial truth. Both these insights threw two assumptions of the totalitarian system in relief: that life may be totally politicized, and that the range of political power may be constantly extended in battling the ever-present enemy. Thus for Schmitt the totalitarian system became the paradigm for all of political life—totalitarianism was the incarnation of his political idea.

[15] Carl Schmitt, *Staat, Bewegung, Volk* (Hamburg: Hanseatische Verlagsanstalt, 1935), p. 33.
[16] Helmut Nicolai, *Rasse und Recht* (Berlin, 1933), p. 5.
[17] Hans Frank, *Nationalsozialistisches Handbuch für Recht und Gesetzgebung* (Munich, 1935), p. xiv.

WOODROW WILSON
1856-1924

SCHOLAR IN THE FIELDS of public law and politics, accomplished essayist and orator, president of Princeton, governor of New Jersey, and president of the United States, Woodrow Wilson stands out not only as a great public figure but also as one of the few men in his time who understood that the old order was passing and that Europe and the United States had gone through irreversible changes. His domestic policies brought consequences as far-reaching as his command during the war and the diplomacy afterward. His program of reform instituted in 1913, called the New Freedom, was the ancestor of the New Deal. Moreover, the emergency measures of 1917–1918, including government control of railroads and the impetus toward economic centralization, ushered in the new era of government-economy interdependence. The New Freedom also stands for a certain form of liberalism, and the following selection from one of Wilson's essays reveals some of its underlying social and political ideas.

[12]   *The Road Away from Revolution*

In these doubtful and anxious days, when all the world is at unrest and, look which way you will, the road ahead seems darkened by shadows which portend dangers of many kinds, it is only common prudence that we should look about us and attempt to assess the causes of distress and the most likely means of removing them.

There must be some real ground for the universal unrest and perturbation. It is not to be found in superficial politics or in mere economic blunders. It probably lies deep at the sources of the spiritual life of our time. It leads to revolution; and perhaps if we take the case of the Russian Revolution, the outstanding event of its kind in our age, we may find a good deal of instruction for our judgment of present critical situations and circumstances.

What gave rise to the Russian Revolution? The answer can only be that it was the product of a whole social system. It was not in fact a sudden thing. It has been gathering head for several generations. It was due to the systematic denial of the great body of Russians of the rights and privileges which all normal men desire and must have if they are to be contented and within reach of happiness. The lives of the great mass of the Russian people contained no opportunities, but were hemmed in by barriers against which they were constantly flinging their spirits, only to fall back bruised and dispirited. Only the powerful were suffered to secure their rights or even to gain access to the means of material success.

It is to be noted as a leading fact of our time that it was against 'capitalism' that the Russian leaders directed their attack. It was capitalism that made them see red; and it is against capitalism under one name or another that the discontented classes everywhere draw their indictment.

There are thoughtful and well-informed men all over the world who believe, with much apparently sound reason, that the abstract thing, the system, which we call capitalism, is indispensable to the industrial support and development of modern civilization. And yet everyone who has an intelligent knowledge of social forces must know that great and widespread reactions like that which is now unquestionably manifesting itself against capitalism do not occur without cause or provocation; and before we commit ourselves irreconcilably to an attitude of hostility to this movement of the time, we ought frankly to put to ourselves the question, Is the capitalistic system unimpeachable? which is another way of asking, Have capitalists generally used their power for the benefit of the countries in which their capital is employed and for the benefit of their fellow men?

Is it not, on the contrary, too true that capitalists have often seemed to regard the men whom they used as mere instruments of profit, whose

From *The Atlantic Monthly*, CXXXII (August, 1923), 145–46. Reprinted by permission.

physical and mental powers it was legitimate to exploit with as slight cost to themselves as possible, either of money or of sympathy? Have not many fine men who were actuated by the highest principles in every other relationship of life seemed to hold that generosity and humane feeling were not among the imperative mandates of conscience in the conduct of a banking business, or in the development of an industrial or commercial enterprise?

And, if these offenses against high morality and true citizenship have been frequently observable, are we to say that the blame for the present discontent and turbulence is wholly on the side of those who are in revolt against them? Ought we not, rather, to seek a way to remove such offenses and make life itself clean for those who will share honorably and cleanly in it?

The world has been made safe for democracy. There need now be no fear that any such mad design as that entertained by the insolent and ignorant Hohenzollerns and their counselors may prevail against it. But democracy has not yet made the world safe against irrational revolution. That supreme task, which is nothing less than the salvation of civilization, now faces democracy, insistent, imperative. There is no escaping it, unless everything we have built up is presently to fall in ruin about us; and the United States, as the greatest of democracies, must undertake it.

The road that leads away from revolution is clearly marked, for it is defined by the nature of men and of organized society. It therefore behooves us to study very carefully and very candidly the exact nature of the task and the means of its accomplishment.

The nature of men and of organized society dictates the maintenance in every field of action of the highest and purest standards of justice and of right dealing; and it is essential to efficacious thinking in this critical matter that we should not entertain a narrow or technical conception of justice. By justice the lawyer generally means the prompt, fair, and open application of impartial rules; but we call ours a Christian civilization, and a Christian conception of justice must be much higher. It must include sympathy and helpfulness and a willingness to forgo self-interest in order to promote the welfare, happiness, and contentment of others and of the community as a whole. This is what our age is blindly feeling after in its reaction against what it deems the too great selfishness of the capitalistic system.

The sum of the whole matter is this, that our civilization cannot survive materially unless it be redeemed spiritually. It can be saved only by becoming permeated with the spirit of Christ and being made free and happy by the practices which spring out of that spirit. Only thus can discontent be driven out and all the shadows lifted from the road ahead.

Here is the final challenge to our churches, to our political organizations, and to our capitalists—to everyone who fears God or loves his country. Shall we not all earnestly coöperate to bring in the new day?

WALTER LIPPMANN
1889-

WALTER LIPPMANN, PUBLICIST AND EDITOR, is one of the most distinguished conservative writers today. He was educated at Harvard, was an editor of the *New Republic* in its infancy, served as assistant secretary of war during World War I, and participated in the planning for the peace conference. Afterward he wrote syndicated columns and worked as an editor of several newspapers. He has written many books on public affairs, including *A Preface to Politics* (1913), *Public Opinion* (1922), *A Preface to Morals* (1929), *The Good Society* (1937), *United States Foreign Policy* (1943), *The Cold War* (1947), and *Essays in the Public Philosophy* (1955). He began his career as a socialist, but moved firmly to the right. Supporting Franklin Roosevelt and the New Deal in its early period, Lippmann changed his views to economic liberalism and political conservatism, becoming a vigorous critic of planned society and collectivism.

[13]   The Good Society

Though liberalism has often been identified with indifference, inaction, and nonresistance, it should now be evident that this is mere confusion. A doctrine which is opposed to all arbitrariness must mean the determination

From *The Good Society* by Walter Lippmann (Boston: Little, Brown & Company–Atlantic, 1947), pp. 355–56, 362–68. Copyright 1936, 1937, 1943 by Walter Lippmann. By permission of Little, Brown & Company–Atlantic.

to resist arbitrariness, to check it, to cut it down, to crush it, wherever and whenever it appears. It cannot mean, for example, that in the seventeenth century the King was under God and the law, but that in the nineteenth century the owners of property were not, that in the twentieth century majorities, pluralities, mobs, or dictators are not, under God and the law. For liberalism all arbitrary power is evil. It matters not what are the titles or the pretensions or the promises of arbitrary power. It must be resisted and brought under control.

So liberalism is not quietism and weak government. That is the corruption of liberalism. In its vigorous periods liberalism has always meant rebellion against oppression and a determination to police aggression and acquisitiveness. Liberalism, therefore, is not the doctrine of laissez-faire, let her rip, and the devil take the hindmost. It does not envisage the demobilization of the police, the repeal of the laws, the disestablishment of legislatures and courts. On the contrary, the effective liberals have always been concerned with the development of the law, with the definition of rights and duties, with the organizing of constitutions, with the absorption of all power to coerce in the hands of duly constituted authorities, with the liquidation or regulation of all kinds of private and petty powers within the community. For the liberal, as distinguished from the anarchist, holds that mere unrestraint does not give the freedom of a voluntary society, that unrestraint merely inaugurates a competitive struggle in which the ruthless will exploit the rest. He insists that the promise of a voluntary life can be realized only as the law is strong enough to restrain aggressors at home and abroad.

*   *   *

ON DESIGNING A NEW SOCIETY

This truth our contemporary authoritarians, whether of the left or of the right, have failed to grasp. They look upon the great sprawling complex of transactions by which mankind lives; seeing that these transactions are in large part still unregulated by law, and that therefore there is much confusion and injustice, they have turned their backs upon the task of regulation by law and have beguiled themselves with the notion that they can plan this economy systematically and administer it rationally. The exact contrary is the truth. The modern economy is perhaps the least systematic of any that has ever existed. It is world-wide, formless, vast, complicated, and, owing to technological progress, in constant change. For that reason it is incapable of being conceived as a system, or of being replaced by another system, or of being managed as an administrative unit.

The hankering for schemes and systems and comprehensive organization is the wistfulness of an immature philosophy which has not come to terms with reality, no less when the conservators of vested interests would stabilize the modern economy in statu quo by protective laws and monopolistic schemes than when the revolutionist makes blueprints of a world composed of planned national economies "coördinated" by a world-planning authority. Neither takes any more account of reality than if he were studying landscape architecture with a view to making a formal garden out of the Brazilian jungle.

For the greater the society, the higher and more variable the standards of life, the more diversified the energies of its people for invention, enterprise, and adaptation, the more certain it is that the social order cannot be planned ex cathedra or governed by administrative command. We live in such an immensely diversified civilization that the only intelligible criterion which political thinkers can entertain in regard to it, the only feasible goal which statesmen can set themselves in governing it, is to reconcile the conflicts which spring from this diversity. They cannot hope to comprehend it as a system. For it is not a system. They cannot hope to plan and direct it. For it is not an organization. They can hope only to dispense lawful justice among individuals and associations where their interests conflict, to mitigate the violence of conflict and competition by seeking to make lawful justice more and more equitable.

It requires much virtue to do that well. There must be a strong desire to be just. There must be a growing capacity to be just. There must be discernment and sympathy in estimating the particular claims of divergent interests. There must be moral standards which discourage the quest of privilege and the exercise of arbitrary power. There must be resolution and valor to resist oppression and tyranny. There must be patience and tolerance and kindness in hearing claims, in argument, in negotiation, and in reconciliation.

But these are human virtues; though they are high, they are within the attainable limits of human nature as we know it. They actually exist. Men do have these virtues, all but the most hopelessly degenerate, in some degree. We know that they can be increased. When we talk about them we are talking about virtues that have affected the course of actual history, about virtues that some men have practised more than other men, and no man sufficiently, but enough men in great enough degree to have given mankind here and there and for varying periods of time the intimations of a Good Society.

But the virtues that are required for the overhead administration of a civilization are superhuman; they are attributes of Providence and not of mortal men. It is true that there have been benevolent despots and that for a little while in a particular place they have made possible a better life than their subjects were able to achieve without the rule of a firm and authoritative guardian. And no doubt it is still true that a community which does not have the essential discipline of liberty can choose only among alternative disciplines by authority. But if a community must have such a guardian, then it must resign itself to living a simple regimented existence, must entertain no hopes of the high and diversified standard of life which the division of labor and modern technology make possible. For despots cannot be found who could plan, organize, and direct a complex economy.

To do that would require a comprehensive understanding of the life and the labor and the purposes of hundreds of millions of persons, the gift of prophesying their behavior and omnipotence to control it. These faculties no man has ever possessed. When in theorizing we unwittingly postulate such faculties, we are resting our hopes on a conception of human nature which has no warrant whatever in any actual experience. The collectivist planners are not talking about the human race but about some other breed conceived in their dreams. They postulate qualities of intelligence and of virtue so unlike those which men possess that it would be just as intelligible to make plans for a society in which human beings were born equipped to fly like the angels, to feed on the fragrance of the summer breezes, and endowed with all possible knowledge.

Thus while the liberal philosophy is concerned with the reform of the laws in order to adapt them to the changing needs and standards of the dynamic economy, while the agenda of reform are long and varied, no one must look to liberalism for a harmonious scheme of social reconstruction. The Good Society has no architectural design. There are no blueprints. There is no mold in which human life is to be shaped. Indeed, to expect the blueprint of such a mold is a mode of thinking against which the liberal temper is a constant protest.

To design a personal plan for a new society is a pleasant form of madness; it is in imagination to play at being God and Caesar to the human race. Any such plan must implicitly assume that the visionary or someone else might find the power, or might persuade the masses to give him the power, to shape society to the plan; all such general plans of social reconstruction are merely the rationalization of the will to power. For that reason they are the subjective beginnings of fanaticism and tyranny. In these utopias the best is the enemy of the good, the heart's desire betrays the interests of man. To think in terms of a new scheme for a whole society is to use the idiom of authority, to approach affairs from the underlying premise that they can be shaped and directed by an overhead control, that social relations can be fabricated according to a master plan drawn up by a supreme architect.

The supreme architect, who begins as a visionary, becomes a fanatic, and ends as a despot. For no one can be the supreme architect of society without employing a supreme despot to execute the design. So if men are to seek freedom from the arbitrary dominion of men over men, they must not entertain fantasies of the future in which they play at being the dictators of civilization. It is the bad habit of an undisciplined imagination. The descent from fantasy to fanaticism is easy. Real dictators raised to power by the fanatics who adore them are only too likely to adopt the fantasy to justify their lust for power.

On the other hand, reasonable and civilized people who would like to make the best of the situation before them, but have no ambition for, or expectation of, the power to reshape a whole society, get no help from these architectural designs. The blueprint, be it as grandiose a work of genius as Plato's *Republic,* cannot hope to fit the specific situation. No a priori reasoning can anticipate the precise formulae which will reconcile the infinitely varied interests of men. The reconciliation has to be achieved by the treatment of specific issues and the solution will appear only after the claims and the evidence have been examined and fairly judged. Thus in Plato's great scheme each man was assigned his station and his duties; any architectural plan is necessarily based on the same presumption. But Plato's scheme worked only in Plato's imagination, never in the real world. No such scheme can ever work in the real world. For the scheme implies that men will remain content in the station which the visionary has assigned to them. To formulate such plans is not to design a society for real men. It is to re-create men to fit the design. For in real life men rest content in their station only if their interests have been successfully reconciled: failing that, they do not fit the design until they have been dosed with castor oil, put in concentration camps, or exiled to Siberia.

That is why the testament of liberty does not contain the project of a new social order. It adumbrates a way of life in which men seek to reconcile their interests by perfecting the rules of justice. No scheme which promises to obliterate the differences of interest can be deduced from it, no architectural design of society in which all human problems have been resolved. There is no plan of the future: there is, on the contrary, the conviction that the future must have the shape that human energies, purged in so far as possible of arbitrariness, will give it. Compared with the elegant and harmonious schemes which are propounded by the theoretical advocates of capitalism, communism, fascism, it must seem intellectually unsatisfying, and I can well imagine that many will feel about liberal society as Emma Darwin felt when she wrote about the *Descent of Man,* "I think it will be very interesting, but that I shall dislike it very much as again putting God further off."

But though it must seem an insufficient ideal both to those who wish to exercise authority and to those who feel the need of leaning upon authority, it is the only practicable ideal of government in the Great Society. When huge masses of men have become dependent upon one another through the division of labor in countless, infinitely complex transactions, their activities cannot be planned and directed by public officials.

Thus it is true that the liberal state is not to be conceived as an earthly providence administering civilization. That is the essence of the matter. To the liberal mind the notion that men can authoritatively plan and impose a good life upon a great society is ignorant, impertinent, and pretentious. It can be entertained only by men who do not realize the infinite variety of human purposes, who do not appreciate the potentialities of human effort, or by men who do not choose to respect them.

The liberal state is to be conceived as the protector of equal rights by dispensing justice among individuals. It seeks to protect men against arbitrariness, not arbitrarily to direct them. Its ideal is a fraternal association among free and equal men. To the initiative of individuals, secure in their rights and accountable to others who have equal rights, liberalism entrusts the shaping of the human destiny. It offers no encouragement to those who dream of what they could make of the world if they possessed supreme power. In the testament of liberty these ambitions have been assessed: the record of all the Caesars from Alexander to Adolf is visible. The world has known many societies in which each man had his station, his duties, and his ordained destiny, and the record shows that it is beyond the understanding of men to know all human needs, to appreciate all human possibilities, to imagine all human ends, to shape all human relations.

Yet if the ambitions of liberalism are more modest than those of authority, its promise is greater. It relies upon the development of the latent faculties of all men, shaped by their free transactions with one another. Liberalism commits the destiny of civilization, not to a few finite politicians here and there, but to the whole genius of mankind. This is a grander vision than that of those who would be Caesar and would set themselves up as little tin gods over men. It is a hope engendered in the human heart during the long ages in which the slowly emerging impulses of civilization, beset by barbarism, have struggled to be free.

JOHN DEWEY*
1859-1952

[14]   The Future of Liberalism

The emphasis of earlier liberalism upon individuality and liberty defines the focal points in discussion of the philosophy of liberalism to-day. This earlier liberalism was itself an outgrowth, in the late eighteenth and nineteenth centuries, of the earlier revolt against oligarchical government, one which came to its culmination in the "glorious revolution" of 1688. The latter was fundamentally a demand for freedom of the taxpayer from government arbitrary action in connection with a demand for confessional freedom in religion by the Protestant churches. In the later liberalism, expressly so called, the demand for liberty and individual freedom of action came primarily from the rising industrial and trading class and was directed against restrictions placed by government, in legislation, common law and judicial action, and other institutions having connection with the political state, upon freedom of economic enterprise. In both cases, governmental action and the desired freedom were placed in antithesis to each other. This way of conceiving liberty has persisted; it was strengthened in this country by the revolt of the colonies and by pioneer conditions.

Nineteenth-century philosophic liberalism added, more or less because of its dominant economic interest, the conception of natural laws to that of natural rights of the Whig movement. There are natural laws, it is held, in social matters as well as in physical, and these natural laws are economic in character. Political laws, on the other hand, are man-made and in that

* For a biographical sketch of Dewey, see pages 52–53.

From *Journal of Philosophy,* XXXII (1935), 225–30. Reprinted by permission of Mrs. John Dewey and *Journal of Philosophy.*

sense artificial. Governmental intervention in industry and exchange was thus regarded as a violation not only of inherent individual liberty but also of natural laws—of which supply and demand is a sample. The proper sphere of governmental action was simply to prevent and to secure redress for infringement by one, in the exercise of his liberty, of like and equal liberty of action on the part of others.

Nevertheless, the demand for freedom in initiation and conduct of business enterprise did not exhaust the content of earlier liberalism. In the minds of its chief promulgators there was included an equally strenuous demand for the liberty of mind, freedom of thought and its expression in speech, writing, print, and assemblage. The earlier interest in confessional freedom was generalized, and thereby deepened as well as broadened. This demand was a product of the rational enlightenment of the eighteenth century and of the growing importance of science. The great tide of reaction that set in after the defeat of Napoleon, the demand for order and discipline, gave the agitation for freedom of thought and its expression plenty of cause and plenty of opportunity.

The earlier liberal philosophy rendered valiant service. It finally succeeded in sweeping away, especially in its home, Great Britain, an innumerable number of abuses and restrictions. The history of social reforms in the nineteenth century is almost one with the history of liberal social thought. It is not, then, from ingratitude that I shall emphasize its defects, for recognition of them is essential to an intelligent statement of the elements of liberal philosophy for the present and any nearby future. The fundamental defect was lack of perception of historic relativity. This lack is expressed in the conception of the individual as something given, complete in itself, and of liberty as a ready-made possession of the individual, only needing the removal of external restrictions in order to manifest itself. The individual of earlier liberalism was a Newtonian atom having only external time and space relations to other individuals, save that each social atom was equipped with inherent freedom. These ideas might not have been especially harmful if they had been merely a rallying cry for practical movements. But they formed part of a philosophy and of a philosophy in which these particular ideas of individuality and freedom were asserted to be absolute and eternal truths; good for all times and all places.

This absolutism, this ignoring and denial of temporal relativity, is one great reason why the earlier liberalism degenerated so easily into pseudo-liberalism. For the sake of saving time, I shall identify what I mean by this spurious liberalism, the kind of social ideas represented by the "Liberty

League" and ex-President Hoover. I call it a pseudo-liberalism because it ossified and narrowed generous ideas and aspirations. Even when words remain the same, they mean something very different when they are uttered by a minority struggling against repressive measures and when expressed by a group that, having attained power, then uses ideas that were once weapons of emancipation as instruments for keeping the power and wealth it has obtained. Ideas that at one time are means of producing social change assume another guise when they are used as means of preventing further social change. This fact is itself an illustration of historic relativity, and an evidence of the evil that lay in the assertion by earlier liberalism of the immutable and eternal character of their ideas. Because of this latter fact, the *laissez-faire* doctrine was held by the degenerate school of liberals to express the very order of nature itself. The outcome was the degradation of the idea of individuality, until in the minds of many who are themselves struggling for a wider and fuller development of individuality, individualism has become a term of hissing and reproach, while many can see no remedy for the evils that have come from the use of socially unrestrained liberty in business enterprise, save change produced by violence. The historic tendency to conceive the whole question of liberty as a matter in which individual and government are opposed parties has borne bitter fruit. Born of despotic government, it has continued to influence thinking and action after government had become popular and *in theory* the servant of the people.

I pass now to what the social philosophy of liberalism becomes when its inheritance of absolutism is eliminated. In the first place such liberalism knows that an individual is nothing fixed, given ready-made. It is something achieved, and achieved not in isolation, but with aid and support of conditions, cultural and physical, including in "cultural" economic, legal, and political institutions as well as science and art. Liberalism knows that social conditions may restrict, distort, and almost prevent the development of individuality. It therefore takes an active interest in the working of social institutions that have a bearing, positive or negative, upon the growth of individuals who shall be rugged in fact and not merely in abstract theory. It is as much interested in the positive construction of favorable institutions, legal, political, and economic, as it is in the work of removing abuses and overt oppressions.

In the second place, liberalism is committed to the idea of historic relativity. It knows that the content of the individual and freedom change with time; that this is as true of social change as it is of individual development

from infancy to maturity. The positive counterpart of opposition to doc-
trinal absolutism is experimentalism. The connection between historic relativity and experimental method is intrinsic. Time signifies change. The
significance of individuality with respect to social policies alters with change
of the conditions in which individuals live. The earlier liberalism in being
absolute was also unhistoric. Underlying it there was a philosophy of history which assumed that history, like time in the Newtonian scheme, means
only modification of external relations; that it is quantitative, not equalita-
tive and internal. The same thing is true of any theory that assumes, like
the one usually attributed to Marx, that temporal changes in society are
inevitable—that is to say, are governed by a law that is not itself historical.
The fact is that the historicism and the evolutionism of nineteenth-century
doctrine were only half-way doctrines. They assumed that historical and
developmental processes were subject to some law or formula outside
temporal processes.

The commitment of liberalism to experimental procedure carries with it
the idea of continuous reconstruction of the ideas of individuality and of
liberty in intimate connection with changes in social relations. It is enough
to refer to the changes in productivity and distribution since the time when
the earlier liberalism was formulated, and the effect of these transformations, due to science and technology, upon the terms on which men associate together. An experimental method is the recognition of this temporal change in ideas and policies so that the latter shall coördinate with
the facts instead of being opposed to them. Any other view maintains a
rigid conceptualism and implies that facts should conform to concepts that
are framed independently of temporal or historical change.

The two things essential, then, to thorough-going social liberalism are,
first, realistic study of existing conditions in their movement, and, secondly,
leading ideas, in the form of policies for dealing with these conditions in
the interest of development of increased individuality and liberty. The first
requirement is so obviously implied that I shall not elaborate it. The second
point needs some amplification. Experimental method is not just messing
around nor doing a little of this and a little of that in the hope that things
will improve. Just as in the physical sciences, it implies a coherent body of
ideas, a theory, that gives direction to effort. What is implied, in contrast to
every form of absolutism, is that the ideas and theory be taken as methods
of action tested and continuously revised by the consequences they produce
in actual social conditions. Since they are operational in nature, they
modify conditions, while the first requirement, that of basing them upon

realistic study of actual conditions, brings about their continuous reconstruction.

It follows finally that there is no opposition in principle between liberalism as social philosophy and radicalism in action, if by radicalism is signified the adoption of policies that bring about drastic instead of piecemeal social changes. It is all a question of what kind of procedures the intelligent study of changing conditions discloses. These changes have been so tremendous in the last century, yes, in the last forty years, that it looks to me as if radical methods were now necessary. But all that the argument here requires is recognition of the fact that there is nothing in the nature of liberalism that makes it a milk-water doctrine, committed to compromise and minor "reforms." It is worth noting that the earlier liberals were regarded in their day as subversive radicals.

What has been said should make it clear that the question of method in formation and execution of policies is the central thing in liberalism. The method indicated is that of maximum reliance upon intelligence. This fact determines its opposition to those forms of radicalism that place chief dependence upon violent overthrow of existing institutions as the method of effecting desired social change. A genuine liberal will emphasize as crucial the complete correlation between the means used and the consequences that follow. The same principle which makes him aware that the means employed by pseudo-liberalism only perpetuate and multiply the evils of existing conditions, makes him also aware that dependence upon sheer massed force as the means of social change decides the kind of consequences that actually result. Doctrines, whether proceeding from Mussolini or from Marx, which assume that because certain ends are desirable therefore those ends and nothing else will result from the use of force to attain them is but another example of the limitations put upon intelligence by any absolute theory. In the degree in which mere force is restorted to, actual consequences are themselves so compromised that the ends originally in view have in fact to be worked out afterwards by the method of experimental intelligence.

In saying this, I do not wish to be understood as meaning that radicals of the type mentioned have any monopoly of the use of force. The contrary is the case. The reactionaries are in possession of force, in not only the army and police, but in the press and the schools. The only reason they do not advocate the use of force is the fact that they are already in possession of it, so their policy is to cover up its existence with idealistic phrases—of

which their present use of individual initiative and liberty is a striking example.

These facts illustrate the essential evil of reliance upon sheer force. Action and reaction are equal and in opposite directions, and force as such is
physical. Dependence upon force sooner or later calls out force on the other
side. The whole problem of the relation of intelligence to force is much
too large to go into here. I can only say that when the forces in possession
are so blind and stubborn as to throw all their weight against the use of
liberty of inquiry and of communication, of organization to effect social
change, they not only encourage the use of force by those who want social
change, but they give the latter the most justification they ever have. The
emphasis of liberalism upon the method of intelligence does not commit
it to unqualified pacifism, but to the unremitting use of every method of
intelligence that conditions permit, and to search for all that are possible.

In conclusion, I wish to emphasize one point implied in the early part
of the paper. The question of the practical significance of liberty is much
wider than that of the relation of government to the individual, to say nothing of the monstrosity of the doctrine that assumes that under all conditions governmental action and individual liberty are found in separate and
independent spheres. Government is one factor and an important one. But
it comes into the picture only in relation to other matters. At present, these
other matters are economic and cultural. It is absurd to conceive liberty as
that of the business entrepreneur and ignore the immense regimentation to
which workers are subjected, intellectual as well as manual workers. Moreover, full freedom of the human spirit and of individuality can be achieved
only as there is effective opportunity to share in the cultural resources of
civilization. No economic state of affairs is merely economic. It has a profound effect upon presence or absence of cultural freedom. Any liberalism
that does not make full cultural freedom supreme and that does not see the
relation between it and genuine industrial freedom as a way of life is a
degenerate and delusive liberalism.

GEORGE SANTAYANA
1863-1952

GEORGE SANTAYANA WAS BORN in Madrid and came to the United States as a child. He was educated at Harvard, taught there until 1912, and then returned to Europe and settled in Italy. Besides many philosophical books, he wrote poetry, a novel, and literary essays. Although his books, which number over three dozen, were written in English, he claimed that he retained his Spanish nationality and sentiment, and that his role in the English-speaking world was that of a permanent guest. His philosophy fashioned a unique synthesis, combining elements as diverse as Platonism, skepticism, and materialism. He said about his point of view that it preserved a spark of pure spirit casting an impartial light over the universe of things. His works exhibited brilliant style and excited strong aesthetic and emotional responses. His political writing, however, was lofty, detached, and, in the most general sense, aristocratic. He was one of the few writers to offer the present age a tranquil response, and from his vantage point the turmoil of the twentieth century, including fascism and communism, represented a minor event in the history of mankind.

[15]   *The Irony of Liberalism*

. . . . what is the direction of change which seems progress to liberals? A pure liberal might reply, The direction of liberty itself: the ideal is that every man should move in whatever direction he likes, with the aid of such as agree with him, and without interfering with those who disagree. Liberty so conceived would be identical with happiness, with spontaneous life,

From George Santayana, *Soliloquies in England* (New York: Charles Scribner's Sons, 1923), pp. 179–89. Reprinted by permission of Constable and Company Limited. This article first appeared in *Dial* in 1921 and was reprinted in a slightly different version in the *New Republic* in 1956.

blamelessly and safely lived; and the impulse of liberalism, to give every-body what he wants, in so far as that is possible, would be identical with simple kindness. Benevolence was one of the chief motives in liberalism in the beginning, and many a liberal is still full of kindness in his private capac-ity; but politically, as a liberal, he is something more than kind. The direction in which many, or even most, people would like to move fills him with disgust and indignation; he does not at all wish them to be happy, unless they can be happy on his own diet; and being a reformer and a philanthropist, he exerts himself to turn all men into the sort of men he likes, so as to be able to like them. It would be selfish, he thinks, to let people alone. They must be helped, and not merely helped to what they desire—that might really be very bad for them—but helped onwards, upwards, in the *right* direction. Progress could not be rightly placed in a smaller population, a simpler economy, more moral diversity between nations, and stricter moral dis-cipline in each of them. That would be progress backwards, and if it made people happier, it would not make the liberal so. Progress, if it is to please him, must continue in the direction in which the nineteenth century progressed, toward vast numbers, material complexity, moral uniformity, and economic interdependence. The best little boy, for instance, according to the liberal ideal, desires to be washed, to go to school, to do Swedish exercises, and to learn everything out of books. But perhaps the individual little boy (and according to the liberal philosophy his individuality is sacred, and the only judge of what is good or true for him is his own consciousness) desires to go dirty, to make mud-pies in the street, and to learn everything by experience or by report from older boys. When the philanthropist runs up to the rescue, this little ingrate sniffles at him the very principle of liberal lib-erty, "Let me alone." To inform such an urchin that he does not know what is good for him, that he is a slave to bad habits and devilish instincts, that true freedom for him can only come of correcting himself, until he has learned to find happiness in virtue—plainly that would be to abandon liberal-ism, and to preach the classical doctrine that the good is not liberty but wisdom. Liberalism was a protest against just such assumptions of authority. . . . In the presence of the little boy liberal philosophy takes a middle course. It is convinced—though it would not do to tell him so prematurely —that he must be allowed to go dirty for a time, until sufficient experience of filth teaches him how much more comfortable it is to be clean; also that he will go to school of his own accord if the books have pictures enough in them, and if the teacher begins by showing him how to make superior mud-pies. As to morals and religion, the boy and his companions will evolve the

appropriate ones in time out of their own experience, and no others would
be genuine.

Liberal philosophy, at this point, ceases to be empirical and British in
order to become German and transcendental. Moral life, it now believes, is
not the pursuit of liberty and happiness of all sorts by all sorts of different
creatures; it is the development of a single spirit in all life through a series
of necessary phases, each higher than the preceding one. No man, accordingly, can really or ultimately desire anything but what the best people
desire. This is the principle of the higher snobbery; and in fact, all earnest
liberals are higher snobs. If you refuse to move in the prescribed direction,
you are not simply different, you are arrested and perverse. The savage must
not remain a savage, nor the nun a nun, and China must not keep its wall.
If the animals remain animals it is somehow through a failure of the will in
them, and very sad. . . . But the transcendental principle of progress
. . . . requires everything to be ill at ease in its own house; no one can be
really free or happy but all must be tossed, like herded emigrants, on the
same compulsory voyage, to the same unhomely destination. The world
came from a nebula, and to a nebula it returns. In the interval, happiness is
not to be found in being a fixed star, as bright and pure as possible, even if
only for a season; happiness is to flow and dissolve in sympathy with one's
higher destiny.

The notion of progress is thus merged with that of universal evolution,
dropping the element of liberty and even of improvement. Nevertheless, in
the political expression of liberalism, liberty took the first innings. Prot-
estants began by asserting the right of private judgment in interpreting scrip-
ture; transcendentalists ended by asserting the divine right of the individual
to impose his own spirit on everything he touched. His duty to himself,
which was also his deepest instinct, was to suck in from the widest possible
field all that was congenial to him, and to reject, down to his very centre,
whatever might thwart or offend. Sometimes he carried his consistency in
egotism to the length of denying that anything he could not digest could
possibly exist. . . . Even when not initiated into these transcendental mys-
teries, he was filled with practical self-trust, the desire to give himself freedom, and the belief that he deserved it. There was no need of exploring anything he was not tempted to explore; he had an equal right to his opinion,
whatever the limits of his knowledge; and he should be coerced as little as
possible in his action. In specific matters, for the sake of expediency, he
might be willing to yield to the majority; but only when his vote had been

counted, and as a sort of insurance against being disturbed in his residual liberty.

There was a general conviction behind all these maxims, that tradition corrupts experience. All sensation—which is the test of matters of fact—is somebody's sensation; all reasoning is somebody's reasoning, and vitally persuasive as it first comes; but when transmitted the evidence loses its edge, words drop their full meaning, and inert conventions falsify the insights of those who had instituted them. Therefore, reform, revision, restatement are perpetually required: any individual, according to this view, who honestly corrected tradition was sure to improve upon it. Whatsoever was not the fresh handiwork of the soul and true to its present demand was bad for that soul. A man without traditions, if he could only be materially well equipped, would be purer, more rational, more virtuous than if he had been an heir to anything. *Weh dir, dass du ein Enkel bist!* Blessed are the orphans, for they shall deserve to have children; blessed the American! Philosophy should be transcendental, history romantic and focussed in one's own country, politics democratic, and art individual and above convention. Variety in religious dogma would only prove the truth—that is, the inwardness—of inspiration.

Yet if this transcendental freedom had been the whole of liberalism, would not the animals, such of them at least as are not gregarious, have been the most perfect liberals? Are they not ruled wholly from within? Do they not enjoy complete freedom of conscience and of expression? Does Mrs. Grundy interfere with their spontaneous actions? Are they ever compelled to fight except by their own impulse and in their private interest? Yet it was not the ideal of liberalism to return to nature; far from it. It admonished the dogs not to bark, even if, in the words of the sacred poet, "it is their nature to." Dogs, according to transcendental philosophy, ought to improve their nature and to behave better. A chief part of the liberal inspiration was the love of peace, safety, comfort, and general information; it aimed at stable wealth, it insisted on education, it venerated culture. It was wholly out of sympathy with the wilder instincts of man, with the love of foraging, of hunting, of fighting, of plotting, of carousing, or of doing penance. It had an acute, a sickening horror of suffering; to be cruel was devilish and to be hardened to pain was brutal. I am afraid liberalism was hopelessly pre-Nietzschean; it was Victorian; it was tame. In inviting every man to be free and autonomous it assumed that, once free, he would wish to be rich, to be educated, and to be demure. How could he possibly fail to covet a way of life which, in the eyes of liberals, was so obviously the best? It must have been a painful surprise to them, and most inexplicable, that hardly anybody who has had a taste of the liberal system has ever liked it.

What about liberty in love? If there is one ingenuous and winged creature among the immortals, it is Eros; the freer and more innocent love is, the more it will flutter, the farther it will range, and the higher it will soar. But at the touch of matter, of conditions, of consequences, how all its freedom shrivels, or turns into tragedy! What prohibitions, what hypocrisies, what responsibilities, what sorrows! The progress of civilization compels love to respect the limits set to it by earlier vows, by age, sex, class, race, religion, blood relationship and even fictitious relationship; bounds of which the impertinent Eros himself knows nothing. Society smothers the imp altogether in the long christening-clothes of domestic affection and religious duty. What was once a sensuous intoxication, a mystic rapture, an enchanted friendship, becomes all a question of money, of habit, of children. British liberalism has been particularly cruel to love; in the Victorian era all its amiable impulses were reputed indecent, until a marriage certificate suddenly rendered them godly, though still unmentionable. And what liberty does even the latest radicalism offer to the heart? Liberty to be divorced; divorced at great expense, with shabby perjuries and public scandal, probably in order to be at once married again, until the next divorce. Was it not franker and nobler to leave love, as in Spain, to the poets; to let the stripling play the guitar as much as he liked in the moonlight, exchange passionate glances, whisper daily at the lattice, and then, dressing the bride in black, to dismiss free fancy at the church door, saying: Henceforth let thy names be charity and fidelity and obedience?

It is not politics that can bring true liberty to the soul; that must be achieved, if at all, by philosophy; but liberalism may bring large opportunities for achievement in a man's outward life. It intensifies—because it renders attainable—the lure of public distinction, of luxury, of love surrounded by refined pleasures. The liberal state stimulates the imagination of an ambitious man to the highest degree. Those who have a good start in the universal competition, or sharp wits, or audacity, will find plenty of prizes awaiting them. With the pride of wealth, when it is great, there comes the pride of munificence; in the suburbs of wealth there is culture, and in its service there is science. When science can minister to wealth and intelligence to dominion, both can be carried on the shoulders of the plutocracy which dominates the liberal state; and they can fill it with innumerable comforts and marvellous inventions. At the same time, nothing will hinder the weaker members of rich families from becoming clergymen or even scholars or artists; or they may range over the five continents, hunt whatever wild beasts remain in the jungle and write books about savages.

Whether these prizes offered by liberal society are worth winning, I cannot say from experience, never having desired them; but the aspects of modern life which anyone may observe, and the analytic picture of it which the novelists supply, are not very attractive. Wealth is always, even when most secure, full of itch and fear; worry about health, children, religion, marriage, servants; and the awful question of where to live, when one may live anywhere, and yet all seems to depend on the choice. For the politician, politics are less important than his private affairs, and less interesting than bridge; and he has always a party, or a wicked opposition, on which to throw the blame if his careless measures turn out badly. No one in office can be a true statesman, because a true statesman is consistent, and public opinion will never long support any consistent course. What the successful man in modern society really most cares about is love; love for him is a curious mixture of sensuality, vanity, and friendship; it lights up all the world of his thought and action with its secret and unsteady flame. Even when mutual and legal, it seems to be three-quarters anxiety and sorrow; for if nothing worse happens to lovers, they grow old. I hear no laughter among the rich which is not forced and nervous. I find no sense of moral security amongst them, no happy freedom, no mastery over anything. Yet this is the very cream of liberal life, the brilliant success for the sake of which Christendom was overturned, and the dull peasantry elevated into factory-hands, shopkeepers, and chauffeurs.

When the lists are open to all, and the one aim of life is to live as much as possible like the rich, the majority must needs be discouraged. . . . There was more encouragement for mediocre people when happiness was set before them in mediocrity, or in excellence in some special craft. Now the mass, hopelessly out of the running in the race for wealth, falls out and drifts into squalor. Since there is liberty, the listless man will work as little and drink as much as he can; he will crawl into whatever tenement he can get cheapest, seek the society in which least effort is demanded and the least shame is felt, have as many children as improvidence sends him, let himself out, at a pinch, for whatever service and whatever wages he can obtain, drift into some syndicated servitude or some great migration, or sink in solitude into the deepest misery. He then becomes a denizen of those slimy quarters, under the shadow of railway bridges, breweries and gas-works, where the blear lights of a public-house peer through the rain at every corner, and offer him the one joy remaining in life; . . . but perhaps God does not see all this, because a pall hangs over it perpetually of impenetrable smoke. The liberal system, which sought to raise the individual, has degraded the masses; and this on so vast a scale and to so pitiable a degree, that the other element in liberalism, philanthropic zeal, has come again to the fore. Liberty go hang, say the new radicals; let us save the people. Liberal legislation, which was to have reduced government to the minimum of police control, now has undertaken public education, social reform, and even the management of industry.

This happy people can read. It supports a press conforming to the tastes of the common man, or rather to such tastes as common men can have in common; for the best in each is not diffused enough to be catered for in public. Moreover, this press is audaciously managed by some adventitious power, which guides it for its own purposes, commercial or sectarian. Superstitions old and new thrive in this infected atmosphere; they are now all treated with a curious respect, as if nobody could have anything to object to them. It is all a scramble of prejudices and rumours; whatever first catches the ear becomes a nucleus for all further presumptions and sympathies. Advertising is the modern substitute for argument, its function is to make the worse appear the better article. A confused competition of all propagandas—those insults to human nature—is carried on by the most expert psychological methods, which the art of advertising has discovered; for instance, by always repeating a lie, when it has been exposed, instead of retracting it. The world at large is deafened; but each propaganda makes its little knot of proselytes, and inspires them with a new readiness to persecute and to suffer in the sacred cause. . . . By giving a free rein to such propagandas, and by disgusting the people with too much optimism, toleration, and neutrality, liberalism has introduced a new reign of unqualified ill-will. Hatred and wilfulness are everywhere; nations and classes are called to life on purpose to embody them; they are summoned by their leaders to shake off the lethargy of contentment and to become conscious of their existence and of their terrible wrongs. These propagandas have taken shape in the blue sky of liberalism, like so many summer clouds; they seem airships sailing under a flag of truce; but they are engines of war; and on the first occasion they will hoist their true colours, and break the peace which allowed them to cruise over us leisurely. Each will try to establish its universal ascendancy by force, in contempt of personal freedom, or the voice of majorities. . . . Liberalism has merely cleared a field in which every soul and every corporate interest may fight with every other for domination. Whoever is victorious in this struggle will make an end of liberalism; and the new order, which will deem itself saved, will have to defend itself in the following age against a new crop of rebels.

For myself, even if I could live to see it, I should not be afraid of the future domination, whatever it may be. One has to live in some age, under some fashion; I have found, in different times and places, the liberal, the Catholic, and the German air quite possible to breathe; nor, I am sure, would communism be without its advantages to a free mind and its splendid emotions. Fanatics, as Tacitus said of the Jews or Christians, are consumed with hatred of the human race, which offends them; yet they are themselves human; and nature in them takes its revenge, and something reasonable and sweet bubbles up out of the very fountain of their madness. Once established in the world the new dispensation forms a ruling caste, a conventional morality, standard of honour; safety and happiness soften the heart of the tyrant. Aristocracy knows how to kiss the ruddy cheeks of its tenants' children; and before mounting its thoroughbred horse at the park gates, it pats him with a gloved hand, and gives him a lump of sugar; nor does it forget to ask the groom, with a kindly interest, when he is setting out for the war. Poor flunkey! The demagogues will tell him he is a fool, to let himself be dragooned into a regiment, and marched off to endure untold privations, death or ghastly wounds, all for some fantastic reason which is nothing to him. It is a hard fate; but can this world promise anybody anything better? For the moment he will have a smart uniform; beers and lasses will be obtainable; many comrades will march by his side; and he may return, if he is lucky, to work again in his master's stables, lounge at the public-house, and bounce his children on his knee amongst the hollyhocks before his cottage. Would the demagoguges give him better prospects, or prove better masters? Would he be happier with no masters at all? Consider the demagogues themselves, and their history. They found themselves in the extreme of misery; but even this is a sort of distinction, and marks off a new species, seizing new weapons in the struggle for existence. The scum of the earth gathers itself together, becomes a criminal or a revolutionary society, finds some visionary or some cosmopolitan agitator to lead it, establishes its own code of ethics, imposes the desperate discipline of outlaws upon its members, and prepares to rend the free society that allowed it to exist. It is astonishing with what docility masses of Englishmen, supposed to be jealous of their personal liberty, will obey such a revolutionary junta, that taxes and commands them, and decrees when they shall starve and when they shall fight. I suspect that the working-people of the towns no longer have what was called the British character. Their forced unanimity in action and passion is like that of the ages of faith; its inspiration, like that of early Christianity, comes from a few apostles, perhaps foreign Jews, men who in the beginning had visions of some millennium; and the cohesion of the faithful is maintained afterwards by preaching, by custom, by persecution, and by murder. Yet it is intelligible that the most earnest liberals, who in so far as they were advocates of liberty fostered these conspiracies, in so far as they are philanthropists should applaud them, and feel the need of this new tyranny. They save liberal principles by saying that they applaud it only provisionally as a necessary means of freeing the people. But of freeing the people from what? From the consequences of freedom.

REINHOLD NIEBUHR 1892-

THE SON OF A MISSOURI PASTOR, Reinhold Niebuhr spent his early years in the Midwest, and completed his theological education at Yale. For 13 years he served as pastor of a small church in Detroit where he was drawn to the problems of "industrial justice" and where his reflections on contemporary society led to a conversion from liberalism. He began teaching at Union Theological Seminary in 1928, and was vice-president when he retired in 1960. In his political views, he abandoned pacifism and socialism for a tough-minded, pragmatic liberalism. His writing covers a vast range of subjects, including theology, social and political thought, moral theory, international politics, and philosophy of history. He has identified himself as a preacher rather than as a theologian, yet it is often declared that he is probably the most influential theological writer of our time.

[16]   Ten Years That Shook My World

I

. . . midway in my ministry which extends roughly from the peace of Versailles to the peace of Munich, measured in terms of Western history, I underwent a fairly complete conversion of thought which involved rejection of almost all the liberal theological ideals and ideas with which I ventured forth in 1915. I wrote a book, my first, in 1927 which when now consulted is proved to contain almost all the theological windmills against which today I tilt my sword. These windmills must have tumbled shortly thereafter for every succeeding volume expressed a more and more explicit revolt against what is usually known as liberal culture.

While my critics accuse me of inconstancy my own biased judgment is that there is no inconstancy in the development of my thought since that day, though there is a gradual theological elaboration of what was at first merely socio-ethical criticism. Since the war was the revelation of the internal anarchy of Western civilization, the existence of which bourgeois culture was inclined to deny, and since the peace of Versailles was the revelation of vindicative passions which liberalism imagined were banished from the world, and since the peace of Munich proves that one cannot simply correct the injustices of conquest by the injustice which results from capitulation to tyranny, I conclude that the whole of contemporary history proves that liberal culture has not seen the problem of mankind in sufficient depth to understand its own history. Its too simple moralism has confused issues at almost every turn.

The contemporary problem is brought into theological focus if it is recognized that liberal Christianity is essentially an appropriation of the genuine achievements, and an accommodation to the characteristic prejudices, of this bourgeois culture which first came to flower in the Renaissance, which gained some triumphs and suffered some checks in the Reformation, which reached its zenith in the early part of this century, which revealed its internal anarchy in the World War and its inability to defend itself against lower forms of civilization in the present hour. In terms of politics and economics the bourgeois world is the world of the business man,

From *The Christian Century*, LVI (April 26, 1939), 542–46. Copyright 1939 The Christian Century Foundation. Reprinted by permission from *The Christian Century* and Reinhold Niebuhr.

of expanding commerce and industry, of economic imperialism, transmuted in a period of decay into economic nationalism.

II

In terms of culture, the bourgeois civilization produced what is generally known as liberalism. This liberalism, I must hasten to add, is something more than either the spirit of tolerance on the one hand or liberal economic theory on the other hand. The liberalism of classical economics, upon which capitalism is built (though it must disavow its own presuppositions in its period of decay) is only one characteristic fruit of the liberal culture. The faith of classical economic theory, that economic activity left to itself, without political interference, would gradually achieve a perfect harmony and justice, was merely one, though a very fateful, error derived from the general liberal assumption that man is essentially a very harmless animal, if only he can be held within the harmonies of nature and of reason from which the fanaticism of religion had beguiled him.

The spirit of tolerance in the liberal culture is of course a real gain. It belongs by right to any profound Christianity which understands the ambiguity of all human actions, the imperfection of all human ideals and the peril of self-righteous fanaticism in all human conflict. It must be admitted, however, that traditional Christianity, both Catholic and Protestant, had so frequently allowed the loyalty and worship, which belongs to God alone, to be appropriated for relative, social, political, economic and theological positions, that it had given rationalists good reason to believe that fanatic cruelty was the chief byproduct, or possibly even the chief product, of religion.

It may be observed, however, that those who move away from a liberal culture have both the obligation and the possibility of proving that they have a securer foundation for the spirit of tolerance than traditional liberalism afforded. In secular liberalism the spirit of tolerance is either rooted in a deep skepticism and pessimism which must finally culminate in the intolerable sneer of Pilate, "What is truth?" or it is based on an untenable optimism which believes, with Professor Dewey, that men of good will must, if they meditate upon the issues of life long and profoundly enough, arrive at a "common faith." Professor Dewey's notion that divisions in the human family are chiefly derived from anachronistic religious dogmas ought, incidentally, to be fairly well refuted now by the force of the tragic events of contemporary history.

In any profound Christianity the spirit of tolerance must be derived from the knowledge that, however necessary it may be to judge one another and even to fight one another on the moral and political level, we are all sinners who stand under God's ultimate judgment. It is this consciousness of a divine judgment which must persuade us to recognize the validity of Christ's admonition, "Judge not that ye be not judged," or of St. Paul's exhortation: "Therefore thou art inexcusable, O man, whosoever thou art that judgest; for wherein thou judgest another, thou condemnest thyself; for thou that judgest doest the same thing."

III

If liberalism as a creed is more than the liberal spirit of toleration on the one hand and more than laissez faire economics on the other, what is it? I should say primarily faith in man; faith in his capacity to subdue nature, and faith that the subjection of nature achieves life's final good; faith in man's essential goodness, to be realized either when man ceases to be spiritual and returns to nature (romanticism), or when he ceases to be natural and becomes rational; and finally, faith in human history which is conceived as a movement upward by a force immanent within it. Whether this faith rests upon Darwin or upon Hegel, that is, whether nature is believed to guarantee progress or whether progress is conceived of as man's "gradual spiritualization" and his emancipation from natural impulses, prejudices and parochial attachments, the optimistic conclusion is the same.

It is instructive to note that liberal culture was always divided against itself on the question whether it should regard human nature and human history primarily from the standpoint of man's relation to nature or from the standpoint of his rational transcendence over nature. In this conflict between the naturalists and idealists, the idealists had something of the Christian doctrine of the dignity of man as made in the image of God, and the naturalists had something of the Christian doctrine of man as a creature who must not pretend to be more than he is. But between them they lost the uneasy conscience of the Christian and expressed themselves in terms of an easy conscience. Whatever was wrong with man, the cause was some defect in his social organization or some imperfection in his education which further social history and cultural development would correct.

I may say that though I express my opposition to liberal civilization politically in terms of Marxian politics, I regard Marxian culture as participating essentially in all the liberal illusions. It also believes in the goodness of man, once capitalism has been destroyed. It also believes in an inevitable progress on the other tide of the revolution. It has a catastrophic view of history, but only provisionally so. The destruction of capitalism is, for it, the final destruction of evil. This error must not be taken lightly, even by those of us who believe that the Marxian analysis of the relation of economics to politics is essentially correct.

The Marxian misunderstanding of man has contributed to the development of a tyranny in Russia which almost, though not quite, rivals fascist tyranny. Objectively it cannot be as bad, because it is impossible to destroy all the universal hopes in communism, which distinguish it from the franker tribal mania of fascism. Subjectively, this decay in Russian may be worse, because it extinguishes a new hope in a world in which all the old lights are going out. I feel genuinely sorry for my friends who seem to be under a spiritual necessity to deny obvious facts about Russian tyranny.

IV

In a sense, the really tragic end of a liberal culture is to be found in the peace of Munich. What was best in that culture was outraged by the peace of Versailles and what was shallowest in it came to the conclusion that the horrors of a peace of conquest could be expiated by a peace of capitulation. Thus it lost its last chance to save what is genuine and universal in its life against the threat of a new barbarism. It fondly imagines that the decay of the modern world may still be healed by belatedly yielding "justice" to Germany, when it is obvious that Germany, and the fascist world in general, is no longer interested in justice, but bent upon the display of its power and the exercise of a dominion which asks no questions about justice in either the Christian or the liberal sense.

Liberal moralism is, in short, unable to cope either with man's immediate political or with his ultimate religious problems. It does not know how to check evil and historical injustice in terms of perfect moral purity. The ultimate religious problem of evil in man does not arise for it, because it is always waiting for the perfect education or perfect social order which will make man moral. It does not understand man in the full dimension of his spirit, and does not see that precisely because he is a child of God and made in God's image, he cannot be contained in, or easily checked by, either the harmony of nature or the prudence of reason.

It would, of course, be grossly unfair not to recognize that liberal Christianity made a genuine contribution to true Christianity by appropriating some of the achievements of this culture. Through some of these appropriations liberal Christianity purified Christian theology of some of its grievous historical errors. One of these was the insistence of Christian orthodoxy that a religious explanation of natural events was also a scientific explanation and obviated the necessity of tracing the natural sequence of events and their secondary causation.

But religion is constitutionally indifferent to the problem of secondary causation. This indifference becomes a sin when theology is made into a bad science and the sense of ultimate meaning and creation is allowed to obscure the problem of natural causation. In accommodating itself to the "scientific spirit," liberal Christianity therefore rightly clarified an ancient confusion, though it must be admitted that it was frequently betrayed thereby into a world view in which its essential theism was transmuted into a vague pantheism.

A second great gain of liberal Christianity, derived from the achievements of modern culture, was the application of the scientific historical method to its own records. Ethically, this emancipated Christianity from the necessity of regarding any moral attitude, fortuitously enshrined in its own canon, as final and authoritative. It permitted the Christian law of love to stand out in Christian ethics as the only final norm. Theologically, this scientific spirit saved Christianity from the corruption of the profound principle, *credo ut intelligam,* into a tyranny of theological authority over human reason. These gains of liberal Christianity must not be imperiled. It would be truer to say that they must not be sacrificed, though they will be imperiled. Frantic and hysterical retreats to orthodoxy are bound to imperil them. This advance must be protected against those who think it a gain to return to theological obscurantism from the shallows of a too simple rationalism.

But liberal Christianity quite obviously accepted the prejudices as well as the achievements of modern culture. It was pathetically eager to justify itself before the "modern mind" and failed to realize that this modern mind was involved in a very ancient human sin. It imagined itself the final mind. It thought of itself as God, the final arbiter of truth and destiny.

V

In seeking to persuade the modern mind that Christianity is respectable and intelligent, the liberals sacrificed most of the essential Christian positions. Christ was transmuted into the good man Jesus, who could charm all men to become as good as he was. The classic Christology of the God-man was repudiated, though innumerable reservations sought to hide the repudiation. It was not recognized that this absurd doctrine of the God-man Christ contains the whole essence of the Christian faith—its belief that God transcends history and yet makes himself known in history; that history measured by Christ is tragic and ends tragically for it crucifies Christ; that only God is able to resolve the conflict between what man is and what he ought to be, a conflict in which all men stand; that God cannot do this by simply wiping out history and transmuting it into eternity, but by redeeming history, but that the redemption of history involves more than persuading man to follow the law of God. It involves God's taking upon himself the inevitable violation of that law.

Liberal Christianity, in short, tended to follow modern culture in estimating both the stature and the virtue of man. It did not recognize that man is a spirit who can find a home neither in nature nor in reason, but only in God. The power of human self-transcendence (the true image of God) is such that man can and does break every restraint set by nature or reason. His very capacities are occasions for sin in him. It is because he is made in the image of God that man can be tempted to make himself God, to seek to overcome his natural insecurity by pretensions of power which involve him in more insecurity; to seek to hide the finiteness of his intelligence by pretensions of absolute truth, which involve him in cruel fanaticisms; to seek to transcend his insignificance by claims of importance which are both ridiculous and dangerous.

All these things man does, not because his pure mind is impeded by the inertia of his animal nature, but because he is the only animal who is involved in history and yet stands outside of it, the only creature who has a glimpse of the eternal beyond the finite and is incited to pretend an eternal significance for all his finite interests, values and ideals.

For this reason, the simple reinterpretations of the Kingdom of God into the law of progress, in the thought of liberal Christianity, is an equally serious betrayal of essential insights of the Christian faith to the prejudices of modern culture. Obviously there is progress of all kinds in human history, including progress in aerial bombing and the effective use of the radio for the dissemination of political lies. There is progress from immaturity to maturity in every field of endeavor. But there is not a single bit of evidence to prove that good triumphs over evil in this constant development of history. History points to a goal beyond itself, and not merely to an eternity which negates history.

This is what all biblical religion tries to say in words and symbols which outrage reason, as they must. For reason cannot contain this idea, though, if it is astute enough, it can uncover the absurdity of alternative propositions. Liberal Christianity sought to efface these irrationalities of biblical apocalypticism by discovering that Jesus had, indeed, some difficulty in freeing his thought about the Kingdom of God from outworn forms of Jewish thought, but that he is to be commended for almost achieving this desirable emancipation in the end and thus approximating what an enlightened modern man believes about history.

Yet from the standpoint of mere history the final story about this Jesus is that he was crucified. That he was raised from the dead and will come again in glory—*that* faith belongs to another dimension which is beyond history, and yet without which history would be either meaningless or filled with tragic meaning only.

VI

Christianity, in short, faces the tremendous task of extricating itself from the prejudices and illusions of a culture which is rapidly sinking with the disruption of the civilization which gave it birth. This is not yet fully realized in America, because the prospects and hopes of our civilization are sufficiently brighter than in Europe to give liberal illusions a tougher vitality and a slower death here. This task of emancipation is a tremendous one, partly because liberalism as a culture is still superior to many of the cultures which threaten to displace it politically. It is certainly superior to the primitive and Nietzschian romanticism which expresses itself in fascist politics. It may even prove superior to socialism, if socialism sacrifices the achievements of democracy as it has done in Russia.

One of the real tragedies of our era is that the very democracy which is the great achievement of liberalism cannot be maintained if liberalism is not transcended as a culture. The problem of achieving economic justice is obviously more difficult than liberalism had imagined. The prerequisite of economic justice is a tolerable equilibrium of economic power, which in a technical age means the socialization of property. The excessive moralism of liberalism makes it impossible to see either the necessity of this end or the rigorous means which will be required to achieve it. Liberalism seems unable to move toward the economic democracy which is required to maintain its political democracy. Nor does it seem able to protect what is still left of its political democracy against the threat of a new barbarism; which is what makes the peace of Munich so significant.

If I believe that the Christian understanding of man could help solve some of these crucial issues and could conserve the best achievements of liberalism better than traditional liberalism can conserve them, I do not for that reason wish merely to hitch Christian faith to this or to that political task. Christianity faces ultimate issues of life which transcend all political vicissitudes and achievements. But the answer which Christian faith gives to man's ultimate perplexities and the hope which it makes possible in the very abyss of his despair, also throw light upon the immediate historical issues which he faces. Christianity is not a flight into eternity from the tasks and decisions of history. It is rather the power and the wisdom of God which makes decisions in history possible and which points to proximate goals in history which are usually obscured either by optimistic illusions or by the despair which followed upon the dissipation of these illusions. Christianity must therefore wage constant war, on the one hand against political religions which imagine some proximate goal and some conditioned good as man's final good, and on the other hand against an otherworldliness which by contrast gives these political religions a seeming validity.

VII

For this reason, any new orthodoxy which seeks to persuade men that because all men must finally be made manifest before the judgment seat of Christ, they are not to regard the momentary judgments, the proximate goals and the relative values of history seriously, must be regarded as a heresy as dangerous as any simple optimism. In every experience of life, Christ appears in many guises to the believer. He is the judge in comparison with whom I am found to fall short and to be an unprofitable servant. He is the redeemer who gives my life a new center of loyalty and a new source of power. He is, however, also the law, the logos, the essential structure of life, which I must seek to obey, even though I fall short in my obedience. He is what I am essentially, and therefore what I ought to be.

Liberal Christianity emphasized that fact rather too simply. The new orthodoxy rightly insists that he is also what I can never be. He is therefore the source of my despair. Only in that despair and in repentance can he become the source of a new hope. This second emphasis is true enough. Only it will tempt us "to continue to sin that grace may abound" if we do not preserve what is genuinely Christian in liberal Christian moralism: the insistence that Christ is our law, our ideal, our norm, and the revelation of our essential being.

All this is not very autobiographical, after all. The only autobiographical note which I can add, in conclusion, is that such theological convictions which I hold today began to dawn upon me during the end of a pastorate in a great industrial city. They dawned upon me because the simple little moral homilies which were preached in that as in other cities, by myself and others, seemed completely irrelevant to the brutal facts of life in a great industrial center. Whether irrelevant or not, they were certainly futile. They did not change human actions or attitudes in any problem of collective behavior by a hair's breadth, though they may well have helped to preserve private amenities and to assuage individual frustrations.

These convictions which dawned in my pastorate have been further elaborated in a teaching position in a theological seminary. Greater leisure has given me opportunity to discover the main currents and emphases of the classical ages of Christian thought, and to find insights there which have been long neglected and which are yet absolutely essential to modern man, or indeed to man of any age.

However, since I am not so much scholar as preacher, I must confess that the gradual unfolding of my theological ideas has come not so much through study as through the pressure of world events. Whatever measure of Christian faith I hold today is due to the gradual exclusion of alternative beliefs through world history. As did Peter, I would preface my confession, "Thou hast words of eternal life," with the question, "Lord, to whom shall we go?" Even while imagining myself to be preaching the gospel, I had really experimented with many modern alternatives to Christian faith, until one by one they proved unavailing.

Socialism

HAROLD J. LASKI
1893-1950

IN SOME WAYS HAROLD LASKI'S political consciousness was a
barometer for the period between the wars: to each crisis he reacted by adopting what he believed was a more radical position. During his
adult life he was successively a pluralist and guild socialist, an orthodox Fabian
socialist, and finally a Marxian socialist.

Laski was born into a fairly well-to-do merchant family in Manchester. He
studied natural science and then history at Oxford University, where he joined
the Fabian Society and was influenced by Ernest Barker and F. W. Maitland.
He lectured at Canadian and American universities in his early twenties and
then joined the London School of Economics, with which he was associated
until his death. As a teacher and friend to thousands of students, Laski will be
long remembered for the excitement he generated about political ideas. His
apparently inexhaustible energy was also directed into his voluminous writings
and his political activity in the leading councils of the British Labour party.

Laski's early works, such as *Studies in the Problem of Sovereignty* (1917)
and *Authority in the Modern State* (1919), reflected the pluralistic theories of
John N. Figgis, Maitland, and Otto von Gierke. The state he viewed as but one
of many associations, and he argued for the decentralization of authority along
functional lines. The tone of these writings was skeptical, open-minded, and
pragmatic, and their scintillating style showed Laski at his best. Between the years
1925 and 1931, in such works as *A Grammar of Politics* (1925) and *Liberty in
the Modern State* (1930), he retained his pragmatic attitude toward the distribu-

tion of state authority but became more concerned with using the power of the state to reduce economic inequality. He also began to veer toward a Marxist conception of politics, a view which he had sharply criticized in earlier years. As he experienced the British Cabinet crisis of 1931, the depression, and the international events of those years, he came to believe that Marxism provided the only key to politics. *The State in Theory and Practice* (1935) and *The Rise of European Liberalism* (1936) are typical of this period of his thought. He prophesied that the capitalist class would not give up its privileges and power without a violent revolution, and he interpreted the British political crises as attempts by that class to use the authority of the state against the workers. At this stage his ideas became dogmatic in tone to complement his pessimistic outlook, and this position became more intransigent after 1943 in such works as *Reflections on the Revolution of Our Time* (1943) and *The American Democracy* (1948). In these last years, his writings celebrated the Soviet system as the basis for "effective freedom." Nonetheless, sufficient criticism of Bolshevik dictatorial policies remained to discourage the Soviets from returning the compliments he bestowed on them.

[17]   *Socialism and Freedom*

I

No accusation against Socialism is more common than the taunt that its exponents do not understand the worth of freedom. It is supposed to be a system under which men will lose all trace of individuality. They will, we are warned, be regimented and dragooned by a powerful bureaucracy which will prescribe each item of their daily lives. The Socialist State is depicted as though it were a Platonic Utopia in which the guardians were replaced by the grim henchmen of Lenin and Trotsky. The indictment varies in its emphasis. Sometimes it is against the family that the Socialist appeal is said to be directed; and we are bidden to compare the proud freedom of Laburnum Villa with the relentless organisation of some nationalised phalanstery. Sometimes it is the artist and the thinker who are said to be in peril; for in a state like the Socialist State the absence of a leisured class is held to involve the necessary disappearance of art and philosophy. Nor, we are told, will the adventurer's risk remain; the boy who is engaged as an ap-

From Harold J. Laski, *Socialism and Freedom,* Fabian Society Tract No. 216 (London: The Fabian Society, 1925), pp. 3–14. Reprinted by permission of Mrs. Harold J. Laski and The Fabian Society.

prentice in a motor factory can never dream of attaining to the eminence of Mr. Ford. A world reduced to plan and system will lose the colour and variety that are the essence of freedom. We shall lose the marks of separate and identifiable personality. We shall become items in a vast card catalogue, marionettes responsive to the control of others. Socialism, so it is said, involves a world of Robots living by the orders of officials. It is a system from which all chance and vividness have gone; in which no man remains, as now, eager and able to be master of the event.

We are advised, accordingly, to cling to what we have. Here, at the worst, is a world in which each man can control his own fate. The fortune that attends him he makes for himself. No barrier stands in the way of his ascent; and the humble engine driver may find himself the cabinet minister of a great empire. Freedom of conscience, freedom of political belief, an educational system which leaves open the high road to the best training society can offer, the power to share in the making of the law, the opportunity, by energy and inventiveness, to attain the eminence of wealth and position, these, we are told, now lie open to all. The prospects of a democratic society built upon the economics of industrialism represent a solid achievement won only after bitter struggle; and we are asked by Socialists to exchange them for a system under which no man can determine his own destiny. The progress of the world, so it is said, is built upon our present method of removing the shackles which fetter the free play of individuality. Socialism would replace that freedom by rigorous control. It would bring down the dead hand of the State upon the priceless initiative now possessed by the ordinary man. It would foster uniformity at the expense of uniqueness. It would fashion a world in the image of mediocrity. To-day, at least, the career is open to the talents, and the sovereign power of the electorate is an assurance that necessary changes will be effected.

It is not, of course, denied that there are disharmonies in the present order. There is disparity of wealth; but since real wages have increased in the last hundred years we have the assurance that the toiler has a larger claim upon the national dividend. There is grievous unemployment; but a system of social insurance has now mitigated its most serious consequences. Educational opportunity is still unequal; but a ladder is being rapidly built whereby all who can take advantage of it may reach its summit. There are slums and infant mortality, preventable accidents in industry, inequality before the law, a harsh penal system. But the conscience of the nation is awakened. Never was charity more widely organised. Never did the essential unity of classes appear more evident to those of our governors who knew the comradeship of the trenches. The spirit of progress permeates every part of the social fabric; and the keynote of our effort is the right of the individual.

It would be an idyllic picture did it possess the single merit of accuracy. But if it is compared with the facts we know, it shrinks at once into ineptitude. The lives of most are not made by themselves. The clerk, the docker, the shop assistant, the factory hand, are driven in each item of their working lives to abide by the behest of other men. They do not share in making the orders under which they live; they are not invigorated by that stimulus to creative effort upon which alone a permanent social order can be built. Most of them fight an unending struggle with poverty, or the penumbra of poverty, in which, almost from the outset, they know they are bound to be defeated. In any sober analysis, the prizes of life are not within their grasp. Materially they are either the possession of men who have never had to do battle for them or have won them by methods often ethically disreputable; intellectually, it is only the rare few who can transcend the limits of an education as mean and narrow as that to which most are condemned. Spiritually, doubtless, they can share not less than others in the gain of living. The splendour of conviction, the mystery of love, the opportunity to share in a great corporate effort lie open to them. But these do not and cannot lie open to them as a natural part of life. Most trade union leaders have had to pay a heavy price for their inability to accept the principles of capitalism; and few working women can hope to be more than unpaid domestic drudges once the first months of love have passed.

The true goods of life, in fact, security, knowledge, the enjoyment of beauty, only a few in the present social order can hope to know. The rest will live a life of unending routine, uncertain of the morrow, and on the threshold of a great spiritual heritage from entrance to which they are debarred. Their homes are mean and devoid of beauty. Their tastes are debauched by immersion in an atmosphere into which the life of the spirit can rarely hope to penetrate. Even if they have the joy of creating beautiful things, they cannot hope to possess them. Even if beautiful things are at their hand, they have seldom been taught to grasp their secret. They have political power; but they view the drama of politics as a play in which they are cast for the part of spectators. They could have economic power; but they have never been trained either to understand its principles, or the complex institutions through which these work. They are forced by the circumstances to remain private persons, whom only unwonted experience compels to report their wants. Their rulers can involve them in war; and they do not know how to judge its rights and wrongs. They are trained to be the recipients of orders which they obey from dumb inertia.

* * *

The community, as Disraeli saw, is divided into the two nations of rich and poor. The one concerns itself in enjoying life while there is yet time, and in seeking to postpone that period when the masses will refuse to suffer in peaceful silence. The other lives in half-impotent wonder at the events it knows of its own experience and those of that other species it sees dimly in the distance. Occasionally, indeed, from its wonder is born indignation, and from indignation thought. It may well be that therein is implied a new social order since thought is a disease against which no specific has been yet discovered. But the period of gestation is slow; and the degree of pain in birth is always a measure of its chance of survival.

Two freedoms we must grant to our own time. In the Western world, it is, on the whole, true that religious toleration is reasonably complete. The cynic might say that it is complete because the religious motive has lost its potency in our civilisation. Men may be what they will, from Atheist to Zoroastrian, only because the life of faith, the passionate communion with things unseen, has for the vast majority, lost its magic; and he might add that the main motive in the coming of religious freedom was the conviction, born of hard experience, that intolerance was commercially unprofitable. He might add, even further, that the acceptance of religious creeds is not held to involve the acceptance of the conduct implied in those creeds. A Dean of the Anglican Church need not preach the Sermon on the Mount so long as he does not doubt too openly the Athanasian Creed. A Nonconformist business man may attain eminence in his denomination; but he is not expected to insist that love of one's neighbour is a principle of business organisation.

There is, also, within the ambit of Western Civilisation, probably a wider degree of political freedom than in the past. Men, on the balance, have ampler room for the expression of intellectual conviction. There are even communities in which no penalty attaches to a belief in Socialism, and there are States which have permitted Socialist parties to hold office for a brief space of time. But, Russia apart, it is to be remembered that Socialism has not, so far, been powerful enough to strike at the heart of the capitalist citadel. Where it has been overemphatic, as in Hungary and Italy, it has suffered appropriate penalty. In America, indeed, the rumour even of what it implies has been sufficient to make its opponents eager to revive every ancient motive of persecution. Yet faith in Socialism does grow, though it must be admitted that the tolerance of its opponents has not yet been put to a serious test. Faith in the power of reason is not the strongest of human impulses; and we shall know more of its tenacity when Socialism begins to move nearer the realisation of its central aim.

Upon one other aspect of freedom under the present order a word may be said. Certainly more amply than at any previous time there exists freedom before the courts of law. But that freedom is limited and hampered by the conditions of the economic régime. A rich woman who steals from a Kensington shop will not get the same sentence as a poor woman who steals from a Whitechapel shop. What is called embezzlement in a junior clerk is often called high finance in a millionaire. What is called high spirits in an Oxford undergraduate is called assaulting the police in Barking and Limehouse. The divorce law bears unequally upon rich and poor. The average prisoner in the dock is attacked by all the legal ability at the command of the State; it is only the wealthy criminal who can afford to pit equal talent against it. A London jury is fairly certain to award damages for libel to a Tory Member of Parliament; but it is also fairly certain to assume that a Labour sympathiser cannot be libelled. Our law, as it is administered, consciously reflects the division of the State into rich and poor; and, unconsciously, the justice it makes assumes a different merit in either part.

For, so the Socialist would emphasise, all freedom is an intimate function of the Property-system which obtains at any given time. At present, outside a small minority, no man has anything to sell except his power to labour. That means, for most, that they must work as the owners of capital permit them to work. They must struggle for each item of improvement in the condition of their labour; and they will find the scales weighted against them in their effort. They will find, for example, that the Press emphasises the wickedness of builders who restrict their output; but does not emphasise the wickedness of employers' trusts formed to limit output. They will find that a strike like the miners' strike of 1921 means wants and hunger and ill-health for them and their wives; but it does not alter one jot or tittle the habits of royalty-owners like the Duke of Northumberland. Long hours of labour at a mechanical routine; an education which ends just as the problems of knowledge begin to exert their fascination; the possibility of dismissal through the caprice or incapacity of the employer; a wage that can rarely mean release from material want at any standard of national adequacy; a knowledge that ill-health or early death means ruin to the family he supports; these are the normal items in the life of the average worker. Upon these things, the system of individual liberty bases its foundations. For the worker, let it be noted again, the compensation is the knowledge, first, that there are prizes to be won, even if he does not win them, and, second, that even the division of the product of industry in terms of a rigorous equality would not make an overwhelming difference to his position. He is bidden, further, to remember that so nice is the equipose of the system that any sudden dislocation of the machinery may destroy even its power to satisfy such wants as it now meets. Its adjustment is so delicate that catastrophe would follow upon any revolt against its inequities.

It is from some such analysis as this that Socialists derive their scepticism of the freedom effected by the present order; and their doubt is intensified by the complete absence of moral principle in the methods by which the division of the State into rich and poor is maintained. For either wealth is the result of inheritance, as from parent to child, or luck; or it is the result of the power to satisfy demand. But the first has no moral basis; I am not entitled to the profits of someone else's exertions. The second takes no account of the moral or even social character of demand. There is no necessary relation between the demands which ought to be satisfied and the demands which have the power to secure satisfaction. For the power to secure satisfaction in its turn depends upon the possession of property; and since freedom means the power to satisfy demands, freedom is a function of property. The scales are therefore weighted in favour of the rich against the poor. The system organises response to demand without regard to human need. It regards wants as significant only at that level where they come armed with purchasing power. Freedom, therefore, in an essential way, is limited to the owners of property. That is why there is one law for the rich and one law for the poor; that is why, also, the education of the poor trains them to habits of command. To speak, therefore, of the present order as one built upon freedom is to regard the interest of the few who can achieve it as coincident with the general well-being of society.

II

The Socialist approaches the problem of freedom from a different angle. The purpose of society, he argues, is to enable each man to be himself at his best. Freedom is the system of conditions which makes that purpose effectively possible. Those conditions define themselves out of the historic record. They are impossible in the presence of special privilege, whether political, or religious, or economic. They are impossible unless I can report fully to those who govern what my experience of life is doing to me. They are impossible, also, unless my education has been of such a kind as to enable me to make articulate the meaning of my experience. They are impossible, further, unless I am safeguarded against the pressure of material want. I must have a wage that gives me a reasonable standard of life. I must work each day only that number of hours which will leave opportunity for creative leisure. And, in the hours of work, I must live under conditions which I assist in making. I must have the sense that they are intelligible in the same way that the orders of a medical man or a sanitary engineer are intelligible; they must be referable, that is to say, to principles which can be established as rational by scientific investigation. I must feel that the State recognises my equal claim with others, in the things essential to the good life; and that no one is admitted to an equal claim save as he pays for it by personal service. There must be equality in these essential things for all before there is superfluity for any; and the differences that exist between the rewards of men must be differences that do not weight the scales unduly in favour of those above the minimum level.

It is the Socialist case that without these things there cannot be freedom. Broadly, they imply equality; and their argument is that freedom and equality are inseparable. It is insisted, further that in an individualist régime like the present anything in the nature of equality is unattainable. For those who own in any society the essential instruments of production are able, in the nature of things, to affect the emphasis of social good towards themselves. It is their view of what is right that prevails; and their view of what is right will, in general, coincide with a policy which makes their own interest the index to what ought to be done. It therefore becomes necessary to socialise the ownership of the essential means of production; and, both within that sphere and without it, so to modify the law of testamentary disposition that no one can acquire, by the efforts of another, a claim upon the national dividend without service proportionate to his reward. The Socialist does not dogmatise as to the forms such social ownership should take. All that he insists is that until they are effectively the possession of the community, they cannot be fully administered in the interest of the community. That means such administration as will realise the system of conditions we call freedom.

It is difficult to see any necessary antithesis between the theory so stated and the freedom at which the individual aims. He would, as now, marry and beget children; he would, as now, enjoy entire freedom of religious belief. He would be certain, as he is not now certain, that his children would be

trained to an understanding of life. He would be released from the fear
that now haunts him of unemployment or of indigence. The rules of industrial life under which he had to live, would be rules in the making of
which he had a right to share. Where he laboured in a socialised industry,
the position he could win would depend, not upon nepotism, or caprice, or
the ability to take advantage of his fellows, but in the capacity he showed
for service. Where he laboured in an industry still left in private hands, the
standards by which he was safeguarded would be far higher than they can
possibly be in a system of which the profit of the employer is the predominating motive. Every political liberty he now enjoys he would possess
in far wider measure than is now possible. He could get elected as now; he
could attain office with the greater opportunity, since the prestige of birth
and wealth would be removed. If he chose, as most men would choose, to
stand apart from an active political life, the process would be intelligible
to him. He would be a significant part of it, because he could, equally with
other persons, hope to press upon it the impact of his experience. He could
live, as now, enfolded within the margins of his little platoon; but he would
have the sense, and he would be trained to act upon the sense, that his
platoon was part of the great regiment of mankind.

It is said that such a régime is impossible for two reasons. It would
need, in the first place, immensely greater productivity than now; and it
would require a skill in management which is invariably absent from
socialised enterprise. The ability to win profit, so it is argued, is the one
sure motive to successful business enterprise; and once that adventurer's
risk is stifled there is sure to be inertia and waste. But the first argument,
so far from being a difficulty in the way of Socialism, is, in fact, one of the
chief reasons for its adoption. The proofs accumulate that we cannot win
either from worker or employer the best that he can give under the present
system. The heart of the first denies his allegiance to it; and the employer,
by the very conditions of the system, is either driven to combination, which
limits output, or is not in a position adequately to grasp the nature of demand. The network of trade union regulations limiting output are the
necessary consequence of capitalism; and they will disappear only with the
establishment of that system of conditions we have called freedom. Under
Socialism the motives to production are far stronger than they are now. The
worker is assured of security. He is safeguarded against unfairness in the
distribution of the product. He is assured that the standards upon which he
depends constitute the first charge on the social income. He is freed that is
to say, from that baulked disposition which is to-day the real barrier against

his effort. He becomes part of an order to which he can give a reasoned allegiance, because it is no longer instinct with injustice.

Nor is there any reason to assume that collective enterprise is uninventive and wasteful. Municipal effort, in electricity for example, compares more than favourably with private effort; and perhaps the most dramatic industrial adventure of the nineteenth century has been that co-operative movement from which the concept of private profit has been eliminated. Nor, it should be insisted, does the socialisation of industry mean that it will be organised on some simple and uniform pattern. Most Socialists demand two things only. They insist, in the first place, that in the essential industries—banking, electric power, coal and railway transport—the only possible source of ownership, granted the claim of the public, is the community; and they insist, in the second place, that the constitution assumed by the government of socialised industries shall leave ample room for the individual worker to feel himself a creative unit in its operation. They do not dogmatise about the form such constitutions should take, since they are aware that the needs of each industry are different. They do not, either, dogmatise about the range over which socialisation shall extend; they admit freely that this is a matter for enquiry and experiment. All that they demand is that when an industry is regarded as so fundamental to the community as no longer to be fit for the hazards of private enterprise, it shall not remain a source of private profit to the owner of capital, and that it shall maximise the creative ability of its working personnel.

It is not a serious argument against the socialisation of essential industries that particular experiments in public ownership have failed. Particular experiments in private ownership fail every day, but the supporters of an individualist system do not urge their failure as a conclusive argument against capitalism. Every defect in the working of public ownership can be paralleled from the working of private enterprise. Every merit in private enterprise has been displayed in the operation of public-owned industries. And no one who knows the history, for example, of the British civil service, can doubt that the opportunity to serve the State is a motive to effort every whit as compelling as the motive to win profit for oneself. The argument that socialised industries would be stifled by their own red tape is merely a gibe, and, at that, an ignorant gibe, taken over from a misunderstanding of the requirements of a modern department of State. Let a business man find a single error in the calculations of the Board of Inland Revenue, and he pants to start a correspondence in *The Times;* but the same man takes it as a matter of course that there should be mistakes in the monthly accounts that he receives from one of those vast emporia the growth of which the modern business man takes as the proof of progress. Most, indeed, of the accusations of bureaucracy brought against public ownership are the crude type of propaganda which seeks to postpone its inevitable victory.

III

Nor is there the slightest reason to suppose that under a Socialist State art and science cannot flourish. If they receive patronage to-day, when only a minority can appreciate them, how much more secure is likely to be their foothold when understanding of their significance is open to the community as a whole? The artist to-day is, hardly less than the worker, the prisoner of the property system. The dealer, the patron, the critic are all affected towards him by his willingness to subordinate himself to the conventions of the time. If, like Byron and Shelley, he finds those conventions outrageous, he is driven into exile; if, like William Morris and Bernard Shaw, he devotes himself to their destruction, it is assumed without discussion that this is merely the madness of the artist. The capitalist state selects for its approval the artist and the thinker who either accept its philosophy or refuse to concern themselves with right and wrong. But in a world where our views of right and wrong either make or destroy freedom the artist and the thinker who are true to themselves can hardly do otherwise than protest against a view of life which makes gain instead of service the main motive of effort. Commercialism has destroyed the true liberty of the individual, by making him the captive of a social philosophy which declares that he is important not for what he is, but for what he has. There can be no true opportunity for the artist in such an atmosphere. He is watching the depression of personality, where his real mission is to secure its release. But in a world where living itself becomes an art, the enormous importance of the artist and the thinker will become apparent. They will cease to be regarded as decorative appurtenancies of the leisured class. They will be recognised as the true leaders of civilisation. The system will not dictate to them the things they should say and the forms they should use, as it does now. Their perceptions and their insight will be their own; and men will have learned to recognise that in the appreciation of their gifts lies the most joyous experience life can offer.

Implied in all this, of course, is the insistence that the true Socialism is a libertarian, and not an authoritarian, socialism. That is, I think, generally agreed among Socialists. Realising as they do more keenly than other people the slavery to which most people are now condemned, they do not propose to remedy its defects by ensuring the slavery of all. They realise that the rules made must be rules to which the average man has consented. They understand that the solutions accepted are solutions that arise naturally out of his experience of life. The record of history is before them to show that laws made by compulsion never win the free assent of men, and that in the end they work only as the allegiance given to them is willing and un-coerced. They do not believe that a social order as vast as our own can be maintained without discipline and plan; freedom, for them, does not mean doing as one likes. But they do believe that the discipline ordained can be made instinct with justice and that it can, accordingly, win the intelligent, and even passionate, allegiance of erect-minded men. They do not suggest that freedom and nonconformity are synonymous. But they do insist that there can be no freedom until those things about which conformity is de-manded have been established only with the common assent of the com-munity.

It is only by freeing ourselves from the tyranny of things that we can enter into our real heritage. That freedom is impossible so long as the di-vision of property is not referable to principles of justice. The absence of these principles under the present system poisons every relation into which we enter. It means that the many are the slaves of the few. It leads some to be angry and sullen rebels. It leaves others little more than dumb animals to whom life is a spectacle without meaning. Others, again, are led by crude convention to waste their effort in producing or enjoying the worthless and insignificant. Fear and hate haunt the margins of our civilisations as pros-pects instinct with disaster. In such an atmosphere freedom has no hope of entrance. For freedom cannot live where there is injustice, since it can flourish only where the souls of men are regarded as of a worth too eminent to be degraded by a mean struggle for bread. A system like our own which leaves men to fight their neighbours for what they can grab from them cannot produce the qualities which give joy to life. It means internal war be-tween classes and external war between nations. It means law as a code of wrongs, instead of law as a code of rights. The qualities that give their hu-manity to men emerge rather as protest than as nature. Aspiration towards the heights is destroyed by the scramble to snatch the chance advantage where, for a brief moment, we can breathe an atmosphere of peace. But it it is for a brief moment only. For the millionaire has the pauper at his door. In the midst of his plenty there penetrates to him the angry murmur, from

Russia and India, from America and France, and England, of men who are embittered by the sense of deprivation. We cannot, whatever our riches, be free save as we seek to be just.

"I feel sure," wrote William Morris, in perhaps the noblest of his lectures, "I feel sure that the time will come when people will find it difficult to believe that a rich community such as ours, having such command over external Nature, could have submitted to live such a mean, shabby, dirty life as we do." But this, it is said, is all Utopian; it forgets the ignobility of human nature. It makes abstraction of the ignorance of men, their laziness, their brutality. It is to expect from them an effort and a quality of effort that they have neither the endurance nor the capacity to undertake.

That is the kind of pessimism that has always been an essential part of the tactic of reaction. We have to build our philosophy on hopes and not on fears. We have to lay the foundations of our systems on what the courage of men has achieved, not on what their cowardice has failed in achieving. Almost every progressive change has met opposition on the ground of its impossibility; and every progressive change has been achieved because a handful of idealists have refused to admit it was impossible. The real sin in social philosophy is lowness of aim. We need not cry for the sun; but, at least equally, we need not deny the possibility of light. Men, whether they will or no, are members of a commonwealth which can be preserved only as they discover the reality of fellowship. They will discover it only as they seek to experiment with the best of themselves. But, so to experiment, we need to be members of a State to which the allegiance of men is given with a passion at once vivid and intelligent, and to that end, it must be a State conceived in justice. For justice is the twin-sister of freedom and and each lives in the victory of the other.

KARL KAUTSKY
1854-1938

WHEN FRIEDRICH ENGELS DIED in 1895, the mantle of Marxist leadership passed to Karl Kautsky, who retained it until World War I. Kautsky was born in Prague and became a socialist in his student days at the University of Vienna. In the year of Marx's death (1883) he founded the Marxist journal, *Die Neue Zeit,* and helped to make it the leading organ of Marxist thought. He was also a key figure in the formulation of the Erfurt Program, adopted in 1891 by the German Social Democratic party.

As revisionism became more and more attractive to socialists during the late years of the nineteenth century, Kautsky led the attack against it. Kantians criticized Marxist theories of morality, or the lack thereof; Kautsky attempted to provide orthodox Marxist responses. When Lenin and Trotsky asserted that violence and terror might be used in seizing and retaining power, Kautsky argued that, in keeping with the humanization of conduct in the past century, Marxism must remain true to its progressive position and abjure brutality. These polemical writings were informed by prodigious studies on economics, religion, philosophy, and the philosophy of history. Kautsky fled before the Nazi invasions of Austria and Czechoslovakia and died in Amsterdam, poor, aged, and comparatively forgotten in the swirl of events that preceded World War II.

In many of his works Kautsky undertook the task of shoring up Marxian socialist theory at its weak points. His monumental *The Materialistic Conception of History* (1927) attempted in part to reconcile the determinist features of the Marxist philosophy of history with the voluntarist characteristics of any revolution. While it did not succeed in solving the problem logically, the work furnished a sharper and more sophisticated analysis of the sociology of revolution than that of any socialist thinker since Marx. In such works as *The Social Revolution* (1903) and *The Road to Power* (1909), Kautsky expounded a theory of socialism that was extensive in scope. He believed that nationalization of the means of production must be accompanied by the vital participation of free trade unions in determining the conditions of work and the goals of industry, and he held that society must be imbued with the democratic ethic if it is to remain truly socialistic.

[18]   Socialism and Democracy

With all his acuteness, Marx was often betrayed by his revolutionary temperament into thinking that the developments of the future, which he foresaw clearly enough, were nearer the point of realization than was actually the case.

Thus in 1852 he could not have been aware that between the great Middle Class Revolution of 1789 and the great Labour Revolution, more than a hundred years of capitalist development would stretch, which would favour the growth of the capitalist class as well as that of the proletariat. Thus the Middle Class Revolution of the eighteenth century was not followed by a Labour revolution until after the dawn of the twentieth century, and in the interval we have more than a century of Labour class struggles, which were necessary to enable the working class to accomplish its revolution.

The conditions of this Revolution are quite different in 1922 from what they were in 1852. Every revolution has two sides, one being political and the other social: the conquest of political power by a new class and the employment of the captured political machinery for the purpose of adapting the economic conditions to the interests of the victorious class, so far as this can be effected by political legislation and administration.

*   *   *

We have every reason to expect that the coming Labour Revolution, that is the conquest of political power, will be achieved on the basis of democracy, and therefore peaceably; that it will not lead to internecine strife, and consequently will not be followed by counter-revolution. It will lack the impetuous progress which characterizes the Middle Class Revolution, but its progress will be all the surer, inasmuch as it will not be checked by serious reactions and setbacks.

From Karl Kautsky, *The Labour Revolution,* trans. H. J. Stenning (London: George Allen & Unwin Ltd., 1925), pp. 16–17, 47, 54–61, 67, 77–78, 81–82, 89, 180–81, 282–83. Reprinted by permission.

Wild-eyed revolutionaries may object to this interpretation. For them a revolution without massacre and terror is not a proper revolution, but merely milk and water reformism. Their notions of the revolution only prove how conservative their minds are, in spite of all their revolutionary utterances. They cannot conceive of a revolution except on the lines of the middle class revolutions of the past. Whatever one may think about the Labour Revolution of the future, one thing is certain: it will assume quite a different form, because it will be accomplished under quite different conditions, from those of the middle class revolutions, whose history has hitherto supplied us with our knowledge and ideas of revolutions in general.

* * *

Between the time when the democratic State has a purely middle class Government and the time when it has a purely Labour Government extends a period when the one is being transformed into the other. To this a political period of transition would correspond, when the Government would generally assume the form of a coalition.

This would apply to all countries where the conquest of political power by Labour is effected by means of democracy, which is the normal method now that the military monarchies have collapsed.

Those who to-day reject the policy of coalition on principle are oblivious to the signs of the times, and incapable of rising to the height of their tasks.

THE STATE IN THE TRANSITIONAL PERIOD

As soon as the workers capture political power, they will use it to transform the State and the economic system, so far as the latter is susceptible to political manipulation, in accordance with their interests.

With respect to the State, we have to distinguish between the period of transition from capitalist to socialist production, and that of complete Socialism, but here we need only deal in detail with the former.

Marx and Engels made only passing references to the problem at the period of complete Socialism. They asserted that, as soon as Socialism was realized and class distinctions obliterated, the State would, in fact, not be abolished, but die out, because it would lose its functions. For, they said, the State is an organization of an exploiting class for maintaining the conditions of its exploitation, and therefore for repressing the exploited class.

With the disappearance of the distinction between exploiting and exploited classes, the State becomes bereft of purpose, and loses its functions one after another.

These pronouncements have caused much head-splitting. Lenin refers to them in his booklet [*State and Revolution*], published in the summer of 1917.

Like many other revolutionaries, Lenin interprets the Marx-Engels' conception of the decay of the State to mean that the anarchist ideal of the complete liberty of the individual will then emerge. "Each person will be voluntarily engaged in work according to his capacities, and each will freely take according to his needs" (Lenin, p. 81).

Such a state of things may exist some day, but there is nothing in the conditions as we know them to-day to indicate that we have reached this point. Lenin himself admits that the "second phase of Communism" will only lead to the decay of the State in the sense of complete anarchy. He appeals to the authority of Marx, who distinguishes two phases of Communism in his programme criticism, from which we have already quoted. In the first phase every worker will be paid according to his needs, and in the second the productivity of labour will be so great that "society will be able to inscribe on its banner: from each according to his capacities, to each according to his needs."

When we come to deal with economics, we shall see how this apparently Utopian pronouncement is to be understood.

To-day we cannot see beyond what Marx designated as "the first phase of Communism." All that we might imagine concerning the second phase would not be inferences from known facts, but conjecture, which might have its value as an intellectual exercise, but would be very unsuitable to serve as a guide to our actions.

We shall achieve a good deal if we obtain clear ideas concerning the functioning of the State during the first phase of Socialism.

To elucidate this question, we must draw a distinction, which is generally overlooked, between the subordination of the individual, and that of the class, to the community.

Man is by nature a social animal, and in the earliest times, long before the formation of the State, we find groups of men united in specific organizations, with specific ordinances and laws, which, although primarily laws of usage, are nevertheless strictly carried out. One need only recall the marriage regulations, the meal customs, the law of inheritance, the laws of hunting, and many other regulations which we find among the Australians,

who are far removed from any political community. Thus the absence of a
State in no wise signifies complete liberty of the individual, but it occurs
in the earliest social conditions accompanied by the subordination of the
individual to the community and its ordinances.

* * *

If class society should be abolished in the period that lies before us, the
consequent decay of the existing forms of the State will by no means signify the complete freedom of the individual. The social process of production will more than ever be organized systematically, and it will not do for
its functioning to be dependent upon individual caprice. Class struggles will
disappear, and with them a number of the tasks of government, but the
economic tasks of the community will multiply. Just as the constitution of
the nascent State assimilated the gentile and Mark constitutions, so the
incipient socialist community will assimilate the political forms surviving
in the period of transition from capitalism to socialism. Whether the community of the future will continue to be called a State or not is essentially
a question of terminology.

In the interests of clear thinking, it is extremely important to distinguish
various phenomena by different designations. But from its beginning the
State has assumed such a variety of forms, all of which are described by the
same name, that to many people the State has come to mean a sovereign
community.

When an oriental despotism and a democratic republic, rigidly centralized France and the loose federation of the British Empire, may all be
called by the same name of "State," it is really not a matter of great moment to refuse this name to the Socialist community.

As a scientific designation, the word "State" says very little if it is not
preceded by an adjective to define the kind of State it is. Consequently all
investigations into the nature of the State *per se* are more or less futile. It
may equally be condemned as a devilish institution and praised to the skies
as the embodiment of the highest social ideal. Thus it is not of considerable
importance to the clarity of social thought whether we invent a special
name for the community of the future, or call it the Socialist State to dif-
ferentiate it from previous types of the State.

One point remains to be discussed concerning the relation of Socialism
to the State. In his preface to the brochure, *Internationales aus dem Volk-
staat,* which appeared in 1894, shortly before his death, Engels speaks of
the political aim which he and Marx pursued. It was:

"The supersession of the entire State, and, therefore, also of democracy."

Engels does not explain what he means by this observation. This sentence was a godsend to Lenin, who exploited it with a vengeance. It does not dispose of my objections. For democracy is older than the State, and is not necessarily bound up with it. Communities anterior to the State were democratically organized, and the State has often proved itself hostile to democracy. Not until the advent of modern capitalism has there been a revival of democracy, which, however, contains the seeds of Socialism, and therefore the seeds of the State's decay in the Marxian sense. On the assumption that Socialism will cause the State to die out, democracy will survive the State.

In advocating the opposite standpoint, Lenin reaches a remarkable conclusion. He says that so long as classes exist a complete democracy is impossible. It will not be possible until classes are abolished, and, therefore, the State ceases to exist. This is to say democracy will not become possible for Lenin until it disappears. Concerning the socialist society, he states: "Only then will a really full democracy be possible and be realized, a democracy without any exceptions. And only then will democracy begin to wither away" (p. 74).

Thus real democracy will emerge for us in the very moment of its disappearance. Lenin calls it "real" evidently because in his opinion it does not exist in reality.

If instead of groping amid the fog of Lenin's "real democracy," we ask ourselves what the constitution of the socialist community will be, it is obvious that no other constitution is conceivable than that of the democratic Republic. This we will maintain. The discovery of the proper name for the new type of community which will arise with the Social Democratic Republic is a task which may be left to the younger generation.

The question we have just discussed as to the type of the community when Socialism is fully realized is an academic question. Yet it is not unimportant, because it is always useful to follow an idea to its logical conclusion.

On the other hand, the question of what constitution is required by the State in the period of transition from capitalist to socialist economy, when the workers have captured political power, although capitalist production is still going on, is of the highest practical and immediate importance.

We would emphasize that we are here speaking of the constitution of the State. Neo-Communism, which has made this question a practical one, confuses the question of the organization which the State ought to have with the social effects which arise from this organization under specific social conditions.

In the passage we have already quoted, Marx spoke of the State of the period of transition from capitalism to socialism, which "could not be anything else than the revolutionary dictatorship of the proletariat."

This leaves undecided the question of the constitution through which this dictatorship would be expressed. Lenin introduces the greatest confusion into this question in his attempts to clarify it. He distinguishes between the form of the State and the form of the Government. The proletarian State form is the dictatorship of the proletariat, the bourgeois State form is the dictatorship of the bourgeoisie. With respect to the State form, he distinguishes between forms of government, or what we should call the political constitution: republic, absolute or constitutional monarchy, etc. These distinctions are for him of very slight account, at least for the period of the "dictatorship of the bourgeoisie." But he takes the greatest pains to elaborate the necessary constitution for the dictatorship of the proletariat.

The description of the middle class State as the "dictatorship of the bourgeoisie" is one of the most absurd fictions that our age has produced. It clearly shows the crudeness of Bolshevist thought, which reduces the totality of the economic and political struggles of our time to the antagonism between the proletariat and the bourgeoisie. Yet Bolshevism itself is always being pulled up short by the reality of the peasantry on its own doorstep.

The bourgeoisie have never been the sole possessors of political power, exercising their dictatorship in this sense. They have constantly been obliged to form a political alliance with various classes, the landlords, the peasantry, the lower middle class, the bureaucracy, and even with the workers, as the English Liberals did for several decades.

What appears as the dictatorship of the bourgeoisie, their dominant influence over Parliament, Governments, the Press, etc., is not the result of a State form, but of their economic and intellectual superiority. Consequently, in advanced capitalist countries this influence is exercised under any political constitution, or, to use Lenin's language, form of government.

The dictatorship of the proletariat is quite a different matter. It cannot arise from an economic or intellectual superiority, which finds expression under all forms of government. It can only be the result of the possession of political power by the workers, which fact presupposes a definite form of government.

* * *

From the Marxian principles we may draw the following inferences without fear of contradiction.

The working classes may not seize any State machinery and operate it for their own purposes. A bureaucratic-militarist State machine is unsuitable to this end. The only suitable instrument is the democratic Republic, which a victorious working class must establish where it is not already in existence. In the year 1871 and for a long time thereafter this seemed to be an essential task of the workers everywhere. The last few years have brought about a fundamental change. Almost everywhere in Europe the victorious workers find the democratic Republic already in existence, and there they have no need completely to destroy the State machinery, but only to remove vestiges of the monarchy as well as bureaucratic and military privileges.

That the Marxian observations concerning the breaking-up of the State apparatus did not apply to every State, but merely to the military monarchies, is pronounced by Engels to be the case in his criticism of the German Social Democratic draft programme of 1891, where he states:

"If anything is certain, it is this, that our Party and the working class can only achieve power under the form of the democratic Republic. This is even the specific form for the dictatorship of the proletariat."

On the other hand, Engels said that the Paris Commune of 1871 was the dictatorship of the proletariat. The constitution of the latter was that of a democratic Republic.

* * *

For the period of transition from capitalism to socialism we most urgently require peace both at home and abroad. Not in the sense of a reconciliation of classes, but in the sense that they will fight out their differences with the agencies of democracy, and not of force. Under these conditions, however, there would not be the slightest reason for combining the executive with the legislative power, and there would be many cogent reasons against it.

Division of labour is the great law of progress. The greater the division of labour that has been effected amongst its organs, the higher an organism stands in the scale of development. It is not every system of division of labour that spells progress, but only that which preserves the harmony of the parts and makes their co-operation subservient to the whole. A division of labour in which a part is perfected at the expense of the whole cannot be regarded as progressive. But where a division of labour is successfully functioning, it would be a retrograde step to abolish it by transferring the functions of various organs to a single organ.

The division of labour that has been effected in the course of a thousand years of social development among the executive, the legislative, and the juridical organs in the State is not an arbitrary growth. It has been increasingly improved because each of those functions require different conditions for their most efficient performance.

The executive power has to act. It has to make rapid decisions for special occasions, and execute them immediately. For this purpose a large body is unsuitable. The most rapid and drastic decisions can be best taken by one person. Consequently war, which renders such decisions most urgently necessary, favours the widest possible supremacy of one person.

*   *   *

Parliaments are distinguished from most other deliberative assemblies by the fact that they provide a platform for all the great classes and parties in society, especially when universal suffrage prevails. This renders parliamentary proceedings important, but it also makes them protracted.

There is no doubt that Parliaments often thresh straw, and do not thereby advance the cause of progress, but the institution is wrongly blamed for a fault which is due to the distribution of class power in society. The character of Parliament reflects the character of the classes and parties which dominate it. If the latter are reactionary or timid, Parliament will be the same. Those revolutionaries who require Parliament to make the revolution for them, irrespective of whether the workers outside Parliament have become strong enough to assert their position in the State, will always be disappointed by parliamentarism.

If Parliament has hitherto given little satisfaction to the workers, this is not due to the institution as such, but to the weakness of the workers in society. The middle class has become conservative, and this explains why Parliament is moribund. This fact would not be altered in the least if Parliament were differently organized, by combining the legislative with the executive power.

The form of an institution is certainly not a matter of indifference. It must be adapted as far as possible to its purposes. But it is preposterous to imagine that a change in structure will bring about an alteration in function.

If we alter the relative strength of parties, and create a compact and determined socialist majority among the people, Parliament will become a "working" body, and the parliamentary mill will supply rich grain, even if it merely exercises legislative functions.

Besides which, it has yet another function. It has not merely to elaborate laws, but also to ensure that they are observed. Thus it has to control the executive power and the employment of the resources of the State.

Where the executive and legislative powers are united in one hand, such control is absent, and the danger arises that the executive power will become all-powerful relative to the population.

*　*　*

Some forms of government are incompatible with a prosperous capitalist development. One of them is Oriental despotism, and another is its most modern proto-type, which masquerades in the garb of the dictatorship of the proletariat.

So long as the dictatorship does not collapse, Russia will continue to go downhill, despite all concessions to the capitalists. But the governmental form of dictatorship is not only incompatible with industrial capitalism, but also with democratic Socialism. For the latter can only arise from a fully developed and flourishing, not a crippled, capitalism, and in the period of transition capitalism will continue to exist in many departments of industry, as we shall see.

From whatever angle we may regard dictatorship, it proves to be an unsuitable means to guide the development of Capitalism into Socialism.

Our examination of the political Labour Revolution may be summarized in the following sentences:

The growth of the Labour movement is accompanied by the growth of democracy. Thus the way of democracy is the normal way for the conquest of political power by the workers.

The democratic Republic is the State form for the rule of the workers.

The democratic Republic is the State form for the realization of Socialism.

*　*　*

Socialization will have to proceed gradually, probably too slowly for the patience of the workers. It will not be able to effect a considerable immediate improvement in the wages of even the workers in the socialized undertakings.

The activities of Governments and Parliaments, after the workers have captured political power, will not therefore be confined to socialization. Measures will have to be adopted which will benefit not single groups of workers, but the whole of the poorer population, and visibly change their condition. The wealthier the society is, the higher the incomes which the capitalist class derives from the productivity of labour, the more drastic these measures will be, and all the heavier will be the burden of taxation which the State and the municipalities will be able to impose upon the possessing classes, in order to extend the scope of the social services.

It will be incumbent on us to create an adequate social health service, both preventive and remedial; to extend the educational system and transfer the cost of feeding and clothing the school children to the community.

The old people as well as the unfit must be properly cared for, and provision must be made for the unemployed which should be productive rather than a drag upon the rest of the community.

Finally, the State must grapple with the housing question, and commence the construction of cheap, healthy, and pleasant dwellings.

Provided they were energetically prosecuted, all these measures would inevitably effect a considerable improvement in the position of the masses, and remove the worst causes of moral degradation and intellectual backwardness. Add to them an ample training of the masses by the Socialist Party, the trade unions, and the works' councils, and the result will be considerably to elevate the workers, to increase their capabilities for industrial self-government, to heighten their feelings of obligation towards national and municipal institutions, to increase their interest in the socialist regime, and to facilitate socialization. At the same time, these measures would curb the impatience of the masses, and enable socialization to be applied without undue haste.

When we say that socialization will necessarily be a slow process, we do not mean that the socialist regime will be lax, or will only proceed at a snail's pace.

Apart from socialization, it will find at hand an abundance of other important problems—we have here only indicated a few of them—which could be solved on a capitalist basis, without any socialization. Failure to solve such problems is not due to the economic conditions, but to the distribution of power in the State, and such problems should prove easy of solution as soon as this distribution of power is fundamentally altered in favour of the workers.

These reforms would have an important social significance. Although they would not abolish the antagonism between Capital and Labour, they would increase the power and intelligence of the workers, who would be more anxious than before to replace capitalist autocracy by industrial democracy.

Not until the socialized type of undertaking has become the dominant type in the process of production will society have found a basis upon which it will be able to develop its life without great class struggles.

* * *

For us, however, even Utopian constructive proposals of a socialist organization offer a certain danger. For life is always richer and more varied than theory, which can only take account of the general and must lose sight of the particular. Every Utopia, therefore, simplifies too much the problems of reality, and if strictly followed, signifies a relapse from variety to monotony.

Society is not a mechanism which may be put together according to arbitrary predetermined plans, but an organism which grows and unfolds according to definite laws. It is an organism whose cells are thinking beings who consciously labour at its construction, but who cannot shape this construction to their own desires. Their freedom consists only in the voluntary execution of what they have recognized as necessary.

This freedom will be accorded us in ampler measure, the better we recognize the laws which govern realities, and this knowledge will be all the more complete, the more we investigate the economic functions of society.

Besides this freedom which is based on scientific perceptions, the modern man possesses another kind of freedom: the freedom of his personality as against other personalities, the greatest possible independence of them in the choice of his mode of life. This is impossible in connection with the production of the material things of life, which necessitates the systematic co-operation of the many. But even under present-day conditions, it is possible as regards most kinds of personal consumption, and it is possible in the realm of personal creativeness through the increasing curtailment of the labour devoted to business, through the constant increase of leisure, which the individual may utilize for his free activity.

Extending scientific knowledge to the reach of all, the greatest possible curtailment of working time, the complete freedom of the individual in all activities outside his business, so far as other individuals or society are not thereby injured—such are the objects which must guide modern Socialism, in contrast to its communistic predecessors who had no suspicion of them, who conceded to the individual sufficient bread and security of existence, without science and without freedom. We want both the latter and the former, for we stand on the shoulders of industrial capitalism, and it is our task to bring to the whole of the people the benefits which have hitherto been monopolized by a small section.

Whatever shape the socialist society may take, it will not be able to maintain its existence or prove adequate to its great historical task—the development of the achievements of capitalism to higher forms of life— unless it brings to the whole of humanity not merely bread and security of existence, but also civilization and freedom.

Integral Nationalism:
The Supremacy of Power

WERNER SOMBART
1863-1941

WERNER SOMBART SUCCEEDED HIS TEACHER Adolf Wagner, a distinguished socialist theorist, in the University of Berlin in 1917. Formally an economist, Sombart did not confine himself to the boundaries of this discipline, but roamed over the borders of several social sciences. A colorful writer, a popularizer as well as a theorist, his lively career moved from the political left (before World War I) to the extreme right.

[19]   A New Social Philosophy

THE AIM AND WAY OF GERMAN SOCIALISM

General Principles

To lead Germany out of the desert of the economic age, is the task which German Socialism has set for itself. In so far as it denies the entire

From Werner Sombart, *A New Social Philosophy*, trans. Karl F. Geiser (Princeton, N. J.: Princeton University Press, 1937), pp. 146–54, 219–21. Reprinted by permission.

spirit of this age, it is far more radical than any other movement, including any other socialistic movement of our time, for example, even proletarian Socialism. The latter has fundamentally . . . accepted the values of the civilization in which we live and has merely demanded that the "blessings" of this age be shared by all men, even the lowest classes. It is a capitalism in an inverted form; German Socialism is anti-capitalism.

The work of deliverance of German Socialism does not extend to any single class or to any particular group of the population, but comprehends all in all their parts. Since peasants, wage-workers, landowners and employers, merchants and manual laborers, officials and intellectuals, in short, all members of society were equally injured by the economic age, they all now must be delivered from these injuries. German Socialism is no proletarian, *petit bourgeois,* or other kind of part-Socialism, but a popular Socialism. And, as it comprehends the entire people, it also includes every branch of culture, not merely the field of economics: it is *totalistic.*

I said that German Socialism aimed to lead the German people out of the desert of the economic age. But the country into which it leads is not the "promised land, flowing with milk and honey," to say nothing of the paradise which is promised to the people by false prophets. We do not believe, and do not wish to believe, in all the promises made by proletarian and other forms of Socialism. There is no perfect happiness on earth for mankind, and there should be none: the wandering in this "vale of tears" is a testing and purifying period for man. We believe in no purification of man; we do not believe in the "natural goodness of man," the *bon sauvage* of the enlightenment period which through bad management was ruined; we believe rather, that man will persist in sin till the end of time. For that reason we do not believe in the self-redemption of man through Socialism, with its claims to bring about a "kingdom of God on earth," a "classless society."

The promise

> "To erect heaven
> Here now on earth . . ."

seems to us blasphemy. There is no salvation in this sinful world. Every attempt to give Socialism a religious stamp is a mistake; it is an attempt to find a substitute for religion, which only those employ who do not have the capacity for religion.

But we do believe that there are conditions of collective life that are more favorable for the fulfillment of man's mission on earth than those which have been set up by the economic age, which permit the better sides of human life to develop, conditions under which the individual will be able to develop his inclinations and capacities more uniformly and thereby contribute more to the good of his community and the service of God. If the protagonists of German Socialism have a vision of an ideal picture it is that of a great, creative period of the human race in which the spirit of unity shall bring the individuals into a more thoughtful whole, wherein each individual, in living the most complete life, thereby renders service to the community. In a word, German Socialists endeavor to bring about a condition—we call it culture—which is destined to change the present state of civilization, and they fully believe that this aim can be achieved. Nor are they led astray by any "theory," however dazzling, about the "Doom of the west." They do not believe in the inevitable "aging" of a people, but rather that with every new generation there is a new-born capacity to be bearers of culture, which is lost only through racial degeneracy—a danger which wise precaution can prevent.

They know, of course, that "culture" cannot be consciously created through action directed to a preconceived purpose, that culture comes by grace. But they wish to make the incursion of culture easier through a thoughtful structure of the social organization; they wish to dig the bed, so to speak, in which a new stream of culture may flow. They have come to this view, above all, through the conviction that our present system of values—our hierarchy of values—are fundamentally wrong. We know from preceding considerations that our own period is characterized by an over-emphasis upon useful and pleasurable values; the economic age resulted, as we saw, in an over-valuation of material goods and thereby gave the primacy to economics. This domination must be broken. We must reconsider the true ranking order of values, we must see that higher values are placed above utility and pleasurable values. We must learn to appreciate the sacred values, the values of the spirit and life (the vital values), which we are obliged to realize before we cultivate the utility and agreeable values. That the new world-values should bear a German stamp is self-evident to those who have accepted German Socialism. For it has set, as its aim, the complete development of the German spirit; that is to say, we recognize, as our problem, the cultivation and unfolding of spirituality, heroism and multiformity.

That we may have the ability for all this, our national resources must be healthy, strong and capable of resistance. Only then can the nation have the assurance of maintaining its peculiar quality and offer effective opposition to the enemy. It must be "united in its racial branches," not merely on paper, but in reality. We shall see how a wise policy will endeavor to realize all this, but in any case it must keep in mind that these aims can be attained only if the bodies and souls of the individuals are sound. It will be easy to train the bodies efficiently; much more difficult to heal the souls.

The first requisite for all this is tranquillity. This baiting and chasing, this unrest, this dissipation, this running hither and yon, must cease: the people must again take time to collect themselves and to rebuild. In place of external mobility and inward torpidity, we must again have inward activity and external calm. The dynamic structure of being must yield to the static. We must convince ourselves that what we so readily accept as an emanation of a strong spirituality and a strong vitality—this senseless fidgeting—is merely a sign of inner weakness and emptiness. We have surrounded our inconstant life, which we have lived, with a halo of glory, in that we have seen in it the manifestation of a "Faustian urge." What an illusion! As the Faustian urge was misapplied to the production of fixed nitrogen, the manufacture of flying apparatus and the conquest of oil-wells, it was drawn away "from its original source." And when capitalistic enterprise came to be regarded as an "idea"—a real German error—and was accepted as "the most desirable calling," worthy of devotion, service and sacrifice, "heroism" became an object of derision. And when every individual is animated by the urge "to rise above his condition," to "be better than his parents and grandparents," when everyone regards an "ascent" and the change to a more profitable and easy calling, as "progress," then the foundations upon which every thoughtful social structure must rest are thereby shattered.

We must free ourselves entirely from the fatal belief in progress, which . . . ruled the ideal world of proletarian Socialism even more than the world of liberalism. Its frailty becomes self-evident in the new order of our scale of values. The (naturalistic) idea of progress is always and only thought of at a time when the central point of values is misplaced from the sphere of the spiritual to that of the civilizing values within which one may speak of progress only in a somewhat suggestive manner, because here the question can only be one, by way of comparison, of more or greater progress. While it would be sheer nonsense to assert that in the fields of religion, politics, art, and philosophic productions the modern period, in comparison with some earlier period, had "progressed," it, of course, may be shown that in our special sciences, our technical knowledge, our wealth of goods, and in the democratization of our society, "progress" has been made. But the moment all these fine things are recognized as having only a peripheral significance, the general belief in progress falls by the wayside through logical reasons.

The notion of progress must also be cast aside, because its effect upon fallen mankind, led astray by it, is fatal, because it regards the present only as a step to a higher, better, more perfect future; the present is to "mediatize," so we are told. It, therefore, depreciates the daily life and ascribes to an eternally new formation a value which it does not possess. To perpetually renew, hinders all culture. And we have today no culture, not the least, because we are "progressing" so rapidly. *Si vitanda est novitas, tenenda est antiquitas.* In case of doubt, the old is always more valuable than the new. Only when in the course of history the traditions of belief, of morals, of education, and of organization are dominant is it possible for a culture to unfold itself. For, in accordance with its very nature, culture is old, rooted, indigenous. For that reason no healthy, strong period has ever subscribed to the mania of progress: it has always rested firmly in itself and was thereby creative.

If the soul again becomes calm, it will also again become free. Free from the thousand constraints and bonds into which the past age has thrown it: free from the exaggerated intellectualism of the forms of our life and our industry, free from servility to material things, free from the weight of undigested knowledge, free from the torturing sense of hatred, of envy, of distrust toward other people who are supposed to fare "better" than we do.

But if the soul is calm and free, then it will also again be able to be happy. It can only be happy if life is significant and formed according to nature. But life acquires a meaning only through its relation to a value which is higher than life itself: to country and to God. And life is formed according to nature only when, pulsating evenly, it moves on rhythmically, when labor and recreation stand in a proper relation to one another and, when in both, the healthy energies of body and soul can find free play and are not forced and stunted by an artificial capriciousness. A peasant and a manual laborer can both be happy in their work, a worker in a blast furnace or a seamstress in a modern shoe-factory cannot, a seaman on a sailing vessel can, a trimmer in a modern steamship cannot; one can be happy in a folk-dance, but not in a foxtrot or a shimmy.

The Social Order

We must now remember that German Socialism is really *Socialism,* that is to say, it is social normativism. Therefore, it seeks an order in which the attainment of predetermined ends are to be realized. It does not wish to leave solely to good will and reasonable intelligence or, in fact, to blind change the formation of collective life and human culture. It sees, all too clearly, the disastrous consequences of the present disorder, as the outgrowth of the economic age. It does not believe in the lasting effect of a "renewal of the spirit." It is not satisfied—it should again be emphasized— with the setting up of socio-ethical principles nor is it exhausted through the awakening of sympathetic feelings or enthusiastic moods. An open spirit must precede—certainly—but it must at once become effective in an objective arrangement which also takes account of daily life with its disenchantments, which guarantees a support for the weak and enchains the wicked.

German Socialism conceives an order which, as we have seen, is a general, a "total" order of life which is not extended only to a single sphere —economics—but which includes all cultural spheres. It must, above all, be uniform, born from a single spirit, and extended from a single central point systematically over the entire social life. There is only one thing that is worse than disorder, and that is a planless order of individual fields from different points of view. Presented and determined in its form, according to the supreme guiding principles of the German spirit, the order should be directed to lead our entire life to a unified base. A general, objective spirit should be embodied in this order, through which the activities of the life of every individual receive their meaning. This has been true of all organic, constructive periods.

The significance of such a Socialism should not be underestimated; nor should it be overestimated; rather, one should keep in mind that a social order does not create spirit or life, that it cannot create culture. That we must await with an open heart.

Socialism cannot open new fountains; it can only direct the waters which flow from the source whose feeding must be left to the disposal of God. But Socialism may seize the sources and protect them from pollution. It may prevent the waters from rushing wildly here and there and devastating meadows and fields, villages and cities. To him who sees his "romantic" joy in the wild-streaming flood prejudiced through such a control of the waters, it may be replied that a taming of wild nature is unavoidable and is of necessity bound up with our life on this earth, and that finally, floods and devastations are not things about which a person of fine sensibilities would have occasion to be enthusiastic.

Still another picture—the forest—may serve to bring to the understanding of the reader the meaning and significance of a social order. Human society will, of course, never be like an original forest in which the hand of man has never interfered. But the interference which we undertake certainly need not have as its aim the dreary "Prussian" forest, the "Toothpick" forest; it should and can fashion a genuine "German" forest, the mixed-forest which grows from its own nature and preserves its own soul. He who has observed the careful management of the forest, as the best German foresters take it in hand today, will be convinced that the wealth and beauty of the forest need not suffer thereby, that, in fact, it comes to its most complete unfolding when a loving and an experienced hand rules over it.

We now come to the question as to *what content* a social order must have to satisfy the idea of German Socialism. . . . Here I will merely recall the determining conceptions of German Socialism, mentioned above, according to which it is to be that system of organization which is "cut according to measure" for *German* conditions at the present time, that is, that all the peculiarities of the German body and soul of which we have spoken may be properly adjusted.

Accordingly, the content of the future social order, as distinguished from the content of all other varieties of Socialism, may be fundamentally defined as follows: The valuable particularities of German society should not be put under any kind of constraint; they should not, for example, impose a definite form upon economics or upon organization, as a substitute for the rest of the existing forms. German Socialism knows that its deepest meaning lies in just this manifold structure of forms. We may express this attitude in a single sentence: German Socialism is not doctrinaire. Doctrinairism is a malignant disease which with the rise of liberalism attacked the spirit of European humanity (and also German humanity, which we could show is peculiarly receptive to this disease) and then came to its real development in the ideal world of proletarian Socialism. By this we mean it proceeds upon a fixed inclination, a "theory" or a "principle," or a demand to have its own will represented. Its attitude seems to be this: for free competition or its abolishment, for private economy, for increasing productivity or profit, for rationalization or some other "principle." And never once is the question asked—Where to? To what purpose? From this attitude, which regards the means as an end in itself, we must carefully guard ourselves. For us there is only one aim—Germany. For the sake of Germany's greatness, power and glory, we will gladly sacrifice every "theory" and every "principle," whether it bears a liberal or any other stamp.

Since German Socialism is not doctrinaire, neither is it monistic or levelling in its tendencies: so far as possible it would preserve, and even intensify, the diversity of the picture which represents present society.

If one were to characterize it with a single word, one might call it "histo-realistic." The peculiarities which it possesses protect it against all kinds of utopianism: all of its reform proposals are to be realized. But for that reason it must refuse to demand an "ideal" social order, that is, one which would do justice to every demand of a reasonable, thoughtful social order. One might prefer to blot out the last one hundred and fifty years of our history and begin again where we were in 1750. But that is simply impossible. We must renounce the idea of building a completely new structure for our society and be satisfied with reshaping and completing the existing structure.

The Means to the End

To attain our end we must clear the way—which in our opinion leads to it—of the dense underbrush of a metaphysics which the past generation of social theorists, especially of the Marxian persuasion, has planted and cultivated. The entire notion of social naturalism, which was proclaimed as scientific, but which, as I have shown, was nothing but bad metaphysics, with all its theories and theses, must be put aside, if we wish to pursue a fruitful policy. We can achieve nothing with philosophical considerations of history, even if these should not lead us so far astray as social naturalism. A positive theory of history only can enlighten the way. Only that which experience and logical evidence can establish in the course of history, may properly be considered. We have already shown that an essential condition to a correct understanding of history is the certainty that our action will be perfectly free. And from this certainty a movement, such as the socialistic, must proceed.

The categories, which we have already established, and by which we are to judge historical events, follow as a logical sequence. There follows, first of all, the understanding that all actions are concerned with the realization of purposes and that these purposes in all great political actions assume the form of ideals. It is a fatal self-deception, also often met with in many non-Marxian circles, to suppose one may succeed without a clearly defined ideal by confining one's self to an examination of the "state of affairs" or the "situation" from which the action to be undertaken will follow "of itself." This tendency in our thinking, which is now called "existenialism," may have its value as a metaphysical interpretation of our existence, but wherever it concerns practical decisions, it leads into the dark. "May Germany never believe that one may enter upon a new period without a new ideal."

But, if we ask, *who* in our case is to complete the work, we must first free ourselves from the false doctrine with which the idea of Socialism seems almost inseparably connected: that is the theory of the (absolute) class struggle, according to which, through an international class, breaking through the bounds of the nation, Socialism is to be obtained by fighting with weapons of hate. This doctrine is born through a wild pairing of the spirit of proletarianism with the naturalistic (materialistic, economic) conception of history. We regard both parents as belonging to an ignoble race and, therefore, cannot accept the child as legitimate.

Since German Socialism is national Socialism, awaiting its realization within the limits of the national union, the forces which are to bring it about are purely political forces; it is wholly a question for the statesman whose duty it is to direct and determine the play of ideas and interests and thereby make history.

* * *

How to Win the Individual for the State
Although we could show that the power and esteem of a nation is as little dependent upon the participation of many or, indeed, of all the people, as is a flower of the community, anxious statesmen and philosophers since Plato have, nevertheless, again and again been concerned about the means which would "bind the state together and make it into one." And even in our own time, when one is so prone to give the state a democratic or—if one shuns that hateful word—a popular appearance, the question has often been raised.

Taking the individual into the state has recently been called—following the example of Rudolf Smend—"integration," and an attempt has been made to set up a whole system of integration-measures. The most important means and methods to arouse the we-consciousness are the following:

1. Meetings of the people for the purpose of making contacts, obtaining expressions of opinion, publishing and praising the aims and tasks of the state: victory celebrations, memorial services with patriotic speeches and songs, processions, historic pageants, "labor camps," children's cele-

brations, dress parades and the like. In these gatherings music plays an important role as an integrating factor.

2. Enlightening, inspiring and inciting propaganda, through word, print and poster, directed to those persons who are not assembled in a single room or who are not assembled for political purposes; pronunciamentos of leaders of the state or government; articles in newspapers and periodicals; portrayal of the leader of the state in all conditions of life; pictorial presentations of significant events in public life in still and movable form; presentation of patriotic theatrical performances; radio speeches, film-propaganda: the most effective means of propaganda at present. Added to all this, is the permanent and enduring effect of a conscious education of the citizen from the public school to the university.

3. Creating a visible and portable common symbol. The head of the state usually serves as an excellent embodiment of such a symbol, as at present the *Führer,* who may be seen in person or whose picture appears on every possible occasion. In this connection one needs only to call to mind the integrating power exercised by the well known picture of Francis Joseph in white uniform with its green-busted double masthead, representing the Austro-Hungarian monarchy. Included under this head are also the flags, the orders and distinctions of honor, the placards, the uniforms, children's toys, the celebrations in honor of "great men," the honoring of heroes, living and dead, and many other things.

And to all this must be added, as integrating factors, the performances and demands of the state, which have already been mentioned, in the form of taxes, laws, elections, the paying of internal revenues, the support of the unemployed and, in the case of enslaved peoples, the paying of tribute, etc.

Now if the question be asked, whether and to what extent these various integrating attempts achieve their end, the answer may not be readily at hand. With a people, such as the Germans, who by their nature are inclined to carry on an individual economy, who are non-political, unwieldy, inclined to be critical, as we know, all attempts at a harmonizing influence will meet with far greater resistance than they would with an easily aroused and credulous people, such as the Italians. But for that reason the effect might be more permanent, if the integrating policy were directed to proper ends. What would be most likely to be developed in our people, is a nationalistic, and at all events, a patriotic feeling, both of which, as we have seen, depend more upon an attitude of reasonable understanding. We are little inclined to enthusiasm. But one thing must always be kept in mind:

a real community cannot be "created" by artificial means. In fact it cannot be created at all. All that we can do is to keep ourselves in readiness to receive it. If it is granted to us at all, it will be an act of grace.

CARL SCHMITT
1888-

CARL SCHMITT WAS EDUCATED in jurisprudence and has written voluminously on a wide variety of political and legal topics. He examined in turn the subjects of political romanticism, dictatorship, sovereignty, parliamentarianism, and international politics, five notable books appearing from 1919 to 1926. By the end of the twenties, works on constitutional, administrative, and international law were added to his authorship. He also wrote a commentary on Catholicism and politics during the brief time in which he permitted religious beliefs to guide him to a political position. He served as a state counselor and as a member of the Academy for German Law during the Nazi period. At present he is in retirement in Germany, where he continues to write and, by some circles, to be admired..

[20]   *The Meaning of Politics*

I

The concept of the state presupposes the concept of the political. According to modern usage the state is the political status of a nation or-

From Carl Schmitt, *Der Begriff des Politischen* in *Wissenschaftliche Abhandlungen und Reden zur Philosophie, Politik und Geistesgeschichte* Heft X (München: Verlag von Duncker und Humblot, 1932), pp. 7–65 passim, by permission of Carl Schmitt. The translation printed here is by David Cooperman. Professor Fred H. Blum generously aided in the translation, but the editors are responsible for its accuracy.

ganized in a territorial unity. But this is only a simple way of paraphrasing; it offers no definition of the state. Such a definition is, however, not necessary here since we are concerned with the nature of the political. We may leave it undecided what the nature of the state really resembles—whether a machine or an organism, a person or an institution, a society or a community, an enterprise or a beehive, or even perhaps a "basic procedural order" (*Verfahrensgrundreihe*). All of these definitions and images anticipate too much meaning, interpretation, illustrations and construction and therefore cannot represent any appropriate point of departure for a simple and elementary statement. In its literal sense and in terms of its historical appearance the state is a special type of status of a nation; and indeed it is ultimately the decisive status and hence, the status par excellence as against the many conceivable individual and collective statuses. It is not possible to say more at this point of the discussion. All characteristics of this conception of status and nation take their meaning from the further characteristic of the political and become incomprehensible when the nature of the political is misunderstood.

One can seldom find a clear definition of the political. Most frequently the word is used merely negatively as a contrast to various other ideas, in such antitheses as politics and economy, politics and morality, politics and law; within the law again there is politics and civil law, and so forth. By means of such negative polemical antithesis it is usually possible to define something with clarity depending upon the context and the concrete situation. However, this is not yet a specific definition. In general, "political" is juxtaposed in one way or another with "state," or at least is referred to the state. The state appears thus as something political; the political, however, as something pertaining to the state—obviously a vicious circle.

* * *

II

The political can only be defined by disclosing and identifying the specifically political categories. The political, that is to say, has its own criteria, which become effective in their characteristic ways in relation to the various, relatively independent spheres of human thought and action, especially the moral, esthetic, and economic. The political must, therefore, rest on its own ultimate distinctions to which all action with specifically political meaning may be referred. Let us assume that in the sphere of morality the final distinctions are good and evil; in esthetics, beautiful and ugly;

in economics, useful and harmful or, for instance, profitable and unprofitable. The question then arises whether there is also a separate simple distinction which can serve as a criterion of the political and of what it might be. Such a distinction is not meant to be similar and analogous to those other distinctions but is to be independent of them, autonomous, and as such is to speak clearly for itself.

The specific political distinction, to which political actions and motives may be traced back, is the distinction of *Friend* and *Foe*. It furnishes a definition in the sense of a criterion, not as an exhaustive definition or as an indication of content. Inasmuch as it is not deducible from other criteria, it corresponds, for the political, to the relatively independent criteria of the other antithesis: good and evil in the moral; beautiful and ugly in the esthetic, etc. In any case, it is independent not in the sense of establishing a separate new realm of discourse, but rather in the manner that it can neither be based on any one, or on any combination of the other antitheses nor can it be traced back to them. If the antithesis of good and evil is not, by itself, simply identical with that of beautiful and ugly, or useful and harmful, and cannot be directly reduced to the others, then the antithesis between Friend and Foe must be confused even less with, or mixed up with, the others. The distinction between Friend and Foe has the meaning of denoting the utmost degree of intensity of a union or of a separation, of an association or a dissociation. It can exist, theoretically and practically, without the necessity of applying simultaneously all those moral, esthetic, economic, or other distinctions. It is not necessary for the political enemy to be morally evil or esthetically ugly; he doesn't have to appear as an economic competitor, and it may even appear profitable to do business with him. He is just the Other, the Stranger, and it is sufficient for his nature that he is, in a specially intense sense, existentially different and a Foe, so that in the final instance, conflicts with him are possible. These conflicts can neither be decided through a previously determined general norm, nor through the judgment of a "disinterested" and therefore "non-partisan" third party. That is to say, the possibility of a correct understanding, and hence the authority to award and adjudge is given only through existential participation. Only the participants themselves, among themselves, can settle the extreme case of conflict. Particularly, each of them can only himself determine whether the "Other-ness" of the Foe implies the negation of one's own kind of existence in the concrete conflict case in question, and therefore whether it must be repulsed or fought in order to preserve one's own inherently natural (*seinsmässige*) way of life. From a psychological point of view the Foe easily becomes treated as evil and ugly because every distinction, most of all the political, as the strongest and most intense of the distinctions and configurations, calls for support by the other distinctions. This does not alter the autonomy of such antitheses. Consequently, the reverse is also correct: the morally evil, esthetically ugly, or economically harmful need not therefore be the Foe; the morally good, esthetically beautiful, and economically useful does not become the Friend in the specifically political sense of the word. The possibility of an autonomous conception of such a specific antithesis and Friend-Foe, separate from other distinction, demonstrates the unique (*seinsmässige*) reality and independence of the political.

III

The concepts Friend and Foe are to be understood in their concrete existential meaning, not as metaphors or symbols, not mixed and weakened by economic, moral, and other conceptions, and least of all in a private-individualistic sense, as the expression of private sentiments and psychological tendencies. They are not normative nor "pure spiritual" antitheses. Liberalism, in what for it is a typical dilemma of intellect and economics . . . has attempted to dissolve the Foe into a competitor from the business point of view, and from the intellectual point of view, into a debating adversary. . . .

What cannot be rationally denied is that nations group themselves according to the antithesis of Foe and Friend, that this antithesis is still real today, and that it exists as an actual possibility for every politically existing nation.

A Foe is thus not the competitor or the adversary in general. Neither is a Foe the private adversary whom we hate. A Foe exists only when one (at least potentially) fighting collectivity of people confronts another collectivity of the same kind. The Foe is only the *public* Foe because everything that has a relationship to such a collectivity of men, especially to a whole nation, becomes *public* by virtue of such a relationship. The Foe is *hostis,* not *inimicus,* in the broader sense. . . . The German language, like other languages, does not distinguish between the private and the political "Foe," so that many misunderstandings and falsifications are possible. The much cited passage "Love your enemies" (Mat. 5, Luk. 6,

27) means "diligite *inimicos* vestros" . . . and not "diligite *hostes* vestros"; the political Foe is not mentioned. Also in the thousand-year struggle between Christianity and Islam, never has a Christian espoused the idea that out of love we must surrender Europe to the Saracens or Turks rather than defend it. It is not necessary to hate the Foe personally in the political sense. And only in the private sphere does it have the meaning to love one's "enemy," that is, one's adversary. The Bible passage just quoted refers to the political antithesis even less than it is intended to dissolve the antithesis of good and evil, or beautiful and ugly. It certainly does not mean that one should love the Foe of one's own nation and support them against one's own.

* * *

The concepts *Friend, Foe,* and *battle* take their meaning from this: that they refer especially to the real possibility of physical killing. War follows from enmity, for this is the existential (*seinsmässige*) denial of another being. War is but the most extreme realization of enmity. It does not have to be common or normal, nor does it have to be experienced as ideal or desirable. Clearly, however, war must remain as a real possibility if the idea of the Foe is to have meaning.

* * *

War is not the aim and purpose or the very content of politics. But as a real possibility it is the leading supposition which determines in a characteristic way human action and thinking, thus creating a specifically political behavior. Therefore, the differentiation between Friend and Foe in no way means that a specific nation must eternally be the Foe or Friend of another specific nation, or that neutrality is not possible or cannot be politically meaningful. The concept of neutrality stands, as does every political concept, under this ultimate supposition of a real possibility of Friend and Foe clustering; and if only neutrality were to prevail in the world, then not only war but even neutrality itself would be abolished. The politics of avoiding war, as all politics, is at an end when the real possibility of fighting generally disappears. What always matters is only the *possibility* of this critical case—of the real war—and the decision whether this occasion arises or not. That the case appears to be an exception does not destroy its decisive character but confirms it all the more. Though today wars are no longer as numerous and common as previously, they have nevertheless in the same, or probably even stronger, proportion intensified their overwhelming total force as their number and commonness have declined. The case of war is still today, the "ultimate case." One can say that here, as in other instances, the very exception has a specially decisive meaning —and one which reveals the heart of the matter. For only real war reveals the utmost implications of the political Friend-Foe relationship. The life of men attains its specifically *political* tension in this most extreme possibility.

A world in which the possibility of such a way is completely eliminated, a definitely pacified globe, would be a world without the distinction between Friend and Foe, and hence, a world without politics.

*   *   *

V

*   *   *

The state as the decisive political unity has an enormous authority concentrated in itself: the possibility of making war and thereby commanding publicly the lives of men. The *jus belli* involves such a disposition; it implies the double possibility: to claim the readiness to die and to kill of the members of the nation.

*   *   *

It is a manifest fraud to curse war as murder of humans and then to demand of men that they make war, kill in wars, and let themselves be killed in order that "no more war prevails." War, the readiness of combatants to die, the physical killing of other men on the Foe's side, all this has no normative, but only an existential meaning. This consists in the reality of actual battle against an actual Foe—not in some sort of ideals, programs, or normatives. There are no rational ends, no norms no matter how right they may be, no program no matter how exemplary, no social ideal no matter how beautiful, no legitimacy or legality for which men on opposite sides would be justified in killing one another. There can be no conceivable justification of such a physical destruction of human life unless it arises from the existential *(seinsmässigen)* affirmation of one's own form of existence against an equally existential *(seinsmässigen)* denial of this form. Neither can war be justified on the basis of ethical and juristic norms. When there are truly Foes in the existential *(seinsmässigen)* sense as is meant here, then it is meaningful, but only politically meaningful, to defend oneself physically against them and to struggle with them when necessary.

* * *

As long as a nation exists in the political sphere it must, even if only in the most extreme case (whether or not it is extreme must be decided by the nation itself), determine the distinction between Friend and Foe itself. In *that* lies the nature of its political existence. When it no longer has the capacity or the will to make this distinction, it ceases to exist politically. When a nation allows a foreign one to prescribe who its Foe is and against whom it is allowed to struggle or not, then it is no longer a free political nation and is absorbed into or subordinated to another political system. The meaning of a war lies not in its being fought for ideals or norms of right, but in its being fought against a real enemy. All obscurities of these categories of Friend and Foe may be explained by the confusion with other abstractions or norms.

* * *

VI

* * *

It would be a dishonest pretension to take a condition of universal peace for granted. And it would be a confusion which can quickly be disposed of to believe that the end of a modern war would lead to "world peace"—thus setting forth the idyllic goal of complete and final "depolitization"—simply because a war between the great powers may easily become a world war today. . . .

Humanity as such cannot fight a war because it has no Foe, at least not on this planet. The concept of humanity excludes the concept of the Foe, because the Foe does not cease to be human—and hence there is no specific differentiation in that concept. The fact that wars are fought in the name of humanity is not a contradiction to this simple truth; quite to the contrary, it has an especially intensive political meaning. When a state fights its political Foe in the name of humanity, it is not a war for the sake of humanity, but a war wherein a specific state seeks to usurp a universal concept against its military opponent. At the cost of its opponent, it thus tries to identify itself with humanity, in the same way as one can misuse peace, justice, progress, civilization in order to claim them for oneself and to deny them to the Foe. "Humanity" is an especially useful ideological instrument of imperialistic expansion and in its ethical-humanitarian form it is a specific vehicle of economic imperialism.

* * *

VII

* * *

Political thought and political instinct validate themselves thus, theoretically and practically, in their capacity to distinguish between Friend and Foe.

* * *

VIII

* * *

[In liberal theory] for the individual as such there is no Foe with whom he must engage in a life-death struggle if he personally does not want to do so. To compel him to fight against his will is in any case, from the point of view of the private individual, lack of freedom and violence. All Liberal pathos turns against violence and lack of freedom. Every encroachment on, every danger to, the individual's freedom (which is on principle unlimited), his private property, and free competition is called "violence" and is *eo ipso* something evil.

* * *

Economy is no longer *eo ipso* freedom; technology serves not only comfort, but equally, the production of dangerous weapons and instruments; its progress does not cause *eo ipso* the humanitarian moral perfection which one thought of as Progress in the eighteenth century. . . .

[An imperialism based on economic methods] might have at its disposal the technical means of violent physical killing—technically perfect modern weapons. These weapons have been made so fabulously practical as a result of an application of capital and intelligence that they actually are to be used if necessary. For the use of such means, a new, essentially pacifistic vocabulary is being formed. This vocabulary does not know war, but only official actions, sanctions, punishing expeditions, pacifications, protection of treaties, international police, measures for securing peace.

The adversary is no longer called Foe, but is decreed to be a breaker of the peace and peace-destroyer and hence ruled *hors-la-loi* and *hors l'humanité*. A war to secure or further economic power positions must be made over into a "crusade" and into a "last war of humanity," with the help of propaganda. This is implicit in the polarity of ethics and economy. This polarity, it is true, is astonishingly systematic and consistent. However, this allegedly unpolitical, and apparently even anti-political, system either serves the existing or leads toward new Friend and Foe clusterings and cannot evade the consequences of the political. . . .

IV

Totalitarian society: a new political world

HISTORY IS FULL of authoritarian governments and autocracies, but, many writers agree, totalitarianism is a creature of the twentieth century. Within a decade and a half after World War I, totalitarian parties gained control of the state in Russia, Italy, and Germany, successfully eliminated opposition movements, and systematically began the construction of a new kind of society.

THE RISE OF THE TOTALITARIAN MOVEMENTS

In each case the totalitarian movement emerged from the crisis of an old regime, destroyed its institutions, and built on the ruins; the leader of the movement appeared as a popular savior and worked through an elitist apparatus; and each dictatorship first defined and then used politics primarily as a weapon for annihilation of opposition and for total social transformation. Each movement wrought not only political revolution but a moral revolution as well; all considered mere social reconstruction a trifling goal and boasted the creation of a new order, a new world with new values, and a new kind of humanity. But all rose from a system ruined by stasis and social exhaustion, fatigued economy, shattered class structure, and an unhinged political apparatus.

The victors as well as the vanquished were affected by the losses and costs of World War I. Fiscal problems multiplied, living standards suffered, and no social institution was spared profound disorganization. Economic transformations of the greatest magnitude provoked malaise and unrest in Russia, Italy, and Germany, and the political machinery lost the strength to cope with economic and social problems. Inflamed class consciousness on the one hand and nationalist excitement on the other heaped abuse on the static political apparatus.

Of the three totalitarian revolutions, the Russian came first. The peasants had chronically suffered from "land hunger," and while the Third Duma had prodded the government to begin some land reforms before 1910, the mass of peasantry were still impoverished at the outbreak of the war. Many of them were stirred by contact with those bearing new ideas in the tsarist army. They were receptive to promises of land, and came to regard the established order as vulnerable to change.

The comparatively small industrial proletariat had learned to distrust the government after the Petrograd revolt of 1905 and the succession of broken promises of social reform which followed it. The famine and inflation of 1916–1917 brought on by the war resulted in demonstrations in Petrograd and then in a major strike, which quickly developed into a full-scale revolution.

In Italy, rising unemployment and an impossible cost of living provoked agitation from the left. Industrial and agricultural workers took "direct action," and Italy writhed in the throes of open class warfare. In Milan and other large industrial cities, workers refused to leave their factories, and some organized councils; the peasants working the large estates rose in wrath, and in September, 1920, it appeared that a Soviet revolution would repeat itself in Italy.

In Germany the inflation of 1922–1923 struck like a catastrophe. *Inflation* is a tepid abstraction unless one has a sense of what it means to live through it. The following vivid passage by Konrad Heiden will help the reader understand why economic disaster destroys human personalities and why some people feared it more than death itself.

On Friday afternoons in 1923, long lines of manual and white-collar workers waited outside the pay-windows of the big German factories, department stores, banks, offices: dead-tired workingmen in grimy shirts open at the neck; gentlemen in shiny blue suits, saved from before the war, in mended white collars, too big for their shrunken necks; young girls, some of them with the new bobbed heads; young men in puttees and gray jackets, from which the tailor had removed the red seams and regimentals, embittered against the girls who had taken their jobs. They all stood in lines outside the pay-windows, staring impatiently at the electric wall clock, slowly advancing until at last they reached the window and received a bag full of paper notes. According to the figures inscribed on them, the paper notes amounted to seven hundred thousand or five hundred million, or three hundred and eighty billion, or eighteen trillion marks —the figures rose from month to month, then from week to week, finally from day to day. With their bags the people moved quickly to the doors, all in haste, the younger ones running. They dashed to the nearest food store, where a line had already formed. Again they moved slowly, oh, how slowly, forward. When you reached the store, a pound of sugar might have been obtainable for two millions; but, by the time you came to the counter, all you could get for two millions was half a pound, and the saleswoman said the dollar had just gone up again. With the millions or billions you bought sardines, sausages, sugar, perhaps even a little butter, but as a rule the cheaper margarine—always things that would keep for a week, until next pay-day, until the next stage in the fall of the mark.

For money could not keep, the most secure of all values had become the most insecure. The mark wasn't just low, it was slipping steadily downward. Goods were still available, but there was no money; there was still labor and consumption, but no economy; you could provide for the moment, but you couldn't plan for the future. It was the end of money. It was the end of the old shining hope that everyone would be rich. The secular religion of the nineteenth century was crumbling amid the profanation of holy property.

Germany had financed her war by means of loans. The state had borrowed from its citizens approximately eighty billion marks, about a third of the so-called national wealth, and shot them into the air—without result, for the war had been lost. Every citizen had been forced to lend, even the propertyless out of their meager wages. Great fortunes and petty savings had been thrown down the gullet of war. And then, suddenly, the mark lost its value. The war loan was worth nothing. Savings of a lifetime were worth nothing. The great radical cure, ruthless equalization, was going into effect. It was a process which would affect the distant future, but most men failed even to suspect its full significance, for they saw only the beginnings, the first symptoms. The great prophecies of the nineteenth century were beginning to be fulfilled. A man who thought he had a small fortune in the bank might receive a politely couched letter from the directors: "The bank deeply regrets that it can no longer administer your deposit of sixty-eight thousand marks, since the costs are out of all proportion to the capital. We are therefore taking the liberty of returning your capital. Since we have no bank-notes in small enough denominations at our disposal, we have rounded out the sum to one million marks. Enclosure: one 1,000,000-mark bill." A cancelled stamp for five million marks adorned the envelope.

The state wiped out property, livelihood, personality, squeezed and pared down the individual, destroyed his faith in himself by destroying his property—or worse: his faith and hope in property. Minds were ripe for the great destruction. The state broke the economic man, beginning with the weakest.[1]

The Collapse of Class Structures

In Germany the inflation destroyed much more than the material security of the middle classes, for it demolished the belief that savings and property provided one with a *Stand*—a station and a stake in German society. The class ideals of hard work and thrift provided a meaning for existence, and savings were cherished as the prize of an honest lifetime. The disappearance of savings with the evaporation of all liquid assets was viewed as personal annihilation, and one faced absorption in the anonymous ranks of the proletariat. Hitler ascended to power on the strength of the desperate yearning of the middle class to be saved from capsizing into a social abyss.

The class structure that collapsed in Russia was more "backward" than that of Italy and Germany. The old system of four estates had been disintegrating for decades. The middle classes had grown in size and influence but, hampered by feudal atavisms and the slow pace of industrialization, had not attained sufficient unity or strength to construct a modern society or to provide effective leadership. The urban workers were small in number but militant and well organized. The largest social group was the formless but restive peasantry. At the time of the revolution no new class was strong enough to lead, the economy was spent and without direction, and the group which had made the important decisions, the old nobility around the throne, could offer only more of the status quo. Lenin arrived after the storm broke with a tactical sense for the correct promises and a gift for improvisation.

The Failure of Politics

Traditional political solutions, even if they had been possible, would have been greeted by popular distrust. Nationalist movements throughout Europe treated conventional politics with scorn, and parliamentary institutions faced contempt from the left as well as from the right. In Italy the Parliament had atrophied during the war and the legislative process afterward broke down entirely under the burden of intransigent party struggles,

[1] Konrad Heiden, *Der Fuehrer: Hitler's Rise to Power,* trans. Ralph Manheim (Boston: Houghton Mifflin Company, 1944), pp. 126–27.

class warfare, and the chauvinistic charge that Italy had been cheated of spoils by the Versailles Treaty.

In Germany, the nationalist movement offered emotional compensation for the sense of loss created by the Versailles Treaty. Many associated the Treaty with the Weimar government; and the nationalist myth that the socialists and democrats who were the heart of that government had betrayed the men in the trenches kept alive a feeling of suspicion and hatred of the Parliament. The Weimar Constitution had constructed a formula for stable government which succeeded through the twenties—a worthy attempt by the bourgeois parties and the social democrats to find a political solution for critical social problems, but this victory of political intelligence never won the full confidence of the people. The economic and social crisis would have shaken the foundations of the most ancient and secure democratic republic, but Germany's prewar experience did not provide the Reichstag with the necessary knowledge, courage, stamina, and obstinacy to cope with an overwhelming crisis.

In Russia parliamentarianism never had an opportunity to disillusion anyone. As Merle Fainsod puts it in *How Russia Is Ruled,* "The history of the Dumas is largely a record of the frustration of parliamentary hopes." [2] The Bolsheviks, who were sure they perceived the strings that manipulated the illusions in Europe, had no patience with the idea that a "bourgeois fraud" might be imported to Russia, and their vehement agitation in the Second Duma of 1907 prefigured their scorn for national assemblies a decade later. The absence of a formal political arena to adjust the conflicting interests of classes and parties left Russia with no institution for their possible resolution by a democratic formula.

In Russia, Italy, and Germany the social and economic systems were in a critical state, placing an impossible burden on weakened political institutions. Carried forward by passion, rage, and discipline, the totalitarian movements, hard and clever in the ways of power, brought an end to the crisis, not by solving it but by destroying the systems that had produced it.

THE SEIZURE OF POWER

The nascent totalitarian parties seized power in different ways: the Bolsheviks by taking advantage of the war and the social revolution, the

[2] Merle Fainsod, *How Russia Is Ruled* (Cambridge: Harvard University Press, 1953), p. 11.

Fascists by a *Putsch* which they themselves had not expected to be successful, and the Nazis by a legal accession which became flimsy and invalid
as soon as the dictatorship established itself and created a revolution from
within.

The Russian Revolution

Despite long theoretical and organizational preparation by Lenin and
the Bolsheviks, the events of March, 1917, took both the government and
the revolutionary groups by surprise.

Popular disgust with the tedious and costly war, loss of faith in the
tsar, hunger riots, and a surprising display of sympathy with the strikers
and demonstrators by large numbers of police and soldiers all combined
to overthrow the monarchy within a few days, from March 8 to 12, 1917.
The Revolution was truly a *levée en masse:* working leadership appeared
only after the popular revolt was obviously successful. The Bolsheviks did
not make the revolution—Lenin was in Switzerland and did not arrive until
April; and neither Trotsky (a theorist of revolution but not yet a Bolshevik)
nor Stalin (a lesser member of the Central Committee) was in Petrograd
at the time.

The tactics of the Bolsheviks after 1917 reflected the general theory
of revolution and the state developed by Lenin and Trotsky since 1905.
The Marxist laws of history, which declared that the initial revolutions
would occur in industrially advanced nations, were amended by the later
prophets. The new "law of combined development" held that in such an
industrially backward nation as Russia, the bourgeois and socialist revolutions might be merged into one cataclysm that would establish socialism
in that nation and pave the way for a worldwide victory.

State and Revolution, written shortly before Lenin led the Bolsheviks
to power, is typical of Lenin's trenchant, polemical style. His language
abounds in militaristic images and in prophecies of Communist victory.
Politics is the art of violent struggle for the ultimate conquest of the enemy.
The state is *nothing but* the organization of violence for the suppression
of some class. Government and law are and ought to be only weapons of
class combat. At the same time Lenin seems to scent revolution in the air,
for the eschatological strains in Marxism ring loudly in this work. It is
full of oracular phrases and visions: the revolt of the downtrodden; History's Chosen People, the Proletariat; the perfect society of childlike simplicity governed by anyone who can read and write, regulated by pure rationality. Tense with revolutionary exhilaration, Lenin scornfully dismisses

traditionally organized parliaments and proclaims the necessity of violent revolution.

Obviously, Lenin was more than a midwife to the Bolshevik Revolution. From the time he arrived in Russia in April, 1917, he set about fulfilling the prophecies announced long before. First by irresistible slogans, then by the extension of Bolshevik power in the Petrograd and Moscow soviets, and finally by insistence at Party meetings that *the* Historical Moment had come, he, more than anyone else, organized the October Revolution. Certainly the Provisional Government through its vacillation had a hand in its own demise. But it was Lenin who exploited its every weakness. And it was Lenin and Trotsky who finally directed the Bolshevik forces in the brief, sharp fighting in Petrograd. On the eve of victory, Trotsky jubilantly consigned the Mensheviks, who had called for a truce and compromise with the Kerenski government, to "the dustbin of history."

The Fascist Coup

In Italy after Versailles, nationalism was heavily inflated with resentment. The old fires of *risorgimento* were fanned by the spirit of such archromantics as Gabriele D'Annunzio (1863–1938). The former firebrand socialist Benito Mussolini, who had turned into a nationalist with the coming of the war, quickly gathered those who sought revenge for something, or anything, into the *Fascio di Combattimento* in North Italy in 1919.

At this time, throughout the Western world, the Bolshevik successes in Russia threw much of the bourgeoisie into political panic. In Italy, Mussolini announced that only the Fascists could prevent communism from engulfing Italy, and his gangs paraded the claim in the streets. Socialists, Communists, liberals, Catholic populists, in fact anyone who was "in the way" became the victims of the Fascist "saviors" wielding instruments of primitive violence.

These events coincided with a period of parliamentary impotence. As cabinet followed cabinet and centrist parties engaged one another in complicated quadrilles, Mussolini "acted."

But now, *action* had a metaphysical, Sorelian halo about it. The word was given a ring of glory, surrounded with the kind of heady political *mystique* that permeated the writings of French romantic, elitist nationalists like Maurice Barrès and Charles Péguy. There is a great difference, however, between Mussolini's opportunistic outbursts and the political musings of the early twentieth-century romantics, and it would be incorrect to suggest that Mussolini was a student of Sorel and the others. The *mystique* of action was a flimsy myth, composed of a call to ancient Roman military virtues mixed with Italian nationalism. Yet it served as the formula that drew the masses and classes alike to the Fascist movement.

The "action" taken by Mussolini belied all the significance attributed by him to that word. Unlike Lenin, he did not set about systematically to overthrow the government. On the very eve of his rise to power, at the end of October, 1922, he shrank from seizing power despite the fact that the monarchy, the government, and the army were either panicking in the face of his threats to march on Rome or conspiring to pave his way to power. After a tragicomedy of events, the black-shirted Fascist *squadristi* swarmed out of their hiding places and straggled toward Rome. Before he knew it, Mussolini found himself named premier.

The Nazi Rise to Power

Postwar conditions in Germany resembled those in Italy. The experience in the trenches, the collapse of the monarchy, the Versailles Treaty as a symbol of defeat all produced an attitude of bitterness among many Germans. When the Spartacists, the militant Communists, attempted to make revolution Bolshevik style in Berlin in January, 1919, they were met by the pent-up hostility and fear of former soldiers, unemployed students and workers, and the shaky, moderate government of the socialist Friedrich Ebert. The attempt by the left was crushed, and Rosa Luxemburg and Karl Liebknecht, the leaders, were murdered; a precedent was set for the use of paramilitary organizations by any group claiming to "save" the nation.

Unlike Italy, however, the newly formed Weimar constitutional democracy managed to hold on for more than a decade in spite of increasing economic and political instability. A climate of conservatism gradually overtook the social and political institutions. The traditional military, bureaucratic, and economic powers regained whatever strength they had lost in 1918. The judiciary too lapsed into the ultra-conservatism of the imperial era.

The National Socialists, at first a handful of assorted *Lumpen*proletarians and intellectual pretenders, failed in their first assaults against the establishment. Adolf Hitler, who had been one of the gray mass of disgruntled veterans, took over the leadership of the small Nazi group by the force of his speech-making abilities alone. The "armed bohemians" within the party and the resentful masses without recognized Hitler as the same *kleiner Mann* that they believed themselves to be. He presented himself as an insignificant man in the face of worldwide conspiracies, an honest

German surrounded by Jews, traitors in government, international socialists, Bolsheviks, Western imperialist nations, wealthy industrialists, and
department store owners, all intent on robbing the ordinary German of
his birthright. He offered heady wine to those who felt themselves humili-
ated by superhuman forces and events.

The Nazi group, thus inflamed, embarked on a program of terror and
assassination which was eventually to reach from top to bottom in German
society. Swept off their feet by an early burst of rage, they attempted a
coup against the Bavarian state government in November, 1923, ill-
planned and clumsily executed. At his trial, Hitler played the part of the
wronged messiah. The nationalistic judges were much impressed, and sentenced him to the minimum prison term of which he served but nine
months. It was probably one of the few occasions in the history of the
modern state when an unsuccessful direct act of treason went so unpun-
ished. In prison Hitler assembled his pronouncements, judgments, and im-
precations uttered on previous occasions, and added some tales of his life.
This collection was later published as *Mein Kampf.*

One looks in vain through the works of the Nazis for a lucid, systematic
account of their doctrines. "National Socialism has no rational political
theory," wrote Franz Neumann in *Behemoth.*[3] Of course, it was not the
purpose of nazism to develop such a theory; on the contrary, to the Nazis
reason represented everything antagonistic to the "German Spirit." Another quasiofficial Nazi document, Alfred Rosenberg's *The Myth of the
Twentieth Century,* attempted to conjure up a primitive, Sorelian type of
myth for the faithful. It might be inaccurate to consider the doctrines political *thought,* for only the blood cry to action, the call of the uprooted, was
welcome in the movement.

But Hitler had learned that impulsive revolution, even charismatically
led, could not overcome the traditional and bureaucratic institutions. On
his release from prison he strengthened his forces with new shock-troop
bands and prepared to come to power legally. He was aided in this effort
by several conditions: the severely depressed economy after 1929 with
millions of unemployed, the internecine warfare among the other parties
of the Republic, and the senility of President Paul von Hindenburg. The
marching columns of determined Nazis and the truculence of the greatest
of all terrible simplifiers provided direction for all who felt themselves lost
or forgotten. Wealthy industrialists looked on this popular upstart as a

[3] Franz Neumann, *Behemoth: The Structure and Practice of National Socialism*
(London: Victor Gollancz Ltd., 1943), p. 379.

barrier against bolshevism; the lower-middle class regarded him as a support for their tumbling destinies; and the "never-employed" youth came to Hitler for the bright future he offered.

In the various elections from 1928 to 1932, the Nazi vote multiplied several fold. After July, 1932, the Nazis were the strongest party in the Reichstag. Through the efforts of the influential banker Kurt von Schroeder and others, Hitler was appointed chancellor on January 30, 1933. The savior of Germany had risen to authority clothed in the legality that made him presentable to more conservative Germans.

TOTALITARIAN MOVEMENTS AS SYSTEMS OF ORDER

Totalitarian ideologies commit the party faithful to perpetual movement—to breaking all traditional bounds—thus making membership in a totalitarian party attractive to many before power is won. Once such a party comes to power, much of the revolutionary *élan* can be taken up in plans for immediate social transformation. But the everyday round of political rule necessarily requires static and repetitive functions. Personnel have to be hired and trained, regulations followed, property assessed, taxes laid and collected. In short, the activities summed up in the commonplace phrase "law and order" are part of any viable government.

Yet the thrust of the three major totalitarian ideologies was directed against such activities. In each of the systems tensions resulted from the contradictions of revolution and rule—tensions which broke out in paroxysms of violence.

The tasks confronting the new regimes were somewhat different, and the differences in each case were due to the varying circumstances of revolution and the different political consciousness of each people. In Germany and Italy, sizable portions of the mass had been drawn to the Nazis and Fascists. The Bolsheviks, on the other hand, were supported by smaller numbers, many of whom expected a libertarian, generous regime or at least eagerly awaited tangible fulfillments of revolutionary promises. Most of the population was distant from the centers of revolution and was overwhelmed by the succession of events of 1917–1921. After seizing power, the Bolsheviks fought a costly civil war to secure it. By that time a frightful famine and a disorganized economy forced them to put off revolutionary transformation until after an initial period of stability.

But Lenin's death in 1924 resulted in further political instability as

Stalin, Trotsky, and the other Bolshevik leaders struggled for the power to determine the future direction of the revolution. When Stalin finally embarked on the task of "building socialism in one country," he had first to undo the order painfully built during the period of the New Economic Policy, a process that was accomplished at the price of liquidating some millions of kulaks. And then the 1930's brought the final communization of the country, effectuated by terror and the further extermination of millions. The Bolsheviks took 20 years to go through the cycle from revolt to complete revolution. The Fascists and Nazis, with fewer obstacles, accomplished their tasks more swiftly.

The Consolidation of Power in Russia

Long before the Bolsheviks gained power they had developed a theory of terror. In 1901, Lenin wrote: "We have never rejected terror on principle, nor can we do so. Terror is a form of military operation that may be usefully applied, or may even be essential in certain moments of the battle. . . ." [4]

At the end of 1917, the first of the several Soviet secret police organizations was organized. The Cheka groups were ordered to seek out and to combat counterrevolutionaries and saboteurs. Any of the following categories qualified for summary arrest by the Cheka: anarchists, left Social Revolutionaries, Mensheviks suspected of antagonism toward the regime, peasants suspected of supporting White armies. During this era the rationale for terror was that the pressure of civil war required extraordinary methods. But after the Stalin-Trotsky struggle, the first Five-Year Plan, and the liquidation of the kulaks, a whole host of new enemies of the people were proclaimed and specters continually raised in order to justify the terror—until Stalin's death.

In Soviet Russia as in the other two totalitarian nations, the official ideology purported to explain all history and promised inevitable success to the believers. Any deflection from a straight course to established goals was explained as malevolent obstruction by willful wreckers. Since the leadership was incapable of error in this closed system, the path to perfection could only be opened by destruction of the enemies. Such was the logic of terror.

The program of social transformation was accompanied by sudden arrests made by the succession of secret police organizations—GPU,

---

[4] Quoted in Bertram D. Wolfe, *Three Who Made a Revolution* (Boston: Beacon Press, 1955), p. 89.

OGPU, NKVD, MVD. During the thirties, the terror whirled in ever-widening circles as engineers, party functionaries, bureaucrats, and military personnel were drawn into the vortex. Individuals were accused with little or no evidence. A secret letter from the Central Committee of the Communist party to all party committees in July, 1936, includes the following sentence: "The inalienable quality of every Bolshevik under present conditions should be the ability to recognize an enemy of the Party, no matter how well he may be masked." [5] Soviet society took on the characteristics of a masquerade in which no one was what he appeared to be and the penalty for being unmasked—and for failing to unmask others one thought to be masked—was immediate imprisonment.

The years of the Great Purge, 1936–1938, were highlighted by the Moscow Trials. The old Bolsheviks Lev Kamenev, Grigori Zinoviev, Ivan Smirnov, Karl Radek, Nikolai Bukharin, Aleksei Rykov, and many others publicly admitted committing treason on a wide scale. The trials vividly portrayed the totalitarian image of man. The instruments of law were given dramatic new political functions and acquired ancient ritualistic ones. Grandiose tales of crime committed by these "anti-Christs" were rehearsed by the prosecutor, Andrei Y. Vyshinsky, who played the role of the defender of "socialist legality." He invoked the vilest names in the Bolshevik vocabulary against the fathers of the revolution—the old heroes now in disgrace before the citizen mass because of allegedly betraying the fatherland. Except for N. M. Krestinsky, they confessed to having committed espionage in the pay of capitalist powers and to having engaged in huge conspiracies under Trotsky's orders. The victims demanded only the heaviest punishment as atonement for their crimes, and mercifully, the state granted them death sentences.

The history of the legal system in Soviet Russia discloses all the paradoxes of totalitarianism in power. The dissolution of the tsarist legal system by the Bolsheviks left only decrees from the new leaders. On the one hand, the revolutionary ideology was contemptuous of law as such. In accord with Lenin's early reductivist views of law, where cases arose that were not covered by decree, the newly appointed—and untrained—judges were ordered to guide themselves by "revolutionary legal consciousness." This was an era of marriage and divorce by mere registry of the fact—an era dominated by a negative view of the substantive values of law. On the other hand, by 1921 the requisites of governing a large nation had led to

[5] Quoted in Merle Fainsod, *Smolensk Under Soviet Rule* (Cambridge: Harvard University Press, 1958), p. 233.

the development of a complex, centrally controlled system of legal institutions.[6] The two contradictory tendencies continued through the 1920's, and the ultimately negative view of law was reflected in the work of Eugen Pashukanis, who expected that law would wither away as the nation's economic base was socialized. In the early 1930's this doctrine ran counter to the requirements of a centrally synchronized economy, and Pashukanis was made to reshape his views. By 1936, Stalin was proclaiming, "We need stability of laws now more than ever," [7] and soon Vyshinsky, the new spokesman for Soviet law, attacked ". . . the rotten theory of the wrecker Pashukanis with its putrid vapor, whereby our enemies sought to sully the pure source of great and truly scientific thought." [8] Pashukanis disappeared without a trace in 1937.

At the same time that Stalin was "stabilizing" the law, terror was raging. The following authoritative attempt was made to distinguish between the work of the ordinary courts and that of the GPU:

The repression of the G.P.U. had its center of gravity in the intimidation of the class enemy, without retreating in separate cases from the responsibility of transforming conscience, while the repression exercised by the Court set before it the end, thanks to publicity in the investigation of the case, of mobilizing proletarian public opinion to fight against the class enemy with all his machinations against Soviet power. In consequence, the G.P.U and the Court constituted different aspects of the class fight against the exploiters who were resisting the dictatorship of the proletariat.[9]

Despite the disorder brought about by the terror, Stalin's talents for organization led to a bureaucratized state and party and to an economy with an initial capacity for the production of heavy industry. To further stabilize his regime, Stalin inaugurated a cultural program to celebrate the traditions of old Russia. By the time World War II broke out, hardly a sector of Soviet life was not under centralized control. Artistic, literary, scientific, and educational efforts were permitted only when in accord with central policy. The society appeared as if magnetized, with individuals or-

---

[6] John N. Hazard, *Settling Disputes in Soviet Society: The Formative Years of Legal Institutions* (New York: Columbia University Press, 1960), pp. 128–75.
[7] J. Stalin, "On the Draft Constitution of the USSR," in *Leninism, Selected Writings* (New York: International Publishers, 1942), p. 402.
[8] Quoted in Harold J. Berman, *Justice in Russia: An Interpretation of Soviet Law* (Cambridge: Harvard University Press, 1950), p. 45.
[9] A. Y. Vyshinsky and V. S. Undrevich, *Course of Criminal Investigation* (Moscow, 1936), I, 28–29, quoted in David Rousset, *Police-State Methods in the Soviet Union* (Boston: Beacon Press, 1953), pp. 21–22.

dered into lines of force commanded by Stalin. His portrait and his name were surrounded with a magical aura, as in theocratic-autocratic societies.

Fascist Rule

In Fascist Italy the devices of terror appeared early in the history of the regime, but total transformation was not achieved with the efficiency the Stalinists showed. After Mussolini's rise to power, the violence done to opponents of fascism, such as the murder of the socialist leader Giacomo Matteotti in 1924, were simply continuations of the previous ruthlessness of the Fascist squads. It was hard to tell the difference between the tyrannical underworld gang and the overworld of the state. Within a decade, however, Mussolini reshaped the constitution, clothing himself in all the habits of the law. But it was clear that a firm dictatorship had been established, with the reins held by the head of government.

As early as 1923, the Fascists began to invade the private realm. Mass youth organizations were established which indoctrinated youngsters from the age of six with the myths of the state, war, and fascism. In addition, to insure the absorption of each moment of the adult's life by the regime, the National Leisure Time Organization (*Opera Nazionale Dopolavoro*) was formed.

The secret police (OVRA) were given discretionary powers, and could declare any person dangerous to the state and punish him by deportation or incarceration in a concentration camp. No judicial appeal was possible from such sentences. A special pseudojudicial tribune composed of high-ranking Fascists dealt with more important political criminals.

Pervading the society was a network of informers and *agents provocateurs*. Some were blackmailed by the OVRA to inform on friends and relatives; others came to believe it was their patriotic duty to do so. In *Bread and Wine,* one of Silone's characters says:

"On this degradation of man into a frightened animal, who quivers with fear and hates his neighbor in his fear, and watches him, betrays him, sells him, and then lives in fear of discovery, the dictatorship is based. He who has had the misfortune to succumb to this shame is condemned to wishing that the dictatorship may endure." [10]

One of the Fascist doctrines which attracted many non-Fascists in Italy was the concept of the corporate state. It appealed to Catholic organic

[10] Ignazio Silone, *Bread and Wine* (New York: Penguin Books, Inc., 1946), p. 268. Originally published by Harper & Brothers, 1937.

theorists and syndicalists alike. As put into practice by Mussolini, however, it became an hierarchical bureaucracy of incredible complexity and proportions which bore little resemblance to any organic ideal. As a political myth, the doctrine of the corporate state was used to rationalize the outlawing of strikes, the repression of free trade-union activity, and the imposition of central economic controls. By 1939, the economy was fully geared for war and the corporative economic structure was integrated with the instruments of political command.

The glorification of war in the Fascist and Nazi ideologies helped to instill in the mass a sense that it was a military column on the march, prepared to overcome all opposition as it swept into the future. Mussolini issued the call for good Italians to emulate their Roman forbears. In 1935 the Fascists attacked the "uncivilized" Ethiopians with bombers and troops equipped with all the devices of modern warfare. Soon afterward, Mussolini and Hitler aided Franco in the Spanish Civil War, marking the end of the peace of 1918 and also the renewal of the war of 1914.

The Nazi Regime

The Nazis had come to power under the cloak of legality; they secured that power by raising the fear of an enemy threat to the safety of the state and then by investing Hitler with extraordinary power to deal with the "distress." Thus, on February 26, 1933, the Reichstag building was burned by the Nazis, and liberals, socialists, and Communists were arrested and charged with having committed the crime. A series of emergency laws were passed in the next month which remained in force while the Nazis were in power. Fundamental liberties were suspended; the government was empowered to confiscate property without compensation and provided with absolute powers to take measures against enemies of the state. Within the next nine months, the federal states and all local governments were brought under the central control of the regime. Trade unions were wrecked and their members organized into a German labor front. All parties except the Nazi were destroyed one by one. The Rechtsstaat [11] was shattered and power concentrated in Hitler's hands.

The successful rise to power of the Nazis was accompanied by inner party tensions. The revolution did not yield sufficient spoils for the competing paramilitary and private terror groups, and it did not fulfill its apocalyptic promises quickly enough. The "political Bovarists" began to

[11] See the opening paragraphs of the selection from Franz Neumann, p. 222.

grumble.[12] Ernst Röhm and his SA (*Sturm-Abteilungen*) leaders and old Nazis like Gregor Strasser became restive, as they feared the revolution was grinding to a stop before they could get all they wanted of spoils and power. Hermann Göring and Heinrich Himmler, on the other hand, were pressing Hitler to cut down the strength of the SA. On June 29–30, 1934, Hitler did so by ordering the purge of those desiring a continued revolution. Besides dealing with Röhm and his top leaders, Strasser and Kurt von Schleicher, the SS (*Schutz-Staffel*) took the opportunity to pay off some old grudges, and over 400 persons were murdered.

Thereafter Germany rapidly became totalitarian. The Nazis used the word *Gleichschaltung,* synchronization, to describe the reorganization of society according to the monolithic Nazi plans. Hitler declared the revolution at an end, meaning that now he had full control. The party was set above the state, and within a few years Hitler was exalted as absolute leader, embodying the Spirit of the *Volk* and the source of all law.

Everything that Hitler had written or said from the time of his appearance on the public scene contained open promises of nihilism. Soon after the Nazis took power, Hitler fulfilled them, partially explaining his initial success in the international arena. It was difficult for his opponents to take direct threats of absolute violence seriously. Hitler had often passionately proclaimed that he had only the welfare of Germany and the world in his heart and that he would not break the peace. At other times he would rant about the *Drang nach Osten* and the necessary war to avenge the defeat of Germany by the traitors and allies in World War I. Hence, when he did unleash his destruction, his opponents were doubly surprised: that one of his apparent lies had come true, and that a self-proclaimed fanatic could gather enough support and power to do such things in Western civilization in the twentieth century.

Hitler seemed to attract all the floating anti-Semitism in Germany and in Europe, and from 1933 to 1945 his fantasies of the Jew-as-enemy created a series of acts designed to make "unpersons" of the "racial enemy." After the Nuremberg laws of 1935 bringing the most private forms of personal relationship among people under state surveillance, there came a series of actions which stripped layer after layer of the "decent drapery of life" from Jews. When World War II began, the climax of the Nazi revo-

---

[12] By political Bovarism we mean an emotional state giving rise to political illusions, held by persons having insatiable romantic cravings for deliverance from the boredom and humdrum oppressions of a stale existence.

lution occurred as this helpless enemy was being systematically destroyed.

Meanwhile, the "master race" was purifying itself in other ways. The inherited legal system was found to bear too many traces of Western Roman law, and so the "healthy" blood calls of the mythical Nordics were substituted. Some scholars contended that large areas of German law were unaffected by Nazi changes, and thus many traditional legal relations remained. Such is the thesis of Ernst Fraenkel in *The Dual State* (1941). This is literally and narrowly true precisely because the Nazis permitted it; but they threatened all branches of law with invasion if the situation warranted. Thus, so far as the legal system was concerned, there was no dual state since there were no boundaries between the untouched area and the area of Nazi prerogative. No one could predict that the regime would not issue new orders for any aspect of life, and hence there was no system of calculable action. Even Hans Frank, a rabid Nazi jurist and official, was deprived of his party posts because he dared suggest that Himmler's SS ought to be limited slightly in its actions by the decrees of Frank's occupation government in Poland.

People's courts were established where criminal cases were decided according to the "healthy racial consciousness" of the judges—many of them newly appointed for the occasion and accredited only with devotion to the Nazi cause. Wherever the traditional law or idea of law was confronted with the will of *der Führer,* it gave way before it. Hence, international law was attacked as a mask for the imperialist designs of the Jews, Marxists, British, and so on. Any international action by the Third Reich was proclaimed legitimate sheerly on grounds of "healthy racial impulse." These racial impulses were publicly rehearsed and rendered more explosive. Many Germans swept themselves up in a political Walpurgis Night, feeling they had recaptured the spirit of the German folk community. What followed was a twentieth-century mechanical fantasy: massed marchers, fiery midnight rituals, immense columns of tanks, planes, and soldiers, all looking alike—all seemingly roaring the name of the One, the Incarnation of Racial Purity, the little Austrian Conductor.

The enormous forces that this civilization-crushing dream brought into play easily cracked the defenses of those nations against which it was first directed. But the dream inevitably extended beyond Germany's capacities to sustain it. Once having declared all others (save Axis friends) absolute foes, the Third Reich exhausted itself and much of the world in its attempt at planetary nihilism.

AN APPRAISAL

While differing in historical and cultural background and in the specific content of their appeals, the three totalitarian dictatorships shared many characteristics. The blending of terror with imposed order is a tour de force which each tried in its own way. All regimes either had the support of the mass from the beginning or else manufactured it, allowing the leaders to claim that their authority was more democratically based than that of the liberal democracies. The retention of the term *democracy* by totalitarians indicates that the language of the Enlightenment is still used to rationalize revolutionary movements, but it also barely conceals the extent to which authoritarian governments rely on the manipulation of the masses in this era. Large-scale organization of mass action was made possible only by the destruction of democratic constitutions or by their absence. Thus, totalitarian elites were able to move large numbers of people and rearrange styles of life comparatively swiftly because they confronted the people directly, unhindered by the time-consuming processes of constitutional government. Yet the very destruction of these formal devices was believed to make possible the construction of "true" democracy. The totalitarian definition of democracy suggested continual stimulation and engagement of the masses—an extension of the revolutionary purposes of the movement throughout the society. Thus understood, democracy was superprogressivistic in meaning: no obstacles were believed to exist to prevent the fulfillment of utopian goals, since it was assumed that the masses were solidly behind the movement. At this point, the gap between ideology and reality becomes apparent. The tasks of an industrial order are not easily accomplished with revolutionary *élan* alone. Neither the authoritarian ideals and extravagant myths of the Fascists and Nazis nor the Bolshevik "hard" utopian visions were capable of defining the problems of wrecked postwar economies without engendering further disorganization. Lenin expected that within 24 hours of the Revolution, "The specific 'commanding' methods of the state officials can and must begin to be replaced . . . by the simple functions of 'managers' and bookkeepers, functions which are now already within the capacity of the average city dweller and can well be performed for 'workingmen's wages.' "[13] The disillusionment that devel-

---

[13] V. I. Lenin, *State and Revolution* (New York: International Publishers Co., 1932), p. 43.

oped during the next decades reflected the unsettling consequences of such simplistic predictions.

From the wealth of analytical literature on totalitarian institutions, we have selected an excerpt from an essay by Franz Neumann dealing with the character and functions of the dictatorship in totalitarian systems. This examination was an important part of Neumann's reflections on the various types of dictatorships in Western history. The selections from the works of Lenin, Trotsky, Stalin, Gentile, and Hitler that follow reveal significant resemblances in precept and character. We also recommend to the reader Hannah Arendt's work *The Origins of Totalitarianism* (1951).

In *"Left-Wing" Communism: An Infantile Disorder,* Lenin ascribed the success of the Bolsheviks to the discipline and firmness of the "vanguard of the proletariat," to their close ties with the masses, and to the conviction among the masses that the party's strategy was correct. This rhetoric of revolutionary success was based on several necessary illusions. First, the party (really its leaders) was equated with the "forefront of the proletariat"; it was considered the leading edge of history. This "fact" itself then justified revolutionary action. The illogical leap from presumed historical condition to principles of right, a part of Marx's legacy, became a matter of faith for his heirs. The argument that it had maintained connections with the masses enabled the party to convince itself that it was more democratic than any parliament could be. Furthermore, if the masses could believe in the party's position, its political truth was thereby confirmed.

Of course, this chain of propositions assumed that there was one and only one vanguard, and that its name was the Communist party, meaning the Bolsheviks. It assumed that there was a singular group, the masses, which might enter into democratic relations with only one "true" party, inferring that all other possible parties or political arrangements were "incorrect."

Lenin was not concerned, in this essay, with proving these propositions, but rather with asserting them and then indicating the proper tactical course for revolutionary action. His argument with the German "left-deviationists" on the issue of whether or not a Communist party should take part in parliaments was made solely on tactical grounds and also revealed how absolutely he considered revolutionary success to be the vindication of his position, an obviously circular argument. More significant for a general view of totalitarian movements, however, was the obsession with "correct" action apparent in the work, where *correct* meant that interpretation of Marxist ideology which would move the party to power.

The logic of Communist morality was extended further in Trotsky's essay "Their Morals and Ours." Despite his political defeat by Stalin and the subsequent decade of playing hare to Stalin's hounds around the world, Trotsky consistently held to the thesis that "Problems of revolutionary morality are fused with the problems of revolutionary strategy and tactics." He addressed himself to such questions more than most Communist theoreticians, and in his work the style and structure of the Bolshevik ethic was unmistakable. It was clearly a doctrine born in battle and impatient with analytic distinctions.

Stalin's gloss on Lenin exhibited the concern for proclaiming Soviet rule democratic noted above, and also demonstrated that Stalin judged questions of national independence solely with reference to whether or not Soviet power was reinforced. But such a course apparently ran counter to the Marxist doctrine that the state would wither away under communism. At the Sixteenth Party Congress in 1930, Stalin justified his handling of the question of nationalities within the Soviet Union and his policy of increasing the power of the state as follows:

We must let the national cultures develop and expand, revealing all their potential qualities, in order to create the necessary conditions for fusing them into one common culture with one common tongue. The flourishing of cultures, national in form and Socialist in content, in the conditions of the proletarian dictatorship in one country, for the *purpose of* their fusion into one common Socialist culture, common both in form and in content, with one common tongue, when the proletariat is victorious throughout the world and Socialism becomes an every-day matter—in this lies the dialectical quality of the Leninist way of treating the question of national culture.

It may be said that such a way of approaching the question is "contradictory." But is there not the same "contradiction" in our treatment of the question of the State? We are in favor of the dying-away of the State, and at the same time we stand for the strengthening of the dictatorship of the proletariat, which represents the most powerful and mighty authority of all the forms of the State which have existed up to the present day. The highest possible development of the power of the State, with the object of preparing the conditions for the dying away of the State: that is the Marxist formula. Is it "contradictory"? Yes, it is "contradictory." But this contradiction is a living thing, and completely reflects Marxist dialectics.[14]

Fascist and Nazi writings were similarly steeped in the language of struggle. But where the Communist style was marked by references to

[14] J. Stalin, *Political Report to the Sixteenth Party Congress of the Russian Communist Party* (London: Modern Books Limited, 1930), pp. 171–72.

strategy and tactics, the Fascists and Nazis were more concerned with military cheerleading and war cries. *Action* did not refer to classes, but suggested rather the impetuous eruption of an inflamed nation. It was a form of conduct best learned by mass imitation of the inflated gestures of a leader.

Benito Mussolini (1883–1945) was one of the first who developed the modern dictatorial style. His ideology and political character were largely composed of truculent outbursts against established democratic institutions and extravagant gestures intended to induce a regeneration of Italy. An essay on fascism attributed to Mussolini published in the *Italian Encyclopedia* was comparatively solemn and was probably sketched out by Giovanni Gentile. The latter's ideas represented an attempt to justify fascism philosophically by resorting to right-wing pseudo-Hegelian interpretations. Hegel's theories had achieved more currency among Italian intellectuals than in most other countries outside of Germany, and several thinkers believed that fascism might be the vehicle by which the World Historical Spirit would favor Italy. It was clear that this doctrine was a misappropriation of Hegel's ideas. As Herbert Marcuse suggests, ". . . the closer Italian idealism drew to Fascism, the more it deviated from Hegelianism. . . ." [15]

Nazism produced the lowest order of political thought in the twentieth century. It was for the most part a patchwork of second- and third-hand popularizations and distortions of several nineteenth-century social Darwinist and decadent romantic writings. No attempt was made to relate the succession of Nazi slogans and blood cries to a traditional line of Western philosophy. Some commentators purport to connect the authoritarian state elements in Nazi thought to Hegel's celebration of the state; the "will to power" has been referred to Nietzsche's influence. If there was any influence of Hegel and Nietzsche on nazism, it was a distant and disfigured one at best. By the turn of the century in Germany, Hegel's Idealist theory of the state and Nietzsche's urgings that man create a new Promethean greatness were dissolved in a general maelstrom of autocratic militarism and Wagnerian fantasies of German greatness.

By the time the Nazis arrived on the scene, it was impossible to establish a clear and proper connection between them and the two great nineteenth-century philosophers. Rather, the Nazi motifs were engendered by the murky atmosphere of *ressentiment* and *anomie* that pervaded Germany

---

[15] Herbert Marcuse, *Reason and Revolution: Hegel and the Rise of Social Theory* (Boston: Beacon Press, 1960), p. 403.

in the 1920's. In any case, the rationalism of Hegel and the transvaluations of Nietzsche are obviously incompatible with the impulsive irrationalism of nazism.

While *Mein Kampf* has often been considered the bible of nazism, it is little more than a megalomaniacal autobiography filled with endless slogans. The fame of the volume in Germany stemmed from mass political sales to party members and to the citizenry. The profits from this best-seller made Hitler an independently wealthy man. So too did Alfred Rosenberg's *The Myth of the Twentieth Century* gain wide recognition and wealth for its author despite its open declarations that it consisted of a mythology deliberately constructed out of a *mystique* of blood and racial spirit. He proclaimed: "This is the task of our century: to create a new human type out of a new life-myth." [16]

These two works and other writings of Nazi leaders reveal the willful irrationalism of this political position. In 1922, the nationalist Moeller van den Bruck had announced the coming of a Third Reich, led by a party rooted in German history and transcending other parties; the Nazis "fulfilled" the prophecy by destroying all parties save theirs, and also destroying all serious political thought in Germany. The selections below presenting Hitler's views have been taken from *Mein Kampf* and from a collection of newspaper articles.

Following the defeat of fascism and nazism and the changes in the Soviet system after Stalin's death, it is tempting to write off the extremes of totalitarianism as a bad dream—a ghost laid to rest, a phantom without power. To do so would be just as unfortunate a misunderstanding of history as to suppose that the roots of totalitarianism go back no further than World War I. This view would suggest that the harshest instruments of totalitarian rule belong, in Engels's words on the state, in a "museum of antiquities, next to the spinning wheel and the bronze ax." [17] However, such is not the way of civilization or of the forces that oppose it. Even if the worst horrors of totalitarianism never reappear, they have carved deeply into the institutions of the present and have etched new lines in the design of the future.

[16] Alfred Rosenberg, *Der Mythus des 20. Jahrhunderts: Eine Wertung der seelisch-geistigen Gestaltenkämpfe unserer Zeit* (Munich: Hoheneichen-Verlag, 1935), p. 2.
[17] Friedrich Engels, *The Origin of the Family, Private Property and the State* (New York: International Publishers, 1942), p. 158.

FRANZ NEUMANN
1900-1954

FRANZ NEUMANN'S DEATH IN 1954 deprived American and European scholarship of a profound analyst of political power. He was among the first to sketch out broad generalizations on the relation between totalitarian politics and the institutional history of the West; his mind ranged with equal skill and integrity over economics, law, and philosophy. Toward the end of his life he brought a mastery of depth psychology to bear on the problems of politics that had always engrossed him.

After his graduation from the University of Frankfurt, he practiced labor law in Berlin and taught at the Academy of Labor and at the Hochschule für Politik. He was a legal adviser to his Social Democratic party and a vigorous foe of nazism, from which he fled in 1933. As a student at the London School of Economics and then in America at the Institute of Social Research and as a professor of politics at Columbia University, his talents as scholar and teacher flourished. During World War II he was an adviser to the Office of Strategic Services and to the State Department, and afterwards he helped in the development of the Free University in Berlin. The events of the postwar years suggested to him that a deeper and more comprehensive theory than was available was required to explain the growing sense of alienation in Western society.

In *Behemoth: The Structure and Practice of National Socialism* (1942), he probed the Weimar Republic and the Nazi regime, and concluded that totalitarianism grew out of the structural faults—especially the economic—of democracy. He argued that the Nazi regime could not be termed a state in the traditional sense since the rational, constitutional apparatus had been ripped away, leaving rulers and masses to confront one another directly. This theme was reiterated in later articles like "Approaches to the Study of Political Power" and "The Concept of Political Freedom," in which he described some of the conditions in which freedom becomes superfluous.

Political theory, Neumann believed, must perform the critical function of seeking out the conditions of political freedom. "A conformist political theory is no theory," he claimed. But this very task required scholars and teachers to discuss "openly and rationally every political action and conception."

[21]   Totalitarian Dictatorship

For the purpose of a brief discussion the modern totalitarian dictatorship may be reduced to five essential factors.

The first of these is the transition from a state based upon the rule of law (the German *Rechtsstaat*) to a police state. The rule of law is a presumption in favor of the right of the citizen and against the coercive power of the state. In the totalitarian state this presumption is reversed. Details need not concern us here, since the power of executive agencies in totalitarian states to interfere at discretion with life, liberty and property may be taken as the best-known feature of this kind of dictatorship.

The second factor is the transition from the diffusion of power in liberal states to the concentration of power in the totalitarian regime. This concentration may vary in degree as well as form. But there is no role in any totalitarian state for the various liberal devices of diffusing power, such as separation of powers, federalism, a functioning multi-party system, bicameralism, etc.

These first two elements, however, are to be found in the absolute monarchy as well as in the totalitarian dictatorship. What distinguishes totalitarianism politically is the third element, namely, the existence of a monopolistic state party. Such a party is required because the traditional instruments of coercion do not suffice to control an industrial society, and all the less so since beaureaucracies and armies may not always be reliable. The monopolistic party is a flexible instrument which provides the force to

From Franz Neumann, *The Democratic and the Authoritarian State* (Glencoe, Ill.: The Free Press, 1957), pp. 244–46, 248–53. Reprinted by permission.

control the state machine and society and to perform the gigantic task of cementing the authoritarian elements within society together.

Morever, the monopolistic party involves a socio-psychological aspect pertaining to what is commonly called a "mass" society. Since modern totalitarian dictatorships arise, almost without exception, within and against democracies (weak though the democratic structures may have been), the totalitarian clique has to assume the shape of a democratic movement and to retain this façade even after it has come to power. In other words, it is forced to practice the ritual of democracy even though the substance is totally denied.

The role of the monopolistic party involves the fourth element of the totalitarian dictatorship: the transition from pluralist to totalitarian social controls. Society ceases to be distinguished from the state; it is totally permeated by political power. The control of society, now as important as the control of the state, is achieved by the following techniques:

(1) The leadership principle—to enforce guidance from the top and responsibility to the top.

(2) The "synchronization" of all social organizations—not only to control them, but to make them serviceable to the state.

(3) The creation of graded elites—so as to enable the rulers to control the masses from within and to disguise manipulation from without, i.e., to supplement bureaucracies in the narrow meaning of the term with private leadership groups within the various strata of the population.

(4) The atomization and isolation of the individual, which involves negatively the destruction or at least weakening of social units based on biology (family), tradition, religion, or co-operation in work or leisure; and positively the imposition of huge and undifferentiated mass organizations which leave the individual isolated and more easily manipulable.

(5) The transformation of culture into propaganda—of cultural values into saleable commodities.

The final factor in totalitarianism is the reliance upon terror, i.e., the use of non-calculable violence as a permanent threat against the individual. Care must be taken, however, not to define a totalitarian dictatorship simply as the rule of violence. Without it, it is true, such regimes could not survive. But they could not endure for any length of time without considerable identification by the oppressed people with its rulers.

These, in brief outline, are the features of the most repressive of political systems. What distinguishes it from absolutism is not primarily the caesaristic element, for this was also characteristic of the absolute monarchy in certain periods of its history, but rather the destruction of the line between state and society and the total politicization of society by the device of the monopolistic party. This is not merely a question of more or less political power. The difference is one of quality, not quantity. Where, as in the absolute monarchy, power is primarily exercised through the traditional bureaucratic instruments of coercion, its operation is governed by abstract, calculable rules, although their execution often may be arbitrary. Absolutism, therefore, already contains the major institutional principles of modern liberalism. Totalitarian dictatorship, on the other hand, is the absolute negation of these principles because the main repressive agencies are not courts and administrative bodies, but the secret police and the party.

A fully developed totalitarian dictatorship is the form an industrial society may adopt if it should become necessary to maximize its repressive elements and eliminate its liberal ones. But totalitarian dictatorship is not the child of modern industrialism alone. Sparta and the regime of Diocletian may be briefly discussed as two illuminating earlier experiments.

* * *

DEMOCRACY AND DICTATORSHIP

If we review the various types of dictatorships . . . , we are forced to conclude that the usual confrontation of liberal democracy vs. dictatorship as an antithesis of good and evil, cannot be maintained from a historical point of view. Moralizing about political systems makes it difficult to understand their functions. The relationship between democracy and dictatorship is not as simple as is sometimes stated.

1. Dictatorships may be an implementation of democracy. But this refers to emergency dictatorships with functions similar to the classical Roman type, which we prefer to classify as a kind of magistracy.

2. Dictatorships may be the preparation for democracy. We may then speak of an educational dictatorship.

3. Dictatorships may be the very negation of democracy and thus be a totally regressive system.

Pisistratus' rule is probably a classical example of an educational dictatorship. As Werner Jaeger puts it: "The masses were still politically inexperienced, so that democracy was far away: it could not come until the aristocracy had been brought low by the Pisistratic tyrants." We may add that the great function of the Pisistratidae was the creation of an Athenian national (or collective) spirit. This was done by facilitating the emergence of a "middle class," which Aristotle believed to be the social prerequisite of democracy. Hence, without the work of Pisistratus the regimes of Cleisthenes and Pericles would hardly be conceivable.

It is well to remember that the Marxist-Leninist conception of a dictatorship of the proletariat was democratic precisely in this sense of a preparatory dictatorship. The concentration of power in the hands of the proletariat was to be used to abolish class rule altogether and to herald a new epoch of freedom in a classless society. That it was not this expectation but the very opposite which materialized cannot be discussed in detail here. However, we may cite the basic reasons why, under modern conditions, every dictatorship tends to be a totalitarian dictatorship and to involve the negation of democracy.

The democratic ideology has become so universal that Guizot's statement seems even truer today than it did in 1848. All modern dictatorships arose from democratic conditions. This is true of Italy, Germany, Spain, Argentina, and perhaps even of the U.S.S.R., although to a lesser degree.

The dictator is therefore compelled to seek mass support and, having obtained it, to practice the ritual of democracy even if its substance is withheld. As Engels already saw, a *coup d'état* seems hopeless against a modern army; the dictator can come to power only with the help or toleration of the army, but to sustain his power, he depends on a mass base.

There is, however, an important distinction between the Fascist-Nazi type and the Bolshevik. In the former, the dictator could rely upon substantial sectors of the traditional ruling groups (industry, finance, agrarians, army, bureaucracy, judiciary) which were committed to a minimum of formal legality since overt rebellion would have jeopardized their own status and security. Consequently, the dictatorship in its rise to power had to play the democratic game (compare Hitler's strategy before his Beer Hall Putsch of 1923 and afterwards). And once it had attained this goal, the requirements of competition with the outside world and the need to secure the active or passive co-operation of industrial labor, led the Nazi-Fascist type of dictatorship to present itself as a higher and nobler form of democracy.

For the Bolsheviks the need for mass support is of a different nature. The original theory of the dictatorship of the proletariat as the dictatorship of the majority over a minority was compatible at least with one version of democracy. But the Russian proletariat was a small minority in 1917, and with the Bolshevik rejection of Trotsky's theory of a permanent revolution, the democratic mass base had to be secured from among the peasants. When this was not voluntarily forthcoming the Bolshevik regime evolved into a full-blown totalitarian dictatorship.

But even in agrarian, colonial, and semi-colonial countries, where democracy did not exist or was inadequately practiced, modern dictatorship tends to become totalitarian. Today every nation experiences democracy vicariously. Due to the world-wide scope of communications, even the most backward peoples have become aware of democracy and want it, awakening mass consciousness usually taking the form of a demand for national emancipation. Consequently, here too a dictator must attempt to be a Caesar by acting out the democratic ritual even if he is compelled to go on towards a totalitarian regime.

THE SOCIAL FUNCTION OF DICTATORSHIP

Neither the attraction of a democratic ideology nor the scope of the dictatorship can fully explain the phenomena of caesarism and totalitarianism. An understanding of the social function of dictatorship would require a comprehensive analysis based upon the following elements:

(a) The economic system;
(b) The class relationship;
(c) The personality structure.

In each historical situation these factors—economic, social, and psychological—must be treated as a unity, not as isolated, independent causes. An index of changes in these elements will frequently—I would even say invariably—be found in the intellectual and artistic trends of a given period, i.e., in philosophy, literature, and the arts. I should like to indicate certain principles that may help in the search for the causes and functions of the various types of dictatorships.

In terms of *class relationships,* the function of dictatorship may be related to three basic and recurring situations:

(1) Disenfranchised and insurgent social classes demand recognition of their interests which the political power-holders refuse to grant. There are two alternatives, depending upon the political maturity of the ascending classes:

If they are politically mature—as the bourgeoisie in England in the seventeenth or in France in the eighteenth century—caesarism will be merely a transitory phenomenon (Cromwell and Robespierre). The new classes, in power and commanding a majority, will for various reasons demand a liberal political system.

But if they are not mature, or too weak, the caesaristic movement will become a dictatorship as in the case of Pisistratus, Cola di Rienzo, or Lenin.

(2) The second case is the attempt of a social class threatened with decline and striving to preserve its status and power. Dictatorship may then arise as an attempt to preserve the *status quo*. The most striking examples are Sparta, to a lesser extent the half-hearted efforts of Napoleon I, and probably the regimes of Franco and Perón.

(3) The third possibility is the attempt of what one might call doomed classes to change radically the socio-economic situation, to reverse it, and to install a political system that would restore them to their old pre-eminence. This is the kernel of the German and Italian Fascist movements.

These class relationships must be studied in the light of changing economic systems. Totalitarianism, although not a new phenomenon, is determined in its modern form by the features of an industrial society. Modern industrialism is politically ambivalent because it contains and intensifies two diametrically opposed trends in modern society: the trend toward freedom and the trend toward repression. Sociologists usually define this as the problem of "moral lag," holding that the growing potentialities of modern technology outstrip the progress of "morality." This may or may not be true, but it is not, in my opinion, the decisive factor.

It is easy to say that technology is neutral politically and socially, so that any desired result can be attained depending upon the persons who use it and upon their aims. Technological optimists (like Georges Sorel and Thorstein Veblen) hold that only the full development of technological resources and their efficient utilization, (e.g., exclusion of "conspicuous consumption") can bring mankind to its highest perfection. We do not challenge this statement, but should like to explore some of its implications.

Large-scale technology on the one hand may imply the total dependence of the industrial population upon a complex, integrated mechanism, which can be operated only in a highly organized, stratified, and hierarchic system. This system must instill the virtues of discipline, obedience and subordination—no matter who owns the means of production. Thus, modern industrialism preaches the very virtues which every authoritarian political system seeks to cultivate. These virtues are repressive because they are opposed to man's self-determination.

On the other hand, the very opposite virtues may also be strengthened by technology: self-reliance, awareness of one's power and, most particularly, the feeling of solidarity—that is, a spirit of co-operation as opposed to authoritarianism.

THE PSYCHOLOGICAL PROCESSES OF DICTATORSHIP

These two antagonistic trends of industrialism are, in my opinion, essential for the understanding of modern dictatorship. The authoritarian element facilitates the rise of a dictatorship. But the co-operative aspect forces the dictatorship to find some way of replacing solidarity based on a rational interest (such as class interest) with some other identification that does not undermine but rather strengthens the dictatorship. Mussolini tried corporatism; Hitler, the doctrine of the folk community; Stalin, that of the classless socialist state. But in varying degrees all these identifications were a fake. That they nonetheless "succeeded" leads us to our final problem: the psychological processes connected with dictatorship. The basic problem is anxiety and fear and their function in political life.

Freud has defined anxiety as an "increase in tensions arising from nongratification of [the individual's] need." Anxiety is thus always present—at least potentially—as a situation or a state of indefiniteness. Fear, in turn, is the recognition of a specific danger.

Therefore, external dangers, arising in specific situations and from specific objects, are experienced in the light of internal anxiety, which then becomes externalized and activated.

But this externalization of anxiety through fear is by no means always dangerous to the personality. One may distinguish three functions of fear:

Fear as a warning;
Fear as protection; and
Fear as destruction.

Thus, an external danger may well have a kind of monitoring function: it may warn the individual that something terrible may happen to him. And the reaction to the threat may then perform a protective or even cathartic function. It may not only remove the concrete danger, but allay the anxiety as well and thus make the individual more free. On the other hand, fear may activate anxiety (particularly neurotic anxiety) to the point of making it destructive. (Indeed there are psychoanalysts who derive anxiety from destructive impulses.) Hence, in some individuals, fear becoming operative or latent anxiety may either paralyze the personality and make it incapable of defense (depressive anxiety) or heighten its aggressive instincts (persecutory anxiety).

This bare (and rather thin) analysis of certain terms of individual psychology may now be put to use in understanding the rise of totalitarian movements and the operation of the totalitarian state.

As an illustration let me again take the Spartan state. Plutarch says, ". . . [T]he Spartans dealt with them [the Helots] very hardly: for it was a common thing to force them to drink to excess, and to lead them in that condition into their public halls, that the children might see what a sight a drunken man is; they made them to dance low dances, and sing ridiculous songs. . . ." Then they assassinated them. There is little difference between the Spartan aristocracy's behavior toward the Helots and the Nazis' treatment of the Jews. The ancients were well aware of the fact that the passive element in the Spartan character was fear, that this fear was systematically cultivated and that the Spartans' famous courage in battle was nothing but fear of being stigmatized if they failed in their military duty. The actual or feigned fear of the Helots is the integrating principle of the Spartan ruling class, their anxieties being activated into aggressiveness and destruction. The totally repressive character of Sparta (as compared to Athens) rests precisely in this fact.

In totalitarian movements (as contrasted with totalitarian states), there appears a similar element. A distinction should be made between the Nazi-Fascist movement and Lenin's party prior to 1917. The Bolshevik party at that time was not a totalitarian movement, nor may Lenin (in contrast to post-1928 Stalin) be considered a totalitarian leader. The Bolshevik party then did not manipulate fear; this is a later development which began with the defeat of the revolutionary movements in Western Europe.

In contrast, the Nazi-Fascist movement activated the anxieties of the middle classes and turned them into channels of destruction which were made legitimate by means of the masses' identification with a leader, the hero. The nature of such identification has already been discussed by Freud. This phenomenon appears in all caesaristic and totalitarian movements, in various degrees, of course, and with varying historical functions.

There can hardly be any doubt as to the essentially repressive implication of overcoming fear through identification with a leader. . . .

VLADIMIR ILYICH LENIN (Ulyanov) 1870-1924

IF EVER AN HISTORIC PERSONAGE was singularly responsible for momentous events, Lenin was such a one. He was the demiurge of the Bolshevik Revolution of 1917 and of the destinies of Soviet Russia in its early stages; but he claimed to act only in the name of "inevitable historical forces."

He was born in Simbirsk (now Ulyanovsk), and came from a respectable middle-class family. His revolutionary career may have been sparked by the execution of his older brother in 1887 by the tsarist government for terroristic conspiracy. Georgi Plekhanov, the founder of Russian Marxism, influenced him in his early years, but after an intense study of Marx's works he began to develop strong views of his own about the adaptation of Marxism to the Russian situation. He hammered out his revolutionary theories in debate with the Narodniks, "Legal Marxists," "Economists," revisionists, Mensheviks, with his old teacher Plekhanov, and with his sometime idol, Karl Kautsky. In all these controversies Lenin held to his views and excoriated his opponents relentlessly. He himself became the archetype for his own conception of the professional revolutionist—he had a genius for underground organization—who would devote his "whole life to working for the Revolution." These same characteristics made him a significant twentieth-century political type: the leader fired with revolutionary zeal, intent on demolishing all the limits of the establishment, and the organizer who has completely rationalized his own acts and who would rationalize and order a whole society—even the world.

Lenin's works are concerned, for the most part, with the strategies and tactics of attaining power. In *What Is to Be Done?* (1902) he set forth his views
on the composition and organization of the party. He declared that ". . . to be-
little Socialist ideology *in any way, to deviate from it in the* slightest degree
means strengthening bourgeois ideology." He insisted that the workers can
only be "educated" to socialism from without by a "small, compact core, con-
sisting of reliable, experienced and hardened workers, with responsible agents
in the principal districts and connected by all the rules of strict secrecy with
the organizations of revolutionists. . . ." *Materialism and Empirio-Criticism*
(1909) was a dogmatic defense of Marx's and Engels's metaphysics against
Idealism and scientific positivism. It has become a model for later Soviet theoreticians in the attack on all non-Soviet Marxist philosophies with the
"method" of dialectic materialism. *Imperialism, The Highest Stage of Capitalism*
(1916–1917) defined imperialism as a final, desperate stage of capitalism. *State
and Revolution* (1917) is an extensive gloss on Engels's political theories. Lenin
hews to the "weapon" theory of the state and prophesies the "withering away
of the state" only when all "capitalists have disappeared." The selection below
was written in a triumphant mood, after the Bolshevik Revolution appeared
secure in 1920. Hence, the "Leninist" tactics are openly described, defended,
and pressed on other Communist parties.

[22]   The Success of the Bolsheviks

Certainly almost everyone now realises that the Bolsheviks could not
have maintained themselves in power for two and one-half years, and not
even for two and one-half months, without the strictest discipline, the truly
iron discipline in our Party and without the fullest and unreserved support
rendered it by the whole mass of the working class, that is, by all those
belonging to this class who think, who are honest, self-sacrificing, influential
and capable of leading and attracting the backward masses.

The dictatorship of the proletariat is the most determined and the most
ruthless war waged by the new class against the *more powerful* enemy,
against the bourgeoisie, whose resistance is increased *tenfold* by its overthrow (even though only in one country) and whose power lies not only in
the strength of international capital, in the strength and durability of the international connections of the bourgeoisie, but also in the *force of habit,* in

From V. I. Lenin, *"Left-Wing" Communism: An Infantile Disorder,* Little Lenin
Library (New York: International Publishers, 1934), pp. 9–12, 39–43. Reprinted by
permission.

the strength of *small-scale production*. For, unfortunately, very, very much of small-scale production still remains in the world, and small-scale production *gives* birth to capitalism and the bourgeoisie continuously, daily, hourly, spontaneously, and on a mass scale. For all these reasons the dictatorship of the proletariat is necessary, and victory over the bourgeoisie is impossible without a long, stubborn and desperate war of life and death, a war which requires perseverance, discipline, firmness, inflexibility, and unity of will.

I repeat, the experience of the victorious dictatorship of the proletariat in Russia has clearly shown to those who are unable to think or who have not had occasion to ponder over this question, that absolute centralisation and the strictest discipline of the proletariat constitute one of the basic conditions for victory over the bourgeoisie.

This has often been discussed. But far from enough thought has been given to the question as to what it means, and under what conditions it is possible. Would it not be better *more frequently* to accompany greetings to the Soviet power and the Bolsheviks by a *very serious analysis* of the reasons *why* the latter were able to build up the discipline necessary for the revolutionary proletariat?

Bolshevism, as a trend of political thought and as a political party, has existed since 1903. Only the history of Bolshevism during the *whole* period of its existence can satisfactorily explain why it was able to build up and maintain, under most difficult conditions, the iron discipline necessary for the victory of the proletariat.

And first of all, the question arises: how is the discipline of the revolutionary party of the proletariat maintained? How is it tested? How is it reinforced? First, by the class consciousness of the proletarian vanguard and by its devotion to the revolution, by its firmness, self-sacrifice, and heroism. Secondly, by its ability to link itself with, to keep in close touch with, and, to a certain degree, if you will, merge itself with the broadest masses of the toilers—primarily with the proletarian *but also with the non-proletarian* toiling masses. Thirdly, by the correctness of the political leadership exercised by this vanguard and by the correctness of its political strategy and tactics, provided that the broadest masses become convinced of this correctness *by their own experience*. Without these conditions discipline in a revolutionary party that is really capable of being a party of the advanced class, whose mission it is to overthrow the bourgeoisie and to transform the whole of society, cannot be achieved. Without these conditions all attempts to establish discipline are inevitably transformed into trifling phrase-mongering and empty gestures. On the other hand, these conditions cannot arise all at once. They are created only through prolonged effort and hard-won experience. Their creation is facilitated only by correct revolutionary theory, which in its turn is not a dogma but assumes complete shape only in close connection with the practical activity of a truly mass and truly revolutionary movement.

If in 1917–1920, under the greatest difficulties, Bolshevism could build up and successfully carry out the strictest centralisation and iron discipline, it was due simply to a number of historical peculiarities of Russia.

On the one hand, Bolshevism arose in 1903 on the very firm foundation of Marxian theory. And the correctness of this—and only this—revolutionary theory has been proved not only by the experience of all countries during the entire nineteenth century but particularly by the experience of the wanderings and vacillations, the mistakes and disappointments of revolutionary thought in Russia. For almost half a century—approximately between the 'forties and 'nineties of the last century—advanced thinkers in Russia, under the oppression of an unprecedented, savage and reactionary tsarism, sought eagerly for the correct revolutionary theory, following each and every "last word" in Europe and America in this sphere with astonishing diligence and thoroughness. Russia achieved Marxism, as the only correct revolutionary theory, virtually through *suffering,* by a half century of unprecedented torments and sacrifice, of unprecedented revolutionary heroism, incredible energy, painstaking search and study, testing in practice, disappointments, checking, and comparison with European experience. Thanks to the emigration enforced by tsarism, revolutionary Russia, in the second half of the nineteenth century, possessed such a wealth of international connections and such excellent information about world forms and theories of the revolutionary movement as no other country in the world possessed.

On the other hand, having arisen on this granite theoretical foundation, Bolshevism passed through fifteen years (1903–1917) of practical history which, in wealth of experience, has had no equal anywhere else in the world. For no other country during these fifteen years had anything even approximating this revolutionary experience, this rapid and varied succession of different forms of the movement—legal and illegal, peaceful and stormy, open and underground, small circles and mass movements, parliamentary and terrorist. In no other country was there concentrated during so short a period of time such a wealth of forms, shades and methods of struggle involving *all* classes of modern society, and, moreover, of a struggle which, owing to the backwardness of the country and the heavy yoke of tsarism, was maturing with exceptional rapidity and assimilating most eagerly and successfully the corresponding "last word" of American and European political experience.

* * *

SHOULD WE PARTICIPATE IN BOURGEOIS PARLIAMENTS?

The German "Left" Communists, very contemptuously, and very frivolously, reply to this question in the negative. Their arguments? . . .

. . . to reject most decisively . . . all reversion to parliamentary forms of struggle, which have become historically and politically obsolete . . .

This is said with absurd pretentiousness, and is obviously incorrect. "Reversion" to parliamentarism! Perhaps a Soviet Republic already exists in Germany? It does not seem so! How, then, is it possible to speak of "reversion"? Is not this an empty phrase?

Parliamentarism has become "historically obsolete." This is correct as regards propaganda. But every one knows that this is still very far from the *practical* overcoming of parliamentarism. Capitalism could have been rightly declared to be "historically obsolete" many decades ago, but this in no way removes the necessity of a very long and very stubborn struggle within capitalism. Parliamentarism is "historically obsolete" in a *world-historical* sense, that is to say, the *epoch* of bourgeois parliamentarism has come to an end, the *epoch* of the dictatorship of the proletariat has *begun*. This is incontestable. But on a world-historical scale one counts in decades. Ten or twenty years sooner or later makes no difference from the point of view of the world-historical scale; from the point of view of world history it is a trifle which cannot be even approximately calculated. But precisely because of this it is a crying theoretical mistake to measure questions of practical politics on a world-historical scale.

Is parliamentarism "politically obsolete?" That is quite another matter. If this were true, the position of the "Lefts" would be a strong one. But it has got to be proved by the most searching analysis, and the "Lefts" do not even know how to set to work to do this. . . .

In the first place, as is known, contrary to the opinion of such prominent political leaders as Rosa Luxemburg and Karl Liebknecht, the German "Lefts" considered parliamentarism to be "politically obsolete" as far back as January 1919. It is well known that the "Lefts" were mistaken. This alone at one stroke utterly destroys the proposition that parliamentarism is "politically obsolete." The obligation falls upon the "Lefts" to prove why their indisputable error at that time has now ceased to be an error. They do not, and cannot produce even the shadow of proof. The attitude of a political party towards its own mistakes is one of the most important and surest criteria of the seriousness of the party and of how it fulfils in *practice* its obligations towards its *class* and towards the toiling *masses*. To admit a mistake openly, to disclose its reasons, to analyse the conditions which gave rise to it, to study attentively the means of correcting it—these are the signs of a serious party; this means the performance of its duties, this means educating and training the *class,* and subsequently, the *masses.* By their failure to fulfil this duty, by failing to give the utmost care, attention, and consideration to the study of their self-evident mistake, the "Lefts" in Germany (and in Holland) have proved that they are not a *class party* but a circle, not a *mass party* but a group of intellectuals and a few workers who imitate the worst features of intellectualism.

Secondly, in the same pamphlet of the Frankfurt group of "Lefts," . . . we read:

. . . the millions of workers who still follow the policy of the Centre (the Catholic 'Centre' Party) are counter-revolutionary. The rural proletarians produce legions of counter-revolutionary troops. . . .

It is quite clear that this statement is too sweeping and exaggerated. But the basic fact set forth is incontrovertible, and its acknowledgement by the "Lefts" very clearly testifies to their mistake. How can one say that "parliamentarism is politically obsolete," when "millions" and "legions" of *proletarians* are not only still in favour of parliamentarism in general but are downright "counter-revolutionary"? It is clear that parliamentarism in Germany is *not yet* politically obsolete. It is evident that the "Lefts" in Germany have mistaken *their desire,* their ideological-political attitude, for objective reality. This is the most dangerous mistake revolutionaries can make. In Russia—where the extremely fierce and savage yoke of tsarism for a particularly long period and in particularly varied forms produced revolutionaries of diverse shades, revolutionaries who displayed astonishing devotion, enthusiasm, heroism and will power—we watched this mistake of the revolutionaries particularly closely, studied it with particular attention, became particularly familiar with it, and hence, we can see it with particular clearness in others. For the Communists in Germany parliamentarism is, of course, "politically obsolete"; but—and this is the whole point—we must *not* regard that which is obsolete *for us* as obsolete *for the class,* as obsolete *for the masses.* It is precisely here that we see that the "Lefts" do not know how to reason, do not know how to conduct themselves as a party of the *class,* as a party of *the masses.* You must not sink to the level of the masses, to the level of the backward strata of the class. This is incontestable. You must tell them the bitter truth. You must call their bourgeois-democratic and parliamentary prejudices—prejudices. But, at the same time, you must *soberly* observe the *actual* state of class consciousness and preparedness of the *whole* class (not only of the Communist vanguard), of *all* the toiling *masses* (not only of its advanced elements).

Even if not "millions" and "legions" but a fairly significant *minority* of industrial workers follow the Catholic priests, and a like number of rural workers follow the landowners and kulaks (*Grossbauern*), it undoubtedly follows that parliamentarism in Germany is *not yet* politically obsolete, that participation in parliamentary elections and in the struggle in parliament is *obligatory* for the Party of the revolutionary proletariat, *precisely* for the purpose of educating the backward strata of *its own class,* precisely for the purpose of awakening and enlightening the undeveloped, downtrodden, ignorant peasant *masses.* As long as you are unable to disperse the bourgeois parliament and every other type of reactionary institution, you *must* work inside them, *precisely* because in them there are still workers who are stupefied by the priests and by the desolateness of village life; otherwise you run the risk of becoming mere babblers.

Thirdly, the "Left" Communists have a great deal to say in praise of us Bolsheviks. One sometimes feels like telling them that it would be better if they praised us less and tried to understand more thoroughly the tactics of the Bolsheviks, to make themselves more familiar with these tactics. We took part in the elections to the Russian bourgeois parliament, the Constitutent Assembly, in September–November, 1917. Were our tactics correct or not? If not, then it should be clearly stated and proved; this is essential for working out the correct tactics for international Communism. If they were correct, certain conclusions must be drawn. Of course, there can be no question of drawing a parallel between Russian conditions and the conditions of western Europe. But as regards the special question of the meaning of the concept "parliamentarism has become politically obsolete" it is absolutely necessary to take exact account of our experience, because unless concrete experience is taken into account, such concepts are very easily transformed into empty phrases. Had not we Russian Bolsheviks, in September–November, 1917, more right than any western Communists to consider parliamentarism politically obsolete in Russia? Undoubtedly we had, for the point is *not* whether bourgeois parliaments have existed for a long or a short period, but to what extent the broad masses of the toilers are *prepared* (ideologically, politically, and practically) to accept the Soviet régime and to dissolve the bourgeois democratic parliament (or allow it to be dissolved). That the urban working class and the soldiers and peasants in Russia in September–November, 1917, owing to a number of special conditions, were exceptionally well prepared for the acceptance of the Soviet régime and for the dissolution of the most democratic bourgeois parliament, is an absolutely incontestable and fully established historical fact. The Bolsheviks did *not* boycott the Constituent Assembly, however, but took part in the elections both before and *after* the conquest of political power by the proletariat. That these elections gave exceedingly valuable (and for the proletariat highly useful) political results I hope I have proved in [a previous] . . . article, which analyses in detail the figures of the elections to the Constituent Assembly in Russia.

The conclusion which follows from this is absolutely incontrovertible: it has been proved that participation in a bourgeois-democratic parliament even a few weeks before the victory of a Soviet Republic, and even *after* that victory, not only does not harm the revolutionary proletariat but actually makes it easier for it to *prove* to the backward masses why such parliaments deserve to be dissolved, *facilitates* their dissolution, and *facilitates* the process whereby bourgeois parliamentarism becomes "politically obsolete." To refuse to take this experience into account and at the same time to claim affiliation to the Communist *International,* which must work out its tactics *internationally* (not narrow or one-sided national tactics but international tactics), is to commit the greatest blunder and actually to reject internationalism in deeds while accepting it in words.

LEON TROTSKY
(Lev Davidovich Bronstein)
1879-1940

A MAN OF MANY REVOLUTIONARY TALENTS—agitator, military organizer, and tactician—Trotsky also developed several important theories of revolution and history. He was born into a middle-class Ukrainian farm family and became a Populist in his teens. A voluminous reader, he wrestled with Marxism before becoming a "devout believer." In 1903, he sided with the Mensheviks against Lenin on the question of party organization. Prophetically, he wrote at this time: "The organization of the Party will take the place of the Party; the Central Committee will take the place of the organization; and finally, the dictator will take the place of the Central Committee. . . ."

He was active in the St. Petersburg Soviet of Workingmen's Representatives during the general strike and revolution of 1905. Before that revolt, he and Parvus (A. I. Gelfand) had advanced the theory of "permanent revolution," that is, because of the particular economic conditions in Russia, the bourgeois and socialist revolutions may be "combined" into one by the proletariat. Once in power, the worker's democracy would spark a whole series of similar revolutions abroad. This theory was the rationale for his struggle with Stalin in later years.

Trotsky took a leading part in the military planning for the Bolshevik Revolution of October–November, 1917, and the civil war that followed. After Lenin's death he was outmaneuvered for control of the Communist party by Stalin, who exiled him, and he sought refuge in France and Norway before settling in Mexico where he was assassinated in 1940, in all probability by a Stalinist agent. Even though he believed Stalin had betrayed the Revolution, up to the end of his life he defended the general principles of Soviet Marxism against the non-Communist West. Here he remained consistent with his own dogmatic belief that in attaining and retaining power, the repressive means used by the Communists are not matters to be judged by "principle" but are matters of expediency. This consistency left him with little moral defense against Stalin's "expediency" in relation to himself.

Among his major works are *Before the Ninth of January* (1905), *History of the Revolution of 1905–06* (1917), and *Dictatorship vs. Democracy* (translated into English in 1922). In *Literature and Revolution* (1924), Trotsky offers a prophetic dream about man in the Communist society of the future, which will be a combination of absolute mechanical mastery of the world, American style; physiological mastery, yoga style; and mastery of feelings and instincts in a bowdlerized Nietzschean-Freudian style. And he ends by writing: "Man will become immeasurably stronger, wiser, and subtler; his body will become more harmonized, his movements more rhythmic, his voice more musical. The forms of life will become dynamically dramatic. The average human type will rise to the heights of an Aristotle, a Goethe, or a Marx. And above this ridge new peaks will rise."

[23] Their Morals and Ours

"MORAL PRECEPTS OBLIGATORY UPON ALL"

Whoever does not care to return to Moses, Christ or Mohammed; whoever is not satisfied with eclectic *hodge-podges* must acknowledge that morality is a product of social development; that there is nothing immutable about it; that it serves social interests; that these interests are contradictory; that morality more than any other form of ideology has a class character.

But do not elementary moral precepts exist, worked out in the development of mankind as a whole and indispensable for the existence of every collective body? Undoubtedly such precepts exist but the extent of their action is extremely limited and unstable. Norms "obligatory upon all" become the less forceful the sharper the character assumed by the class struggle. The highest form of the class struggle is civil war which explodes into mid-air all moral ties between the hostile classes.

Under "normal" conditions a "normal" man observes the commandment: "Thou shalt not kill!" But if he kills under exceptional conditions for self-defense, the jury acquits him. If he falls victim to a murderer, the court will kill the murderer. The necessity of courts as well as that of self-

From Leon Trotsky, *Their Morals and Ours* (New York: Pioneer Publishers, 1939), pp. 15–17, 31–33, 45–47. Reprinted by permission.

defense, flows from antagonistic interests. In so far as the state is concerned, in peaceful times it limits itself to legalized killings of individuals so that in time of war it may transform the "obligatory" commandment, "Thou shalt not kill!" into its opposite. The most "humane" governments, which in peaceful times "detest" war, proclaim during war that the highest duty of their armies is the extermination of the greatest possible number of people.

The so-called "generally recognized" moral precepts in essence preserve an algebraic, that is, an indeterminate character. They merely express the fact that man, in his individual conduct, is bound by certain common norms that flow from his being a member of society. The highest generalization of these norms is the "categorical imperative" of Kant. But in spite of the fact that it occupies a high position in the philosophic Olympus this imperative does not embody anything categoric because it embodies nothing concrete. It is a shell without content.

This vacuity in the norms obligatory upon all arises from the fact that in all decisive questions people feel their class membership considerably more profoundly and more directly than their membership in "society." The norms of "obligatory" morality are in reality filled with class, that is, antagonistic content. The moral norm becomes the more categoric the less it is "obligatory upon all." The solidarity of workers, especially of strikers or barricade fighters, is incomparably more "categoric" than human solidarity in general.

The bourgeoisie, which far surpasses the proletariat in the completeness and irreconcilability of its class consciousness, is vitally interested in imposing *its* moral philosophy upon the exploited masses. It is exactly for this purpose that the concrete norms of the bourgeois catechism are concealed under moral abstractions patronized by religion, philosophy, or that hybrid which is called "common sense." The appeal to abstract norms is not a disinterested philosophic mistake but a necessary element in the mechanics of class deception. The exposure of this deceit which retains the tradition of thousands of years is the first duty of a proletarian revolutionist.

*   *   *

Civil war is the most severe of all forms of war. It is unthinkable not only without violence against tertiary figures but, under contemporary technique, without killing old men, women and children. Must one be reminded of Spain? The only possible answer of the "friends" of republican Spain sounds like this: Civil war is better than fascist slavery. But this completely correct answer merely signifies that the *end* (democracy or socialism) justifies, under certain conditions, such *means* as violence and murder. Not to speak about lies! Without lies war would be as unimaginable as a machine without oil. In order to safeguard even the session of the Cortes (February 1, 1938) from fascist bombs the Barcelona government several times deliberately deceived journalists and their own population. Could it have acted in any other way? Whoever accepts the end: victory over Franco, must accept the means: civil war with its wake of horrors and crimes.

But, after all, do not lying and violence "in themselves" warrant condemnation? Of course, even as does the class society which generates them. A society without social contradictions will naturally be a society without lies and violence. However there is no way of building a bridge to that society save by revolutionary, that is, violent means. The revolution itself is a product of class society and of necessity bears its traits. From the point of view of "eternal truths" revolution is of course "anti-moral." But this merely means that idealist morality is counter-revolutionary, that is, in the service of the exploiters.

"Civil war," will perhaps respond the philosopher caught unawares, "is however a sad exception. But in peaceful times a healthy socialist movement should manage without violence and lying." Such an answer however represents nothing less than a pathetic evasion. There is no impervious demarcation between "peaceful" class struggle and revolution. Every strike embodies in an unexpanded form all the elements of civil war. Each side strives to impress the opponent with an exaggerated picture of its resoluteness to struggle and its material resources. Through their press, agents, and spies the capitalists labor to frighten and demoralize the strikers. From their side, the workers' pickets, where persuasion does not avail, are compelled to resort to force. Thus "lying and worse" are an inseparable part of the class struggle even in its most elementary form. It remains to be added that the very conception of *truth* and *lie* was born of social contradictions.

* * *

DIALECTICAL INTERDEPENDENCE OF END AND MEANS

A means can be justified only by its end. But the end in its turn needs to be justified. From the Marxist point of view, which expresses the historical interests of the proletariat, the end is justified if it leads to increasing the power of man over nature and to the abolition of the power of man over man.

"We are to understand then that in achieving this end anything is permissible?" sarcastically demands the Philistine, demonstrating that he understood nothing. That is permissible, we answer, which *really* leads to the liberation of mankind. Since this end can be achieved only through revolution, the liberating morality of the proletariat of necessity is endowed with a revolutionary character. It irreconcilably counteracts not only religious dogma but all kinds of idealistic fetishes, these philosophic gendarmes of the ruling class. It deduces a rule for conduct from the laws of the development of society, thus primarily from the class struggle, this law of all laws.

"Just the same," the moralist continues to insist, "does it mean that in the class struggle against capitalists all means are permissible: lying, frame-up, betrayal, murder, and so on?" Permissible and obligatory are those and only those means, we answer, which unite the revolutionary proletariat, fill their hearts with irreconcilable hostility to oppression, teach them contempt for official morality and its democratic echoers, imbue them with consciousness of their own historic mission, raise their courage and spirit of self-sacrifice in the struggle. Precisely from this it flows that *not* all means are permissible. When we say that end justifies the means, then for us the conclusion follows that the great revolutionary end spurns those base means and ways which set one part of the working class against other parts, or attempt to make the masses happy without their participation; or lower the faith of the masses in themselves and their organization, replacing it by worship for the "leaders." Primarily and irreconcilably, revolutionary morality rejects servility in relation to the toilers, that is, those characteristics in which petty-bourgeois pedants and moralists are thoroughly steeped.

These criteria do not, of course, give a ready answer to the question as to what is permissible and what is not permissible in each separate case. There can be no such automatic answers. Problems of revolutionary morality are fused with the problems of revolutionary strategy and tactics. The living experience of the movement under the clarification of theory provides the correct answer to these problems.

Dialectical materialism does not know dualism between means and end. The end flows naturally from the historical movement. Organically the means are subordinated to the end. The immediate end becomes the means for a further end. In his play, *Franz von Sickingen,* Ferdinand Lassalle puts the following words into the mouth of one of the heroes:

> ". . . Show not the *goal*
> But show also the *path.* So closely interwoven
> Are path and goal that each with other
> Ever changes, and other *paths* forthwith
> Another *goal* set up."

Lassalle's lines are not at all perfect. Still worse is the fact that in practical politics Lassalle himself diverged from the above expressed precept —it is sufficient to recall that he went as far as secret agreements with Bismarck! But the dialectical interdependence between means and end is expressed entirely correctly in the above quoted sentences. Seeds of wheat must be sown in order to yield an ear of wheat.

Is individual terror, for example, permissible or impermissible from the point of view of "pure morals"? In this abstract form the question does not exist at all for us. Conservative Swiss bourgeois even now render official praise to the terrorist William Tell. Our sympathies are fully on the side of Irish, Russian, Polish or Hindu terrorists in their struggle against national and political oppression. The assassinated Kirov, a rude satrap, does not call forth any sympathy. Our relation to the assassin remains neutral only because we know not what motives guided him. If it became known that Nikolayaev acted as a conscious avenger for workers' rights trampled upon by Kirov, our sympathies would be fully on the side of the assassin. However, not the question of subjective motives but that of objective expediency has for us the decisive significance. Are the given means really capable of leading to the goal? In relation to individual terror, both theory and experience bear witness that such is not the case. To the terrorist we say: It is impossible to replace the masses; only in the mass movement can you find expedient expression for your heroism. However, under conditions of civil war, the assassination of individual oppressors ceases to be an act of individual terror. If, we shall say, a revolutionist bombed General Franco and his staff into the air, it would hardly evoke moral indignation even from the democratic eunuchs. Under the conditions of civil war a similar act would be politically completely expedient. Thus, even in the sharpest question—murder of man by man—moral absolutes prove futile. Moral evaluations, together with those political, flow from the inner needs of struggle.

JOSEPH STALIN
(Djugashvili)
1879-1953

IN MARCH OF 1917 Stalin impressed an independent socialist jour-
nalist, N. N. Sukhanov, as a "grey blur, looming up now and
then dimly and not leaving any trace. There is really nothing more to be said
about him." His life before that date likewise offered no hint that this man
would command an apparatus that was to transform a society completely.

He was born into a poor Georgian family and studied for the priesthood.
In the late 1890's he joined underground revolutionary groups in his native
region; he was probably a Menshevik before he became a Bolshevik. Like
Lenin and Trotsky, he was exiled to Siberia briefly by the tsarist government.
Stalin played a comparatively small role in the Bolshevik Revolution, but after
1922, when he became general secretary of the Russian Communist party,
the organizational talents and tactical skill he displayed in intraparty factional
disputes won him top power positions. He argued against Trotsky that socialism
must be established and strengthened in one country, Russia, from which base
world revolution could *later* be made. The "strengthening" of Russia was undertaken in 1928, and involved the sacrifice of human and material resources to
the swift development of heavy industry.

During the 1930's, Stalin attained the status of charismatic autocrat and
proceeded to rewrite all revolutionary history to endow himself with godlike
qualities from the beginning. "Paper will put up with anything that is written
on it," he once wrote. It was as if he were not content with being the spirit of
the present and future, but had resolved to become the spirit of the past as well.

In the two decades before his death, Stalin succeeded in Russianizing the
Communist Revolution and in nationalizing Soviet Russia. More than the other
Bolshevik leaders, Stalin turned his back on European civilization. After World
War II and until his death, his moodiness and suspiciousness became more pro-
nounced; the resulting flashes of terror against groups and individuals whom

the leader viewed as heretically "un-Russian" kept many leading circles in the Soviet Union in a state of constant apprehension.

Stalin contributed very little to the theoretical exegesis of Marxism, and his style is notable for its lack of brilliance. Under the tutelage of Lenin he wrote *Marxism and the National Question* in 1913, in which he simply articulated the developing Bolshevik precept that ethnic "self-determination" was legitimate only when subordinated to the purposes of the Revolution. This same line was taken in his "On Marxism in Linguistics," which appeared in *Pravda* on June 20, 1950, and was acclaimed by Soviet linguists as a work of scholarly genius in linguistics, history, and philosophy. The article emphasized the importance of the national rather than the class characteristics of a language. In his last published work, *Economic Problems of Socialism in the U.S.S.R.,* Stalin attempted to resolve some knotty questions of interpretation concerning the status of the Soviet economy in the period of transition from "socialism to communism." He denied that any *contradictions* existed between various sectors and classes of the economy; only *differences* had survived. But he also implied that contradictions between productive forces and productive relationships remained, and were likely to continue in the future.

[24]   *Foundations of Leninism*

Briefly: [according to Lenin] *the dictatorship of the proletariat is the rule—unrestricted by law and based on force—of the proletariat over the bourgeoisie, a rule enjoying the sympathy and support of the labouring and exploited masses. (The State and Revolution.)*

From this follow two main conclusions:

FIRST CONCLUSION: The dictatorship of the proletariat cannot be "complete" democracy, democracy for *all,* for the rich as well as for the poor; the dictatorship of the proletariat "must be a state that is democratic *in a new way—for* the proletarians and the propertyless in general—and dictatorial *in a new way—against* the bourgeoisie. . . ." (Lenin, *Selected Works,* Vol. VII, p. 34.)   The talk of Kautsky and Co. about universal equality, about "pure" democracy, about "perfect" democracy, and the like, is but a bourgeois screen to conceal the indubitable fact that equality between exploited and exploiters is impossible. The theory of "pure" democracy is the theory of the upper stratum of the working class, which has

From Joseph Stalin, *Foundations of Leninism* (New York: International Publishers, 1939), pp. 53–56, 78–82, 90–99, 119–20, 122–23, 125–27. Reprinted by permission.

been broken in and is being fed by the imperialist robbers. It was brought into being for the purpose of concealing the ulcers of capitalism, of touching up imperialism and lending it moral strength in the struggle against the exploited masses. Under capitalism there are no real "liberties" for the exploited, nor can there be, if for no other reason than that the premises, printing plants, paper supplies, etc., indispensable for the actual enjoyment of "liberties" are the privilege of the exploiters. Under capitalism the exploited masses do not, nor can they, really participate in the administration of the country, if for no other reason than that, even under the most democratic regime, governments, under the conditions of capitalism, are not set up by the people but by the Rothschilds and Stinneses, the Rockefellers and Morgans. Democracy under capitalism is *capitalist* democracy, the democracy of the exploiting minority, based on the restriction of the rights of the exploited majority and directed against this majority. Only under the dictatorship of the proletariat are real "liberties" for the exploited and real participation in the administration of the country by the proletarians and peasants possible. Under the dictatorship of the proletariat, democracy is *proletarian* democracy, the democracy of the exploited majority, based upon the restriction of the rights of the exploiting minority and directed against this minority.

SECOND CONCLUSION: The dictatorship of the proletariat cannot arise as the result of the peaceful development of bourgeois society and of bourgeois democracy; it can arise only as the result of the smashing of the bourgeois state machine, the bourgeois army, the bourgeois bureaucratic machine, the bourgeois police.

In a preface to *The Communist Manifesto* Marx and Engels wrote, quoting from *The Civil War in France:*

"The working class cannot simply lay hold of the ready-made state machine and wield it for its own purposes." (Marx, *Selected Works,* Vol. I, p. 190.)

In a letter to Kugelmann (1871) Marx wrote that the task of the proletarian revolution is

"no longer as before, to transfer the bureaucratic military machine from one hand to another, but to *smash* it, and that is a preliminary condition for every real people's revolution on the Continent." (Marx, *Selected Works,* Vol. II, p. 528.)

Marx's qualifying phrase about the Continent gave the opportunists and Mensheviks of all countries a pretext for proclaiming that Marx had thus conceded the possibility of the peaceful evolution of bourgeois democracy into a proletarian democracy, at least in certain countries outside the European continent (England, America). Marx did in fact concede that possibility, and he had good grounds for conceding it in regard to England and America in the 'seventies of the last century, when monopoly capitalism and imperialism did not yet exist, and when these countries, owing to the special conditions of their development, had as yet not developed militarism and bureaucracy. That was the situation before the appearance of developed imperialism. But later, after a lapse of thirty or forty years, when the situation in these countries had radically changed, when imperialism had developed and had embraced all capitalist countries without exception, when militarism and bureaucracy had appeared in England and America also, when the special conditions for peaceful development in England and the United States had disappeared—then the qualification in regard to these countries necessarily could no longer hold good.

"Today," said Lenin, "in 1917, in the epoch of the first great imperialist war, this qualification made by Marx is no longer valid. Both England and America, the greatest and the last representatives—in the whole world—of Anglo-Saxon 'liberty,' in the sense that militarism and bureaucracy were absent, have slid down entirely into the all-European, filthy, bloody morass of military-bureaucratic institutions to which everything is subordinated and which trample everything underfoot. Today, both in England and in America, the 'preliminary condition for every real people's revolution' is the smashing, the *destruction* of the 'ready-made state machine' (brought in those countries, between 1914 and 1917, to general 'European' imperialist perfection)." (*Selected Works,* Vol. VII, p. 37.)

In other words, the law of violent proletarian revolution, the law of the smashing of the bourgeois state machine as a preliminary condition for such a revolution, is an inevitable law of the revolutionary movement in the imperialist countries of the world.

Of course, in the remote future, if the proletariat is victorious in the most important capitalist countries, and if the present capitalist encirclement is replaced by a socialist encirclement, a "peaceful" path of development is quite possible for certain capitalist countries, whose capitalists, in view of the "unfavourable" international situation, will consider it expedient "voluntarily" to make substantial concessions to the proletariat. But this supposition applies only to a remote and possible future. With regard to the immediate future, there is no ground whatsoever for this supposition.

Therefore Lenin is right in saying:

"The proletarian revolution is impossible without the forcible destruction of the bourgeois state machine and the substitution for it of a *new one*. . . ." (*Selected Works,* Vol. VII, p. 124.)

*   *   *

Lenin rightly says that with the appearance of the Soviet power "the era of bourgeois-democratic parliamentarism has come to an end, and a new chapter in world history—the era of proletarian dictatorship—has commenced."

What are the characteristic features of the Soviet power?

The Soviet power has a most pronounced mass character and is the most democratic state organization of all possible state organizations while classes continue to exist; for, being the arena of the bond and collaboration between the workers and the exploited peasants in their struggle against the exploiters, and basing itself in its work on this bond and on this collaboration, it represents, by virtue of this, the power of the majority of the population over the minority, it is the state of the majority, the expression of its dictatorship.

The Soviet power is the most internationalist of all state organizations in class society, for, since it destroys every kind of national oppression and rests on the collaboration of the labouring masses of the various nationalities, it facilitates, by virtue of this, the amalgamation of these masses into a single state union.

The Soviet power, by its very structure, facilitates the task of leading the oppressed and exploited masses for the vanguard of these masses— for the proletariat, as the most consolidated and most class-conscious core of the Soviets.

*   *   *

THE NATIONAL PROBLEM

. . . Leninism has proved, and the imperialist war and the revolution in Russia have confirmed, that the national problem can be solved only in connection with and on the basis of the proletarian revolution, and that the road to victory of the revolution in the West lies through the revolutionary alliance with the liberation movement of the colonies and dependent countries against imperialism. The national problem is a part of the general problem of the proletarian revolution, a part of the problem of the dictatorship of the proletariat.

The question presents itself as follows: Are the revolutionary possibilities latent in the revolutionary liberation movement of the oppressed countries *already exhausted* or not; and if not, is there any hope, any ground to expect that these possibilities can be utilized for the proletarian revolution, that the dependent and colonial countries can be transformed from a reserve of the imperialist bourgeoisie into a reserve of the revolutionary proletariat, into an ally of the latter?

Leninism replies to this question in the affirmative, *i.e.,* it recognizes the latent revolutionary capacities of the national liberation movement of the oppressed countries and the possibility of utilizing these capacities for the purpose of overthrowing imperialism. The mechanics of the development of imperialism, the imperialist war and the revolution in Russia wholly confirm the conclusions of Leninism on this score.

Hence the necessity for the proletariat to support—resolutely and actively to support—the national liberation movement of the oppressed and dependent peoples.

This does not mean, of course, that the proletariat must support *every* national movement, everywhere and always, in every single concrete case. It means that support must be given to such national movements as tend to weaken, to overthrow imperialism, and not to strengthen and preserve it. Cases occur when the national movements in certain oppressed countries come into conflict with the interests of the development of the proletarian movement. In such cases support is, of course, entirely out of the question. The question of the rights of nations is not an isolated, self-sufficient question; it is a part of the general problem of the proletarian revolution, subordinate to the whole, and must be considered from the point of view of the whole. In the 'forties of the last century Marx supported the national movement of the Poles and Hungarians and was opposed to the national movement of the Czechs and the South Slavs. Why? Because the Czechs and the South Slavs were then "reactionary nations," "Russian outposts" in Europe, outposts of absolutism; whereas the Poles and the Hungarians were "revolutionary nations," fighting against absolutism. Because support of the national movement of the Czechs and the South Slavs was at that time equivalent to indirect support for tsarism, the most dangerous enemy of the revolutionary movement in Europe.

"The various demands of democracy," writes Lenin, "including self-determination, are not an absolute, but a *small part* of the general democratic (now:

general socialist) *world* movement. In individual concrete cases, the part may contradict the whole; if so, it must be rejected." (*Collected Works,* Russian edition, Vol. XIX, pp. 257–58.)

This is the position in regard to the question of certain national movements, of the possible reactionary character of these movements—if, of course, they are appraised not from the formal point of view, not from the point of view of abstract rights, but concretely, from the point of view of the interests of the revolutionary movement.

The same must be said of the revolutionary character of national movements in general. The unquestionably revolutionary character of the overwhelming majority of national movements is as relative and peculiar as is the possible reactionary character of certain particular national movements. The revolutionary character of a national movement under the conditions of imperialist oppression does not necessarily presuppose the existence of proletarian elements in the movement, the existence of a revolutionary or a republican program of the movement, the existence of a democratic basis of the movement. The struggle the Emir of Afghanistan is waging for the independence of Afghanistan is objectively a *revolutionary* struggle, despite the monarchist views of the Emir and his associates, for it weakens, disintegrates and undermines imperialism; whereas the struggle waged by "desperate" Democrats and "Socialists," "revolutionaries" and republicans, such as, for example, Kerensky and Tsereteli, Renaudel and Schneidemann, Chernov and Dan, Henderson and Clynes, during the imperialist war was a *reactionary* struggle, for its result was the whitewashing, the strengthening, the victory of imperialism. For the same reasons the struggle the Egyptian merchants and bourgeois intellectuals are waging for the independence of Egypt is objectively a *revolutionary* struggle, despite the bourgeois origin and bourgeois title of the leaders of the Egyptian national movement, despite the fact that they are opposed to socialism; whereas the fight the British Labour Government is waging to perpetuate Egypt's dependent position is for the same reasons a *reactionary* struggle, despite the proletarian origin and the proletarian title of the members of that government, despite the fact that they are "for" socialism. I need not speak of the national movement in other, larger, colonial and dependent countries, such as India and China, every step of which along the road to liberation, even if it runs counter to the demands of formal democracy, is a steam-hammer blow at imperialism, *i.e.,* is undoubtedly a *revolutionary* step.

Lenin was right in saying that the national movement of the oppressed countries should be appraised not from the point of view of formal democracy, but from the point of view of the actual results obtained, as shown by the general balance sheet of the struggle against imperialism, that is to say, "not in isolation, but on . . . a world scale." (*Collected Works,* Russian edition, Vol. XIX, p. 257.)

* * *

STRATEGY AND TACTICS

Stages of the Revolution, and Strategy

Strategy is the determination of the direction of the main blow of the proletariat at a given stage of the revolution, the elaboration of a corresponding plan for the disposition of the revolutionary forces (the main and secondary reserves), the fight to carry out this plan throughout the given stage of the revolution.

Our revolution already passed through two stages, and after the October Revolution it has entered a third stage. Our strategy changed accordingly.

FIRST STAGE.   1903 to February 1917. Objective: to overthrow tsarism and completely wipe out the survivals of mediaevalism. The main force of the revolution: the proletariat. Immediate reserves: the peasantry. Direction of the main blow: the isolation of the liberal-monarchist bourgeoisie, which was striving to win over the peasantry and liquidate the revolution by *compromising* with tsarism. Plan for the disposition of forces: alliance of the working class with the peasantry.

"The proletariat must carry to completion the democratic revolution, by allying to itself the mass of the peasantry in order to crush by force the resistance of the autocracy and to paralyse the instability of the bourgeoisie." (Lenin, *Selected Works,* Vol. III, p. 110.)

SECOND STAGE.   March 1917 to October 1917. Objective: to overthrow imperialism in Russia and to withdraw from the imperialist war. The main force of the revolution: the proletariat. Immediate reserves: the poor peasantry. The proletariat of neighbouring countries as probable reserves. The protracted war and the crisis of imperialism as the favourable factor. Direction of the main blow: isolation of the petty-bourgeois democrats (Mensheviks and Socialist-Revolutionaries), who were striving to win over the toiling masses of the peasantry and to terminate the revolution by *compromising* with imperialism. Plan for the disposition of forces: alliance of the proletariat with the poor peasantry.

"The proletariat must accomplish the socialist revolution by allying to itself the mass of the semi-proletarian elements of the population in order to crush by force the resistance of the bourgeoisie and to paralyse the instability of the peasantry and the petty bourgeoisie." (*Ibid.*, p. 111.)

THIRD STAGE.   Commenced after the October Revolution. Objective: to consolidate the dictatorship of the proletariat in one country, using it as a base for the overthrow of imperialism in all countries. The revolution is spreading beyond the confines of one country; the period of world revolution has commenced. The main forces of the revolution: the dictatorship of the proletariat in one country, the revolutionary movement of the proletariat in all countries. Main reserves: the semi-proletarian and small-peasant masses in the developed countries, the liberation movement in the colonies and dependent countries. Direction of the main blow: isolation of the petty-bourgeois democrats, isolation of the parties of the Second International, which constitute the main support of the policy of *compromise* with imperialism. Plan for the disposition of forces: alliance of the proletarian revolution with the liberation movement in the colonies and the dependent countries.

Strategy deals with the main forces of the revolution and their reserves. It changes with the passing of the revolution from one stage to another, but remains essentially unchanged throughout a given stage.

The Flow and Ebb of the Movement, and Tactics
    Tactics are the determination of the line of conduct of the proletariat in the comparatively short period of the flow or ebb of the movement, of the rise or decline of the revolution, the fight to carry out this line by means of replacing old forms of struggle and organization by new ones, old slogans by new ones, by combining these forms, etc. While the object of strategy is to win the war against tsarism, let us say, or against the bourgeoisie, to carry the struggle against tsarism or against the bourgeoisie to its end, tactics concern themselves with less important objects, for they aim not at winning the war as a whole, but at winning a particular engagement, or a particular battle, at carrying through successfully a particular campaign or a particular action corresponding to the concrete circumstances in the given period of rise or decline of the revolution. Tactics are a part of strategy, subordinate to it and serving it.

Tactics change according to flow and ebb. While the strategic plan remained unchanged during the first stage of the revolution (1903 to February 1917) tactics changed several times during that period. In the period from 1903 to 1905 the Party pursued offensive tactics, for the tide of the revolution was rising, the movement was on the upgrade, and tactics had to proceed from this fact. Accordingly, the forms of struggle were revolutionary, corresponding to the requirements of the rising tide of the revolution. Local political strikes, political demonstrations, the general political strike, boycott of the Duma, insurrection, revolutionary fighting slogans—such were the successive forms of the struggle during that period. These changes in the forms of struggle were accompanied by corresponding changes in the forms of organization. Factory committees, revolutionary peasant committees, strike committees, Soviets of workers' deputies, a workers' party operating more or less openly—such were the forms of organization during that period.

In the period from 1907 to 1912 the Party was compelled to resort to tactics of retreat; for we then experienced a decline in the revolutionary movement, the ebb of the revolution, and tactics necessarily had to take this fact into consideration. The forms of struggle, as well as the forms of organization, changed accordingly: Instead of boycott of the Duma there was participation in the Duma; instead of open, direct revolutionary action outside the Duma, there were parliamentary speeches and work in the Duma; instead of general political strikes, there were partial economic strikes, or simply a lull in activities. Of course, the Party had to go underground during that period, while the revolutionary mass organizations were superseded by cultural, educational, cooperative, insurance and other legal organizations.

The same must be said of the second and third stages of the revolution, during which tactics changed dozens of times, whereas the strategical plans remained unchanged.

Tactics deal with the forms of struggle and the forms of organization of the proletariat, with their changes and combinations. During a given stage of the revolution tactics may change several times, depending on the flow and ebb, the rise and decline, of the revolution.

Strategic Leadership

The reserves of the revolution can be:

DIRECT: (a) the peasantry and in general the intermediate strata of the population within the country; (b) the proletariat of the neighbouring countries; (c) the revolutionary movement in the colonies and dependent countries; (d) the gains and achievements of the dictatorship of the proletariat—part of which the proletariat may give up temporarily, while retaining superiority of forces, in order to buy off a powerful enemy and gain a respite; and

INDIRECT: (a) the contradictions and conflicts among the non-proletarian classes within the country, which can be utilized by the proletariat to weaken the enemy and to strengthen its own reserves; (b) contradictions, conflicts and wars (the imperialist war, for instance) among the bourgeois states hostile to the proletarian state, which can be utilized by the proletariat in its offensive or in manoeuvering in the event of a forced retreat.

* * *

The task of strategic leadership is to make proper use of all these reserves for the achievement of the main object of the revolution at the given stage of its development.

What does making proper use of reserves mean?

It means fulfilling certain necessary conditions, of which the following must be regarded as the principal ones:

FIRST: the concentration of the main forces of the revolution at the enemy's most vulnerable spot at the decisive moment, when the revolution has already become ripe, when the offensive is going full-steam ahead, when insurrection is knocking at the door, and when bringing the reserves up to the vanguard is the decisive condition of success. The Party's strategy during the period from April to October 1917 well illustrates this manner of utilizing reserves. Undoubtedly, the enemy's most vulnerable spot at that time was the war. Undoubtedly, it was on this question, as the fundamental one, that the Party rallied the broadest masses of the population around the proletarian vanguard. The Party's strategy during that period was, while training the vanguard for street action by means of manifestations and demonstrations, to bring the reserves up to the vanguard through the medium of the Soviets in the rear and the soldiers' committees at the front. The outcome of the revolution has shown that the reserves were properly utilized.

Here is what Lenin, paraphrasing the well-known theses of Marx and Engels on insurrection, says about this condition of the strategic utilization of the forces of the revolution:

"Never *play* with insurrection, but when beginning it firmly realize that you must *go to the end.* You must concentrate a *great superiority of forces* at the decisive point, at the decisive moment, otherwise the enemy, who has the advantage of better preparation and organization, will destroy the insurgents. Once the insurrection has begun, you must act with the greatest *determination,* and by all means, without fail, take the *offensive.* 'The defensive is the death of every armed rising.' You must try to take the enemy by surprise and seize the moment when his forces are scattered. You must strive for *daily* successes, even if small (One might say hourly, if it is the case of one town), and at all costs retain *'moral ascendancy.'* " (Lenin, *Collected Works,* Vol. XXI, Russian edition, pp. 319–20.)

SECOND: the selection of the moment for the decisive blow, of the moment for starting the insurrection, so timed as to coincide with the moment when the crisis has reached its climax, when it is fully apparent that the vanguard is prepared to fight to the end, the reserves are prepared to support the vanguard, and maximum consternation reigns in the ranks of the enemy.

The decisive battle, says Lenin, may be deemed to have fully matured *when*

"all the class forces hostile to us have become sufficiently entangled, are sufficiently at loggerheads with each other, have sufficiently weakened themselves in a struggle which is beyond their strength"; *when* "all the vacillating, wavering, unstable, intermediate elements—the petty bourgeoisie and the petty-bourgeois democrats as distinct from the bourgeoisie—have sufficiently exposed themselves before the people, have sufficiently disgraced themselves through their practical bankruptcy"; *when* "among the proletariat a mass sentiment in favour of supporting the most determined, supremely bold, revolutionary action against the bourgeoisie has arisen and begun vigorously to grow. Then, indeed, revolution is ripe; then, indeed, if we have correctly gauged all the conditions indicated above . . . and if we have chosen the moment rightly, our victory is assured." (*Selected Works,* Vol. X, pp. 137–38.)

The manner in which the October insurrection was carried out may be taken as a model of such strategy.

Failure to observe this condition leads to a dangerous error called "loss of tempo," when the Party lags behind the movement or runs far ahead of it, courting the danger of failure.

*   *   *

THIRD: undeviating pursuit of the course adopted, no matter what difficulties and complications are encountered on the road towards the goal; this is necessary in order that the vanguard may not lose sight of the main goal of the struggle and that the masses may not stray from the road while marching towards that goal and striving to rally around the vanguard. Failure to observe this condition leads to a grave error, well known to sailors as "losing the course." As an example of this "loss of course" we may mention the erroneous conduct of our Party when, immediately after the Democratic Conference, it adopted a resolution to participate in the Pre-parliament. For the moment the Party, as it were, forgot that the Pre-parliament was an attempt of the bourgeoisie to switch the country from the path of the Soviets to the path of bourgeois parliamentarism, that the Party's participation in such a body might result in mixing up all the cards and confusing the workers and peasants, who were waging a revolutionary struggle under the slogan: "All power to the Soviets." This mistake was rectified by the withdrawal of the Bolsheviks from the Pre-parliament.

FOURTH: manoeuvering the reserves with a view to effecting a proper retreat when the enemy is strong, when retreat is inevitable, when to accept battle forced upon us by the enemy is obviously disadvantageous, when, with the given alignment of forces, retreat becomes the only way to ward off a blow against the vanguard and to keep the reserves intact.

"The revolutionary parties," says Lenin, "must complete their education. They have learned to attack. Now they have to realize that this knowledge must be supplemented with the knowledge how to retreat properly. They have to realize—and the revolutionary class is taught to realize by its own bitter experience—that victory is impossible unless they have learned both how to attack and how to retreat properly." (*Selected Works*, Vol. X, pp. 65–66.)

The object of this strategy is to gain time, to demoralize the enemy, and to accumulate forces in order later to assume the offensive.

*   *   *

Tactical Leadership

Tactical leadership is a part of strategic leadership, subordinated to the tasks and the requirements of the latter. The task of tactical leadership is to master all forms of struggle and organization of the proletariat and to ensure that they are used properly so as to achieve, with the given alignment of forces, the maximum results necessary to prepare for strategic success.

What does making proper use of the forms of struggle and organization of the proletariat mean?

It means fulfilling certain necessary conditions, of which the following must be regarded as the principal ones:

FIRST: to put in the forefront precisely those forms of struggle and organization which are best suited to the conditions prevailing during the flow or ebb of the movement at a given moment, and which therefore can facilitate and ensure the bringing of the masses to the revolutionary positions, the bringing of the millions to the revolutionary front, and their disposition at the revolutionary front.

The point here is not that the vanguard shall realize the impossibility of preserving the old order of things and the inevitability of its overthrow. The point is that the masses, the millions, shall understand this inevitability and display their readiness to support the vanguard. But the masses can understand this only from their own experience. The task is to enable the vast masses to realize from their own experience the inevitability of the overthrow of the old regime, to promote such methods of struggle and forms of organization as will make it easier for the masses to learn from experience to recognize the correctness of the revolutionary slogans.

*   *   *

THE PARTY

The Party as the Embodiment of Unity of Will, Incompatible with the Existence of Factions

The achievement and maintenance of the dictatorship of the proletariat is impossible without a party which is strong by reason of its solidarity and iron discipline. But iron discipline in the Party is inconceivable without unity of will, without complete and absolute unity of action on the part of all members of the Party. This does not mean, of course, that the possibility of contests of opinion within the Party is thereby precluded. On the contrary, iron discipline does not preclude but presupposes criticism and contest of opinion within the Party. Least of all does it mean that discipline must be "blind." On the contrary, iron discipline does not preclude but presupposes conscious and voluntary submission, for only conscious discipline can be truly iron discipline. But after a contest of opinion has been closed, after criticism has been exhausted and a decision has been arrived at, unity of will and unity of action of all Party members are the necessary condition without which neither Party unity nor iron discipline in the Party is conceivable.

* * *

The Party Is Strengthened by Purging Itself of Opportunist Elements

The source of factionalism in the Party is its opportunist elements. The proletariat is not an isolated class. It is constantly replenished by the influx of peasants, petty bourgeois and intellectuals who have become proletarianized by the development of capitalism. At the same time the upper stratum of the proletariat, principally trade union leaders and labour members of parliament who are fed by the bourgeoisie out of the super-profits extracted from the colonies, is undergoing a process of decay.

"This stratum of bourgeoisified workers, of the 'labour aristocracy,' " says Lenin, "who are quite philistine in their mode of life, in the size of their earnings, and in their outlook, serves as the principal prop of the Second International, and, in our days, the principal social (not military) *prop of the bourgeoisie*. They are the real *agents of the bourgeoisie in the labour movement*, the labour lieutenants of the capitalist class, real channels of reformism and chauvinism." (*Selected Works,* Vol. V, p. 12.)

In one way or another, all these petty-bourgeois groups penetrate into the Party and introduce into it the spirit of hesitancy and opportunism, the spirit of demoralization and uncertainty. It is they, principally, that constitute the source of factionalism and disintegration, the source of disorganization and disruption of the Party from within. To fight imperialism with such "allies" in one's rear means to expose oneself to the danger of being caught between two fires, from the front and from the rear. Therefore, ruthless struggle against such elements, their expulsion from the Party, is a prerequisite for the successful struggle against imperialism.

The theory of "overcoming" opportunist elements by ideological struggle within the Party, the theory of "outliving" these elements within the confines of a single Party, is a rotten and dangerous theory, which threatens to condemn the Party to paralysis and chronic infirmity, threatens to make the Party a prey to opportunism, threatens to leave the proletariat without a revolutionary party, threatens to deprive the proletariat of its main weapon in the fight against imperialism.

* * *

STYLE IN WORK

Leninism is a school of theory and practice which trains a special type of Party and state worker, creates a special Leninist style in work. What are the characteristic features of this style? What are its peculiarities?

It has two specific features: (a) the Russian revolutionary sweep and (b) American efficiency. The style of Leninism is a combination of these two specific features in Party and state work.

The Russian revolutionary sweep is an antidote to inertness, routine, conservatism, mental stagnation and slavish submission to ancestral traditions. The Russian revolutionary sweep is the life-giving force which stimulates thought, impels things forward, breaks the past and opens up perspectives. Without it no progress is possible. But there is every chance of it degenerating in practice into empty "revolutionary" Manilovism if it is not combined with American efficiency in work. . . .

The combination of the Russian revolutionary sweep with American efficiency is the essence of Leninism in Party and state work.

This combination alone produces the finished type of Leninist worker, the style of Leninism in work. . . .

GIOVANNI GENTILE
1875-1944

UNLIKE NAZISM, FASCISM ATTRACTED philosophers who exercised their talents in its behalf. Gentile was foremost among these. Born in Castelvetrano, Sicily, he studied literature and philosophy at the University of Pisa. He met Benedetto Croce in 1896 and collaborated with him in editing the periodical *La Critica* until 1924, when Croce's antagonism to fascism split them apart. He taught at the universities of Naples, Palermo, Pisa, and Rome. In the early years of the Fascist regime he held several offices in the government, helped plan the reorganization of education, and was the president of a commission for constitutional "reform." Mussolini appointed him to the Fascist Grand Council from 1923 to 1924 and from 1925 to 1929. Gentile was the leading spirit and major editor of the *Italian Encyclopedia* from 1925 to 1944. He was assassinated in Florence by anti-Fascists.

Like Croce, he was a critical neo-Hegelian. His Idealist leanings were discernible in his emphasis on the unity of mind, or spirit. By *education* he meant the dialectic process whereby the pure spirit may be apprehended and then expressed in a pure act. His philosophy is sometimes called *actualism*. Mussolini's talk about the organically unified state and his clamor about action attracted Gentile to Fascism.

His works covered a wide array of subjects: he wrote commentaries on Marx, Hegel, Scholastic and Renaissance philosophers, religion, art, the philosophy of history, logic, and education. English translations of his works include *Theory of Mind as Pure Act* (1922) and *The Reform of Education* (1923).

[25]   The Philosophic Basis of Fascism

In the definition of Fascism, the first point to grasp is the comprehensive, or as Fascists say, the "totalitarian" scope of its doctrine, which concerns itself not only with political organization and political tendency, but with the whole will and thought and feeling of the nation.

There is a second and equally important point. Fascism is not a philosophy. Much less is it a religion. It is not even a political theory which may be stated in a series of formulae. The significance of Fascism is not to be grasped in the special theses which it from time to time assumes. When on occasion it has announced a program, a goal, a concept to be realized in action, Fascism has not hesitated to abandon them when in practice these were found to be inadequate or inconsistent with the principle of Fascism. Fascism has never been willing to compromise its future. Mussolini has boasted that he is a *tempista,* that his real pride is in "good timing." He makes decisions and acts on them at the precise moment when all the conditions and considerations which make them feasible and opportune are properly matured. This is a way of saying that Fascism returns to the most rigorous meaning of Mazzini's "Thought and Action," whereby the two terms are so perfectly coincident that no thought has value which is not already expressed in action. The real "views" of the *Duce* are those which he formulates and executes at one and the same time.

Is Fascism therefore "anti-intellectual," as has been so often charged? It is eminently anti-intellectual, eminently Mazzinian, that is, if by intellectualism we mean the divorce of thought from action, of knowledge from life, of brain from heart, of theory from practice. Fascism is hostile to all Utopian systems which are destined never to face the test of reality. It is hostile to all science and all philosophy which remain matters of mere fancy or intelligence. It is not that Fascism denies value to culture, to the higher intellectual pursuits by which thought is invigorated as a source of action. Fascist anti-intellectualism holds in scorn a product peculiarly typical of the educated classes in Italy: the *letterato*—the man who plays with knowledge and with thought without any sense of responsibility for the

From *Foreign Affairs,* VI (January, 1928), 299–304. Reprinted by special permission from *Foreign Affairs,* January, 1928. Copyright by Council on Foreign Relations, New York.

practical world. It is hostile not so much to culture as to bad culture, the culture which does not educate, which does not make men, but rather creates pedants and aesthetes, egotists in a word, men morally and politically indifferent. It has no use, for instance, for the man who is "above the conflict" when his country or its important interests are at stake.

By virtue of its repugnance for "intellectualism," Fascism prefers not to waste time constructing abstract theories about itself. But when we say that it is not a system or a doctrine we must not conclude that it is a blind praxis or a purely instinctive method. If by system or philosophy we mean a living thought, a principle of universal character daily revealing its inner fertility and significance, then Fascism is a perfect system, with a solidly established foundation and with a rigorous logic in its development; and all who feel the truth and the vitality of the principle work day by day for its development, now doing, now undoing, now going forward, now retracing their steps, according as the things they do prove to be in harmony with the principle or to deviate from it.

And we come finally to a third point.

The Fascist system is not a political system, but it has its center of gravity in politics. Fascism came into being to meet serious problems of politics in post-war Italy. And it presents itself as a political method. But in confronting and solving political problems it is carried by its very nature, that is to say by its method, to consider moral, religious, and philosophical questions and to unfold and demonstrate the comprehensive totalitarian political character peculiar to it. It is only after we have grasped the political character of the Fascist principle that we are able adequately to appreciate the deeper concept of life which underlies that principle and from which the principle springs. The political doctrine of Fascism is not the whole of Fascism. It is rather its more prominent aspect and in general its most interesting one.

The politic of Fascism revolves wholly about the concept of the national State; and accordingly it has points of contact with nationalist doctrines, along with distinctions from the latter which it is important to bear in mind.

Both Fascism and nationalism regard the State as the foundation of all rights and the source of all values in the individuals composing it. For the one as for the other the State is not a consequence—it is a principle. But in the case of nationalism, the relation which individualistic liberalism, and for that matter socialism also, assumed between individual and State is inverted. Since the State is a principle, the individual becomes a consequence—he is something which finds an antecedent in the State: the State limits him and determines his manner of existence, restricting his freedom, binding him to a piece of ground whereon he was born, whereon he must live and will die. In the case of Fascism, State and individual are one and the same things, or rather, they are inseparable terms of a necessary synthesis.

Nationalism, in fact, founds the State on the concept of nation, the nation being an entity which transcends the will and the life of the individual because it is conceived as objectively existing apart from the consciousness of individuals, existing even if the individual does nothing to bring it into being. For the nationalist, the nation exists not by virtue of the citizen's will, but as datum, a fact, of nature.

For Fascism, on the contrary, the State is a wholly spiritual creation. It is a national State, because, from the Fascist point of view, the nation itself is a creation of the mind and is not a material presupposition, is not a datum of nature. The nation, says the Fascist, is never really made; neither, therefore, can the State attain an absolute form, since it is merely the nation in the latter's concrete, political manifestation. For the Fascist, the State is always *in fieri*. It is in our hands, wholly; whence our very serious responsibility towards it.

* * *

The Fascist State, on the contrary, is a people's state, and, as such, the democratic State *par excellence*. The relationship between State and citizen (not this or that citizen, but all citizens) is accordingly so intimate that the State exists only as, and in so far as, the citizen causes it to exist. Its formation therefore is the formation of a consciousness of it in individuals, in the masses. Hence the need of the Party, and of all the instruments of propaganda and education which Fascism uses to make the thought and will of the *Duce* the thought and will of the masses. Hence the enormous task which Fascism sets itself in trying to bring the whole mass of the people, beginning with the little children, inside the fold of the Party.

On the popular character of the Fascist State likewise depends its greatest social and constitutional reform—the foundation of the Corporations of Syndicates. In this reform Fascism took over from syndicalism the notion of the moral and educational function of the syndicate. But the Corporations of Syndicates were necessary in order to reduce the syndicates to State discipline and make them an expression of the State's organism from within. The Corporation of Syndicates are a device through which the

Fascist State goes looking for the individual in order to create itself through the individual's will. But the individual it seeks is not the abstract political individual whom the old liberalism took for granted. He is the only individual who can ever be found, the individual who exists as a specialized productive force, and who, by the fact of his specialization, is brought to unite with other individuals of his same category and comes to belong with them to the one great economic unit which is none other than the nation.

This great reform is already well under way. Toward it nationalism, syndicalism, and even liberalism itself, were already tending in the past. For even liberalism was beginning to criticize the older forms of political representation, seeking some system of organic representation which would correspond to the structural reality of the State.

The Fascist conception of liberty merits passing notice. The *Duce* of Fascism once chose to discuss the theme of "Force or Consent?"; and he concluded that the two terms are inseparable, that the one implies the other and cannot exist apart from the other; that, in other words, the authority of the State and the freedom of the citizen constitute a continuous circle wherein authority presupposes liberty and liberty authority. For freedom can exist only within the State, and the State means authority. But the State is not an entity hovering in the air over the heads of its citizens. It is one with the personality of the citizen. Fascism, indeed, envisages the contrast not as between liberty and authority, but as between a true, a concrete liberty which exists, and an abstract, illusory liberty which cannot exist.

Liberalism broke the circle above referred to, setting the individual against the State and liberty against authority. What the liberal desired was liberty as against the State, a liberty which was a limitation of the State; though the liberal had to resign himself, as the lesser of the evils, to a State which was a limitation on liberty. The absurdities inherent in the liberal concept of freedom were apparent to liberals themselves early in the Nineteenth Century. It is no merit of Fascism to have again indicated them. Fascism has its own solution of the paradox of liberty and authority. The authority of the State is absolute. It does not compromise, it does not bargain, it does not surrender any portion of its field to other moral or religious principles which may interfere with the individual conscience. But on the other hand, the State becomes a reality only in the consciousness of its individuals. And the Fascist corporative State supplies a representative system more sincere and more in touch with realities than any other previously devised and is therefore freer than the old liberal State.

ADOLF HITLER
1889-1945

BORN IN BRAUNAU, AUSTRIA, directly across the Bavarian border, Adolf Hitler came from back-country peasant stock. His father was a minor customs official who tried to give his son a respectable education, but apparently lack of interest in school foiled the father's plans. The young man dreamed of becoming an artist, but was refused entry into the Academy of Fine Arts in Vienna; the professors claimed the dreamer had no artistic talent.

From 1909 to 1913 he moved about Vienna, barely making a living as a casual laborer and crude sketcher of post cards and posters. He went to Munich and undertook the same life, but was rescued by World War I, about which he wrote: "For me, as for every other German, the most memorable period of my life now began." He fought in the front lines and, like hundreds of thousands of others, was wounded. Like many more, he found coming "home" difficult.

Back in Munich, not having discovered any other talents than the ones he had before the war, he turned to politics. There, in this century, he found his vocation. His flair for propaganda and his virtuosity as a haranguer of mobs thrust him to the top of the German Workers' Party. The failure of the *Putsch* of November 8–9, 1923, only convinced him that he needed more training in organization and better-laid plans to be a success. Released from prison after nine months of a five-year sentence, he set to work refounding the National Socialist party, and attracted funds from wealthy industrialists like Emil Kirdorf and Fritz Thyssen. In 1933 he came to power and proceeded to transform

Germany into the utopia of his fantasies. He committed suicide on April 30, 1945, as his empire crashed around him.

What follows is a systematization of Hitler's thought for the purpose of concise presentation. Even such a simple classification of ideological themes imposes a logical order on the stream of slogans that is absent in the original.

[26]   The Führer's Words

STRUGGLE—THE SOURCE OF STRENGTH *

Politics is nothing else than the struggle of a people for its existence in this world; it is the eternal battle of a people, for better or for worse, for its existence on this planet. How does this struggle take place? Great men of world history have described it. Frederick the Great said that politics is the art of serving one's people with all the means at one's disposal; according to Bismarck, politics is the art of the possible. . . . Clemenceau declared that the politics of peace was nothing else than the continuation of war with other means. Clausewitz asserted that war was nothing else than the continuation of politics with other weapons to the limit of its power for its existence on this earth.

With what question is struggle primarily related? It is the drive for self-preservation which leads to struggle—that is, the question of love and hunger. These are the two fundamental primitive forces around which everything on this earth centers. The total space on which life is carried on is circumscribed. This leads to a struggle of one against the other for this limited area. In addition, this area is more restricted for certain groups than for others so that their existence is dependent upon the preservation of the particular region which they inhabit.

Thus, the struggle for daily bread becomes in reality a struggle for the soil which produces this daily bread; that is, for space itself. It is an iron principle: the weak fall in order that the strong may live. . . . From all the innumerable creatures a complete species rises and becomes the master

This reading is based on selections from two sources: Gordon W. Prange, ed., *Hitler's Words* (Washington: Public Affairs Press, 1944) and Ralph Manheim, trans., Adolf Hitler's *Mein Kampf* (Boston: Houghton Mifflin Company, 1943). Reprinted by permission.

* Prange, pp. 6–7.

of the rest. Such a one is man—the most brutal, the most resolute creature on earth. He knows nothing but the extermination of his enemies in the world. . . . This struggle, this battle has not been carried on by all men in the same way. Certain species stand out, and at the top of the list is the Aryan. The Aryan has forged the weapons with which mankind has made itself master of the animal world. There is scarcely anything in existence when traced back to its origin cannot claim an Aryan as its creator. . . . Never have votes and majorities added one iota to the culture of mankind. Every accomplishment is solely the result of the work and energy of great men, and as such, a flaming protest against the inertia of the masses.

How does this process then take place? It is an eternal struggle. Every achievement is nothing else than the result of a struggle of give-and-take. Every new invention is a triumph over an old one. Every record is a struggle against that which exists. Every championship performance is a conquest of that which prevailed previously.

Hence the following principles result: The value of man is determined in the first place by his inner racial virtues; second, by the ability of the race to bring forth men who in turn become leaders in the struggle for advancement; third, this entire process takes place in the form of eternal struggle. As a consequence struggle is the father of all things in this world. (Munich, Nov. 21, 1927; *Voelkischer Beobachter,* Nov. 23, 1927.)

RACIAL PURITY *

The main plank in the National Socialist program is to abolish the liberalistic concept of the individual and the Marxist concept of humanity and to substitute therefor the folk community, rooted in the soil and bound together by the bond of its common blood. This is a very simple statement, but it involves a principle that has tremendous consequences. This is probably the first time and this is the first country in which the people are being taught to realize that, of all tasks which we have to face, the noblest and most sacred for mankind is that each racial species must preserve the purity of the blood which God has given it. . . . The greatest revolution which National Socialism has brought about is that it has rent asunder the veil which hid from us the knowledge that all human failures and mistakes are due to the conditions of the time and therefore can be remedied, but that there is one error which cannot be remedied once men have made it, namely,

* Prange, p. 80.

the failure to recognize the importance of conserving the blood and the race free from intermixture and thereby the racial aspect and character which are God's gift and God's handiwork. It is not for men to discuss the question of why Providence created different races, but rather to recognize the fact that it punishes those who disregard its work of creation. . . . (Berlin, Jan. 30, 1937; *Voelkischer Beobachter,* Jan. 31, 1937.)

RACE AND HISTORY *

Everything we admire on this earth today—science and art, technology and inventions—is only the creative product of a few peoples and originally perhaps of *one* race. On them depends the existence of this whole culture. If they perish, the beauty of this earth will sink into the grave with them.

However much the soil, for example, can influence men, the result of the influence will always be different depending on the races in question. The low fertility of a living space may spur the one race to the highest achievements; in others it will only be the cause of bitterest poverty and final undernourishment with all its consequences. The inner nature of peoples is always determining for the manner in which outward influences will be effective. What leads the one to starvation trains the other to hard work.

All great cultures of the past perished only because the originally creative race died out from blood poisoning.

The ultimate cause of such a decline was their forgetting that all culture depends on men and not conversely; hence that to preserve a certain culture the man who creates it must be preserved. This preservation is bound up with the rigid law of necessity and the right to victory of the best and stronger in this world.

Those who want to live, let them fight, and those who do not want to fight in this world of eternal struggle do not deserve to live.

Even if this were hard—that is how it is! Assuredly, however, by far the harder fate is that which strikes the man who thinks he can overcome Nature, but in the last analysis only mocks her. Distress, misfortune, and diseases are her answer.

The man who misjudges and disregards the racial laws actually forfeits the happiness that seems destined to be his. He thwarts the triumphal march of the best race and hence also the precondition for all human progress, and

* Manheim, pp. 288–89, 295–96, 328.

remains, in consequence, burdened with all the sensibility of man, in the animal realm of helpless misery.

* * *

The progress of humanity is like climbing an endless ladder; it is impossible to climb higher without first taking the lower steps. Thus, the Aryan had to take the road to which reality directed him and not the one that would appeal to the imagination of a modern pacifist. The road of reality is hard and difficult, but in the end it leads where our friend would like to bring humanity by dreaming, but unfortunately removes more than bringing it closer.

Hence it is no accident that the first cultures arose in places where the Aryan, in his encounters with lower peoples, subjugated them and bent them to his will. They then became the first technical instrument in the service of a developing culture.

Thus, the road which the Aryan had to take was clearly marked out. As a conqueror he subjected the lower beings and regulated their practical activity under his command, according to his will and for his aims. But in directing them to a useful, though arduous activity, he not only spared the life of those he subjected; perhaps he gave them a fate that was better than their previous so-called 'freedom.' As long as he ruthlessly upheld the master attitude, not only did he really remain master, but also the preserver and increaser of culture. For culture was based exclusively on his abilities and hence on his actual survival. As soon as the subjected people began to raise themselves up and probably approached the conqueror in language, the sharp dividing wall between master and servant fell. The Aryan gave up the purity of his blood and, therefore, lost his sojourn in the paradise which he had made for himself. He became submerged in the racial mixture, and gradually, more and more, lost his cultural capacity, until at last, not only mentally but also physically, he began to resemble the subjected aborigines more than his own ancestors. For a time he could live on the existing cultural benefits, but then petrifaction set in and he fell a prey to oblivion.

Thus cultures and empires collapsed to make place for new formations.

Blood mixture and the resultant drop in the racial level is the sole cause of the dying out of old cultures; for men do not perish as a result of lost wars, but by the loss of that force of resistance which is contained only in pure blood.

All who are not of good race in this world are chaff.

And all occurrences in world history are only the expression of the races' instinct of self-preservation, in the good or bad sense.

*   *   *

All really significant symptoms of decay in the pre-War period can in the last analysis be reduced to racial causes.

Whether we consider questions of general justice or cankers of economic life, symptoms of cultural decline or processes of political degeneration, questions of faulty schooling or the bad influence exerted on grownups by the press, etc., everywhere and always it is fundamentally the disregard of the racial needs of our own people or failure to see a foreign racial menace.

And that is why all attempts at reform, all works for social relief and political exertions, all economic expansion and every apparent increase of intellectual knowledge were futile as far as their results were concerned. The nation, and the organism which enables and preserves its life on this earth, the state, did not grow inwardly healthier, but obviously languished more and more. All the illusory prosperity of the old Reich could not hide its inner weakness, and every attempt really to strengthen the Reich failed again and again, due to disregarding the most important question.

ANTI-SEMITISM *

The Jewish Peril

Is there still a racial problem in this "modern" world? The yellow race is denied the permission to settle in America. But this peril, comparatively speaking, is not nearly so great as the peril which today stretches its hand over the entire world—the Jewish peril. Many people do not regard the Jews as a race, but is there another people that is as determined to perpetuate its race everywhere in the world as the Jews? As a matter of fact, the Jew can never become a German. If he wanted to become a German he would have to give up being a Jew. That he cannot do. The Jew cannot become a German at heart for a number of reasons: First, because of his blood; second, because of his character; third, because of his will; and fourth, because of his actions. His actions remain Jewish and he works for the "greater idea" of the Jewish people. Since that is so and cannot be otherwise, the mere existence of the Jew is a colossal lie. The Jew is a past master at lying, for his existence as such in the organism of other peoples is only

* Prange, pp. 77–78.

possible because of falsehood. This already was the opinion of the great Arthur Schopenhauer. The Jew lies to the other peoples when he pretends to be German, French, or the like.

What are the aims of the Jews? They aim to expand their invisible state as a supreme tyranny over the whole world. The Jew is therefore a destroyer of nations. In order to realize his domination over peoples he has to work in two directions. Economically he dominates the peoples, politically and morally he subjugates them. Politically he accomplishes his aims through the propagation of the principles of democracy and the doctrine of Marxism, which makes the proletarian a terrorist in domestic matters and a pacifist in foreign policy. From the ethical point of view the Jew destroys the peoples in respect to religious and moral considerations. Any one who is willing to see that, can see it; and no one can help the person who refuses to see it. The Jew, voluntarily or involuntarily, consciously or unconsciously, undermines the foundation on which alone a nation can exist.

Thus, the following question comes up: Are we still in a position to resist an enemy who is our deadly enemy? The prime consideration is whether we want to save Germany. If so, then we must first save her from her destroyer. I confess, it is a severe struggle that must be fought out on this score. We National Socialists, however, occupy an extreme position in this regard. We know only one people for which we fight, and that is our own people. We may be inhuman, but if we save Germany we will have righted the greatest wrong on earth. We may be immoral, but if we save our people, morality will have been given a new lease on life.

It is said that we are only making a lot of noise about anti-Semitism. Yes indeed, we want to stir up a storm. The people must not sleep, they should know that a storm is gathering. We have therefore laid down the principle in our program that only Germans can be citizens of the state. We could tolerate Jews only as guests, providing they did us no harm. But they are harmful. (Munich, April 20, 1923; *Voelkischer Beobachter,* April 22/23, 1923.)

THE NAZI ATTACK ON TRADITIONAL INSTITUTIONS *

Democracy Is Jewish Domination

Democracy is Jewish domination, for the people do not rule; public opinion is manufactured by the press, which is owned by Jews. At the same

* Prange, pp. 37, 42–44.

time democracy is not an end in itself, but the means to an end. The end is the achievement of Jewish domination through education for democracy —that is, through the creation of a lethargic mass of people who thinks that it rules through its elected representatives. The achievement of Jewish domination is facilitated by the determination of a minority and the cowardice of the majority in the ranks of the middle class, where, in addition, a great deal is accomplished by the threat of terror. . . .

Parliaments will not help the German people. We can hope for a change in our predicament only when we realize that the Jewish Revolution of 1918 was made by a small determined group, which, like shocktroops, swept the broad lethargic majority with it. That is the way great changes have always been accomplished. In realization of this Bismarck as a single individual once raised up the German people. We National Socialists want to adopt this "political" law of nature and want to be the shocktroops which will guide the destiny of the nation in order to lead it out of depression into a better future. It is our task to gather about us those dissatisfied with parliamentarianism in order to give our people the place it deserves. (Munich, Oct. ? [sic], 1922; Voelkischer Beobachter, Nov. 1, 1922.)

* * *

The Mediocrity of Numbers

In all ages it was not democracy that created values, it was individuals. However, it was always democracy that ruined and destroyed individuality. It is madness to think and criminal to proclaim that a majority can suddenly replace the accomplishment of a man of genius. . . . Every people must see in its most capable men the greatest national value, for this is the most lasting value there is. One single inventor, one genius, can mean more for a people than hundreds or even a billion in capital.

Nations have always gone to ruin on the principle of democracy. If Germany has declined in the last fourteen years, it is because the advocacy of the principle of democracy had gone so far that its patrons and representatives in Germany were actually subject to the mediocrity of numbers, whose very sovereignty they preached. They themselves had become so inferior, so puny and dwarfish, that they did not even possess the right to lift themselves above the masses. There has never yet been a regime or a government which gave up the ghost in a more dismal, more lamentable, and more inferior manner than the representatives of the recent system. (Berlin, March 2, 1933; Voelkischer Beobachter, September 2, 1933.)

* * *

Parliamentary Perversion

In that we deny the principle of parliamentary democracy we strike the strongest blow for the right of the nation to the self-determination of its own life. For in the parliamentary system we see no genuine expression of the nation's will—a will which cannot logically be anything else than a will to the maintenance of the nation—but we do see a distortion, if not a perversion, of that will. The will of a nation to the self-determination of its being manifests itself most clearly and is of most use when its most capable minds are brought forth. They form the representative leaders of a nation, they alone can be the pride of a nation—certainly never the parliamentary politician who is the product of the ballot box and thinks only in terms of votes. The constructive development of the future leadership of the nation through its most able men will take years; the intelligent education of the German people will take decades. (Nuremberg, September 1, 1933; *Voelkischer Beobachter,* September 2, 1933.)

* * *

Democratic Dictatorship

From the Anglo-Saxon countries I often hear expressions of regret that Germany should have departed from just those principles of democratic government which such countries consider as specially sacred. This opinion is based upon a serious error. Germany too has a "democratic" constitution. The present German Government of the National Socialist State has also been elected by the people and feels itself in the same way responsible to the people. It does not matter how many votes a deputy must have in the individual countries. There are countries which consider 20,000 votes necessary for a deputy, others consider 10 or 5,000 sufficient, while in others again the number is 60,000 or more.

The German people has elected a single deputy as its representative with 38,000,000 votes. This is perhaps one of the most important differences between our conditions and those existing in other countries. It means that I feel myself just as responsible to the German people as would any Parliament. I act on the trust it has placed in me and I carry out its mandate. (Berlin, May 21, 1935; *Voelkischer Beobachter,* May 22, 1935.)

THE STATE *

The state is a means to an end. Its end lies in the preservation and advancement of a community of physically and psychically homogeneous creatures. This preservation itself comprises first of all existence as a race and thereby permits the free development of all the forces dormant in this race. Of them a part will always primarily serve the preservation of physical life, and only the remaining part the promotion of a further spiritual development. Actually the one always creates the precondition for the other.

States which do not serve this purpose are misbegotten, monstrosities in fact. The fact of their existence changes this no more than the success of a gang of bandits can justify robbery.

We National Socialists as champions of a new philosophy of life must never base ourselves on so-called 'accepted facts'—and false ones at that. If we did, we would not be champions of a new great idea, but the coolies of the present-day lie. We must distinguish in the sharpest way between the state as a vessel and the race as its content. This vessel has meaning only if it can preserve and protect the content; otherwise it is useless.

Thus, the highest purpose of a folkish state is concern for the preservation of those original racial elements which bestow culture and create the beauty and dignity of a higher mankind. We, as Aryans, can conceive of the state only as the living organism of a nationality which not only assures the preservation of this nationality, but by the development of its spiritual and ideal abilities leads it to the highest freedom.

But what they try to palm off on us as a state today is usually nothing but a monstrosity born of deepest human error, with untold misery as a consequence.

We National Socialists know that with this conception we stand as revolutionaries in the world of today and are also branded as such. But our thoughts and actions must in no way be determined by the approval or disapproval of our time, but by the binding obligation to a truth which we have recognized. Then we may be convinced that the higher insight of posterity will not only understand our actions of today, but will also confirm their correctness and exalt them.

*   *   *

* Manheim, pp. 393–94, 397–98, 403–4.

Anyone who speaks of a mission of the German people on earth must know that it can exist only in the formation of a state which sees its highest task in the preservation and promotion of the most noble elements of our nationality, indeed of all mankind, which still remain intact.

Thus, for the first time the state achieves a lofty inner goal. Compared to the absurd catchword about safeguarding law and order, thus laying a peaceable groundwork for mutual swindles, the task of preserving and advancing the highest humanity, given to this earth by the benevolence of the Almighty, seems a truly high mission.

From a dead mechanism which only lays claim to existence for its own sake, there must be formed a living organism with the exclusive aim of serving a higher idea.

The German Reich as a state must embrace all Germans and has the task, not only of assembling and preserving the most valuable stocks of basic racial elements in this people, but slowly and surely of raising them to a dominant position.

* * *

The folkish state must make up for what everyone else today has neglected in this field. *It must set race in the center of all life. It must take care to keep it pure. It must declare the child to be the most precious treasure of the people. It must see to it that only the healthy beget children; that there is only one disgrace: despite one's own sickness and deficiencies, to bring children into the world, and one highest honor: to renounce doing so. And conversely it must be considered reprehensible: to withhold healthy children from the nation. Here the state must act as the guardian of a millennial future in the face of which the wishes and the selfishness of the individual must appear as nothing and submit. It must put the most modern medical means in the service of this knowledge. It must declare unfit for propagation all who are in any way visibly sick or who have inherited a disease and can therefore pass it on, and put this into actual practice. Conversely, it must take care that the fertility of the healthy woman is not limited by the financial irresponsibility of a state regime which turns the blessing of children into a curse for the parents. It must put an end to that lazy, nay criminal, indifference with which the social premises for a fecund family are treated today, and must instead feel itself to be the highest guardian of this most precious blessing of a people. Its concern belongs more to the child than to the adult.*

Those who are physically and mentally unhealthy and unworthy must not perpetuate their suffering in the body of their children. In this the folk-ish state must perform the most gigantic educational task. And some day this will seem to be a greater deed than the most victorious wars of our pres-ent bourgeois era. By education it must teach the individual that it is no disgrace, but only a misfortune deserving of pity, to be sick and weakly, but that it is a crime and hence at the same time a disgrace to dishonor one's misfortune by one's own egotism in burdening innocent creatures with it; that by comparison it bespeaks a nobility of highest idealism and the most admirable humanity if the innocently sick, renouncing a child of his own, bestows his love and tenderness upon a poor, unknown young scion of his own nationality, who with his health promises to become some day a powerful member of a powerful community. And in this educational work the state must perform the purely intellectual complement of its practical activity. It must act in this sense without regard to understanding or lack of understanding, approval or disapproval.

THE MASSES AND THE LEADER *

The nationalization of the broad masses can never be achieved by half-measures, by weakly emphasizing a so-called objective standpoint, but only by a ruthless and fanatically one-sided orientation toward the goal to be achieved. That is to say, a people cannot be made 'national' in the sense understood by our present-day bourgeoisie, meaning with so and so many limitations, but only nationalistic with the entire vehemence that is inherent in the extreme. Poison is countered only by an antidote, and only the shal-lowness of a bourgeois mind can regard the middle course as the road to heaven.

The broad masses of a people consist neither of professors nor of diplo-mats. The scantiness of the abstract knowledge they possess directs their sentiments more to the world of feeling. That is where their positive or negative attitude lies. It is receptive only to an expression of force in one of these two directions and never to a half-measure hoving between the two. Their emotional attitude at the same time conditions their extraordinary stability. Faith is harder to shake than knowledge, love succumbs less to change than respect, hate is more enduring than aversion, and the impetus to the mightiest upheavals on this earth has at all times consisted less in a

* Manheim, pp. 337–38, 343–45, 478–79.

scientific knowledge dominating the masses than in a fanaticism which inspired them and sometimes in a hysteria which drove them forward.

Anyone who wants to win the broad masses must know the key that opens the door to their heart. Its name is not objectivity (read weakness) but will and power.

. . . The soul of the people can only be won if along with carrying on a positive struggle for our own aims, we destroy the opponent of these aims.

The people at all times see the proof of their own right in ruthless attack on a foe, and to them renouncing the destruction of the adversary seems like uncertainty with regard to their own right if not a sign of their own unright.

The broad masses are only a piece of Nature and their sentiment does not understand the mutual handshake of people who claim that they want the opposite things. What they desire is the victory of the stronger and the destruction of the weak or his unconditional subjection.

The nationalization of our masses will succeed only when, aside from all the positive struggle for the soul of our people, their international poisoners are exterminated.

* * *

. . . The goal of a political reform movement will never be reached by enlightenment work or by influencing ruling circles, but only by the achievement of political power. Every world-moving idea has not only the right, but also the duty, of securing, those means which make possible the execution of its ideas. Success is the one earthly judge concerning the right or wrong of such an effort, and under success we must not understand, as in the year 1918, the achievement of power in itself, but an exercise of that power that will benefit the nation. Thus, a coup d'état must not be regarded as successful if, as senseless state's attorneys in Germany think today, the revolutionaries have succeeded in possessing themselves of the state power, but only if, by the realization of the purposes and aims underlying such a revolutionary action, more benefit accrues to the nation than under the past regime. Something which cannot very well be claimed for the German revolution, as the gangster job of autumn, 1918, calls itself.

If the achievement of political power constitutes the precondition for the practical execution of reform purposes, the movement with reform purposes must from the first day of its existence feel itself a movement of the masses and not a literary tea-club or a shopkeepers' bowling society.

* . . . The young movement is in its nature and inner organization anti-parliamentarian; that is, it rejects in general and in its own inner structure, a principle of majority rule in which the leader is degraded to the level of a mere executant of other people's will and opinion. In little as well as big things, the movement advocates the principle of unconditional authority of the leader, coupled with the highest responsibility.

The practical consequences of this principle in the movement are the following:

The first chairman of a local group is appointed by the next highest leader; he is the responsible leader of the local group. All committees are subordinate to him and not, conversely, he to a committee. There are no electoral committees, but only committees for work. The responsible leader, the first chairman, organizes the work. The first principle applies to the next higher organization, the precinct, the district or county. The leader is always appointed from above and at the same time vested with unlimited powers and authority. Only the leader of the whole party is elected, in a general membership meeting compatible with the laws governing associations. But he is the exclusive leader of the movement.* All committees are subordinate to him and not he to the committees. He makes the decisions and hence bears the responsibility on his shoulders. Members of the movement are free to call him to account before the forum of a new election, to divest him of his office in so far as he has infringed on the principles of the movement or served its interests badly. His place is then taken by an abler, newer man, enjoying, however, the same authority and the same responsibility.

It is one of the highest tasks of the movement to make this principle determining, not only within its own ranks, but for the entire state.

Any man who wants to be leader bears, along with the highest unlimited authority, also the ultimate and heaviest responsibility.

Anyone who is not equal to this or is too cowardly to bear the consequence of his acts is not fit to be leader; only the hero is cut out for this.

The progress and culture of humanity are not a product of the majority, but rest exclusively on the genius and energy of the personality.

To cultivate the personality and establish it in its rights is one of the

* [The passage between the asterisks, on the organization of the party, is taken from the second edition of *Mein Kampf* rather than from the first. The passage reprinted above appears as a footnote in the Houghton Mifflin edition. Ralph Manheim's explanation for the differences between the passages is that by the time the second edition appeared, "Hitler had emerged victorious from the factional conflicts within the party." Hence, where the first edition suggested that the leader is elected, in the second, Hitler centralizes power by directing that "The leader is always appointed from above. . . ." Ed. Note.]

pre-requisites for recovering the greatness and power of our nationality.

Hence the movement is anti-parliamentarian, and even its participation in a parliamentary institution can only imply activity for its destruction, for eliminating an institution in which we must see one of the gravest symptoms of mankind's decay.

* * *

The mass meeting is . . . necessary for the reason that in it the individual, who at first, while becoming a supporter of a young movement, feels lonely and easily succumbs to the fear of being alone, for the first time gets the picture of a larger community, which in most people has a strengthening, encouraging effect. The same man, within a company or a battalion, surrounded by all his comrades, would set out on an attack with a lighter heart than if left entirely on his own. In the crowd he always feels somewhat sheltered, even if a thousand reasons actually argue against it.

But the community of the great demonstration not only strengthens the individual, it also unites and helps to create an *esprit de corps.* The man who is exposed to grave tribulations, as the first advocate of a new doctrine in his factory or workshop, absolutely needs that strengthening which lies in the conviction of being a member and fighter in a great comprehensive body. And he obtains an impression of this body for the first time in the mass demonstration. When from his little workshop or big factory, in which he feels very small, he steps for the first time into a mass meeting and has thousands and thousands of people of the same opinions around him, when, as a seeker, he is swept away by three or four thousand others into the mighty effect of suggestive intoxication and enthusiasm, when the visible success and agreement of thousands confirm to him the rightness of the new doctrine and for the first time arouse doubt in the truth of his previous conviction—then he himself has succumbed to the magic influence of what we designate as 'mass suggestion.' The will, the longing, and also the power of thousands are accumulated in every individual. The man who enters such a meeting doubting and wavering leaves it inwardly reinforced: he has become a link in the community.

THE IDEOLOGY AS MYTH *

The greatness of every mighty organization embodying an idea in this world lies in the religious fanaticism and intolerance with which, fanatically

* Manheim, pp. 351, 458–59.

convinced of its own right, it intolerantly imposes its will against all others. If an idea in itself is sound, and, thus armed, takes up a struggle on this earth, it is unconquerable and every persecution will only add to its inner strength.

The greatness of Christianity did not lie in attempted negotiations for compromise with any similar philosophical opinions in the ancient world, but in its inexorable fanaticism in preaching and fighting for its own doctrine.

The apparent head start which movements achieve by fusions is amply caught up with by the steady increase in the strength of a doctrine and organization that remain independent and fight their own fight.

. . . On principle the movement must so educate its members that they do not view the struggle as something idly cooked up, but as the thing that they themselves are striving for. Therefore, they must not fear the hostility of their enemies, but must feel that it is the presupposition for their own right to exist. They must not shun the hatred of the enemies of our nationality and our philosophy and its manifestations; they must long for them. And among the manifestations of this hate are lies and slander.

* * *

If the folkish idea wants to arrive at a clear success from the unclear will of today, it must pick out from the broad world of its ideas certain guiding principles, suited in their essence and content to binding a broad mass of men, that mass which alone guarantees the struggle for this idea as laid down in our philosophy.

Therefore, the program of the new movement was summed up in a few *guiding principles, twenty-five* in all. They were devised to give, primarily to the man of the people, a rough picture of the movement's aims. They are in a sense a political creed, which on the one hand recruits for the movement and on the other is suited to unite and weld together by a commonly recognized obligation those who have been recruited.

Here the following insight must never leave us: Since the so-called *program of the movement* is absolutely correct in its ultimate aims, but in its formulation had to take psychological forces into account, in the course of time the conviction may well arise that in individual instances certain of the guiding principles ought perhaps to be framed differently, given a better formulation. Every attempt to do this, however, usually works out catastrophically. For in this way something which should be unshakable is submitted to discussion, which, as soon as a single point is deprived of its dogmatic, creedlike formulation, will not automatically yield a new, better, and above all unified, formulation, but will far sooner lead to endless debates and a general confusion. In such a case, it always remains to be considered which is better: a new, happier formulation which causes an argument within the movement, or a form which at the moment may not be the very best, but which represents a solid, unshakable, inwardly unified organism. And any examination will show that the latter is preferable. For, since in changes it is always merely the outward formulation that is involved, such corrections will again and again seem possible or desirable. *Finally, in view of the superficial character of men, there is the great danger that they will see the essential task of a movement in the purely outward formulation of a program.* Then the will and the power to fight for an idea recede, and the activity which should turn outward will wear itself out in inner programmatic squabbles.

With a doctrine that is really sound in its broad outlines, it is less harmful to retain a formulation, even if it should not entirely correspond to reality, than by improving it to expose what hitherto seemed a granite principle of the movement to general discussion with all its evil consequences. Above all, it is impossible as long as a movement is still fighting for victory. For how shall we fill people with blind faith in the correctness of a doctrine, if we ourselves spread uncertainty and doubt by constant changes in its outward structure?

PROPAGANDA *

Propaganda in the War was a means to an end, and the end was the struggle for the existence of the German people; consequently, propaganda could only be considered in accordance with the principles that were valid for this struggle. In this case the most cruel weapons were humane if they brought about a quicker victory; and only those methods were beautiful which helped the nation to safeguard the dignity of its freedom.

This was the only possible attitude toward war propaganda in a life-and-death struggle like ours.

If the so-called responsible authorities had been clear on this point, they would never have fallen into such uncertainty over the form and application of this weapon: for even propaganda is no more than a weapon, though a frightful one in the hand of an expert.

* Manheim, pp. 178–81, 589.

The second really decisive question was this: To whom should propaganda be addressed? To the scientifically trained intelligentsia or to the less educated masses?

It must be addressed always and exclusively to the masses.

* * *

The function of propaganda does not lie in the scientific training of the individual, but in calling the masses' attention to certain facts, processes, necessities, etc., whose significance is thus for the first time placed within their field of vision.

The whole art consists in doing this so skillfully that everyone will be convinced that the fact is real, the process necessary, the necessity correct, etc. But since propaganda is not and cannot be necessity in itself, since its function, like the poster, consists in attracting the attention of the crowd, and not in educating those who are already educated or who are striving after education and knowledge, its effect for the most part must be aimed at the emotions and only to a very limited degree at the so-called intellect.

* * *

The more modest its intellectual ballast, the more exclusively it takes into consideration the emotions of the masses, the more effective it will be. And this is the best proof of the soundness or unsoundness of a propaganda campaign, and not success in pleasing a few scholars or young aesthetes.

The art of propaganda lies in understanding the emotional ideas of the great masses and finding, through a psychologically correct form, the way to the attention and thence to the heart of the broad masses. The fact that our bright boys do not understand this merely shows how mentally lazy and conceited they are.

Once we understand how necessary it is for propaganda to be adjusted to the broad mass, the following rule results:

It is a mistake to make propaganda many-sided, like scientific instruction, for instance.

The receptivity of the great masses is very limited, their intelligence is small, but their power of forgetting is enormous. In consequence of these facts, all effective propaganda must be limited to a very few points and must harp on these in slogans until the last member of the public understands what you want him to understand by your slogan. As soon as you sacrifice this slogan and try to be many-sided, the effect will piddle away, for the crowd can neither digest nor retain the material offered. In this way the result is weakened and in the end entirely cancelled out.

Thus we see that propaganda must follow a simple line and correspondingly the basic tactics must be psychologically sound.

* * *

A movement which in a time of majority rule orients itself in all things on the principle of the leader idea and the responsibility conditioned by it will some day with mathematical certainty overcome the existing state of affairs and emerge victorious.

Part Two

THE POSTMODERN WORLD

SINCE 1945 THE SLOGANS and symbols of the cold war have shaped the patterns of political thought, truncating the range of ideas, diminishing the variety of argument, and stiffening the political imagination. Conceptions are tending to polarize: civilizations conceived as Eastern or Western, political systems as either totalitarian or democratic. The image of the future tends to be confined to the bleak alternatives of survival or annihilation.

The technology of weapons and missiles has advanced to the stage where within minutes of an outbreak of hostilities the number of lives lost would probably equal the number of persons killed in the entire five years and eight months of World War II. If a war were to last beyond a few minutes, it could totally extinguish all forms of life in large areas of the world. Furthermore, the longer the cold war persists, the more probable mass destruction becomes as the result of further advances in weapon technology on both sides; and the more intense it becomes, the greater the chances that underdeveloped societies, having learned the passions of nationalism, will also be swept into the vortices of polarized politics.

The international situation magnifies the significance of what might otherwise be minor events, and any political change may act as a trigger. The secession of a province in a newly independent African state, a *coup d'état* in a Southeast Asian country, a revolution in the Caribbean are all calculated as gains or losses in the continuing struggle. A pebble falling anywhere in the world may ultimately be transformed into the assassination at Sarajevo in 1914.

Domestic policies often take their cue from the cold war. In both camps, questions like the desirable rate of economic growth, the proper age to teach children higher mathematics, and the degree of decentralization in the administration of agricultural programs are considered to be part of the cold-war strategy. It is as if Carl Schmitt's conception of the ultimate political condition [1] had ironically found its place in this desperate era.

With each side watching the other so intently, interpreting the moves of the other so closely, and reacting so swiftly to the other's actions, parallel features in the forms of popular ideology and national purpose have appeared. In both one finds pronouncements concerning the necessity for collective unity. In both, the inclination to issue dogmatic claims concerning the absolute truth of their ideals is heightened. The posture of each tends to resemble that of the other. The greatest fear that haunts leaders and citizens of each is that the other system will outdistance their own in missiles, submarines, economic growth, school construction, and labor productivity.

Of course, substantial differences between the totalitarian systems and the Western democracies prevent any exact duplication. The multiplicity of nonpolitical groups in the West of itself offers continual resistance to politically induced attempts at synchronizing reactions to totalitarian gestures. In the liberal democracies, moreover, the cold-war situation is generally regarded as tragic, whereas a single-minded sense of conquering optimism pervades most Soviet pronouncements. Aside from the larger sense of humanity the sober outlook fosters, it may impel leaders to search more determinedly for alternatives; in its absence, Communist man is hard put to consider his antagonist as anything but a doomed enemy.

The comparative openness of Western democratic societies and the larger areas of freedom available to the individual prevent a completely uniform vision of the enemy from taking hold. The pluralistic character of social life retains many elements of "modern" civilization. On the other hand, new characteristics have emerged since World War II that define the

[1] See pp. 119, 190 ff. of this volume.

following years as the *postmodern* era. Other writers have also observed that the atomic age has put an end to modernism. Hannah Arendt, for instance, does not use the term *postmodern,* but makes a similar distinction between the modern age and the modern world:

> . . . the modern age is not the same as the modern world. Scientifically, the modern age which began in the seventeenth century came to an end at the beginning of the twentieth century; politically, the modern world, in which we live today, was born with the first atomic explosions.[2]

As the power centers of the world shifted to what were formerly the outposts of Europe, or the peripheral states as Raymond Aron calls them, traditional cultural patterns have tended to disintegrate. The idea of a single civilization, European in character, with regional variations, has given way to the conception of two mutually antagonistic congeries, each with internal patterns of variation. The change has speeded the fragmentation of formerly universal intellectual systems, commonly understood standards of morality, widely shared art forms, and the generally respected values and ideals of the modern period. The emergence of new power centers even more "peripheral"—in Asia and in Africa—promises to accelerate the fragmentation, even though the new nations in these regions of the world hope to learn how to "modernize" themselves.

What tends to become universal in the postmodern period is a pattern of military-industrial symbiosis and a form of extensive division of labor, shaped by the forces of industrial development and international conflict. Similar bureaucratic patterns of organization appear, together with similar hierarchies of formal power and prestige allocation.

Moreover, the trinity of reason, liberty, and progress, key ideas of the modern era, wither as ideals. They persist as shadows of their former incarnations, lacking the spirit that first imbued them. The idea of reason remains as rationalization through technology and social organization. The idea of progress, which carried in it some conception of moral goodness, now becomes simply the acceleration of technological change, with the pace and direction of social change following wherever technology leads.

Here too the political division of the world provides the major impulses for new research and ultimately for economic allocation and social development. Thus, scientific reflections on the possibilities of escaping from the earth's gravitational field and of transforming matter into energy persisted

---

[2] Hannah Arendt, *The Human Condition* (Chicago: University of Chicago Press, 1958), p. 6.

throughout the modern age, and were given flesh by the development of higher logic and mathematics from Newton to Einstein. Those reflections became visions of space exploration and ceaseless service to man as they were incorporated into the ideals of progress held in the late-modern age. But in postmodern times they take on different functions. A lag in technological application by one of the cold-war camps is interpreted by the other as possible disaster—hence the rush on both sides to explore the macro- and the microcosmos. The social consequences of such action are not questioned extensively by either side. Nor is it popularly understood that the dramatic advances in recent years are part of a revolution in technology and engineering—but not in science.

Both the Hobbesian, bourgeois conception of liberty as individual freedom from restraint and the Idealist view as fulfillment of personal potentiality [3] lose their force. The middle classes of Western civilization, beset for almost a century by the fear of revolutionary movements, can be driven into convulsive responses to the Communist threat. The fear of "softness" and the determination to take a "realistic" position in world politics produces a climate of opinion which tends to reject dissent and nonconformity —especially political—as a potential danger to the national interest. Yet at the same time, the large public budget required for successful maneuvering in the international arena and the increasing functions of the central government to coordinate such activity are interpreted as deprivations of freedom.

Fulfillment of human potential has come to be popularly equated with ever-increasing consumption of goods, or with the satisfaction of new desires which the industrial civilization creates as fast as it satisfies old ones.[4]

The perplexing questions of human freedom shrink to the proportions of puzzles that require only technical solutions. These shifts in the meaning of political language have resulted from changes in the relation between social and political institutions in contemporary systems. The distinction between state and society made by thinkers of the modern era was reflected in the actual structure of institutions. Hence the issue of individual freedom *versus* state authority was comparatively clear, and the nineteenth-century arguments between liberals and conservatives referred to different evaluations of state and society. In the postmodern era the distinctions between state and society have been removed in totalitarian systems, while in the

---

[3] See Isaiah Berlin, *Two Concepts of Liberty* (Oxford, England: The Clarendon Press, 1958).

[4] Raymond Aron, *The Century of Total War* (Boston: Beacon Press, 1955), p. 361.

democratic societies the lines have been blurred by the impact of war and preparation for total war. Cherished conceptions of the natural and proper relation between social and political development have been mocked by the actual course of events. We have been brought to suspect that there is no natural course of general social development—no obvious social or economic foundations which determine "secondary" political ideas and institutions. Not only are the laws of history considered to be much more subtle than the olympians had supposed, but the very possibility of defining such general laws has been seriously questioned.

Constructing political theories in the grand manner has become an anachronistic calling. Modern theorists from Hobbes to Marx were penetrating interpreters of political change who, willfully or not, spelled out the ethics of social control and individual obligation for emergent groups. But the context to which those questions so clearly and broadly pertained has shifted. It meant one thing to consider the conditions that would legitimate individual rebellion against a sovereign; it means quite another to deal with contending systems that have absolute monopolies of physical force. Cries of liberty (which may be distorted and faint echoes of the Enlightenment) tend to be interpreted outside their own borders as potential disturbances of the balance of terror.

Max Weber noted that the rationalization and disenchantment of the world was accompanied by the retreat of grand values from public life and art, and he warned against pressing such ideals on civilizations that could not sustain them. Political thought in the postmodern era is critical, analytical, and full of anxiety about the increasing rigidities of contemporary life. Its vision and persuasions are modest at best and timid at worst. With respect to the grand values, it seems to have fulfilled Weber's words.

V

The future of totalitarianism

BY THE END OF WORLD WAR II, the Nazi and Fascist systems
were crushed. Five years later, it was obvious that totalitarianism in its Communist form was more militant and vigorous than had
been foreseen by those optimists who believed that tyrannical regimes inevitably collapse under the weight of their own oppression. Moreover, of
the theorists who envisioned each stage of history as a necessary unfolding
of the latent forces in the previous stage, few could have predicted the rise
to power of the Chinese Communists and the extension of Soviet Russian
control. Certainly orthodox Marxists, insistent that the material foundations of society determine historical processes, could not have perceived
how the political "superstructure" determined the socioeconomic "base"
in these Communist systems. Today it is much more difficult to believe
that social and economic institutions are more "real" than political ones.
Stalin stood Marx on his head, giving the totalitarian state a turn that had
not been anticipated by Marx and Engels. Richard Lowenthal analyzes the
Stalinist theoretical revolution and its relevance for totalitarianism as
follows:

It was only Stalin who, casting aside all doubt, boldly proclaimed that this
apparent reversal of the Marxian relation between "basis" and "superstruc-

ture," the use of political power as a lever for *creating* the new "relations of production" (and if need be even the productive forces), was the very criterion of a true "proletarian revolution," and the ultimate reason why the socialist transformation could not be accomplished in *any* country without violent revolution and dictatorship. . . .

At first sight, this difference thus appears as a straight reversal of the respective roles of state and society: in contrast to the democratic revolutions and to the Marxian theories founded on them, it now seems to be the state that initiates the process of change, and the social structure which suffers passive adjustment. But while this paradoxical formula helps to bring out the radically new character of the totalitarian revolutionary process, it is too superficial to give a correct picture of either the modus operandi or the historical origin of the totalitarian regime.

In fact, it is the totalitarian movement—the ruling party—and not the state as such which maintains the initiative of social transformation in the totalitarian regime, just as it was the totalitarian movement that created the regime in the first place. Moreover, the totalitarian ruling party always makes its specific impact on the social order by combining domination of the state with its all-pervading penetration of society founded on a monopoly of organization and information. While using the state machine as an apparatus of repression, it simultaneously manipulates all legally permitted channels of information and all social organizations so as to "mobilize" the active cooperation of the "masses" in the transformation of their lives. So far from simply transferring the initiative of change from society to the state, the totalitarian revolution thus tends to obliterate the relative mutual autonomy of state and society characteristic of modern Western history: both are now made to develop in unison not according to their autonomous laws, but to the "Laws of History" laid down in the doctrine of the totalitarian party.[1]

SUCCESSION AND NEW MYTHS OF LEADERSHIP

The totalitarians' "laws of history" do not solve the problem of succession to political leadership. The very claim of the leader to be the sole interpreter of those "laws," founded on the power he commands in the hierarchical synchronization of party and government, makes him a severely jealous political god while he is alive and creates a sharp crisis when he dies or is deposed. Latent antagonisms or mutual suspicions among rulers and cliques are likely to erupt when power is transferred. At such moments elites often form shaky alliances to strengthen their positions; and if they are successful they resort to the purge to remove opponents from the arena.

[1] Richard Lowenthal, "Totalitarianism Reconsidered," *Commentary*, XXIX (June, 1960), 511.

The field of forces during this period is extremely unstable and highly unpredictable.

The period between the end of World War II and Stalin's death was a time of increasing anxiety for the dictator's lieutenants. Stalin made no attempt to open the path for a successor to the vast power he held. Extensive purges occurred at lower party levels. The jockeying for position was apparent as early as 1946 when A. A. Zhdanov outmaneuvered Georgi Malenkov. For the next twelve years the whole pattern of inner-circle power relations was clearly unsettled. Any distinct change in the situation, like Zhdanov's death in 1948 or Stalin's in 1953, was marked by fantastic charges of plot and counterplot, making it difficult for both actors and audience to unravel the actual skein of events. To complicate matters further, since the Communist ideological style calls for rationalistic, deterministic explanations, the antagonists attempted to justify their acts by weaving favorable legends about their own political histories—even short-term success in such struggles for leadership requires deception and manipulation. The myth of heroic totalitarian leadership constrains the would-be leader to demonstrate his priestly purity; his past sins must be justified if he would build holy temples. Hence, a recurrent theodicy appears, composed of useful remnants of the previous leaders' Marxist dogmas reinterpreted in accord with the demands of strategic power moves.

Like Stalin, Nikita Khrushchev bided his time at first, having gained control of the important post of first secretary of the party. From this superior ground, he was able to build a loyal following at the lower levels of leadership in the outlying party centers. From there he moved to control over higher and more central groups. As he gained strength, he bargained more and more effectively. He demonstrated how completely he had superseded the Stalinist era leaders when he suppressed the attempt of Malenkov, V. M. Molotov, and L. M. Kaganovich (his former protector) to curb his power in June, 1957.

The climax of Khrushchev's rise to power came in February, 1956, when at the Twentieth Party Congress the "eldest son" and formerly self-proclaimed "comrade-in-arms" of the "great father" Stalin revealed to the elite how the *Vozhd* had exercised naked power. The myth of Stalin's heroic virtues was punctured and the end of the personality cult proclaimed.

In the passages from the secret speech that appear in the reading below, it is clear that Khrushchev was attempting to displace Stalin as a direct successor to Lenin. In this way his own ideological purity and strength could be enhanced; but one cannot help feeling that the vehemence of some sections of the report and the revelation of many aspects of the Stalinist terror represent an outburst of unspoken indignation that Khrushchev had harbored for years. In the parts of the speech that follow those reprinted in this volume, Khrushchev described some of the events of the years of terror. He noted the Stalin directive of December 1, 1934, ordering that the investigation of actions against the regime be speeded up. Then he said:

This directive became the basis for mass acts of abuse against Socialist legality. During many of the fabricated court cases the accused were charged with "the preparation" of terroristic acts; this deprived them of any possibility that their cases might be re-examined, even when they stated before the court that their "confessions" were secured by force, and when, in a convincing manner, they disproved the accusations against them.[2]

After suggesting that the actual number of Trotskyites was relatively small even in 1927 and hence could not have endangered the country as Stalin claimed, Khrushchev said, "It is clear . . . there was no basis for mass terror in the country." He quoted from Lenin's report to the All-Union Central Executive Committee on February 2, 1920, to the effect that terror was to be used only against the exploiting classes and was to cease with the end of the civil war, and he concluded that Stalin had obviously deviated from this Leninist policy. He noted that many of those arrested as spies and saboteurs in 1937 and 1938 were falsely accused and their confessions achieved "with the help of cruel and inhuman tortures." [3] The details disclosed by Khrushchev coincide with the description of terror given by many of its victims who managed to survive. In the Khrushchev speech, the following quotation from an NKVD man, one Zakovsky, to an arrested party worker, Rozenblum, appeared:

The NKVD will prepare for you a ready outline for every branch of the center; you will have to study it carefully and to remember well all questions and answers which the Court might ask. This case will be ready in 4–5 months, or perhaps a half year. During all this time you will be preparing yourself so that you will not compromise the investigation and yourself. Your future will depend on how the trial goes and on its results. If you begin to lie and to testify

[2] Nikita S. Khrushchev, *Speech to the XXth Party Congress of the Communist Party of the Soviet Union, February 25, 1956* (Washington: U.S. Department of State, 1956), p. 15.
[3] For an account and interpretation of the techniques of terror used in the Stalin period, see the remarkable book, F. Beck and W. Godin, *Russian Purge and the Extraction of Confession,* trans. Eric Mosbacher and David Porter (New York: The Viking Press, Inc., 1951).

falsely, blame yourself. If you manage to endure it, you will save your head and we will feed and clothe you at the government's cost until your death.[4]

Khrushchev's next words were: "This is the kind of vile things which were then practiced." He underscored the harm done to the nation by the arrests of economic and military personnel, and attributed the primary blame to Stalin.

Facts prove that many abuses were made on Stalin's orders without reckoning with any norms of party and Soviet legality. Stalin was a very distrustful man, sickly suspicious; we knew this from our work with him. He could look at a man and say: 'Why are your eyes so shifty today,' or 'Why are you turning so much today and avoiding to look me directly in the eyes?' The sickly suspicion created in him a general distrust even toward eminent Party workers whom he had known for years. Everywhere and in everything he saw 'enemies,' 'two facers' and 'spies.'[5]

Khrushchev then excoriated Stalin for his wartime conduct. The Stalin-inspired view of the *Vozhd* as omniscient military tactician was debunked, and Stalin's orders deporting whole peoples from their homelands were officially declared to be cruel facts. He shattered the icon itself by hurling invectives at Stalin's self-worship in the form of thousands of memorials, the fantastically idealized films, and the rewritten histories of the Stalin era. In the course of his tirade, Khrushchev referred to the leader's hostility toward Marshal Zhukov, Molotov, and others who since have been downgraded by Khrushchev himself. Finally, he called for the abolition of the cult of the individual and for a return to "the most important theses of Marxist-Leninist science about the people as the creator of history and as the creator of all material and spiritual good of humanity, about the decisive role of the Marxist Party in the revolutionary fight for the transformation of society, about the victory of Communism."[6]

The Twentieth Party Congress report can be termed a political counter-myth. It prepared the way for the construction of the new myths more appropriate to Soviet Russia in the postmodern era. The outlines of these are to be seen in the Twenty-first Party Congress report, where the emphasis is on Khrushchev as new leader pointing the way to the classless society and as prime manager of the technological and strategic conflict with the West. The report celebrates Khrushchev's person to some degree, and

[4] Khrushchev, *op. cit.,* p. 23.
[5] *Ibid.,* p. 25.
[6] *Ibid.,* p. 57.

contains only faint references to the ideal of "collective leadership" ad·
vanced so boldly by Stalin's heirs soon after his funeral. At the Twenty·
second Party Congress which opened on October 17, 1961, Khrushchev
further exorcised Stalin's spirit by removing his body from the mausoleum
housing Lenin's remains to a lesser place at the Kremlin wall. By so doing,
Khrushchev hoped to solidify his internal position against the "anti-party
group" led by Molotov and to reenforce his external leadership of world
communism. But that Congress was marked by an open show of antagonism
between the Soviet and Chinese Communist leaders. When Stalin helped
to change the nature of communism from a supranational movement to a
Russian-led imperium, he also made possible national struggles for hegemony within the Communist camp. The manifest points of issue in such
quarrels are the correctness of Stalin's policies and the proper interpretation of the future course of communism. In coming to power by declaiming
Stalin, Khrushchev has committed himself to a less extremist international
line than the Chinese Communists. He then had to justify this policy by
proclaiming it singularly necessary to attain the ultimate Communist victory. The *Draft of the Party Program* submitted to the Twenty-second
Congress of the Party contains a sketch of Soviet society twenty years
hence, when, purportedly, the final stage of communism will come into
being. The sketch includes a list of the "free" goods and services that will
be provided to each according to his needs. Thus the new vision seems to
justify the policies and leadership of Khrushchev by concretely linking his
era, if not his name, to the inauguration of the "final days." [7]

SOCIAL AND CULTURAL CHANGES

Stalin's emphasis on heavy industrial investment continued after the
war. Plant facilities and equipment destroyed during the fighting were re-
built, and the former justification for these policies—the theory of capitalist
encirclement—was proclaimed with ever greater force as the Truman doctrine, the Marshall Plan, and the formation of NATO appeared to frustrate
the extension of communism westward.

This intensification of Stalinist policies coincided with the damping of
all cultural initiative under the direction of Zhdanov. In 1950, two years

[7] "Draft of the Party Program of the Communist Party of the Soviet Union,"
Pravda and *Izvestia*, July 30, 1961, p. 1; *Current Digest of the Soviet Press*, XIII,
Nos. 28, 29, 30 (August 9, 16, 23, 1961). See also Merle Fainsod, "The 22nd Party
Congress," *Problems of Communism*, X, No. 6 (Nov.–Dec., 1961), Special Supple-
ment.

after the "culture leader's" death, Zhdanovism was still the official line, and his speech calling for literature that would "promote the development of our country's national economy" was widely quoted. The expressions that poured from the Soviet presses could have been written by a Soviet heavy-industry myth machine. The characters were stylized heroes and villains, lacking all depth, riding through stock, melodramatic crises; the hero, exhilarated by his Communist teaching, was inevitably victorious. As Ernest Simmons says:

> Contrary to the prevailing image of the hero type in Western fiction, who is a lonely man, alienated from society, insisting upon his individuality in opposition to the encroachments of the crowd upon his freedom, the Soviet hero fulfills his personality only by completely identifying himself with society in the joys of collective labor. . . . It is largely though not entirely an idealized life that is portrayed in this fiction, for "socialist realism" justifies a presentation of life in the Soviet Union not as it is but as it should be or must be—the life of the hoped-for socialist future.[8]

Spontaneity in Soviet music and art was smothered during the Zhdanovist period. Only "socialist realist" programmatic music and folk music were designated as acceptable for Communist man. Such composers as Serge Prokofiev, Dmitri Shostakovich, Aram Khachaturian, and Vano Muradeli were made to renounce any tendencies toward Western music. Muradeli, whose opera *The Great Friendship* had triggered a blast by the party against "antipopular" elements in composition, recanted his errors and atoned by writing the prize-winning composition *The Party, Our Rudder*.[9]

Soviet "philosophy" continued to follow the style laid down by Stalin in *Marxism and Questions of Linguistics*. There was no question about the direction philosophical writing could take. An editorial in *Kommunist* in 1955 held that

> . . . philosophers must be militant materialists, "assisting the party in every way to educate the workers in the spirit of communism, Communist morality . . . tirelessly propagandizing the masses with a scientific, materialistic, atheistic world view." Philosophers must make plain the decisive role of the masses in the shaping of history, and this "in indissoluble connection with the root questions of party politics, strategy, and tactics. . . ." Soviet philosophers are castigated for "failing to exhibit the scientific foundations of party policy." [10]

    [8] Ernest J. Simmons, "Soviet Literature, 1950–1955," *Annals of the American Academy of Political and Social Science*, CIII (January, 1956), 91–92.

    [9] Robert M. Slusser, "Soviet Music Since the Death of Stalin," *Annals of the American Academy of Political and Social Science*, CIII (January, 1956), 116.

    [10] Quoted by George L. Kline, "Recent Soviet Philosophy," *Annals of the American Academy of Political and Social Science*, CIII (January, 1956), 129.

Work in the natural sciences had to cope with tensions and contradictions between ideological requirements and technical needs. On the one hand, the party hailed Marxism as a superscience and urged its application to every branch of knowledge in the belief that this would assure progressive success. On the other hand, the swift industrialization and the theoretical work in fields far removed from those into which Marx and Lenin had ventured demanded a highly rational language unhindered by Marxist intrusions.

The Lysenko controversy of the thirties is an example of how severely scientific work can be hampered in a totalitarian system where the ideology is seriously introduced into research. I. V. Michurin (1855–1935), a Russian plant breeder, had asserted a neo-Lamarckian theory of evolution: that acquired characteristics are inherited, especially those acquired under the influence of new environmental conditions which shatter the hereditary constitution of living things. Lysenko espoused this doctrine and vigorously argued its case against such neo-Mendelians as N. I. Vavilov, who finally perished in Siberia for his "crime" of opposition.[11] T. D. Lysenko's views were consistent with the strongly environmentalist Marxist assertions and conceivably provided genetic support for the transfiguration of human nature envisaged in Communist goals. In 1948, by decision of the party's Central Committee, Lysenkoism was declared the official dogma for studies in genetics, whereupon many of the neo-Mendelians went through the purification ritual of public recantation. Although Lysenko's influence and power declined somewhat after Stalin's death, he has since found favor again.

In the other natural sciences serious work continues while party ideologues hail Soviet successes as victories for Marxist philosophy. As long as lip service is paid to Soviet interpretations of dialectical materialism, the regime hesitates to demand complete transformation of thought. Scientific and technological success is considered proof that Marxist doctrines inspired such work.

THE THAW

The brief period known as "the thaw" coincided with Malenkov's short reign (1953–1955).

The sigh of relief at Stalin's death produced several amnesty decrees

[11] Julian Huxley, *Soviet Genetics and World Science: Lysenko and the Meaning of Heredity* (London: Chatto and Windus Ltd., 1949), p. 32.

freeing small classes of criminals. Soon thereafter, jurists were once more set to work to produce a revision of the criminal code, a task which had been alternately started and halted for 25 years. The discussion that followed in the Soviet law journals and the code itself, promulgated at the end of 1958, indicated an increased concern for formal rationality in criminal law: some procedural rules were tightened, and an attempt was made to clarify such juridical concepts as "the criminal suspect." These reforms together with the absence of mass terror tactics have lasted, despite the freeze which ended the thaw in other fields.

The declarations of freedom from the rigid confines of "socialist realism" made by Khachaturian, Shostakovich, Ehrenburg and others elicited hope that since Stalin's death the totalitarian system was becoming more flexible; Shostakovich's *Tenth Symphony* and Ilya Ehrenburg's novel *The Thaw* were discussed more openly than any artistic endeavors had been in years. Malenkov had relaxed many economic controls and had begun to emphasize consumer goods production more than any previous leader. But from the end of 1954 until Malenkov was deposed in February, 1955, and his Minister of Culture, G. F. Aleksandrov, a month later the system showed signs of returning to its rigid form. Khrushchev attacked Malenkov's "new course" as a betrayal of communism to the bourgeois West, and the culture hardened once more.

DREAM AND IDEOLOGY IN KHRUSHCHEV'S RUSSIA

In Khrushchev's report to the Twenty-first Party Congress, part of which appears below, one may find the ideological justification for policies and leadership in the new era. The future is brought closer to the masses, and the initial stage of Communist construction is proclaimed. After a little more intensive development of basic industry, the future will bring in the "mature returns" of consumer goods in abundance. Equal distribution of the fruits of production or the removal of "socialist incentives" from work would destroy Communist goals. Like Stalin, Khrushchev holds that the present is a necessary sacrifice to the future.

The symbol of the future plays a similar role in movements or intellectual systems that set up harmonious utopias: it legitimates and gives consolation for sacrifice. The urge to bring in the final days evokes fantasies of glory and reward to the faithful—if they sacrifice sufficiently.

The combination of olympian ideas of progress, speculations about the productive potential of the industrial revolution, and horror of the suffering that accompanied early industrialization contributed to the latent content in the extravagant dreams of Saint-Simon and Fourier. Marx and Engels then rationalized the vision, but did not diminish the hope of achieving it. They did not discuss the shape of the future society, considering such speculation to be utopian and unscientific. Nevertheless, their work was used as the source of scientific guarantees for true believers who expected a share in the world to come. These believers assumed that the axiom of classical economics—that human needs exceed the means to fulfill them—would not apply to the Communist era, depending on statements such as the following from Engels:

Instead of generating misery, overproduction will reach beyond the elementary requirements of society to assure the satisfaction of the needs of all; it will create new needs and at the same time the means of satisfying them. It will become the condition of and stimulus to new progress. . . .[12]

In the final days, the material reality principle itself, which according to Freud and other psychologists provides the frustrations from which mature selfhood is created, would disappear. Some publicists, writing in Soviet newspapers and journals, went so far as to describe the future society as something like a communal nursery and a dreamlike state of constant wish-fulfillment.

In the first thirty years of the regime, the shocks of war, terror, and heavy economic sacrifices made the dream appear distant and legendary to the Russian people. But impressed by a newly expanded economy and the staggering amounts predicted for mass production and mass consumption in the near future, citizens and officials began to take the vision more seriously. As Erich Goldhagen observes, their fantasies presented a problem:

The eschatological imagination threatens to become a source of indiscipline, a breeder of "dangerous" expectations incompatible with the total claims of the State. Totalitarian order has to be imposed upon the anarchic vision without, however, robbing it of the enthusiasm and purposefulness that it imparted to its bearers. As early as October 13, 1952, Poskrebyshev, Stalin's secretary and éminence grise of the Soviet system, denounced in Pravda "those among us who await the coming of communism as if it were some heavenly paradise. They sit there and ask themselves: 'When will communism finally be proclaimed? Will we soon be getting things from society according to our needs?' " . . . And

[12] Friedrich Engels, *Principles of Communism,* trans. Paul M. Sweezy (New York: *Monthly Review* Pamphlet Series No. 4, 1952), p. 59.

Khrushchev, at the 21st Party Congress, sought to dispel with oracular authority the "vulgar" conception of communism "as a formless, unorganized and anarchic mass of people. No, it will be a highly organized and arranged co-operation of workers. In order to direct machines, everybody will have to fulfill his functions as a laborer and his *social duties* at a determined time and in an established order." [13]

A skillful leader adjusts and balances the public dream life. If the dream loses vividness, then the necessary sacrifices have no emotional props; if the dream becomes too fantastic, mass disillusionment follows. Khrushchev has achieved balance, but his picture of the future society is quite different from the original Marxist vision. According to the Twenty-first Congress report, sports societies will be founded, free from state control; children will be given free lunches; and the individual will be subsidized from cradle to grave. But there are other promises as well. Free choice of vocation is to be restricted, and the processes of production are to determine the organization and allocation of labor. The rhythm of the machine will provide the standard for human work. Marx's prophecy that machine-imposed alienation would come to an end under communism is abandoned.

At the same time that consumption increases and the standard of living improves, drawing Soviet life closer to the culture of bourgeois welfare capitalism, ideological pressure mounts to stress the differences between the two types of system. The values of collectivism are praised and individualism is condemned. Collective patterns of consumption are publicly approved. The cooperatively built apartment house and the car pool are invested with virtue, in contrast to the privately owned dacha and automobile. A government offensive against private property and personal savings is always possible, and with it, perhaps, a "redistribution." In the final stage of communism, publicists reiterate, all private property will have disappeared, and such vestiges of the past must be eradicated before the new world is established. [14]

So far, totalitarian society has been perceived as either of two dominant images based on two different models. The first, emphasized in Chapter IV, is that of an armed camp permanently mobilized against a permanent enemy—a society organized for battle and conquest. The other image is of a society organized for work—an industrious, disciplined association of

[13] Erich Goldhagen, "The Glorious Future–Realities and Chimeras," *Problems of Communism,* IX (November–December, 1960), 13–14.
[14] See Herbert Ritvo, "Totalitarianism without Coercion?" *Problems of Communism,* IX (November–December, 1960), 27–28.

comrades producing and consuming in perfect harmony. The internal conflict among those who control Soviet society goes beyond the mere struggle for power in the narrow sense. It is also a conflict between these two great images—a struggle for the power to design a civilization.

In studying ideological pronouncements, it is important to understand what leaders and publicists say, but it is also important to notice how they say it. Metaphors convey a great deal. In the speeches of Stalin, military metaphors predominated. In Khrushchev's speeches, military images are still abundant, but they coexist with others that represent toil and industry. Khrushchev has conveyed his image of Soviet society vividly: "Just like bees toiling from dawn to dusk, creating a new building and filling it with honey, so our people fulfill their obligations and functions in society." [15]

Khrushchev also has officially proclaimed the end of the doctrine of capitalist encirclement. Thus he opened the way for more flexible statements of foreign policy. He announced that armed conflict between the capitalist and socialist camps was not inevitable. But this pronouncement did not relax the "hard, realistic" posture of Leninism. "By the final victory of socialism Marxists mean its triumph on an international scale," he declared.

CHINESE COMMUNISM

Khrushchev's concern to accommodate the Chinese Communists within the framework of Leninism is evident in the concluding sections of the report to the Twenty-first Party Congress. Their rise to the stature of a great power has changed Russia's position as undisputed leader of the Communist camp.

Chinese civilization had been exposed to the influence of the Occident for several centuries, and had resisted the pressures of Western ideals; but in the postmodern era, directed by leaders who avowed allegiance to the theories of Marx (who relegated traditional peasant societies to the tail end of history), the institutions and values of Chinese civilization were uprooted and the nation was transformed into a totalitarian collective.

As the selection from Mao Tse-tung's writings below indicates, the Chinese Communist party was formed soon after World War 1. At that

---

[15] *Pravda*, November 18, 1959, quoted by Erich Goldhagen, *op. cit.,* p. 15. In this article, Goldhagen notes the similarity between Khrushchev's vision of Soviet society and Plutarch's description of Sparta as a company of bees.

time, while yet a student, Mao was converted to Marxism and helped organize labor unions among the urban proletariat. Early in 1926, he showed
himself strongly impressed by the latent revolutionary strength of the peasantry. In a report of his visit to rural areas, he wrote:

> In a very short time, in China's central, southern, and northern provinces,
> several hundred million peasants will rise like a tornado or tempest, a force
> so extraordinarily swift and violent that no power, however great, will be able
> to suppress it. They will break all trammels that now bind them and rush for-
> ward along the road to liberation. They will send all imperialists, warlords, cor-
> rupt officials, local bullies and bad gentry to their graves. All revolutionary
> parties and all revolutionary comrades will stand before them to be tested, and
> to be accepted or rejected as they decide.
>   To march at their head and lead them? Or to follow at their rear, gesticulat-
> ing at them and criticising them? Or to face them as opponents?
>   Every Chinese is free to choose among the three alternatives, but circum-
> stances demand that a quick choice be made.[16]

Operating from the vantage point of revolutionized peasant-militia
soviets (often against the ideological lines of Stalin), Mao skillfully ma-
neuvered through the factional splits in the Chinese Communist party to
a leading position by 1932–1933. When Chiang Kai-shek's Nationalist
armies threatened to exterminate the Communist units in 1934, Mao led
the successful transfer of their base of operations 6000 miles to the north.
At the end of World War II the Communists led the most extensive, tightly-
knit fighting force in China, and within a few years they controlled all of
the mainland.

The development of Communist ideology in China presents a particularly clear example of the tortuous relationships between reality and thought
that haunt modern totalitarianism. The political-economic situation in
post-World War I China bore no resemblance whatever to a Marxist conception of a society ripe for Communist or even bourgeois revolution. But
the confusion created by struggles for power among armed opportunists as
well as idealists of every political hue made it possible for skilled and
dedicated revolutionaries to seize control. Theories of the prerequisites for
Communist success abounded. Where a swift turn of events apparently negated a theory, rationalizations were constructed to "prove" the validity of
the theory while explaining the events away. Hence, Chiang Kai-shek's attack on the Communist alliance with the Kuomintang in 1927 did not result in an immediate shift of policy by Stalin and the Comintern. Rather,

---

[16] "Report of an Investigation into the Peasant Movement in Hunan," *Selected
Works of Mao Tse-tung* (London: Lawrence and Wishart, Ltd., 1954), I, 21–22.

for the sake of preserving the façade of Marxist-Leninist-Stalinist historical correctness (and in order to preserve a Soviet foothold in China), Stalin and his followers in China insisted that the Kuomintang was yet the "correct" organization through which communism might succeed. This, however, required a further elaboration of Marxism, which was already distorted from previous "explanations" of apparent exceptions to "Historical Law."

Mao Tse-tung's espousal of the peasantry rested on flimsy ideological grounds from an orthodox Marxist point of view, and he too was forced to justify his position by appending sweeping subtheories to Marxist revolutionary concepts. In his own terms, this meant that the party had to adopt a "zigzag" approach to strategy and ideology. But more than this, Maoism eventually amounted to a justification of "zigzaggism" itself, couched in the usual Marxist-Leninist terms. The selections from the writings of Mao show the effects of these twists and turns. His ideas seem to move like random cannon fire, in explosive parabolic arcs, apparently disconnected, and directed against real and illusory enemies without discrimination.

Although the official view attributed communism's success in China to the pressure of historical forces, a more realistic appraisal is given by Benjamin I. Schwartz: "The Chinese Communist Party under the leadership of Mao Tse-tung has been, I would suggest, neither 'the vanguard of the proletariat' in the Marxist-Leninist sense, nor a 'peasant party' in the Marxist-Leninist sense, but an elite of professional revolutionaries which has risen to power by basing itself on the dynamic of peasant discontent." [17]

In the decade from 1949 to 1959, China underwent a transformation that telescoped 40 years of the Russian Revolution. Initial leniency toward "necessary capitalist elements," bursts of expropriation, massive doses of heavy industry investment, sudden party purges—all followed one another swiftly and intensely. There was even a vague resemblance to the Soviet thaw in the events that followed Mao's proclamation: "Let a hundred flowers bloom, let a hundred schools of thought contend." During the brief thaw in the spring of 1957, professors and university students and many non-Communist leaders vigorously attacked the party, the bureaucracy, and the dictatorship. The nature of one such attack may be seen in the following official denunciation of a speech attributed to a female student:

[She said] True socialism is highly democratic but the socialism we have here is not democratic. I call this society a socialism sprung from a basis of

[17] Benjamin I. Schwartz, *Chinese Communism and the Rise of Mao* (Cambridge: Harvard University Press, 1951), p. 199.

feudalism. We should not be satisfied with the Party's rectification and reformist methods and the slight concessions made to the people. . . . We must find
genuine solutions to our problems and master our difficulties and the only way
to do this is to rouse and mobilize the people. . . .

. . . these two countries [the Soviet Union and China] had not yet eliminated class differences. In particular, both the countries exercise the dictatorship of the proletariat. Moreover, quoting Engels' theory that one country
cannot construct socialism and Lenin's dictum that socialism is the elimination
of classes, she arrived at the conclusion that present day China and the Soviet
Union are not socialist. She loudly demanded a search for "true socialism"
and advocated using explosive methods to reform the present social system.
She also declared "I do not approve of reformism and demand thoroughgoing
transformation."

She rumored it that the movement against counter-revolutionaries had
wronged 720,000 persons. . . .

. . . In China there is no freedom of the press. . . . She said, "There is
a limit on the ruling classes and that is the law." She said last year [1956] she
went from Peking to Yumen and saw "with her own eyes" men on strike at the
side of the road. . . .[18]

In the beginning of June, the freeze set in once more and recantations
followed one another in a familiar pattern. The special style required for
"self-criticism" appears poignantly in the following excerpts from the "confession" of Chang Po-chun, one of the alleged leaders of the "rightist"
forces:

I am an offender guilty of serious political mistakes. . . . With all my
heart I accept . . . the denunciation and exposure by deputies in the last few
days who brought to light my ugly and absurd words and actions. . . . I have
a deep feeling that in reprimanding and criticizing me the people . . . are
rescuing me . . . and are giving me a chance of rebirth. I wish to express my
heartfelt thanks once again to the whole nation and all the deputies.

My erroneous thinking and crime have their historical root . . . I came
from the landlord class and for a long time received feudal and bourgeois education. After betraying the glorious Communist Party of China in 1927, I degenerated into . . . following the middle-of-the-road course and "being 30
per cent against the Communists and 70 per cent against Chiang. . . ." Although on the occasion of the 30th anniversary of the birth of the great and
glorious Communist Party of China on July 1, 1951, I published my self-
criticism headed "The Communist Party Has Saved Me" showing my repen-

[18] *Jen Min Jih Pao,* June 30, 1957, p. 5, translated for this volume by Edward
Friedman. See also Roderick MacFarquhar, *The Hundred Flowers Campaign and
the Chinese Intellectuals* (New York: Frederick A. Praeger Inc., 1960), pp. 140,
141.

tance, I did not pull out the root of my bad thoughts. Consequently, my stand was not firm, vacillating between the "left" and the "right" and frequently showing myself to be a double dealer. I hankered after the old things; outwardly I accepted new things but actually I kept myself away from them. The latent bad thought reasserted itself after the 20th Congress of the Soviet Communist Party criticized Stalin's cult of individuality. I went too far to subject Stalin to vicious criticism. As to the great socialist construction in the Soviet Union, I sometimes under-rated its achievements and sometimes emphasized its drawbacks. . . . I even belittled the basic theories of Marxism-Leninism and I never gave them a serious study. This gave rise to the so-called revisionist thinking opposed to Marxism-Leninism. This new bad thought was a continuation of my old rightist opportunism. . . .

[My] mistakes show that my political and ideological degeneration has reached such a shameful, detestable and dreadful state in the past year. . . . I cannot shirk the responsibility for this serious crime. I am willing to ask punishment from the whole nation, from the Party and the government.

The whole nation is demanding stern punishment of me, a rightist. This is what should be done and I am prepared to accept it. I hate my wickedness. I want to kill the old and reactionary self so that he will not return to life. I will join the whole nation in the stern struggle against the rightists, including myself. The great Chinese Communist Party once saved me, it saved me once more today. I hope to gain a new life under the leadership and teaching of the Party and Chairman Mao and to return to the stand of loving the Party and socialism. I will mend my way and whole-heartedly serve socialism.[19]

The rituals of confession and self-humiliation recall scenes from George Orwell's *1984*.

Although the picture is not clear and there is much we do not know, it appears that in China the possibilities of the totalitarian control of personality have been considerably extended. In the fall of 1958 an announcement was made to the effect that Chinese society would be completely reorganized in communes. The communes were declared to be a short cut to full communism that would provide the basic form of the classless society while industrialization was taking place and even before the era of abundance would begin. Every vestige of private concern was to be eliminated. Labor, military service, family roles, and education were all to be arranged in centrally administered division of labor patterns for the purpose of increased productivity and more efficient control.

By December of 1958, however, the communization drive was behind schedule and the leaders retreated from the glowing predictions of the

[19] Chang Po-chun, "I Bow My Head and Admit My Guilt before the People" (written statement to the 4th session of the 1st National People's Congress), Peking *Jen Min Jih Pao*, July 16, 1957, trans. in *Current Background* (Hong Kong: American Consulate General, 1957), No. 470, pp. 28, 32–33.

march to communism within five years. The idea of the communal unit as the fundamental social group still persists, and it stands as a model for the possibilities that may be achieved by political transformation from above.[20] Communist China today is more of a Marxist anomaly than even Soviet Russia. It seems odd that a disorganized, quasifeudal society, torn by a succession of civil wars within and attacks from Japan without, should become a major industrial power in so short a time. One explanation is to be found, once again, by "turning Marx on his head." W. W. Rostow notes:

> The fact is that Communism as a technique of power is a formidable force. Although it was an un-Marxist insight, it was a correct insight of Lenin's that power could, under certain circumstances, be seized and held by a purposeful minority prepared to use a secret police. Although it was an un-Marxist insight, it was a correct insight that societies in the transition from traditional to modern status are peculiarly vulnerable to such a seizure of power.[21]

If a skilled Leninist elite takes advantage of such vulnerability and manages to unify a large, strategic land mass, it may utilize modern technology to become a leading industrial nation under forced draft. The human costs of heavy capital accumulation in the nineteenth-century liberal democracies may be measured in terms of mass poverty; the costs of the twentieth-century totalitarian systems are counted in greater sacrifices of lives and values.

THE FUTURE OF TOTALITARIANISM

What are the similarities between prewar Communist totalitarianism and its postwar forms, and what are the differences? Can any predictions be made about the nature of communism in the future? It would be hazardous to make prophetic claims, but there is no reason to ignore clues or to fear hypotheses.

One significant factor in the shifting frictions of the systems is the use to which ideology is put. We have already seen how Marxism was transmuted from a revolutionary intellectual system into power-seeking ideolo-

[20] Early in 1961, the *Jen Min Jih Pao,* the official organ of the Chinese Communist party, hailed recent experiments in growing human embryos in a laboratory. "If children can be had without being conceived 'working mothers need not be affected by childbirth,' the article said, and added, 'This is happy news for women.'" (*New York Times,* March 19, 1961, p. 6.)

[21] W. W. Rostow, *The Stages of Economic Growth: A Non-Communist Manifesto* (Cambridge: Cambridge University Press, 1960), pp. 162–63.

gies by Communist dictators. But one cannot set about turning ideas to pragmatic use without paying a price; modern totalitarian ideologies are not "mere rationalizations." The very same seductive appeals of traditional communism—those inherited from Enlightenment humanism—also placed special burdens on Communist tactics. The apocalyptic aspects of the ideology (its announcement that the state would wither away in the class-less society), its appeal to all proletarians of the world, and its insistence that it is more democratic than bourgeois ideologies strained credulity when actualities ran counter to these conceptions. Furthermore, because communism claims to be rational, some attempt had to be made to justify all action by the application of "Marxist science," even if the attempt was a tour de force. The appeals of communism were more humanistically seductive but also more sensitive to serious challenge than were Nazi and Fascist ideologies.

With the successes of the Chinese Communists, the secession of the Yugoslavs in 1948, the Hungarian rebellion of 1956, and the quasiindependent line taken by the Poles in the late 1950's, even the appearance of ideological uniformity was strained. Thus, Khrushchev had to cope with a different pattern of international Communist relationships and power problems than Stalin had faced. Under these conditions the Stalinist construction of Communist ideology was a handicap, and Khrushchev found himself in a difficult position when he attempted to maintain ideological hegemony over the Communist bloc. It was only by upsetting Stalinist ideas in the Twentieth, Twenty-first, and Twenty-second Party congresses and by substituting a set of his own that he was able to justify his actions and maintain a position of security within his own regime and with the Chinese Communists.

The new ideology is not without possible dangers to the security of Khrushchev's future rule. In the first place, the de-Stalinization campaign is not likely to be forgotten. The very fiction of rationality carried in the Communist ideology operates against the firm establishment of a personality cult around Khrushchev. Second, the same may be said about the use of mass terror: having openly announced what was known to all privately, if Khrushchev wanted to apply terroristic methods, he could not very well do so under the old ideological guises. Finally, the conflicts and the near-breaking of ties with Communist China, meaning that the way to "socialism" adopted by the Soviet Union is no longer regarded as the mechanical model for all countries, opens a wedge for other Communist nations to deviate from the Soviet path while claiming to remain true to Marxism.

RATIONALIZATION

In assessing the nature of totalitarian systems, many commentators have considered the relationships between rational modes of thought and the rationalization of the economy and the society to be highly significant factors.[22] It is an exceedingly complicated matter, not lending itself to facile analysis. Isaac Deutscher, on the other hand, reviewing the de-Stalinization campaign, noted the changes occurring in the direction of more rational and equalitarian forms of control and wrote, in 1957, "It is the twilight of totalitarianism that the U.S.S.R. is living through." [23] This thesis tends to identify rationalization with democracy, whereas, as Bertram Wolfe and others have indicated, more rationalized codes of law and forms of administration may only increase the efficiency with which party controls are carried out. Rationalization by itself, as Herbert Marcuse suggests in the selection from his Soviet Marxism, can give rise to varying political forms. Whether it will stimulate more individual autonomy or more rigid party control is partly related to the problems of succession and to other factors outside the system.

Within the system, several developments are notable. Many branches of research and study in the Soviet Union are characterized by the same kinds of empirical research and rational theory construction that are found in the West; but such uses of reason are fenced off from other areas. Legal thought since Stalin's death has exhibited more of the characteristics Max Weber called "formally rational." Like lawyers and jurists everywhere, those in the Soviet Union have developed a professional outlook which makes their own vocational behavior more systematic and intelligible to them and endows their work with higher status than that accorded it by revolutionary Marxism.[24] Of course their arguments are often reinforced by the proper slogans and the prescribed rhetoric. Authors who argued for a clearer and more logical distinction among classes of criminals or who urged that the vague, whimsical category of "suspect" be refined

[22] See, for example, Zbigniew Brzezinski, "Totalitarianism and Rationality," American Political Science Review, L (September, 1956), 751–63. Brzezinski holds that "The rationalist tomorrow, if it ever comes, will . . . not be an introduction to a democratic form of government, but rather a stage in further totalitarian evolution, accentuating features present from the start and minimizing some of the irrational outbursts . . ." (p. 761).

[23] Isaac Deutscher, Russia in Transition (New York: Grove Press, 1960), p. 50.

[24] See, for example, some of the statements made by Soviet judges, as quoted in Rudolf Schlesinger, "Soviet Lawyers on the Problems of their Legal System—I," Soviet Studies, VII (October, 1955), 164–82; and ibid., for the second part of the article, VII (January, 1956), 332–42.

claimed that such reforms would advance "socialist legality." Furthermore, the arguments would be recognized by any Western jurist as desirable from a juridical point of view. The appearance of such views in the Soviet Union indicates that nonpolitical centers of change can arise in the post-Stalin era. This may never lead to the democratization of the system politically, but it suggests that rational, nontotalitarian sectors of thought are possible.

Offsetting these trends in the law, however, is the renewed emphasis on the "comrades' courts." Khrushchev hailed them as one of the pathways to entry into the kingdom of communism; but their projected general use currently indicates that they are meant to aid in the exercise of more disciplined party control at the lower levels. They are part of the built-in impulse toward irrationality which characterizes all the totalitarian movements and which has broken out sporadically in Soviet society.

The legal developments are linked to the further rationalization of the economy and of public administration. Stalin's dictatorship was rational only in the sense that all possible means that would attain the end of swift industrialization were adopted, regardless of consequences to the other sectors of society. The pattern of rationalization thus far introduced by Malenkov and Khrushchev is more pragmatic in its regard for avoiding inefficient consequences of overcentralization. Lower policy-making authority has been decentralized to regional economic councils, and Soviet trust and factory managers appear to have more flexibility in making decisions than before. The goal of such moves—higher production at less cost—is simply more and better rationalization than Stalin's brand. Also, in recent years the lines of force have shifted slightly from state coercive organs to persuasive, quasipublic, and parajudicial party organizations. This does not mean the loosening of political controls. Rather, more subtle methods have been introduced for the uses of the post-Stalin era.

In the Communist camp at large, Poland, Yugoslavia, and China at present are variations on the older, more rigid theme. They indicate that different combinations of power and control are developing in postmodern totalitarianism. Whether any single type, known or new, or a combination of types comes to predominate ultimately depends on whether the present bipolarization of the world continues and on how China will wield her power.

THE COMMUNIST VIEW OF MAN

Marx expected that the flow of history would result in the end of man's alienation from himself and his work in the final Communist period. Juxtaposed with this we have already noted the presence of childlike visions of omnipotence in communism. Given the rigid, authoritarian social structure which has been imposed on Russia and China, these visions have been institutionalized in the name of growth and progress. The Soviet or Chinese Communist citizen is viewed as a child, and often his behavior is marked as that of a naughty or uneducated one by his rulers. The communication media constantly scold; good (obedient) citizens are exhorted to watch for and report any antisocial behavior of their misbehaving siblings; judges consider it their official duty to teach backward adults the rudiments of Soviet morality. Harold Berman suggests, "The subject of law, legal man, is treated less as an independent possessor of rights and duties, who knows what he wants, than as a dependent member of the collective group, a youth, whom the law must not only protect against the consequences of his own ignorance but must also guide and train and discipline." [25]

The manipulation of childhood anxiety, a technique of the self-righteous parent, becomes a model for the handling of citizens. Khrushchev's revelations about Stalin's terroristic behavior may imply that the people should feel grateful for the rescue from the tyrant father—but at the same time should repay the new parent by being completely obedient.

The extreme model of the totalitarian universe is the concentration camp. There, as Bettelheim has noted, an underlying purpose and effect is the regression of the inmate to the status of a helpless infant.[26] While the comparison is not wholly valid for contemporary totalitarian societies, the social processes of both forms of organization are strikingly similar. An ironic paradox of this development is that the absorption of the child's personality by the parent, a nightmare familiar to many private bourgeois households, now prevails in the public stronghold of totalitarian systems.

The society is not completely closed to individual autonomy, however. Some few personalities drew sustenance from private worlds and managed to protect themselves from public onslaught. One of the most startling experiences of recent years was the publication of *Doctor Zhivago* outside the Soviet Union. The immediate reaction was one of surprise that an artist's consciousness could survive beneath the snows of the Stalin and Khrushchev regimes and produce such a robust novel. Nicola Chiaromonte has said that Pasternak's work portrays the conditions of existence that have confronted the West since 1914—and on a tragic scale. It is indeed remarkable to see a man preserve his identity and endure in the face of

[25] Harold J. Berman, *Justice in Russia* (Cambridge: Harvard University Press, 1950), p. 204.
[26] Bruno Bettelheim, "Individual and Mass Behavior in Extreme Situations," *Journal of Abnormal and Social Psychology*, XXXVIII (1943), 417–52.

overwhelming events without bitterness or rancor. At the same time there is a haunting quality about the work which almost suggests that it may be the last of its kind from that environment. On the other hand, perhaps Zhivago teaches that despite the attempts of the totalitarian system to make a new creature and a new world, underground survives one of the oldest figures of Western thought and action: the stoic hero. He suffers, endures— and remains a man.

NIKITA S. KHRUSHCHEV
1894-

BORN OF "POOR BUT HUMBLE FOLK" in a small village near Kursk, Khrushchev spent his early years as a shepherd and locksmith and was drafted into the tsarist army during World War I. Afterward he joined the Bolsheviks and fought in the Red Army during the civil war; he took up his father's trade of mine worker briefly after the war, and soon chose party work as a career. Gradually he worked his way up through Communist party posts. In the late 1920's he was in Kiev, where he came under the tutelage of Lazar Kaganovich. In 1929, he was transferred to Moscow and in the following years advanced in party circles until he succeeded Kaganovich as first secretary of the Moscow Regional Committee in 1935. By 1938, he had become first secretary of the Ukranian Communist party, was responsible for planning agricultural production, and was a member of the Presidium of the USSR Supreme Soviet as well as of the Politburo of the party. During World War II, he was head of a political department of the Red Army; after the war he resumed his party career.

Khrushchev was named to the party's Central Committee in 1949, and in the following year he took charge of merging collective farms into larger units. His plan for the reorganization of rural population into *agrogorods* (rural towns) was opposed by the Party leadership and was dropped. Khrushchev's rise to power was not seriously affected, however, and in 1952 he was instrumental in the reorganization of the party. When Stalin died, he was chairman of the commission on the leader's funeral, becoming first secretary of the party in 1953. From that important post, he repeated Stalin's feat of moving into complete political power.

Merle Fainsod notes that "Khrushchev was the harbinger of a new Politburo generation. He was the first member to be admitted to the inner circle who had entered the Party after the Revolution." As a leader of the second wave of elite, Khrushchev had to develop his techniques in the uses of power by rising slowly in the party apparatus, unlike Stalin; but he has shown that control of the party is still the key to power in the Soviet system.

[27]   The Direction of the Soviet System

I. THE CULT OF THE INDIVIDUAL *

Comrades! In the report of the Central Committee of the Party at the XXth Congress, in a number of speeches by delegates to the Congress, as also formerly during the plenary CC/CPSU sessions, quite a lot has been said about the cult of the individual and about its harmful consequences.

After Stalin's death the Central Committee of the Party began to implement a policy of explaining concisely and consistently that it is impermissible and foreign to the spirit of Marxism-Leninism to elevate one person, to transform him into a superman possessing supernatural characteristics akin to those of a god. Such a man supposedly knows everything, sees everything, thinks for everyone, can do anything, is infallible in his behavior.

Such a belief about a man, and specifically about Stalin, was cultivated among us for many years.

* * *

In December 1922 in a letter to the Party Congress Vladimir Ilyich [Lenin] wrote: "After taking over the position of Secretary General Comrade Stalin accumulated in his hands immeasurable power and I am not certain whether he will be always able to use this power with the required care."

This letter—a political document of tremendous importance, known in the Party history as Lenin's "testament"—was distributed among the dele-

---

* From secret speech of Khrushchev concerning the "cult of the individual," delivered at the Twentieth Congress of the Communist Party of the Soviet Union, February 25, 1956. U.S. Department of State release, June 4, 1956, pp. 1, 3–4, 5–6, 8–9, 10, 13.

gates to the XXth Party Congress. You have read it, and will undoubtedly read it again more than once. You might reflect on Lenin's plain words, in which expression is given to Vladimir Ilyich's anxiety concerning the Party, the people, the State, and the future direction of Party policy.

Vladimir Ilyich said: "Stalin is excessively rude, and this defect, which can be freely tolerated in our midst and in contacts among us Communists, becomes a defect which cannot be tolerated in one holding the position of the Secretary General. Because of this, I propose that the comrades consider the method by which Stalin would be removed from this position and by which another man would be selected for it, a man, who above all, would differ from Stalin in only one quality, namely, greater tolerance, greater loyalty, greater kindness and more considerate attitude toward the comrades, a less capricious temper, etc."

* * *

As later events have proven, Lenin's anxiety was justified: in the first period after Lenin's death Stalin still paid attention to his [i.e., Lenin's] advice, but later he began to disregard the serious admonitions of Vladimir Ilyich.

When we analyze the practice of Stalin in regard to the direction of the Party and of the country, when we pause to consider everything which Stalin perpetrated, we must be convinced that Lenin's fears were justified. The negative characteristics of Stalin, which, in Lenin's time, were only incipient, transformed themselves during the last years into a grave abuse of power by Stalin, which caused untold harm to our Party.

We have to consider seriously and analyze correctly this matter in order that we may preclude any possibility of a repetition in any form whatever of what took place during the life of Stalin, who absolutely did not tolerate collegiality in leadership and in work, and who practiced brutal violence, not only toward everything which opposed him, but also toward that which seemed to his capricious and despotic character, contrary to his concepts.

Stalin acted not through persuasion, explanation, and patient co-operation with people, but by imposing his concepts and demanding absolute submission to his opinion. Whoever opposed this concept or tried to prove his viewpoint, and the correctness of his position, was doomed to removal from the leading collective and to subsequent moral and physical annihilation. This was especially true during the period following the XVIIth Party Congress, when many prominent Party leaders and rank-and-file

Party workers, honest and dedicated to the cause of Communism, fell victim to Stalin's despotism.

We must affirm that the Party had fought a serious fight against the Trotskyites, rightists and bourgeois nationalists, and that it disarmed ideologically all the enemies of Leninism. This ideological fight was carried on successfully, as a result of which the Party became strengthened and tempered. Here Stalin played a positive role.

The Party led a great political ideological struggle against those in its own ranks who proposed anti-Leninist theses, who represented a political line hostile to the Party and to the cause of Socialism. This was a stubborn and a difficult fight but a necessary one, because the political line of both the Trotskyite-Zinovievite bloc and of the Bukharinites led actually toward the restoration of capitalism and capitulation to the world bourgeoisie. Let us consider for a moment what would have happened if in 1928–1929 the political line of right deviation had prevailed among us, or orientation toward "cotton-dress industrialization," or toward the kulak, etc. We would not now have a powerful heavy industry, we would not have the Kolkhozes, we would find ourselves disarmed and weak in a capitalist encirclement.

*   *   *

Lenin's wisdom in dealing with people was evident in his work with cadres.

An entirely different relationship with people characterized Stalin. Lenin's traits—patient work with people; stubborn and painstaking education of them; the ability to induce people to follow him without using compulsion, but rather through the ideological influence on them of the whole collective—were entirely foreign to Stalin. He [Stalin] discarded the Leninist method of convincing and educating; he abandoned the method of ideological struggle for that of administrative violence, mass repressions, and terror. He acted on an increasingly larger scale and more stubbornly through punitive organs, at the same time often violating all existing norms of morality and of Soviet laws.

Arbitrary behavior by one person encouraged and permitted arbitrariness in others. Mass arrests and deportations of many thousands of people, execution without trial and without normal investigation created conditions of insecurity, fear and even desperation.

This, of course, did not contribute toward unity of the Party ranks and of all strata of working people, but on the contrary brought about annihilation and the expulsion from the Party of workers who were loyal but inconvenient to Stalin.

Our Party fought for the implementation of Lenin's plans for the construction of Socialism. This was an ideological fight. Had Leninist principles been observed during the course of this fight, had the Party's devotion to principles been skillfully combined with a keen and solicitous concern for people, had they not been repelled and wasted but rather drawn to our side—we certainly would not have had such a brutal violation of revolutionary legality and many thousands of people would not have fallen victim of the method of terror. Extraordinary methods would then have been resorted to only against those people who had in fact committed criminal acts against the Soviet system.

*   *   *

Lenin used severe methods only in the most necessary cases, when the exploiting classes were still in existence and were vigorously opposing the revolution, when the struggle for survival was decidedly assuming the sharpest forms, even including a civil war.

Stalin, on the other hand, used extreme methods and mass repressions at a time when the revolution was already victorious, when the Soviet state was strengthened, when the exploiting classes were already liquidated and Socialist relations were rooted solidly in all phases of national economy, when our Party was politically consolidated and had strengthened itself both numerically and ideologically. It is clear that here Stalin showed in a whole series of cases his intolerance, his brutality and his abuse of power. Instead of proving his political correctness and mobilizing the masses, he often chose the path of repression and physical annihilation, not only against actual enemies, but also against individuals who had not committed any crimes against the Party and the Soviet government. Here we see no wisdom but only a demonstration of the brutal force which had once so alarmed V. I. Lenin.

*   *   *

In practice Stalin ignored the norms of Party life and trampled on the Leninist principle of collective Party leadership.

Stalin's willfulness vis-a-vis the Party and its Central Committee became fully evident after the XVIIth Party Congress which took place in 1934.

Having at its disposal numerous data showing brutal willfulness toward Party cadres, the Central Committee had created a Party Commission under the control of the Central Committee Presidium; it was charged with investigating what made possible the mass repressions against the majority of the Central Committee members and candidates elected at the XVIIth Congress of the All-Union Communist Party (Bolsheviks).

The Commission has become acquainted with a large quantity of materials in the NKVD archives and with other documents and has established many facts pertaining to the fabrication of cases against Communists, to false accusations, to glaring abuses of Socialist legality—which resulted in the death of innocent people. It became apparent that many Party, Soviet and economic activists who were branded in 1937–1938 as "enemies," were actually never enemies, spies, wreckers, etc., but were always honest Communists; they were only so stigmatized, and often, no longer able to bear barbaric tortures, they charged themselves (at the order of the investigative judges—falsifiers) with all kinds of grave and unlikely crimes. The Commission has presented to the Central Committee Presidium lengthy and documented materials pertaining to mass repressions against the delegates to the XVIIth Party Congress and against members of the Central Committee elected at that Congress. These materials have been studied by the Presidium of the Central Committee.

It was determined that of the 139 members and candidates of the Party's Central Committee who were elected at the XVIIth Congress, 98 persons, i.e., 70 percent, were arrested and shot (mostly in 1937–1938). [*Indignation in the hall.*]

II. PROBLEMS OF THEORY *

New Stage in Communist Construction
and Some Problems of Marxist-Leninist Theory

Comrades! Now that our country has entered a new historical period of its development, special importance attaches to problems of Marxist-Leninist theory connected with the transition from socialism to communism.

First of all, the question of *the two phases of communist society—of*

---

* From speech of Khrushchev delivered at the Twenty-first Congress of the Communist Party, January 28, 1959. Reprinted from *Current Soviet Policies III,* ed. Leo Gruliow *et al.* (New York: Columbia University Press, 1960), pp. 64–69. Copyright by the Joint Committee on Slavic Studies, publisher of the *Current Digest of the Soviet Press,* New York.

the laws governing the evolution of socialism into communism—should be mentioned.

The founders of scientific communism—Marx, Engels and Lenin—indicated that, following the overthrow of capitalist and landlord domination, society would pass through two stages. The first would be socialism, and the second, higher stage would be a classless communist society.

The development of Soviet society has confirmed the Marxist-Leninist prediction of two phases of communism. Having built a socialist society, the Soviet people have entered a new period of historical development in which socialism grows into communism.

Marxist-Leninist theory and the practical experience of building socialist society provide grounds for some important conclusions concerning the nature of society's advance to communism.

First, the transition from the socialist stage of development to the higher phase is a logical historical process that one cannot arbitrarily violate or bypass. The Marxist-Leninist parties consider the building of communist society to be their ultimate goal. But society cannot leap from capitalism to communism, skipping the socialist stage of development. "From capitalism," said V. I. Lenin, "mankind can pass directly only to socialism, i.e., to public ownership of the means of production and the distribution of goods according to the work performed by each individual. Our party looks farther ahead: Inevitably, socialism must gradually turn into communism, upon the banner of which is inscribed the motto, 'from each according to his ability, to each according to his needs' " ["Works" (in Russian), Vol. XXIV, p. 62].

Of course, some comrades may say that the principles of communism should be introduced sooner. But to pass prematurely to distribution according to needs when the economic conditions for this have not yet been created, when an abundance of material goods has not yet been achieved and when people have not been prepared to live and work in a communist way would harm the cause of building communism. It must be borne in mind that with the present level of development of production there is still not enough to satisfy fully the requirements of all the people. Such "equalitarian communism" would only eat up accumulated funds and make impossible the further successful development of the economy and expanded production.

We must advance step by step, creating the material and spiritual requisites for a planned transition to communism.

Second, notwithstanding all the differences between communism and the socialist stage, there is no wall separating these two stages of social development. Communism grows out of socialism and is its direct continuation. It would be wrong, erroneous, to assume that communism will somehow appear suddenly. Communist forms of labor and industrial organization as well as such forms of satisfying the requirements of our people as public catering, boarding schools, kindergartens and day nurseries are already developing more and more widely. Our society has many tangible and visible communist features which will be developing and improving.

There is no calendar date marking the entry into communism. There will be no given moment at which we shall shut one door and announce: "The building of socialism is completed," then open another door and say: "We have now reached communism." The transition from socialism to communism is a continuous process. We are already opening the door to communist society, we are now engaged in building communism. Our country has now entered a period of extensive communist construction, one in which all the material and spiritual requirements for communism are being created. Communist construction will be completed when we shall have provided a complete abundance of everything needed to satisfy the requirements of all the people, when all the people learn to work according to their ability, so as to multiply and accumulate communal wealth.

Third, gradual transition to communism should not be understood as a slowed movement. On the contrary, it is a period of rapid development of modern industry and large-scale mechanized agriculture, rapid progress in all of the economy and culture with the active and conscious participation of the millions upon millions of builders of communist society. This law-governed evolution of socialism into communism can be accelerated on the basis of the high level of material production attained in the period of socialism. One cannot hurry and hastily introduce what is not yet ready for introduction. This would lead to distortions and to discrediting our work. But one cannot rest content with what has been achieved; this would lead to stagnation.

Is the time far off when it will be possible fully to satisfy the essential requirements of all Soviet persons? Evidently not so far off, considering our immense potentialities for increasing social production and raising the cultural standards of society. But this will be accomplished not all at once, but step by step; not by a single act, but progressively, as the material production conditions are prepared.

Full satisfaction, within necessary and reasonable limits, of all the Soviet people's requirements of food, housing and clothing can probably be attained in the near future. Not very much time is needed before, say, free lunches and dinners are provided for school children and all children can be accommodated in kindergartens, nurseries and boarding schools with full maintenance at the expense of society. As for the adult population, it must be borne in mind that man's requirements of means of existence are not limitless. A person cannot, for instance, consume more bread and other foods than his organism needs. There are also definite limits to the amounts of clothing and housing that can be used. Of course, when we speak of satisfying people's requirements, we have in mind not whims or claims to luxuries, but the wholesome consumption of a cultured person.

It will take a longer time for people to acquire the inner need to work in accordance with their abilities. As long as this is lacking, society cannot dispense with definite regulation of working time in order that every able-bodied person contribute a definite amount of labor to the production of the goods and services that the community needs.

Our country's basic practical task at this time is *to establish the material and technical base of communist society, to secure a great new expansion of socialist productive forces.*

Why is this now our principal task in economic development of the country? At the present level of socialist production we are still unable to create the full abundance of material goods and cultural benefits necessary to satisfy the growing requirements of our people, necessary for their full development. But communism is impossible without this. Consequently, it is necessary first of all to develop the productive forces further and to increase the production of goods. Communism can be achieved only if we surpass the level of production in the developed capitalist countries and raise labor productivity to a new level far above that of capitalism.

Creation of the material and technical base of communism presumes, first of all, a highly developed, modern industry, complete electrification of the country, scientific and technical progress in all branches of industry and agriculture, complex mechanization and automation of all production processes, maximum utilization of new power sources and of our wealth of natural resources, new synthetics and other materials, a higher cultural and technical level of all the working people, further improvement in the organization of production, and higher labor productivity.

It would be an oversimplification to assume that if we overtake the

United States economically, that will signify completion of communist construction. No, that is not the final limit of our advance, only a decisive stage in the competition with capitalism.

While competing with America, we do not regard America as our yardstick of economic development. Although the U.S.A. has a highly developed economy, the defective capitalist mode of production and distribution prevails there. Along with a profusion of every kind of goods, there are millions of unemployed and millions poorly provided for, who cannot satisfy their most elementary needs. The Communists do not want to imitate this order, but, on the contrary, to put an end to such injustice on earth. And if America's production level is taken as a yardstick for the growth of our economy, it is only in order to compare this economy with the most developed capitalist economy. When we win the economic competition with the U.S.A., we shall only have completed the first stage of communist construction. The level of economic development reached at this stage will not be the end of our road, but only a way station at which we shall be able to overtake the most highly developed capitalist country, leave it behind and push ahead. [*Stormy applause.*]

As our productive forces grow, socialist production relations, which are based on principles of comradely cooperation, friendship and mutual assistance of all the toilers of society, will be perfected. In our country social labor has already become the expression of new, socialist relationships among people and an index of the lofty moral qualities of man.

As socialist production develops further on a new material and technical base and as education is steadily more closely linked with work, the essential distinctions between mental and manual labor will gradually disappear. The rounded development of our people will turn into a prime need of man. The contemplated reduction of working hours and further improvement of working conditions will facilitate this. When all branches of industry are automated, when man becomes a commander of machines, he will have to spend less time and energy to produce the means of existence. Labor, which is now at times still arduous and tiring, will become a source of joy and pleasure for the healthy, rounded man.

In laying prime emphasis in the coming period on the creation of the material and technical base of communism we proceed completely from Marxism-Leninism and the experience of the Soviet Union and all the socialist countries.

The development of society presents another major problem of scientific communism, the problem of *distribution of society's material and cultural product among all of society's members.* Marxism—Leninism teaches that in social development distribution is not a determining but a derivative factor and that its forms and principles depend on the mode and volume of production.

In socialist society distribution is based in the main on the principle "from each according to his abilities, to each according to his labor." This means that the greatest part of the material and cultural product is distributed among society's members in accordance with their labor contribution to social production.

It must be borne in mind, of course, that even under socialism a considerable and ever increasing portion of the material and cultural product is distributed among the members of society independently of the quantity and quality of their work—that is, gratis. Society carries immense costs of free education, free health services, pensions, grants to large families, free club services, free libraries, etc. . . .

As we advance toward communism society's care of each individual from the cradle to old age will increase more and more.

At the present stage the chief yardstick of the share each citizen receives from society in the distribution of the social product is the quantity and quality of his labor. Lenin said "Until a higher phase of communism arrives, socialists demand the most *stringent* control by society *and by the state* over the amount of labor and the amount of consumption . . ." ["Works" (in Russian), Vol. XXV, p. 441].

The history of the development of our country included a period of "war communism," when we were temporarily obliged to depart from the principle of distribution according to work and adopt equalitarian "distribution according to the number of mouths." This was not due to abundance, but to an acute shortage of food and consumer goods. By the most stringent discipline in food distribution, the state was able to avert mass famine and to supply the fighters of the Red Army and the urban population with regular, if meager, rations, at times only an eighth of a pound of bread a day.

This method of distribution, however, could not be a normal economic system. Its defects became evident as soon as the country set about reconstruction and development of the economy. V. I. Lenin most directly stated then that, without a material stake for all personnel in the results of their work, the country's productive capacity could not be raised, a socialist economy could not be built and the millions of people could not be led toward communism.

With the change to peaceful construction, monetary pay for workers and employees was introduced. Its underlying principle was distribution according to work. With the triumph of the system of collective farming this principle of distribution was established in the collective-farm countryside as well.

In articles and lectures, some social scientists voice the view that distribution according to work signifies application of bourgeois law to socialist society. They ask whether the time has not come to shift from this principle to equalitarian distribution of the social product among all personnel. One cannot agree with this view.

True, Marx and Lenin spoke of survivals of "bourgeois law" that are inevitable under socialism, but what they had in mind was juridical forms which were left over from the old society and will disappear under communism.

Socialist distribution on the principle of equal pay for equal work means that one and the same legal yardstick is applied to different people. That single, equal yardstick is labor. Socialism excludes class inequality; there remains only the inequality of the share received in the distribution of goods. Inasmuch as different people have different skills, talents and working ability and different sized families, it is natural that with equal pay for equal work they have in fact unequal incomes. But this system is inevitable in the first phase of communist society.

We should not confuse legal forms with the substance of the social relationships which they express. Bourgeois law recognizes individual private ownership of the means of production, whereas socialism makes them public property and in this respect completely breaks with bourgeois law. Under socialism all people stand in equal relationship to the means of production and are paid according to their work. In socialist society the rule applying to all able-bodied members of society is: He who does not work, neither shall he eat.

Under capitalism distribution is in fact based not on work, but primarily on capital, and is regulated by the laws of value, profit and rent. For that reason greater income is received not by those who work more, but by those who have more capital.

As we see, there is a fundamental difference between capitalism and socialism in the distribution of the values produced.

The socialist principle of distribution according to work is based on the recognition that equalitarian distribution is impossible in the socialist period. Distribution according to work is the only reasonable and just principle under the given conditions. One cannot fail to see that leveling would lead to unjust distribution. The bad worker and the good one would receive an equal share, which would be to the advantage of the slackers only. The material incentive for people to work better, to raise productivity and produce more, would be undermined. Leveling would signify not transition to communism, but discrediting of communism.

Distribution according to work provides a material stake for people in the results of production, stimulates labor productivity, the acquisition of higher skills, and technical progress. It also performs an important educational function by accustoming people to socialist discipline and making labor universal and obligatory. In socialist society labor enthusiasm rises higher and higher and the moral incentives to work acquire even greater importance. Thanks to the material incentive, as a result of higher consciousness and through habit work becomes a vital inner need for the millions of working people of socialist society.

The need for regulating the distribution of goods among the members of society disappears only under communism, when the productive forces will have expanded so much that an abundance of all the necessary consumer goods will be attained and when all people, voluntarily and irrespective of the share of material goods that they receive, will work to the full of their ability, knowing that this is necessary for society.

Communist society will of course have a planned and organized allocation of labor among the various branches of production and social regulation of working time in accordance with the specific requirements of various production processes. Production by machine has a definite rhythm that is impossible without a corresponding scheduling of people's work.

Some persons have a vulgarized conception of communist society as a loose, unorganized, anarchic mass of people. No, it will be a highly organized and closely coordinated community of men of labor. Operation of machinery requires that each person perform his job and meet his social obligations at definite times and in definite ways. The highly mechanized and automated industry of the future will not require long hours of work; there will be a great deal of free time for study, art, literature, sports, etc.

The question of *the ways of developing and bringing closer together the collective-farm and public forms of socialist ownership* acquires great theoretical and practical importance in resolving the tasks of communist construction.

It is quite clear that in the future the collective-farm-cooperative and state forms of ownership will merge completely into a single form of communist ownership. Why, then, it may be asked, are we not pressing for their merger now, why do we consider that at the present stage it is necessary to develop collective-farm-cooperative ownership in every way, along with state ownership?

Forms of ownership are not changed arbitrarily, but develop on the basis of economic laws and depend on the nature and level of development of the productive forces. The collective-farm system fully accords with the present level and developmental requirements of today's productive forces in agriculture. It permits the most effective use of modern farm machinery, which is impossible with fragmented, small-scale peasant holdings. Now that powerful modern machinery is going directly to the collective farms, their communal output is increasing more rapidly.

Some branches of agriculture lagged in the recent past not because the collective-farm form hampered development of the productive forces, but because inadequate use was made of the potentialities and advantages offered by the collective-farm system. The successes achieved in agriculture in the past five years are most convincing evidence that the collective-farm-cooperative form of production relations, far from having exhausted its potentialities, serves and for a long time can continue to serve the development of agriculture's productive forces.

With the further development of the productive forces there will be a rise in the degree of socialization of collective-farm production, and collective-farm-cooperative ownership will come to approximate public ownership more closely; gradually the line dividing the two will be obliterated. . . .

Along with the problems of economic development, there likewise urgently arise *problems of the political organization of society, the state structure and government in the period of extensive building of communism.*

Marxism-Leninism teaches that under communism the state will wither away and that the functions of public administration will lose their political character and will turn into management of society's affairs directly by the people. But one cannot oversimplify and conceive of the process of the withering away of the agencies of state as something like the turning of leaves in autumn, when the branches are left bare as the leaves fall.

If we approach it dialectically, the question of withering away of the state is a question of evolution of the socialist state toward communist public self-government. Under communism, too, there will remain certain public functions similar to those now performed by the state, but their nature and the methods by which they will be accomplished will differ from those obtaining in the present stage.

The chief trend in the development of the socialist state is the utmost unfolding of democracy, the enlisting of the broadest strata of the population in the management of all affairs of the country, enlistment of all citizens in participation in the management of economic and cultural construction.

The Social-Democratic theoreticians and revisionists try every variation to discredit and vilify socialist democracy. In their view, "democratization" should mean renunciation of the leading role of the working class and its party under socialism, a return to the forms of bourgeois democracy. Without this, in their view, there is neither democracy nor socialism. To them democracy is the opportunity to engage in glittering parliamentary oratory, to play at political deals among the parties, to set up a flowery screen of "free elections" behind which capital is omnipotent and the people are actually disenfranchised. To us, democracy is genuine rule by the people, the fullest development of the initiative and activity of the masses of working people, self-government of the people. [*Applause.*]

It is already clear that many functions performed by government agencies will gradually pass to public organizations. Take, for instance, certain aspects of cultural services. It is not at all essential that they remain in the hands of government organizations. Public organizations can deal with them successfully.

Life suggests also that it is necessary to change the organization of health services and resort facilities. Evidently the conditions are ready for turning over more and more public health matters in the cities to the trade unions and in the countryside, at the present stage, directly to the local Soviets.

Up to now the physical culture movement in our country has been directed by a government agency, the Committee on Physical Culture and Sports. Now a more expedient structure for the physical culture movement has been formed; public organizations participating in this movement will play the decisive role in it. A Federation of Public Sports Societies, not a governmental but a public organization, is being set up.

Problems of enforcing public order and the rules of the socialist community should likewise come increasingly under the jurisdiction of public organizations. There are now no cases in the Soviet Union of people being tried for political crimes. This is undoubtedly a great achievement. It testifies to an unprecedented unity of political convictions of our entire people, to their solidarity with the Communist Party and Soviet government. [*Prolonged applause.*]

But there are still many instances of violation of public order, and a resolute struggle must be waged against them. Can the Soviet public cope with the violators of socialist law and order? Of course it can. Our public organizations have no less adequate capacities, means and forces for this than the militia, the courts and the Prosecutor's Office!

Matters are approaching a situation in which public organizations, alongside and parallel with such state agencies as the militia and the courts, will perform the functions of safeguarding public order and security. This process is now under way. The size of the militia has been sharply reduced; the state security agencies in particular have been considerably reduced.

Socialist society forms such voluntary organizations for safeguarding public order as the people's militia, comrades' courts, and the like. They all employ new methods and find new ways of performing public functions. The voluntary detachments of people's militia should undertake to keep public order in their respective communities and to see that the rights and interests of all citizens are respected and protected.

The time has come when more attention should be paid to the comrades' courts, which should seek chiefly to prevent assorted kinds of law violations. They should hear not only cases concerning behavior on the job but also cases of everyday deportment and morality, cases of improper conduct by members of the group who disregard the standards of social behavior.

When the comrades' public courts function actively, and the public itself delegates persons to ensure public order, it will be much easier to combat transgressors. It will be possible to spot a transgressor before he commits a misdemeanor or crime, when he first shows a departure from the standards of public behavior that might lead him into antisocial acts. People could exert timely influence on such a person to curb his evil propensities. Measures are required that will prevent and subsequently completely preclude individuals' commission of acts harmful to society. The chief thing is preventive, educational work.

Of course, definite functions will remain with the courts, the militia and the Prosecutor's Office. These agencies will continue to function in order to exert influence on persons who maliciously refuse to submit to socialist society's standards of behavior and are not amenable to persuasion.

The transfer of some functions of state agencies to public organizations should be carried out without undue haste. In some circumstances it should be done more resolutely; in others only the first, exploratory steps should be taken in order to accustom people to safeguard public order themselves. . . .

The tasks of the socialist state in safeguarding peace, in the sphere of defense against the threat of armed attack by the imperialist powers, are especially important and great. As long as the Western powers' aggressive military blocs exist, we are obliged to strengthen and improve our glorious Armed Forces, which stand guard over the great achievements and peaceful labor of the Soviet people. [*Stormy, prolonged applause.*] The state security agencies, which direct their spearhead primarily against agents sent into the country by imperialist states, must be strengthened, as must other agencies which have the mission of blocking the provocational actions and intrigues of our enemies from the imperialist camp. Our enemies are spending enormous sums on subversive work against the socialist countries. How, then, can we abolish agencies which have the duty of safeguarding the security of the socialist state! That would be foolish and criminal.

The Yugoslav revisionists criticize us for the fact that our party devotes great attention to strengthening the Soviet state, alleging that this does not accord with the Marxist-Leninist doctrine on the withering away of the state.

As I have already stated, we do not now have prisoners who have been jailed for political reasons. It would be a good thing if the Yugoslav leaders, who like to talk about the withering away of coercive agencies, were to release all the Communists now languishing in Yugoslav prisons for disagreeing with the new program of the League of Communists of Yugoslavia, for holding dissenting views on the building of socialism and the role of the Party. [*Stir in the hall. Stormy, prolonged applause.*]

Leninism teaches that the state will wither away with the complete triumph of communism. To weaken the socialist state in present conditions would be to help our enemies. The imperialists cannot crush us now, but the revisionists are inviting us, in effect, to disarm, abolish the state agencies that ensure defense of the country and thus leave ourselves to the mercy of our enemies. The functions of defending the socialist Fatherland, now performed by the state, can wither away only when the danger of an imperialist attack on our country or on countries allied with ours is completely removed.

Now that the building of socialism is no longer confined to one country and a world socialist system has been formed, *new theoretical problems of the struggle for the victory of socialism and communism* have arisen.

Not so long ago the Communist movement was facing and discussing the question of whether socialism could be built in one country separately, the question of its complete and final victory.

When the Soviet land had only just set about building socialism and when for many the country's path ahead was hidden in the mist of the future, V. I. Lenin opened up clear and broad vistas before the country. He said that we have ". . . everything necessary for building a complete socialist society" ["Works" (in Russian), Vol. XXXIII, p. 428]. Unswervingly guided by Lenin's instructions, the Soviet peeople, inspired by the Communist Party, worked perseveringly, amid the constant menace of armed attack by capitalist states, to build a socialist society; advanced along uncharted paths, and achieved the complete triumph of socialism in our country. [*Prolonged applause.*]

But this victory was not final. By the final victory of socialism Marxists mean its triumph on an international scale. Having built socialism, our country for a long time remained the world's only socialist state, in a hostile capitalist encirclement. It could not consider itself fully guaranteed against armed intervention and the danger of a forcible restoration of capitalism by international reaction. The capitalist states then surrounding the land of socialism were much stronger economically and militarily.

Now the world situation has changed fundamentally. The capitalist encirclement no longer exists for our country. There are two world social systems: capitalism, living out its day, and socialism, filled with growing, vital forces and enjoying the support of the working people of all lands. [*Applause.*]

The Soviet country, like any other socialist country, is not guaranteed against the possibility of aggression by the imperialist states. But the correlation of real forces in the world now is such that we shall be able to repel any attack by any enemy. [*Stormy applause.*]

There are no forces in the world now that could re-establish capitalism in our country or crush the socialist camp. The danger of capitalist restoration in the Soviet Union is ruled out. This means that *the triumph of socialism is not only complete but final.* [*Stormy, prolonged applause.*]

Thus it can be considered that the questions of building socialism in one country and its complete and final victory have been decided by the world-historic course of social development.

The victory of socialism in the USSR and the formation of the world socialist system immeasurably strengthen the forces of the international workers' movement and open up new vistas for it. The brilliant scientific prediction made by Vladimir Ilyich Lenin in his last pronouncement is now coming true. "In the final analysis," he said, "the outcome of the struggle will be determined by the fact that Russia, India, China, etc., represent the overwhelming majority of the population. And it is precisely this majority that in recent years has been drawn into the struggle for emancipation with extraordinary rapidity, so that in this sense there cannot be the slightest shadow of doubt about the final outcome of the world struggle. In this sense the final victory of socialism is fully and absolutely assured" ["Works" (in Russian), Vol. XXXIII, p. 458]. [*Stormy applause.*]

How will the further development of the socialist countries toward communism proceed? Can one imagine one of the socialist countries attaining communism and introducing the communist principles of production and distribution, while other countries are left trailing somewhere behind in the early stages of building socialist society?

This prospect is highly improbable if one takes into account the laws governing the economic development of the socialist system. From the theoretical standpoint it would be more correct to assume that by successfully employing the potentialities inherent in socialism, the socialist countries will enter the higher phase of communist society more or less simultaneously. We base ourselves on the fact that new laws of development, laws unknown to human society in the past, operate in the socialist economic system. For instance, the law operating under imperialism is that of uneven economic and political development of different countries. The course of development under that system is such that some countries push ahead at the expense of others and oppress and exploit these others. The ones that have pushed ahead take care to safeguard their privileged position so as to keep the backward countries in dependence and subjugation.

The law of planned, proportional development operates in the socialist economic system, with the result that formerly economically backward countries rapidly make up for lost time and raise their economic and cultural levels by drawing on the experience of other socialist countries and on cooperation and mutual assistance. Thus the common line of the economic and cultural development of all the socialist countries is evened out.

There is no doubt that, with the further growth and strengthening of the world socialist system, all the socialist countries will develop with in-

creasing success. The conditions necessary for the transition from the first
phase of communism to its second phase will be established at an increasingly faster pace in these countries. . . .

In surveying the prospect of mankind's advance to communism, we
must bear in mind the tremendous diversity of historical conditions in the
different countries. Hence inevitably there arises a diversity of methods,
ways and forms of applying the common laws of mankind's advance to
communism. But, for all this, it must be emphasized that the principal, determining aspect in the development of all countries along the path to communism is the laws common to all of them, not the particular ways in which
these laws are manifested. Marxism-Leninism requires the ability to apply
the theory of scientific communism to the specific conditions of each individual country at the various stages of its development.

The Yugoslav leaders talk a great deal now about the alleged fact that
the Communist Parties are speaking out against them because they, the
Yugoslav leaders, take as their starting point in building socialism the
features peculiar to their own country and do not follow the example and
experience of other socialist countries. That, of course, is a distortion of
the truth. The Marxist-Leninist parties recognize that each country has
its own specific features of development. But this does not mean that one
can reach socialism by some other road that lies to the side of the common
path indicated by Marxism-Leninism. The particular features of the situation and period in which one country or another is developing—these must
be taken into consideration. For example, some measures applied in socialist construction in the Soviet Union in the past cannot be mechanically
applied in other countries. All the socialist countries are building socialism,
but they do not do it by stereotype.

The Communist Party of China is employing many original forms of
socialist construction. But we have no disagreements with this party, nor
can there be any disagreements.

The Yugoslav revisionists are now concentrating their fire on the Chinese People's Republic, disseminating all sorts of inventions about alleged
differences between the Communist Parties of the Soviet Union and China.
As the Russian saying puts it, "the hungry man dreams of bread." The
revisionists are searching for discord among our Communist Parties, but
their illusory hopes are doomed to failure. [*Stormy, prolonged applause.*]
We are in full and complete agreement with the fraternal Communist Party
of China, although in many respects its methods of building socialism do
not resemble our own. We know that China has its specific features of his-

torical development, size of population, level of production and national culture. Therefore it would be a mistake to ignore these specific features and to copy what is good for one country but unsuitable for another.

Why have we no differences with the Communist Party of China? Because we share the same class approach and class conception. The Chinese Communist Party stands firmly on Marxist-Leninist class positions. It is waging a struggle against the imperialists and exploiters, a struggle to refashion life along socialist lines; it abides by the principle of international proletarian solidarity and is guided by Marxist-Leninist theory.

The chief thing is to maintain and strengthen class solidarity in the struggle against capitalism, for the liberation of the working class, for the building of socialism. And on this score there is no divergence, there are no conflicting conceptions, among Communists, nor can there be. This is the main point that divides us from revisionists. [*Stormy applause.*]

Questions of the methods and practice of socialist construction are the domestic affair of each individual country. We have no controversy with the Yugoslav leaders on the establishing of workers' councils or other matters of their domestic affairs. When the declaration of the conference of representatives of the Communist and Workers' Parties of the socialist countries was being signed, there were no arguments and no controversies on such matters.

One can say to the Yugoslav revisionists: Don't look for cracks where they don't exist. Presumably, you want to encourage yourselves and mislead the Yugoslav people by asserting that there are differences not only between us and you, but also between the Soviet Union and the Chinese People's Republic. It won't work. You will never see such differences, any more than you can see your own ears. [*Stir in the hall. Applause.*] The Communist Party of the Soviet Union and the Communist Party of China are doing everything to strengthen the friendship of the two great socialist countries. [*Stormy, prolonged applause.*]

For the international workers' movement, for the triumph of communism, the ideas of Marxism-Leninism have the same life-giving power as sunshine and warmth have for plants, for life on earth. As life itself is boundless in its progress, in its diverse manifestations, so Marxism-Leninism is limitless in its development and enrichment by new experience and new propositions.

MAO TSE-TUNG
1893-

MAO IS SOMETIMES COMPARED to Lenin in his application of Marxism to novel historical situations. Both came from families with petit bourgeois aspirations, and reached maturity during periods of turbid transition in the history of their homelands. Like Lenin, Mao channeled his personal energies into revolutionary struggle.

Mao was born of a poor peasant family in Hunan province. Reports of his early life suggest that he was treated harshly by his father and at school, where he studied modern subjects and the classics. He attended middle school at Changsha, where he became involved in "antiforeign-capital" movements. He joined Sun Yat-sen's revolutionary groups in 1911 and began to study modern Western writers—Darwin, Adam Smith, Spencer, Rousseau. Of his own thinking during his formative political years, he said: "At this time my mind was a curious mixture of ideas of liberalism, democratic reformism, and Utopian Socialism." He worked for a time as an assistant librarian in Peking University, and then returned to his own province to edit a small literary-political review.

Mao's public activities began in the early 1920's, when he helped to found the Chinese Communist party, and continued with increasing force in the following years. He was successively a trade union organizer, Kuomintang party bureaucrat, peasant union founder, and revolutionary army chief. He knew both how to set his course successfully, even against prevailing party opinion, and how to sacrifice his own personal life and that of others for the ends to which he was committed. In the late 1920's he developed a form of soviet government appropriate to rural guerrilla areas, and within two years he was elected chairman of the first All-China Congress of Soviets. From then until recently he was the master strategist and tactician for the Red Chinese Army and in the organization and administration of the new governments that were established.

Mao is known to have some poetic talents, which links him to the Chinese poet-warrior tradition. But perhaps his poetic imagination soars beyond political realities. His Faustian visions of communal collectives, thoroughly organized and "reclaimed" from a surrounding sea of hostile forces, have fallen short of success.

[28]   The People's Democratic Dictatorship

This date, the first of July 1949, shows that the CCP has passed through twenty-eight years. Like a man, it has its childhood, youth, manhood, and old age. The CCP is no longer a child, nor is it a youth in his teens; it is an adult. When a man reaches old age he dies; it is the same with a [political] party. When classes are eliminated, all the instruments of class struggle, political parties and the state apparatus, will, as a result, lose their functions, become unnecessary and gradually wither away; and their historical mission accomplished, [mankind] will move to a higher plan of human society. We are just the opposite of the political parties of the bourgeoisie. They are afraid to talk of the elimination of classes, state authority, and party, while we openly declare that we struggle hard precisely for the creation of prerequisites [which will] achieve the elimination of these things. The CP and the state authority of the people's dictatorship constitute such prerequisites. Anyone who does not recognize this truth is no Communist. Young comrades who have just joined the Party and have not read Marxism-Leninism may not yet understand this truth. They must understand this truth before they can have a correct world outlook. They must understand that all mankind have to go through the process of eliminating classes, state authority, and party; the question is only one of time and conditions. The Communists in the world are more intelligent than the bourgeoisie in that respect. They understand the law governing the existence and development of things. They understand dialectics and thus see farther ahead. The bourgeoisie do not welcome this truth because they do not want to be overthrown by the people. To be overthrown—as in the case of the KMT reactionaries who are being overthrown by us along with peoples of various countries in the past—is painful and is inconceivable to the persons overthrown. But for the working class, labouring people, and Communists, the question is not one of being overthrown but of working hard and creating

Reprinted by permission of the publishers from Conrad Brandt, Benjamin Schwartz, and John K. Fairbank, *A Documentary History of Chinese Communism* (Cambridge, Mass.: Harvard University Press, 1952), pp. 449–50, 451–53, 456–61.

conditions for the natural elimination of classes, state authority, and political parties, so that mankind will enter the era of universal fraternity. We have here touched on the perspectives of the progress of mankind in order to explain the following questions.

Our Party has passed through twenty-eight years. Everybody knows that [they were] not passed peacefully but amid difficult surroundings. We had to fight against enemies at home and abroad, and within and outside the Party. We owe thanks to Marx, Engels, Lenin, and Stalin, who gave us weapons. These weapons are not machine-guns but Marxism-Leninism.

Lenin in his book *"Left Wing" Communism—An Infantile Disorder*, written in 1920, described how the Russians sought for revolutionary theory. After several decades of hardships and tribulations they eventually discovered Marxism. There are many things which are the same or similar between China and Russia before the October Revolution. The feudal oppression was the same. The economic and cultural backwardness was similar. Both countries were backward, China even more backward. Progressive people endured hardships and struggled to seek the revolutionary truth, so as to bring about national recovery; this was the same [in both countries].

*   *   *

OCTOBER REVOLUTION AND CHINA

Imperialist aggression shattered the Chinese dream of learning from the West. They wondered why the teachers always practised aggression against their pupils. The Chinese learned much from the West, but what they learned could not be put into effect. Their ideals could not be realized. [Many struggles, including the Revolution of 1911, had all failed.] Meanwhile, conditions in the country worsened day by day, and the environment was such that the people could not live. Doubt sprang up, it grew and developed. The First World War shook the whole world. The Russians carried out the October Revolution, creating the first socialist country in the world. Under the leadership of Lenin and Stalin the revolutionary energy of the great Russian proletariat and labouring people, which had lain hidden and could not be seen by foreigners, suddenly erupted like a volcano. The Chinese and all mankind then began to look differently at the Russians. Then, and only then, did there appear for the Chinese an entirely new era both in ideology and in living. The Chinese found the universal truth of Marxism-Leninism which holds good everywhere, and the face of China was changed.

It was through the introduction of the Russians that the Chinese found Marxism. Before the October Revolution the Chinese not only did not know Lenin and Stalin, but also did not know Marx and Engels. The gunfire of the October Revolution sent us Marxism-Leninism. The October Revolution helped the progressive elements of the world and of China to use the world outlook of the proletariat as the instrument for perceiving the destiny of the country, and for reconsidering their own problems. Travel the road of the Russians—this was the conclusion. In 1919, the May Fourth movement took place in China, and the CCP was formed in 1921. In his moment of despair Sun Yat-sen came across the October Revolution and the CCP. He welcomed the co-operation of the CCP; Sun Yat-sen died [March, 1925] and Chiang Kai-shek came into power. During the long period of twenty-two years [since 1927] Chiang Kai-shek has dragged China into hopeless straits.

During this period the anti-fascist Second World War, with the Soviet Union as its main force, defeated three big imperialist powers, weakened two other big imperialist powers, leaving only one imperialist country in the world—the United States of America, which suffered no loss. However, the domestic crisis in America is very grave. She wants to enslave the entire world and she aided Chiang Kai-shek with arms to slaughter several millions of Chinese. Under the leadership of the CCP, the Chinese people, after having driven away Japanese imperialism, fought the people's war of liberation for three years and gained a basic victory. Thus the civilization of the Western bourgeoisie, the bourgeois democracy, and the pattern of the bourgeois republic all went bankrupt in the minds of the Chinese people. Bourgeois democracy has given way to the people's democracy under the leadership of the proletariat, and the bourgeois republic has given way to the people's republic. A possibility has thus been created of reaching socialism and Communism through the people's republic, of attaining the elimination of classes and universal fraternity. K'ang Yu-wei wrote the book *On Universal Fraternity* [*Ta-t'ung shu*], but he did not, and could not, find the road to it. The bourgeois republic has existed in foreign countries but cannot exist in China, because China is a country oppressed by imperialism. The only [way for us] is to travel the road of the people's republic under the leadership of the proletariat and attain the elimination of classes and universal fraternity.

THE BIRTH OF THE COMMUNIST PARTY

All other things had been tried and had failed. Of those who yearned for other things, some had fallen, some had awakened to their mistake, and others are in the process of changing their minds. Events developed so swiftly that many people felt surprised and the need to learn anew. This state of mind is understandable, and we welcome such a well-intentioned attitude, that asks to learn things anew.

Having learnt Marxism-Leninism after the October Revolution, the vanguard of the Chinese proletariat established the CCP. Following this, it entered into the political struggle and had to travel a zigzag path for twenty-eight years before it could gain a basic victory. From the experiences of twenty-eight years, just as from the "experiences of forty years" as Sun Yat-sen said in his will, a common conclusion has been reached, namely: "The firm belief that to attain victory we must awaken the masses of the people and unite ourselves in a common struggle with those peoples of the world who treat us on the basis of equality" [quoted from Sun's famous testament]. Sun Yat-sen had a different world outlook from us, and started out from a different class standpoint in observing and dealing with problems, but in the twenties of the twentieth century, on the problem of how to struggle against imperialism, he arrived at a conclusion which was fundamentally in agreement with ours.

Twenty-four years have elapsed since Sun Yat-sen's death, and under the leadership of the CCP, Chinese revolutionary theory and practice have made big forward strides, fundamentally changing the realities of China. Up to the present, the Chinese people have gained the following two major and basic [lessons from] experiences: (1) [We must] awaken the masses in the country. This is to unite the working class, the peasant class, the petty bourgeoisie, and national bourgeoisie into a national united front under the leadership of the working class, and develop it into a state of the people's democratic dictatorship led by the working class with the alliance of workers and peasants as its basis. (2) [We must] unite in a common struggle with those nations of the world who treat us on the basis of equality and with the people of all countries. This is to ally ourselves with the Soviet Union, to ally ourselves with all the New Democratic countries, and to ally ourselves with the proletariat and the broad masses of the people in other countries, to form an international united front.

PEOPLE'S DEMOCRATIC DICTATORSHIP

"You are dictatorial." Dear sirs, you are right; that is exactly what we are. The experience of several decades, amassed by the Chinese people, tells us to carry out the people's democratic dictatorship. That is, the right of reactionaries to voice their opinions must be abolished and only the people are allowed to have the right of voicing their opinions.

Who are the "people"? At the present stage in China, they are the working class, the peasant class, the petty bourgeoisie, and national bourgeoisie. Under the leadership of the working class and the CP, these classes unite together to form their own state and elect their own government [so as to] carry out a dictatorship over the lackeys of imperialism—the landlord class, the bureaucratic capitalist class, and the KMT reactionaries and their henchmen representing these classes—to suppress them, allowing them only to behave properly and not talk and act wildly. If they talk and act wildly their [action] will be prohibited and punished immediately. The democratic system is to be carried out within the ranks of the people, giving them freedom of speech, assembly, and association. The right to vote is given only to the people and not to the reactionaries. These two aspects, namely, democracy among the people and dictatorship over the reactionaries, combine to form the people's democratic dictatorship.

Why should it be done this way? Everybody clearly knows that otherwise the revolution would fail, and the people would meet with woe and the State would perish.

"Don't you want to eliminate state authority?" Yes, but we do not want it at present, we cannot want it at present. Why? Because imperialism still exists, the domestic reactionaries still exist, and classes in the country still exist. Our present task is to strengthen the apparatus of the people's state, which refers mainly to the people's army, people's police, and people's courts, for the defence of the country, and the protection of the people's interests; and with this as a condition, to enable China to advance steadily, under the leadership of the working class and the CP, from an agricultural to an industrial country, and from a New Democratic to a Socialist and Communist society, to eliminate classes and to realize the state of universal fraternity. The army, police, and courts of the state are instruments by which classes oppress classes. To the hostile classes the state apparatus is the instrument of oppression. It is violent, and not "benevolent." "You are not benevolent." Just so. We decidedly will not exercise benevolence towards the reactionary acts of the reactionaries and reactionary classes. Our benevolence applies only to the people, and not to the reactionary acts of the reactionaries and reactionary classes outside the people.

The (function of the) people's state is to protect the people. Only when there is the people's state, is it possible for the people to use democratic methods on a nationwide and all-round scale to educate and reform themselves, to free themselves from the influence of reactionaries at home and abroad (this influence is at present still very great and will exist for a long time and cannot be eliminated quickly), to unlearn the bad habits and ideas acquired from the old society and not to let themselves travel on the erroneous path pointed out by the reactionaries, but to continue to advance and develop towards a Socialist and Communist society accomplishing the historic mission of completely eliminating classes and advancing towards a universal fraternity.

The methods we use in this field are democratic; that is, methods of persuasion and not coercion. When people break the law they will be punished, imprisoned, or even sentenced to death. But these are individual cases and are different in principle from the dictatorship over the reactionary class as a class.

FUTURE OF THE REACTIONARIES

After their political régime is overthrown the reactionary classes and the reactionary clique will also be given land and work and a means of living; they will be allowed to re-educate themselves into new persons through work, provided they do not rebel, disrupt, or sabotage. If they are unwilling to work, the people's state will compel them to work. Propaganda and educational work will also be carried out among them, and, moreover, with care and adequacy, as we did among captured officers. This can also be called "benevolent administration," but we shall never forgive their reactionary acts and will never let their reactionary activity have the possibility of a free development.

Such re-education of the reactionary classes can only be carried out in the state of the people's democratic dictatorship. If this work is well done the main exploiting classes of China—the landlord and bureaucratic capitalist classes—will be finally eliminated. [Of the exploiting classes] there remain the national bourgeoisie among many of whom appropriate educational work can be carried out at the present stage. When socialism is realized, that is, when the nationalization of private enterprises has been carried out, they can be further educated and reformed. The people have in their hands a powerful state apparatus and are not afraid of the rebellion of the national bourgeois class.

The grave problem is that of educating the peasants. The peasants' economy is scattered. Judging by the experience of the Soviet Union, it requires a very long time and careful work to attain the socialization of agriculture. Without the socialization of agriculture, there will be no complete and consolidated socialism. And to carry out the socialization of agriculture a powerful industry with state-owned enterprises as the main component must be developed. The state of the people's democratic dictatorship must step by step solve this problem [of the industrialization of the country]. The present article does not intend to deal with the economic problem, so I shall not discuss it in detail.

In 1924 a well-known manifesto was passed by the KMT First National Congress, which was directed personally by Sun Yat-sen and participated in by Communists. The manifesto stated: "The so-called democratic system in countries of modern times is often monopolized by the bourgeois class and turned into an instrument for oppressing the common people. But the democracy of the KMT belongs to the people in general and is not the private possession of a few." Except for the question of who is to lead whom, the democracy mentioned here, when viewed as a general political programme, is consistent with the people's democratic dictatorship practised at present by us. [If to the state system, which is only allowed to be the common possession of the common people and not the private possession of the bourgeoisie, is added the leadership of the working class, this state system is that of the people's democratic dictatorship.]

Chiang Kai-shek betrayed Sun Yat-sen and used the dictatorship of the bureaucratic capitalist class and the landlord class as an instrument for oppressing the common people of China. This counter-revolutionary dictatorship remained in force for twenty-two years, and not until now has it been overthrown by the Chinese common people under our leadership.

DICTATORSHIP AND TOTALITARIANISM

The foreign reactionaries who vilify us for carrying out "dictatorship" and "totalitarianism" are in fact the very people who are carrying out dictatorship and totalitarianism of one class, the bourgeoisie, over the proletariat and other people. They are the very people referred to by Sun Yat-sen as the bourgeois class in countries of modern times who oppress the common people. Chiang Kai-shek's counter-revolutionary dictatorship was learnt from these reactionary fellows.

Chu Hsi, a philosopher of the Sung dynasty [A.D. 960–1260], wrote many books and said many things which we have forgotten, but there is one sentence we have not forgotten and this is "Apply to anyone the method he has first used on others." This is what we are doing. That is, to apply to imperialism and its lackeys, the Chiang Kai-shek reactionary clique, the same method with which they treated others. Simply this and nothing else!

The revolutionary dictatorship and the counter-revolutionary dictatorship are opposite in nature. The former learns from the latter. This process of learning is very important, for if the revolutionary people do not learn the methods of ruling over counter-revolutionaries, they will not be able to maintain their régime, which will be overthrown by the reactionary cliques at home and abroad. The reactionary cliques at home and abroad will then restore their rule in China and bring woe to the revolutionary people.

The basis of the people's democratic dictatorship is the alliance of the working class, peasant class, and the urban petty-bourgeois class, and is mainly the alliance of the working class and the peasant class because they constitute eighty to ninety per cent of the Chinese population. It is mainly through the strength of these two classes that imperialism and the KMT reactionary clique were overthrown. The passing from New Democracy to Socialism mainly depends on the alliance of these two classes.

THE LEADERSHIP OF THE WORKING CLASS

The people's democratic dictatorship needs the leadership of the working class, because only the working class is most far-sighted, just and unselfish and endowed with revolutionary thoroughness. The history of the entire revolution proves that without the leadership of the working class, the revolution is bound to fail, and with the leadership of the working class, the revolution is victorious. In the era of imperialism no other class in any country can lead any genuine revolution to victory. This is clearly proved by the fact that the Chinese national bourgeoisie had led the revolution many times and each time had failed.

The national bourgeoisie is of great importance at the present stage. Imperialism is still standing near us and this enemy is very fierce. A long time is required for China to realize true economic independence and become free from reliance on imperialist nations. Only when China's industries are developed, and she no longer depends economically on powerful nations, can there be real independence. The proportion of China's modern industry in the entire national economy is still very small. There are still no reliable figures at present, but according to certain data it is estimated that modern industry only occupies about ten per cent of the total productive output in the national economy of the whole country. To cope with imperialist oppression, and to raise our backward economic status one step higher, China must utilize all urban and rural factors of capitalism which are beneficial and not detrimental to the national economy and the people's livelihood, and unite with the national bourgeoisie in a common struggle. Our present policy is to restrict capitalism and not to eliminate it. But the national bourgeoisie cannot be the leader of the revolutionary united front and should not occupy the main position of state power. This is because the social and economic status of the national bourgeoisie has determined its feebleness; it lacks foresight, lacks courage, and in large part fears the masses.

Sun Yat-sen advocated "awakening the masses" or "helping the peasants and workers." Who is to awaken and help them? Sun Yat-sen meant the petty bourgeoisie and the national bourgeoisie. But this is in fact not feasible. Sun Yat-sen's forty years of revolutionary work was a failure. Why? The reason lies precisely here, in that in the era of imperialism it is impossible for the bourgeoisie to lead any true revolution towards success.

Our twenty-eight years are entirely different. We have plenty of invaluable experience. A party with discipline, armed with the theories of Marx, Engels, Lenin, and Stalin, employing the method of self-criticism, and linked up closely with the masses; an army led by such a party; a united front of various revolutionary strata and groups led by such a party; these three are our main (lessons of) experience. They all mark us off from our predecessors. Relying on these three things, we have won a basic victory. We have traversed torturous paths and struggled against rightist and leftist opportunistic tendencies within the Party. Whenever serious mistakes were committed in these three matters, the revolution suffered set-backs. The mistakes and set-backs taught us and made us wiser. Thus we were able to do better work. Mistakes are unavoidable for any party or person, but we ask that fewer mistakes be committed. When a mistake is committed, correction must be made, the quicker and the more thoroughly the better.

FIRST STEP OF THE 10,000-MILE MARCH

Our experience may be summarized and boiled down into one single thing, namely, the people's democratic dictatorship based on the alliance of workers and peasants led by the working class [through the CP]. [This dictatorship must unite in concert with international revolutionary forces.] This is our formula, our main experience, our main programme.

In the twenty-eight long years of the Party we have done only one thing, and that is, we have won the basic victory. This is worth celebrating, because it is the people's victory and a victory in a large country like China. But there is plenty of work before us, and, as on a march, what work has been done in the past is like the first step on a ten-thousand-mile long march. Remnants of the enemy have still to be wiped out, and the grave task of economic reconstruction still lies before us. Some of the things with which we are familiar will soon be laid aside, and we are compelled to tackle things with which we are unfamiliar. This means difficulty. The imperialists are positive that we are incapable of tackling our economic work. They look on and wait for our failure.

We must overcome difficulties, and must master what we do not know. We must learn economic work from all who know the ropes [no matter who they are]. We must acknowledge them as our teachers, and learn from them respectfully and earnestly. We must acknowledge our ignorance, and not pretend to know what we do not know, nor put on bureaucratic airs. Stick to it, and eventually it will be mastered in a few months, one or two years, or three or five years. At first some of the Communists in the U.S.S.R. also did not know how to do economic work, and the imperialists also waited for their failure. But the CP of the Soviet Union won. Under the leadership of Lenin and Stalin they not only could do revolutionary work but also reconstruction work. They have already built up a great and brilliant socialist state. The CP of the U.S.S.R. is our best teacher from whom we must learn. [The international and domestic situation is favourable to us.] We can rely wholly on the weapon of the people's democratic dictatorship to unite all people throughout the country, except the reactionaries, and advance steadily towards the goal.

HERBERT MARCUSE
1898-

HERBERT MARCUSE, A DISTINGUISHED political philosopher whose
work ranges over the boundaries of philosophy, sociology, psychology, and politics, has shown that the traditional borderlines between the
separate disciplines and politics "have been made obsolete by the condition of
man in the present era." Formerly autonomous areas of private existence, he
argues, are being absorbed by public existence.

Educated at the universities of Berlin and Freiburg, he has been one of
the inner circle of the Institute of Social Research (New York and Frankfurt).
He has worked as a research fellow in the Russian Institute at Columbia University and in the Russian Research Center at Harvard, lectured at both universities, and at present is Professor of Politics and Philosophy at Brandeis
University. He is the co-author of *Studies in Authority and the Family* and
the author of *Hegel's Ontology,* both in German. In English he has written
Reason and Revolution (1941), a significant work on the development of social theory since Hegel, and *Eros and Civilization* (1955), an inquiry into the
relationship between psychoanalysis and the institutions of contemporary society. He is working on a new book on the patterns of thought and behavior
in advanced industrial societies.

[29]   *Transition from Socialism to Communism*

We have seen that, in the Stalinist conception, the disappearance of the
state as repressive machinery is made conditional on the strengthening of

From Herbert Marcuse, *Soviet Marxism* (New York: Columbia University Press,
1958), pp. 179–91. Reprinted by permission.

the socialist state, and that the latter is to continue into the second phase. There are no indications that this conception has been altered since Stalin's death. Although Stalin's "erroneous formula" on the aggravating class struggle during the progress of socialism is rejected, although a considerable "democratization" of the state, decentralization, and self-government is proclaimed and even implemented, the continued strengthening of the state and of the party agencies remains on the agenda. Nor—and this is far more important—are there any objective factors or tendencies which would allow such alteration. The reorientation in international strategy, and the corresponding domestic reorientation, especially in the field of agriculture, confront the regime with problems of such a magnitude that intense regimentation from above seems to be required for the very success of the new efforts. Relaxation no less than hardening of the system necessitates planned control. The gulf, in terms of privileges and of power, between the bureaucracy and the underlying population is still great enough to make for the self-perpetuation of the former. Moreover, education and training of the people are geared to a well-functioning mass of competitive subjects of administration. According to the doctrine itself, the very nature of the state as an independent power over and above the individuals must sustain the separation of the "immediate producers" from control over the means of production: social unfreedom reproduces political unfreedom. The trend we have suggested is toward alleviating the latter; but only if it affects the former, or, in Stalin's terminology, only if the contradictions between the growing productive forces and the production relations have really been solved, would the entire structure change. This solution is reserved for the "final victory of socialism," and the "final" victory of socialism is still linked to the international revolution. In this respect, the initiative in the turn toward the "withering away" of the state is not with the Soviet leadership—the turn depends on the break in the "capitalist environment" and its effects on Soviet society.

The sustained power of the state sustains the controls over the ideological sphere. The relaxation might be considerable; individual liberties are likely to increase with increasing economic benefits—but quantity will not turn into quality unless the economic benefits have themselves become political ones, that is to say, have led to the control of production by the "immediate producers," or, according to the progress of automation, by the "immediate consumers." As long as this is not the case, the post-Stalinist welfare state will remain the direct heir of the Stalinist state. And for just as long, the basic "spirit" of socialism will remain the same. Soviet society in this case pays tribute to the dialectic of ideology and reality, consciousness and societal relations. According to this dialectic, a genuinely socialist base is reflected in an ideology which is *free* in a strict sense. The mental development in all its manifestations is freed from the blind determination by the "realm of necessity" and tends toward a free play of humane individual faculties. Materialism is canceled through its realization; as the economy is brought under the control of the associated individuals whose material needs are fulfilled, their mental development is released from control. The rational regulation of the necessities, of the struggle for existence and the struggle with nature, enables society to dispense with the regulation of the instinctual and intellectual life of its members. Reason appears as individual freedom. In Soviet society, however, the progressing control of the base continues to be accompanied by a progressing control of the ideology, and by the regulation of the realm of freedom gained by conquest of the necessity. In the very passage where Stalin calls for the reduction of the working day "at least to six and then to five hours" (a measure in which Marx saw the basic prerequisite for freedom), he states that this reduction is necessary "in order that members of society may receive the leisure time necessary for a thorough education." Thus the time saved will not be *free* time—it will have to be spent in education.

To be sure, education is the prerequisite for liberation: only the freedom to learn and to know the whole truth, to grasp the arrested, violated, and destroyed potentialities of man and nature can guide the building of a free society. What kind of education did Stalin envisage? He demanded the introduction of "universal, compulsory, polytechnical education, so that a member of society may be able to make a free choice of occupation and not be shackled for life to any one occupation." Following up this program, the Twentieth Congress again places all emphasis on "training"—the training of "specialists on the basis of a close cooperation between studies and production" and calls for "strengthening the ties of the country's scientific establishments with production, with the concrete demands of the national economy." The exchangeability of functions, the elimination of the institutionalized division of labor, is indeed in Marxian theory the characteristic of a socialist society—as a precondition for the all-sided development of the genuinely human faculties *outside* the process of material production. But in Stalin's context the Marxian idea appears as that of a society in which all men are technicians and engineers. For Marx and Engels, the goal of communism was the "abolition of labor," in the Soviet Marxist conception, all will be laborers of the one communist society. With the free time transformed into education time for polytechnical training, with the work morale anchored in the instinctual structure of man, administrative control is secured, and the past is safely transferred into the future. Stalin could thus quote without danger Engels's statement that labor will change from a burden into enjoyment. The enjoyment, however, will not be qualitatively different from that permitted under repression.

The ideological perspective parallels the political perspective. The state will continue into the period of communism—as will the "capitalist environment." For the state is the "collective subject" of the national economy which organizes the whole of society, and this organization has become the objectified representative of society over and above the individuals. Since societal production is systematically directed by the state and since the basic decisions are imposed upon the society by the state, progress itself, that is to say, the use of the growing productivity for the needs and aspirations of the individuals, must pass through the agencies of the state. The continuity of the administration thus bridges the gap between necessity and freedom, and assimilates the first and the second phase, socialism and communism. And the administration, as we have tried to show, depends on the ever more effective growth and utilization of the productivity of labor: it tends to drive society to a higher stage. Industrialization and rationalization, carried through according to standards of competitive efficiency at the national and international level, and developing human beings as ever better functioning instruments of material and intellectual labor, are likely to bear economic as well as political fruits—overruling the diverging interests and intentions of particular groups and individuals.

The reward will not be the end of domination of man by man; administration of things is not likely to replace the administration of men in any foreseeable future. Marx stressed the essentially "neutral" character of technology: although the windmill may give you a feudal society, and the steammill an industrial capitalist society, the latter may just as well give you another form of industrial society. Modern machinery is susceptible to capitalist as well as socialist utilization. This amounts to saying that mature capitalism and socialism have the same *technical* base, and that the historical decision as to how this base is to be used is a *political* decision. During the period of coexistence, the economic factors are political factors; it is the period of political economy with respect not only to the state's role in the economy, but also to the political implications of the development of consciousness. The consciousness of the underlying population, permeated with the power of ever growing productivity, with the efficiency of an ever better mechanized and coordinated apparatus, and with the rewards of an ever more indispensable compliance, does not attain any other political level than that of the apparatus itself. Thus it is barred from developing the political consciousness which may serve as a guide to political change.

The two antagonistic social systems here join in the general trend of technical progress. It has been noted . . . how much the present "communist spirit" resembles the "capitalist spirit" which Max Weber attributed to the rising capitalist civilizations. The Soviet state seems to foster the disciplining, self-propelling, competitive-productive elements of this spirit in a streamlined and politically controlled form. "Businesslike management," directorial initiative and responsibility, and scientific rationalization of the human and material resources have remained the consistently imposed demands throughout both the Stalinist and post-Stalinist period, in times of both "hard" and "soft" policy, of both personal and collective leadership. And "businesslike management" has also been applied to grand international strategy, to the conduct of foreign affairs. The change in the type of leader, from the professional revolutionary to the manager (a change which began as early as 1922, with the development of the New Economic Policy), now seems to be consummated. In 1922 Lenin proclaimed preference for the merchant, the trader, the administrator over the loyal revolutionary communist who did not know how to trade, how to sell, how to do business. He went further than that: "We are not afraid to say that the character of our work has changed. Our worst internal enemy is the Communist who occupies a responsible (or not responsible) Soviet post and enjoys universal respect as a conscientious man."

However, the spirit of businesslike politics and competitive efficiency in the twentieth century is no longer that described by Max Weber. Developed industrial society requires a different organization and a different behavior. Soviet society, in the position of a "latecomer" telescoping entire phases of growth, meets its antagonist in a common situation. At the "atomic" stage of the mastery of man and nature, societal productivity surpasses the traditional forms of control and utilization. The cohesion of society is no longer left to the free play of economic forces and their individual evaluation and calculation; they have to be supplemented by more powerful regulation. The fusion between economic, cultural, and political controls is an international phenomenon, cutting across differences in economic, cultural, and political institutions. In the Soviet Union, this fusion is an avowed ideological as well as economic goal: at the very time when

Soviet industry is again to be revamped in accordance with the standards of business efficiency, the government emphasized that this program is to be implemented by strengthening the "industrial leadership" of the Communist Party!

There is no prospect that this fusion of economic and political controls in a self-perpetuating state will dissolve; it is doubly grounded, in the nationalized but not socialized Soviet economy, and in the international situation of large-scale industry. This framework of the state leaves room for many changes within the administration: the top rule may pass from one group to the other, from party to army predominance, from "committee rule" back to personal rule, and so forth. However, these changes would not fundamentally alter the basis of Soviet society, nor the basic direction in which this society is moving. Unless another world war or similar catastrophe occurs which would change the situation, the direction is toward a growing welfare state. Rising standards of living up to a practically free distribution of basic goods and services, steadily extending mechanization of labor, exchangeability of technical functions, expanding popular culture —these developments constitute the probable trend. It is likely to lead to the gradual assimilation of urban and agricultural, intellectual and physical labor—brought under the common denominator of technology. Technical progress will overtake the repressive restrictions imposed at earlier stages —they will become technically obsolete. This will lead to further changes in the political structure: it will make for a spread of the bureaucracy and its privileges, for a reduction of the gap between the top strata and the underlying population, for the transformation of political into technological controls. Personal rule will increasingly be replaced by collective administration, even if a new dictator should concentrate the leadership at the top. Social mobility within the system will grow. But these changes themselves will take place within the framework of universal control, universal administration. Whether or not the growth of the welfare state will ultimately bring the administration under direct popular control, that is to say, whether or not the Soviet state will develop into a socialist or communist democracy, is a question for which the prevailing facts and tendencies do not provide a workable hypothesis. Negatively, it seems that nothing in the structure of Soviet society would exclude such a long-range development, and that it would depend neither on a "decision" of the Soviet leadership nor on the internal situation of the Soviet orbit alone. From our analysis, it follows that the emergence of a socialist democracy in the USSR would be conditional upon two main prerequisites, which in turn are interrelated:

(1) a level of social wealth which would make possible the organization of production according to individual needs and thus cancel the prerogatives of privileged powers; and (2) an international situation in which the conflict between the two social systems would no longer define their economy and their policy.

We have suggested that such qualitative change is no longer an economic but a political problem: the technical-economic basis for the change is there. It is not the still terrifying scarcity and poverty which prevents "socialist democracy," that is, the control of production and distribution "from below." In Marxist terms, distribution of scarcity and the concerted struggle for its abolition pertain to the content of socialism from the very beginning—even during the first phase. On the basis of the nationalized economy, establishment of this control remains a political act. As such, it involves the abolition of the repressive state and its repressive machinery —which does not necessarily mean violent overthrow in civil war. However, the political act itself seems to be dependent on the second prerequisite. The rising welfare state may render life more comfortable and more secure, but as long as the East-West conflict remains a determining economic and political factor, it precludes the decisive transformation, for it serves to justify—subjectively and objectively—repressive competition and competitive mobilization on a totalitarian scale. The history of Soviet society seems to be fatefully linked to that of its antagonist. Over and above the construction of socialism or communism in one country and in one orbit, the essentially international element of socialism seems to prevail.

But in this constellation, the prospective development of the Soviet state stands under the dialectical law which it invokes. The qualitative change can never be envisaged as an automatic one. No matter how high the level of technical progress and material culture, of labor productivity and efficiency, the change from socialist necessity to socialist freedom can only be the result of conscious effort and decision. The maintenance of repressive production relations enables the Soviet state, with the instrumentalities of universal control, to regiment the consciousness of the underlying population. We have suggested that the bureaucracy may not have a vested interest in perpetuating the repressive state machinery. However, this does not dispose of the question as to whether or not the "spirit" of Soviet socialist construction, the specific "rationality" of the system, tends to perpetuate repression by and in the underlying population itself—in other words, whether repression from above does not meet repression from below. The Soviet system would then repeat and reproduce that determinism which Marx attributed to the basic processes of capitalist society. There, Marxian theory and practice themselves were to be the lever which would break this determinism and free the subjective factor, that is, the class consciousness of the proletariat. We have tried to show that, in Soviet society, Marxism no longer has this function. Left without a conceptual level for the "determinate negation" of the established system, for comprehending and realizing its arrested potentialities, the ruled tend not only to submit to the rulers but also to reproduce in themselves their subordination. Again, this process is not specific to Soviet society. The means and rewards of highly advanced industrial society, the work and leisure attitudes called forth by its organization of production and distribution, establish a human existence which makes for a change in basic values—for a transformation of freedom into security. Such a transformation in turn would counteract the development of a "negative" political consciousness and thus counteract qualitative political change. The basic value system, the prevalent "spirit" of the society, would then assume the role of an active factor determining the direction of the societal development. . . .

VI

Democracy reconsidered

THE SOCIAL THOUGHT of the late-modern period was full of
speculation about the future of democracy. Ranging from scientific plans to poetic images, democratic vistas were rich in adventure and
new possibilities. Today, in contrast, one is struck by the narrow span of
alternatives presented by contemporary writers. The realities of the cold
war have dimmed their vision. They feel that unless nuclear weapons dev-
astate the world or unless fundamental changes take place in the Soviet
Union and in Communist China, the democratic states will continue to face
a permanent enemy, and the problems of security, mobilization, and industrial output will dominate society.

THE EFFECT OF INTERNATIONAL CONFLICT

Already World War II and the cold war, requiring two decades of
mobilization, have brought a new relationship between government and
economy and a new pattern of civil-military relationship. In 1940, Harold
Lasswell wrote "The Garrison State," which appears in the reading below.
He intended to sketch not an empirical reality but an abstraction based on

tendencies—an "ideal type," in Max Weber's terminology. If the tendencies were to continue uncomplicated and unchecked, Lasswell suggested, future societies would develop according to his model of the garrison state. Indeed, the tendencies have not been checked, and they are more complex than they appear in Lasswell's sketch. Nevertheless, his idea has been incorporated in the critical literature on American society. C. Wright Mills, for example, accepts the notion of the garrison state but fuses it with other elements in his conception of the power elite.[1]

INTERNAL TRANSFORMATIONS

The effect of international politics on democracy is not more important than the pangs of its great social changes. Around the time of World War I it was not unusual to read that democracy in the twentieth century was very different from the picture drawn by the democratic writers of the American and the French Revolutions. Now one may read that democracy in the postmodern world is entirely different from what it was at the beginning of this century.

The debate over democracy has also changed in our time. Many writers question whether the familiar conceptions of democracy have any relevance to political institutions today. Previously, the apologists for democracy lauded its institutions and values, and argued that their abuses were correctable errors not inherent in democratic society. Their opponents argued either that democracy was not possible—that in reality the people could not ever really control their leaders, or that it was not desirable—that leaders should not be controlled by the people.[2] This dispute still goes on, but today it is displaced by another one, and usually both sides of the present debate are themselves committed to democratic values.

The question is not whether democracy is possible or desirable, but rather how to interpret the facts of twentieth-century life. Some writers contend that the conditions of social life have in fact changed in such a way that democratic institutions are nothing more than a façade to mask a hidden oligarchy; although democracy retains its form, economic, social, and political forces have produced a society in which the control of major

[1] C. Wright Mills, *The Power Elite* (New York: Oxford University Press, 1956).
[2] See David Spitz, *Patterns of Anti-democratic Thought* (New York: The Macmillan Company, 1949).

decisions have passed to a select few. The identity of the oligarchy varies with the argument: in *The Managerial Revolution,* James Burnham claims that it is a managerial class, both political and economic; others declare that it is the governmental bureaucracy; Harold Lasswell in the selection below points to the military; C. Wright Mills argues it is a tripartite elite drawn from corporation executives, the military establishment, and the political directorate.

In opposition to this point of view, other writers argue that the great transformations of our era have altered but not destroyed democracy, and that democratic institutions have the flexibility and the vitality to adjust to contemporary life.[3] In his essay below, Louis Hartz demonstrates that every political system harbors a discrepancy between myth and fact, and he warns us not to be shocked by the contrast between democratic ideals and realities.

The readings in this chapter explore some of the aspects of postmodern democracy that contemporary writers are trying to interpret. E. H. Carr identifies three main propositions upon which democracy has rested from the time of its origins in modern Europe. He discusses the changes in industrial civilization and shows how the old democratic conceptions did not fit "the mass civilization of the twentieth century." He demonstrates the novelty of "mass democracy," exploring ways in which democracy might be preserved and suggesting how the older conceptions might be adapted to present conditions.

DEMOCRATIC VALUES

Anxiety over the fate of democracy has stimulated discussion of democratic values and has brought forth attempts to reinspire democratic thought. Sidney Hook's essay below illustrates many characteristics of postmodern secular and naturalistic democratic theory. Hook denies the relevance of optimistic assumptions about universal goodness associated with popular democratic thought in the past. This denial is coupled with a carefully reasoned skepticism about any absolute doctrines of human nature; it also rejects deterministic views of history. Human existence is indeterminate, Hook claims, and its possibilities may be explored most hon-

---

[3] See David Spitz, *Democracy and the Challenge of Power* (New York: Columbia University Press, 1958).

estly in a democratic setting. The argument accepts only inferences from experience, and is reluctant to move beyond the framework of empirical knowledge.

Hook's naturalistic theory of democracy is opposed by religious points of view.[4] Hook's essay below and Jacques Maritain's in Chapter VII can be looked upon as a dialogue on the relation between democracy and values. Maritain argues that democracy originated from religious sources, from the Gospel working in history, and has lived on the spiritual capital of Christianity. Hook, in contrast, says that there is no necessary connection between democracy and religion, and that democracy is deduced neither from the nature of man nor from general principles of justice and morality, as Maritain contends. Democracy, according to Hook, depends on nothing more than empirical procedures leading from the hypothesis of human equality. The lines of argument are clear: Maritain insists that the weakness of democracy is due to the loss or the neglect of its "real" spiritual base; Hook maintains that the logic of democratic thought has been weakened by supernatural appeals, and he insists that it be grounded on secular premises.

Both arguments have been trivialized and vulgarized. Naturalists and secularists have not understood the complexities of the religious viewpoint and have missed its perception of the important link between social institutions and religious ideals. On the other hand, the religious argument has been diluted and diminished in a similar way. Impressed into the service of the cold war, the democratic appeal to divine inspiration has been used as a riposte to the Communist claim of historical invincibility. In this capacity it becomes a countermyth in the international struggle, nourished for its effect on morale rather than for its truth. Trivialized in this manner and used by leaders for mass inspiration, this point of view may eventually look upon secular and naturalistic defenses of democracy as heretical and dangerous.

[4] Cf. John H. Hallowell, *The Moral Foundation of Democracy* (Chicago: University of Chicago Press, 1954).

HAROLD D. LASSWELL
1902-

HAROLD D. LASSWELL IS a distinguished political scientist whose work has often been unorthodox and innovating. He was born in Donnellson, Illinois, and was educated at the University of Chicago, where he also taught for many years. He is a past president of the American Political Science Association (1955), and is a professor of law and politics at Yale University. At the beginning of his career he studied psychoanalysis, and in the early 1930's published works such as *Psychopathology and Politics* (1930), which claimed that political events may be explained by the character structure and unconscious motivations of participants in public life. He next investigated the distribution of power among elites in such works as *Politics: Who Gets What, When, How* (1936). This phase of his writing was marked by an attempt to construct a "realistic" and objective science of politics. During and after World War II his views changed, and he conceived of political science as a "policy science" devoted ultimately to the preservation of democratic values. In *Power and Personality* (1948), for example, he suggested that "social self-observatories of personality formation" be established in the nation in order to aid in the formation of democratic character and personality. He considered social scientists as "scientists of democracy" and urged that they "aid the progressive transformation of human society into a free man's commonwealth." In the past decade his work has shown an increased emphasis on the construction of formal concepts and categories of political action as part of his attempt to synthesize an increasingly broad range of phenomena.

[30]   The Garrison State

The purpose of this article is to consider the possibility that we are moving toward a world of "garrison states"—a world in which the specialists on violence are the most powerful group in society. From this point of view the trend of our time is away from the dominance of the specialist on bargaining, who is the businessman, and toward the supremacy of the soldier. We may distinguish transitional forms, such as the party propaganda state, where the dominant figure is the propagandist, and the party bureaucratic state, in which the organization men of the party make the vital decisions. There are mixed forms in which predominance is shared by the monopolists of party and market power.

*　*　*

To speak of a garrison state is not to predict something wholly new under the sun. Certainly there is nothing novel to the student of political institutions about the idea that specialists on violence may run the state. On the contrary, some of the most influential discussions of political institutions have named the military state as one of the chief forms of organized society. Comte saw history as a succession (and a progression) that moved, as far as it concerned the state, through military, feudal, and industrial phases. Spencer divided all human societies into the military type, based on force, and the industrial type, based on contract and free consent.

What is important for our purposes is to envisage the possible emergence of the military state under present technical conditions. There are no examples of the military state combined with modern technology. During emergencies the great powers have given enormous scope to military authority, but temporary acquisitions of authority lack the elements of comparative permanence and acceptance that complete the garrison state. Military dictators in states marginal to the creative centers of Western civilization are not integrated with modern technology; they merely use some of its specific elements.

The military men who dominate a modern technical society will be very

From *The American Journal of Sociology*, XLVI (January, 1941), 455, 457–60, 461–63, 465, 466. Reprinted by permission of the author.

different from the officers of history and tradition. It is probable that the specialists on violence will include in their training a large degree of expertness in many of the skills that we have traditionally accepted as part of modern civilian management.

The distinctive frame of reference in a fighting society is fighting effectiveness. All social change is translated into battle potential. Now there can be no realistic calculation of fighting effectiveness without knowledge of the technical and psychological characteristics of modern production processes. The function of management in such a society is already known to us; it includes the exercise of skill in supervising technical operations, in administrative organization, in personnel management, in public relations. These skills are needed to translate the complicated operations of modern life into every relevant frame of reference—the frame of fighting effectiveness as well as of pecuniary profit.

This leads to the seeming paradox that, as modern states are militarized, specialists on violence are more preoccupied with the skills and attitudes judged characteristic of nonviolence. We anticipate the merging of skills, starting from the traditional accouterments of the professional soldier, moving toward the manager and promoter of large-scale civilian enterprise.

In the garrison state, at least in its introductory phases, problems of morale are destined to weigh heavily on the mind of management. It is easy to throw sand in the gears of the modern assembly line; hence, there must be a deep and general sense of participation in the total enterprise of the state if collective effort is to be sustained. When we call attention to the importance of the "human factor" in modern production, we sometimes fail to notice that it springs from the multiplicity of special environments that have been created by modern technology. Thousands of technical operations have sprung into existence where a few hundred were found before. To complicate the material environment in this way is to multiply the foci of attention of those who live in our society. Diversified foci of attention breed differences in outlook, preference, and loyalty. The labyrinth of specialized "material" environments generates profound ideological divergencies that cannot be abolished, though they can be mitigated, by the methods now available to leaders in our society. As long as modern technology prevails, society is honeycombed with cells of separate experience, of individuality, of partial freedom. Concerted action under such conditions depends upon skilfully guiding the minds of men; hence the enormous importance of symbolic manipulation in modern society.

The importance of the morale factor is emphasized by the universal fear which it is possible to maintain in large populations through modern instruments of warfare. The growth of aerial warfare in particular has tended to abolish the distinction between civilian and military functions. It is no longer possible to affirm that those who enter the military service take the physical risk while those who remain at home stay safe and contribute to the equipment and the comfort of the courageous heroes at the front. Indeed, in some periods of modern warfare, casualties among civilians may outnumber the casualties of the armed forces. With the socialization of danger as a permanent characteristic of modern violence the nation becomes one unified technical enterprise. Those who direct the violence operations are compelled to consider the entire gamut of problems that arise in living together under modern conditions.

There will be an energetic struggle to incorporate young and old into the destiny and mission of the state. It is probable that one form of this symbolic adjustment will be the abolition of "the unemployed." This stigmatizing symbol will be obsolete in the garrison state. It insults the dignity of millions, for it implies uselessness. This is so, whether the "unemployed" are given a "dole" or put on "relief" projects. Always there is the damaging stigma of superfluity. No doubt the garrison state will be distinguished by the psychological abolition of unemployment—"psychological" because this is chiefly a matter of redefining symbols.

In the garrison state there must be work—and the duty to work—for all. Since all work becomes public work, all who do not accept employment flout military discipline. For those who do not fit within the structure of the state there is but one alternative—to obey or die. Compulsion, therefore, is to be expected as a potent instrument for internal control of the garrison state.

The use of coercion can have an important effect upon many more people than it reaches directly; this is the propaganda component of any "propaganda of the deed." The spectacle of compulsory labor gangs in prisons or concentration camps is a negative means of conserving morale—negative since it arouses fear and guilt. Compulsory labor groups are suitable popular scapegoats in a military state. The duty to obey, to serve the state, to work—these are cardinal virtues in the garrison state. Unceasing emphasis upon duty is certain to arouse opposing tendencies within the personality structure of all who live under a garrison regime. Everyone must struggle to hold in check any tendencies, conscious or unconscious, to defy authority, to violate the code of work, to flout the incessant demand for sacrifice in the collective interest. From the earliest years youth will be trained to subdue—to disavow, to struggle against—any specific opposition to the ruling code of collective exactions.

The conscience imposes feelings of guilt and anxiety upon the individual whenever his impulses are aroused, ever so slightly, to break the code. When the coercive threat that sanctions the code of the military state is internalized in the consciences of youth, the spectacle of labor gangs is profoundly disturbing. A characteristic response is self-righteousness—quick justification of coercive punishment, tacit acceptance of the inference that all who are subject to coercion are guilty of antisocial conduct. To maintain suspended judgment, to absolve others in particular instances, is to give at least partial toleration to countermores tendencies within the self. Hence, the quick substitute responses—the self-righteous attitude, the deflection of attention. Indeed, a characteristic psychic pattern of the military state is the "startle pattern," which is carried over to the internal as well as to the external threat of danger. This startle pattern is overcome and stylized as alert, prompt, commanding adjustment to reality. This is expressed in the authoritative manner that dominates military style—in gesture, intonation, and idiom.

* * *

For the immediate future . . . ruling élites must continue to put their chief reliance upon propaganda as an instrument of morale. But the manipulation of symbols, even in conjunction with coercive instruments of violence, is not sufficient to accomplish all the purposes of a ruling group. We have already spoken of the socialization of danger, and this will bring about some equalitarian adjustments in the distribution of income for the purpose of conserving the will to fight and to produce.

In addition to the adjustment of symbols, goods, and violence, the political élite of the garrison state will find it necessary to make certain adaptations in the fundamental practices of the state. Decisions will be more dictatorial than democratic, and institutional practices long connected with modern democracy will disappear. Instead of elections to office or referendums on issues there will be government by plebiscite. Elections foster the formation and expression of public opinion, while plebiscites encourage only unanimous demonstrations of collective sentiment. Rival political parties will be suppressed, either by the monopolization of legality in one political party (more properly called a political "order") or by the abolition of all political parties. The ruling group will exercise a monopoly of opinion in public, thus abolishing free communication of fact and interpre-

360 DEMOCRACY RECONSIDERED

tation. Legislatures will be done away with, and if a numerous consultative body is permitted at all it will operate as an assembly; that is, it will meet for a very short time each year and will be expected to ratify the decisions of the central leadership after speeches that are chiefly ceremonial in nature. Plebiscites and assemblies thus become part of the ceremonializing process in the military state.

As legislatures and elections go out of use, the practice of petition will play a more prominent role. Lawmaking will be in the hands of the supreme authority and his council; and, as long as the state survives, this agency will exert effective control ("authority" is the term for formal expectations, "control" is the actual distribution of effective power).

This means that instrumental democracy will be in abeyance, although the symbols of mystic "democracy" will doubtless continue. Instrumental democracy is found wherever authority and control are widely dispersed among the members of a state. Mystic "democracy" is not, strictly speaking, democracy at all, because it may be found where authority and control are highly concentrated yet where part of the established practice is to speak in the name of the people as a whole. Thus, any dictatorship may celebrate its "democracy" and speak with contempt of such "mechanical" devices as majority rule at elections or in legislatures.

What part of the social structure would be drawn upon in recruiting the political rulers of the garrison state? As we have seen, the process will not be by general election but by self-perpetuation through co-option. The foremost positions will be open to the officers' corps, and the problem is to predict from what part of the social structure the officers will be recruited. Morale considerations justify a broad base of recruitment for ability rather than social standing. Although fighting effectiveness is a relatively impersonal test that favors ability over inherited status, the turnover in ruling families from generation to generation will probably be low. Any recurring crisis, however, will strengthen the tendency to favor ability. It seems clear that recruitment will be much more for bias and obedience than for objectivity and originality. Yet, as we shall presently see, modern machine society has introduced new factors in the military state—factors tending to strengthen objectivity and originality.

In the garrison state all organized social activity will be governmentalized; hence, the role of independent associations will disappear, with the exception of secret societies (specifically, there will be no organized economic, religious, or cultural life outside of the duly constituted agencies of government). Government will be highly centralized, though devolution may be practiced in order to mitigate "bureaucratism." There is so much outspoken resistance to bureaucratism in modern civilization that we may expect this attitude to carry over to the garrison state. Not only will the administrative structure be centralized, but at every level it will tend to integrate authority in a few hands. The leadership principle will be relied upon; responsibility as a rule will be focused upon individual "heads."

* * *

Although the rulers of the garrison state will be free to regularize the rate of production, they will most assuredly prevent full utilization of modern productive capacity for nonmilitary consumption purposes. The élite of the garrison state will have a professional interest in multiplying gadgets specialized to acts of violence. The rulers of the garrison state will depend upon war scares as a means of maintaining popular willingness to forego immediate consumption. War scares that fail to culminate in violence eventually lose their value; this is the point at which ruling classes will feel that bloodletting is needed in order to preserve those virtues of sturdy acquiescence in the regime which they so much admire and from which they so greatly benefit. We may be sure that if ever there is a rise in the production of nonmilitary consumption goods, despite the amount of energy directed toward the production of military equipment, the ruling class will feel itself endangered by the growing "frivolousness" of the community.

* * *

The tendency to ceremonialize rather than to fight will be particularly prominent among the most influential elements in a garrison state. Those standing at the top of the military pyramid will doubtless occupy high positions in the income pyramid. During times of actual warfare it may be necessary to make concessions in the direction of moderating gross-income differences in the interest of preserving general morale. The prospect of such concessions may be expected to operate as a deterrent factor against war. A countervailing tendency, of course, is the threat to sluggish and well-established members of the upper crust from ambitious members of the lower officers' corps. This threat arises, too, when there are murmurs of disaffection with the established order of things on the part of broader components of the society.

It seems probable that the garrison state of the future will be far less rigid than the military states of antiquity. As long as modern technical society endures, there will be an enormous body of specialists whose focus of attention is entirely given over to the discovery of novel ways of utilizing nature. Above all, these are physical scientists and engineers. They are able to demonstrate by rather impersonal procedures the efficiency of many of their suggestions for the improvement of fighting effectiveness. We therefore anticipate further exploration of the technical potentialities of modern civilization within the general framework of the garrison state.

E. H. CARR
1892-

EDWARD HALLETT CARR, BRITISH HISTORIAN and political scientist, was educated in Trinity College, Cambridge University, and served for 20 years in the diplomatic service before he entered academic life. He was also an editor of the London *Times* from 1941 to 1946. He has been a professor in the University College of Wales, a tutor in Balliol College, Oxford, and, since 1955, a fellow in Trinity College, Cambridge. His major work is the comprehensive six-volume *History of Soviet Russia,* most of his earlier books having been biographical studies of men who played important roles in Russian revolutionary history.

Carr has also written several books on international relations. In the monumental history of Russia, his purpose was not to write about the events of the Revolution, "but of the political, social and economic order which emerged from it." In 1951 he delivered a series of BBC lectures on the theory and practice of democracy in the twentieth century. They were collected and published in *The New Society* (1951).

[31]   From Individualism to Mass Democracy

The problem of political organization in the new society is to adapt to the mass civilization of the twentieth century conceptions of democracy formed in earlier and highly individualistic periods of history. The proclamation by the French revolution of popular sovereignty was a serious challenge to institutions which had grown up under quite different auspices and influences. It is no accident that Athenian democracy, which has been commonly regarded as the source and exemplar of democratic institutions, was the creation and prerogative of a limited and privileged group of the population. It is no accident that Locke, the founder of the modern democratic tradition, was the chosen philosopher and prophet of the eighteenth-century English Whig oligarchy. It is no accident that the magnificent structure of British nineteenth-century liberal democracy was built up on a highly restrictive property franchise. History points unmistakably to the fact that political democracy, in the forms in which it has hitherto been known, flourishes best where some of the people, but not all the people, are free and equal; and, since this conclusion is incompatible with the conditions of the new society and repugnant to the contemporary conscience, the task of saving democracy in our time is the task of reconciling it with the postulate of popular sovereignty and mass civilization.

Modern democracy, as it grew up and spread from its focus in western Europe over the past three centuries, rested on three main propositions: first, that the individual conscience is the ultimate source of decisions about what is right and wrong; second, that there exists between different individuals a fundamental harmony of interests strong enough to enable them to live peacefully together in society; third, that where action has to be taken in the name of society, rational discussion between individuals is the best method of reaching a decision on that action. Modern democracy is, in virtue of its origins, individualist, optimistic and rational. The three main propositions on which it is based have all been seriously challenged in the contemporary world.

In the first place, the individualist conception of democracy rests on

From E. H. Carr, *The New Society* (New York: St. Martin's Press, Inc., 1957), pp. 61–63, 64–76. Reprinted by permission of Macmillan & Company, Ltd., St. Martin's Press, Inc., and The Macmillan Company of Canada, Ltd.

a belief in the inherent rights of individuals based on natural law. According to this conception, the function of democratic government is not to create or innovate, but to interpret and apply rights which already exist. This accounts for the importance attached in the democratic tradition to the rights of minorities within the citizen body. Decision by majority vote might be a necessary and convenient device. But individuals belonging to the minority had the same inherent rights as those belonging to the majority. Insistence on the rule of law, preferably inscribed in a written and permanent constitution, was an important part of the individualist tradition of democracy. The individual enjoyed certain indefeasible rights against the society of which he was a member; these rights were often regarded as deriving from a real or hypothetical "social contract" which formed the title-deeds of society. Just as the individualist tradition in *laissez-faire* economics was hostile to all forms of combination, so the individualist tradition in politics was inimical to the idea of political parties. Both in Athenian democracy and in eighteenth-century Britain, parties were regarded with mistrust and denounced as "factions".

The French revolution with its announcement of the sovereignty of the people made the first serious assault on this view of democracy. The individualism of Locke's "natural law" was replaced by the collectivism of Rousseau's "general will". Both Pericles and Locke had thought in terms of a small and select society of privileged citizens. Rousseau for the first time thought in terms of the sovereignty of the whole people, and faced the issue of mass democracy. He did so reluctantly; for he himself preferred the tiny community where direct democracy, without representation or delegation of powers, was still possible. But he recognized that the large nation had come to stay, and held that in such conditions the people could be sovereign only if it imposed on itself the discipline of a "general will". The practical conclusion drawn from this doctrine, not by Rousseau himself, but by the Jacobins, was the foundation of a single political party to embody the general will. Its logical conclusions were still more far-reaching. The individual, far from enjoying rights against society assured to him by natural law, had no appeal against the deliverances of the general will. The general will was the repository of virtue and justice, the state its instrument for putting them into effect. The individual who dissented from the general will cut himself off from the community and was a self-proclaimed traitor to it. Rousseau's doctrine led directly to the Jacobin practice of revolutionary terror.

*   *   *

While, however, the beginnings of mass democracy can be discerned in the doctrines of Rousseau and in the practice of the French revolution, the problem in its modern form was a product of the nineteenth century. The Industrial revolution started its career under the banner of individual enterprise. Adam Smith was as straightforward an example as could be desired of eighteenth-century individualism. But presently the machine overtook the man, and the competitive advantages of mass production ushered in the age of standardization and larger and larger economic units. And with the mammoth trust and the mammoth trade union came the mammoth organ of opinion, the mammoth political party and, floating above them all, the mammoth state, narrowing still further the field of responsibility and action left to the individual and setting the stage for the new mass society. It was the English Utilitarians who, by rejecting natural law, turned their backs on the individualist tradition and, by postulating the greatest good and the greatest number as the supreme goal, laid the theoretical foundation of mass democracy in Britain; in practice, they were also the first radical reformers. Before long, thinkers began to explore some of the awkward potentialities of mass democracy. The danger of the oppression of minorities by the majority was the most obvious. This was discerned by Tocqueville in the United States in the 1830's and by J. S. Mill in England twenty-five years later. In our own time the danger has reappeared in a more insidious form. Soviet Russia has a form of government which describes itself as a democracy. It claims, not without some historical justification, to stem from the Jacobins who stemmed from Rousseau and the doctrine of the general will. The general will is an orthodoxy which purports to express the common opinion; the minority which dissents can legitimately be suppressed. But we are not concerned here with the abuses and excesses of the Soviet form of government. What troubles us is the question how far, in moving from the individualism of restrictive liberal democracy to the mass civilization of today, we have ourselves become involved in a conception of democracy which postulates a general will. The question is all around us today not only in the form of loyalty tests, avowed or secret, or committees on un-American activities, but also in the form of the closed shop and of increasingly rigid standards of party discipline. In a speech made to a regional Labour party conference at the time of Mr. Aneurin Devan's resignation in April, the Minister of Defence denounced "absence of loyalty" in the party: "The loyalty of our party", exclaimed Mr. Shinwell, "is superior to any exhibition of political private enterprise. . . . No person, I don't care who he is, can be allowed to interfere with the democratic structure of this party." Lenin used strikingly similar phrases at the Bolshevik party congress in March 1921. We have moved far from the conception of truth emerging from the interplay of divergent individual opinions. Loyalty has come to mean the submission of the individual to the general will of the party or group.

The second postulate of Locke's conception of society, the belief in a fundamental harmony of interests between individuals, equally failed to stand the test of time, and for much the same reason. Even more than natural law, the harmony of interests was essentially a conservative doctrine. If the interest of the individual rightly understood coincided with the interest of the whole society, it followed that any individual who assailed the existing order was acting against his own true interests and could be condemned not only as wicked, but as short-sighted and foolish. Some such argument was, for instance, often invoked against strikers who failed to recognize the common interest uniting them with their employers. The French revolution, an act of self-assertion by the third estate against the two senior estates of nobility and clergy, demonstrated—like any other violent upheaval—the hollowness of the harmony of interests; and the doctrine was soon also to be powerfully challenged on the theoretical plane.

The challenge came from two quarters. The Utilitarians, while not making a frontal attack on the doctrine, implicitly denied it when they asserted that the harmony of interests had to be created by remedial action before it would work. They saw that some of the worst existing inequalities would have to be reformed out of existence before it was possible to speak without irony of a society based on a harmony of interests; and they believed in increased education, and the true liberty of thought which would result from it, as a necessary preparation for establishing harmony. Then Marx and Engels in the *Communist Manifesto* took the class struggle and made out of it a theory of history which, partial though it was, stood nearer to current reality than the theory of the harmony of interests had ever done. Social and economic pressures resulting from the break down of *laissez-faire* illustrated in practice what Marx had demonstrated in theory. But in Great Britain it was reformist Utilitarianism rather than revolutionary Marxism that set the pace. The flagrant absence of a harmony of interests between competing and conflicting classes more and more urgently called for state intervention. The state could no longer be content to hold the ring; it must descend actively into the arena to create a harmony which did not exist in nature. Legislation, hitherto regarded as an exceptional function required from time to time to clear up some misunderstanding or to rectify some abuse, now became normal and continuous. It no longer sufficed to interpret and apply rights conferred on the individual by the laws of nature. What was expected of the state was positive and continuous activity—a form of social and economic engineering. The substitution of a planned economy for *laissez-faire* capitalism brought about a radical transformation in the attitude towards the state. The functions of the state were no longer merely supervisory, but creative and remedial. It was no longer an organ whose weakness was its virtue and whose activities should be restricted to a minimum in the interests of freedom. It was an organ which one sought to capture and control for the carrying out of necessary reforms; and, having captured it, one sought to make it as powerful and effective as possible in order to carry them out. The twentieth century has not only replaced individualist democracy by mass democracy, but has substituted the cult of the strong remedial state for the doctrine of the natural harmony of interests.

The third main characteristic of Locke's conception of society—a characteristic which helped to give the eighteenth century its nicknames of the Age of Reason or the Age of Enlightenment—was its faith in rational discussion as a guide to political action. This faith provided the most popular nineteenth-century justification of the rule of the majority as the basis of democracy. Since men were on the whole rational, and since the right answer to any given issue could be discovered by reason, one was more likely, in the case of dispute, to find right judgment on the side of the majority than on the side of the minority. Like other eighteenth-century conceptions, the doctrine of reason in politics was the doctrine of a ruling oligarchy. The rational approach to politics, which encouraged leisurely argument and eschewed passion, was eminently the approach of a well-to-do, leisured and cultured class. Its efficacy could be most clearly and certainly guaranteed when the citizen body consisted of a relatively small number of educated persons who could be trusted to reason intelligently and dispassionately on controversial issues submitted to them. The prominent rôle assigned to reason in the original democratic scheme provides perhaps the most convincing explanation why democracy has hitherto always seemed to flourish best with a restrictive franchise. Much has been written in recent years of the decline of reason, and of respect for reason, in human affairs, when sometimes what has really happened has been the abandonment of the highly simplified eighteenth-century view of reason in favour of a subtler and more sophisticated analysis. But it is none the less true that the epoch-making changes in our attitude towards reason provide a key to some of the profoundest problems of contemporary democracy.

First of all, the notion that men of intelligence and good will were likely by process of rational discussion to reach a correct opinion on controversial political questions could be valid only in an age when such questions were comparatively few and simple enough to be accessible to the educated lay-man. It implicitly denied that any specialized knowledge was required to solve political problems. This hypothesis was perhaps tenable so long as the state was not required to intervene in economic issues, and the questions on which decisions had to be taken turned on matters of practical detail or general political principles. In the first half of the twentieth century these conditions had everywhere ceased to exist. In Great Britain major issues of a highly controversial character like the return to the gold standard in 1925 or the acceptance of the American loan in 1946 were of a kind in which no opinion seriously counted except that of the trained expert in possession of a vast array of facts and figures, some of them probably not available to the public. In such matters the ordinary citizen could not even have an intelligent opinion on the question who were the best experts to consult. The only rôle he could hope to play was to exercise his hunch at the election by choosing the right leader to consult the right experts about vital, though probably still unformulated, issues of policy which would ultimately affect his daily life.

At this initial stage of the argument reason itself is not dethroned from its supreme rôle in the decision of political issues. The citizen is merely asked to surrender his right of decision to the superior reason of the expert. At the second stage of the argument reason itself is used to dethrone reason. The social psychologist, employing rational methods of investigation, discovers that men in the mass are often most effectively moved by non-rational emotions such as admiration, envy, hatred, and can be most effectively reached not by rational argument, but by emotional appeals to eye and ear, or by sheer repetition. Propaganda is as essential a function of mass democracy as advertising of mass production. The political organizer takes a leaf out of the book of the commercial advertiser and sells the leader or the candidate to the voter by the same methods used to sell patent medicines or refrigerators. The appeal is no longer to the reason of the citizen, but to his gullibility. A more recent phenomenon has been the emergence of what Max Weber called the "charismatic leader" as the expression of the general will. The retreat from individualism seemed to issue at last—and not alone in the so-called totalitarian countries—in the exaltation of a single individual leader who personified and resumed within himself the qualities and aspirations of the "little man", of the ordinary individual lost and bewildered in the new mass society. But the principal qualification of the leader is no longer his capacity to reason correctly on political or economic issues, or even his capacity to choose the best experts to reason for him, but a good public face, a convincing voice, a sympathetic fireside manner on the radio; and these qualities are deliberately built up for him by his publicity agents. In this picture of the techniques of contemporary democracy, the party headquarters, the directing brain at the centre, still operates rationally, but uses irrational rather than rational means to achieve its ends—means which are, moreover, not merely irrational but largely irrelevant to the purposes to be pursued or to the decisions to be taken.

The third stage of the argument reaches deeper levels. Hegel, drawing out the philosophical implications of Rousseau's doctrine, had identified the course of history with universal reason, to which the individual reason stood in the same relation as the individual will to Rousseau's general will. Individual reason had been the corner-stone of individualist democracy. Marx took Hegel's collective reason to make it the corner-stone of the new mass democracy. Marx purported to reject the metaphysical character of Hegel's thought. But, equally with Hegel, he conceived of history pursuing a rational course, which could be analysed and even predicted in terms of reason. Hegel had spoken of the cunning of reason in history, using individuals to achieve purposes of which they themselves were unconscious. Marx would have rejected the turn of phrase as metaphysical. But his conception of history as a continuous process of class struggle contained elements of determinism which revealed its Hegelian ancestry, at any rate on one side. Marx remained a thorough-going rationalist. But the reason whose validity he accepted was collective rather than individual.

Marx played, however, a far more important part in what has been called "the flight from reason" than by the mere exaltation of the collective over the individual. By his vigorous assertion that "being determines consciousness, not consciousness being", that thinking is conditioned by the social environment of the thinker, and that ideas are the superstructure of a totality whose foundation is formed by the material conditions of life, Marx presented a clear challenge to what had hitherto been regarded as the sovereign or autonomous human reason. The actors who played significant parts in the historical drama were playing parts already written for them: this indeed was what made them significant. The function of individual reason was to identify itself with the universal reason which determined the course of history and to make itself the agent and executor of this universal reason. Some such view is indeed involved in any attempt to trace back historical events to underlying social causes; and Marx—and still more Engels—hedged a little in later years about the rôle of the individual in history. But the extraordinary vigour and conviction with which he drove home his main argument, and the political theory which he founded on it, give him a leading place among those nineteenth-century thinkers who shattered the comfortable belief of the Age of Enlightenment in the decisive power of individual reason in shaping the course of history.

Marx's keenest polemics were those directed to prove the "conditioned" character of the thinking of his opponents and particularly of the capitalist ruling class of the most advanced countries of his day. If they thought as they did it was because, as members of a class, "being" determined their "consciousness", and their ideas necessarily lacked any independent objectivity and validity. Hegel, as a good conservative, had exempted the current reality of the Prussian from the operation of the dialectic which had destroyed successively so many earlier historical forms. Marx, as a revolutionary, admitted no such absolute in the present, but only in the future. The proletariat, whose victory would automatically abolish classes, was alone the basis of absolute value; and collective proletarian thinking had thus an objectivity which was denied to the thinking of other classes. Marx's willingness, like that of Hegel, to admit an absolute as the culminating point of his dialectical process was, however, an element of inconsistency in his system; and, just as Marx was far more concerned to dissect capitalism than to provide a blue-print for socialism, so his use of the dialectic to lay bare the conditioned thinking of his opponents lay far nearer to his heart, and was far more effective, than his enunciation of the objective and absolute values of the proletariat. Marx's writings gave a powerful impetus to all forms of relativism. It seemed less important, at a time when the proletarian revolution was as yet nowhere in sight, to note his admission of absolute truth as a prerogative of the proletariat. The proletariat was for Marx the collective repository of Rousseau's infallible general will.

Another thinker of the later nineteenth century also helped to mould the climate of political opinion. Like Darwin, Freud was a scientist without pretensions to be a philosopher or, still less, a political thinker. But in the flight from reason at the end of the nineteenth century, he played the same popular rôle as Darwin had played a generation earlier in the philosophy of *laissez-faire*. Freud demonstrated that the fundamental attitudes of human beings in action and thought are largely determined at levels beneath that of consciousness, and that the supposedly rational explanations of those attitudes which we offer to ourselves and others are artificial and erroneous "rationalizations" of processes which we have failed to understand. Reason is given to us, Freud seems to say, not to direct our thought and action, but to camouflage the hidden forces which do direct it. This is a still more devastating version of the Marxist thesis of substructure and superstructure. The substructure of reality resides in the unconscious: what appears above the surface is no more than the reflexion, seen in a distorting ideological mirror, of what goes on underneath. The political conclusion from all this— Freud himself drew none—is that any attempt to appeal to the reason of the ordinary man is waste of time, or is useful merely as camouflage to conceal the real nature of the process of persuasion; the appeal must be made to those subconscious strata which are decisive for thought and action. The debunking of ideology undertaken by the political science of Marx is repeated in a far more drastic and far-reaching way by the psychological science of Freud and his successors.

By the middle of the nineteenth century, therefore, the propositions of Locke on which the theory of liberal democracy were founded had all been subjected to fundamental attack, and the attack broadened and deepened as the century went on. Individualism began to give way to collectivism both in economic organization and in the forms and practice of mass democracy: the age of mass civilization had begun. The alleged harmony of interests between individuals was replaced by the naked struggle between powerful classes and organized interest groups. The belief in the settlement of issues by rational discussion was undermined, first, by recognition of the complex and technical character of the issues involved, later and more seriously, by recognition that rational arguments were merely the conditioned reflexion of the class interests of those who put them forward, and, last and most seriously of all, by the discovery that the democratic voter, like other human beings, is most effectively reached not by arguments directed to his reason, but by appeals directed to his irrational, subconscious prejudices. The picture of democracy which emerged from these criticisms was the picture of an arena where powerful interest-groups struggled for the mastery. The leaders themselves were often the spokesmen and instruments of historical processes which they did not fully understand; their followers consisted of voters recruited and marshalled for purposes of which they were wholly unconscious by all the subtle techniques of modern psychological science and modern commercial advertising.

The picture is overdrawn. But we shall not begin to understand the problems of mass democracy unless we recognize the serious elements of truth in it, unless we recognize how far we have moved away from the conceptions and from the conditions out of which the democratic tradition was born. From the conception of democracy as a select society of free individuals, enjoying equal rights and periodically electing to manage the affairs of the society, a small number of their peers, who deliberate together (the assumption being that the course which appeals to the majority is likely to be the most rational), we have passed to the current reality of mass democracy. The typical mass democracy of today is a vast society of individuals, stratified by widely different social and economic backgrounds into a series of groups or classes, enjoying equal political rights the exercise of which is organized through two or more closely integrated political machines called parties. Between the parties and individual citizens stand an indeterminate number of entities variously known as unions, associations, lobbies or pressure-groups devoted to the promotion of some economic interest, or of some social or humanitarian cause in which keen critics usually detect a latent and perhaps unconscious interest. At the first stage of the democratic process, these associations and groups form a sort of exchange and mart where votes are traded for support of particular policies; the more votes such a group controls the better its chance of having its views incorporated in the party platform. At the second stage, when these bargains have been made, the party as a united entity "goes to the country" and endeavours by every form of political propaganda to win the support of the unattached voter. At the third stage, when the election has been decided, the parties once more dispute or bargain together, in the light of the votes cast, on the policies to be put into effect; the details of procedure at this third stage differ considerably in different democratic countries in accordance with varying constitutional requirements and party structures. What is important to note is that the first and third stages are fierce matters of bargaining. At the second stage, where the mass persuasion of the electorate is at issue, the methods employed now commonly approximate more and more closely to those of commercial advertisers, who on the advice of modern psychologists, find the appeal to fear, envy or self-aggrandizement more effective than the appeal to reason. Certainly in the United States, where contemporary large-scale democracy has worked most successfully and where the strongest confidence is felt in its survival, experienced practitioners of politics would give little encouragement to the idea that rational argument exercises a major influence on the democratic process. We have returned to a barely disguised struggle of interest-groups in which the arguments used are for the most part no more than a rationalization of the interests concerned, and the rôle of persuasion is played by carefully calculated appeals to the irrational subconscious.

This discussion is intended to show not that mass democracy is more corrupt or less efficient than other forms of government (this I do not believe), but that mass democracy is a new phenomenon—a creation of the last half-century—which it is inappropriate and misleading to consider in terms of the philosophy of Locke or of the liberal democracy of the nineteenth century. It is new, because the new democratic society consists no longer of a homogeneous closed society of equal and economically secure individuals mutually recognizing one another's rights, but of ill co-ordinated, highly stratified masses of people of whom a large majority are primarily occupied with the daily struggle for existence. It is new, because the new democratic state can no longer be content to hold the ring in the strife of private economic interests, but must enter the arena at every moment and take the initiative in urgent issues of economic policy which affect the daily life of all the citizens, and especially of the least secure. It is new, because the old rationalist assumptions of Locke and of liberal democracy have broken down under the weight both of changed material conditions and of new scientific insights and inventions, and the leaders of the new democracy are concerned no longer primarily with the reflexion of opinion, but with the moulding and manipulation of opinion. To speak today of the defence of democracy as if we were defending something which we knew and had possessed for many decades or many centuries is self-deception and sham.

It is no answer to point to institutions that have survived from earlier forms of democracy. The survival of kingship in Great Britain does not prove that the British system of government is a monarchy; and democratic institutions survive in many countries today—some survived even in Hitler's Germany—which have little or no claim to be called democracies. The criterion must be sought not in the survival of traditional institutions, but in the question where power resides and how it is exercised. In this respect democracy is a matter of degree. Some countries today are more democratic than others. But none is perhaps very democratic, if any high standard of democracy is applied. Mass democracy is a difficult and hitherto largely uncharted territory; and we should be nearer the mark, and should have a far more convincing slogan, if we spoke of the need, not to defend democracy, but to create it.

LOUIS HARTZ
1919-

LOUIS HARTZ WAS EDUCATED at Harvard, where he is now professor of government. In his published work he has explored the fields of American political thought and intellectual history. He searches for the realities underlying political ideas and myths, revealing their origins, logical and historical development, and social functions. His analysis probes conventional thinking on historical development, for, as he has put it, "History has its strategic uses. An image of the past can be worth a score of arguments based on the present." In his book *Economic Policy and Democratic Thought: Pennsylvania, 1776–1860* (1948), he examines conceptions of the relation between government and economic life, and punctures the myth that laissez-faire was an early American doctrine, demonstrating that it was fashioned instead in the age of the "corporate revolution" after the Civil War. *The Liberal Tradition in America* (1955) is a perceptive study of the relation between thought and institutions, and a lively reinterpretation of the place of liberalism in the unique development of American society.

[32]   Democracy: Image and Reality

The system of democracy works by virtue of certain processes which its theory never describes, to which, indeed, its theory is actually hostile.

From W. N. Chambers and R. H. Salisbury, eds., *Democracy in the Mid-Twentieth Century* (St. Louis, Mo.: Washington University Press, 1960), pp. 13–18, 22–29. Reprinted by permission of Louis Hartz and Washington University Press.

But we identify the system with the theory, as if we actually lived by the ancient Jeffersonian image of democracy we cherish, so that when we are confronted with some of the practices which make democracy work we become terrified that the system is breaking up. In large measure the internal "crisis of democracy," heralded since the age of E. L. Godkin, is of this fantastic sort, an agony of the mind rather than of the real world. We have been in the position of the Victorian who, discovering sex, feels that the human race is about to vanish. Biologically this reaction is fantastic, but psychologically there is plenty of evidence to prove that it exists.

Democracy has always worked through group coercion, crowd psychology, and economic power, yet for fifty years these factors have sent a tremor through democratic hearts. It would be absurd, of course, to argue that none of these factors poses a problem for the democratic process. Quite obviously they all do. The tyranny of party and group, if carried beyond a certain point, can begin to nullify the decision of an electorate. Mass opinion, if it reaches a point where it is completely manipulable by a monopolistic force, will also make a sham of the democratic system. And a powerful economic minority clearly has certain bounds within which it must function if democracy is to retain its meaning. But it is one thing to define these problems as problems of "excess," of the necessary machinery of the democratic world somehow getting out of hand, and it is quite another to define them as an apocalyptic "exposure" of democratic institutions. They do indeed expose our theory, which has room for none of them, but they do not expose the real processes by which democracy has always worked.

What I am suggesting, then, is that during the last half century, with respect to domestic factors, we have had a surplus of pessimistic excitement about the "fate of democratic institutions," and that this in turn derives from the discovery of things which challenge the *image* of democracy much more than they do its *practice*. But how does such a situation come about? How can it happen that the theory of a system will leave out so much of the real machinery by which it lives? And why should men so confuse the theory with the machinery that they are led in the end to suffer unreal anxieties?

These questions drive us back to the larger issue of the historic development of political systems, and they lead us finally to a new problem facing democracy on the world plane which is more subtle and difficult than any discovered by the familiar theorists of domestic pessimism.

The truth is, no modern political system as it has risen to power has ever developed an image which corresponds to the real procedures by which it works. Nor has this been due to any trick, any conscious hypocrisy of mind. It has been due to the inevitable perspectives of political controversy, which compel a system to define itself in terms of the one it seeks to undermine. Its image of itself is a negation of what it seeks to destroy. Thus Marxism, instead of being a picture of socialist society, the nature of which we are only now beginning to discover, is a negative picture of capitalism. And in the same sense the doctrine of liberal democracy, instead of being a description of democratic life, is a negative description of life in the old European world that democracy destroyed. Locke, Rousseau, and Bentham are in this sense not "theorists of democracy" at all: they are the inverted theorists of the "corporate society" of the Seventeenth and Eighteenth centuries.

Once we go back to that society, it is clear enough why the democratic image these men gave us should be hostile to half of the machinery that was later invented in order to make democracy work. The points at which they assailed the old corporate system were precisely the points at which that machinery was destined to appear: this is one of the crucial correlations involved in our whole problem, the link between the institutions of the corporate world that the classical thinkers denounced and the new inventions of the democratic age that they did not bother to mention. Seeking to emancipate men from the rigid pluralism of church, guild, and province, those thinkers were bound to be "individualists." How could they say, even if they understood the fact, that democracy itself would function through a new pluralism of associations, parties, and groups? Anxious to shatter the claims of revelation, to dissolve the hierarchies based on the notion of mass incompetence, they were bound to be "rationalists." Could they say also that the electorate of a large state, if only to unify itself sufficiently to function, would have to forge a common opinion largely through the use of stereotypes and symbols, and that herein would lie the possibilities of manipulation? Nor is the issue less clear with respect to economic power. The men who gave us our image of democracy were associated with the rise of the middle class, and where there has been no such class democracy has had its difficulties. But seeking to shatter the rule of another older class they could not fail to be universalists, to form an image of pure "equality."

Thus Locke, Bentham, and Jefferson were bound to coin clichés which contradicted half of the institutional reality which has made them triumph in the modern world. The bond between the old institutions of the corporate age and the new institutions of the democratic age, a bond of group pluralism, mass emotion, and elite rule, had, in the nature of things, to remain as hidden as possible. This does not mean, of course, that democracy is really the same as the dying feudalism of the Seventeenth and Eighteenth centuries, that no progress in the direction of individualism, real popular decision, and the equal state has actually taken place. The English worker today has much more of all of these things than he had in the earlier era. But he has them precisely because he is related to a party machine that Locke never described, involved with mass media that Bentham does not mention, the heir of a bourgeois development that finds no place in the "state" of such a late Nineteenth century liberal as T. H. Green. So that what happens in the case of an ascendant social and political system is that it strikes in fact some middle ground between the blazing negative ideals of its origin and the operational necessities of actual life. As a living thing it turns out to be a mad anomaly, a set of ideals half realized through institutions which contradict them, which no one has ever described. And it is always productive, at a certain stage in its later history, of a crowd of thinkers who suddenly discover that no one has ever described it. This is the age of "realism," which mixes with new anxiety a vast amount of empirical research.

But why should the facts be so hard to face? Why, if we see ourselves as we have always been, should we feel that our existence is suddenly threatened? There is really nothing mysterious about this, nothing excessively subtle. We have projected onto the real world the moral difficulties we have actually experienced in perceiving the realities of democratic life. Surely no one will deny that, since the first World War when Walter Lippmann nearly gave up hope for public opinion, we have sustained a considerable shock. The mood of the "muckraker" has become a permanent aspect of our lives, shifting from party machines to the mass media to social or "power elites," forever refueling our Victorian sense of impending doom. And yet it would be a mistake to assume that our anxieties have derived wholly from this false mechanism. Many of the modern "exposures" of democracy have come from Fascism and Communism, or have at least been seconded by them. These ideologies have represented external threats to Western democracy of a most real kind, backed up by guns and bombs, by the territorial power of opposing nations. There has been nothing imaginary about these challenges to our survival. So that what has happened is that the fantastic has somehow gained strength from the real, the fear of "elites" from the fear of Hitler's bombs. There is a type of emotional rationality which can argue as follows: "How can we deny the Communist exposure of democracy? After all Communism has conquered half the world."

So far I have spoken of our mood of anxiety and realism as if it were itself detached from the empirical world—a response to that world, as horror is the Victorian response to sex, but not a participant in it. Actually, of course, this is far from being true. On the world plane, especially, where democracy meets Fascism and Communism, our current mood has great operational relevance. For these ideologies are utopian, have behind them the driving negative images that democracy had in the day of its origin out of the feudal order. Strictly speaking this was not true of Fascism. Negative it was, a revolt against the whole Enlightenment complex which produced both democracy and Communism, but negative it remained until the end. Communism, however, is a different matter. Rooted itself in the Enlightenment, its battle against capitalism has produced even more vivid promises of emancipation than those produced by democracy in its struggle against the old corporate order: statelessness, abundance, the end of all natural coercion. And there is a sense in which the modern democrat, when he confronts the Communist, is half struck with an image of his earlier, driving, utopian self. But how, in the age of his unillusionment, is he to argue with the Communist? How, burdened with the sadness of self-knowledge, is he to compete with him for the uncommitted world?

This question has given a new dimension to our sense of "crisis," and in the response which it has yielded, has dramatized pathetically the whole development I have been discussing. We have told ourselves again and again that we must "recapture the revolutionary spirit," that we must somehow flog ourselves backward into the halcyon and simplistic age of Paine and Jefferson. But this recommendation, which appears in so many of our political speeches and Chamber of Commerce utterances, we have never been able to follow. It has been the secular analogue to the plea for a religious revival, a political rather than a clerical fideism, and it has suffered the same major disappointments. We should be able to minimize the anxieties which have come from our realism; but the realism itself, for good or for bad, is as irrevocable as the spirit of science in the modern world. In the Twentieth century democracy will never yield another Locke to belabor the claims of the Soviet Union.

But this ought not to leave us with a sense of gloom, the feeling that all is lost. There is another aspect to this situation in which the modern democrat can take a kind of ironic satisfaction. Communism is itself subject to the same process of disenchantment that democracy has experienced, the same principle of rising realism, the same crisis of anxiety. And because its negative ideals are in fact broader than those of democracy, and in certain areas its institutions are a more glaring contradiction of them, its shock of disenchantment is bound to be even more severe than any we have sustained. Have we not already seen this process at work in Communism, from the Western "God That Failed" to the "New Class" of Milovan Djilas? There is mounting evidence to prove that Communism is susceptible to an even more frightful version of the unillusionment we have experienced, the hidden anticlimax which the Enlightenment imposes on all of its children.

I do not mean to say that the Soviet Union will collapse because of the cynicism of its inhabitants, however great the proof of that cynicism may be. Systems work, despite the anguish men have when they discover how they work. But I do mean to say that in the argument with Communism we have more to hope from an inexorable disenchantment on its part than from an impossible attempt to recapture the Eighteenth century on our part. Indeed to repeat with a manufactured passion the simplisms we have outgrown is merely to multiply the anxieties they ultimately generate, and to prolong into the era of Communism's disenchantment the problem of our own. Today democracy has nothing to lose, and everything to gain, from a frank and unfrightened recognition of itself.

* * *

The rationalism which emerged out of the ruins of the old European order is a complex matter, and in the sense of crisis we have had about democracy, no factor has been more significant than our disillusionment with it. The horror of lobbies and party machines has been somewhat dissipated over the course of time; we have learned to live with them, even if uneasily. But the horror of crowd psychology, of the mass media, of the irrational depths in the electorate, is keener today than ever. And yet the principle we have seen at work in the first case is also at work in the second. There has always been a large dash of collective emotion in democracy, and the notion that democracy is about to disappear because we have at last discovered it is more irrational than anything in the emotion itself.

But why should the attack on the old order have yielded so vivid an image of mass rationality? I have already hinted at a phase of the answer to this question: "reason" was the link which made possible a common judgment among individuals emancipated from the old group establishments. It was a kind of social cement. But more than this, it made possible the right judgment, according to God and nature, which meant that there was no longer a role for the old elites, for kings and aristocrats and priests. It united individuals, and it justified their government of themselves. Finally there was a third role that it played: it dissolved the whole mythology, from religion to monarchical heredity, which held the old order together. Not all critics of that order, of course, were extremists on all of these counts, and if Voltaire assailed the church with a simple rationalism, he still believed in monarchy. But as modern rationalism flowed into the democratic image it ultimately served all of these purposes. The Jacksonian "will of the people" glowed with a sense of community, democracy, and utility.

From the outset these principles were betrayed in the process of their realization. Whatever "reason" might mean, in order to develop democracy over the large extent of a nation state you needed much more than a utilitarian version of it to unite the people involved. You needed a myth fully as emotional in substance as the myth of the church or the myth of the king. And this is what, by an ironic twist which the French Revolution and its "cult of reason" shows in almost satiric fashion, democracy itself became: even "rationalism" became emotional. Here is the source of our modern anxieties in the face of the real democratic world, the fact that the historic ideas of democracy are as sensitive as religious symbols. But the problem of organizing "public opinion" over a large territory involved more than the transformation of democracy into a faith. Rousseau is our classic thinker here, and if we take his concern out of its immediate moral context, we will see again the sharpness of his empirical perception. What troubled Rousseau was that the intimacy of the general will might not be susceptible of projection over the wide territory of the nation, so he fell back, as we know, on the small community, the Greek city. Now whatever might be said about the collective symbiosis Rousseau desired to achieve, one thing is clear: even the most primitive kind of public opinion, the kind that is needed to execute an election, to define an issue, to organize a party, was hard to come by in the Eighteenth century. The isolation of individuals and localities, physical and psychic as well, posed a real problem for the unifying function even of "natural law." In this sense Rousseau was concerned with a plain problem of communication, and it was a very important one indeed.

It was solved by a series of technical developments which have never quite been given their due in treatments of the rise of democracy. There was the growth of cities, which brought people together on a larger scale than ever before. There was the expansion of transport, which shrank the dimension of the nation state. There was, above all the rise of cheap journalism, of newspapers that every man could buy. When the penny press was invented in Philadelphia by Christopher Conwell in 1830, and soon spread throughout the country, a cry went up on the part of genteel critics like Tocqueville. Its standards were low, its political invective almost incredible, and there is no doubt that the temper of our journalism has risen rather than fallen since that time. But this popular press, with its analogues in England and France, was indispensable for organizing the very essentials of a public opinion. Whatever its slogans were, whether "the Bank" or "the Corn Law" or the "will of the people" or *"la république,"* they provided (for all their emotionalism) the only fixed points around which popular decisions could be made.

Was the rationalism then which assailed the older order completely perverted by democracy? Was there no "progress" as men moved from the one to the other? These are subtle questions, more subtle than those involved in measuring old corporate pluralism as against democratic pluralism. For it would indeed be hard to argue, especially in light of the anxieties they have generated in our own time, that the rituals of democracy are any less ritualistic, any less superstitious, to use a more brutal word, than those of monarchy and aristocracy. The coronation of kings, Bentham to the contrary notwithstanding, was never charged with more emotional content than the reification of the people. But after this has been said, is there not surely one major difference? The symbols of monarchy are the symbols of popular submission, while those of democracy are the symbols of popular participation. The power of myth is used in radically different ways in the two cases. Nor in arriving at decisions, can we say that the rationality of interest, the Benthamite factor, has remained unchanged as we have moved into the democratic world. Whatever the emotional hullabaloo may be by which popular participation has to be implemented, out of it have come real calculations of democratic interest. It would be absurd to say, in light of all the popular social reforms of the last century, that democracy has not produced more decisions in the popular interest than the will of Eighteenth century aristocracies. "Reason" in this sense has been at work through the very medium of popular emotion.

It is unnecessary to minimize our difficulties here. The power of a great electorate to understand the technical questions of modern policy is, as Walter Lippmann and Graham Wallas began to lament after the first World War, bound to be limited. There must be a heavy reliance on the knowledge of elites. The expansion of the mass media, if it has yielded a razor-edge closeness between public opinion and government policy, has yielded also manipulative possibilities that are serious. The newspaper of the Jacksonian era could be started on a shoe-string; the newspaper of today is a big business, as is the broadcasting station as well. To prevent monopoly from functioning here is a major aspect of democratic policy. But our modern anxieties over the "mass mind" do not derive in a major sense from the realistic aspect of these policy questions. They derive instead from the collapse of our images of "rationality." From theorists of mass "contagion" and anti-individualistic irrationalism like Gustave Le Bon and Vilfredo Pareto, to mass-manipulators like Hitler, the spectre of the "crowd" has frightened the Western democrat. This is because he has never conceded to himself that without some sort of crowd his democracy could not work.

The Communist here is in the same boat, though rather a more leaky one, as was true in the case of the "general will." The Communist shares with the democrat a remarkable notion of public rationality, derived from the same Enlightenment source, but in his case several additional things are at work. In the first place he has triumphed in the backward East, where even modern media of communication have had a hard time activating populations. It is not enough to have a myth of democracy, one must have as well people who are ready to embrace it. But more than this, the centralization of communications in the hands of the state produces a frightfully overt monopoly for the manipulation of opinion in the Communist world. And that opinion is backed up by force. Under these circumstances the image of popular "rationalism" as a determinant of public policy has vastly more to hide than it does elsewhere. If we are speaking of the anxieties yielded by disenchantment on this score, surely Western democracy has reason to congratulate itself.

Political equality, the idea of a state dominated by no elite and no class, has probably been "exposed" more often than any other aspect of the democratic image. Indirectly the exposure of it is related to every other phase of the anti-democratic criticism, the idea being in the case of pluralism that "pressures" and "machines" really run the state, and in the case of mass irrationalism that "demagogues" do. But the most significant muckraking on this count in the Twentieth century has undoubtedly been done by the Marxists, who have insisted that democracy is ultimately an instrument of the capitalist minority, and that the effort to use it for fundamental social reform will lead inevitably to a fascist reaction. The high point of anxiety here was reached during the 1930s, when critics like Harold J.

Laski ended practically every book they wrote on a note of deep gloom.

Certainly the image of an equal state, as it evolved in the struggle against the old aristocracies of Europe, was as pure and shining a symbol as any other in the democratic myth. It was, indeed, related to the others by a logic which argument could not break. In the theory of Locke the individuals emancipated from the old group establishments, governed by a common principle of reason, had to "contract" on an equal basis to create the state apparatus. The whole theory would have been meaningless if the parties to the contract derived inequitable results from it. Nor for our purposes does it matter whether there are one or two contracts in Locke, whether there is only a social contract and the relationship between society and government is merely fiduciary. Whatever political commitments flow from the original pact must, by virtue of everything antecedent to them, be universal in their consequence. In the democratic mind, "special privilege" is the worst of political crimes.

Now when Marx framed his attack on democracy, when he announced that the state was the "executive agency of the ruling class," there was a good deal of wisdom in his view. He was writing of France under Louis Philippe, of England after the first Reform Act of 1832, and whereas these states had expanded the suffrage to some degree, there can be no question that they were heavily under the domination of capitalist power in land and industry. Nor as suffrage was extended even further in the Nineteenth century is it easy to deny that economic might was influential beyond proportion in the determination of public policy. In America the very pattern of democratic "exposure" was set during the Progressive Era of the early Twentieth century, when the cry against the "interests," not merely as they choked off opportunity but as they influenced the action of the state, was raised throughout the land.

But the situation has changed since the early Nineteenth century in Europe or the late Nineteenth century in America: the state has become more universal, and under the impact of reform movements, even differences in private income have been flattened out remarkably. What has happened is that the democratic state, originally distorted by the impact of capitalist power, has achieved a measure of universality which Marx never anticipated. The notion that our party competition is a myth because of the ulterior grip of "capitalism" on all of the parties involved, is a notion which has been dramatically refuted by the social gains of the Twentieth century. Of course the Marxist can always fall back on the argument that the "fundamentals" of capitalism have not yet been touched by the party system, as he did so often in the 1930s, and predict a Fascist catastrophe when the proletariat makes an effort to touch them. But what is "fundamental?" If the New Deal and the British Labor Party are excluded from the "fundamental" category, there is a real question as to whether we need interest ourselves in that category at all.

The truth is, as the experience of Spain and Germany and Italy show, Fascism has appeared in precisely those countries which either lacked a capitalist tradition or were late in developing one. And as we move farther East, where the authoritarianism of the left rather than the right has emerged as a problem in our time, it is again the historic absence of a capitalist middle class which forces itself upon our attention. Thus capitalism contributed enormously to democracy by helping to create a state which could ultimately transcend capitalist interest and become a genuine vehicle of popular liberty. One is reminded here of Eduard Bernstein, of late Nineteenth century Marxian "revisionism," of all the modifications of Marxian doctrine hated so much in the Leninist tradition. For it was this trend of thought, within socialism, which insisted that democracy could universalize itself through the action of the working class. Bernstein said that democracy was originally a "partnership," a queer echo of the "contract" of Locke, but that it was not a real partnership until the mass of the people had exploited the political rights which it gave them. His socialist utopia has nowhere appeared in the West, if only because capitalism has proved itself vastly more viable than any Marxist imagined. But the record of welfare legislation is proof enough that his faith in the ultimate universality of the democratic state was a sound one.

But can we say the same thing of the Marxist state as it has actually materialized in the East? In orthodox Marxism there is, of course, no symbolism of contract, itself a hated memory of the bourgeois order. The "dictatorship of the proletariat" emerges organically out of the decay of capitalism, ultimately withering away into a world where no state is needed. A stateless world is indeed a wild promise, one which the symbolism of democracy, for all of its claims, happily does not make. The concept of a stateless time is to be found in Locke and Rousseau, but they wisely place it at the beginning of things rather than at their end. But even within the context of the Marxian proletarian dictatorship as we know it in Russia and China, the dream of popular rule is matched by the fact of party despotism. Realism here is thus very explosive indeed. For if a man gives up his faith in a coercionless future, he has nothing to face but an authoritarian present.

Is it any wonder that, at least in our own time, the bitterness of the alienated Communist exceeds by far the passion of the disenchanted democrat?

The competition between democracy and Communism that I have sketched in this essay is, I admit, a curious one, a kind of reverse competition in the process of disillusionment. There are many levels on which that competition proceeds today, military, economic, and political, and it is not my purpose to say that this one is in any sense "ultimate." But insofar as ideas play a part in the struggle, I believe that the factor we must watch is not how glowing the utopias are but how drastic are the consequences of disenchantment—what remains when the fires are out.

Compared to pleas that we "recapture the revolutionary spirit" of the Eighteenth century, this view is bound to seem unsatisfying in certain ways. For one thing it seems to give us little to do but wait until troubles have beset the Communist world. Actually this is not true. Apart from the major task of conquering our own anxieties, of defending democracy in a realistic sense (in terms of the functioning system rather than the classical image), it does not preclude the "exposure" of Communism. The realism of opposing movements is always a factor in the precipitation of insight on the part of any system. If Marx helped to make democracy aware of the power of the bourgeoisie, certainly democracy ought not to forego the pleasure of making Khrushchev aware of the tyranny of the Communist party.

Here, however, we must guard against a certain kind of disappointment. For the intellectual competition between systems proceeds by its own historic logic, which is often independent of the charges they hurl against one another. We ought not to hope for too much from "disproving" the claims of our opponents. The power of a rising system is manifest, not in the arguments it can refute, but in the arguments it can ignore. Most of the modern "exposures" of democracy were developed by the early conservatives, from Edmund Burke to Vicomte Louis de Bonald, but their arguments rarely received a reply. Democracy ignored them, simply repeated its slogans with a wilder fury. Communism has been in the same position in the Twentieth century, and if a thousand people have joined the Communist ranks for every pamphlet which conclusively "disproves" Communism, we ought to remember, on the basis of our own experience, that this situation cannot last. It is itself, in a kind of Greek fashion, the prelude to more difficult times.

When a system has become established, when it faces enemies from within and without, gradually it begins to feel the need to reply, and the age of realism appears. The replies are matched by a deepening insecurity, and there is an odd aspect of whistling in the dark, for together with the tired affirmations there are the fantastic anxieties of self discovery. Democracy reached this point some time ago, and Communism is reaching it now.

But why should both of these systems, so antagonistic to one another in the modern world, experience the same process? I have spoken of a common Enlightenment root. The truth is, intellectually we have only experienced *one* revolution in modern times, and that is the revolution of the Enlightenment. The negative idealism that liberalism forged in the fight against feudalism, with its images of individuality, rationality, and the popular will, were adapted by Marxism to the fight against liberalism. Democracy and capitalism overthrew the old corporate order with a new set of images, but Communism has tried to overthrow them with their own. The consequence has been all manner of semantic confusion in the polemic of our time, which did not take place in the polemic of the Eighteenth century —where after all a king could pretty well be distinguished from a common man. Now we have to argue over what is "real democracy," what is "real equality." But more significant than this is the fact that when Communism appropriated the Enlightenment it appropriated also, as if in compensation for its theft, the same mechanism of idealism and self-discovery that democracy contained.

And yet: not quite the same mechanism. The triumph of Communism in the East has meant that it has taken place in an area which had no long tradition of popular participation in government. This has meant that the distance between the Communist slogans of "democracy" and the actual world has been much greater on every count than in the case of Western democracy. It has meant that the sternest despotisms have been joined to the slogans of the Eighteenth century. Moreover Marxism made some improvements on the theory of democracy in the process of taking it over: a classless, stateless, coercionless world. And so in a situation where few political promises could be fulfilled, it has multiplied their number.

Viewed against this background, the anxieties that we have experienced over witnessing democratic institutions as they actually function in the West are peculiarly fantastic. We have made the Enlightenment work in spite of itself, and surely it is time that we cease to be frightened of the mechanisms we have devised to do so. We have implemented popular government, democratic judgment, and the equal state on a scale that is remarkable by any earthly standard. There are problems here, but no "crisis," no question of "survival." In the post-Enlightenment era into which we are inevitably moving, Western democracy, if it has the courage to face itself, need not fear facing others.

SIDNEY HOOK
1902-

SIDNEY HOOK IS an American philosopher whose work includes political and social philosophy, logic, and the philosophy of history. He was educated at the College of the City of New York and Columbia University. He taught in the New York City school system and then joined the department of philosophy at New York University where he is now chairman of the graduate department of philosophy.

Early in his career he was known as an interpreter of Marx and John Dewey. His works include *From Hegel to Marx* (1935), *The Ambiguous Legacy, Marx and the Marxists* (1955), and *John Dewey, an Intellectual Portrait* (1939). In such books as *Reason, Social Myths and Democracy* (1940) and *Political Power and Personal Freedom* (1959), he argued the case for liberal democracy.

Among his other writings are *Education for Modern Man* (1946), *The Hero in History* (1943), *Heresy, Yes—Conspiracy, No!* (1953), and *Common Sense and the Fifth Amendment* (1953).

[33] *Naturalism and Democracy*

. . . for our purposes we may say that a democratic state is one in which the basic decisions of government rest upon the freely given consent

From Y. H. Krikorian, ed., *Naturalism and the Human Spirit* (New York: Columbia University Press, 1944), pp. 48–52, 53–59, 61–63, 64. Reprinted by permission.

of the governed. This obviously is only a beginning. For as soon as we begin to investigate the conditions which must be present before we grant that a state lives up to this principle, we are carried beyond the sphere of political considerations into the domain of ethics. Thus, if information has been withheld or withdrawn before consent is assessed; if the opposition is muzzled or suppressed so that consent is as unanimous as a totalitarian plebiscite; or if economic sanctions are threatened against a section of the community in the event that consent takes one form or another, we declare that the "spirit" or "logic" or "rationale" of democracy is absent from its political forms. If birth does not give divine right, neither do numbers. We are all acquainted with situations in which we say that a political democracy has traduced its own ideals. Whenever we criticize existing states which conform to the political definition of democracy on the ground that they are not democratic enough; whenever we point out that Athenian democracy was limited only to free men or that in some parts of the American South it is limited only to white men, or that in some countries it is limited only to men, we are invoking a broader principle of democracy as a controlling reference in our judgments of comparison. This principle is an ethical one.

What is this principle of ethical democracy? It is the principle of equality —an equality, not of status or origin, but of opportunity, relevant functions, and social participation. The enormous literature and bitter controversy which center around the concept of equality indicate that it is only a little less ambiguous than the concept of democracy. It is necessary, therefore, to block it off from some current notions before developing the argument.

1. The principle of equality is not a *description* of fact about men's physical or intellectual natures. It is a *prescription* or policy for treating men.

2. It is not a prescription for treating men in identical ways who are unequal in their physical or intellectual nature. It is a policy of equality of concern or consideration for men whose different needs may require differential treatment.

3. It is not a mechanical policy of equal opportunity for everyone at any time and in all respects. A musical genius is entitled to greater opportunities to develop his musical talents than someone who is tone deaf. It is equality of opportunity for all individuals to develop whatever personal and socially desirable talents they possess and to make whatever unique contributions their capacities permit.

4. It is not a demand for absolute uniformity of living conditions or even for arithmetically equal compensation for socially useful work. It de-

mands that when the productive forces of a society makes possible the gratification of basic human needs (which are, of course, historical variables), no one should be deprived of necessities in order to provide others with luxuries.

5. It is not a policy of restricting the freedom of being different or becoming different. It is a policy of *encouraging* the freedom to be different, restricting only the exercise of freedom which converts talents or possessions into a monopoly that frustrates the emergence of other free personalities.

6. It is not a demand that all people be leaders or that none should be. It does demand that the career of leadership, like all other careers, be open to all whose natural or acquired talents qualify them; that everyone have a say in the process of selecting leaders; that the initiative of leaders operate within a framework of basic laws; and that these laws in turn ultimately rest upon the freely given consent of the persons who constitute the community.

7. It does not make the assumption of sentimental humanitarianism that all men are naturally good. It does assume that men, treated as equals in a community of persons, may become better. The emphasis upon respect for the personality of all individuals, the attitude which treats the personality, not as something fixed, but as a growing, developing pattern, is unique to the philosophy of democracy.

What I have been trying to show is that the logic of the democrat's position compels him to go beyond the limited conception of political democracy—the equality of freedom—to a broader attitude extending to those other phases of social existence that bear upon the effective exercise of equality of freedom. This in fact has been the historical tendency observable wherever democratic principles and programs are permitted to operate. Perhaps the synoptic phrase "social equality," whose connotations encompass political, educational, and economic democracy, may be taken as the most appropriate expression of the meaning of democracy in the broadest sense.

It is clear that the principle of equality, like any principle of justice, cannot by itself determine what is specifically right or good in each concrete case. But whatever the right is discovered to be, from the point of view of democracy it is the result of an analysis which considers equally the needs of all the persons involved in the situation; and, furthermore, whatever the good is, it becomes better to the extent that it is shared among other members of the community. It is also clear that in concrete situations there will be conflicts between various demands for equality and that in negotiating these conflicts the methods of intelligence are indispensable for a functioning democracy. If "naturalism" and "scientific empiricism" be generic terms for the philosophic attitude which submits *all* claims of fact and value to test by experience, then scientific empiricism as a philosophy is more congenial to a democratic than to an antidemocratic community, for it brings into the open light of criticism the interests in which moral values and social institutions are rooted. *Empiricism so conceived is commitment to a procedure, not to a theory of metaphysics.*

*   *   *

We now come to the problem which is of primary concern to philosophers. What are the grounds upon which acceptance of democracy in contradistinction to other modes of social life can be justified? So far as I can see, there are four generic types of justification which have been or can be offered.

The first asserts that the rational foundation of democratic belief consists in a set of supernatural religious truths in the sense that there can be no intelligent ground for choosing between democracy and other forms of society which does not logically commit us to some kind of theology.

The second asserts the same thing about metaphysics understood as a theory of "reality." Usually these two approaches go hand in hand.

The third maintains that the choice of democracy is a nonrational preference rooted in the constitution of our natures and brought to flower by nurture and education.

The fourth affirms that the belief in democracy is an hypothesis controlled by the same general pattern of inquiry which we apply to any scientific hypothesis, but referring to different subject matter, that is, our evaluations.

DEMOCRACY AND RELIGION   Does democracy as a way of life rest upon belief in supernatural religious truths in the sense that if the latter are denied, the former must necessarily be denied? It is becoming increasingly fashionable to maintain this. Were historical considerations relevant here, I think it could be conclusively established that the great institutional religions, with the possible exceptions of some forms of Protestantism, have tended in fact to support theocratic forms of government. Nor is this surprising if the Kingdom of Heaven be taken as a model or inspiration for the Kingdom of Earth. Whoever heard of a democratically organized Paradise? Walt Whitman in heaven would meet with the same fate as Lucifer, but for different reasons. Not only is the notion of a democratically organized heaven blasphemous, but the proposal to reform along democratic

lines a hierarchically organized church would lead to excommunication. If
we examine the actual behavior which has been sanctified by the maxim:
"Render unto Caesar what is Caesar's and to God what is God's," we will
discover that historical, institutional religion has always been able to adapt
itself to any form of government or society which will tolerate its existence.

But our concern is not with historical questions, fascinating as they are,
but with the logic of the position. We must consequently rephrase the question to read: Does belief in democracy logically rest upon any theological
propositions in the sense that the denial of the second entails the denial of
the first? And for this discussion I shall take as illustrative of theological
propositions the two cardinal propositions of natural theology, namely,
"God exists" and "Man has an immortal soul." To assert that whoever has
no grounds for affirming the existence of God and immortality has no
grounds for affirming the validity of democracy is to claim that the former
are at least necessary conditions of the latter. I shall argue that they constitute neither necessary nor sufficient conditions.

*   *   *

Aside from the difficulties of establishing God's existence, how can we
get from the fact of his existence to the desirability of the democratic way
of life? None of the attributes of God, save the moral attributes, can serve as
a premise justifying one way of life rather than another. And if the moral
attributes of God can serve as premises, necessary or sufficient, for the democratic way of life, it is only because we regard them as worthy, that is, as
truly moral. Obviously any theology which makes God's power the justification or source of his goodness is worse than useless for purposes of deriving
democracy. The attribution of moral qualities to God is an expression of
what we think his qualities ought to be. And this is a problem of precisely
the same order as that which we are called upon to answer when we ask
for the grounds of our democratic allegiance.

The situation is the same if we grant that human beings have immortal
souls. In what way is this a necessary or sufficient presupposition of democracy? The brotherhood of man may be a theological fact as it is a
biological fact, but what makes it wrong for Cain to kill his brother Abel
and right, under certain circumstances, for us to kill Cain is a moral principle which can no more be derived from theology than from biology—
unless, of course, the moral principle is one of the premises of our theological (or biological) system. In this case we are no further along than we
were when we raised the question about the democratic way of life. In
passing it should be observed that belief in the immortality of the soul can

be, and has been, used (in the Hindu doctrines of *samtra* and *karma*) to sanctify the tightest system of antidemocratic social stratification the world has ever seen.

DEMOCRACY AND METAPHYSICS   The problem of the metaphysical foundation of democracy is more difficult because of varying conceptions of metaphysics. By "metaphysics" I shall understand the discipline designated by the term "ontology" or any theory of "being *überhaupt*." The evidence seems to me to be overwhelming that there is a definite historical connection between the social movements of a period and its dominant metaphysical teachings; furthermore, I am prepared to defend as a historically true proposition that systems of idealistic metaphysics, because of the semi-official roles they have played in their respective cultures, have been more generally employed to bolster antidemocratic social movements than systems of empirical or materialistic metaphysics. Whether there is *always* an intrinsic personal or psychological relation between a philosopher's metaphysics and his ethics or politics is a more difficult question, but one which seems to me to require an answer in the negative. More germane to our present concern is my contention that there is no necessary logical connection between a theory of being or becoming and any particular theory of ethics or politics. Stated more accurately, it seems to me demonstrable that no system of metaphysics *univocally* determines a system of ethics or politics. There may be certain facts about man and nature which might have a bearing upon our judgment about what social system is of the highest worth, but, as I shall argue later, these are facts concerning which the empirical sciences are qualified to report without benefit of metaphysics.

Two species of metaphysics are most often invoked in behalf of democracy. One asserts that the value of democracy or the values from which it may be derived are "grounded in reality," a phrase which is interpreted to mean that the universe "justifies" or "guarantees" both the validity and the ultimate supremacy of basic human ideals. I must confess that it is difficult for me to understand this view except as a shame-faced kind of theology. However that may be, there is no agreed-upon denotation of *the* universe. There are many universes. Nor is there any one basic human ideal, but there are many human ideals which are often in conflict with one another, even though they all invoke the universe as a ground of their validity and as a guaranty of their triumph. Finally, and most important, no matter what character the universe is alleged to have, no matter what the nature of the far-off event toward which it is moving, no matter who wins or loses, nothing logically compelling in the way of judgment follows unless *we* have already morally evaluated the character of events. For most metaphysicians the very word "reality" is an implicit value term. To be sure, history may be conceived as a struggle between the Prince of Darkness and the Prince of Light, but the latter is so named because he carries *our* moral flag.

The second metaphysical view to which resort is often made is at the same time a kind of rejoinder to our position. It distinguishes between a metaphysical realm of being and a metaphysical realm of values and grounds the democratic way of life in the latter. Just as the spectrum of colors is there to be beheld by all who are not color blind and would still be there even if man's ancestors had climbed no higher than the mole in the tree of evolution, so the spectrum of values is there to be beheld by all who are not value blind and would still be there even if human beings had never existed at all. The view that colors would still be there even if human beings had no eyes is not without its difficulties. But they do not begin to compare in difficulty with the view that values are essentially unrelated to an evaluator and his interests. Santayana has quite aptly remarked of this doctrine that there is much sense in saying that whiskey "is pervaded as it were, by an inherent intoxication, and stands dead drunk in its bottle."

The subject is vast, but it is enough to show that this view is question-begging in precisely the same way as other theological and metaphysical derivations. The existence of these absolute norms is presumably certified or authenticated at some point by an act of immediate intuition. If the testimony of the intuition is construed not merely from what individuals *say* they intuit but also from the conduct that flows from their intuition—and conduct counts more in any moral scheme than mere words—then it is clear that individuals intuit or "see" *different* values. The "great" visions are not all compatible with one another in what they command, not to mention the visions that we do not call great. Which visions are the authentic ones? Prior to every conclusion that these are the objective values of all eternity, or even of all time and existence, is the assumption that *this* is the trustworthy seer. In a dispute between two men, one of whom asserts that the other is color blind and the other that the first is "just seeing things," there are definite ways of determining who is right. In a dispute between two seers whose immediate intuitions report conflicting news about the nature and hierarchy of absolute values, there is no rational way of reaching a consensus. The true prophet cannot be distinguished from the false by invoking absolute values whose validity depends upon a prior assumption of the reliability of prophetic testimony. The complacency with which some writers have cut the Gordian knot by introducing reference to the intuitions of "the best people" of "the most cultured people" or "the saving remnant" is evidence either of parochialism or of snobbery.

The record of human error and cruelty shows what ghastly consequences often result from the conviction that one's moral insight cannot possibly be wrong and that it needs no further justification than its own incandescent purity. No more than a solipsist can make plausible on his own assumptions the existence of another solipsist, can an absolutist find a rightful place for another absolutist who disagrees with him. Absolutists face each other over an abyss which cannot be bridged even by their weapons of war.

DEMOCRACY AND PREFERENCES   The view that an acceptance of democracy is an expression of a preference does not carry us far until the kind of preference is indicated. A preference may express a passing whim or a deep natural bent; it may be impulsive or reflective. Preferences are rooted in our natures. Their forms, occasions, and objects are supplied by education, that is, broadly speaking, by social habits and intelligence. But either our natures can be changed, or the educators can be re-educated. If neither is possible, then the fact of moral choice becomes unintelligible. If we can offer no justification of a preference except that it is ours, obviously no point of intellectual or moral issue is raised; nor, a fortiori, can any be settled by the trial of arms. If we offer a justification of a preference, it will take one of the generic forms already discussed or about to be discussed.

DEMOCRACY AS A HYPOTHESIS   When democracy is taken strictly as a form of political government, its superiority over other forms of government can be established to the extent to which it achieves more security, freedom, and co-operative diversity than any of its alternatives. If we test the workings of political democracy by Paul's scheme of virtues or by Nietzsche's, we may perhaps reach another conclusion. So long as there is no dispute about observable effects and so long as we raise no question about the moral ideals by which we evaluate these effects, we have clear sailing.

But, as has already been made plain, by democracy as a way of life we mean a way of organizing human relationships which embodies a certain complex of moral ideals. Can these ideals be treated as hypotheses? The conventional reply has always been that no moral principle can be regarded as a hypothesis, for we must already have certain knowledge of what is good before we can evaluate the consequences of acting upon it. If any position is question-begging, surely this seems to be.

Were this a symposium on value theory, I would devote all my time to developing the general theory of moral ideals as hypotheses. But here I can only barely indicate that the notion is not viciously circular. A moral ideal is a prescription to act in a certain situation or class of situations in determinate ways that will organize the human needs and wants involved so as to fulfill a set of other values which are postulated as binding in relation to the problem in hand. No more than in other cases of inquiry do we start with an empty head. The cluster of values we bring to the situation is the result of prior experience and reflection. *They are not arbitrarily postulated.* The consequences of acting upon the hypothesis may lead us to challenge a postulated or assumed value. This in turn can become the subject of a similar investigation. Terminal values are always related to specific contexts; there is no absolute terminal value which is either self-evident or beyond the necessity of justifying itself if its credentials are challenged. There is no vicious infinite regress involved if we take our problems concretely and one at a time. Nor is the procedure narrowly circular. For if after a long history of raising and solving moral problems we postulate as a value in solving a later problem a value which had itself to be certified in an earlier problem, this would testify to the presence of a fruitful set of systematically related values in the structure of our moral behavior. New values would emerge or be discovered in the course of our attempt to act upon our ideals and from the necessity of mediating the conflict between the postulated values as they bear on concrete human needs in specific situations.

I should like, however, to make the general position take form out of the discussion of the theme before us. That theme is: *Why should we treat individuals of unequal talents and endowments as persons who are equally entitled to relevant consideration and care?* Short of a treatise, I can state only the reasons, without amplification of the concrete needs of the social situation which democracy seeks to meet and the institutional practices by which it must meet them.

1. This method of treating human beings is more successful than any other in evoking a maximum of creative, voluntary effort from all members of the community. Properly implemented, it gives all persons a stake in the community and elicits a maximum of intelligent loyalty.

2. It enlarges the scope of our experience by enabling us to acquire insight into the needs, drives, and aspirations of others. Learning to understand how life is organized by other centers of experience is both a challenge and a discipline for our imagination. In aiding the growth of others, we aid our own growth.

3. The willingness to understand another man's point of view without necessarily surrendering to it makes it more likely that different points of view may negotiate their differences and learn to live peacefully with one another. A democratic community cannot be free from strife in a world where inequalities will always exist, but its ethics, when intelligently acted upon, makes more likely the diminution of strife or its transference to socially harmless forms than is the case when its principle of equality is denied. The consequences are less toadying, less fear, and less duplicity in the equalitarian community than there are in the non-equalitarian society.

4. In nurturing the capacities of each individual so that they may come to their greatest fulfillment we can best share our existing stores of truth and beauty and uncover new dimensions in these realms. How can anyone dedicated to the values of science and art consistently oppose a policy which maximizes the possibility of the discovery and widest dispersion of scientific truths and artistic meanings?

5. Regard for the potentialities of all individuals makes for less cruelty of man toward man, especially where cruelty is the result of blindness to, or ignorance of, the needs of others. A community organized along democratic lines is guilty of cruelty only at those points where it has failed to live up to its own ideals. A totalitarian community is systematically insensitive to the personal needs not only of members of the outlawed scapegoat group but also of the majority of its subjects who are excluded from policy-making discussions. At best, there is no way of determining these personal needs except by the interpretation of the dictator and his experts who act on the fateful dogma that they know the true interest of their subjects better than the subjects themselves. At worst, the dictator assumes not only that he speaks for his subjects but that in some mystic way he feels and thinks for them too. Despite the great limitations—limitations from the point of view of their own ideals—under which the nineteenth- and twentieth-century democracies of the Western world suffered, I think it is indisputable, on the evidence, that by and large their social life, in so far as this was the consequence of policy, displayed less cruelty than the social life of any other historical period.

6. Reasonableness of conclusions, where attitudes and interests conflict, depends upon the degree of mutual consultation and free intellectual communication between the principals involved. The democratic way of life makes possible the widest forms of mutual consultation and communication. Conclusions reached by these processes have a quality that can

never be found where conclusions are imposed by force or authority—even if they are our own.

* * *

We now turn to the question, Is democracy feasible? We can imagine someone who has accepted the tentative ends by which we evaluate ways of life criticizing us as follows: "If only the assertions made in the previous section could be established as true, the case for democracy would be convincing. But the nature of man as we know him, of history as scientifically understood, and of the larger world we live in precludes the possibility of ever achieving democracy. It runs counter to the facts. Although you may still choose to live or to die for democracy, the attempt to realize it, like any attempt to realize an ideal which has no natural basis, will be a ghastly failure. Its natural consequences will be worse than the evils it sets out to cure, and it will subvert the very ideals to which you have appealed in your argument. Democracy is an infirmity of noble but innocent minds who have never understood the world. It is not an intelligent option."

I have to consider briefly three types of objection to the feasibility of the democratic ideal.

1. The first is based upon the alleged psychological impossibility of democracy. It maintains that democracy is too good for men who are essentially evil, fallen creatures, dominated by the lust for power, property, and self. In less theological form it asserts that democracy makes too high a call upon human intelligence and disinterestedness.

It is true that the psychological nature of man is quite relevant to our problem. If most human beings were idiots or infantile or permanently incapable of self-development, the democratic ideal could hardly be defended on plausible grounds. But there is no evidence that most human beings are such, and *an intelligent attempt to find out whether they are would require that equalization of social opportunity which is of the essence of democracy.* Even without such an experiment, if we surrender the utopian expectation of the complete realization of the democratic ideal and bear in mind that the forms of democracy may be direct as well as indirect and that democracy is compatible with the delegation of powers and responsibilities, the evidence at hand could hardly justify the belief either in universal cretinism or in man's permanent ineducability. Nor do we have to counter with the assertion that men are *infinitely* perfectible to make our option for democracy reasonable. We require merely that they be sufficiently plastic, sufficiently capable of learning, improvement and intelligent self-criticism, to choose responsibility between alternatives of action whenever—and here is the rub—they have alternatives of choice. It is only the democratic community which will systematically give them the alternatives of choice on basic decisions. It is not without significance that no free people has ever voluntarily relinquished its democratic forms in favor of a government which has openly proclaimed as its aim the establishment of a permanent dictatorship. Principled dictatorships, as distinct from those that come in through the unguarded doors of democracy, always triumph by usurpation. As low as the human estate is today, there is no reason to believe that human beings belong to a psychological species inferior to that of their ancestors. Although history is rich in human stupidities and lost opportunities, in the face of men's achievements in the arts and sciences it would be simply foolish to read history as nothing but the record of human error.

The theological doctrine of man's essentially evil nature metaphorically expresses the truth that he is always limited, always tempted, and never free from his animal origins. But, taken literally, it makes any kind of moral virtue inconceivable except by interposition of divine grace or mystery. Here, too, we do not have to counter with a contrary theological proposition that man is essentially good. He is neither one nor the other, but he becomes good or evil depending upon his society, his habits, and his intelligence.

2. The most powerful arguments against the feasibility of democracy, strangely enough, have been neglected by most social philosophers. These are developed in the writings of Gaetano Mosca, Vilfredo Pareto, and Roberto Michels. Their common thesis, formulated on the basis of vast, detailed studies of political and social history, is that all historical change whether reform or revolution, consists of the substitution of one ruling minority for another. This rule rests upon three pillars: vital myths which cement human relationships and conceal differences of interest; fraud or manipulation which negotiates differences of interests; and force which ultimately settles differences of interest. The nature of social organization, they maintain, is such that democrats may be victorious, but democracy never. So it has been; so it is; and so it will be.

. . . Three basic errors, it seems to me, vitiate their conclusion. The first is that the amount of freedom and democracy in a society is determined by a law *already known,* or, as some would say today, by a historical wave. The truth is that the amount of freedom and democracy in the present and the future depends as much upon human willingness to fight for them as upon anything else. The second error is the belief, common not only to these thinkers but also to countless others, that human nature is unchangeable. In so far as this is neither a proposition of biology or of theology nor a logical tautology, but refers to psychological and social traits, it can be shown to be false. The third is their confusion between an organizing principle and the individual members of the series organized. Since no identification is possible between the principle of democracy and any one member of the series, they go from the true conclusion that the principle is incompletely realized in any one case to the false conclusion that there are no degrees of realization in the series of cases.

* * *

That the cosmic home of man limits his power, if not his dreams, is, of course, true. It is a perennial source of his humility before the intractabilities of things and the transient character of what he builds. But it is also true that this limitation is the source of his opportunities and a necessary condition for all achievement. From these truths we cannot infer that nature is the guarantor of man's ideals, certainly not of the democratic ideal. But neither is it the enemy of human ideals. Man's friends and enemies are other men. To forget this is to go from natural piety to superstition. The cosmic scene against which men live out their lives will not be affected by Hitler's victory or by his defeat. Democracy needs no cosmic support other than the *chance* to make good. That chance it has, because man is part of nature. To ask for more is unreasonable, even if it is not unworthy. The way in which man acts upon his chances is additional evidence of the objective possibilities and novelties of existence. In so far as he is caught up in the flux of things, the intelligent democratic man honestly confronts the potentialities of existence, its futurities, its openness, its indeterminateness. He is free from the romantic madness which would seek to outlaw the truths of science and of the quaint conceit, permissible only as poetry, that nature is a democratic republic. He takes the world as science describes it. He employs his knowledge of the world to increase man's power over things, to decrease man's power over man, and to enlarge the fellowship of free and equal persons striving to achieve a more just and happier society.

VII

The political spectrum

POLITICAL DISCOURSE in the forties and fifties contrasted with that of the twenties and thirties. Fatigue was now more typical than high-spirited debate, and men were reluctant to discuss the moral dimensions of politics. Some writers applauded "the end of ideology," others lamented it—but most acknowledged it.

Even though large sections of Europe had been exhausted by the war, within a decade the welfare state and the appearance of affluence cast a haze of comfort over the unresolved problems of political economy. Moreover, the spectre of global war reinforced a feeling of individual helplessness. Government policy seemed bound to an inexorable track; debate seemed futile, and reasoned alternatives to government policy were declared to be political illusions.

It was not the first time a listless mood had descended on the West. H. Stuart Hughes points out that the years after World War I were marked by a similar "spiritual disarray." [1] However, those years were followed by a resurgence of energies which were to be channeled into several different forms of political action.

[1] H. Stuart Hughes, *Consciousness and Society* (New York: Alfred A. Knopf, Inc., 1958), p. 391.

In the postmodern era, despite an abundance of causes and rebels, many opportunities for reconstruction and reform have closed down. Furthermore, political thought and action have been sapped by the frustration of partial achievement. Some old ideals, such as perpetual peace, are remote, but others are half-achieved and half-thwarted, presenting the representatives of several political positions with the alternatives of celebrating partial victory or of protesting partial frustration. It is possible, of course, to celebrate the gains and hope for even more, but the very institutions which have brought partial success seem also to exclude ultimate victory.

Many goals of the late-modern socialists (social security, wages-and-hours laws, workmen's compensation, to mention a few) have been achieved by the welfare state, but the welfare state has also created institutions which make the ultimate conquest of socialism impossible. Therefore, socialists are divided between revisionists who think of a union with the liberal parties and who believe in consolidating progressive social gains, and intransigents who condemn the welfare state for frustrating socialism. Similarly, conservatives, though they dislike the changes in postmodern society, recognize and approve the strong and unmistakable conservative mood these changes have brought with them. Likewise, the liberals rejoice in many social, economic, and political changes of the past decades and yet recognize that a fully rational, enlightened, and free society is as far off as ever. What should one do, rejoice and support a society with freedom in it or reject present institutions because of their political evils and engage in a radical struggle for a free society?

The reading selections below illustrate how postmodern events and social conditions have affected the traditional political stances. It is clear, also, how divided is the intention of some political writers: though they try to leave the grooves of their old positions, they also seek to revive antebellum issues and even the climate.

Almost all the writers now respond to the present by proclaiming a state of crisis and by offering a diagnosis. Such an approach was common, as we have shown in Part One, after World War I as well, but now the diagnoses and the recommendations for therapy seem to become more similar, despite the differences in political position. Liberals, socialists, and conservatives share more than they are willing to admit. And underlying their laments and hopes, resolution and resignation, rebellion and disquietude, they are all engaged in an ancient quest that has been intensified in recent years—the search for community.

Diagnoses are never self-evident, although they are often presented as such. Any judgment of crisis or sickness becomes clear only if the value from which it is drawn is known. There are important differences as well as similarities between medical and political-social diagnoses that should be held in mind considering the political spectrum of the present era. The physician, like the social critic, implies a value when he declares a person ill. He means that the patient has changed from his usual state of health or from the "normal" human condition. The illness which brings physical or mental suffering is judged to be bad; it might also bring death, which is considered to be worse. These opinions on physical illness are almost universally acceptable, which makes the value judgment a suppressed or silent premise that goes unnoticed. On the other hand, claims of political crisis or social illness are founded on judgments that are not universally held. They depend on alternative conceptions of a good society, and the very lack of agreement among these conceptions charges politics with tension. What is diagnosed as social illness by one critic may be judged as a manifestation of health by another. Political thought often expresses the conflict raging among political ideals and social needs.

The difference between medical and social diagnosis is even greater when one considers the cures that are offered. Therapy of body and mind is one thing—developed through pragmatic applications of many remedies, or following from scientific theories which explain and predict the course of illness. But societies are not the same as individual humans; and they are not organisms, or machines, or galaxies. Aside from the question of whether or not structural models are useful, the terms employed to describe abnormal conditions in biological, mental, or mechanical systems apply only as analogies in societies and polities. Nonetheless, we hear a great deal about sick societies, about disintegrated social orders, and about imbalance, dysfunction, and disequilibrium. At best, these terms are suggestive metaphors; the pronouncements of illness dinned into postmodern ears certainly indicate the deep concern with which political and social writers assess their time—but too often they mislead and confuse.

LIBERALISM

Changing circumstances have altered the sense of political labels. The idea of liberalism has continued to lose rigor and clarity and is now associated with "positive" political thinking or with a generalized concern for extending social welfare. The opponents of liberalism, conservatives as well as totalitarians, use the term as a synonym for "unrealism."

Several thinkers have attempted to retrieve half-forgotten values in order to restore them for new uses in liberal thought. Edward Shils has attacked the rationalistic, utilitarian elements in liberalism, and has contended that tradition must be rescued from the distortions suffered at the hands of liberals and conservatives alike. Liberty flourishes when the traditions that gave it birth are preserved, he argues, and it is injured equally by unreflective traditionalism and by the individualism that has condemned tradition.[2]

Others have tried to resolve the dilemmas of liberal thought by reconsidering the function of public power in society. Hans Morgenthau notes that nineteenth-century liberalism conceived of liberty as individual freedom from state control; yet, when social and economic groups accumulated great power, "The state, which had just been relegated to the inconspicuous and relatively innocuous role of a night watchman by a society fearful of its power, was now restored to power as the protector of individual rights." [3] He claims that the contradiction may be resolved by revising certain conceptions. Individual freedom, he suggests, may depend on how successfully public intervention limits and controls the interaction of business enterprises and other social organizations. This way of looking at the role of public power has appeared before in the liberal political tradition, and may appropriately be called "the day-watchman state."

Writers concerned with rational defenses against arbitrary power have depended, in the past, on the guardianship of various institutions—the constitutional order, the law, the party system, the balance of interests and social groupings—to tame arbitrary power and bring it under rational control. David Riesman in *The Lonely Crowd* developed a theory of veto groups in America composed of interest clusters and pressure blocs that tend to balance and restrain one another, preventing any single ruling group from gaining control.

Likewise, Adolph A. Berle and John K. Galbraith have presented theories of countervailing power. In *The Twentieth-Century Capitalist Revolution* (1954), Berle argues that whenever great centers of power have emerged in history, they have tended to be counterbalanced by other in-

[2] Edward Shils, "Tradition and Liberty: Antinomy and Interdependence," *Ethics*, LXVIII (1958), 153–65.

[3] Hans J. Morgenthau, "The Dilemmas of Freedom," *American Political Science Review*, LI (1957), 714–23.

stitutions, and that this tendency will probably continue in the United States and in other modern capitalist states. Similarly, Galbraith believes that the huge concentrations of economic power in the United States have providentially developed in such a way as to balance and limit one another. Government intervention now insures that power will not be monopolized by any single group. The government also performs the function of redistributing a proper portion of national wealth through agencies of welfare and public service.[4] Both Berle and Galbraith identify liberalism with the doctrine of distributive justice and with the search for ways to prevent political power from becoming irresponsible.

Other "new liberals" concentrate on the technical details of reform and are reluctant to associate themselves with ideologies or philosophical systems. Writing on political economy, Dahl and Lindblom declare that both "socialism and capitalism are dead." Socialism as a general theory and capitalism as a universal method of producing and distributing goods have given way to systems which select strategically the social techniques necessary to accomplish specific tasks. Moreover, this *ought to be* the way in which political and economic matters are handled. No longer should we bother with "mythical grand alternatives"; we must devise specific techniques and adopt the ones that prove, experimentally, to solve problems. The social sciences are the most promising source of new techniques, they argue.[5]

This type of liberalism is still in the tradition of John Stuart Mill and John Dewey. It is skeptical about ultimate ends and uses the term *rationality* to refer to means. It insists on achieving reform by reducing large-scale predicaments to smaller, manageable problems, and it has a great deal in common with what was formerly called "piecemeal social engineering."

Morris R. Cohen was often associated with this point of view in the United States. Beneath his optimism about the success of applying reason to social ills, however, one finds a tragic reserve. In *The Faith of a Liberal,* he suggested that liberalism might be defined as a "rationalism that is rational enough to envisage the limitations of mere reasoning." [6] Although he called for the progressive liberation of human energies and urged the continual questioning of political assertions advertised as self-evident truths, he noted

[4] John K. Galbraith, *American Capitalism: The Concept of Countervailing Power* (Boston: Houghton Mifflin Company, 1952); *The Affluent Society* (Boston: Houghton Mifflin Company, 1958).

[5] R. A. Dahl and C. E. Lindblom, *Politics, Economics, and Welfare* (New York: Harper & Brothers, 1953).

[6] Morris R. Cohen, *The Faith of a Liberal* (New York: Henry Holt and Company, 1946), p. 437.

that the traditions that once had produced a liberal attitude in the United States were dying out. As for faith in progress, he declared that we still may have faith in the possibility of progress, but not in its inevitability. These attitudes portend a deeper concern with the dilemmas and paradoxes of political life than was characteristic of earlier generations of liberals.

Intimations of such a mood are also present in literary criticism. For example, Lionel Trilling believes that "The word liberal is a word primarily of political import, but its political meaning defines itself by the quality of life it envisages, by the sentiments it desires to affirm." [7] He is apprehensive of the tendency in liberalism, when aims are being carried out concretely, to neglect the nuances of emotion and imagination—even though the aims themselves include the appreciation of variety and the cultivation of sensibility.

Some socialists, sobered by the apparently retrograde direction of recent events, have found within liberalism—an ideology many of them once despised—values to temper the populist democratic ideal which was at the heart of most forms of modern socialism. Familiar in the writing of Rousseau, that ideal implies that in true governments *of* the people, there is no need to protect the citizens from the agents of their own will. At one time, most socialists assumed that the restraints of law and other institutions of order were to be identified with the bourgeois state, and that the socialist state, without a ruling class to oppress the people, would no longer concern itself with the problem of arbitrary power.

But Paul Ricoeur points out in his essay below that power wielders almost inevitably have interests apart from those of the community. The liberal idea of responsible power, he argues, is not restricted to bourgeois society, and in a socialist state—if there were such a state—the issue of political responsibility would be even more important than in capitalist society. "Liberal politics carried an element of universality because it was attuned to the universal problem of the state, beyond that of its specifically bourgeois form." For this reason, "the revival of liberal politics is possible within a socialist context." The state, Ricoeur explains, is a reality not reducible to economic forces, and the central problems of the state are liberty and the control of power.

So many traditional elements of liberal thought are accepted by postmodern thinkers that there has been no steady call for a resurgence, such as the conservative revival. Yet one may discern, if not different values,

[7] Lionel Trilling, *The Liberal Imagination* (New York: Doubleday Anchor Books, 1953), p. 7.

at least a different mood in some liberal writing which might be called tragic liberalism. It is more sensitive to the ironies of politics, to the way in which resolutions of certain problems create new problems, and to the unanticipated consequences of good intentions. It does not conclude, however, as conservatism often does, that because of the irony and complexity of social life, reform should not be attempted, but insists that whatever the odds the effort be made to ameliorate the conditions under which men live and to broaden their destinies by creating new possibilities. This viewpoint hews to the canons of logical argument in political discourse, but no longer assumes that the adversary will respond in the same way or that he even listens in a rational spirit. The liberal is thus committed to engage in public action, since he recognizes the interdependence of men and the impact that individual conduct has on others today; yet he expects to find in the public realm not the niceties of an idealized democratic process but the forces of mass action. While he would deny that there is an iron law of cultural decline in democratic states, he would affirm that there is no guarantee that democracy will produce lives of intelligent purpose or great civilizations, or that it will inevitably conquer tyrannical regimes.

SOCIALISM

As totalitarian communism adapted to postmodern conditions and grew stronger, democratic socialism suffered severe setbacks and grew weaker, both intellectually and politically. Briefly, when the British Labour party came to power in 1945, the victory of socialism seemed possible. A decade later, however, few would deny that socialism was in retreat.

The doctrine of progress, once the very foundation of socialist theories, is no longer taken seriously. As a leader of the left wing of the British Labour party, who is also a prominent socialist theorist, declared:

The evolutionary and the revolutionary philosophies of progress have both proved false. Judging by the facts, there is far more to be said for the Christian doctrine of original sin than for Rousseau's fantasy of the noble savage, or Marx's vision of the classless society.[8]

The conceptions of rationality and freedom, as crucial for socialist theory as they were for liberalism, have received the same criticism. As the

[8] R. H. S. Crossman, "Towards a Philosophy of Socialism," in *New Fabian Essays* (London: Turnstile Press, 1953), pp. 7–20. Italics in the original.

olympian theoretical structure collapsed, socialism was left without an explanation of reality and a basis for hope and prediction. At the same time, the strength of the welfare state damaged the socialist critique of capitalism. Socialists hovered between approving and condemning the welfare state.

Yet, one should not conclude that socialism is dead. As Irving Howe and Lewis Coser put it, socialism "is a vision which, for many people throughout the world, provides moral sustenance, but also . . . it is a vision which objectifies and gives urgency to their criticism of the human condition in our time." Its moral vitality keeps it alive, though the apocalyptic vision and the progressive confidence are gone. Socialists today are more modest in their claims:

> Socialism is not the end of human history, as the deeply-held identification of it with perfection must mean. There is no total fulfillment, nor is there an "end to time." History is a process which throws up new problems, new conflicts, new questions; and socialism, being within history, cannot be expected to solve all these problems or, for that matter, to raise humanity at every point above the level of achievement of previous societies. . . . What socialists want is simply to do away with those sources of conflict which are the cause of material deprivation and which, in turn, help create psychological and moral suffering.[9]

In politics, however, the socialist parties cannot reach agreement about what they want. They discuss what has happened to the socialist movement interminably and they debate the question of the future. This kind of debate among British socialists has tended to dissipate the energies of the Labour party. The question of unilateral disarmament, which so dramatically divided the party recently, is far from the only source of internal division. C. A. R. Crosland, speaking for the "revisionist" wing, has proclaimed that the task of the British Labour party is "to adapt itself, without in any way surrendering basic principles, to the realities of social change, and to present itself to the electorate in a mid-Twentieth-century guise," though retaining such traditional socialist ideals as social welfare, distribution of wealth according to effort, social equality, and, ultimately, a classless society.[10] The leaders, following revisionist counsel, have tried to amend the party program by eliminating the clause that calls for public ownership of the means of production, but so far without success, for the clause is a powerful symbol. Even the left wing of the party has abandoned the idea of

[9] Lewis Coser and Irving Howe, "Images of Socialism," *Dissent,* I (1954), 130.
[10] See C. A. R. Crosland, *The Future of Socialism* (London: Jonathan Cape, 1956).

total nationalization, and the extent to which property should be collectivized is no longer a burning issue.

Left-wing socialists like R. H. S. Crossman have criticized the party for its revisionist policies and for surrendering to welfare capitalism. The appearance of affluence is an illusion, Crossman says, and welfare policies merely disguise the real weaknesses of capitalism. He charges that when the Labour party was in power it betrayed its socialist responsibilities, and instead of socializing the economy merely bureaucratized the nationalized industries. For him, authentic socialism necessarily implies full public control of economic decisions—but at the same time decentralization.

Standing in a critical relation to the Labour party, groups of socialist intellectuals, many of them associated with British universities, have tried to revitalize socialism and find new directions for it. They are interested in general questions such as the drift of capitalist society and the politics of culture as well as immediate problems such as city planning. They see that questions about the quality of life are also issues of power. The work of Raymond Williams [11] and the essays collected in the volume *Conviction* (1958) contain this perspective. A recent group known as the New Left affirms its socialist identity, though it tries to escape from the stereotypes of both communism and social democracy as it searches for ways to cope with the problems of the sixties.[12]

Socialism on the Continent has followed the course of revisionism. In West Germany the social democrats, who had formed the major opposition party during the entire postwar era, revised the Weimar socialist program. Private property and religion were highly regarded in the new program, and the question of nationalizing industry was virtually ignored. The Italian and French socialists, who were filled with great expectations at the end of the war, declined in power and spirit. Yet the position is not extinct. In France, for example, Pierre Mendès-France announced his commitment to democratic socialism, and his testimonial indicates the attraction the moral and idealistic elements of socialism retain and attests to its survival as a political force.

The times have left behind the theories of G. D. H. Cole, Eduard Bernstein, Harold Laski, Karl Kautsky, and Léon Blum, together with the socialist blueprints discussed in Chapter III. Some argue that in order to

[11] Raymond Williams, *Culture and Society 1780–1950* (London: Chatto and Windus, Ltd., 1958); *The Long Revolution* (New York: Columbia University Press, 1961).
[12] The first in a projected series of New Left books is E. P. Thompson, ed., *Out of Apathy* (London: Stevens and Sons Ltd., 1960).

revive, socialism must first find a new philosophic foundation. Iris Murdoch, in the reading below, explores the reasons for its theoretical decline and suggests sources for revitalizing the socialist imagination.

In contrast to the writers who consider socialism as nothing more than a troubled political movement, Martin Buber in the selection below declares that it is the only solution to the world crisis. Modern societies, over-centralized and overpoliticized, must be transformed by the cooperative communal principle if they are to survive. Socialism means to Buber the common management of community property, but in small, organic communities. Nations and commonwealths must be reconstructed as communities of communities. Society, Buber writes, can be saved from destruction not by political solutions but only by the renewal of its cell tissue.

CONSERVATISM

The idea of the small community as a solution to the contemporary crisis is advanced by conservatives as well; though these differ from communal socialists in their rationales for power and in their conceptions of civilization, they share a reaction to technology and centralization that extends from the eighteenth century and may be found in the work of the brothers Grimm, Thomas Carlyle, and William Morris, as well as the living writers Wilhelm Röpke, T. S. Eliot, and Aldous Huxley. These negative sentiments are in themselves politically ambiguous—they may move to the left or right. On the left they inspire the political thought of anarchists and syndicalists, and on the right, a laissez-faire conservatism that finds its ideal society in unregulated early capitalism or a more poetic conservatism that goes back still further to a precapitalist past.

The poems and essays of T. S. Eliot have influenced conservative thought a great deal. In a recent lecture he claimed that his own talents are employed in "the *pre-political* area," which would place him with those subtle minds that exercise a literary, philosophical, and imaginative influence on politics. He argued, "My defense of the *pre-political* is simply this, that it is the stratum down to which any sound political thinking must push its roots, and from which it must derive its nourishment." In this area, politics is linked to ethics and theology:

For the question of questions, which no political philosophy can escape, and by the right answer to which all political thinking must in the end be judged, is simply this: What is Man? what are his limitations? what is his misery and what his greatness? and what, finally, his destiny? [13]

Eliot's work reflects the deeper spiritual needs of conservatism and the nature of its response to the postmodern world. His poetry reveals in profound and moving images the fragmentation of civilization, the despair of modern men, and the conviction that the past lives in the present. Historical changes tend to be seen as mere appearances, disguising the eternal struggle between good and evil. Eliot's political essays are really part of his poetic authorship.[14] Taken directly and literally they seem merely to claim that the modern age is no more than a grave error, and to suggest that men somehow return to a premodern way of life. Since he does not take secular history seriously, Eliot does not worry about the irreversibility of historical changes. Yet Eliot's political writing should not be dismissed as fantasy or a hankering after a lost world. Taken indirectly—or prepolitically—his political essays are prose poems, infusing politics with the images and ideals of art. The "organic Wholes" of art are the models for community in political life. "Between the true artists of any time there is, I believe, an unconscious community," one that resembles the society Edmund Burke conceived, enriched by tradition, uniting the living with the dead. Tradition is more than repetition of the behavior of previous generations, for it depends on the "historical sense," meaning

. . . perception not only of the pastness of the past, but of its presence; the historical sense compels a man to write not merely with his own generation in his bones, but with a feeling that the whole of the literature of Europe from Homer and within it the whole of the literature of his own country has a simultaneous existence and composes a simultaneous order. This historical sense, which is a sense of the timeless as well as of the temporal, and of the timeless and of the temporal together, is what makes a writer traditional.[15]

In America in the fifties a group of writers stimulated a conservative revival and searched for an intellectual tradition to provide a source of conservative principles. These "new conservatives" were less concerned with policy than with what it means to be a conservative, and attempted to establish standards for conservative thinking, feeling, and acting. Their

[13] T. S. Eliot, *The Literature of Politics* (London: Conservative Political Centre, 1955), p. 22.

[14] T. S. Eliot, *Notes Toward the Definition of Culture* (first American ed.; New York: Harcourt, Brace & Co., 1949); *The Idea of a Christian Society* (London: Faber and Faber, Ltd., 1939).

[15] Quoted by Yvor Winters in Leonard Unger, ed., *T. S. Eliot: A Selected Critique* (New York: Rinehart & Co., 1948), p. 94.

ideas were eclectic, drawn from the work of writers as diverse as Edmund Burke, Irving Babbitt, Paul Elmer More, and Winston Churchill, and their attack was directed against liberalism and socialism from John Locke through Marx to John Dewey. Russell Kirk, one of the most prominent writers in this group, frequently intoned funeral rites for liberalism:

. . . the American liberal would be quite content with a universal suburbia. It is the genuine conservative, nowadays, who speaks out against an overween-ing complacency and a world that would be a life-in-death. It is the conserva-tive who asserts the claims of Justice and Order and Liberty against the demand for a featureless Security. . . . The liberal imagination has run out; the lib-eral myth, feeble in its beginnings, is now exhausted; and what is best in our society will have to be saved, if it is to be saved at all, by the advocates of some older and more stalwart system of thought. . . .[16]

Kirk's outlook has been influenced by Eliot, but his greatest debt is to Edmund Burke, and he leaves the impression that he believes his own task is to present Burke's ideas in postmodern dress. In his essay below, Kirk argues that Burke is the "founder of modern conservative thought," and traces out the conservative principles his work contains.[17]

In another selection below, Wilhelm Röpke represents a more prosaic form of conservative thought, resembling nineteenth-century Manchester liberalism. However, like other thinkers in our time, he asks, "What un-canny disease has invaded our world?" The answer is that dogmatic ra-tionalism has pervaded Western thought and institutions since the French Revolution. The solution is a return to the liberty of "precollectivistic" so-ciety. Others holding this position include Bertrand de Jouvenel [18] and Friedrich Hayek.[19] Hayek claims that "planning leads to dictatorship be-cause dictatorship is the most effective instrument of coercion and the en-forcement of ideals. . . ." [20] This charge unites these writers, sometimes called the Ordo group. Although they have been called liberal or con-servative-liberal, their relation to the past and to the present resembles that of the other conservatives.

[16] Russell Kirk, "The Dissolution of Liberalism," *Commonweal,* Jan. 7, 1955, p. 377.
[17] See also Russell Kirk, *The Conservative Mind* (Chicago: Henry Regnery Co., 1953).
[18] Bertrand de Jouvenel, *On Power,* trans. J. F. Huntington (New York: The Viking Press, 1949); *Sovereignty,* trans. J. F. Huntington (Chicago: University of Chicago Press, 1957).
[19] Friedrich Hayek, *The Road to Serfdom* (Chicago: University of Chicago Press, 1960), first published 1944.
[20] *Ibid.,* p. 70.

Like others before them, today's conservatives designate the rise of the masses as a crucial factor in the postmodern crisis. Walter Lippmann, who appears in Chapter III, is close to the Ordo group in his views on political economy, but he brings out more clearly the aristocratic strain in classical liberalism. Effective government is impossible, he argues, when irresponsible masses try to run the state. Political decisions must be made by leaders who govern subject to natural law, which may be learned through reason and which limits power and defends civilization. The principles of natural law are embodied in the wisdom of the past and contained in the "traditions of civility." [21] How may they be recognized? By the fact that wise elites defend them. How may we recognize wise elites? By their comprehension of the traditions of civility.

RECUSANT RADICALISM

In the past, radicalism has been associated with movements to transform society by revolution, education, or some other means to some entirely new design, inspired by a moral judgment that condemned existing institutions and by a faith in inevitable victory. One form of radicalism in the postmodern period has maintained its moral fervor, but has no faith in revolution or in historical progress. This kind of radicalism, Dwight Macdonald once declared, applies

. . . to the as yet few individuals—mostly anarchists, conscientious objectors, and renegade Marxists . . . who reject the concept of Progress, who judge things by their present meaning and effect, who think the ability of science to guide us in human affairs has been overrated and who therefore redress the balance by emphasizing the ethical aspect of politics. They . . . think it is an open question whether the increase of man's mastery over nature is good or bad in its actual effects on human life to date, and favor adjusting technology to man, even if it means—as may be the case—a technological regression, rather than adjusting man to technology. . . . the firmest ground from which to struggle for that human liberation which was the goal of the old Left is the ground not of History but of those non-historical Absolute Values (truth, justice, love, etc.) which Marx has made unfashionable among socialists.[22]

To define the radical position taken by George Woodcock and Mulford Sibley in the reading selections below, we have revived an old political

[21] Walter Lippmann, *Essays in the Public Philosophy* (Boston: Little, Brown & Co., 1955).
[22] Dwight Macdonald, "The Root Is Man," *Politics,* III (April, 1946), 100.

term. *Recusancy* is a seventeenth-century word that suggests not with-drawal from politics, but intransigent refusal. Recusants and dissenters originally refused to take part in the rites of the Established Church in England, but the terms took on a more general meaning and applied to those who, on moral or religious grounds, refused to acknowledge authority or to obey commands.

Woodcock refuses to give moral assent to the practices of the modern state, and indeed denies the authority of any state. Centralization, culminating in totalitarianism, is not the result of bad or mistaken state policy, he argues, but inherent in the nature of government itself. Power destroys civilization, Woodcock suggests, and "The vitality of human culture appears to run in inverse proportion to the strength of the state." His anarchism implies the rejection of politics.

Sibley argues that an implicit radical political philosophy is contained in pacifist thought. He accepts the state as a human necessity, but refuses to participate in its war-making activities. Woodcock would contend that such a distinction is unreal, and that any involvement in the state's activity is necessarily an involvement in violence and injustice. Sibley would accept the necessity for political coercion, but would draw the line at violence and war. The logical extension of his position is unilateral disarmament. It is often considered a utopian position, but it claims to be more realistic than cold-war politics, which flirt with universal destruction.

RELIGIOUS PERSPECTIVES

The olympians, discussed in Chapter I, in the main excluded religion from political and social thought. As the olympian system gave way, religion once again moved into the sphere of political discourse. Now that men are impressed with the limits of reason, faith and dogma receive new attention; now that everyone is aware that the best intentions often turn out badly, the doctrine of original sin acquires fresh relevance. The process of secularization, once hailed as a force of liberation, now seems to destroy the most cherished values of Western civilization. Moreover, viewed in historical perspective, religious institutions are seen as checks on arbitrary state power. Religion is also associated with moral responsibility, and religious thinkers view the problem of power ultimately as the problem of a society which has gone out of moral control.

As in the past, Roman Catholic political theory applies the "unchanging principles" of Catholic philosophy to the new social and political conditions. The question for Catholic theory is not what the principles are, but how they are to be applied. Hence it never offers a single political theory but a range of political positions, extending from extreme conservatism to anarchism and pacifism. Order and justice are central values in Catholic thought. However, those thinkers who have emphasized order tend to fall into right-wing categories, in some cases supporting concordats with authoritarian regimes. Those who have emphasized justice tend to reject the status quo and to call for radical change, appealing to the authority of the social encyclicals issued by Leo XIII and Pius XI. The Catholic Worker movement, located in the slums of lower Manhattan, is a radical Catholic group which, like its leaders, Dorothy Day and Ammon Hennacy, is anarchist and pacifist in its politics.[23]

Heinrich Rommen writes that since Catholic social thought coordinates nature and grace, it avoids the optimism of the liberals and the pessimism of those who believe in total depravity. Salvation depends on action in this world; therefore the Church cannot be indifferent to social conditions. The state, however, is not the only master of moral life; it is a relative value, never absolute.[24]

The essay below by Jacques Maritain represents a position that may be called Catholic humanism. Maritain argues that the only true humanism lives on the spiritual capital of the Gospel. He believes that to consider the work of reform and social reconstruction in solely material terms is a dangerous misconception; moral and spiritual regeneration must come first. Even the success of the Russian Revolution, he claims, depended on an unconfessed spiritual commitment. Revolution and political crises, moreover, are not the work of the devil—they are the divine judgment on the nations for having failed in their spiritual mission. Atheistic communism today functions as a scourge, demolishing the blasphemous identification of social order and religion to be found in bourgeois society.

For Maritain, both civilization and democracy are the fruits of Christianity, which has been a leaven in the Western world even though ruling classes have falsely tried to buttress unjust regimes with religious authority. Democracy is the best approximation of religious ideals in political life; however, it must be a democracy which limits the role of the state and which is not blinded by the liberal secular illusions of the past.

In recent years there has been a great deal of discussion in Protestant

[23] See Dorothy Day, *The Long Loneliness* (New York: Harper & Brothers, 1952); Ammon Hennacy, *The Autobiography of a Catholic Anarchist* (New York: Catholic Worker Books, 1954).

[24] H. A. Rommen, *The State in Catholic Thought* (St. Louis: Herder Book Co., 1955).

circles of social and political problems. Notably, the ecumenical movement of the World Council of Churches in several international conferences has made it possible for leading theologians to make significant contributions to social and political thought. Their work has appeared in several volumes of the Amsterdam Assembly Series, *Man's Disorder and God's Design*. In the third volume of this series, the Assembly's social and political position is summarized.[25] The breakdown of religion, it is proclaimed, led to society's going out of moral control, and men have lost their sense of responsibility to God. Tradition and family sanctions are weakened; secular ideologies have propagated a false view of man; changes in social systems have brought fresh evils. Society now is afflicted by the inertia of huge organizations. But it is possible for the churches to help man control his technology. Justice demands that economic activity be subordinated to social ends, and there is no longer any necessity for hunger and depressions. The ideal of the small community is extolled; above all the churches must call for a responsible society, meaning a social order in which economic and political leaders are responsible to God and to the people.

The Assembly holds that churches should reject the ideologies both of communism and of laissez-faire capitalism, for each has made promises which it could not redeem. Communism emphasizes economic justice and says that freedom will follow the revolution. Capitalism emphasizes freedom and promises that justice will follow as a by-product of free enterprise. "It is the responsibility of Christians to seek new, creative solutions which never allow either justice or freedom to destroy the other." The goal of the churches must continue to be the responsible society.

The article by Paul Tillich which concludes this chapter was written in 1937, but its spirit is appropriate to the postmodern climate. It sets out the principles and the method for many religious approaches to the problems of power and the social order, and illuminates the antinomies, tensions, and ambiguities of both political and religious life.

CONCLUSION

From the positions represented in this chapter, the reader will note that postmodern writers tend to be hesitant and to make few demands. Liberals claim that the ideals of the Enlightenment still have a fighting chance; so-

---

[25] *The Church and the Disorder of Society* (New York: Harper & Brothers, 1948), pp. 197–205.

cialists assert that they cannot transform humanity, but at least can make life a little better; conservatives maintain that rational intervention in social processes brings disaster, and that therefore quietism is a virtue and following tradition the only wholesome political action. Even religion, formerly the stimulant to clearly formulated positions and to unequivocal action, now contributes to the mood of indecisiveness. Dialectical theology has made a great impression on the present generation of religious thinkers. From Paul Tillich's essay, one discovers that, according to this form of thought, in every human realm each yes coexists with a no, every action is ambiguous, and behind each idea lurks a demon.

In contemporary philosophy, existentialism contributes to the atmosphere of ambiguity. We have not included selections from secular existentialist writers, but we should point out that existentialist philosophy does not imply any single political position. Its moral and metaphysical principles may support the humanist liberalism of Albert Camus, the revolutionary socialism of Jean-Paul Sartre, or even a thoroughgoing nihilism. In any of its political forms, however, it expresses a conviction that human behavior is paradoxical and unpredictable.

If one examines the *relation* between opposing positions, one cannot but notice that true dialogue and even polemic have diminished. The great issues are dim, and each writer seems more concerned with expressing his convictions and his reactions to events than with arguing or persuading. The function of political thought during the interbellum had seemed to be to find ways to change the world, or at least to improve the social order. Perhaps the postmodern social order really is immeasurably more resistant to ideas. It seems clear in any case that although writers have not given up the hope of changing society for the better, political writing has taken on another function that was much less important in the previous generation: since opportunities for significant political action have become so limited, theoretical political and social expression is a form of effort through which men may still affirm a political identity.

CHARLES FRANKEL
1917-

CHARLES FRANKEL WAS EDUCATED at Columbia and Cornell, and
now teaches philosophy at Columbia. Besides *The Case for Modern Man* (1956), he has written *The Faith of Reason* (1948) and edited *The
Golden Age of American Philosophy* (1960).

[34]   *Liberalism and the Imagination of Disaster*

An intellectual revolution, however we may define it, is at least a revolution among intellectuals. Sometimes it may consist in a sweeping change
in the theories they hold about the nature of the universe—the sort of
thing that has happened, for example, in modern physics. Sometimes, however, it may cut deeper morally and intellectually. It may involve a change
in the intellectual's beliefs about the intellectual life itself—its conditions

From Charles Frankel, *The Case for Modern Man* (New York: Harper & Brothers, 1955), pp. 23–44. Copyright 1955, 1956 by Charles Frankel. Reprinted by permission of Harper & Brothers.

and prospects, the objectives it serves, and the standards which should govern it. It represents a shift in prevalent conceptions of intellectual method, and of the relation of reason to other human interests and to society at large.

We are all nervous now, and it is easy to mistake the tick of fashion for the crack of doom. But the evidence is growing that we are living in the incipient stages of such a revolution. The signs are all about us—in the search for faith, or orthodoxy, or peace of mind, in the growing appeal of new philosophies of Anguish and the resurgence of old philosophies of Sin, in the confidence with which large historical prophecies are pronounced, and in the fear or apathy with which concrete proposals for doing something about our problems are greeted. In the sense that it contemplates a change in the methods and values that govern the life of reason, this nascent revolution is like the revolution which took place in the sixteenth and seventeenth centuries, when intellectuals emerged from the cloister, when their values became secular, and when they took the new sciences of nature as the models of proper intellectual method. It resembles, again, the sort of large uneasiness of mind which came over the intellectuals of the newly industrialized nineteenth century, facing, on one side, the social challenge of the emergence of new and apparently rootless classes, and on the other, the intellectual challenge of Darwin's new theory of natural selection.

Like these other revolutions among intellectuals, the present revolution is a response to larger disturbances in the minds and bodies of men who are not professionally concerned with words or ideas. But it is quite unlike these other intellectual revolutions of the modern era in one fundamental respect. It rests upon a conscious rejection of what, until very recently, most educated men in the modern world have regarded as the tested methods for gaining reliable knowledge. It is an intellectual revolution whose main note seems to be the limitations of intellect, a revolution which, with only a few important exceptions, is quite frankly and directly an attempt to get back to things more fundamental than reason, or to conceptions of reason and argument that antedate the rise of modern science. It does not, in a word, accept the idea which the eighteenth century hammered out with such difficulty, and which has been a central, regulating ideal in the perspective and aspirations of modern men—the idea that reason stands above sect and party, and that it can be an independent agency in the organization of a culture. To say that this revolution contemplates a reversal of the liberal and humanist trends which have been the hopes of modern culture is not an overstatement; it is a sober paraphrase of what its leading spokesmen say.

For the historical analogue of the intellectual revolution which now seems to be taking shape, we must go back, not to Mill or Marx or Thomas Hobbes, but to Saint Augustine, or to that "failure of nerve" which overtook the Mediterranean world when the Greek city-states collapsed. It represents a deliberate shift in the focus of intellectual attention. It is an attempt to restore sobriety and humility in human affairs by the remarkable technique of fixing men's minds on transcendent and unattainable ideas. In place of confidence in what man can achieve, it emphasizes the limits of his possible achievement. Where there was a sense of the independence and neutrality of intelligence, it would substitute a sense of the dependence of intelligence on other things—on the heart within or the Mystery above—and its rightful subordination to these things. It speaks of the "treason of the clerks," but it does not mean the intellectual's betrayal of intellectual standards (which is what Julien Benda, who coined the phrase, meant), but his treason to what is outside or above intelligence. It no longer would conceive of reason primarily as an instrument of understanding and control, but as an instrument of therapy and consolation. It proposes a new orientation for the inquiring mind—where once it started with limited doubts and ended with probable beliefs, it is now to move between the poles of ultimate skepticism and absolute dogma. It seems, in short, to contemplate one of those polar shifts in perspective which have periodically overtaken the Western mind in its career.

This intellectual revolution speaks with a peculiar relevance and poignancy to the present mood—to the sense, so endemic to our times, that the old assurances have disappeared and the old limits of life have vanished. Anxiety, the feeling that one must wait impotently for some nameless doom, could at one time be taken as the sign of individual neurosis. It is now a pervasive state of mind, supported by impersonal institutions, the invisibility and anonymity of social power as we experience it, the tremendous pace of events, and the failure of our intellectual defenses. Yeats' lines, written forty years ago, express the contemporary mood almost perfectly:

> . . . Somewhere in sands of the desert,
> A shape with a lion body and the head of a man,
> A gaze blank and pitiless as the sun,
> Is moving its slow thighs, while all about it
> Reel shadows of the indignant desert birds. . . .

And what rough beast, its hour come round at last,
Slouches towards Bethlehem to be born?

This mood, and the intellectual revolution it supports, are embodied
in the new philosophies of history. Like illiberal minds, the liberal mind
in the contemporary world has been subjected to a series of mounting
shocks; and, unlike illiberal minds, its hopes were large. It is natural, therefore, that it should be something known as "the liberal outlook" which
should be the main object of our current disenchantment; and it is ex-
plicable, too, that it should be sensitive and liberal minds that have turned
most articulately against this outlook. If there is now a new assurance on
the part of the illiberal, and a failure of assurance on the part of the liberal,
the source of these feelings is the increasingly widespread conviction that
the liberal outlook on human affairs and the liberal vision of history have
demonstrated their incapacity to guide us. To believe in human progress,
to measure that progress by secular values, to believe that it is mainly implemented by scientific techniques—these have become the shibboleths that
tell us who has failed to learn anything from recent history.

For it is a philosophy of history, philosophers of history are telling
us, which is responsible for most of our present troubles. For a period
ranging from two hundred to six hundred years, it is being said, Western
society has been laboring under a fundamental misconception of the nature
and possibilities of human history. It has been pathetically trying to understand events in terms of categories that do not fit them, and indeed could
not fit any possible world in which human beings might live; it has been
blindly seeking to achieve ideals which no human beings could achieve, or
which are deeply corrupting when they are achieved. In Fascism and Communism, in the broken hopes of modern men, in the sheer darkness and
terror of our times, the emptiness and mischievousness of this view of
history has been brought home to us.

This theme has become the standard point of departure for our present
thinking about politics and society. It has brought together theologians,
historians, and social scientists, has created new schools of literary criticism,
and has established an unspoken understanding between the anxious man of
affairs and the *avant guarde* intellectual. It has been taken up, not only in
conservative and ecclesiastical circles where it has always been popular,
but in liberal and secular circles as well. It is a liberal historian who writes
that the belief in human perfectibility left liberalism unprepared for Hitler.
It is liberal literary critics who tell us that liberalism has a dangerous

penchant for abstractions, for over-simplifying, for denying the indelible mystery and ambiguities of human experience. The source and center of the intellectual revolution which seems now to be taking shape is the conviction that liberalism's approach to human affairs is empty, moribund, and responsible for most of our troubles. And it is this idea which constitutes the central theme of nearly all the new philosophies of history. The weaknesses of the liberal view of history are their point of departure; its replacement is their common objective. The essence of their message is that we cannot make headway against our present problems unless we get rid of the liberal philosophy of history and put a better one in its place.

"Liberalism" is a troublesome word, and men have used it to hide their views as well as to define them. One of Ibsen's characters remarks: "He has neither character nor convictions nor social position. So liberalism is the most natural position in the world for him." I had better say something to characterize the movement which is now so much under attack, and to indicate how I will use the term.

"Liberalism," as I intend to use the term, stands for a distinctive social movement in the modern world. For approximately two-thirds of the nineteenth century, liberalism in the United States and Great Britain stood for the espousal of the economic doctrine of *laissez faire,* and this doctrine is sometimes said to be its essence. However, this was in fact only a passing phase. Between 1905 and 1915, for example, a Liberal party in Great Britain introduced social security and labor legislation and gave the final blow to the power of the House of Lords; between 1933 and 1939 a liberal government in the United States made large-scale government action in economic affairs a permanent part of the American system. As the experience of the last seventy-five years suggests, liberalism has had certain guiding principles and attitudes which were much more fundamental than *laissez faire*.

One of them, quite simply, is what might be called an engineering approach to social action. The Eighteenth Proposition of Oxford Liberalism announced to the Victorian age: "Virtue is the child of Knowledge: Vice of Ignorance: therefore education, periodical literature, railroad travelling, ventilation, and the arts of life, when fully carried out, serve to make a population moral and happy." "The objects of this Society," declared the prospectus of the Rochdale pioneers, "are the moral and intellectual advancement of its members. It provides them with groceries, butcher's meat, drapery goods, clothes and clogs." Liberalism has regularly proceeded on the assumption, in short, that while increase in material well-being may not guarantee virtue, it removes the principal source of vice. Long before Marx's economic interpretation of history, liberalism was the social movement that spoke most distinctively for modern man's sense of the new powers which technology and science had brought him. It is a movement associated with the industrial classes and industrial outlook engendered by modern society, a movement that expresses the experience of the restless, mobile inhabitants of cities rather than of the settled, stratified country dweller. It goes with the sense that men tend to have in cities—that man makes his environment; and it expresses the peculiarly modern conviction that man can remake his life more effectively by the material reconstruction of his environment than by changing the philosophy he verbally professes. The vision behind liberalism is the vision of a world progressively redeemed by human power from its classic ailments of poverty, disease, and ignorance.

Again, liberalism has consistently taken a secular approach to political and social affairs. Except in countries where there has been a long tradition of clerical control, liberalism has not been antireligious or anticlerical as such. But it has usually stood for the doctrine of the separation of Church and State, and for antipathy to ecclesiastical control of key social activities like education or politics. From Locke and Voltaire on, liberals have argued that it is sufficient to consult human interests in this world when evaluating a social proposal or a political order. It has treated religious and philosophical beliefs as private affairs, of ultimate moment, perhaps, to the individual's salvation and to his sense of the meaning of life, but without political significance as such. In discussing the foundations of political authority it has confined itself to purely secular and naturalistic considerations—the minimizing of violence, the protection of property, the maximizing of pleasure—which might have equal cogency for men of any denomination, or of none.

This suggests, very briefly, the general perspective of liberalism, the social experience and moral climate that sustain it. But within this general perspective, which is not unlike the perspective that has animated other social movements in the modern world, liberalism has been distinguished by certain persistent principles of social action. On its political side, liberalism has stood first and foremost for parliamentary institutions and civil liberties. And behind this insistence on a permanent legal framework for disagreement and negotiation has stood a fundamental conviction about the nature of social power. Liberalism inherited from Thomas Hobbes the belief that the struggle for power is the persisting fact about political life, and it is a belief which has remained a fundamental assumption for the long line of liberal writers on politics, from John Locke to James Mill to Bertrand Russell to so recent an exponent of the philosophy of American liberalism as Professor J. K. Galbraith. Competition for power cannot be eliminated from human affairs; there is no perfect society which can guarantee that one man's interest will never collide with the interest of another man. The pursuit of a just society, therefore, is not the pursuit of an absolute which, when attained, will allow a liberal social movement to close up shop. The business of liberalism is a recurrent one—to correct imbalances of power, and to organize social institutions in such a way that no one has too much power. For the major source of social injustice is the monopoly of power by any group, political, economic, or ecclesiastical; and the only way to prevent social injustice is to counter power with power. Only by diffusing power in the community does one expand the area in which men act by free choice and not by coercion.

This concern for expanding the area of voluntary behavior is exemplified in another principle which has characterized liberalism. This has to do with the conditions which surround membership by individuals in groups. The liberal social philosophers of the seventeenth and eighteenth centuries characteristically argued that civil society rested on a "social contract"—an agreement on the part of individuals to come together and observe common rules for the sake of certain definite advantages such as the preservation of life and the protection of property. This conception of a "social contract" has been criticized on a number of counts, legitimate and illegitimate, and it has now been dropped from the liberal lexicon. But the idea of a "social contract" was at bottom a metaphor, and a peculiarly apt one. It expressed a social ideal, and the ideal persists. From the point of view of liberalism, membership in any association should never be absolutely irrevocable. The individual should always have a choice about his social affiliations.

What does this mean in concrete terms? It has meant, in the first place, a remarkable change in the relationship between the individual and the social groups to which he belongs. List a series of reforms which have contributed to the making of the modern world: the struggle against the medieval guild; the campaign to make it possible for men to be legally born, educated, and married outside the Church; the relaxation of laws governing divorce; the encouragement of secular charity; the lifting of restrictions on emigration and immigration; the progressive adoption of the policy that full employment and minimum economic security are obligations of the State to its citizens: in all of these men of liberal principles have been predominantly on the side that would release men from being tied down immovably by any social affiliation. This is the heart of what is meant, I think, when liberalism is spoken of as "individualistic."

In the second place, this drive to release the individual from unalterable dependence on any particular social group has changed the nature of most of the social groups that characterize modern society, and changed men's style of thought about society. Such liberal reforms as those mentioned above have had an effect on the structure of Western society, and on the fundamental social attitudes of Western man, which surpasses the more obvious and dramatic political upheavals in terms of which the history and progress of liberalism are usually told. A single individual now belongs to many social groups—a family, a labor union, a business, a church, a parent-teachers' association, a professional society, a political club. No one of these groups protects all his interests. Many of them overlap in the interests they protect, and compete for the individual's loyalty. A man can turn to the Church or to the State, for example, for the education of his children, to the local political clubhouse, to a veterans' society, or to a social service agency when he needs the doctor's bills paid in an emergency. And most important, each of these groups functions with a considerable degree of independence from the others. As a result, it is more difficult for any of these groups to exercise really final power over the individual. And as a further result, each of these groups tends to take on a definitely functional character. Men come to take a business-like attitude toward their membership in a group, to approach it with certain clear and definite purposes in mind, and to appraise it in terms of how it serves these purposes.

The consequences for the shape of modern society, and for men's everyday experience within it, have been profound. Groups ranging from families to churches have come to be regarded as having restricted purposes, their existence is looked upon as contingent and provisional, and the loyalty men feel toward them is limited. Piety in social attitudes has come progressively to be displaced by the habit of asking for results; fixed patterns of authority have been loosened. It is by no means accidental, indeed, that the first objective of totalitarian movements has been to break up these independent groups, to make them all appendages of a single party, and to subject them all to the influence of a single, encompassing myth. Nor is it accidental that the path to totalitarianism has been prepared by the gradual disintegration and devitalization of these independent groups under the impact of uncontrolled urbanization and industrial developments. For the sort of social groups which liberalism once fostered has been the real support for individual liberty, the effective base from which it could operate; and it created a kind of social experience which made a "show-me" attitude normal.

We come, therefore, to a certain characteristic bias or emphasis that goes with liberalism and "the liberal outlook." It is something which is suggested by our ordinary usage of the term "liberal." Liberalism stands for a general predisposition in favor of reform. When men suffer, it is the defenders of the *status quo* who must bear the burden of proof, and not those who propose to see how this suffering can be avoided. Indeed, the great and distinctive contribution of modern liberal philosophers, from Voltaire to Bertrand Russell, was to domesticate the idea of reform in Western society, to make social reform an established habit for which deliberate provision has been made in Western institutions. To put it starkly, but I think exactly, liberalism invented the idea that there are such things as "social problems."

More generally, liberalism has characteristically stood for the principle that the actions of the State are subject to a higher moral standard. To take a liberal view of politics has meant to see that political values are not final values, and that politics is not an end in itself. And although the language liberalism has employed to make this point has changed, it has been the well-being of individuals, the advantages which they immediately enjoy, to which liberals have recurrently turned for the final estimate of the worth of a social policy. Neither early liberals nor later liberals have recognized any justification for social policies that do not in the end make a difference which the individual who is at the receiving end can feel and approve.

This brings us, finally, to the more purely intellectual aspects of liberalism. Political and social liberalism have been practical movements of reform. They have been carried on by working alliances composed of diverse social elements. Far from requiring an official ideology, these alliances have done better without one. But if there has been no official liberal ideology, liberal thinkers have nevertheless tended to focus on certain themes, to emphasize certain methods, and to aim at certain broad intellectual and cultural objectives.

The belief in a society composed of a variety of groups struggling for power obviously presupposes that there will also be present certain widely shared interests, and certain attitudes that favor negotiation, mutual concession, and the nonpartisan solution of social conflicts. Among the social movements that have appeared on the stage of human history, liberalism stands distinctively for the view that it is possible to take something like an objective view of human problems, and that such an objective view is the major instrument for keeping a society at once fluid and cohesive. The development of the intellectual tools that are necessary for engendering and disseminating an objective intelligence has been a major concern of the modern liberal intellectual.

This has generally taken a distinctive turn. Empirical science, depending finally on public observation for the verification of its conclusions, has been taken as the model of objectivity in all fields. With the triumphs of modern science, intellectual liberals have distinctively emphasized, men can finally hope with some realism to remake their society by objective and nonpartisan methods of inquiry. The notion that science can be the central organizing agency for modern society is thus a distinctive feature of intellectual liberalism. Conversely, the story of intellectual liberalism is the story of a progressively more emphatic denial that scientific methods can be limited in what they study or in what they disturb. In its largest terms, intellectual liberalism has been the outlook of men who have felt that, with the emergence of science, modern society has a fox in its bosom—a dynamic institution which will allow nothing else to remain unchanged; and intellectual liberalism has been the outlook of men who have been prepared to live with science, and who have felt that its consequences can be turned to human advantage.

This relation between the social objectives of practical liberalism and intellectual liberalism's attachment to the empirical methods of science is a peculiarly intimate one. For liberalism has been a reform movement, and empirical methods are natural weapons for the reformer. "The practical reformer," as John Stuart Mill remarked,

has continually to demand that changes be made in things which are supported by powerful and widely-spread feelings, or to question the apparent necessity and indefeasibleness of established facts; and it is often an indispensable part of his argument to show, how those powerful feelings had their origin, and how those facts came to seem necessary and indefeasible. There is therefore a natural hostility between him and a philosophy which discourages the explanation of feelings and moral facts by circumstances and association, and prefers to treat them as ultimate elements of human nature; a philosophy which is addicted to holding up favorite doctrines as intuitive truths, and deems intuition to be the voice of Nature and of God, speaking with an authority higher than that of our reason.

The belief that science represented the triumphant consolidation of empirical methods was the great spur to the liberal outlook on history and liberal confidence in the future. Philosophical liberals believed until recently that they had a peculiarly powerful instrument on their side, and that reform could finally be said to be in the saddle. Mill's dictum is central to the liberal theory of history: "The state of the speculative faculties, the character of the propositions assented to by the intellect, essentially determines the moral and political state of the community. . . ." And since empirical science, with its built-in methods for correcting and enlarging its own findings, was bound to bring progress in knowledge, the moral and political progress of mankind could reasonably be expected to follow: the indefinite improvement of mankind had become a plausible ideal. In the emergence of science mankind had come upon the turning point in its career—the point at which it could finally take control of its destiny, and free itself from a slavish dependence on its past.

These liberal attitudes and ideals came together, and were supported by, a general view of human destiny. It was a view of history which was occasionally expressed in systematic form—most notably in Condorcet's classic *Outline of the Progress of the Human Mind,* written at the end of the eighteenth century. More often, however, it was something which stood behind the spoken words and explicit arguments of liberals, and has to be inferred from what they say. In its main lines, however, it is continuous from Voltaire, Gibbon, and Condorcet in the eighteenth century to Bertrand Russell and John Dewey in the twentieth. It provided a coherent framework for liberal social thinking and an impelling vision to liberal social action. The details of this view will emerge as we proceed. But its main outlines are clear.

To hold the liberal view of history meant to believe in "progress." It meant to believe that man could better his condition indefinitely by the application of his intelligence to his affairs; it meant, further, to measure the improvement of man in secular terms, in terms of his growth in knowledge, the diminution of pain and suffering, the increase of joy, the diffusion and refinement of the civilized arts; and it meant that such improvement in the condition—and, indeed, in the nature—of man could be brought about by deliberately adopted legislative and judicial techniques which would gradually change the institutions that framed men's lives. The liberal view of history was associated with the doctrine—sometimes couched in terms of "natural rights," sometimes in terms of the utilitarian principles of pleasure and pain—that in matters of morals every man might be his own priest, judging the final worth of things for himself. It looked to public education and to the developing techniques of communication to spread intelligence in the community; and it looked for the steady elimination of socially inherited inequalities, which prevented men from defending themselves against exploitation, and were responsible for most of the crimes and follies that had dominated the record of human history. It expected, therefore, to see political authority dispersed in the community at large, and to see a steady movement away from government by coercion and toward government by rational consent. And at the basis of all this, supporting and propelling it, it saw the fact of intellectual progress, now assured by the advent of science—an intellectual progress which would move the human mind away from animistic and mythological modes of thought toward definite, positive knowledge of fact, and which would substitute this knowledge of fact for tradition or revelation as the new foundation for moral and political behavior.* This picture of the human race, advancing with firm steps towards the attainment of truth, virtue, and happiness," wrote Condorcet, "presents the philosopher with a spectacle that consoles him for the errors, the crimes, the injustice, with which the earth is still polluted." The liberal vision of history did this for generations of liberals; and it brought illumination and warmth to liberal politics.

The liberal approach to the problems of the modern world has never, of course, been universally shared. But the power and appeal it exercised until recently, particularly in the United States, can hardly be questioned. For more than a century, something like this view of history provided most Americans with roughly consistent attitudes toward the past, with a conception of the overall direction in which history was—or ought to be—moving, and with ideas about the nature and conditions of human betterment. And no other view of history has been more peculiarly appropriate to American experience, or better able to provide Americans with an image of the place of their most modern, technological, and democratic of countries in the total design of world history. We have had fewer fixed traditions than other countries, and more room to make decisions on the grounds of efficiency and individual happiness. Applying human skill to the mastery of nature has been our principal occupation for a century and a half. Social engineering and applied social science, as exemplified in our advertising, our organization of factories, our military institutions, and our

---

* If anyone thinks I am unduly adorning the liberal outlook, he should go back and consider what its subtlest critic had to say about it. In this characterization of the central features of that outlook, I take my cue from Edmund Burke.

schools, have flourished here as nowhere else. "No author, without a trial," Hawthorne once wrote, "can conceive the difficulty of writing a romance about a country where there is no shadow, no antiquity, no mystery, no picturesque and gloomy wrong, nor anything but a commonplace prosperity, in broad and simple daylight, as is happily the case with my native land." It may be bad for the novelist. But it is good for a belief in free-ranging intelligence, good will, and the idea of progress.

Indeed, if many Americans have been suspicious of history and unconcerned with the past, it is perhaps because they have had a rough philosophy of history all along without quite knowing it. Because they believed in progress, the past, they knew, was, if not gone, at any rate best forgotten. The inherent superiority of the new over the old, the right of each generation to make its own way without being limited by what had gone before, its capacity in fact to do so—these have been the unspoken assumptions of ordinary men, their way of initially approaching experience and of acting and reacting upon it. It was these unexpressed assumptions that made America in particular a natural habitat for the more articulate views of liberal philosophers on the nature and meaning of history, the perfectibility of man, and the role of emancipated scientific intelligence in human affairs. The liberal outlook on history was backed up until recently by a sort of check which Americans regularly cashed at the bank of experience. And if Americans have now lost their bearings, and are in search of a philosophy of history, it is because an attitude toward history which was so much a part of the national life has obviously collapsed.

For the bank now seems to have returned the check, marked "no funds." Writing after the outbreak of World War I, Leonard Hobhouse, the British liberal, observed: "It turned out to be in sober truth a different world from that which we knew, a world in which force had a greater part to play than we had allowed, a world in which the ultimate securities were gone, in which we seemed to see of a sudden through a thin crust of civilisation the seething forces of barbaric lust for power and indifference to life." A long depression and a second war, followed by anxieties about another depression and another war, have brought this mood to this country.

There is much to support it, and to support the feeling that the liberal outlook on history was a piece of pathetic foolishness. One by one, on every crucial point it seems to have been refuted. The disasters already accomplished by technology, and the greater disasters that are threatened, have undermined the genial assumption that there is a simple connection between engineering and happiness. The belief that there is a necessary connection between progress in knowledge and progress in morality has been shattered by the spectacle which the Fascists and Communists have placed before us of bestiality joined with technical efficiency. We see that disinterested science is not necessarily beneficent. And the idea that progress in science means the gradual elimination of mythological modes of thought has been challenged by the emergence, in this most "scientific" of ages, of mythologies whose intellectual quotients are in inverse proportion to the primitive character of the passions they evoke.

Further, the belief that the growth of democratic equality would cause moral intelligence to be generally diffused in the community at large has been challenged by the vulgarization and standardization of culture, and by the heightened susceptibility of masses of men to intellectual manipulation. A sort of Gresham's law of culture has come to be exemplified—a situation in which bad ideas drive out good ones, and in which social passions have an epidemic character while social information moves sluggishly and distortedly through the social structure. The hope that political power would be diffused has been dampened by the growth of tight bureaucratic structures in business, politics, and government which concentrate decision-making authority at the top. And the ideal of an enlightened and spirited public has been obscured by the image of the mob on one side and the anonymous, powerless individual on the other. An urban and technological civilization has progressively isolated individuals from one another, making their relations more formal and impersonal, their experience more private and lonely.

Most immediately, the naïvely or shrewdly misnamed "Russian experiment" has been a traumatic experience, chilling the sensitive minds of two generations. In countries where liberal traditions are strong, Communist parties have been ineffective as practical political movements, and have stood as half-amusing, half-shocking monuments to organized foolishness and fanaticism. But they have nevertheless usurped and perverted the traditional vocabulary of liberalism, and their calculated double-talk has left no clear and unambiguous language for stating the liberal case—a contribution to semantic corruption in which our advertising men and patrioteers have joined. Even more important, Soviet imperialism has done something which no other modern imperialism has been able to do: it has moved to power by exploiting the generous impulses and large hopes that have gone with the liberal tradition. The Nazis showed us the depths of which human beings are capable; the Communists have shown us the same depths while manipulating a social vision. The faith in science, the belief in progress, the ideals of liberty, equality, and fraternity, have all been paraded before us in a murderers' masquerade. "I have the imagination of disaster," Henry James wrote in 1896, "and see life as ferocious and sinister." In the sixty years since he wrote the imagination of disaster has overwhelmed the liberal vision.

But we had better see whether we are being reasonable and prudent in being overwhelmed, or merely scared out of our wits—the only wits we have. Can we, amidst the collapse of our hopes, still maintain the essential elements of the liberal outlook on history? I think we can. And it is important to see if we can. For the liberal outlook on history was bound up with, and gave idiomatic expression to, the most distinctive features of modern history—its secularism, its dependence on science and technology, its attempt to organize society without appeal to any moral or political orthodoxy, and its faith in social mobility and free communication as the dissolvents of prejudice and error. It is possible that these things will be preserved with some other outlook on human affairs. But it is not at all certain that it will be easier.

In fact, the disasters of recent history are not enough to explain the present decline of the liberal outlook. It is not these disasters alone, but the *imagination* of disaster, and the attempt to convert that imagination from an historical circumstance into a metaphysical necessity. For there have always been reasons, after all, why liberals should feel surrounded by hostile forces, and alienated from the main drift of their times. Stupidity, fanaticism, the impatience of starving or desperate men, the inertia of old habits, and the stubbornness of vested power are not modern inventions. They are merely things which we are now able to organize more efficiently. But if we have new techniques for organizing stupidity or for exploiting fear and ignorance, then, at least in principle, we also have techniques for controlling or mitigating these things.

What is peculiar about the present situation is not simply the pressure upon liberalism, but the peculiar sort of response which liberals are making to this pressure. Instead of having a program, practical, working liberalism now seems to be reduced to a series of defensive holding actions, to containment abroad and complaint at home. Strangely, the liberal now seems to be the man who has his head turned backward, and who is anxious to see things merely kept as they were. He can work himself up to fighting for what he has, but he listens skeptically to any suggestions that he might have something more. He has courage, but it is dogged courage. He has intelligence, but it merely holds the line. The last folly of which he wishes to appear guilty is the folly of hope.

The reason, I think, is the curiously split attitude which now prevails in liberal circles toward the liberal heritage. On the level of fundamental principles, everything in liberalism seems to be in solution; on the level of practical program everything is fixed. On one side, none of the old answers is accepted; on the other, no new questions are being asked. No coherent framework pulls problems together; no exciting vision suggests new goals that might be sought. Liberalism is riding with events. It does not convert them into opportunities, as a movement which knew where it was going, and had a comprehensive program for getting there, might do. It is meeting the issues as they come up, but it exercises very little influence over what these issues are.

It is not surprising, to be sure, that liberalism should now be under reconsideration by liberals; it has been reconsidered and revised by successive generations of liberals, from Jeremy Bentham's criticisms of Locke's "natural rights," through John Stuart Mill's criticisms of Bentham, to John Dewey's criticisms of Mill. And liberalism, it need hardly be said, has never needed criticism more than now. But what is unprecedented is that liberal voices should be speaking, as they now are, in such strange accents, in the accents of Burke and Kierkegaard and Dostoevsky and Heidegger. It is what gives substance to the feeling that something like an intellectual revolution is taking place. A current of criticism that runs back to the reaction against the French Revolution has touched the American shore and the liberal mind, and is being taken seriously for perhaps the first time in our history.

The contemporary liberal, in short, is negative and defensive in his attitudes not only because he is under pressure from without, but because he has no push from within. What has gone out of practical liberalism is the liberal imagination, once so affirmative and flexible, now so nostalgic and rigid. A quality which was once the great distinction of liberalism is no longer discernible in it—the capacity to project programs that were more than merely stopgap devices, and less than utopian dreams. For, despite everything that is now being said about the classic liberals—the "doctrinaire" *philosophes* of the Enlightenment, the "narrow" and "mechanistic" Bentham, the "cold" and "intellectual" Mill—their great quality as social thinkers was a quality of imagination. They had the ability to create a fairly determinate image of what a better society would contain, to make that image large and exciting, and to think seriously and responsibly of programs for attaining it.

Why did they have this ability? At least part of the answer is plain. It is because of the view of history which they held, and because they believed in the meaning and possibility of progress. They were not just fools who believed that everything was bound to go well: it was Voltaire, after all, who wrote *Candide,* and Mill who discovered that not even the achievement of all his social projects was enough to define or to bring happiness. But neither did they believe that intellectual obscurity was a form of higher wisdom, or that suffering must be accepted for its alleged educational advantages. The present cosmic hypochondria, the creation of a metaphysics which makes anguish and sin, mystery and frustration, the plan of the universe and the keys to history, has, it seems to me, chilled the liberal imagination. And it is to help take it out of cold storage that it is worth examining what the new philosophies of history have to say, and worth considering whether there is anything left that is desirable or defensible in that liberal view of history which, when the record is examined, will be seen to have stood behind the most viable and permanent social programs instituted in the West in the past two hundred years. Certainly, it would be a grisly impertinence to try to revive the old complacent faith in the automatic progress of mankind through the steady advance of the free market, technological invention, and enlightened public opinion. But clearly it is one thing to deny that the language of reason and progress, the ideals of liberty and equality, the ethic of the questioning mind and the emancipated spirit, have the special benediction of nature; and it is quite another thing to deny that they have at least a fighting chance.

PAUL RICOEUR
1913-

A PROFESSOR OF PHILOSOPHY at the Sorbonne, Paul Ricoeur is also an editor of the well-known liberal Christian monthly periodical *Esprit*. His chief interests are philosophy of religion, ethics, phenomenology, existentialism, symbolism, and the link between psychopathology and religious interpretations of the human condition. His books include *Gabriel Marcel et Karl Jaspers* (1948); *Histoire et Vérité* (1955); and three volumes on the philosophy of the will: *Le Volontaire et l'Involontaire* (1950), and *Finitude et Culpabilité* in two volumes (1960).

[35]   The Control of Power

Every political theory which does not recognize the autonomy of politics *vis à vis* socio-economic history rejects out of hand the following propositions:

that the problem of political power in a socialist economy is not fundamentally different from the same problem in a capitalist economy;

that political power in a socialist economy offers comparable or even greater possibilities for tyranny;

and therefore that public controls as strict as, if not stricter than, those imposed in capitalist societies are necessary under socialism.

The autonomy of politics—for which I shall argue in this essay— seems to me to consist of two characteristics. On the one hand, politics embodies a human relationship which is not reducible to class conflict or socio-economic tensions in general. Even the state that is most in subjection to a dominating class is also a state precisely to the extent that it expresses the fundamental will of the nation as a whole. Moreover, the state as such need not be radically affected by major changes in the economic sphere. Through this primary characteristic, man's political existence develops a specific type of rationality which cannot be reduced to economics.

On the other hand, politics develops evils of its own—evils specific to the exercise of power. These evils cannot be reduced to others, particularly not to economic alienation. Consequently, economic exploitation can disappear while political evil persists. The very means developed by the state to end economic exploitation can provide the occasion for abuses of power, abuses which while new in expression or effect are nonetheless essentially the same in their irrational force as those perpetrated by previous states.

Specific rationality, specific evil: such is the double and paradoxical character of politics. It is the task of political philosophy to educidate the paradox. . . .

From *Dissent*, V (Winter, 1958), 43–49. Translated by Leonard Prager. Reprinted by permission.

I

If the State is simultaneously both more rational and more irrational than the individual, then the great problem of democracy is that of control of the state by the people. Just as the rationality of the state may not simply be derived from socio-economic history and its evils attributed to class contradictions, so must the problem of the control of the state be viewed as an irreducible one. The problem of controlling the state consists in developing institutional techniques specially designed to make the exercise of power possible and the abuse of power impossible. The concept of "control" proceeds directly from the central paradox of man's political existence, being the *practical* resolution of this paradox. The state should exist, but not in excess; should direct, organize and decide, so that the political animal himself may exist; but the tyrant must not be allowed to rise to power.

Only a political philosophy which has recognized the specific function and specific evil of politics is in a position to state the problem of political control correctly.

It is for this reason that the reduction of political alienation to economic alienation seems to me the weak point in Marxist political thinking. This reduction of political alienation has, in effect, led Marxism-Leninism to substitute for the problem of controlling the state that of its withering away. Even as it projects the end of the evil of the state into an indeterminate future, it underestimates the practical problem of limiting that evil in the present. In promising too much tomorrow, the thesis of the withering away of the state also tolerates too much today.

This notion can also serve as cover and pretext for the perpetuation of terrorism. By a malevolent paradox the thesis of the provisional character of the state becomes the best justification for the endless prolongation of the "dictatorship of the proletariat," thus paving the way for totalitarianism. But it is essential to notice that the theory of the withering away of the state is a logical consequence of the reduction of political alienation to economic alienation. For if the state is solely an organ of repression which arises from class antagonisms and expresses the domination of a class, then the state will disappear when the class division of society is no more. The problem, however, is to know whether the end of private ownership of the means of production will or can entail the end of *all* forms of alienation. Perhaps private ownership is in itself but one form of man's power over man; perhaps money itself is but one among other means of domination; perhaps the same spirit of domination expresses itself in exploitation through money, bureaucratic tyranny, intellectual dictatorship and clerical-ism.

It is true that Marx, Engels and Lenin attempted to relate to experi-ence the theory of the withering away of the state. They interpreted the Paris Commune as showing that the dictatorship of the proletariat can be something quite different from the simple transfer of the state's repressive power into other hands, that it can actually mean the destruction of the state machine as a "special force" of repression. If the armed people takes the place of the permanent army, if the police can be dismissed at any moment, if the bureaucracy is dismantled as an organized body and reduced to the lowest salaried condition, then the general force of the majority of the people replaces the repressive special force of the bourgois state and the beginning of the withering away of the state coincides with the dictator-ship of the proletariat. As Lenin said, *"It is impossible to pass from capital-ism to socialism without some return to primitive democracy."* And Marx could even say: *"The commune was no longer a state in the proper sense of the word."*

In the thinking of Marx and Lenin the withering away thesis was not hypocritical but sincere. Few men have so discounted the state as have the great Marxists: "As long as the proletariat still needs the state," reads the *Letter to Bebel,* "it needs it not to guarantee freedom, but to suppress its enemies, and the day when it will become possible to speak of freedom, the State as such will have ceased to exist."

II

My working hypothesis, by contrast, is that the state cannot wither away; it must be controlled by special institutional techniques.

One must go still further and assert that the socialist state requires a more vigilant popular control than the bourgeois state. And this precisely because the socialist state is the more rational, extending design and plan-ning to areas of human existence that had previously been left to chance or improvisation. Since the rationality of a state which plans to end class division is greater than that of its predecessors, its potential power and the opportunities offered to tyranny are also greater.

The task of a critique of socialist power is to show, lucidly and honestly, the new possibilities of political alienation which are linked to the very struggle against economic alienation and to the increase in state power which that struggle entails.

Here are some directions in which research on the problem of power under socialism might move:

1) One must examine to what degree "the administration of things" is necessarily "a government of persons" and to what degree progress in the administration of things gives rise to an increase in the political power of man over man.

Planning implies choice of an economic character concerning order of priority in the satisfaction of needs and in the utilization of the means of production. But immediately this choice becomes more than economic. It is a function of a general politics, that is, of a long-term project concerning the orientation of the human community. The ratio of part reinvested to part consumed, the proportion of cultural to material goods in the general equilibrium of the plan derives from a total strategic vision in which economics injects itself into politics. A plan is a technique put at the service of a project animated by implicit values, of a project which in the last analysis concerns the very humanity of man. That is why politics is the soul of economics insofar as it expresses both will and power.

Thus, an administration of things cannot be substituted for a government of persons, because the rational technique of ordering man's needs and works on the macroscopic scale of the state cannot wholly free itself from the ethical-cultural context. Moreover, it is political power which in the final instance mediates between the latent aspirations of the human community and the technological means derived from knowledge of economic laws. This linkage of ethics and technique in the planning "task" is the fundamental reason why an administration of things implies a government of persons.

2) It must also be shown how reinforcement of state power, linked to the growth of the socialist state's spheres of action, develops *possibilities of abuses intrinsic to it as a socialist state*. This will be putting to use the idea developed above that the most rational state has the greatest opportunities for being irrational.

Engels has clearly demonstrated in his *Anti-Dühring* that, as long as there persist the old division of labor and the other alienations which make of work a burden rather than a joy, the organization of production will remain authoritarian and repressive even after the expropriation of the expropriators. The allotment and the choice of work, when the latter is not spontaneous, still arises from coercion and that coercion is linked to the transition from chance to rationalization.

The temptation of forced labor thus becomes one of the greatest available to the socialist state. Since planning gives this state the *economic* monopoly over psychological coercion (culture, press and propaganda are comprehended in the plan and thus *economically* determined by the state), it will have at its disposal a whole arsenal of means, ranging from stimulation and emulation to deportation.

To opportunities for abuse which thus arise must be added the temptation to overcome irrational opposition by means more rapid than those of discussion and education. The rational state, in effect, encounters resistance of all sorts. There is, for example, the resistance characteristic of the peasantry and the petty bourgeoisie who cannot adapt to the rhythm of the technocrats but remain adjusted to former conditions. This may be dismissed as merely an habituation to outmoded economic conditions; but not all forms of resistance are so readily explained. The planning state, which thinks in terms of generations, has a project more vast and more remote than has the individual, whose interest is more immediate, usually limited to the horizon of his own life-span or that of his children. The state and the individual do not share the same time scheme and thus the individual develops interests which are not easily reconciled to the needs of the state. We are aware of at least two manifestations of this dichotomy between the state's goal and that of the citizen. One concerns the division between investment and immediate consumption, the other the determination of norms and tempo in production. The micro-interests of individuals and the macro-decisions of power are in constant tension, and this tension develops a dialectic of individual demand and state compulsion which makes misuse of power possible. . . .

In short, the socialist state is more "ideological" than the "liberal" state. It can reclaim for itself the old dreams of unifying the domain of truth in an orthodoxy encompassing all the manifestations of knowledge and all expressions of the human word. Under the pretext of revolutionary discipline and technocratic efficiency, the socialist state can justify the complete regimentation of human minds. It can do this, because it enjoys a monopoly over the means of subsistence.

All these thoughts converge towards the same conclusion: If it is true that the socialist state rather than abolishing the power problem, renews it; if it is true that it advances its rationality and increases opportunities for perversion, then the problem of democratic control of the state is even more urgent in a socialist than in a capitalist regime and the myth of the withering away of the state is an obstacle to a systematic treatment of this problem.

3) The third task of a critique of power in a socialist regime would be to reassess the critique of the liberal state in the light of this idea of democratic control. The aim here would be to distinguish which of the institutional arrangements of the liberal state are independent of the phenomenon of class domination and specifically adapted to limiting abusive power. Almost inevitably the liberal state had to appear as a hypocritical medium for permitting economic exploitation. But today, after the bitter experience of Stalinism, the distinction between an instrument of class domination and democratic control in general thrusts itself upon us. Perhaps the principle of this revaluation is contained within Marxism itself, in that it teaches us that a class in its ascendant phase fulfills a universal function. In discovering the problem of democratic controls, the *philosophes* of the 18th century discovered true liberalism, which doubtless transcends the destiny of the bourgeoisie. Liberal politics carried an element of universality because it was attuned to the universal problem of the state, beyond that of its specifically bourgeois form.

This is why the revival of liberal politics is possible within a socialist context.

III

I should like to give several examples of this discrimination between the "universal" and "bourgeois" aspects of the liberal State:

1) Is not the independence of the judge the very first means of recourse against the abuse of power? It seems to me that the judge is a personage who, by the consent of all, must be voluntarily placed on the border of fundamental conflicts of society.

Some will say that the independence of the judge is an abstraction. Precisely! Society requires for its human respiration an "ideal" function, a willed abstraction in which it projects the idea of legality which legitimates the reality of power. Without this projection, in which the state represents itself as lawful, the individual is at the mercy of the state and power itself is unprotected against its own arbitrariness. It is clear that, among other reasons, the trials of Moscow, Budapest and Prague were possible because the independence of the judge was not technically insured nor ideologically established in a theory of the judge as man above class, as abstraction in human guise, as law incarnate. Stalin was possible because there were always judges to judge according to his decree.

2) Is not the second condition for permanent appeal against the mis-

use of power that citizens should have access to sources of information, of knowledge and science, independent of those of the state? We have seen that the modern state, from the time that it economically orients all man's choices through the large decisions of its planners, determines his way of life. *And if the citizens cannot by themselves form opinions concerning these massive decisions,* this power will be less and less distinguishable from totalitarian power.

The planning state, more than any other, requires the counter force of public opinion in the true sense of the term, that is, a public which has opinions and opinion which has public expression. This implies a press which belongs to its readers and not to the state, and whose freedom of inquiry and expression are constitutionally and economically guaranteed. Stalin was possible because no public opinion could begin to criticize him. And even now it is the post-Stalinist state alone which has condemned Stalin; the people have not been allowed to speak.

These two concepts are so important that it is upon them that Stalinism foundered. The revolts in eastern Europe crystallized around the "abstract" ideas of *justice* and *truth*. If the intellectuals, writers and artists played a decisive role in these events, it was because the stake—despite poverty and low salaries—was not economic and social; the stake was political: the new "alienation" which infected political power. Now the problem of political alienation, as we know it since Plato's *Gorgias,* is the problem of *non-truth;* we have also learned of it through the Marxist critique of the bourgeois state founded on non-truth, on seeming, mystifying and lying. It is precisely here that the intellectual as such is involved in politics. He finds himself pressed to the very fore of the revolution, not merely into the ranks, when its motive force is more political than economic, when it concerns the relationship of power to truth and justice.

3) Thus it seems to me that a labor democracy requires a certain dialectic between the state and the independent workers' organizations. We have seen that the long-range interests of the state, even aside from economic problems, do not coincide immediately with those of the workers. This is evident in a socialist period in the precise sense of the term, that is a period of inequality of salaries and professional specialization which places workers, managers, intellectuals in opposition to one another. It is also apparent in a period of rapid and even forced industrialization. Consequently, only a legitimated structuring of the tensions between the state and the trade unions representing the diverse interests of the workers can guarantee the groping search for a viable equilibrium, one which is both

economically profitable and humanly tolerable. The right to strike in particular seems to me to be the only recourse of the workers against the state, even against the workers' state. The postulate that the will of the socialist state and the interests of all the workers directly coincide is a pernicious illusion and a dangerous pretext for the abuse of state power.

4) In short, the key is that of control of the state by the people, by the democratically organized base. Do a plurality of parties, the technique of "free elections," and parliamentary government arise from the "universality" of the liberal state or do they belong irremediably to the bourgeois period of that state? One need not have a preconceived idea. It is certain that planning techniques demand that the socialist form of production be as irrevocable as the republican form of our [French] government. Carrying out a plan demands plain powers, a stable government and a long-term budget. Now our [French] parliamentary techniques of alternating majorities in power does not seem very compatible with the tasks of the new state rationality. On the other hand it is no less certain that free discussion is a vital necessity for the state: discussion gives it impetus and orientation, discussion curbs its abuses. Democracy is discussion. Thus in one way or another discussion must be *organized,* and it is here that the question of parties poses itself. The case for the multiple parties system is advanced by the fact that in the past this system has not only reflected tensions between social groups as determined by class division, but has also furnished an organization for political discussion as such, thus having "universal" and not only "bourgeois" meaning. Analysis of the concept of the party solely in terms of socio-economic interests seems to me dangerously simplistic. This is why the notions of multiple parties and single party must not be judged solely from the point of view of class dynamics, but also from the point of view of techniques for controlling the state.

I do not know if the term "political liberalism" can be saved from discredit. Perhaps it has been definitively compromised by linkage with economic liberalism. But if the term can be saved, it will express that which must be said: whether the state establishes liberty through its rationality or whether liberty, through resistance, limits the irrationality of power, the central problem of politics is liberty.

Socialism

IRIS MURDOCH
1919-

IRIS MURDOCH, PHILOSOPHER AND NOVELIST, was educated at Oxford, where she has been a fellow of St. Anne's College since 1948 and a tutor in philosophy. In both her fiction and her philosophical writing she explores the imaginative and the logical dimensions of themes such as appearance and reality, freedom and responsibility. She has written a philosophical study, *Sartre, Romantic Rationalist* (1953), and several novels, the most recent of which are *The Bell* (1958) and *A Severed Head* (1961).

[36]   A House of Theory

The Socialist movement in this country is suffering from a loss of energy: and this is a misfortune which touches the whole community. The Tories are, by their nature, not a party of ideals and moral inventions. It is rather their function, a function which liberal-minded Socialists must

From Norman MacKenzie, ed., *Conviction* (London: Macgibbon and Kee, 1958), pp. 218–33. Reprinted by permission.

welcome in general even if they often deplore it in particular, to check and criticize the more abstract visions of the Left. But now the salt itself seems to have lost its savour. The more progressive section of society seems able, in this time, to provide very little in the way of guidance and inspiration. There is a certain moral void in the life of the country. How has this come about?

It does not seem difficult to analyse the sources of moral energy which fed the Socialist movement in the past. First and most primitive was the desire for human equality, the valuing of the poorest he with the richest he: a desire made more intense by the miseries of the Industrial Revolution. Developing later, and giving to the movement its most characteristic and probably most profound motive, was the conception of exploitation, whose technical form was the Labour Theory of Value. Joined with this was what one might call Benthamite efficiency, the desire to tidy up society, sweeping away metaphysical obscurantism and out-dated tradition, and plan rationally for the happiness which was so patently lacking. To be compared and contrasted with this was Marxist efficiency, closely knit theoretical scientific Socialism, offering a more complex philosophy and a more revolutionary vision. A product of this confident science was a certain determinism whose appeal was religious as well as scientific: the apocalyptic belief that capitalism was doomed, the Messianic belief in the role of the proletariat. Independent of these sources of power but mingled with all of them was a general revolt against convention, the resistance to the nineteenth-century father-figure in his many guises, the revolt against sexual taboos and restrictions, the movement for the liberation of women. With this one may connect the hatred of industrial civilization which certainly moved many people and which sometimes led to nostalgia for the apparent simplicity of the medieval world: all that poor Morris had in mind when he cried that 'Shoddy is king!' Consolation and promise were, however, to be found in the sheer energy generated by the working men's associations themselves, the discovery of active community and common purpose, the warmth of proletarian solidarity. While common in some way to almost all, and equally Christian, Marxist and anarchist in its inspiration, was the vision of an ideal community in which work would once again be creative and meaningful, and human brotherhood would be restored; whereas now the working classes were deracinate and disinherited, human nature both in them and in their masters mutilated and divided: all that could be summed up in the Hegelian concept of 'alienation'. These —and the list could doubtless be extended and the items subdivided in different ways—were the complex and various ideals and motives of Socialism.

Nearly all this great accumulation of energy has now been dissipated, by the achievement of goals which satisfied the desires in question, or by the achievement of something which made the desires less sharp. As a result largely of the working-class movement itself together with the development of new economic techniques we have the Welfare State. Many of the most obvious injustices and deprivations have been remedied. The rich are not so rich nor the poor so poor, and there has been a serious attempt to create equality of opportunity. The sense of exploitation has faded and the struggle for equality tends to take the form of the struggle for higher wages. It now seems possible that capitalism is not doomed after all, or at least not doomed in the dramatic manner once envisaged. On both the theoretical and the practical plane economists have led us to believe that capitalism can (perhaps) overcome its tendency to periodic crises, and does not inevitably (and, as was thought, increasingly) grind the faces of the poor: thus removing the sense of impending cataclysm, destroying the attraction of the Labour Theory of Value, and blunting the Socialist claim to provide the only true science of society.

The appeal of Marxism as a body of doctrine, never strong in this country, has diminished with the lengthening history of the U.S.S.R. Marx and Marxist theorizing have been left to the Communists. The revolt against convention which was a sacred duty in the nineteenth century and between the wars was at least still fun, is now, as a result of the greater flexibility of society, not obviously either. Shoddy remains king, but nobody bothers much. The vision of the ideal society, which, outside Marxism, was often associated with opposition to parliamentary methods, lingered a while in Guild Socialism, and perished with the development of the parliamentary Labour Party. The sentiments of 'proletarian solidarity' have given way to the sentiments of the trade union movement. Socialism no longer seems (as it seemed to certain favoured spirits) something essentially and profoundly Christian. The anarchists are gone. What has triumphed (with many results for which we are profoundly thankful) and what is still largely with us is Benthamite efficiency, the spirit of the Fabians. Socialism, in the course of its rapid and successful development, has lost even the oddments of theory with which it started out.

It will be argued that the absence of Socialist theory is neither surprising nor deplorable. The British were never ones for theory in any case. We have always been empiricist, anti-metaphysical in philosophy, mistrustful of theoretical systems. It is true, indeed, that our political thought has been almost entirely sceptical, and could be summed up under the three heads of Tory scepticism, scientific scepticism, and Liberal humanist scepticism. Hume and Burke would represent the first. (Don't theorize: let habit and tradition solve your problems.) Bentham, with some assistance from Hobbes, would represent the second. (Don't theorize: theories are troublesome metaphysical nonsense. What matters in society is the mechanics of satisfaction.) Locke and Mill, with Kant in the background, would represent the third. (Don't theorize: empirical truths are unsystematic and moral truths can't be demonstrated; so be an undogmatic but rational respecter of persons.) However, all these thinkers were themselves theorists in the minimal sense that they invented certain concepts, presented certain schemes and pictures, in terms of which we can understand their differences and conceive them as constituting a conversation. The Liberals particularly set before us, unsystematically but with a power which has kept its hold upon our imagination, certain spiritual values 'fixed' in concepts such as that of Natural Rights.

Now 'Socialist theory', in so far as it existed here, was not directly a product of academic thinkers. It was not in its nature to be. It consisted rather of overlapping sets of ideas argumentatively put together by bodies such as the Socialist League and the Fabian Society. We have never produced a great Socialist philosopher, and we have paid very limited attention to the one whom we had in our midst. However, our Socialist thinking was strongly nourished by philosophical ideas which had become to some extent common property: the ideas of Locke and Utilitarians, as well as modified versions of Marxism and Utopian theories imported from France. A Socialist philosophy does not, and should not, grow independently of the main stream of philosophical ideas. With this in mind, we turn from the 'conceptual conversation' of the past to look at the contemporary scene, where we notice, of course, a marked contrast. Developments in mathematical logic, the influence of scientific method, the techniques of linguistic analysis, have combined to produce a new philosophy even more antitheoretical than its sceptical predecessor. The creative aspect of philosophy is reduced almost to nil, or rather tends to be limited to the invention of what one might call 'logical gadgets'. (Russell's Theory of Descriptions would be a distinguished example.) The instrument that results is for its purposes excellent, and the critical task of philosophy, of great importance in a liberal society, has never been performed with greater exactness and rigour. Many persistent philosophical problems have been solved by the new method, which represents a genuine advance and discovery. One con-sequence, however (and I shall argue an unnecessary one), is that a cer-tain area of thought which was formerly influential is becoming denuded. As philosophy is steadily drawn in the direction of logic and becomes in-creasingly a matter for highly trained experts, it separates itself from, and discourages, the vaguer and more generally comprehensible theorizing which it used to nourish and be nourished by; and the serious student who is either studying philosophy or is influenced by it (and there are many of the latter) develops an almost excessive fear of imprecision. 'Everything that can be said can be said clearly'. Outside the small area of possible clarity lies the dangerous region of 'mushy' thinking from which attention is averted. The ideal is a demonstration, however tiny, which is clean, sterile and con-clusive.

In considering the way in which the modern techniques have affected moral and political theory, and through them affected a range of less specialized theorizing, it is necessary to consider in more detail the 'elimi-nation of metaphysics'. In the past philosophers had invented concepts expressive of moral belief and presented them as if they were facts con-cerning the nature of the mind or of the world. Philosophy since Hume has, in opposing dogmatic rationalist metaphysics in general, been critical of this tendency, but in varying ways. Briefly, criticism of metaphysics may proceed along Humian, Kantian, or Hegelian lines. Hume, who wished to maintain as rigorously as possible that we know only what our senses tell us, denied the existence of moral 'facts' or 'realities', analysed moral con-cepts into non-rational feelings and imaginative habits, and was prepared to let basic empirical concepts suffer the same fate. Kant, anxious to de-fend both the reality of our empirical knowledge and the dignity of our moral intimations, changed Hume's habits of imagination into 'categories', or fixed formal modes of apprehension which if directed upon empirical data would yield knowledge. Other matters, such as the moral law and the destiny of the soul, could only be objects of belief, although the reality and something of the nature of the spiritual realm were suggested by the de-mands of conscience. Hegel altered Kant's criticism in a fundamental way when he conceived the categories as the forms not only of our knowledge of empirical objects, but also of our apprehension of social, psychological and spiritual realities, and subjected them to historical treatment, taking the pattern of their development initially from the history of the changing ideas of the human race.

These philosophers were all critical of dogmatic rationalist metaphysical arguments (such as those used by St. Thomas) and so put a question mark beside moral beliefs (ethical, political, religious) which rested formerly on such arguments; but they differed significantly in the place which they assigned to beliefs of this kind under the new regime. Neither Hume nor Kant had any interest in variety of belief, nor, for these purposes, any historical sense; and they virtually removed from the scene of rational discourse all theories except those specifically accredited by their own philosophical methods. Hume, whose 'elimination' followed the simple lines of atomic empiricism, regarded all beliefs as equally irrational, but some as inevitable and convenient. Civilized life after all rested on moral instincts, and Hume described those of his own society. Kant more systematically attempted to show why our knowledge was limited to certain kinds of object, and in doing so pictured the mind as solely concerned with the objects of empirical observation and science. He allowed in addition one belief (the belief in Reason, with the related and tentative belief in God); and all other theories were classed together as superstition. Hegel differed from Hume and Kant in that he did not regard the fact that a belief or theory had rested upon a discredited type of philosophical argument as automatically denuding the theory of philosophical interest or even of truth. He did not class theories as either whole truths or total errors, but allowed to all the influential beliefs that men have held the status of interpretation and discovery of the world. All three philosophers are, of course, vulnerable themselves, though not in the essentials of what they have to say, to attacks by modern critics; all three, in different ways, can lay claim to the title of 'empiricist'.

Modern British philosophy is Humian and Kantian in inspiration. It follows Hume and Kant in regarding sense experience as the only basis for knowledge, and it follows Kant in attempting more specifically to show that concepts not so based are 'empty'. Moral and political philosophies, never the centre of modern developments, have followed in the wake. Attention was concentrated upon the error by which former philosophers imagined themselves to be making quasi-factual discoveries when really they were preaching. Since morality could not be 'proved' by philosophical argument, philosophy now aimed at studying it in a non-partisan manner, analysing the 'logic' of moral discourse in general, and leaving moral exhortation to others. Moral judgements, since they did not admit of empirical verification, were first said to be 'emotive' (a Humian position). Later they were likened to imperatives (a Kantian position). In this second and more subtle phase Kant's single belief in Reason was re-fashioned into a formula which purported to give the defining characteristics of any moral judgement as such. A certain rationality, universality, consistency, was thought of (with minor variations) as defining the *form* of morality irrespective of its *content*. The variegated area of moral belief or ideology (the special religious and social concepts which guide choice, and which are in many cases a legacy from the metaphysical philosophers) was usually treated, together with the actual patterns of choice, as part of the *content*, the region of morality which is a matter of personal decision and not a proper subject for analysis. Such beliefs were not, of course, demonstrable by philosophical argument (it was the mistake of the old philosophers to think that they were) and they came to be seen as the idiosyncratic 'colour' of a moral attitude, something nebulous and hazy, which for purposes of exposition and example was best analysed away into actual choices at the empirical level. The moral agent is thus pictured, in a manner which remains essentially Kantian, using his reason to survey the ordinary factual world, and making decisions therein which he will defend by reference to facts and to simple principles offered as patently rational. He is *not* pictured as using his reason to explore the intermediate area of concepts. Moral action, in short, is seen as the making of sensible choices and the giving of sensible and simple reasons. It is not seen as the activity of theorizing, imagining, or seeking for deeper insight.

Such a situation could hardly be promising for the department of ethics which deals with political concepts; and indeed whereas moral philosophy survives by the skin of its teeth, political philosophy has almost perished. Whereas some sense (misleading perhaps but just comprehensible) can be made of the idea of the 'fundamental logical form of a moral judgment', very little sense can be made of the idea of the 'fundamental logical form of a political judgment'. The 'form' of political thinking cannot be thus plausibly divided from its 'content'. It is impossible not to regard political philosophy in an historical manner; and it is very difficult to extract from it the type of compact philosophical problem whose statement and attempted solution now alone count as really 'doing philosophy'. Exercises in political philosophy consist usually in carefully restricted discussion of a well-known concept (such as the General Will), attempting with brief and undetailed historical reference to illustrate the nature and 'function' of the concept. These discussions are often valuable; but they are not popular because they necessarily lack precision of a logical or near-logical variety, and their atmosphere is such as to suggest that 'political concepts' are things of the past. They are, after all, metaphysical beliefs, or, to be more exact, they are personal evaluations and social recommendations disguised as truths about the nature of man. It is the (logical and morally neutral) task of the philosopher to pierce this disguise, and to separate the solid recommendation from the conceptual mask which comes away, as it were, empty. The giving of actual political advice and the suggestion of moves in definite political dilemmas are, of course, not the business of philosophy. Here again, political activity, like moral activity, is thought of as the making of empirical choices, and not as itself an activity of theorizing. The most consistent exposition of this generally favoured view is in T. D. Weldon's *The Vocabulary of Politics*. A curious result of this development is that liberal and progressive thinkers who are touched by modern philosophy come on what they take to be logical grounds to the same conclusions about political theorizing to which conservative thinkers come on frankly moral grounds. Berlin and Weldon and Popper agree with T. S. Eliot and Michael Oakeshott that systematic political theorizing is a bad thing. The former think it so because it is 'metaphysical' and opinionated and obscures the scientific business of altering our society for the better. The latter think it so because it interferes with the deep operation of traditions which should not be tampered with by critical reflection. Bentham and Hume are still with us; but we are losing touch with Locke and Mill.

The discrediting of theory has, then, taken place as a result of a combination of different tendencies: Tory scepticism, Benthamite scepticism, a Kantian protestant fear of 'superstitions', and more recently a dislike of Marxism, all apparently supported by the anti-metaphysical destructive techniques of modern philosophy. It is moreover felt that theorizing is anti-liberal (an idea which it is easy to extract from Kant) and that liberal-minded persons should surround their choices with a minimum of theory, relying rather on open above-board references to facts or to principles which are simple and comprehensible to all. Here it is important, in accordance indeed with the clear-headed methods of analytical philosophy, in order to see what one is doing, to separate neutral arguments from evaluations. The point, briefly made, is that the 'elimination of metaphysics', though it shows that moral beliefs were often supported by erroneous arguments, does not *ipso facto* 'discredit' the area of moral belief, properly understood as an area of conceptual moral exploration. All that the anti-metaphysical arguments make clear (and one would not wish to deny this) is that moral theorizing is not the discovery of bogus 'facts', but is an activity whose purpose and justification are moral. Hegel understood and displayed this, though he also sinned by picturing moral exploration dogmatically within a rigid hierarchy of ideas. There is no philosophical (or scientific) reason why there should not be an area of theory, reflection, meditation, contemplation, *between* ourselves and the simple empirical levels of action, so long as certain arguments are eschewed, and so long as it is clearly recognized that the purpose of the theorizing is moral clarification and understanding: and moral, political, and religious theories have, after all, often served this purpose in the past and have not always been 'mere superstitions'. It therefore emerges that the choice made by our intellectuals against the development of theories is a moral choice.

Is it a right choice? I think not. There is a serious and growing void in our thinking about moral and social problems. This void is uneasily felt by society at large and is the more distressing since we are now perhaps for the first time in our history feeling the loss of religion as a consolation and guide; until recently various substitutes (Socialism itself, later Communism, Pacifism, Internationalism) were available: now there seems to be a shortage even of substitutes. The claim of Socialism to be a 'science' has become, after many setbacks, a trifle less confident, and has certainly lost the spiritual appeal which it once had. Of course, Socialism will continue to attempt to constitute itself a science, in the sense of a highly organized investigation of the mechanics of society. But, and especially since it cannot now claim to be the scientific study of an inevitable quasi-biological development, it should, in my view, also far more frankly and more systematically declare itself a morality. Our Socialist ancestors had ideals but no techniques. We are often amazed at their naïveté. We have the techniques: *these* we can explain clearly. But we can give only a rather brief and denuded explanation of our ideals. We have reached a stage where the amount of theory is decreasing while the social need for it increases. The danger represented by what is called the 'managerial society' is the danger (already diagnosed by Marx as characteristic of capitalism) of the division of the population into experts and ignorant (though perhaps contented) masses with no communication between them; and we have now the additional spectacle of the division of the experts into mutually non-comprehending groups. What is needed is an *area of translation,* an area in which specialized concepts and recommendations can be seen and understood in the light of moral and social ideas which have a certain degree of complexity and yet are not the sole property of technicians. There is a Tory contention that theorizing leads to violence, and there is a liberal contention that theories are obscurantist and blinding. Now on the contrary it is the absence of theory which renders us blind and which enables bureaucracy, in all its sense, to keep us mystified; and as for violence, the absence of civilized theorizing can also lead in that direction. It is dangerous to starve the moral imagination of the young. We require, in addition to our 'science', a social analysis which is both detailed and frank in its moral orientation. A more ambitious conceptual picture, thought out anew in the light of modern critical philosophy and our improved knowledge of the world, of the moral centre and moral direction of Socialism would enable those of us who are not experts to pick up the facts of our situation in a reflective, organized and argumentative way: would give us what Shelley called the power to imagine what we know. Socialist thought is hampered, and the appeal of Socialism is restricted, because our technical concepts are highly esoteric and our moral concepts are excessively simple and there is nothing in between. We need, and the Left should provide, some refuge from the cold open field of Benthamite empiricism, a framework, a house of theory.

In response to these ambitious desires it may be coldly argued that 'Socialist theory' was a product of the working-class movement, and that the working-class movement no longer exists, whereas the trade union movement does; and that it is impossible to call up moral visions in a situation in which there is no material incentive to make people lift their eyes to the hills. Further, it will be said that a perfectly good Socialist theory of a down-to-earth kind does exist and indeed fills many volumes. Those who ask for information about Socialism are not left unanswered: what more is required? If it is a 'philosophy' that is wanted, that can hardly be produced on the spur of the moment and would in any case be itself something esoteric and technical.

It is doubtless true in a sense that the working-class movement as a dynamic theory-generating body with immediate objectives does not at present exist. There is less appetite for ideas. Education is no longer seen as the road to freedom; it is seen as the road to a higher salary. However, the working class exists, and with it many of the ills of capitalist society which were a scandal to our forefathers, and a large body of increasingly vague but loyal Socialist opinion exists, too. The question must be continually asked: how are we to keep *thought* about Socialism and *moral concern* about Socialism alive in a Welfare State? Spiritual unrest and even decisive moral reactions are not lacking. 'Public opinion' is the name of a force which should control and check the development of bureaucracy; and public opinion has shown itself of late, to the dismay of certain Tories, to be still both lively and powerful. Its activity, however, has been limited to the sudden assertion of some absolute value (usually in the field of foreign affairs), obscurely grasped, without any connection of a theoretical kind being established between the occasions. A religious and moral vocabulary is the possession now of a few; and most people lack the words with which to say just what is felt to be wrong is wrong.

If in the hope of finding such words we turn to the available Socialist 'literature' we are likely to be disappointed. In the old days professional and amateur philosophizing fed the public mind with ideas. Now, for a larger vision, we have to look back to Laski or Tawney, or search for hints in eccentric and little-known works by Christians or Marxists. What we have plenty of, and what we find officially in the centre of the picture, are detailed technical books and pamphlets in which the author tells us briefly that we need public ownership in order to bring about equality, and then hurries on to the details of investment policy. The motive, the passion, in much of this literature is patently that of an expert making an efficient plan. Needless to say one is glad of such experts, and it would be an impertinence in the uninitiated to criticize what they cannot understand. But what one requires as well is a little more pausing at the first stage, a little more analysis, in terms which are not those of the economist, of an idea such as that of equality: which is, in fact, in danger of becoming the only influential 'general idea' of contemporary Socialism. More theoretical exploration of the aims of Socialism, those aims to which all techniques are properly subordinate, would benefit both sides of the specialist barrier. The expert would gain that unifying vision which is needed to prompt more inspired and imaginative uses of technique. He would be less isolated, more responsible, more often compelled to explain; and having to explain, to connect, to translate, deepens understanding: while the average person would gain a more complex and hence, more influential, grasp upon what is being done on his behalf, instead of coming straightaway up against the blank wall of economics.

It is not true that 'everyone knows what is wrong with our society' and differs only over a simple choice of solutions. What we see as wrong, and our ability to express what is wrong in a profound, subtle and organized way, will influence our conception of a solution as well as providing us with the energy to seek it. We have not mended our society since its mutilation by nineteenth-century industrialism. There is less poverty but no more (in some ways less) true community life. Work has become less unpleasant without becoming more significant. The gulf remains between the skilled and creative few and the unskilled and uncreative many. What was formerly called the proletariat has lost what culture it once had, and gained no true substitute. A stream of half-baked amusements hinders thought and the enjoyment of art and even of conversation. Equality of opportunity produces, not a society of equals, but a society in which the class division is made more sinister by the removal of intelligent persons into the bureaucracy and the destruction of their roots and characteristics as members of the mass. In short, a proletariat in the fundamental sense intended by Marx still exists: a deracinate, disinherited and excluded mass of people. Only this mass is now quiescent, its manner of life largely suburban and its outlook 'petty bourgeois', and it increasingly lacks any concept of itself as deprived.

This list of grievances, whose items would be regarded as obvious in some quarters and eccentric in others, suggests to me the following, which again will seem obvious to some. The Socialist movement should most explicitly bring back into the centre of its thinking its original great source of inspiration and reflection, the problem of labour: the problem, that is, of the transformation of labour from something senseless which forms no real part of the personality of the labourer into something creative and significant. To do this would involve a re-thinking and re-grouping on the theoretical plane of concepts such as 'exploitation' and 'alienation' which were formerly gathered about the Labour Theory of Value. The familiar ideas of 'equality', 'democracy', 'freedom' need to be understood anew in the light of the problem of labour and not treated as independent 'absolutes' whose meaning is taken for granted. To treat them so is ultimately to imperil them. Theory is needed to refresh the tired imagination of practice. Our available techniques seem uninteresting because we lack the vision to grasp their possibilities. A line of thought such as I have in mind leads very directly to problems that have been immensely discussed and considered. Can we maintain educational standards while making education more 'democratic'? Can we make technical training more universal and more humane while still meeting the demands of industry? Is the 'opposition' role of the trade unions a hindrance to 'industrial democracy'? It is not that these matters have not been studied; it is rather that they have been studied on too severely practical a level and without a sufficient consultation of our final aims. We should profit by widening the area in which they could be discussed with intelligence and interest.

A study of nationalization, such as *Industry and Society*, for instance, representing an official attitude, combines complexity at the technical level with question-begging simplicity at the moral and theoretical level. 'Nationalization' is spoken of in terms of redistribution of wealth, making important powers socially responsible, and enabling the State to profit from the present structure of our economy. 'Equality' is envisaged as the abolition of private shareholding and inherited position. Keynes is quoted to show that with the dissociation of ownership of industry from its control there is a 'natural line of development' in the direction of State Socialism. There is a momentary reference to 'joint consultation'. Nothing whatever is said about conditions and nature of work. Whereas critics (the authors of *The Insiders,* for instance) who rightly suggest that 'public ownership must be seen in the context of the original Socialist goal of industrial democracy', and who point out the extent to which *Industry and Society* takes our present economic and social structure for granted, still conceive the problem in terms of 'the democratization of power', rather than in terms of what such a shift of power would be designed to achieve. But the fascination of the means should not obscure the end; and to *see* the end we must to some extent separate it from the often seemingly barren complexities of the means; we must to some extent lend it the remoteness and flexibility of a 'theory'. The problem of the transformation of labour is not only the original centre of Socialist thought, it is the problem of the managerial society. Even to pose it with enough clarity would help to counteract the movement of talent and interest toward the levels of bureaucratic control and to send it back toward the levels of the unskilled. But for such an idea to be fruitful, a source of inspiration and controversy, it needs to be presented as an autonomous moral conception, independent of, and ultimately sovereign over, the mere notions of efficiency and rational 'tidying up' of capitalist society into which Socialism is in danger of degenerating.

If we seek here for inspiration in our own tradition we have not far to look. The Guild Socialists dissented on precisely this point from their less ambitious and more purely Benthamite colleagues, in that the latter were concerned with the damage done to the consumer and the former with the damage done to the producer. The Guild Socialists were deeply concerned with the destruction of community life, the degradation of work, the division of man from man which the economic relationships of capitalism had produced; and they looked to the transformation of existing communities, the trade unions, the factories themselves, for the restoration of what was lost. Such ideas were and are easy targets for mockery, and in the old Guild Socialist form were doubtless quite impracticable; and they faded from the scene partly because they were tied to inadequate techniques, and partly because the conception of the Welfare State presented an easier and more obviously urgent and attractive target. With its achievement it is necessary to renew our study of the more difficult and fundamental problems of capitalism. We cannot live without the 'experts'. But the true 'open society' in the modern world is one in which expertise is not mysterious; and the only way to prevent it from becoming mysterious is continually to subordinate its activities to a lively and *interested* public opinion: and this in turn will languish without 'theories'. The Welfare State marks the successful end of the first road along which the Socialist movement in this country elected to travel. It is time now to go back and explore the other road, to go back to the point of divergence, the point not so very far back at which we retained as a living morality ideas which were common to Marx and to William Morris.

MARTIN BUBER
1878-

MARTIN BUBER WAS BORN in Vienna, raised in Galicia, and studied philosophy and art history at the universities of Vienna and Berlin. He became active in Jewish cultural and educational affairs in his early twenties and was quickly recognized as a creative and imaginative leader and thinker. His early published works, such as *Daniel* (1913), reveal a blending of mystical and German neo-Idealist thought. After World War I, however, his writing focused more and more on the concrete categories of personal existence. In his famous volume *I and Thou* (1923) Buber brought the sacred into personal relations, suggesting that encounters between men should recreate the confrontation of man and God. He wrote, "The relation with man is the real simile of the relation with God." He joined with several Catholic and Protestant thinkers to found the religious journal *Die Kreatur*. With Franz Rosenzweig, he translated the Hebrew Bible into a German version of majestic power and beauty. He was also associated with Rosenzweig and others in leading a cultural renaissance among Jews until he was forced to leave Germany in 1938.

Buber was a professor of social philosophy at the Hebrew University in Jerusalem until his retirement in 1951, and during the formative struggles of Israel was a leading member of a small group who called for cooperation between Arab and Jew to form a binational state. His views on religious and political questions have often stirred much controversy. He has received such notable honors as the Goethe Prize and the Peace Prize of the German book industry. His prolific outpouring of writings include *Between Man and Man* (1947), *Eclipse of God* (1952), *For the Sake of Heaven* (1945), *Good and Evil* (1953), *Moses* (1946), *The Prophetic Faith* (1949), *Tales of the Hasidim* (1947–1948), and *Two Types of Faith* (1951).

Although many of Buber's interpreters put him in the existentialist tradition and although he has some affinities with such writers as Kierkegaard and Dostoevsky, he himself has denied being an existentialist, and the mainstream of his work bears him out. Unlike the essentially subjectivist tenor of such writers as the young Sartre, Buber's basic categories extend logically to social and political thought. In such works as *What is Man?* (1938) and *Paths in Utopia* (1949), he has called for the construction of communities that would reinforce the life of dialogue and personal responsibility. He believes that both modern individualism and collectivism are destructive of these ends.

[37]   The Renewal of Society

For the last three decades we have felt that we were living in the initial phases of the greatest crisis humanity has ever known. It grows increasingly clear to us that the tremendous happenings of the past years, too, can be understood only as symptoms of this crisis. It is not merely the crisis of one economic and social system being superseded by another, more or less ready to take its place; rather all systems, old and new, are equally involved in the crisis. What is in question, therefore, is nothing less than man's whole existence in the world.

Ages ago, far beyond our calculation, this creature "Man" set out on his journey; from the point of view of Nature a well-nigh incomprehensible anomaly; from the point of view of the spirit an incarnation hardly less incomprehensible, perhaps unique; from the point of view of both a being whose very essence it was to be threatened with disaster every instant, both from within and without, exposed to deeper and deeper crises. During the ages of his earthly journey man has multiplied what he likes

From Martin Buber, *Paths in Utopia* (New York: The Macmillan Company, 1950), pp. 129–38. Reprinted by permission of Routledge and Kegan Paul Ltd.

to call his "power over Nature" in increasingly rapid tempo, and he has borne what he likes to call the "creations of his spirit" from triumph to triumph. But at the same time he has felt more and more profoundly, as one crisis succeeded another, how fragile all his glories are; and in moments of clairvoyance he has come to realize that in spite of everything he likes to call "progress" he is not travelling along the high-road at all, but is picking his precarious way along a narrow ledge between two abysses. The graver the crisis becomes the more earnest and consciously responsible is the knowledge demanded of us; for although what is demanded is a deed, only that deed which is born of knowledge will help to overcome the crisis. In a time of great crisis it is not enough to look back to the immediate past in order to bring the enigma of the present nearer to solution; we have to bring the stage of the journey we have now reached face to face with its beginnings, so far as we can picture them.

The essential thing among all those things which once helped man to emerge from Nature and, notwithstanding his feebleness as a natural being, to assert himself—more essential even than the making of a "technical" world out of things expressly formed for the purpose—was this: that he banded together with his own kind for protection and hunting, food gathering and work; and did so in such a way that from the very beginning and thereafter to an increasing degree he faced the others as more or less independent entities and communicated with them as such, addressing and being addressed by them in that manner. This creation of a "social" world out of persons at once mutually dependent and independent differed in kind from all similar undertakings on the part of animals, just as the technical work of man differed in kind from all the animals' works. Apes, too, make use of some stick they happen to have found, as a lever, a digging-tool or a weapon; but that is an affair of chance only: they cannot conceive and produce a tool as an object constituted so and not otherwise and having an existence of its own. And again, many of the insects live in societies built up on a strict division of labour; but it is just this division of labour that governs absolutely their relations with one another; they are all as it were tools; only, their own society is the thing that makes use of them for its "instinctive" purposes; there is no improvisation, no degree, however modest, of mutual independence, no possibility of "free" regard for one another, and thus no person-to-person relationship. Just as the specific technical creations of man mean the conferring of independence on things, so his specific social creation means the conferring of independence on beings of his own kind. It is in the light of this specifically human idiosyncrasy that we have

to interpret man's journey with all its ups and downs, and so also the point
we have reached on this journey, our great and particular crisis.

In the evolution of mankind hitherto this, then, is the line that pre-
dominates: the forming and re-forming of communities on the basis of
growing personal independence, their mutual recognition and collaboration on that basis. The two most important steps that the man of early
times took on the road to human society can be established with some certainty. The first is that inside the individual clan each individual, through
an extremely primitive form of division of labour, was recognized and
utilized in his special capacity, so that the clan increasingly took on the
character of an ever-renewed association of persons each the vehicle of a
different function. The second is that different clans would, under certain
conditions, band together in quest of food and for campaigns, and consolidated their mutual help as customs and laws that took firmer and firmer
root; so that as once between individuals, so now between communities
people discerned and acknowledged differences of nature and function.
Wherever genuine human society has since developed it has always been
on this same basis of functional autonomy, mutual recognition and mutual
responsibility, whether individual or collective. Power-centres of various
kinds have split off, organizing and guaranteeing the common order and
security of all; but to the political sphere in the stricter sense, the State with
its police-system and its bureaucracy, there was always opposed the organic, functionally organized society as such, a great society built up of
various societies, the great society in which men lived and worked, competed
with one another and helped one another; and in each of the big and little
societies composing it, in each of these communes and communities the
individual human being, despite all the difficulties and conflicts, felt himself
at home as once in the clan, felt himself approved and affirmed in his functional independence and responsibility.

All this changed more and more as the centralistic political principle
subordinated the de-centralistic social principle. The crucial thing here was
not that the State, particularly in its more or less totalitarian forms, weakened and gradually displaced the free associations, but that the political
principle with all its centralistic features percolated into the associations
themselves, modifying their structure and their whole inner life, and thus
politicized society to an ever-increasing extent. Society's assimilation in
the State was accelerated by the fact that, as a result of modern industrial
development and its ordered chaos, involving the struggle of all against all
for access to raw materials and for a larger share of the world-market,

there grew up, in place of the old struggles between States, struggles between whole societies. The individual society, feeling itself threatened not only by its neighbours' lust for aggression but also by things in general, knew no way of salvation save in complete submission to the principle of centralized power; and, in the democratic forms of society no less than in its totalitarian forms, it made this its guiding principle. Everywhere the only thing of importance was the minute organization of power, the unquestioning observance of slogans, the saturation of the whole of society with the real or supposed interests of the State. Concurrently with this there is an internal development. In the monstrous confusion of modern life, only thinly disguised by the reliable functioning of the economic and State-apparatus, the individual clings desperately to the collectivity. The little society in which he was embedded cannot help him; only the great collectivities, so he thinks, can do that, and he is all too willing to let himself be deprived of personal responsibility: he only wants to obey. And the most valuable of all goods—the life between man and man—gets lost in the process; the autonomous relationships become meaningless, personal relationships wither; and the very spirit of man hires itself out as a functionary. The personal human being ceases to be the living member of a social body and becomes a cog in the "collective" machine. Just as his degenerate technology is causing man to lose the feel of good work and proportion, so the degrading social life he leads is causing him to lose the feel of community—just when he is so full of the illusion of living in perfect devotion to his community.

A crisis of this kind cannot be overcome by struggling back to an earlier stage of the journey, but only by trying to master the problems as they are, without minimizing them. There is no going back for us, we have to go through with it. But we shall only get through if we know *where* we want to go.

We must begin, obviously, with the establishment of a vital peace which will deprive the political principle of its supremacy over the social principle. And this primary objective cannot in its turn be reached by any devices of political organization, but only by the resolute will of all peoples to cultivate the territories and raw materials of our planet and govern its inhabitants, *together*. At this point, however, we are threatened by a danger greater than all the previous ones: the danger of a gigantic centralization of power covering the whole planet and devouring all free community. Everything depends on not handing the work of planetary management over to the political principle.

Common management is only possible as socialistic management. But if the fatal question for contemporary man is: Can he or can he not decide in favour of, and educate himself up to, a common socialistic economy? then the propriety of the question lies in an inquiry into Socialism itself: what sort of Socialism is it to be, under whose aegis the common economy of man is to come about, if at all?

The ambiguity of the terms we are employing is greater here than anywhere else. People say, for instance, that Socialism is the passing of the control of the means of production out of the hands of the entrepreneurs into the hands of the collectivity; but again, it all depends on what you mean by "collectivity". If it is what we generally call the "State", that is to say, an institution in which a virtually unorganized mass allows its affairs to be conducted by "representation", as they call it, then the chief change in a socialistic society will be this: that the workers will feel themselves represented by the holders of power. But what is representation? Does not the worst defect of modern society lie precisely in everybody letting himself be represented *ad libitum?* And in a "socialistic" society will there not, on top of this passive political representation, be added a passive economic representation, so that, with everybody letting himself be represented by everybody else, we reach a state of practically unlimited representation and hence, ultimately, the reign of practically unlimited centralist accumulation of power? But the more a human group lets itself be represented in the management of its common affairs, and the more it lets itself be represented from outside, the less communal life there is in it and the more impoverished it becomes as a community. For community—not the primitive sort, but the sort possible and appropriate to modern man—declares itself primarily in the common and active management of what it has in common, and without this it cannot exist.

The primary aspiration of all history is a genuine community of human beings—genuine because it is *community all through.* A community that failed to base itself on the actual and communal life of big and little groups living and working together, and on their mutual relationships, would be fictitious and counterfeit. Hence everything depends on whether the collectivity into whose hands the control of the means of production passes will facilitate and promote in its very structure and in all its institutions the genuine common life of the various groups composing it—on whether, in fact, these groups themselves become proper foci of the productive process; therefore on whether the masses are so organized in their separate organizations (the various "communities") as to be as powerful as the common economy of man permits; therefore on whether centralist representation only goes as far as the new order of things absolutely demands. The fatal question does not take the form of a fundamental Either-Or: it is only a question of the right line of demarcation that has to be drawn ever anew—the thousandfold system of demarcation between the spheres which must of necessity be centralized and those which can operate in freedom; between the degree of government and the degree of autonomy; between the law of unity and the claims of community. The unwearying scrutiny of conditions in terms of the claims of community, as something continually exposed to the depredations of centralist power—the *custody of the true boundaries,* ever changing in accordance with changing historical circumstances: such would be the task of humanity's spiritual conscience, a Supreme Court unexampled in kind, the right true representation of a living idea. A new incarnation is waiting here for Plato's "custodians".

Representation of an idea, I say: not of a rigid principle but of a living form that wants to be shaped in the daily stuff of this earth. Community should not be made into a principle; it, too, should always satisfy a situation rather than an abstraction. The realization of community, like the realization of any idea, cannot occur once and for all time: always it must be the moment's answer to the moment's question, and nothing more.

In the interests of its vital meaning, therefore, the idea of community must be guarded against all contamination by sentimentality or emotionalism. Community is never a mere attitude of mind, and if it is *feeling* it is an inner disposition that it felt. Community is the inner disposition or constitution of a life in common, which knows and embraces in itself hard "calculation", adverse "chance", the sudden access of "anxiety". It is community of tribulation and only because of that community of spirit; community of toil and only because of that community of salvation. Even those communities which call the spirit their master and salvation their Promised Land, the "religious" communities, are community only if they serve their lord and master in the midst of simple, unexalted, unselected reality, a reality not so much chosen by them as sent to them just as it is; they are community only if they prepare the way to the Promised Land through the thickets of this pathless hour. True, it is not "works" that count, but the work of faith does. A community of faith truly exists only when it is a community of work.

The real essence of community is to be found in the fact—manifest or otherwise—that it has a centre. The real beginning of a community is when its members have a common relation to the centre overriding all other relations: the circle is described by the radii, not by the points along its circumference. And the originality of the centre cannot be discerned unless it is discerned as being transpicuous to the light of something divine. All this is true; but the more earthly, the more creaturely, the more attached the centre is, the truer and more transpicuous it will be. This is where the "social" element comes in. Not as something separate, but as the all-pervading realm where man stands the test; and it is here that the truth of the centre is proved. The early Christians were not content with the community that existed alongside or even above the world, and they went into the desert so as to have no more community save with God and no more disturbing world. But it was shown them that God does not wish man to be alone with him; and above the holy impotence of the hermit there rose the Brotherhood. Finally, going beyond St. Benedict, St. Francis entered into alliance with all creatures.

Yet a community need not be "founded". Wherever historical destiny had brought a group of men together in a common fold, there was room for the growth of a genuine community; and there was no need of an altar to the city deity in the midst when the citizens knew they were united round— and by—the Nameless. A living togetherness, constantly renewing itself, was already there, and all that needed strengthening was the immediacy of relationships. In the happiest instances common affairs were deliberated and decided not through representatives but in gatherings in the market-place; and the unity that was felt in public permeated all personal contacts. The danger of seclusion might hang over the community, but the communal spirit banished it; for here this spirit flourished as nowhere else and broke windows for itself in the narrow walls, with a large view of people, mankind and the world.

All this, I may be told, has gone irrevocably and for ever. The modern city has no agora and the modern man has no time for negotiations of which his elected representatives can very well relieve him. The pressure of numbers and the forms of organization have destroyed any real togetherness. Work forges other personal links than does leisure, sport again others than politics, the day is cleanly divided and the soul too. These links are material ones; though we follow our common interests and tendencies together, we have no use for "immediacy". The collectivity is not a warm, friendly gathering but a great link-up of economic and political forces inimical to the play of romantic fancies, only understandable in terms of quantity, expressing itself in actions and effects—a thing which the individual has to belong to with no intimacies of any kind but all the time conscious of his energetic contribution. Any "unions" that resist the inevitable trend of events must disappear. There is still the family, of course, which, as a domestic community, seems to demand and guarantee a modicum of communal life; but it too will either emerge from the crisis in which it is involved, as an association for a common purpose, or else it will perish.

Faced with this medley of correct premises and absurd conclusions I declare in favour of a rebirth of the commune. A rebirth—not a bringing back. It cannot in fact be brought back, although I sometimes think that every touch of helpful neighbourliness in the apartment-house, every wave of warmer comradeship in the lulls and "knock-offs" that occur even in the most perfectly "rationalized" factory, means an addition to the world's community-content; and although a rightly constituted village commune sometimes strikes me as being a more real thing than a parliament; but it cannot be brought back. Yet whether a rebirth of the commune will ensue from the "water and spirit" of the social transformation that is imminent— on this, it seems to me, hangs the whole fate of the human race. An organic commonwealth—and only such commonwealths can join together to form a shapely and articulated race of men—will never build itself up out of individuals but only out of small and ever smaller communities: a nation is a community to the degree that it is a community of communities. If the family does not emerge from the crisis which to-day has all the appearance of a disintegration, purified and renewed, then the State will be nothing more than a machine stoked with the bodies of generations of men. The community that would be capable of such a renewal exists only as a residue. If I speak of its rebirth I am not thinking of a permanent world-situation but an altered one. By the new communes—they might equally well be called the new Co-operatives—I mean the subjects of a changed economy: the collectives into whose hands the control of the means of production is to pass. Once again, everything depends on whether they will be ready.

Just how much economic and political autonomy—for they will of necessity be economic and political units at once—will have to be conceded to them is a technical question that must be asked and answered over and over again; but asked and answered beyond the technical level, in the knowledge that the internal authority of a community hangs together with its external authority. The relationship between centralism and decentralization is a problem which, as we have seen, cannot be approached in principle, but, like everything to do with the relationship between ideal and reality, only with great spiritual tact, with the constant and tireless weighing and measuring of the right proportion between them. Centralization—but only so much as is indispensable in the given conditions of time and place. And if the authorities responsible for the drawing and re-drawing of lines of demarcation keep an alert conscience, the relations between the base and the apex of the power-pyramid will be very different from what they are now, even in States that call themselves Communist, i.e. struggling for community. There will have to be a system of representation, too, in the sort of social pattern I have in mind; but it will not, as now, be composed of the pseudo-representatives of amorphous masses of electors but of representatives well tested in the life and work of the communes. The represented will not, as they are to-day, be bound to their representatives by some windy abstraction, by the mere phraseology of a party-programme, but concretely, through common action and common experience.

The essential thing, however, is that the process of community-building shall run all through the relations of the communes with one another. Only a community of communities merits the title of Commonwealth.

The picture I have hastily sketched will doubtless be laid among the documents of "Utopian Socialism" until the storm turns them up again. Just as I do not believe in Marx's "gestation" of the new form, so I do not believe either in Bakunin's virgin-birth from the womb of Revolution. But I do believe in the meeting of idea and fate in the creative hour.

RUSSELL KIRK
1918-

RUSSELL A. KIRK WAS BORN in Plymouth, Michigan; he attended
Michigan State University and Duke University, and received a
D.Litt. from St. Andrews University, Scotland. He has taught and lectured at
several American universities. As the editor of *Modern Age: A Conservative
Review* and many books and articles on conservatism, he has become a major
spokesman for that position.

He has not claimed to present any "new" conservative ideas. Rather, in
such works as *The Conservative Mind* (1953) and *A Program for Conservatives* (1954) he represents the views of past generations of conservative thinkers, and asserts that if we made them the mainstays of Western thought, our
major perplexities would be resolved. In *The Conservative Mind,* he defined
these troubling questions as (1) the problem of a spiritual and moral regeneration which would restore the ethical system and the religious sanction upon
which worthwhile lives are founded; (2) the problem of leadership, or of preserving "some measure of veneration, discipline, order, and class"; (3) the
problem of the proletariat, or of restoring to the masses status, hope, respect
for the past, and responsibility for the future; and (4) the problem of economic
security, that is, "the establishment of a rational relationship between endeavor
and reward." He is averse to the treatment of these questions by the methods
of most contemporary social scientists. In a recent article in *The New York
Times* he wrote, "Modern society, in many ways sick, needs, not the short-
sighted manipulations of the research technician, but the artist's touch."

[38]   *How Dead Is Edmund Burke?*

Walk beside the Liffey in Dublin, a trifle west of the dome of the Four Courts, and you come to Number 12, Arran Quay. This is a brick building of three stories, which began as a gentleman's residence, some time since became a shop, and now is a governmental office of the meaner sort— symbolic of changes on a mightier scale during the generations since 1729. For here in that year Edmund Burke was born. Across the river you see what once was the town house of the Earls of Moira and is now the office of a society for suppressing mendicity; and beyond that, the great Guinness brewery. Back of Burke's house, toward the old church of St. Michan in which, they say, he was baptised, stretch tottering brick slums where bare-foot children scramble over broken walls. If you turn toward O'Connell Street, an easy stroll takes you to the noble façade of Trinity College and the statues of Burke and Goldsmith; to the north, near Parnell Square, you may hear living Irish orators proclaiming through amplifiers that they have succeeded in increasing sevenfold the pensions of widows, a mere earnest of their intent. And you may reflect, with Burke, "What shadows we are, and what shadows we pursue!"

Since Burke's day there have been alterations in Dublin. Yet to the visitor, Ireland appears a refuge of tradition amidst the flux of our age, and Dublin a conservative old city; and so they are. Burke might not be pleased with the state of his native place; but were his ghost to rise from under the stones of the church at Beaconsfield, that spirit would be trebly vexed at the spectacle of modern England—though not, perhaps, greatly surprised. A world that damns tradition, lauds equality, and welcomes change; a world that has clutched Rousseau, swallowed him down, and demanded prophets yet more radical; a world scarred by industrialism, standardised by the common man, consolidated by government; a world harrowed by war, trembling between the colossi of East and West, and peering over the brink into a gulf of dissolution. So Burke would see us, and know he had failed.

Burke failed. During the greater part of his career, he stood among

From *Queen's Quarterly*, LVII (Summer, 1950), 160–71. Reprinted by permission of the author and *Queen's Quarterly*.

the opposition—stood grandly, but in opposition, not in power. In the hour of his death, 1797—"a terrible moment in the history of England and of Europe", Morley writes—he beheld the triumph of his denunciations of the Revolution, but only a triumph of dubious battle. The passing of a mere fifty years was to bring the Communist Manifesto. And from the day of his death onward, history was to record the trampling of Burke's society beneath the feet of our epoch.

We do not draw the moral lessons we might from history. On the contrary, without care it may be used to vitiate our minds and to destroy our happiness. In history a great volume is unrolled for our instruction, drawing the materials of future wisdom from the past errors and infirmities of mankind. It may, in the perversion, serve for a magazine, furnishing offensive and defensive weapons for parties in church and state, and supplying the means of keeping alive, or reviving, dissensions and animosities, and adding fuel to civil fury. History consists, for the greater part, of the revenge, lust, sedition, hypocrisy, ungoverned zeal, and all the train of disorderly appetites, which shake the public with the same

> . . . troublous storms that toss
> The private state, and render life unsweet.

Thus Burke himself. It might be unwise to summon up the reflection of a defeated politician and his followers renewing old quarrels interred by time. But Burke was more than a defeated politician. He was the founder of modern conservative thought; and most of what genuine conservatism survives among us, in the English-speaking world, is the shadow of Burke's creation; and so he is not wholly dead. We have had an interesting succession of radicalisms since 1797; but none of them seems to have satisfied the mind of man. It is time to ask what Burke's conservatism is, and whether we have anything to learn from it.

Men of conservative impulse are numerous in every society; they are among us to-day, but most of them are perplexed for guidance, the popular prophets of this century being advocates of change. Many of them are looking for a conservative's decalogue—groping in this twilight hour. If ever they find it, it may be in the pages of Burke. Spend some hours in a bookshop frequented by young men, and you observe that some of them are after The Book—the book which holds the clue to life with principle, particularly social principle. Many have ceased to search, having found Freud or Marx or some other mighty name. But some go on browsing, turning over Spengler and Berdyaev, Ortega and Belloc, dissatisfied. Prejudice, interest, conscience have told this remnant that their Idea resides elsewhere. But where? Not many come upon Burke.

For in North American bookshops, at least, little of Burke is in stock; and there are few teachers or preachers or intimates who tell them even the name of the great liberal conservative; he is recorded, respected, ignored. John Morley prophesied more than half a century ago that Burke "will be more frequently and more seriously referred to within the next twenty years than he has been within the whole of the last eighty"; Paul Elmer More, a quarter of a century ago, remarked that Morley had been in error; and certainly Burke's fame has not increased since More wrote. A scholar of German birth recently observed to me that among literati in the United States exists a curious ignorance of Burke—who, with his beauty and power of style, the varied aspects of his genius, and the breadth of his intellect, might be supposed to attract the attention of those circles which pride themselves upon their grasp of modern thought; and my German friend attributed this condition to a vague popular impression that Burke "was wrong about France" and somehow not quite the right reading for a Liberal. Of course 'liberal' has been the word to conjure with in American academic circles, until very recently. But it is interesting to observe, in 1950, how Mr. Lionel Trilling doubts the efficacy of liberal ideas, and how Mr. Arthur Schlesinger, Jr., confesses, "We find Burke more satisfying to-day than Paine, Hamilton or Adams than Jefferson, Calhoun than Clay or Webster."

Possibly the people who neglect Burke are right in assuming that his system is a world away from theirs. Yet many of them are discontented with their own principles, and Burke's ideas should interest anyone, even men bitterly opposed to his conclusions. It would be more courageous to refute Burke than to ignore him. Most conservatives of the twentieth century are no more fit to combat *intelligent* advocates of the Left than were Falstaff's recruits to meet the Percys: but most radicals are in no better discipline, and both schools can profit from an examination of Burke's concepts. Serious debate requires preliminary definition. If conservatives would know what they defend, Burke is their touchstone, and if radicals want to test the temper of their opposition, they should turn to Burke. Having done this, some conservatives may find that their previous footing is insecure, or that they are not sterling conservatives at all; while some radicals may admit that the position of traditionalists is tenable or that Burke, too, was a liberal—if liberalism be in any degree associated with liberty.

Our age ought to make these inquiries: What is the nature of Burke's thought? Why was his conservatism vanquished by the forces of change? And what meaning has it for our guidance? Although there never was a formal school of Burke, great names are found in the list of Burke's British followers: Coleridge, Scott, Macaulay, Disraeli, Stephen, Maine, Bagehot, Lecky. Although America never has admitted to the existence of a conservative party (and almost no American politician acknowledges the influence of any political thinker but Jefferson) we find the mark of Burke on Americans of several persuasions: the Adamses, John Randolph, Calhoun, Lowell, the New Humanists. And although Burke has been in his grave these hundred and fifty years, we hear his disciples raising their voices from out the Comus' rout of twentieth-century politics. Though the odds seem opposed, when Time has given the historical kaleidoscope another twist Burke's name may eclipse those of Rousseau and Bentham and Marx.

What a spin the kaleidoscope of history has had from Burke's declining years to our passionate hour! A decade before *Reflections on the Revolution in France* came from the press, American troops at Yorktown had greeted Cornwallis with the tune of *The World Turned Upside Down;* and that air, mingling now and then with the Carmagnole, has been blaring ever since. The gloomy vaticinations of Burke, which seemed to liberals of Buckle's generation the follies of a deranged old genius, have come to pass; the gods of the copy-book headings with fire and sword return. Nations dissolving into mere aggregations of individuals; property reapportioned by the political power; great European states ground into powder; tranquil Britain transformed into a socialist commonwealth; the ancient beauty of the Orient ravaged and the empire of India gnawing at her own vitals; the colonial world vomiting out its Europeans, although already metamorphosed by them; the rising on the eastern confines of Europe of a levelling frenzy fierce enough to make Jacobins pale; the passing of riches and might to the Western republic Burke aided—but prosperity acquired in haste and linked with arrogance. Where is the divine guidance Burke discerned in history? Beheld, perhaps, in the punishment of disobedience: "The Lord made all things for himself—yea, even the wicked for the day of evil." This horror may have been inevitable; but the last decade of the eighteenth century resounded to Burke's warning, and we still hear its echo, and, perhaps, can profit. We can salvage: salvaging is a great part of conservatism.

To be sure, not all men found in the modern conservative camp are

the intellectual heritors of Burke. Some hold by the old ways because of
religious orthodoxy—a movement of origins largely independent of Burke,
although sometimes tinged with Burke's ideas. Some are descendants of
the Utilitarians, driven by the fortunes of war within the conservative
ramparts. Some come from Herbert Spencer. Some in America retain a
trace of Federalist or Old Republican ideas. Yet throughout the nineteenth
century and this, when the intellectual struggle between new and old was
most fierce the ablest partisans among the conservatives were of Burke's
lineage. Many of the adherents of tradition since Burke have been men of
thought rather than of action. This may help explain their failure to win
the vast public of our times, so different in its impulses from Burke's solid,
propertied 'public' of a few hundred thousand men; but it is not *per se*
a just reproach. Action and conservatism are by nature often inconsonant;
moreover, the world of thought endures. The *idea* of Marx, not the power
of Moscow, is the sword of modern communism; imagination, Napoleon
tells us, rules the world.

What is conservatism? The term is not Burke's. It does not deserve some
of the epithets pinned upon it by reformers, nor yet the fealty of certain
influences leagued with it. It is not big business nor bourgeois supremacy;
it is neither Toryism nor Whiggery; it is not autocratic power and feudal
privilege. It *is* a belief in saving—preserving features of society and spirit
that have long held the affection of man. Most conservatives are such
through prejudice, not through persuasion—which would not perturb
Burke—and they cannot tell you clearly for what they stand. Perhaps the
words of Randolph of Roanoke may help us here: "This is a great cardinal
principle, that should govern all statesmen—never, without the strongest
necessity, to disturb that which is at rest." Or as Falkland put it: "When
it is not necessary to change, it is necessary *not* to change."

We may be more specific, without presuming to enter deeply into
definition, and draw up a summary of the chief articles in the creed of
Burke and his disciples—these:

(1) A belief in a divine intent ruling society as well as conscience,
which purpose it is the duty of man to venerate—an eternal chain of duty
linking great and obscure, living and dead—

As the ends of such a partnership cannot be obtained in many generations,
it becomes a partnership not only between those who are living, but between
those who are living, those who are dead, and those who are to be born. Each
contract of each particular state is but a clause in the great primæval contract

of eternal society, linking the lower with the higher nature, connecting the visible and invisible world, according to a fixed compact sanctioned by the inviolable oath which holds all physical and all moral natures, each in their appointed place.

(2) A faith in prescription and a distrust of "sophisters and calculators"—

Prejudice is of ready application in the emergency; it previously engages the mind in a steady course of wisdom and virtue, and does not leave the man hesitating in the moment of decision, skeptical, puzzled, and unresolved. Prejudice renders a man's virtue his habit; and not a series of unconnected acts.

(3) A conviction that civilised society requires orders and classes—

You would have had a protected, satisfied, laborious, and obedient people, taught to seek and to recognize the happiness which is to be found by virtue in all conditions; in which consists the true moral equality of mankind, and not in that monstrous fiction, which, by inspiring false ideas and vain expectations into men destined to travel in the obscure walk of laborious life, serves only to aggravate and embitter that real inequality, which it never can remove; and which the order of civil life establishes as much for the benefit of those whom it must leave in an humble state, as those whom it is able to exalt to a condition more splendid, but not more happy.

(4) A persuasion that property and freedom are inseparably linked, and that economic levelling is not economic progress—

In this partnership all men have equal rights; but not to equal things.

(5) A recognition that change and reform are not identical, and that innovation is a devouring flame more often than it is a torch of progress—

By this wise prejudice we are taught to look with horror on those children of their country, who are promptly rash to hack that aged parent in pieces, and put him into the kettle of magicians, in hopes that by their poisonous weeds, and wild incantations, they may regenerate the paternal constitution, and renovate their father's life.

These passages are drawn from *Reflections on the Revolution in France,* but they will serve for our generation. We need not consider these canons absolute. All the same, the odds are that an alleged conservative who cannot subscribe to most of these declarations is in the wrong camp, and that a radical whose sympathies are aroused by some of them should inquire into the state of his conscience.

Our age has beheld the literal disintegration of the notion of irresistible social progress—gone in a vortex of blazing dust. Even the dogged confidence of the Marxist begins to look in upon itself. "It's not a question of whether you believe communism is right" says an acquaintance of mine; "it's simply that you have to go along with the stream." But after this Hegelian dictum he hesitates oddly, as if a doubt had occurred—perhaps the reflection "that even the weariest river winds"—why, to the great deep. For a man in a small boat, the sea is death. If progress appears to have led to a precipice and such quavers as my friend's are becoming daily more frequent, perhaps it is time we began to conserve rather than to covet. Against the overweening assurance of modern man, Burke fought. He failed; but as Burke himself tells us, the past is not truly dead. If ever we are to learn from it, we had best now descend, Ulysses-like, to query the shades; otherwise we may be numbered among them. Burke can be our Tiresias.

Conservatism begins with Burke. Upon the basis of the conservative canons listed above, we must reject Bolingbroke and Hobbes as conservatives, for they were theological and metaphysical radicals; the true conservative believes in Providence. Montesquieu, among modern thinkers, influenced Burke more than any other philosopher he read; but half of the Frenchman's mantle went to Rousseau. Similarly, Locke was a philosophical innovator. Whether or not there *might* have been an earlier founder for conservatism, it was left for a man of versatile genius, who reached the height of his powers just as industrialism, democracy, and nationalism loured, to build Whiggery and Toryism into a rampart against radicalism. Burke was a modern man, and his concern was with our modern perplexities. "The gift of prophecy", a recent reviewer in the *Times Literary Supplement* observes, "Burke possessed in abundance."

There is no Age of Burke. In literature, we call Burke's period the Age of Johnson; in philosophy and politics, we ought to call it the Age of Rousseau.

The Age of Rousseau: the era of abstraction, feeling, emancipation, expansion, equality, the people absolute, the kiss bestowed upon the universe, the deity impotent. The system of Burke: prescription, experience, duty, old ties, social gradation, the reign of law, the love engendered by association, Jehovah omniscient. Rousseau and Burke stand at the antipodes, despite the curious theory of some writers that they are two peas in a libertarian pod. Though Rousseau cannot be credited, like Burke, with the foundation almost single-handed of an intellectual system, the movement of which he was the most influential representative can boast of the fealty of ten devotees for every one of Burke's, perhaps: the romantic gaze of Jean Jacques darts out, at intervals, from behind a variety of masks—behind the flushed face of Paine, the grim brow of Marx, the scholarly visage of John Dewey. Indeed, the disciples of Burke himself, in the generation after his death, are the heirs of Rousseau as well—Coleridge, Southey, Wordsworth. Let us confess that a knowledge of the mind of Rousseau is even more important than a comprehension of Burke's, if one seeks to find the roots of modern ideas. Admit this, and ask who else, in Burke's lifetime, eclipsed him in significance.

I do not find anyone else. Pitt, a man of practicality; Fox, a man of emotion—their names must perish before Burke's, since he was a man of thought. Pitt and Fox have been more fortunate in their chroniclers, for each has several respectable biographies, while lives of Burke are scant. Having left us a long shelf of treatises, speeches, and letters, perhaps Burke has needed no biographer. During the past two years, however, we have seen a revival of the study of Burke—Hoffman's and Levack's *Burke's Politics,* Copeland's *Our Eminent Friend, Edmund Burke,* even a piece in *Fortune.* After all the accounts of Pitt and Fox and a great many others have crept down to the obloquy of booksellers' bargain-tables, Burke will continue to exert the power of the word, the word upheld by principle.

Yes, the most influential man of his day, Rousseau excepted: and the most influential man of his stamp, down to our day. Of the terrors of sudden change, the *Reflections* endures as the best warning; of the duties of a popular representative, the speech at Bristol still is the best word; concerning price-fixing, *Thoughts on Scarcity* continues to be the most lucid retort of the advocates of free enterprise.

"See my pageant passing," says the French dramatist apropos of the revolutionary torrent raving past his window. To attempt the unravelling of intertwined philosophical origins is a thankless task. Few statesmen acknowledge even to themselves the source of their prejudices. There are not many politicians so conscious of the guiding hand of Burke as was

Disraeli, or of that of Jefferson as was Woodrow Wilson. All the same, a debt to Burke is confessed frequently enough from Canning to Churchill for us to know that Burke's blood continues to flow in the body social. "Burke has endured as the permanent manual of political wisdom without which statesmen are as sailors on an uncharted sea." It was not Mr. Churchill who said this, nor Mr. Taft, but the late Harold Laski.

Edmund Burke was original. Foreseeing a pillaging of the world by the forces of flux and change, he determined to save the best of the traditional order within barricades of thought. He was the first conscious conservative of our time of troubles. He endeavoured to perpetuate the ideas that have converted the brute into the civil social man, to ensure their conservation while the world blazes. To find his compeers, we must make our way back to Aristotle and Cicero, true conservatives both. In modern politics the function of *saving* begins with him. Mistaken an intelligent critic may honestly believe Burke to be; but to deny him the gift of originality is hardly possible.

In the keep of conservatism, Burke is sitting yet. Alive or dead? That depends upon the spirit of the age. For one partisan, the warder of the keep may be Giant Despair; for another, Barbarossa waiting the trump. Young truth lies just under the wrinkled skin of myth, and a trumpet-blast, or one of those flaming clouds which we deny to the Deity but arrogate to our own purposes, still can efface our elaborate constructions. The tocsin in the Faubourg St. Germain in 1789 was such a trump. We may hear another; there is a great deal in the old Greek concept of cycles. History, instead of being a kaleidoscope, may resemble a roulette-wheel; round again may come the number which signifies a conservative order. Both these similes would be repugnant to Burke, who knew history to be the unfolding of a Design; and Burke, could he see our century, would hardly concede that our consumption-society, so very near to suicide, is the end for which Providence has prepared man. If a conservative order is indeed to return, we ought to know Burke's thoughts that we may rebuild society; if it is not, we still ought to know them, that we may rake from the ashes what scorched fragments of civilisation we can.

WILHELM RÖPKE
1899-

WILHELM RÖPKE was a professor of economics at the universities of Jena, Graz, and Marburg before being dismissed by the Nazis in 1933. From 1933 to 1937 he taught at the University of Istanbul, and later at the University of Geneva. He was an adviser to the West German government in 1950. He has published many articles dealing with problems of international economics, and such books as *Solution of the German Problem* (1947), *Mass und Mitte* (1950), and *The Problem of Economic Order* (1951).

Röpke is an eloquent advocate of a humane, bourgeois civilization, a pure capitalist economy, and a weak, decentralized democratic government. Those nations which exhibit such characteristics are "healthy," he believes; those which encounter continual crises of order, which are "over-rationalized and over-organized," where the market economy is destroyed, and where governments intervene extensively in the economy, are "sick." In tones that recall Ortega y Gasset, he condemns the "congestion and proletarianization" of society —the rise to power of disorganized, propertyless masses. He is critical of Keynesian policies for maintaining full employment, arguing that these are bound to lead to collectivism. In *Civitas Humana* (1944), he asserted that any policy of economic stabilization should include "anchoring human beings in self-provisionment and property and strengthening the healthy middle classes, thus achieving an inner regeneration of the nation. . . ."

[39] Collectivism and the Human Spirit

On the steps of the scaffold the hapless Louis XVI is supposed to have said: "I have seen all this coming for the past ten years. How was it pos-

Reprinted from *The Social Crisis of Our Time* by Wilhelm Röpke (Chicago: The University of Chicago Press, 1950), pp. 1–3, 176–80, 181–83, 184–86, 191–94, by permission of The University of Chicago Press. Copyright in the International Copyright Union. All rights reserved.

sible that I never wanted to believe it?" There are but few people in the world today who would not wholeheartedly say the same of themselves; there are, in fact, none except those who saw nothing of the sort coming because they lived blindly from day to day, and those who not only saw the disaster approaching but also disdained to silence their own pessimism with cheap words of comfort. Sooner or later, however, they were bound to be seized by the feeling that the ground was rocking under their feet and thus all became ready for the question which had since long occupied the thoughts of those whose soul or body had first been affected by the convulsions of our civilization: what uncanny disease has invaded our world and what exactly has been happening in those countries which have already succumbed to it?

As nothing happens without sufficient cause it must surely be possible to find an interpretation and explanation for this catastrophe, offering sounder reasons than just coincidence, stupidity and malevolence. As the vast dimensions of the rupture became increasingly evident and one could no longer avoid the impression that the fissures reached deep down into the foundations, it appeared necessary and natural to detach oneself from the ever changing vicissitudes of the moment and to consider oneself more consciously the heir of an age-old civilization which now seemed more and more openly jeopardized. Becoming accustomed to seeing ourselves in perspective against the majestic background of history we have learned to turn our thoughts to ultimate values, origins and "constants," and to ask ourselves: Where do we stand? Whence do we come? Whither are we drifting? What are we? What is, and even more, what should be our goal?

In this manner a growing number of people have learned to view this world of ours, so sadly out of joint, from a viewpoint which lets the incidentals recede behind the essential, the variables behind the constants, the ephemeral behind the permanent, the fluctuating behind the durable, the fleeting moment behind the era; and our own unimportant personality behind the responsibility which we bear towards society, towards the heritage of the past and the promises of the future. We are experiencing the despair of one who has gone astray, and to be told the way is almost more important to us than to be given bread.

Just as the space surrounding us has shrunk and we are constantly aware of the earth as a whole, as something familiar and intimately affecting us, the historical distances, too, have been foreshortened in our minds, so that the distant past seems to reach forward into the present and more than ever before do we consider ourselves the last member of a continuous chain. "The Burden of Three Thousand Years" (Goethe) has become an integral part of the life of every thinking person today. We are continually looking back on the various stages of our civilization, Miletus, Jerusalem, Athens, Rome, Florence, Paris, London or Weimar; we thrill to the dramatic spectacle of the ship of progress threatening to founder on so many rocks and yet, by a veritable miracle, always regaining its course, and anxiously we ask whether this miracle will be repeated today, or whether the inevitable end is now approaching for the development which began with the Ionians during one of the greatest moments of world history. On the other hand, we can now recognize more clearly the cross roads in the course of history where the wrong path was taken which finally led us to the present. To the same extent to which we are consciously re-living the passage of our own civilization through the ages, we gain a clearer understanding of the general possibilities and prerequisites for human civilization and society by studying the experience of other civilizations and the remotest origins of mankind that prehistoric research, ethnology, and anthropology are gradually revealing to us. What we learn here tends to strengthen in us a feeling which divides us as much from the nineteenth century, drunk with progress, as it links us with the eighteenth which is constantly growing in our estimation, a feeling, namely, that we represent by no means the dizzy summit of a steady development; that the unique mechanical and quantitative achievements of a technical civilization do not disembarrass us of the eternal problems of an ordered society and an existence compatible with human dignity; that these achievements complicate rather than facilitate the solution of these problems; that other civilizations have come nearer to the answer than we, and that throughout the centuries and civilizations the range of human potentialities has remained surprisingly small notwithstanding radio and motion pictures. The sun which shone on Homer is still smiling on us, and all the essentials around which life revolves have remained equally unchanged—food and love, work and leisure, religion, nature and art. Children still have to be born and raised, and we may surely be permitted to presume that other times, without radio and motion pictures, have done better than we in this respect.

The shock would hardly have been so great if it had merely been a question of a slow and gradual decline. Ours has, however, this in common with most historical crises, and even with an ordinary economic crisis, that we have suffered a headlong downfall from heights never reached before and considered completely safe. The saying, "It is only a step from the Capitol to the Tarpeian Rock" also applies in history. It is first of all true in a narrower and more familiar sense in that the outbreak of the economic and political catastrophe at the end of 1929 had been preceded by a period during which the postwar hangover had been effectively displaced by exceptional world-wide recovery and an excess of optimism. But the maxim is also true in a much wider sense if we consider this crisis as a general crisis of civilization beginning in August 1914, and then look back on the preceding hundred years. We shall then realize with astonishment that this unique period between 1814 and 1914 was predominantly a century of peace and at the same time the century of liberal capitalism, and this century, whose spirit of progress, order, stability, and increasing prosperity is unequalled in history, is succeeded by a period of disruption which in turn surpasses most of its historical predecessors. Truly a sudden descent from the proud pinnacle on which the nineteenth century—despite the predictions of a few far-sighted prophets—had felt so secure!

* * *

THE ROUTE—"THE THIRD WAY"

Let us glance back once more at the road of collectivism which we are under no circumstances prepared to take and do not even want to approach along the deceptive by-paths which we have just mentioned. Its details are sufficiently known: abolition of freedom and of the sphere of private personality, extreme mechanization, rigid hierarchies and proletarization, the kneading of society into a dough-like lump, unrelieved dependency of each on the dominant group with its arbitrary and changing plans and programs where man in his uniqueness and dignity means nothing, power and the bureaucratic machine everything. Human dignity, freedom and justice have completely vanished there and, to round off the picture, even material productivity leaves much to be desired.

But we also know that this is not an entirely new and revolutionary state of affairs which has succeeded an idyllic non-collectivist existence. What we are facing is rather the last stage of a long pre-collectivist development which smoothed the way for total collectivism: the increasing mechanization and proletarization, the agglomeration and centralization, the growing dominance of the bureaucratic machinery over men, monopolization, the destruction of independent livelihoods, of modes of living and working which satisfy men, the disruption of the community by ruthless group interests of all kinds and the dissolution of natural ties (the family, the neighborhood, professional solidarity, and others). Of course, important differences of degree become apparent between the various countries, differences which show at the same time how far a particular country has remained sound and healthy.

Now it cannot well be denied that this process of the progressive hardening of the arteries which finally ends in the apoplexy of collectivism, has taken place in the era of a world order which—rightly or wrongly—is called liberal. The apologists of this world order cannot offer the excuse that this development must solely be attributed to the fact that economic liberty, one of the points on the liberal program, has not been realized with sufficient seriousness and radicalism. Our previous investigation of the perversions and malformations of capitalism has already shown us that this excuse is not adequate. The exclusive emphasis placed on economic liberty as a postulate—which is certainly important, but by no means sufficient and in any case necessitates further elaboration—tends to divert attention from other equally weighty matters. That becomes quite clear when we realize that laissez-faire and economic liberty are by no means antipodal to collectivism, that they are, rather, quite compatible with many shortcomings of the pre-collectivist stage. A return to domestic and foreign economic liberty would very likely lead to the disappearance of many—we even believe, of most—monopolies, and in other respects, too, there might be a turn for the better, but in some respects also for the worse. Above all: would the remaining aspects of the disease of our time be altered to any great extent? For example, would a country now without peasants and craftsmen be able to get them back by returning to a system of comprehensive economic freedom? Would the proletariat vanish? Would society acquire a stable economic and social equilibrium? Would it become, in a very elementary sense, a just society? Would it invest work and life of the individual once more with meaning and dignity? But if a return to economic freedom is insufficient to achieve all this, can we really advocate it with a good conscience? And how can we expect men to warm to this postulate? Where is the vitality necessary for carrying out such a revision of our economic policy?

This once more places before us—in a new perspective—the problem which has accompanied us . . . and whose solution, we hope, is gradually taking more definite shape: the problem of an anti-collectivist alternative program which meets the real situation and the justified desires of men. We saw again and again that the fight against collectivism only holds promise of tangible success if we succeed in revitalizing the liberal principle in such a manner that satisfactory solutions will be found for all the now obvious defects, the breakdowns and deficiencies of historical liberalism and capitalism, without interfering with the structure of the market economy's competitive system and our whole economic system's ability to function. The non-collectivist world will only be able to deal with the dangers of collectivism successfully when it knows how to deal in its own way with the problems of the proletariat, large scale industrialism, monopolism, the multitudinous forms of exploitation and the mechanizing effects of capitalist mass civilization.

Economic freedom as an essential form of personal liberty and as a premise of everything that follows belongs undeniably to the total picture of a society which is diametrically opposed to collectivism. While this social order is necessarily based on economic freedom, other factors are also essential. In order to recognize the true antithesis of a collectivist society we must look far beyond economic freedom. We shall find it in a society in which the greatest possible number of people leads a life based on private property and a self-chosen occupation, a life that gives them inward and, as much as possible, outward independence, which enables them to be really free and to consider economic liberty as a matter of course. It is at the same time a form of society whose arbiters are not the proletarians—with or without white collars—not the vassals of a new industrial feudalism and retainers of the state, but men who, thanks to their way of working and living, depend on no one but themselves and do not allow the affairs of the world to touch them; these are to be found among the best types of peasants, artisans, small traders, small and medium-sized businessmen in commerce and industry, members of the free professions and trusty officials and servants of the community. They set the tone not because they are a minority which has usurped power, but because their number will be so great that they will determine the character of society. Whatever one may think of it, no one will dispute that only such a society and not one which is herded together in large cities, giant enterprises, tenements, mass associations, trusts and monopolies of all kinds, represents the true antithesis of collectivism. The conditions enumerated here have already taken us half or three quarters of the way along the road to collectivism—in spite of all the remnants of economic freedom—and it will not take long to cover the rest of the way. The misery of "capitalism," we must point out to the socialists, is not due to some men owning capital, but rather to others not owning any, and thus being proletarians. Sufficient millennia have passed into recorded history for us to have learned in a most convincing manner that whenever the lamp of freedom, of the enquiring mind and of humanity has illuminated the darkness, it was in times when a sufficient number of people had a modicum of private property and were therefore in a position to shake off their economic dependence on the state or the feudal lord. It rests with us whether one of the most magnificent of these periods, which started with the rise of the cities in the Middle Ages and reached its peak in the liberation of the peasants, is now again to come to a close.

These remarks are intended to show once more the kind of measures with which the defense and re-establishment of economic liberty and the accompanying battle against selfish vested interests must be conducted in order to fulfil our counter-program of the "Third Way"; they are also intended to show the more important aspects of this program, the character of the philosophy behind it, and with which of the more or less clearly felt grievances of the under-privileged we concern ourselves. Economic liberty and competition are self-evident postulates where the arch evils of collectivism and monopolism are involved, but they are only part of a many-sided and comprehensive general program. This program lays down the firm frame which will give the necessary support to the freedom of the market. Decentralization, promotion of smaller production and settlement units and of the sociologically healthy forms of life and work (after the model of the peasant and the artisan), legislation preventing the formation of monopolies and financial concentration (company law, patent law, bankruptcy law, anti-trust laws, &c.), strictest supervision of the market to safeguard fair play, development of new, non-proletarian forms of industry, reduction of all dimensions and conditions to the human mean ("à la taille de l'homme," as the Swiss poet Ramuz put it so well); elimination of over-complicated methods of organization, specialization and division of labor, promotion of a wide distribution of property wherever possible and by all possible means, sensible limitation of state intervention according to the rules of, and in keeping with, the market economy (compatible state interventions instead of incompatible interference à la planned economy), while care is exercised to reserve a sphere for the actual planned economy—these are some of the main points which we would mention, though for the time being only in the form of headings open to misunderstanding. We add, however, that perhaps the Swiss reader is the least likely to misunderstand these since he has the example of his own country before his eyes, a country whose economic and social structure corresponds in decisive respects largely to our program. How much still remains to be done in that country, too, in order to make the imperfect more perfect and the diseased healthy again, we need not go into here. All the more should we stress, however, that the fundaments are still sound, that what has become subject to disease and disintegration seems relatively easy to cure, compared with the gravely pathological state of the big industrial nations. It therefore seems advisable to us to recommend not only, as is frequently done today, the political but also the economic and social constitution of Switzerland as a model for the rehabilitation of the world after this war. Switzerland, in any case, refutes by its mere existence every cynical doubt regarding the possibility of realizing our program.

Our program is to be one in which everything is balanced. It must therefore appeal more than any other to the willingness of the reader to follow our thoughts with sympathy and understanding and not to pick out this or that point for premature praise or criticism. However, in the case of some readers we have to reckon with the possibility of being misunderstood as siding with trends which are foreign to us. All endeavors would be in vain if we were to be misunderstood on one decisive point: the necessity of competition. That is why we shall add a few words on this subject.

However unsatisfactory and even misleading a program of reform seems to us which has to offer nothing but the postulate of economic freedom, we nevertheless hope that we have left no doubt that economic freedom—to be more exact, competition—is indeed the *conditio sine qua non* of any recovery of our sick society. How to maintain the freedom of the market and of competition happens to have become the crucial problem of the non-collectivist world, and if we fail to solve it everything else will be pointless. But—and that is the other side of the problem—we are bound to fail in this task if we devote ourselves solely to this problem and neglect everything else or push it aside with gentle sarcasm. However radical our thoughts and demands should be concerning the questions so far discussed, we must be on our guard not to transcend the limits set to us, if we are really concerned with the essentials of the economic order of a free society. Such an economic order, we recall, is the opposite of collectivism, monopoly and—in the field of agriculture—of peasant serfdom (including serfdom to the state). In saying this we have—with the exception of the sphere of agricultural self-sufficiency—defined this constitution as a competitive economy. But has that term not already become in our eyes somewhat ambiguous? Is it not often associated with matters which seem to be at variance with the rest of our program?

* * *

Finally, we must stress most emphatically that we have no intention to demand more from competition than it can give. It is a means of establishing order and exercising control in the narrow sphere of a market economy based on the division of labor, but not a principle on which a whole society can be built. From the sociological and moral point of view it is even dangerous because it tends more to dissolve than to unite. If competition is not to have the effect of a social explosive and is at the same time not to degenerate, its premise will be a correspondingly sound political and moral framework. There should be a strong state, aloof from the hungry hordes of vested interests, a high standard of business ethics, an undegenerated community of people ready to co-operate with each other, who have a natural attachment to, and a firm place in society.

Those who have already agreed with us in our defense of competition, may perhaps find it somewhat wearisome that we cannot yet decide to leave this extremely important subject. As, however, there is a possibility that there are a few readers who are not yet fully convinced and cannot yet overcome their mental resistance against the principle of competition, we will go further by strongly emphasizing two points. In the first place we once more feel called upon to deal with an idea which many may have been pondering without expressing it: that competition is most uncomfortable and wearing, whereas we long for the peace of a secure position in the market, where we do not have to fear every day that the better and cheaper services of another may perturb us, and we hope to enjoy this peace the more tranquilly the more successful we are in finding a nicer word for the crude term "monopoly." That is quite human and excusable as long as one keeps this feeling within certain bounds. Our sympathy even extends so far that we would like to see competition shaped and controlled in such a manner that it loses all traces of its cut-throat and nerve-racking character. In saying this we must stress with even more emphasis that the efforts which the competitive principle demands from us will never become unnecessary, particularly not if we decide to choose collectivism. All those who today groan under competition and would employ any means to protect their position in the market against inconvenient competitors, cannot be shown convincingly enough that the collectivist state would be a much harder taskmaster than competition. Collectivism knows perfectly well that its success will be all the greater, the more it succeeds in insuring that discipline and effort with which the competitive system burdens the producers, and under collectivism there will be fewer chances than before of clinging in unmanly fashion to comfortable nests. If competition has chastized us with whips, the collectivist state will chastize us with scorpions (I Kings, 12, 11). Indeed, in economic life we can never do without that pitiless, yet beneficent discipline, if we do not want to make the acquaintance of that anarchy which we know only too well from the recent history of great countries. However, there are only two kinds of such discipline, i.e., that of competition, or that of the state as task-master. Between these two lies our choice. To speak against competition and to evade the problem of monopolist and interventionist industrial feudalism with all the only too familiar phrases, simply means taking the side of collectivism.

The above also answers the objection that, if one rejects unadulterated competition, one need not necessarily accept collectivism, since there exists, after all, what we are impolite enough to call, monopolism. Monopolist-interventionist capitalism can only exist as a relatively short intermediate phase, just as in the political field the distortion of democracy through the anarchy of group interests (pluralism) can never be permanent. We want to print this sentence in italics and impress it again and again on all who openly or secretly flirt with the monopoly principle: *our economic system and everything else that we defend in it against collectivism, can in the long run only be maintained as a competitive system which continually ensures discipline, hard work, decency, harmony, balance and a just relation between performance and payment.* We cannot honestly and effectively defend what is so near to our hearts if, instead of employing the same strong words against monopoly and subsidy capitalism as we do against collectivism, we agree to weak compromises and a dishonest play on words, and we can hardly blame people if in the end they come to the conclusion: then let us rather have collectivism.

* * *

THE TOOLS OF ECONOMIC POLICY

After having decided on the general direction reform should follow and having outlined what we mean by the program of the "Third Way," we must now make a few general observations concerning the various methods which should be chosen in order to reach this goal. First and foremost, we must make the distinction between compatible and incompatible intervention with which we are already familiar. After what we have said above, there is no need to state once more that we have very sound reasons for preferring the compatible to the incompatible interventions in all circumstances. If we wish to avoid the downhill path to collectivism it will always be in our interest to realize our economic aims by attempting changes in the framework of the economic system, but not by interfering with the actual mechanism of the market economy itself which is characterized by the price mechanism and by competition. Such a procedure requires foresight, thought and an intimate knowledge of the economic mechanism, but if we try hard enough we shall always find that there is scarcely any problem in the economic sphere which does not offer some opportunity for compatible adjustment.

In saying this, we really only paraphrase what one of the fathers of political economy, Léon Walras, the famous head of the so-called Lausanne School expressed in the following words in his *Etudes d'économie sociale* (1896):

"I bow down before the holy name of liberty and declare that it would be contrary to all order, if the state, interfering in my private affairs, began to weigh, select and apportion my food, my clothing and my accommodation, and to watch and control my inclinations and thoughts. . . . But I should like to be told whether the name of authority is less lofty and whether it is more in keeping with order, when individuals take the function of the state upon themselves. . . . In the first case we have despotism and in the second, anarchy. The one must be avoided as much as the other and for this purpose a line must be drawn between the individual's sphere of initiative and action, i.e., liberty, and the state's sphere of initiative and actions, i.e., authority. We can establish this line by simply distinguishing between two things. There is an order of the integrated whole [*ordre d'ensemble ou d'unité*] and the order of varied detail [*ordre de détail ou de variété*]. The former causes all the musicians in a concert to play in time, the latter sees to it that they all play different parts. If the various parts as well as the measure were to be subjected to the order of the integrated whole, an unbearable consonance would result with all harmony destroyed. But if, conversely, the measure together with the different parts is subjected to the order of varied detail, a horrible discordance is the result and harmony is destroyed again. If we apply this differentiation to the problem of the social order we can see at once the line of demarcation between the field of liberty and that of authority. Man is a moral being, i.e., a being that fulfils its destiny in freedom. It is therefore completely against the order of detail if the state interferes in every action by which the individual achieves and maintains the position appropriate to it in society, because thereby it would suppress the moral personality of each individual. On the other hand, man is a moral being only within society, i.e., within the natural environment in which human destiny is fulfilled. It is therefore entirely opposed to the order of the integrated whole if the individual assumes the function of the state in any action which concerns the delineation, maintenance and improvement of the social frame, because thereby the moral personality of man is again suppressed through the destruction of the elements absolutely necessary to it. Freedom of the individual as regards his position, authority of the state as regards the conditions—that is the formula according to which we can distinguish and adjust to each other the spheres of rights and duties of the individual and of the state."

If one wants to express the matter even more clearly—and perhaps in a more felicitous way, in some respects, one might take advantage of the well-known simile of traffic control. As long as traffic control is confined to laying down and enforcing traffic regulations, backed by the whole force and incorruptibility of the state—by licensing vehicles and drivers, marking traffic routes, controlling traffic itself and giving instructions for the proper conduct on the road—it fulfils an absolutely necessary task whilst every individual is still quite at liberty to decide whether and where and how he is going to drive. This control of traffic—which is all the more necessary the more complex and intensive the traffic becomes—represents our compatible interventions and the official determination of conditions, of which Walras spoke. However, it would be an entirely incompatible intervention and thus akin to planned economy if the traffic police would, absurdly enough, attempt to determine the "position" (Walras) of each individual on the road and to direct every move as an officer directs a column on the march. Incompatible interventionism, planning and collectivism mean in fact nothing but the transfer of military principles to economic life.

It is a permanent task of economic policy to lay down and enforce the norms and standards of economic life. There must always be certain laws and institutions which form the framework in which the economic process takes place. The major part of the reform which we have to accomplish is to change, extend and strengthen this permanent framework in accordance with the program of the "Third Way." In addition, there is another no less important task. Within the legal and institutional permanent framework the economic process will always produce certain frictions which are temporary by nature, changes which will bring hardship to certain groups, states of emergency and difficulties of adjustment. This is where special dynamic problems arise concerning which we shall always have to ask ourselves two questions: firstly, whether or not economic policy should interfere and, secondly, what is the best method to be adopted.

* * *

POLITICAL AND MORAL PREREQUISITES

Of course, the more we burden the state with various tasks, the more insistent becomes the question: how about the state itself? Are we not perhaps committing the frequent mistake of turning the state into an ideal which does not correspond to sober reality? *Quis custodiet ipsos custodes?* Who is to guard the guardians?

It would indeed be very unrealistic if we were to call for an economic policy which presupposed such a moral and intellectual perfection of the organs of the state that in practice it could never be attained. In this respect, too, one should not overburden human beings but should rather confront them with simple and straightforward tasks and keep temptations away from them. For this very reason it is advisable to base economic policy on definite rules and fixed principles and to restrict the sphere of arbitrary action as much as possible. The economic system must, so to speak, be an unbreakable toy—"fool-proof" is the telling English expression. In that consists the unsurpassable strength of the market economy and, vice versa, the great danger of collectivism. For this same reason we should beware of artificial monetary systems and give preference to a quasi-automatic system such as the gold standard. It is easy to criticize the gold standard and to draft—on paper—a more perfect monetary system. Nevertheless, we adhere to the gold standard because it is distinguished particularly by the fact that it preserves the stability of the currency, as one of the most precious possessions of the national economy, against the inevitable imperfections of conscious governmental manipulations. We must further realize quite clearly that an economic policy which makes intervention for preservation (through protective tariffs and subsidies of all kinds) its rule, must, according to unalterable sociological laws, lead to open or disguised corruption and generate a poison which in the end will spell ruin for the nation. Ordinary interventionism and pluralism (i.e., the disruption of the state by group interests), are in fact, as everyone should know, very close relatives.

By renouncing this interventionism and the ruthless exploitation of the state by the mob of vested interests, we can create the prerequisites for a trust-worthy state and a clean public life. But on the other hand, this same renunciation presupposes a really strong state, a government with the courage to govern. A strong state is by no means one that meddles in everything and tries to monopolize all functions. On the contrary, not busyness but independence from group interests and the inflexible will to exercise its authority and preserve its dignity as a representative of the community, mark the really strong state, whereas the state that acts as a maid of all work, finally degenerates into a miserable weakling and falls victim to the vested interests. A market economy and our economic program presuppose the following type of state: a state which knows exactly where to draw the line between what does and what does not concern it, which prevails in the sphere assigned to it with the whole force of its authority, but refrains from all interference outside this sphere—an energetic umpire whose task it is neither to take part in the game nor to prescribe their movements to the players, who is, rather, completely impartial and incorruptible and sees to it that the rules of the game and of sportsmanship are strictly observed. That is the state without which a genuine and real market economy cannot exist. Benjamin Constant envisaged it when he wrote the words . . . . "Le gouvernement en dehors de sa sphère ne doit avoir aucun pouvoir; dans sa sphère il ne saurait en avoir trop."

Of course it is not sufficient just to demand such a state. One must rather develop the structure of the state in such a fashion that it meets our demands as far as possible. This poses a problem whose extent and importance can hardly be exaggerated. To deal with it properly would require a book of its own so that here, too, we are forced to restrict ourselves to a few pointers and hints. We have to start with the negative observation—not unfamiliar to us—that there is no more disastrous way to obstruct the desired development than by erecting one of the types of the corporate state, so much discussed today, to make the vested interests themselves the masters of the state and thereby assign them a legitimate place in its structure. It is our plain duty not to solidify and legalize the political influence of the vested interests, but reduce it. The means to be employed for this end require careful and expert investigation which we do not feel competent to make here. But this much is certain, if the authority of the state is to be strengthened it is absolutely necessary that it should be headed by a qualified civil service small in numbers but equipped with the highest standard of professional ethics and a pronounced *esprit de corps*. At this point, too, the difficult questions of political constitutions, administration and party rules should be discussed.

It must always be remembered that nowhere in the political sphere is the authority of the state expressed as directly as in the administration of justice. Nowhere else are integrity and impartiality of the civil service usually of such a high quality as among judges. And, therefore, confidence is nowhere as great as here, nor the readiness to accept the decision made as final. And lastly, we find nowhere else such reluctance to influence decisions illegitimately. Indeed, the law courts of a country are the last citadel of the authority of the state and of trust in the state, and no state is completely lost where this citadel is still intact. This leads us to urge more insistently than has ever been done before that the law courts should be made organs of national economic policy and that they should be given jurisdiction over matters which up to now have been left to the administrative agencies. How such a judicially directed economic policy is likely to work in practice can best be learned from the example of the American anti-trust legislation (since the Sherman Act of 2nd July, 1890) according to which the highest courts of the land decide in civil or criminal proceedings whether an act of a monopolistic nature, prohibited by the law and listed as an offense, has been committed. Such an economic policy presupposes, of course, that the law schools afford more opportunities to future judges to acquire a knowledge of the principles of our economic order than has so far been the case—to the great disadvantage, alas, of the highly important commercial law practice.

But where shall we find the people who desire this kind of state? To which group should we turn in order to form a vanguard for carrying out our program? We have asked this question already . . . : we do not appeal to any single group and its special interests at all, because it seems to us to have been the great mistake of the past to appeal to the "interest" of people, rather than to what is common to them all, i.e., reason and an elementary sense of decency, justice, order, community spirit, chivalry and a conciliatory disposition. Man is a being with many facets—*ni ange, ni bête,* to quote Pascal's famous words—and everything depends on the side of his nature to which we appeal, to the better or to the worse, to that which makes him vicious like a chained cur or to that which makes him friendly and peaceable. If the author may be permitted to close with a personal anecdote, he must confess that he will always remember a small event in his life which took place more than twenty years ago in the main railroad station in Hamburg. About to consign his baggage, he saw the official behind the counter trying to persuade an American negro to take out baggage insurance, hoping thereby to earn the commission paid by the

insurance company. Unfairly exploiting the fact that the negro was unfamiliar both with the language and local customs, the official was trying
to tell him that such an insurance was practically a necessity, when suddenly his colleague interfered and, flushed with anger, shouted at him in
front of the public: "Don't you see he is a foreigner who can't understand
you? You ought to be ashamed to take advantage of him." The other was
shame-facedly silent, and the incident was closed. Whenever we are asked
who are the people to whom we address ourselves, we cannot help thinking of that honest railroad official in Hamburg, and we believe that there
is something in most men which one need only arouse and encourage in
order to make them the brethren and comrades of our friend.

GEORGE WOODCOCK
1912-

GEORGE WOODCOCK HAS WRITTEN several biographies, including
studies of William Godwin, Peter Kropotkin, Oscar Wilde, and
Pierre Joseph Proudhon, all of whom were political or literary radicals. He
has also written political essays, among them *The Writer and Politics* (1948).
The following extracts are from his book *Anarchy or Chaos* (1944), a work
with which for many reasons he is dissatisfied and which as a whole he has
withdrawn from circulation. The selection that appears below has been revised
by the author for this volume. He is now engaged in writing a history of
anarchism in which his views on that subject will be presented more fully and
more critically. At present, Mr. Woodcock teaches at the University of British
Columbia.

[40]   *Anarchism: The Rejection of Politics*

Politically, modern society is based on the system of government; economically, on the system of property concentrated in the hands of the few.

From George Woodcock, *Anarchy or Chaos* (London: Freedom Press, 1944),
pp. 6–7, 19–24, 108–9. Reprinted by permission of the author and with his changes
prepared for this volume.

Its political manifestation is the state; its economic manifestation is the capitalist system of production. Its tendency is centripetal, so that political power becomes more and more concentrated in the state and economic power tends to progress from the system of many small capitalists to monopoly capitalism, which in its turn becomes state capitalism. So the totalitarian state is achieved by the coalescence of political and economic power in the same body. But this identity of the state and capitalism is no new thing. For the state may be regarded as the translation into social terms of the economic form of society. It serves as the executive instrument of those who, by virtue of the economic power conferred by property, are the real ruling class of a country. And as property comes, through the growth and amalgamation of large business trusts, under the effective control of a class which grows progressively smaller and smaller, so the state itself becomes more and more concentrated until the apparent parallels of political and economic life meet in the totalitarian state. . . .

Anarchism, which presents the extreme opposition to this contemporary development, is not a creed of terror and destruction, of social chaos and turmoil, of perpetual war between the individuals within society; it is not nihilism. On the contrary, it is the opposite to all these; a doctrine based on the idea of natural order within society, and of peace between individuals who respect their mutual freedom and integrity. It is the faith of the complete man, growing to fulfilment through social, economic and mental freedom. It is a social philosophy, but it is also a philosophy of individual aspirations.

Anarchism is the only logically complete doctrine of freedom, because it denies all external authority, all domination of man by man. It proclaims the sufficiency of the individual human mind and spirit, and the inborn tendency of men towards peace and co-operation when their natural feelings have not been twisted and frustrated by the oppression of authority.

Socially, anarchism is the doctrine of society without government. It teaches that the major economic and social injustices are intimately associated with the principle of government, which inevitably, in whatever form it takes, creates privilege, and a class hierarchy, and, however much it may call itself democratic, must base itself on the coercion of the individual, at best to the will of the majority, most often to that of the governing minority. An authoritarian society—and every kind of society that bases itself on government is, in virtue of that fact, authoritarian—cannot survive if it does not create a governing class and a series of gradations of responsibility in its hierarchy which must inevitably destroy all forms of equality, whether of wealth, status or opportunity. The governing class, once created, will tend to harden into a caste and to gather to itself privileges which give its members substantial advantages over the other members of society. These privileges will first be granted in the name of expediency, but will be continued as an usurped right. Though rulers may set out with the most sincere intentions, the very necessities of maintaining the power they hold will force them to injustice, and the privileges they obtain will accomplish their inevitable corruption. The evidence of history is unvaried on these points.

True democracy cannot exist outside the imagination in a society based on coercion. Yet, even were democracy possible, the anarchist would still not support it, for democracy puts forward the will of the majority as the supreme law, and declares that society must be governed, and the individual, whether he agrees or not, be coerced by that will. Democracy then, is not based on freedom and differs only in degree from despotism in its negation of the individual. To the individual whose life is frustrated by the law of the State, it does not matter whether that law is the will of one man or the will of a million. What matters to him is that through its existence he is not free and therefore cannot become complete.

The anarchist seeks neither the good of a minority, nor the good of the majority, but the good of all men considered as individuals. He believes that a society based on the great super-individual myth of the State must in the end enslave all its members in the interests not even of the majority but of the privileged few who form its ruling class. Anarchists have often been up-braided as impractical visionaries for their denial of the institution of government. But they contend that impracticality belongs to those who, in the face of the irrefutable historical verdict, still believe that some day a form of government will appear which will not involve the exploitation of the ruled and the corruption of the rulers. These attributes are as natural to government as venom to the viper.

All anarchists believe that the institutions of government and the state and all other coercive instruments of administration should be abandoned, and many believe they can only be ended by the direct action of the op-pressed. This destructive side of anarchism has received undue prominence among its enemies and among some of its more irresponsible friends, and has given rise to certain misconceptions, some frivolous and some serious, which have been deliberately fostered by those in authority.

Of the more frivolous is the idea that the anarchist is a man who throws bombs and wishes to wreck society by violence and terror. That this charge should be brought against anarchists now, at a time when they are among the few people who are not throwing bombs or assisting bomb throwers, shows a curious purblindness among its champions. It is true that a few individual anarchists have in the past, and particularly during the last two decades of the nineteenth century, used the weapon of terrorist assassination as a means of carrying on the social revolution. Some anarchists, therefore, certainly have thrown bombs. But so, also, have members of other political groups, and so have governments. And the difference in responsibility lies in this, that while the bombs thrown by anarchists were very few and were always directed against those who were considered guilty of the oppression and murder of their subjects, the bombs thrown by governments in war can be numbered in their millions and have slain hundreds of thousands of men and women innocent of crime against their fellows. And it must be remembered that the practice of individual terrorism was virtually abandoned by the anarchists some forty years ago, when the advent of anarchist syndicalism opened up the possibility of the more satisfactory tactic of revolutionary mass economic action.

The anarchist believes that a political or governmental organisation of society is incompatible with justice and liberty. He contends that society should be based on the free co-operation of individual men and women in fulfilment of their common functional and economic needs.

Here we reach a second and more serious misconception concerning anarchism, which has arisen among many people with a superficial knowledge of the movement; that anarchism is individualism carried to its extreme conclusion, and therefore admits of no organisation of society. A certain support would appear to be given to this notion by the fact that a few anarchist intellectuals have preached this extreme form of individualism by which a man would live independent of all ties with his fellows and concern himself solely with the development of his own personality and his own happiness.

Where, however, anarchism has existed as a social movement, its exponents have always envisaged the necessity for organisation, but a free organisation rising organically from the needs of man. Anarchism does indeed preach freedom of the individual man, but freedom cannot be isolated in society. An individual's freedom is reciprocal, depending on the freedom of others, and therefore anarchism preaches that the concept of justice is as necessary as the concept of freedom, for without justice there can be no true freedom, just as without freedom there can be no real justice.

Furthermore, work in common achieves more in a shorter time than solitary work, and a sane division of labour provides both plenty and leisure where a man dependent on his own two hands would have to toil all his hours for a miserable standard of life. But the benefits of common work and common life cannot be enjoyed in full measure if the vital functions of production are not organised by the people who perform them.

This necessity for social organisation has been argued by these leading anarchist theoreticians, who have refuted the contentions of the "pure" individualist anarchists. In 1872 Michael Bakunin, the founder of the historical anarchist movement, wrote the following defence of participation in the First International:

"To whoever might pretend that action so organised would be an outrage on the liberty of the masses, or an attempt to create a new authoritative power, we would reply that he is a sophist and a fool. So much the worse for those who ignore the natural, social law of human solidarity, to the extent of imagining that an absolute mutual independence of individuals and of masses is a possible or even desirable thing. To desire it would be to wish for the destruction of society, for all social life is nothing else than this mutual and incessant dependence among individuals and masses. All individuals, even the most gifted and strongest, indeed most of all the most gifted and strongest, are at every moment of their lives, at the same time, producers and products. Equal liberty for every individual is only the resultant, continually reproduced, of this mass of material, intellectual and moral influence exercised on him by all the individuals around him, belonging to the society in which he was born, has developed and dies. To wish to escape this influence in the name of a transcendental liberty, divine, absolutely egoistic and sufficient to itself is the tendency to annihilation. To refrain from influencing others would mean to refrain from all social action, indeed to abstain from all expressions of one's thoughts and sentiments and simply become non-existent. This independence, so much extolled by idealists and metaphysicians, individual liberty conceived in this sense would amount to self-annihilation.

"In nature, as in human society, which is also part of the same nature, all that exists lives only by complying with the supreme conditions of interaction, which is more or less positive and potent with regard to the lives of other beings, according to the nature of the individual. And when we vindicate the liberty of the masses, we do not pretend to abolish anything of the natural influences that individuals or groups of individuals exert upon one another. What we wish for is the abolition of artificial influences, which are privileges, legal and official."

This extract represents the attitude of most militant anarchists. They accept the voluntary limitations necessary for reciprocal freedom. What they do not accept are the limitations imposed from above by coercive bodies such as the state.

Instead of accepting the government of men, the anarchist wishes, in the words of Saint-Simon, to base society on the administration of things. It is on the economic plane alone, in the necessary production of goods consumed by men and in the provision of necessary social service, that he sees the need for organisation, not from above but on a voluntary and co-operative basis, among the individuals whose work actually produces the necessities of a civilised life.

From this point the anarchist proceeds to the contention that the functions of the modern state, represented by its paraphernalia of legal codes, bureaucracy, army and police, would be unnecessary in a society where common ownership had ended privilege and social economic inequalities. All these appendages of the modern state are intended ultimately not for the well-being of all men and women, but for the protection of the ruling class and the property by whose virtue it rules. In a society without inequality of property, where every man's needs were satisfied, there would be no incentive to crime, except among the pathological, who in any case are no subjects for prison or law courts. Where property rights had vanished there would be no need for codified laws. Customs and not regulations are the natural manifestations of men's ideas of justice, and in a free society customs would adapt themselves to the constant growth and testing of ideas of that society. Under a society of anarchy every man, once he had fulfilled his economic functions, would be free to live as he liked, provided he did not interfere with the lives of his fellows. A free people could be relied on to see that peace maintained under such circumstances without the need of police or magistrates.

The economic ideas of the anarchists have found a concrete expression in anarcho-syndicalism. Anarcho-syndicalism . . . is both a technique of social revolution and a theory of the organisation of a free society after that revolution. It advocates the organisation of workers under capitalism in voluntary economic organisations, the syndicates, which differ from trades unions in being controlled directly by the workers themselves and in having as their purpose, not the winning of reforms under capitalism, but the achievement of radical social change by economic means. The withdrawal of economic co-operation, in the form of the general strike, is the basis of the anarchist conception of the revolution, and in this economic struggle the syndicates would play the vital role of uniting the efforts of the workers. After the social revolution the syndicates would be the basic units of the network of economic and functional bodies intended to organise the satisfaction of the common needs of men and to replace the system of administration by authority and coercion.

Anarchism, it must be emphasised, is not a static and unchangeable social system. It is rather a dynamic philosophy which recognises the importance of evolution in human society, and the consequent futility of any attempt to plan social advancement on rigid lines.

The anarchist, therefore, deprecates the idea that a just revolution can be planned and carried out through the seizure of power by a disciplined party organisation. Instead he contends that the social revolution can arise only out of the spontaneous movement of the people against their rulers, and that in any ensuing struggle the role of the revolutionary would be to maintain in the minds of men the nature of the goal for which they strive. The anarchist may preach freedom, but he considers that the people must take it for themselves.

In the same way, although many anarchists consider syndicalism a practical means of organising society after a hypothetical revolution, they recognize that it may not present a perfect social pattern. Indeed, they envisage no static blueprint of a future world. For, when men have been freed from social and economic oppressions, the evolution of human institutions will undoubtedly attain forms we cannot conceive. Proposals for future organisation must not therefore be regarded as permanent and hence dead, but as the bases of further social evolution.

The anarchist does not expect to achieve a society without flaw. But he does think that anarchism offers the only possibility of a society based on freedom and justice, which will function efficiently and produce a degree of spiritual and material comfort far higher than men enjoy to-day. Anarchism may seem Utopian to those who are embittered by the corruption and injustice of modern society. But, as Wilde said, "Progress is the realisation of Utopias". . . .

Anarchists do not advocate political freedom. What they advocate is freedom from politics, freedom from the institution of government, freedom from coercion, freedom from the law's interference in the lives of individual men and women, freedom from economic domination and inequality. The last is perhaps the most important, in that economic freedom, the satisfaction of man's physical needs for food, clothing, shelter, and all the other material necessities of a civilized life, is necessary before any man can begin to be free.

By the elimination of property, vested either in individuals or in corporate ruling classes, by the destruction of the state, by the substitution, for a society based on the mechanical and artificial institutions imposed by the dictates of propertied and governing interests, of a society based on institutions rising organically from the needs of men, the anarchist sees the need for the suppression of individual freedom brought to an end. Only a society based on control from above has need of coercion. A society based on co-operation can do without oppression and restriction because it is based on the voluntary agreement between its members. Indeed, it *must* do without coercion, if it is to retain its co-operative basis, and avoid relapsing into a political institution controlled by a governing cabal.

Freedom is as much a necessity for society as it is for the individual men and women who comprise it. Restrictions on liberty naturally produce oppositions within a society. No political unit in the history of civilisation has existed without carrying within itself the disruptive forces of discontent —precisely because no political unit has existed which did not base itself ultimately on the ability to force the individuals within it to obey the will of the controlling elements. On the other hand, social units operated by co-operative and voluntary means have often succeeded in surviving over long periods without destructive internal strife. Their failure has resulted either from the attack of overpoweringly strong external forces or from the co-operative units themselves adopting the authoritarian pattern of external political bodies. (The decline of the English trade unions to subordinate control institutions of the state is a notable example of the decay of an originally co-operative institution which adopted a centralised authoritarian pattern).

An examination of history, the real history of concrete human achievements and institutions as against the semi-mythical history of political institutions, shows that the development of the corporate and individual achievements of men is strongest and assumes its most significant forms in periods and places where political organisation is weakened and least centralised. The vitality of human culture appears to run in inverse proportion to the strength of the state. Periods of political stabilisation, when authority is held firmly by an efficient centralised government, when the state is deified and the free action of the individual is impeded, are most often periods of sterility, both in the development of organic institutions and the cultural achievements of individual artists and scientists. Times of political disintegration, when social forms are in flux, when the power and efficiency of the government are weak, when the state is regarded lightly and the individual finds room and freedom for development, are periods of institutional and cultural growth. One need only compare Sparta with Athens, the Italy of Mussolini with the Italy of the Renaissance. . . .

MULFORD Q. SIBLEY
1912-

MULFORD Q. SIBLEY IS a political philosopher and a leading
American pacifist as well as an active socialist. Born in Marston,
Missouri, he attended the University of Oklahoma and the University of Minnesota. He has taught at the universities of Illinois, Oklahoma, and Stanford,
and is now professor of political science at the University of Minnesota. *Con-
scription of Conscience: The American State and the Conscientious Objector,
1940–1947,* which he wrote with Philip E. Jacob, was published in 1952 and
received the Franklin D. Roosevelt Foundation award for the best book in government and welfare of the year.

Sibley is the author of articles on a variety of political subjects, including
utopian thought and movements. He is editing a volume on the theory and
practice of nonviolent resistance, and is the author of a forthcoming work on
the history of political theory.

[41]   *Pacifism: The Rejection of Violence*

Any critical evaluation of the political theories of modern pacifism
must begin with an emphasis on the divergencies in content and varieties
of approach within those theories themselves. As is true of any vital tendency in political thought, differences of statement and emphasis within the
pacifist stream seem only less great than those which separate it from other

From Mulford Q. Sibley, *The Political Theories of Modern Pacifism,* The Pacifist
Research Bureau Pamphlet Series V (July, 1944), pp. 24–28, 30, 31–32, 34–36, 39,
42–46, 49–50, 51–54. Reprinted by permission of the author and The Pacifist Research Bureau (Philadelphia).

analyses. Hindu pacifism roots in presuppositions which see "matter" as evil and "spirit" as good; and in its statement there remains an acute tension produced by the idea, perfectly consistent with its own assumptions, that even the process of living in a "material" body is an act of violence and hence to be condemned. Christian pacifism, in contrast, is in the main non-dualistic. It sees good, as well as evil, attached to the "material" and evil, as well as good, inhering in "spirit." But even in Christian pacifism there is a dualistic strain, which becomes particularly marked in Christian anarchists such as Tolstoy, for whom any physical force—that is, "matter" —is in essence evil.

As for non-religious revolutionary pacifism, it roots itself in a kind of utilitarianism for which problems of natural and divine law, so vital to the Hindu and Christian pacifist, do not exist. Violence is to be condemned and a theory of revolutionary action developed with that condemnation as its base, not because violent action is contrary to the will of God or to the rational nature of man, but rather because violence produces undesired results. This utilitarian approach is not lacking in Hindu and Christian pacifism, which can easily be understood since both are in fact revolutionary, but it constitutes only part of the religious approach.

Then again, within the whole broad current of modern pacifist thought there is a constant difficulty in regard to the problem of differentiation between non-resistance and non-violent resistance. Some emphases contend that the two are to be sharply distinguished, the former implying renunciation of power in any form, the latter an endeavor to change "the world" by a "right" method of acquiring and using power. Yet other analyses would minimize the distinction, and some even deny it altogether. On the whole, "non-violent resistance" has tended to eliminate "non-resistance" in the ideology of modern pacifism.

This latter tendency may be due to the fact that modern pacifism is much more explicitly political than were doctrines of non-violence before the twentieth century. Many in the historic current of pacifist thought have looked upon the ethics of pacifism as essentially personal and without any particular relation to the problem of conquest of power. Non-resistance was associated with the idea of renunciation of the "world," not with the conception of a conquest of the city of Man by methods characteristic of the city of God. One became a non-resistant, not with the hope of attaining political power, but in a sense for the contrary reason: a Christian was not interested in political power—had he been so interested, he would have fought and used all the methods of this world. This conflict between an individualistic pacifism, which holds to the belief that political power is to be totally rejected, and a political pacifism, which seeks to attain political power for the purpose of changing "the world," is very much alive in twentieth-century pacifist thought. It accounts in considerable measure for many inconsistencies which appear in the political doctrines which we have, in a rather broad sense, denominated "pacifism."

Finally, there is a sharp conflict between those who adopt frankly anarchistic views with reference to the State and those who, while attacking the modern State, would yet retain it and with it a measure of coercion within strictly prescribed limits. Within very wide limits, indeed, it might be said that all pacifism is tinged with anarchism; but those limits are so far apart that it would be grossly mis-representative to fail to make very specific distinctions. Most pacifists would undoubtedly repudiate the anarchism of Berkman and DeLigt. Yet the anarchist eddy in the current of modern pacifism is extremely important and cannot be neglected in a critical evaluation.

But these widely varying interpretations of meaning and implications should not blind the analyst to unifying elements. The general tendency of pacifist political philosophies moves in one direction, in negative and positive senses alike. There are a large number of common arguments, particularly at the political level. And even where the divergence is so sharp that it is impossible to discern any common ground, it is often possible to examine the predominating thesis and then turn to the dissents.

Thus, on the theological level, Hindu and Christian pacifism seem far apart at points. But a close examination will disprove this appearance. For Hindu doctrine feels constrained, in the political area at least, to modify its strict dualism by accepting as inevitable a large element of the "material" and admitting the impossibility of dissociating "spirit" from "body"; while Christian pacifism, refusing to admit the essentially evil character of the "material," is yet led to agree that sensual corruption as well as "pride of spirit" is a factor in the problem of violence. The "body-force" which Hindu pacifism attempts to repudiate completely in its dualistic presuppositions is accepted over a certain area in its ethics and politics; while Christian distrust of any sharp dichotomy between body and spirit does not lead it to deny that there is an ethical distinction between types of pressure associated with what Gandhi calls "body force" and methods of coercion termed "soul force." In the political area, the problem for both Hindu and Christian pacifism thus becomes one of allocating to both "body force" and "soul force" their proper spheres of action.

Again, while most secular pacifism is utilitarian or pragmatic in approach, and religious pacifism has non-pragmatic elements, this difference should not blind one to their essential likenesses on the social level. Some religious pacifist doctrines do, indeed, deny that non-violence has anything to do with success in this world, but most affirm that the pragmatic criterion is entirely legitimate when used as an element in the validation of a tentative religious insight.

Similar observations could be made in relation to the controversy between those who advocate non-resistance and those who see the pacifist ethic fructifying in non-violent resistance. While differences between the two interpretations should not be minimized, there is at least one unifying factor: both non-resistance and non-violent resistance deny the ethical right of any State to claim complete and unquestioning obedience. When the non-resistant refuses to be conscripted for war service, he is, in the very act of refusing to fight the "enemy," resisting the demands of the State that he do so. At this point, at least, he is not acquiescing, any more than the non-violent resister. And on this common ground, if on no other, the two approaches—one ostensibly an extreme attempt to renounce power of all kinds, and the other an effort to gain power by methods which will more nearly frustrate the will to power—can unite. Some renunciation of "this world" is implicit in both doctrines. But at the same time, neither view can avoid the problem of power and its use—the non-violent resistant not attempting to do so; the non-resistant forced by the exigencies of life in society to concede the inevitability of power in the very act of choosing to resist the State rather than the State's "enemy." For even individual disobedience of political authority is a very real act of power; and unless the non-resistant is to become an exponent of passive obedience to all the commands of all those who assume authority over him, he must join the non-violent resister in acts of resistance.

More specifically, the main currents of modern pacifist thought which have been examined in this essay hold five propositions in common. A critical examination of each will reveal most clearly both the strength and weakness of pacifism considered as a political theory. The tenets are:

A. TENET ONE: *Violence Hinders the Achievement of a Democratic and Peaceful Order.*

Violence—including war, violent revolt, verbal misrepresentation, and much of the characteristic activity of the modern State—can never hasten, but only hinder, the achievement of a democratic and peaceful order. This principle is seen to be valid regardless of the fact that violence may be administered by those who look forward to a coercionless order. It is applicable in all instances and is not a matter of mere expediency. In larger perspective, violence is seen to inhere in any political system or action which hinders the free expression of divergent views of truth. Implicit in this conception, in turn, is the idea that a society which, either because of its defective organization or by reason of the ideologies of its rulers, fails to make possible a free and unhampered expression of clashing views of truth is a society reposing on violence. Reversing the statement, the existence of violence in its obvious political expressions—as in war and State propaganda—is evidence that the rulers of that society either fear the truth or believe that they have complete knowledge and therefore possess the ethical right to impose their views on others.

The pacifist is contending that violence is power which can never be controlled and which always "corrupts," not only its user but also the end for which it was ostensibly used. A society in which violence is utilized to maintain public authority, whether in the form of war, or suppression of "revolt" or the habitual violence of a ruling caste against its "subjects," can never consider the public welfare, if only because the means which constitute its weapons swallow up the end to be attained. The means cannot be isolated from the end to be achieved. They *determine* the end. Spanish progress was impeded not only by the violence of General Franco and the Nazis, but also by that of Largo Caballero and the Stalinite communists.

*   *   *

Moreover, the thrust of all modern politics, the pacifist contends, is in the direction of making violence the ethical norm of existence. Always in past history power has tended to be the end, but there have been areas in which one might escape the ubiquity of violence. In the twentieth century, on the other hand, those areas are rapidly closing because of a centralized economic order and a politics associated with it.

*   *   *

. . . When Aldous Huxley maintains in the course of his argument that "the end cannot justify the means, for the simple and obvious reason that the means employed determine the nature of the ends produced," he subjects himself to several critics, of whom [Max] Lerner is . . . one. "If the end does not justify the means," Lerner demands, "then what does?" It is a legitimate question and one about which the pacifist argument has been all too ambiguous. A not infrequent answer is to contrast the principle "the end justifies the means" with the dictum "the means determine the ends." The assumption often seems to be that one principle is the antithesis of the other. On close examination, however, no such contradiction can be seen to exist. The end justifies the means only if and when the end is actually achieved—then, indeed, the means selected can receive approval. But a projected end, as contrasted with one achieved, can never "justify" any and all means. The very statement of an end automatically excludes certain types of means.

It would be more nearly correct to say that a projected end dictates its own means just as our desire to see a forest of oak trees flourish on what is now bare earth dictates that we plant acorns and only acorns. The acorn is not the oak nor the oak the acorn. But the oak is embryonic in the acorn; and, with proper conditions, the acorn will always become an oak and never a beech or pine. In politics, of course, the problem is extremely complex, due to the multiplicity of factors involved. But the principle would seem to be the same.

* * *

B. TENET TWO: *Modern States Are Built on Violence and Only Revolution Can Effect a Pacifist Order.*

Any sober analysis of modern political and economic history would seem to corroborate a second commonly held assertion of pacifist doctrine: that all modern states are built upon a large substratum of violence and that only a political and economic revolution can effect a pacifist world-order. The whole literature of Marxian speculation also is an assertion of the validity of this contention. What Barthelemy de Ligt called the "horizontal violence" of international war and the "vertical violence" implicit in modern class structure are phenomena so obvious as scarcely to require comment. Whether the State be looked upon as dominated by capitalists or by a rising class of bureaucrats or "managers," as Burnham would have it, the use of naked bayonets or officially sponsored verbal manipulations is indispensable to any minority domination. That the degree to which this statement is applicable varies from State to State does not alter its fundamental conformity to fact. The utilization of violence may be more overt in States like Germany and Japan than in political structures like those of Great Britain and the United States, where economic exigencies have thus far not called for its more brutal manifestations. But that the modern State *per se,* however the expression may vary in particular instances, is suffused with violence, is surely difficult to deny. Even so-called democratic States exhibit increasingly what Michels once so aptly termed "the iron law of oligarchy"—the tendency in an ostensibly democratic society for the forms of democracy alone to remain, the substance of power shifting to small groups of self-designing men whose end is power. The movement of history seems to be inevitably in that direction, unless checked by an almost super-human capacity for resistance and a widespread knowledge of the structure and dynamics of society.

To a degree never surpassed in any former age the State today tends to approach St. Augustine's conception of a commonwealth without justice. Such a "State," the bishop of Hippo avowed, more nearly resembled a rob-ber band than an ordered polity. The modern State, on the whole, does more to promote disorder than to destroy it, any order it achieves ministering strictly to the disorder characteristic of war. Internally, it elicits obedience often by overt, more often by covert, violence; and when its subjects be-come restive despite its propaganda ministries, economic doles, private police systems, industrial use of tear gas, and elaborate bureaucracies, it opens up an avenue for human energy externally by engaging in war. In either case its essential aim is to destroy as much as necessary for retention of power by its rulers and to cloak its motives in as much plausible decep-tion as possible. Within what other framework is it possible to explain the Second World War? Here the pacifist argument would appear to be but-tressed by an amazing amount of evidence.

C. TENET THREE: *This Revolution Must Develop and Employ a Technique Embodying a Non-Violent Ethic.*

There is a powerful argument to be made out, then, for the third propo-sition common to the most articulate stream of twentieth-century pacifist thought. That is a plea for a technique of revolution which will conform and conduce to the end of a non-violent political order. Pacifism discovers the answer to this problem in the conscious infusion of politics with a non-violent ethic. Specifically, it asks for the adoption of a technique modeled on that of modern Hindu pacifism. A highly disciplined body of relatively ascetic individuals, inured to suffering and ready to undergo death or im-prisonment in the process of civil disobedience as non-cooperators—such is the picture presented.

*   *   *

D. TENET FOUR: *Decentralization in Politics and in the Economic Order Is Sought.*

Another element common to all pacifist political thought is its emphasis on decentralization in politics and the economic order. Accompanying this tendency is a strong distrust of industrialism and a parallel belief in a semi-agrarian society. Gandhi, as our analysis of Hindu pacifism showed, is strongly in favor of a large degree of economic self-sufficiency and local autonomy for all political entities—not primarily, as has been so frequently asserted, because he is a political and economic reactionary (however "conservative" his politics may be), but rather because he sees in centralization and extreme industrialization great impediments to a non-violent order. Complex organization loses sight of the individual and, because it is intricate, necessitates a large number of experts, who in the end become a ruling class using violence and terrorism to sustain their power. Huxley reinforces this argument by emphasizing the dangers of large-scale reform, which likewise plays always into the hands of the violent unless rigorously checked by a group embracing a definitive philosophy of non-violence.

*　*　*

Being distrustful of all organization, it [pacifism] combines with its plea for decentralization and simplicity the proposal for a systematic education in non-violence and in all that non-violence implies politically. It sees, as so much modern political speculation has not, that while the system may and does manipulate the individual, no genuine revolution is possible in the absence of regenerated individuals.

But although it is thus true that pacifist theory in its decentralist and agrarian phases contributes not a little to a well-rounded criticism of life and politics in the twentieth century, there are undoubtedly certain dangers in its emphases. The first is that it will tend to over-idealize rural life and forget that for the most part an agrarian existence has in the past been considered intolerable by vast multitudes of human beings. And justifiably so. To some, the reek of manure, days of grinding toil, and the sheer boredom involved in much rural living, are far from conducive to the development of those qualities of mind and heart which pacifist doctrine exalts. No wonder many of the most intelligent have sought refuge in the over-crowded cities and chained themselves to machines in order to escape the monotony of farm life. It is true that technological developments promise to make an agrarian existence far more preferable. But technology is the very phenomenon against which pacifist agrarians so often protest.

Then, again, greater autonomy for small communities and regions can be grossly exaggerated. The pacifist, whether anarchist or non-anarchist, is right in protesting against the swallowing up of the individual personality by the Leviathan State. His is a valid criticism, both implicit and explicit, of what Hilaire Belloc, in the opening years of the twentieth century, called the "servile State"—one where the individual increasingly becomes a slave dependent upon the State for his very existence, whether he be a recipient of the State's doles, or takes the State's old age pensions and "unemployment insurance," or simply becomes one more member of an ubiquitous State bureaucracy which battens upon the land. Such a State can govern only by chicane, force, and violence. Quite often the pacifist does not see, however, that the very evils which he discerns in the modern State because of its centralization and emphasis on technology would arise were the contrary principles, decentralization and agrarianism, pushed too far. A world in which the binding tie of political cohesion is practically severed would be a poor setting for social harmony and non-violence. Yet that is exactly where the argument of anarchist, and even of some non-anarchist, pacifism, ultimately would lead us.

A balanced view of the problem of violence would seem to warn us against both the Scylla of extreme centralization and industrialization and the Charybdis of extreme social and political decentralism and agrarianism. The first course would separate most men from the primary means of subsistence, enhance their dependence upon central political authority, and hence minimize chances of effective resistance to any tyranny which might gain control of the political machinery. The second course, if pushed to extremities, would tend to eliminate the principle of order and planning altogether, and in so doing give birth to a violence of chaos as destructive as the violence of centralization. It would be the story of fourteenth and fifteenth century Italian City-States repeated. It is the situation of the twentieth-century international order, a fact well recognized in pacifist writings. From one point of view, indeed, twentieth-century politics may be looked upon as an interacting of both first and second courses—the first reflected in the internal structure of the national State, while the latter is manifest in its external relations. The violence inherent in each principle stimulates the other so that the effect is cumulative. The tendency toward internal oligarchy in all areas of life is reflected most dramatically in that oligarchy's manipulation of its subjects for purposes of external war; and the power thus exemplified in war is utilized as a springboard for perpetuation of the oligarchy's power internally. Peace becomes the problem of so articulating centralizing and decentralizing elements as to allow neither to become the paramount principle. The answer in terms of statesmanship is not an easy one.

If pacifist speculation could elaborate a new synthesis of the two prin-

ciples, in terms of political organization, it would be contributing vastly to
the major problem of twentieth-century politics. Starting from its premise of
non-violence, it could attempt to show in specific terms, how, given the
facts of industrialism, the structure of the modern State, and the development of an ethos of violence, the political world might be transformed. It
would show, perhaps in the form of a utopia, how the balance between
central planning and local autonomy is to be maintained. It would re-
emphasize what Alexander Hamilton and James Madison pointed out long
ago—that political entities as such cannot by arms be effectively coerced.
It would attempt to blend the virtues of an agrarian existence with the very
real contributions made by industrial technology. It would understand that
a non-violent order can never be attained and preserved, in the last analysis,
solely by a reconstructed social and political organization; that such an
order, once approximated, is always made immediately subject to destruction once more through the eruption of violence. It would refine and develop its doctrine of non-violent resistance, so that the weapons of non-
violence could be brought to bear effectively at any point in the social and
political structure where the principles of a non-violent and non-parasitic
social order were disregarded. A positive statement of this kind would go
far in answering those who maintain that pacifist criticism of centralism
and the industrial order is merely negative and unconstructive.

E. TENET FIVE: *The Ideology of Non-Violence Has a Direct Relevance to Politics.*

A fifth element underlying most modern pacifist philosophy, one implicit
in the previous four, is the belief that an ideology of non-violence has a
direct relevance to politics. Pacifism, its proponents aver, is not an endeavor
to escape from a sordid world—a pietistic or neo-platonic aloofness from
the power struggles of the human race. It believes, whether it be Hindu,
Christian, revolutionary, anarchist, or non-anarchist, that its conception of
the universe is pertinent to history here and now. It holds that, if acted
upon, its philosophy of politics can constitute the basis of a framework
within which power will more often, if not always, remain subordinate to
non-power values. It argues that seemingly impossible ideals are the very
ones which often, on closer inspection, reveal the only strategies of political
action which can possibly be successful. It maintains, indeed, that the very
width of the gulf subsisting between an "impossible" ideal and the practice
of the world will not infrequently generate the power that will make ideal
and practice more nearly coincident.

It is these fundamental assertions of twentieth-century pacifist doctrine which have constituted the target for its most redoubtable critic's charges. For Reinhold Niebuhr has maintained that pacifist political theory falls within the category of what he terms "ethical utopianism." Perfectionist, it does not understand that an ethics such as it advocates cannot be operative in the political sphere. The political area is one in which power is the keynote. Here the love-ethic of the New Testament can find but little place; and to attempt to practice it, as pacifist political theory would have us do, can result only in giving power to autocrats and tyrants. Niebuhr criticizes pacifist doctrine on the ground that it would attempt to emancipate reason from force. It assumes, he contends, the separation of spirit from body. It upholds the thesis that reason, freed, can act without the implementation of force. Failing in this endeavor, as he asserts it must fail, pacifism tends to be escapist and to renounce politics altogether. Indeed, Niebuhr apparently holds that there can be no middle ground between complete world-renunciation, on the one hand, and a willingness to see all types of power without distinction as ethically legitimate.

This latter element in his argument seems to be specifically confirmed in his analysis of the nature of God and of God's relation to history. The characteristic feature of the Divine is for him a "perfect coincidence of power and goodness." Divine love is selfless love. But no love on the plane of history can be selfless or disinterested. It must always be concerned about its own. If expressed at all, it expects reciprocation. Justice on the level of history is a nice balancing of mutually contradictory interests, and any love which was genuinely selfless would soon find itself extinguished in politics. Men, in other terms, who deliberately refuse to participate in the power struggles of history—who give and do not seek, and who offer no resistance —will find their lives ending "tragically."

The non-resistance taught in the Sermon on the Mount is, therefore, the only way by which this conception of divine love can be realized in history —but the essence of history is negated if the ethics of non-resistance be exalted. The pacifist theory of politics, on the other hand, believes it is possible to embody the principles of non-resistance in history. In this, being necessarily and inevitably frustrated, it emerges with an entirely different principle: non-violent resistance. But this latter is not to be differentiated ethically from all politics—it, too, is power seeking and a repudiation of the Sermon on the Mount.

In its political theory, Niebuhr maintains, pacifism is afflicted with the same disease as Marxism, which he denounces as "too superficial to plumb the depths of evil illumined by a profound religion." No perpetual guarantee of peace or justice in society is possible, because of the tendency to oligarchical control and because no self can be disinterested without surrendering its ability to live on the plane of history. From this phenomenon proceed revolts and violence; and while a time of relative peace may some day be assured, always there will be "periods of decay and destruction, such as our own, in which it is necessary to risk the very destruction of civilization for the sake of preventing a tyrannical unification of western Christendom." Force can be the only answer to those who would seek the reins of power for tyrannical purposes, although that force, as Niebuhr admits, may itself create greater destruction than the havoc wrought by tyrants.

* * *

When Niebuhr terms pacifist political theory "perfectionist" or "ethically utopian," he is undoubtedly correct, if by those terms he means to say that no conduct in the world of political relativity can possibly measure up to the ideal. Whether expressed in religious or non-religious terms, the pacifist ideal of conduct in politics represents an "impossible" goal in one sense. It implies the liquidation of politics as it has been understood in history. It is, as Gandhi emphasizes, the negation of that history. But from all this Niebuhr draws the wrong inference. He implies that because the ideal has not been embodied in the politics of the present, men ought to discard it and not so act as to protest historic political ethics. To follow that advice, however, would be to remove completely the tension between the "city of the world" and the "city of God"—a tension indispensable if power politics are to be controlled at all. Niebuhr, in general, would admit that this tension is essential if the political world is to remain under judgment for failure to raise its ethical practice to a higher level; and yet, inconsistently, he denies to pacifism any role in making this gulf between the ideal and the real vivid and meaningful. Pacifist apologetics would not contend that individual "perfection" in political and social action could be attained so long as the contemporary political structure subsists; but that does not mean that a "perfectionist" ideal, frustrated as it may be in a political order where men do not follow it, should not be laid down as the standard for action of those who wish to see it ultimately prevail in all areas. The social role of utopias is exactly this—to constitute the ideological cement for those small groups who refuse to identify prevalent practice with ideal right and who hold that, at points, they should deliberately dissociate

themselves from those acts of a society which most clearly and unequivo-
cally violate the ideal.

* * *

. . . to question the ethical justification of overt violence is to raise
immediately the problem of all the covert violences which stand at the very
center of modern life. Disparities in power as among individuals and groups
can no doubt be defended so long as those disparities have some relation
to function performed in the community; but if no such relation can be
clearly shown, they become acts of sheer violence. Now any cursory investigation of the contemporary State will show an astounding array of examples illustrating this non-functional, and hence violent, quality of power
in twentieth century politics and economic organization. War is merely the
most vivid and dramatic destruction of the finer qualities of human personality and the values which all the universal religious and humanist philosophies have exalted. The grinding toil of the tenant farmer, the wage
slavery of the city worker, the forcible surrender of political privileges by
the minor civil servant, the persistence of a profit economy placing the
emphasis on scarcity rather than abundance, and the increasing subjection
of the "lower orders" of men to a State machine which patronizes them
through doles and "social security" in lieu of genuine justice—all these
phenomena, when seen clearly, indicate a wide infusion of the ethos of
violence. It is precisely against this all-pervasiveness of the cult of violence
in the modern world that pacifism directs its criticism.

But all this means that any political analyst who has the slightest regard
for consistency and coherence and who begins with pacifist assumptions,
cannot possibly emerge with any other than a radical social philosophy.
Implicit in the pacifist view of things is always the anarchist, socialist, or
communist world outlook. The fact that some pacifist thinkers have not
pushed their argument to its furthermost limits does not argue against the
contention that every pacifist is implicitly either an anarchist, or a socialist,
or a communist; it merely raises the further query as to why some pacifists
and not a few of their critics have failed to see this.

From the other side, it would seem that any anarchist, socialist, or communist social theory would have to embody the pacifist perspective as a
part of its own. The goals laid down for an anarchist, socialist, or communist society dictate the means which the pacifist insight exalts, just as
the pacifist emphasis on means would seem clearly to indicate the ends of
socialism or communism.

An adequate social and political philosophy, then, would see with pacifism the dangers lurking in centralization of power and would question the possibility, given the raw human stuff upon which political and economic structures must repose, of any lasting resolution of the problem of power becoming violence. It would maintain, again with pacifism, that the imminence of violence will confront any future society; but that it is possible through the development of training for non-violent resistance to keep the tendency to violence within much narrower limits than in the past. It would give emphatic assent to the pacifist analysis of the problem of ends and means in politics. But it would also insist, with socialism and communism, upon a radically altered perspective in relation to the phenomena of property. With socialism and communism, it would argue that no world of peace and harmony can be even approximately achieved in the absence of an economic organization whose whole thrust is in the direction of economic equality—not necessarily exact equality in incomes (although a much more powerful argument for this can be made out than is generally assumed), but equality in the sense that every human being shall be equally assured that he will have the material goods essential to perform his proper function in society.

It is the thesis of this essay that just such a philosophy is clearly implicit, and often explicit, in the leading doctrines of twentieth-century pacifism. When Niebuhr criticizes the pacifist argument because it places violence, and particularly war, in the central place of its analysis, it is not difficult to reply, then, that such an emphasis is perfectly legitimate. If the State could be prevented by organized effort such as pacifists advocate from engaging in the wholesale and dramatic form of violence called war, it could not long maintain the covert and often more insidious violences which stand at the base of modern society. For the modern State and its ruling oligarchy, war is an escape from the constant pressure from below which menaces all oligarchs. The twentieth century State cannot live without exploitation and to attack it at the point of most obvious violence would be to remove the props upholding the whole system.

But Niebuhr also fails to apprehend clearly the theological assumptions of at least non-anarchist religious pacifism. They are much closer to his own beliefs than he will admit. It is precisely because it is aware of what he terms the "demonic" element in human nature—the tendency, under all conditions to glorify force and seek power as an end in itself—that the ethical and political theory of pacifism is so concerned about the quality of the means used to implement political ideals. Its object is to make more nearly certain that those means do not encourage and enhance this very tendency which Niebuhr so rightly discerns in the very nature of human society.

Political theories of non-violence do indeed envision the possibility of a measure of progress, in the sense that they do not believe it beyond the wit of man to make more shallow the valleys of "decay and destruction" and to level down the peaks of power. Therein they constitute an attempt to refute the contention of Niebuhr and Oswald Spengler that because the past seems with regularity to demonstrate cycles of progress and decay, the future must also necessarily exhibit such a pattern. Pacifism is a belief that it is possible to break into what Gandhi has called this "chain of destruction," by invoking a political ethic, which, if valid at all, is revolutionary in its implications. By seeking to base its politics upon the systematized use of what it looks upon as an ethically higher and politically more efficacious type of power—while recognizing with Niebuhr that at any level power contains within itself "demonic" qualities—it believes it has discovered the key to this revolution.

But with non-anarchistic pacifist approaches at least, it is the key to partial success in the future inevitable struggles of political society—not the open sesame to the elimination of struggle, as with the Marxian and many Liberal views of progress. For the struggle will remain, as with Niebuhr. On this hard inner core of human nature and destiny, a large body of pacifists and their critics will agree. Contrary to Niebuhr's whole interpretation of what it holds, there is no evidence that the main stream of religious pacifism, with the exception of Tolstoyan currents, looks forward to an easy triumph of that divine love or *agape*, which it seeks to infuse into politics. Certainly there is nothing in Gandhi's doctrine to support such a contention. There is to be no apocalyptic descent of the Kingdom of God, no swift transformation of the whole into a classless society, no imminent end of history.

JACQUES MARITAIN
1882-

JACQUES MARITAIN IS ONE of the outstanding Catholic philosophers of our time. His spiritual journey has taken him from Protestantism and Bergson's intuitionism to neo-Thomist Catholicism. He has skillfully woven together a systematic theory of man and society, based on modern Scholastic theological assumptions.

Maritain received his degree in philosophy from the Sorbonne in 1905. He had been strongly influenced by Léon Bloy, and in 1905–1906 was converted to Catholicism. At first he attempted to reconcile Bergsonian views with Catholic doctrine, which only produced in him a state of turbulent dissatisfaction. He gradually turned to Thomism, which had been reasserted by Popes Leo XIII and Pius X in the late nineteenth and early twentieth centuries as the philosophic foundation for the Catholic approach to the modern world. Maritain became a professor at the Institut Catholique in Paris in 1914, and soon gained a reputation as a leading religious thinker.

One of the fundamental tenets of Maritain's position is that the human person is to be valued above worldly concerns and that social-political systems should be judged according to how well they serve as instruments to sustain the sanctity of the person. He expanded this view into a general ethical theory which he called *personalism*. When he applied it to fascism, communism, and bourgeois individualism, he found them all spiritually destructive. He has argued that political life universally is becoming *technically* rationalized, whereas it should be brought under the sway of *moral* reason. Only a democracy inspired by the Gospel "can progressively carry out its momentous task of the moral rationalization of political life."

Maritain's major writings are *Art and Scholasticism* (1930), *Introduction to Philosophy* (1930), *True Humanism* (1938), *Scholasticism and Politics* (1939), *The Rights of Man and Natural Law* (1943), and *Man and the State* (1951). He has lectured and lived in the United States for many years.

[42]   *Christianity and Democracy*

The tragedy of the modern democracies is that they have not yet succeeded in realizing democracy. The causes of this failure are many. First, the enemies of democracy never laid down their arms, and their resentment, hatred of the people and of freedom, have only grown in proportion as the weaknesses and mistakes of the modern democracies gave them more pretexts. Finally there was a coalition made between the interests of the leader classes, corrupted by money, desperately clinging to their privileges, and crazed by a blind fear of Communism (the spread of which could have been prevented only by a clear-sighted policy of social reform), between the interests of the leader classes and the ambitions of sordid adventurers, as well as the slave philosophy taught in all the countries of Europe by utopians eager to see their ideas realized through any possible means, or by sadistic racists, drunk with the joy of using the spirit to betray the spirit. At the very time when all the artifices of intellectual intimidation were bringing this sham ideology to its greatest efficacy, the youth of the democratic countries was engaging in an examination of conscience from which it would have come forth a few years later with renewed strength. But the first effect of this was to develop doubt and hesitancy, and that youth was to finish its examination of conscience in prisons and concentration camps, and in heroic resistance to the beast trampling Europe.

Another great reason for the failure of modern democracies to realize democracy is the fact that such a realization demands necessarily to take place in the social order as well as in the political order, and that this requirement has not yet been fulfilled. The irreducible antagonisms inherent in an economy founded upon the self-propagating power of money, the selfishness of the monied classes, and the secession of the proletariat, erected

From *Commonweal*, LX (June 11, 1954), 239–42. Reprinted by permission of the author and *Commonweal*.

by Marxism into a mystic principle of the revolution, all have kept the democratic tenets from passing into the life of the society: and the impotence of modern societies in the face of poverty and the dehumanization of work as well as their inability to overcome the exploitation of man by his fellows have been a bitter failure for them.

But the main reason is one of a spiritual nature. It resides in the inner contradiction and tragic misunderstanding of which the modern democracies have been the victims, particularly in Europe. In its essential principle, the form and ideal of democracy is inspired by the spirit of the Gospel and cannot subsist without it. In virtue of the blind logic of historical conflicts and of social memory, which has nothing to do with the logic of thought, we saw the leading forces in modern democracies repudiating both the Gospel and Christianity in the name of human liberty. On the other hand, we saw the leading forces in specifically Christian strata combatting democratic aspirations in Europe for over a century in the name of religion.

In France, the labor movement of 1848 was animated by a flame of Christian feeling, however smoky this flame may have been. The freethinking bourgeoisie simultaneously smothered both the movement and the flame. The nineteenth century saw the consummation of the great scandal of which Pius XI spoke. The working classes were seeking their salvation in the denial of Christianity; conservative Christian circles were seeking theirs in the denial of the material foundations and temporal requirements of justice and love. Soon, throughout Europe, panic-stricken leaders were to hold up an absurdly false dilemma before their followers. They claimed that men must choose between Communism, which sought to expel God, and fascism which sought to enslave and regiment Him, to corrupt religion in souls, and to "de-Christianize the Church herself."

This state of affairs was to reveal the frightful paralysis, caused by the contradiction of which I have spoken, both in the Christian spirit and the democratic spirit in the temporal life of peoples. It also made clear the disaster brought about in modern democracies, by the divorce between Christian and the democratic principles.

What then are those thoughts and profound aspirations awakened in the depths of the conscience of peoples by the Christian message, and which have traveled underground for centuries before coming to light? However badly understood or distorted they may have been during their hidden journey in the secular conscience, just what are those truths of evangelical origin which the secular conscience henceforth connected and identified with the very idea of civilization?

If we seek to consider them in themselves, freeing them from any erroneous context, we shall say that, by virtue of this hidden work of evangelical inspiration, the secular conscience has understood that human history does not turn in a circle, but is directed toward a goal, and proceeds in a certain direction. Progress is not automatic and necessary, but threatened and thwarted; it is not due to an advent of pure reason which would invalidate all that was inherited from the past, but that heritage itself is what increases, groaning under the labor of all the human and divine energies in man. What has been gained for the secular or profane conscience, if it does not swing to barbarism, is faith in the onward movement of mankind.

Under evangelical inspiration, often ignored but nevertheless active, the secular conscience has understood that the human person, while being part of the state, yet transcends the state because of the inviolable mystery of his spiritual freedom, and because he is called to the attainment of goods which are absolute. The state's reason for existing is to help the human person achieve the conquest of these goods and of a life truly human. What has been gained for the secular conscience, if it does not swing to barbarism, is faith in the rights of man, as a human person, as a person engaged in social and economic life, and as a working person; and it is faith in justice as being the basis of communal life and as being an essential property of the law, which is not a law if it is unjust.

Under the inspiration of the Gospel at work in history, the secular conscience has learned the dignity of the people and of the common man. The people are not God, the people do not possess an infallible reason, the will of the people or the spirit of the people is not the rule which decides what is just or unjust. But the people are the slowly prepared and formed body of common humanity, the living patrimony of the common gifts and promises made by God to His creatures—which are deeper and more essential than all additional privileges and social differentiations—and of the like dignity and like weakness of all members of the human race. It is only by existing in the communion of the people that any effort can bear fruit, or that the inspiring leadership which the people needs, can keep both its vitality and legitimacy.

Awakened by the movement of civilization to a consciousness of himself, the common man knows that his day has dawned, provided only that he triumph over totalitarian corruption and be not devoured by it; he knows that the idea of a class or race hereditarily constituted to be the master and dominator, must make way for the idea of a community of men equal in rights and in work, and of an élite of the mind and of work which will arise out of the people, without cutting itself off from the people, and will be, so to speak, the flowering and luxury of its energies. What has been gained for the secular conscience, if it does not swing to barbarism, is the sense of the basic equality of men in nature, and of the relative equality which justice must create amongst them, in the participation of everyone, according to his capacities and deserts, in the common task, and in the common heritage of civilization.

In virtue of the hidden work of the evangelical inspiration, the secular conscience has understood that the authority of those who govern (by the very fact that it derives from the author of human nature) is meant for free men and is exercised by virtue of the consent of the governed. For the Christian the dictates of authority bind in conscience because authority has its source in God; but from the very fact that authority has its source in God and not in man, no man or special group of men has in itself the right to command others. The leaders of the people receive that right from the principle which creates and preserves nature, and receive this right through the channels of nature itself, that is to say through the consent or will of the people or of the body of the community, through which authority always passes before it is invested in the leaders; and it is as vicars or representatives of the multitude that the holders of authority lead the multitude; and it is toward the common good of the multitude that they must lead it.

What has been gained for the secular conscience, if it does not swing to barbarism, is the conviction that authority, or the right to wield power, is held by the governments of the earthly commonwealth only because this authority manifests the common consent in them, and because they have received their trust from the people; and it is the conviction that the normal state toward which human societies must tend is a state in which the people act as an adult person, or one come of age in the political life.

In virtue of the hidden work of the evangelical inspiration, the secular conscience has learned that the political domain and the flesh and blood paraphernalia of the things that are Caesar's must nevertheless be subject to God and to justice. It has understood that all the art of dominating and all the crimes used by princes and leaders of nations to conquer and consolidate their power can indeed give them power, but always turn out for the misfortune of the peoples.

Once man has understood that in reality politics depends on morality because its end is the human good of the community, he sees at the very same moment that to want justice and law in politics is to want a great revolution which will replace the politics of power for the masters, men, states or nations by the politics of the common good, over which the people itself must watch, as being the main party interested. A community of free men cannot live if its spiritual foundation is not, essentially, law. Machiavellianism and the politics of domination, which consider justice and law as sure means of losing everything, are the born-enemies of a community of free men. What is gained for the secular conscience, if it does not swing to barbarism, is its condemnation of the politics of domination and of iniquitous and perverse means of ruling nations; it is the profound feeling that justice fosters order, and that injustice is the worst disorder, and that the cause of the well-being and freedom of the people and the cause of political justice are substantially connected.

Under the evangelical inspiration, often ignored, but nevertheless active, the secular conscience has awakened not only to the dignity of the human person, but also to the aspirations and the urge which are at work in the depths of man. The person, in itself a root of independence, but plunged into the constraints that come from material nature within and outside of man, tends to overcome these constraints and achieve its freedom of autonomy. When it is known that we are all created for blessedness, death no longer holds any terror; but then it is impossible to become resigned to the operation and enslavement of one's brother, and one aspires, for the very life of mankind on earth, to a state of emancipation in conformity with man's dignity. What has been gained for the secular conscience, if it does not swing to barbarism, is the conviction that the forward march of human societies is progress toward the conquest of a freedom conformable to the vocation of our human nature.

Finally, under the inspiration of the Gospel at work in history, the secular conscience has understood that amidst the misfortunes and sufferings of our existence, crushed as it is by the iron laws of biological and economic necessity, and by the weight of men's pride, injustice and wickedness, one single principle of liberation, one single principle of hope, one single principle of peace can stir up the mass of servitude and iniquity, and can triumph over it, because this principle descends into us from the creative source which created the world and is stronger than the world: namely that brotherly love whose law, a scandal to the mighty, was promulgated by the Gospel, and which is, as the Christian well knows, the charity of God poured out into the hearts of men.

Once the heart of man has felt the sweetness of this awesome hope, it is troubled for all time. The human race was exalted by this hope, and can lose it only by becoming more fierce than before. This hope is holy in itself.

It answers the deepest, most solidly rooted desires of human nature. It places souls in a communion of suffering and impatience with all who are oppressed and persecuted. It calls for heroism. It has a divine power for transforming human history. What has been gained for the secular conscience, if it does not swing to barbarism, is faith in the brotherhood of man, a sense of that social duty which demands compassion for man in the person of the weak and suffering, and the conviction that the political task par excellence is that of rendering common life better and more fraternal, and of working to make the structure of laws, customs and institutions of this common life into a house for brothers.

It is in its radical opposition to the philosophy of enslavement, in other words, to the totalitarian philosophy, that the democratic philosophy of man and society most clearly reveals its essential characteristics. Though personally involved in the traditions of the great landowners who possessed slaves, Thomas Jefferson sought to abolish slavery as a general practice. And this condemnation of slavery is at the very heart of democratic philosophy. This philosophy can be recognized in the traits to which I alluded a while ago; inalienable rights of the person; equality; political rights of the people whose consent is implied in any political regime, and as vicars of whom the leaders govern; absolute primacy of those relationships of justice and law at the basis of society; an ideal, not of war, prestige or power, but of improvement and emancipation of human life, and of brotherhood.

For that philosophy, the political task par excellence is one of civilization and culture. It tends primarily to bring about the common good of the multitude, in such a way that the concrete person, and not merely a privileged class, but the whole mass of the population, will really accede to the measure of independence suitable to civilized life, and which is ensured at the same time by the economic guarantees of work and property, by political rights, by civic virtues and the cultivation of the mind. Democratic philosophy does not admit that the state is a transcendent power which gathers up within itself every authority and imposes it from above onto human life; it demands that autonomous organs, enjoying an authority proportionate with their functions, spontaneously emanate from the civic community and the tension that exists between its various activities; and that the state be merely the highest organ of regulation, the object of which is the common good taken in what concerns the whole as a whole.

After that shall we make a point of defining the form of government to which the principles of the democratic political philosophy naturally tend? This philosophy maintains that the human person as such is called to participate in political life and that the political rights of a community of free men must be solidly guaranteed. That is why it claims the right of suffrage for every adult citizen of whatever race or social condition and likewise demands that a juridically formulated constitution establish the fundamental laws of the regime to which the people have expressly decided to submit their political life. The principles of the democratic philosophy of man and society can be satisfied by a constitutional form of monarchy or oligarchy, but it is toward the republican form that they tend, as being their most natural expression: a form of government in which the legislative power must be exercised by the representatives of the people, and the executive power by delegates directly or indirectly designated by the people and supervised by the people.

According to a familiar formula, democracy is described as the sovereignty of the people. This expression is ambiguous, for, in truth, there is no sovereign or absolute master in a democracy. It would be better to say that democracy is that regime in which the people enjoy social and political majority, and use it to direct their own affairs, or again that it is the "government of the people, by the people and for the people," which means that the people are then governed by men they themselves designated for functions of a determined type and duration, and over whose management they retain specific control by means primarily of their representatives and assemblies.

The error of individualistic liberalism has been, in principle, to deny the elected officers of the people any real right to command, under the pretext that everyone should obey only himself. These elected officers then became the holders of power without real authority, and at the very moment when they were governing the people, they had to make the people believe that they were merely its passive tools. In reality the elected officers receive their trust from the people and must govern in conjunction with the people, but, within the limits of their functions, they are invested with real authority. They enjoy a real right to be obeyed. In emphasizing this point, I wonder whether I am not departing from some ideological tendencies of Jefferson, who sometimes seemed to distrust the very idea of government; but I am sure I am not departing from his practical conviction as a statesman.

Another error of Rousseau's political philosophy and of subsequent pseudo-individualism was that of reducing the community to a myriad of individuals in the face of an all-powerful state in which the individual will is supposed to be annihilated in order to be mystically reborn in the form of a general will; of excluding the existence and autonomy, initiative and rights proper to any group or community of a rank inferior to that of the state, and, finally, of suppressing the very notion of common good and common task. These errors which corresponded to the rise of the bourgeois class and ideology, far from being closely linked with democracy are destructive to democracy. They paved the way for totalitarianism. In freeing itself from them, democracy will return to the authentic principles of democratic philosophy.

Democracy must not only proclaim in a more or less symbolic manner, but foster in reality, and be really animated by, trust in the people, in the plain people. Such trust does not proceed from the rationalistic and romanticist optimism which prevailed at the end of the eighteenth century. It proceeds from a realistic and sober appreciation of the aims and conditions of political life. One of the distinctive features of American civilization is that, despite the power in fact enjoyed by the groups of men or of families which control economic life, these groups do not constitute a class in the European sense, that is to say, deep-rooted in history, hereditarily stable and possessing a powerful moral and social cohesion. Because, in coming over to this country and leaving the Old World, men also leave the past, and, so to speak, blot out the nightmare of history; they doubtless get rid of a treasure of historical experience, but they also get rid of the poisonous resentments, hatreds, rivalries and prejudices conveyed by the century-old history of social groups and nations.

The considerations I have just laid down proceed from another conception of Christianity than Jefferson's. Yet I believe that taken in themselves these considerations are in agreement with his political philosophy. I am not pretending that they give a complete picture of all the particular features of this philosophy—far from it! But I believe that they correspond to its basic principles and to the lasting substance it conveys to us. And in this very fact I find a stimulating lesson—I mean a proof that the genuine democratic philosophy of man and society, which is a fruit and achievement of our Judeo-Christian civilization, can agree on its basic statements as well as cooperate in the common task, men sharing in quite different religious inspirations, from the most orthodox forms of Christianity to the merely natural outlook of those "ethical culture societies" of which Thomas Jefferson, as Professor Francis Philbrick put it, would almost certainly have been a member today.

PAUL TILLICH
1886-

PAUL TILLICH, THEOLOGIAN AND PHILOSOPHER, was born in Prus-
sia, and was educated and taught in several European universities. An outspoken critic of the Nazi movement, he was deprived of his
post at Frankfurt-am-Main, and in 1933 came to the United States. He taught
at the Union Theological Seminary in New York, and since 1955 has been a
University Professor at Harvard.

Tillich's main interests have been philosophical theology, the moral foundations of culture, and the reinterpretation of Christianity for the twentieth century. He has said about the conditions of his vocation: "We are not scholars
according to the pattern of our teachers at the end of the nineteenth century.
We were forced into history in a way which made the analysis of history and
of its contents most difficult. Perhaps we have had the advantage of being nearer
to reality than they were. . . ." He has attempted to define the ways in which
Christianity is related to secular culture, and he also searches for a *rapproche-
ment* between religious and secular thought. His work indeed has helped fashion an existentialist vocabulary for religious thought which is at the same time
congenial to many secular-minded students of history and society. His many
books include *The Interpretation of History* (1936), *The Protestant Era* (1948),
the two-volume *Systematic Theology* (1951, 1957), *The Courage to Be* (1952),
Love, Power and Justice (1954), and *Theology of Culture* (1959).

[43]   *The Gospel and the State*

If the dialectical method has any field in philosophy and theology where
it must be applied, it is the relationship between the Gospel and the State.

From *Crozer Quarterly*, XV (1938), 251–61. Reprinted by permission.

All relations of the Gospel to the State contain a Yes and a No, an affirmation and a negation, a likeness and a contrast. But not only this. Both concepts, the Gospel as well as the State, are dialectical in themselves. They contain innumerable tensions, contrasting possibilities, paradoxical elements. This is the reason for the tremendous amount of possible interpretations of each of these concepts and of their relation to each other. Therefore, if the word "dialectic" has still any meaning and methodological value, if this main discovery of Plato which has been used by the Greek philosophers as well as by the Christian theologians, is still important for us, the dialectical method must be applied to our problem.

I know that the word dialectical today is suspect to many people, partly because they connect it with the so-called "dialectical theology" of our day (which in reality is not dialectical at all) partly because the kind of thinking which rightly is called dialectical is strange to those who are accustomed to mere empirical and statistical methods. Therefore it is significant to realize that the whole New Testament is dialectical in its explanation of the relationship of God and man, of sin and justification, of the Kingdom of God and history, in its attitude toward the State, expressing different sets of Yes and No.

But, obviously, it is not only the complexity of the concepts and the necessity of applying the dialectical method which makes our problem so difficult. It is also the great variety in the interpretation of the Gospel through the different churches and denominations, and the abundance of forms and self-interpretations of the State in the course of history. In order to limit our task we shall concentrate our interest on the recent developments of the State in the totalitarian countries. But in order to understand them we must understand the State itself and its main characteristics, and we must, first of all, have a clear concept of what the Gospel means.

I. THE DIALECTICAL INTERPRETATION OF THE GOSPEL

The Gospel is a message coming from *beyond* man and coming *to* man. In order to be Gospel, Good News, to me it cannot be *from* me. What I already have is neither new nor message to me. "Me," means human existence generally, and, since man is the center of his world, it means the world universal. The Gospel is by its very definition transcendent, from beyond the world. But at the same time it is a message *to* me; I must receive it; it must concern me in my very existence and in my world. I must understand it, my existence must be transformed by it. Therefore it is immanent, it belongs to my world.

The Gospel pronounces the transcendent fulfilment which cannot be found on earth, the Kingdom which is beyond the historical kingdoms, which is "not of this world." Here must be found the reason for the complete detachment from all the affairs of State, law, politics, culture which we find in Jesus. Here is the root of the eschatological flavor in all sayings and actions of Jesus; for his complete unconcern for Jewish nationalism as well as for Roman imperialism; for Pilatus as well as for Herodes.

No Christian doctrine of the State is possible which does not start with this radical detachment. The Gospel comes from another realm and leads to another than that in which the State is powerful. But the kingdom of God is not only of another world; it is also *in* this world. It has appeared in it through Christ; it is struggling in it against the kingdoms of earth and their demonic power; it is represented in the history of the Church, and our hope is that it may "come to us." It is an immanent reality although it is not of this world.

Therefore, the detachment in principle must be followed by a concern in actuality. In the New Testament we find two main affirmative attitudes towards the State—the Paulinian and the Apocalyptic. Paul acknowledges the State as a divine order for the sake of suppressing the social evil and of preventing complete chaos. He demands, from this point of view, that the Christian acknowledge the legality of State-power by subjecting himself to it—a word which implies the refusal of enthusiastic anarchism (a danger of primitive Christianity) but which does not imply any support of conservativism and bad government, as it was abused in Church history. The other attitude is the struggle against the Roman Empire because of the persecution of the Christians by it and because of its demonic arrogance in making itself God and commanding divine adoration. This attitude is expressed in the Revelation of Saint John and means something quite different from detachment and unconcern.

Beyond mentioning these two attitudes (in which all problems of later Church history to the present are anticipated) we may point to the fact that the use of symbols like the "Kingdom of God," the "Reign of Christ and his apostles," as well as the demand for order and leadership within the Church itself, indicate that the idea of some statelike structure even in the perfect community is maintained. But all this does not mean an explained doctrine of the State. The situation of early Christianity made a complete affirmative attitude toward the State impossible. What we can learn from the New Testament with respect to our problem is first and mainly the complete detachment of Jesus himself; secondly, the very limited and hesitating affirmation of the State by Paul and, thirdly, the radical criticism of a demonized State by John.

II. THE FIRST DIALECTICAL TENSION OF THE STATE AND THE GOSPEL

The State is that institution which creates social unity by power and law. Both elements, power and law, belong essentially to the State. It is the ultimate power and therefore the bearer of law. Consequently the first dialectical tension in the State is that between power and law. The naturalistic interpretation, most radically explained in orthodox Marxism, considers the State essentially as power, namely as the power which is necessary to establish class rule. Laws are laws only for the subjected groups or classes. The ruling class adapt themselves to it as far as it is necessary in order to maintain order and through order their power. The idealistic interpretation, on the contrary, considers law as a reality in itself which, unfortunately, needs power and compulsion in order to be realized but which is self-sufficient and which should become more and more independent of power. This is the main ideal of the democratic interpretation of the State.

The Christian attitude toward this tension is dependent on the following points: As far as the transcendent character of the kingdom of God is emphasized, as far as its realization is seen beyond human possibility, as far as the cleavage between God and man is recognized, as far as the realities of sin and tragedies are taken seriously, Christian theology must be inclined to share the naturalistic and even the materialistic interpretation of the State. So Augustine has explained in his City of God that States are the name for the successful groups of pirates and burglars. The demonic will to power is connected with everything which has State character. Therefore, the earthly kingdom necessarily is a demonic kingdom. Here as in many other points Christian and Marxian realism are much more in agreement than Christianity and some types of an ideological bourgeois idealism.

On the other hand Christianity asserts that the kingdom of God is appearing and struggling in history. From this point of view Christianity must emphasize the idealistic element in the nature of the State. Augustine agrees with Cicero that Justice is the special quality of the State and he includes the State in his universal idea of peace which consists in unity, order and justice. "The peace between men consists in the ordered concord: and especially the peace in the family in the ordered concord of its members with respect to commanding and obeying; the peace in the State in the ordered concord of the citizens with respect to commanding and obeying; the peace of the heavenly city in the perfect and united fruition of God and the mutual fruition of each other in God, the peace of all things in the quietness of order. Order means the division of equal and non-equal things which gives to each of them its proper place." In positing the State between the family and the kingdom of God, Augustine attributes to it an essential perfection which, of course, is completely distorted in the existential actuality of the earthly State.

Considering these two qualifications of the State, the essential and the existential, we have to ask what is the judgment of the Gospel about the real State in which both qualifications are united. Augustine has two answers, corresponding to the two poles of the tension between power and law. He answers much as did Paul, that the State even in its demonized reality is better than chaos. The compulsory action of the State, which in itself is sinful, at the same time suppresses sin and makes possible all social life, even that of the Church. "We too use the peace of Babel." This was the answer also of Luther who, however, gave a more positive meaning to the State in teaching that its compulsory acts are an expression of the love of God, although indirectly, in a veiled and paradoxical form. And the same is the attitude of the present Reformed theology which emphasizes (for example in Brunner) that the State must suppress human arbitrariness by compulsion. It was and is the prevailing attitude of the Greek Orthodox Church.

The danger of this attitude is that it prevents any critical judgment against the State. If in any case the State has demonic qualities and if just this character, namely its unrestricted power, makes it, although paradoxically, the tool of God, then no criticism of the State is meaningful. For the sake of realizing *some* order the *just* order is neglected. But order without justice finally defeats itself. The unchallenged demon is a bad servant of God. The tragedy of European history and the servility of the Christian churches toward the State-powers in Central and Eastern Europe is rooted in this attitude.

The other element in Augustine has become predominant in Catholicism and Anglo-Saxon Calvinism: The State can be sanctified by its subjection to the will of God which, in Roman Catholicism, is represented by the Church; in theocratic Calvinism, by the Bible. The divine law, imposed on the Christian States, must be enforced by Christian rulers. American denominationalism has not much changed this attitude since sectarian and Calvinistic theology agreed to a great extent on this point. And even secular democracy has maintained the same attitude. The law of the State must represent the divine law. The State-powers have to serve this law or must be overthrown. Order must be *just* order. The State must realize as much as possible the justice of the kingdom of God. The State has to work on earth for the peace of the kingdom of God. The danger of this attitude is that the Christian detachment disappears, that, therefore, a relatively democratic and peaceful state of things seems to be the kingdom of God; that the depth of sin and tragedy in any human power, especially State-power, becomes invisible and that the height of the justice of the kingdom of God becomes lowered.

The same problem exists in the relationship of States to one another, and the same principles are valid for the Christian interpretation of world politics. There is no possible world peace without a law to which all nations are subject. And there is no possible international law without a power beyond the nations which is able to enforce this law. World peace is dependent on a world-state, and no other form of world peace can be imagined. This means that from the point of view of the Gospel as long as there are sovereign nations which act according to their natural will to power, it is idealistic utopianism to assume that those States could be subjected to law without an embracing power strong enough to enforce the law. On the other hand, there is no reason for denying the possibility of a development toward an embracing power in which the sovereignty of the single national States is transferred to the sovereignty of a united State for all nations. Only in such a final unity of universal power and universal law the political goal of human history is reached—to become, not the realization, but the representation of the kingdom of God.

III.   THE SECOND DIALECTICAL TENSION IN THE STATE AND THE GOSPEL

The State is a unity of human beings, who are individuals. This leads to the problem whether each individual is the purpose of the State or whether the State is the purpose of each individual belonging to it. Whether the individuals who are united in the State or the State as the unity of those individuals is decisive for the structure and activity of the State. The modern liberal and democratic State has chosen the first way. The main task of its theory of the State is to determine the limitations of the State. The liberal State tries to give as much independence as possible to every individual. It is more interested in giving rights than in requesting duties. The philosophical background of this theory is medieval "Nominalism," namely, the doctrine that the only reality is the reality of the individual and that universals are mere names or terms for institutional tools to be used for the satisfaction of each individual.

The opposite answer also is dependent on medieval thought, namely, on the mystical realism in medieval philosophy. It considers the individual as a merely contingent bearer of the universal. The State as a universal has more reality than any individual belonging to it. Therefore its power and growth are more important than the happiness and improvement of the individual. There are no "rights of man" as the rights of individual man. Justice is the expression of the needs of the State or the group united in the State. In modern times the idea of organism was used in order to describe the superiority of the State as a whole over each of its members. The so-called "State-reasons" became a weapon in the hands of ruling groups for suppressing justice and personal rights for the sake of the assumed happiness of the whole. In State-totalitarianism this tendency has reached its most radical expression, unbroken by the religious restrictions of medieval realism.

Christianity never has admitted a complete mystical realism and universalism, not even in a period in which the State was supposed to be a Christian State. The idea of personality and of the infinite value of each individual soul before God makes the submerging of the individual in a totalitarian community, even a Christian one, impossible. The kingdom of God is a community of personalities who have a direct relationship to God. This separates Christianity from any kind of pagan mysticism and totalitarianism. God has appeared in a personal life. The idea of the God-Man is the idea of a personal reality. Love in the sense of "Agape" is a personal relationship in distinction to love in the sense of "Eros" which means mystical identification. The individual personality stands directly before God, subject to his judgment, his salvation or damnation. A state, which attempts to create a representation of the kingdom of God on earth, must acknowledge the infinite value of each individual personality as a potential image and child of God. In this respect Christianity and humanism are in full agreement. Both, for example, have worked together toward the abolition of slavery, humanism more directly in the political sphere, Christianity more indirectly in destroying the pagan assumption that the slave must be considered as a thing and not as a person. The same prophetic presupposition and the same humanistic demand are effective in the protest of Marxism against a social order which uses human beings as working power to be calculated and measured instead of being considered as the real purpose of all collective work. This also can be expressed in terms of freedom. The freedom of the individual in a state is not, of course, identical with the "freedom of the children of God." This transcendent freedom is possible even in chains. But this is the exception and should not be considered as the rule. Man as the image of God must be able to participate in God's creative freedom. Not an abstract, merely negative, idea of freedom can be derived from the interpretation of man in the Gospel. But a freedom for everybody to share the creative work of the State is an unmistakable demand of the Christian doctrine of man. It is the fundamental right of man to be considered as personality. And all especial rights must be derived from it. The denial by a state of the rights of man in this sense is tyranny and must be attacked as tyranny by Christian prophetism. It must be challenged as a demonic destruction of justice. Hobbes was right in calling this State by the name of the mythological portent "Leviathan."

But Christianity never has and never should neglect the other pole of dialectical tension. The Christian churches, in long periods of history, have favored authoritarian forms of the State. Catholicism even today favors Fascism although it is threatened by it. Greek orthodoxy has supported Czarism. Lutheranism favors absolute monarchy, the Anglican Church is allied with aristocracy. The authoritarian form of church administration in Catholicism and to a certain extent in Lutheranism makes those churches inclined to support State-authoritarianism. The idea that the eternal order of things has hierarchical character is an expression of the demand for an hierarchical order in Church and State. For Augustine, even in the genuine creation and in the final fulfilment, hierarchical differentiations exist. No beings are equally near to God and therefore equal in power and grace. The Kingdom of God and the Reign of Christ are monarchic symbols and have consequences, consciously and unconsciously, for political theory.

Another impulse in this direction comes from the sacramental character of Christianity: First the divine gift, then human activity; first the assembly of God which as such is holy, then the individuals, who belong to it; first the people of God, then those who are elected to it; first the body of Christ, then the single members and organs. All this works strongly in the direction of mystical realism. This feeling is deepened by the evil in human existence, in the lack of actual personality in the majority of men, in the arbitrariness and disintegration of souls and groups. The Christian pessimism with respect to human nature has helped a great deal to bring about the alliance between Christianity and authority.

So the second dialectical tension in the State becomes very important for the relationship of the Gospel and the State. A solution must be sought in the direction of a doctrine of the State, in which community is the first and individuality is the second, but in which not the State as such and not the individual as such are the ultimate goal of history but the honor and glory of the Kingdom of God.

IV. THE THIRD DIALECTICAL TENSION IN THE STATE AND THE GOSPEL

The State appears as an external form of life; but no external form can exist without something which gives meaning to it, without a content in which its power of being and growing is rooted. This leads to a tension between the interpretations of the State from the point of view of form and of content. Where the State is considered as a mere form, its task is to protect the real life which is independent of it. Where the State is considered as a meaningful life in itself, its task is to create life by its own activities. In the extreme form of this latter interpretation the State is called the "God on Earth" embracing and fulfilling all sides of human life. The "God-on-Earth-State" against the mere "Police-State"—this is the tension with which we have to deal finally and which leads us into the center of the State-Church-problem in our present situation.

There is no doubt that any State needs a spiritual substance, an ultimate meaning of life on which it is based. No devotion to a State is possible without it. Even the liberal State has such a substance: The national idea. It never could exist without it. And this substance has always religious or semireligious character. It is connected with the ultimate meaning of human existence. This becomes manifest by an historical survey on the different stages in which form and content of the State have developed in relationship to each other. We can distinguish four great periods of this development. In the first, pre-Christian period of the relationship between religion and State there are three main stages. The primitive tribal stage in which State and religion were completely identical, king and priest had the same function, State-activities were, without distinction, religious activities.

In the second polytheistic stages mythology as well as rites are the expression of the State-life and are serving the State-purpose. The priests are cult-officials in the service of the State. The latest and highest development of this pre-Christian period is the abstract State of the Roman Empire which is beyond the concrete life of its subject and at the same time an object of adoration in the personality of the emperor. Here the form of the State itself has become sacred.

The second period in the development of State and religion in relation to each other is marked by the prophetic protest against any identification of State and religion. Religion in the prophetic message is related to any personality without mediation of the State and, consequently, has universal character without limitation by any national State. The great Jewish prophets, making the distinction between God and national politics, created an entirely new relationship between State and religion. This line was followed by Christianity in its absolute detachment from the State, in its message to each individual in all States and nations and consequently in its supernational universalism.

The third period of the development of State and religion in their relationship to each other begins with the foundation of the Christian State by Constantine. Three lines of development must be mentioned in this period. First, the Greek which is nearest to Constantine's interpretation of his function as Christian emperor and which is not very far removed from the State-religion of the pagan emperors. This form of a Christian State must be characterized as Cesaro-papism. The emperor as emperor is at the same time representative of the Church; so it was in the Byzantine empire and in Czarist Russia. The second line of development is the Roman-Catholic, which must be characterized as Papo-Cesarism: The Pope as the successor of Christ is at the same time the universal monarch, from which all other monarchs must receive their power. The medieval history can be considered as a struggle between these two lines: On the one side the pope aspiring to be emperor, on the other side the emperor of the Holy German Empire aspiring to have papal powers. The third line of the idea of the Christian State is expressed in both main groups of Protestantism, namely the demand for a Christian government but for a government which has no direct religious functions. This demand was directed to the Christian prince in the period of absolutism as well as to the elected governments in democracy. The Christian State in this manifold sense of the word was a reality, not because the authorities were personally Christians but because there was no other substance of life in these States. Even the humanistic epoch did not change the situation because modern humanism was Christian humanism.

The fourth period of the development of State and religion in relation to each other began in this twentieth century only. Christian humanism became more and more secular and empty. It lost the power of giving a meaning and a spiritual substance to human life. A feeling of complete meaninglessness conquered the souls of many groups of people, first of all of the younger generation. The Christian churches were not able to show a new meaning and to give a spiritual substance to State and society. This, in connection with the tremendous growth of nationalism, led to the rebirth of the old tribal powers of the first period. Nation, blood and soil became the real content and the spiritual substance of many States. The fundamental identification of religion and State in the pre-Christian period was resumed. And the final outcome of all this was the totalitarian tribal State as represented first of all by national socialism.

This historical survey has shown that the Gospel is the fundamental and everlasting protest against tribal religion, religious nationalism and State adoration. There is no possible compromise between Christianity and the religious philosophy of national-socialism; there is no possible compromise between Christianity and the religious glorification of race, soil and blood. Therefore, the struggle between Church and State in Germany must be considered as the renewal of the struggle between the Roman Empire and the old Christian Church. The struggle cannot be solved by a clear-cut separation between State-power and Church-power. When the State itself assumes Church character the fight becomes inescapable. The demand of the national socialist State-authorities that the Church restrict itself to the transcendent realm, is only a method of replacing the Christian Church by the German racial community, its creed and its cult. Neither is there a possible compromise with the nationalist-socialist State, since the alternative is exclusive: either nation and race are the ultimate values for which the sacrifice of soul and body is duty, or the salvation of the soul is the ultimate duty and meaning of human existence, equally in all nations and races. Therefore only the third way is left, the way used by the old Church in the days of persecution, to become an underground church in order to save the Christian message for its members and for coming generations. This way is used today by the radical wing of the Confessional Church in Germany. It is unavoidable but it also is dangerous. It works in the direction of a sectarian seclusion, of dogmatism, pharisaism and hierarchical dictatorship. These dangers already have become visible in the life of the Confessional Church.

The democratic countries cannot remain neutral in the long run in this struggle. The more secularized the democratic States become, the more danger of an entire loss of Christian substance is imminent. But since any State needs a spiritual substance nationalism would more and more replace Christianity, thus assuming a semireligious character itself. And whenever the national idea has become the ultimate meaning of life, racial fanaticism, the adoration of blood and soil, the hatred of the foreigner and the adoration of State power are the final outcome. Nationalism as the substitute for Christianity necessarily leads to some form of State totalitarianism. Only a few people in the present democratic countries realize this tremendous danger. The insight into the dialectical tension between form and content in every State may force the realization upon all. If Christianity is no more able to give a spiritual substance to the State and an ultimate meaning of life to its subjects, other powers will break into this vacuum, powers which always are dwelling in the depth of the human soul, which are overcome in principle by the Gospel, but which may rise again and wage a life-and-death struggle against the Gospel.

VIII

Predicaments of
thought and action

THE REMAINING TWO READINGS in this volume discuss the
factors that make it difficult for new political conceptions to
emerge at this point in history. Yet at the same time, the very discussion of
the limits of thought reveals its possibilities.

Günther Anders suggests that the most formidable obstacle to thought
and imagination is the threatened annihilation of history itself. The sense of
impending apocalypse paralyzes creative thought; and the conditions of
postmodern life have created a "gulf between our emotional capacity and
our destructive powers, [which] aside from representing a physical threat to
our lives, makes us the most divided, the most disproportionate, the most
inhuman beings that have ever existed." The capacity for action has gone
beyond the limits of our emotional, imaginative, and moral capacities. Men
are "confronted with situations and things with which they cannot cope by
definition, to which they are unequal linguistically, intellectually, and emotionally . . . ."

Taken one way, this essay sounds like the knell of doom; in that case,
there is nothing more to say. But taken another way, it suggests that the
twenty-first century may be a world that we cannot imagine, that the mind
may stretch to meet its ultimate challenge, and that the remaining half of

the twentieth century will bring moral and spiritual surprises to match the technical surprises of the first half. If as postmoderns we are serious and resolute in our conviction that action always has unanticipated consequences, then we must recognize that it is not unrealistic to think that things may turn out better than we expect. For certainly according to the dominant mood, we expect the worst.

Isaiah Berlin, in the concluding selection, declares that the peril to thought stems from the almost universal pressure for conformity. It is not an age of dissolving values and standards, he argues, but on the contrary is "stiff with rigid rules and codes and ardent, irrational religions." Heterodoxy is treated as the supreme danger in such a world. Social and economic requirements have demanded a perpetual tightening of discipline and repression of the discontented. Faith or leadership or organization, as it is often maintained, is not what the world needs at the present moment, but rather the opposite—less ardor, more skepticism, more heterodoxy, more spontaneous, individual variation.

In contrast to Berlin, who sees the world stiff with ideological norms, some writers have proclaimed "the end of ideology," recognizing, however, that the fatigue of ideologies in the West is matched by their vitality in the rest of the world. As Daniel Bell states it:

The extraordinary fact is that while the old nineteenth-century ideologies and intellectual debates have become exhausted, the rising states of Asia and Africa are fashioning new ideologies with a different appeal for their own people. These are the ideologies of industrialization, modernization, Pan-Arabism, color, and nationalism. In the distinctive difference between the two kinds of ideologies lies the great political and social problems of the second half of the twentieth century. . . .

Thus one finds, at the end of the fifties, a disconcerting caesura. In the West, among the intellectuals, the old passions are spent. The new generation, with no meaningful memory of these old debates, and no secure tradition to build upon, finds itself seeking new purposes within a framework of political society that has rejected, intellectually speaking, the old apocalyptic and chiliastic visions. . . .

The trajectory of enthusiasm has curved East. . . .[1]

Nevertheless, even if we admit the fatigue of old ideological formulas, it may be misleading to speak of the end of ideology, even in the West. If we grant that ideology serves not the mind but the passions, then we have no reason to expect that the "lesson" postmodern men have learned from

[1] Daniel Bell, *The End of Ideology* (Glencoe: The Free Press, 1960), pp. 373–74.

their immediate past will defend them from the energies released by the next wave of fury and delusion. Benjamin Nelson, a sociologist and historian of culture, observes:

. . . we have barely scratched the surface of the relations of politics and passion. Recently acclaimed writings such as *Eros and Civilization, The Sane Society,* and *Life Against Death* have not carried us a step beyond Freud in understanding the problems of civilization and its discontents. It is disheartening to note that not one of the current efforts to resolve Freud's Sphinx-like riddles promotes the urgent task assigned to this century, of demythologizing politics. Indeed, Narcissus and Prometheus are now given the greatest license possible to masquerade as world-redeeming Saviors who will deliver us from ever again bowing to the yoke of repression, sublimation, alienation, political obligation, finitude and death.

All the resources of modern logic, social science and psychoanalysis will need to be harnessed if we are to preserve our bearings in the midst of this outburst of "historiosophic" mythologies decked out as new and ultimate roads to lasting freedom. The variety and lushness of the new utopias should warn us that we are very far, indeed, from the "end of ideology," whose obsequies have been portentously announced in the eye-catching title of another recent volume. At this rate, one wonders whether men in any number shall be able before the hour grows too late to tell the difference between creative political action and its myriad nihilistic counterfeits.[2]

The urgent task of the twentieth century, we would add, is not only to demythologize politics, but also to understand it and to bring it under human control. As we have already suggested, understanding partly depends on our ability to work free of the stereotypes of the cold war. In a time when, as Isaiah Berlin points out, all social systems tend to demand ideological conformity as a part of political discipline, the effort to think independently becomes a political act. Thus the gap between thought and action, which we shall discuss in the concluding chapter, tends to close. Merely to live as a human person should live involves choices that become increasingly drawn into the political sphere. To live and to think is also to act.

[2] Benjamin Nelson, "Contemporary Politics and the Shadow of De Sade," *Psychoanalysis and the Psychoanalytic Review,* XLVIII (1961), 31–32.

GÜNTHER ANDERS
1902-

GÜNTHER ANDERS WAS EDUCATED at the universities of Hamburg and Freiburg. He is known as a philosophical writer, an art historian, and a critic of music and literature, and he has also written many social and political essays for German literary and philosophical periodicals. His books include a work on epistemology, *Über das Haben, sieben Kapitel zur Ontologie der Erkenntnis* (1928); a literary study, *Kafka, Pro und Contra* (1951), translated into English as *Franz Kafka* (1960); and a social-philosophic essay, *Die Antiquiertheit des Menschen* (1956).

[44]   *Reflections on the H Bomb*

1. The modern infinite. Faust is dead

If there is anything that modern man regards as infinite, it is no longer God; nor is it nature, let alone morality or culture; it is his own power. *Creatio ex nihilo,* which was once the mark of omnipotence, has been supplanted by its opposite, *potestas annihilationis* or *reductio ad nihil;* and this power to destroy, to reduce to nothingness lies in our own hands. The Promethean dream of omnipotence has at long last come true, though in an unexpected form. Since we are in a position to inflict absolute destruction on each other, we have apocalyptic powers. It is we who are the infinite.

From *Dissent,* III (Spring, 1956), 146–55. Translated by Norbert Guterman. Reprinted by permission.

To say this is easy, but the fact is so tremendous that all historically re-corded developments, including epochal changes, seem trifling in compari-son: all history is now reduced to prehistory. For we are not merely a new historical generation of men; indeed, we are no longer what until today men have called "men." Although we are unchanged anatomically, our com-pletely changed relation to the cosmos and to ourselves has transformed us into a new species—beings that differ from the previous type of man no less than Nietzsche's superman differed from man. In other words—and this is not meant as a mere metaphor—we are Titans, at least as long as we are omnipotent without making *definitive* use of this omnipotence of ours.

In fact, during the short period of our supremacy the gulf separating us Titans from the men of yesterday has become so wide that the latter are beginning to seem alien to us. This is reflected, to take a salient example, in our attitude toward Faust, the hero in whom the last generations of our forefathers saw the embodiment of their deepest yearnings. Faust strives desperately to be a Titan; his torment is caused by his inability to transcend his finitude. We, who are no longer finite, cannot even share this torment in our imagination. The infinite longing for the infinite, which Faust symbol-izes, and which for almost a thousand years was the source of man's greatest sufferings and greatest achievements, has become so completely a thing of the past that it is difficult for us to visualize it; at bottom we only know that it had once existed. What our parents, the last humans, regarded as the most important thing is meaningless to us, their sons, the first Titans; the very concepts by means of which they articulated their history have become ob-solete.*

The infinite longing some of us still experience is a nostalgia for finitude, the good old finitude of the past; in other words, some of us long to be rid of our Titanism, and to be men again, men like those of the golden age of yesterday. Needless to say, this longing is as romantic and utopian as was that of the Luddites; and like all longings of this kind, it weakens those who indulge in it, while it strengthens the self-assurance of those who are suffi-ciently unimaginative and unscrupulous to put to actual use the omnipotence they possess. But the starving workmen who early in the nineteenth century rose against the machines could hardly have suspected that a day would come when their longing for the past would assume truly mythological

---

* For instance, the antithesis between the Apollonian and the Dionysiac principle. The former denoted the happy harmony of the finite; the latter, the intoxication found in exploding the boundaries of the finite. Since we are no longer finite, since we have the "explosion" behind us, the antithesis has become unreal.

dimensions—when man could be appropriately described as the Titan who strives desperately to recover his humanity.

Curiously enough, omnipotence has become truly dangerous only after we have got hold of it. Before then, all manifestations of omnipotence, whether regarded as natural or supernatural (this distinction, too, has become unimportant), have been relatively benign: in each instance the threat was partial, only particular things were destroyed—"merely" people, cities, empires, or cultures—but we were always spared, if "we" denotes mankind.

No wonder that no one actually considered the possibility of a total peril, except for a few scientific philosophers who toyed with the idea of a cosmic catastrophe (such as the extinction of the sun), and for a minority of Christians who took eschatology seriously and expected the world to end at any moment.

With one stroke all this has changed. There is little hope that we, cosmic parvenus, usurpers of the apocalypse, will be as merciful as the forces responsible for former cataclysms were out of compassion or indifference, or by accident. Rather, there is no hope at all: the actual masters of the infinite are no more imaginatively or emotionally equal to this possession of theirs than their prospective victims, i.e., ourselves; and they are incapable, and indeed must remain incapable, of looking upon their contraption as anything but a means to further finite interests, including the most limited party interests. Because we are the first men with the power to unleash a world cataclysm, we are also the first to live continually under its threat. Because we are the first Titans, we are also the first dwarfs or pygmies, or whatever we may call beings such as ourselves who are mortal not only as individuals, but also as a group, and who are granted survival only until further orders.

2. The proposition, All men are mortal, has been superseded by the proposition, Mankind is exterminable

We have just emerged from a period in which for Europeans natural death was an unnatural or at least an exceptional occurrence. A man who died of old age aroused envy: he was looked upon as one who could afford the luxury of a peaceful and individual death, as a kind of slacker who had managed to escape from the general fate of extermination, or even as a sort of secret agent in the service of cosmic foreign powers through which he had been able to obtain such a special favor. Occasionally natural death was viewed in a different light—as evidence of man's freedom and sovereignty, as a twin brother of Stoic suicide—but even then natural death was felt to be unnatural and exceptional. During the war, being killed was thus the most common form of dying: the model for our finitude was Abel, not Adam.

In the extermination camps natural death was completely eliminated. There the lethal machines operated with absolute efficiency, leaving no uneconomical residues of life. There the venerable proposition, All men are mortal, had already become an understatement. If this proposition had been inscribed on the entrance gates to the gas chambers, instead of the usual misleading, "Shower Baths," it would have aroused jeers; and in this jeering laughter the voices of the victims would have joined in an infernal unison with the voices of their guards. For the truth contained in the old proposition was now more adequately expressed in a new proposition— "All men are exterminable."

Whatever changes have taken place in the world during the ten years since the end of the war, they have not affected the validity of the new proposition: the truth it expresses is confirmed by the general threat hanging over us. Its implications have even become more sinister: for what is exterminable today is not "merely" all men, but mankind as a whole. This change inaugurates a new historical epoch, if the term "epoch" may be applied to the short time intervals in question. Accordingly, all history can be divided into three chapters, with the following captions: (1) All men are mortal, (2) All men are exterminable, and (3) Mankind as a whole is exterminable.

3. Ecclesiastes's, "There is nothing new under the sun," will be replaced by, "Nothing ever was"

Under the present dispensation, human mortality has acquired an entirely new meaning—it is only today that its ultimate horror is brought home to us. To be sure, even previously no one was exempt from mortality; but everyone regarded himself as mortal within a larger whole, the human world; and while no one ever explicitly ascribed immortality to the latter, the threat of its mortality stared no one in the face either. Only because there was such a "space" within which one died, could there arise that peculiar aspiration to give the lie to one's mortality through the acquisition of fame. Admittedly the attempt has never been very successful: immortality among mortals has never been a safe metaphysical investment. The famous men were always like those ship passengers of the *Arabian Nights,* who enjoyed the highest reputation aboard, but whose reputation enjoyed no reputation, because the very existence of the ship was totally unknown on land. Still, as compared with what we have today, fame was something. For today our fear of death is extended to all of mankind; and if mankind were to perish leaving no memory in any being, engulfing all existence in darkness, no empire will have existed, no idea, no struggle, no love, no pain, no hope, no comfort, no sacrifice—everything will have been in vain, and there would be only that which had *been,* and nothing else.

Even to us, who are still living in the existing world, the past, that which merely *was,* seems dead; but the end of mankind would destroy even this death and force it, as it were, to die a second time, so that the past will not even have been the past—for how would that which merely had been differ from that which had never been? Nor would the future be spared: it would be dead even before being born. Ecclesiastes's disconsolate, "There is nothing new under the sun," would be succeeded by the even more disconsolate, "Nothing ever was," which no one would record and which for that reason would never be challenged.

4. Lack of conscience today is no moral defect, but an objective condition; hence all the more fatal

Let us assume that the bomb has been exploded.

To call this "an action" is inappropriate. The chain of events leading up to the explosion is composed of so many links, the process has involved so many different agencies, so many intermediate steps and partial actions, none of which is the crucial one, that in the end no one can be regarded as the agent. Everyone has a good conscience, because no conscience was required at any point. Bad conscience has once and for all been transferred to moral machines, electronic oracles: those cybernetic contraptions, which are the quintessence of science, and hence of progress and of morality, have assumed all responsibility, while man self-righteously washes his hands. Since all these machines can do is to evaluate profits and losses, they implicitly make the loss finite, and hence justifiable, although it is precisely this evaluation that destroys us, the evaluated ones, even before we are actually destroyed. Because responsibility has been displaced on to an object, which is regarded as "objective," it has become a mere response; the Ought is merely the correct chess move, and the Ought Not, the wrong chess move. The cybernetic machines are interested only in determining the means that can be advantageously used in a situation defined by the factors $a, b, c \ldots n$. Nothing else matters: after all, the continued existence of our world cannot be regarded as one of the factors. The question of the rightness of the goal to be achieved by the mechanically calculated means is forgotten by the operators of the machine or their employers, i.e., by those who bow to its judgment the moment it begins to calculate. To mistrust the solutions provided by the machine, i.e., to question the responses that have taken the place of responsibility, would be to question the very principle of our mechanized existence. No one would venture to create such a precedent.

Even where robots are not resorted to, the monstrous undertaking is immensely facilitated by the fact that it is not carried out by individuals, but by a complex and vastly ramified organization. If the organization of an undertaking is "all right," and if the machines function smoothly, the performance too seems "all right" and smooth. Each participant, each intermediary, performs or has insight into only the job assigned to him; and certainly each works conscientiously. The specialized worker is not conscious of the fact that the conscientious efforts of a number of specialists can add up to the most monstrous lack of conscience: just as in any other industrial enterprise he has no insight into the process as a whole. In so far as *conscientia* derives from *scire*, i.e., conscience from knowledge, such a failure to become conscious certainly points to a lack of conscience. But this does not mean that any of the participants acts against his conscience, or has no conscience—such immoral possibilities are still comfortingly human, they still presuppose beings that might have a conscience. Rather, the crucial point here is that such possibilities are excluded in advance. We are here beyond both morality and immorality. To blame the participants for their lack of conscience would be as meaningless as to ascribe courage or cowardice to one's hand. Just as a mere hand cannot be cowardly, so a mere participant cannot have conscience. The division of labor prevents him so completely from having clear insight into the productive process, that the lack of conscience we must ascribe to him is no longer an individual moral deficiency.

And yet it may result in the death of all mankind.

5. The effect transcends both the cause and the end

The "action" of unleashing the bomb is not merely irresponsible in the ordinary sense of the term: irresponsibility still falls within the realm of the morally discussible, while here we are confronted with something for which no one can even be held accountable. The consequences of this "action" are so great that the agent cannot possibly grasp them before, during, or after his action. Moreover, in this case there can be no goal, no positive value that can even approximately equal the magnitude of the means used to achieve it.

This incommensurability of cause and effect or means and end is not in the least likely to prevent the action; on the contrary, it facilitates the action. To murder an individual is far more difficult than to throw a bomb that kills countless individuals; and we would be willing to shake hands with the perpetrator of the second rather than of the first crime. Offenses that transcend our imagination by virtue of their monstrosity are committed more readily, for the inhibitions normally present when the consequences of a projected action are more or less calculable are no longer operative. The Biblical "They know not what they do" here assumes a new, unexpectedly terrifying meaning: the very monstrousness of the deed makes possible a new, truly infernal innocence.

The situation is not entirely unfamiliar. The mass exterminations under Hitler could be carried out precisely because they were monstrous—because they absolutely transcended the moral imagination of the agents, and because the moral emotions that normally precede, accompany, or follow actions could not arise in this case. But can one speak here of "agents"? The men who carry out such actions are always coagents: they are either half-active and half-passive cogs in a vast mechanism, or they serve merely to touch off an effect that has been prepared in advance to the extent of 99 per cent. The categories of "coagent" and "touching off" are unknown in traditional ethics.*

Let us sum up the main points of our arguments. Shocking as this may sound, the murder of an individual is a relatively human action—not because the effect of an individual murder is quantitatively smaller than that of a mass murder or a total extermination (for deaths cannot really be added; the very plural form of the noun "death" is absurd, for each individual death is qualitatively unique), but because the individual murderer still can react to his crime in a human way. It is possible to mourn one victim of murder, not a million victims. One can repent one murder, not a million murdered. In other words, in the case of an individual murder,

---

* This is not to be interpreted as a justification of the German crimes. The concept of collective guilt was morally indispensable: something had to be done to prevent these crimes from being quickly forgotten. But the concept proved inadequate because the crime in question transcended the ordinary dimensions of an immoral act; because a situation in which all perpetrators are merely co-perpetrators, and all non-perpetrators are indirectly perpetrators, requires entirely new concepts; and above all because the number of dead was too great for any kind of reaction. Just as men can produce acoustic vibrations unperceivable by the human ear, so they can perform actions that lie outside the realm of moral apperception.

man's emotional, imaginative, and moral capacities are congruent or at least commensurable with his capacity for action. And this congruence, this condition in which man is more or less equal to himself, is no doubt the basic prerequisite of that which is called "humanity." It is this congruence that is absent today. Consequently, modern unmorality does not primarily consist in man's failure to conform to a specific more-than-human image of man; perhaps not even in his failure to meet the requirements of a just society; but rather in his half-guilty and half-innocent failure to conform to himself, that is to say, in the fact that his capacity for action has outgrown his emotional, imaginative, and moral capacities.

6. Our incapacity for fear marks the freezing point of human freedom

We have good reason to think that our fear is by far too small: it should paralyze us or keep us in a continual state of alarm. It does not because we are psychically unequal to the danger confronting us, because we are incapable of producing a fear commensurate with it, let alone of constantly maintaining it in the midst of our still seemingly normal everyday life.

Just like our reason, our psyche is limited in the Kantian sense: our emotions have only a limited capacity and elasticity. We have scruples about murdering one man: we have less scruples about shooting a hundred men: and no scruples at all about bombing a city out of existence. A city full of dead people remains a mere word to us.

All this should be investigated by a Critique of Pure Feeling, not for the purpose of reaching a moral verdict, but in order to determine the boundaries of our emotional capacity. What disturbs us today is not the fact that we are not omnipotent and omniscient, but the reverse, namely, the fact that our imaginative and emotional capacities are too small as measured against our knowledge and power, that imaginatively and emotionally we are so to speak smaller than ourselves. Each of us moderns is an inverted Faust: whereas Faust had infinite anticipations and boundless feelings, and suffered because his finite knowledge and power were unequal to these feelings, we know more and produce greater things than we can imagine or feel.

As a rule, then, we are incapable of producing fear; only occasionally does it happen that we attempt to produce it, or that we are overwhelmed and stunned by a tidal wave of anguish. But what stuns or panics us at such moments is the realization not of the danger threatening us, but of the futility of our attempts to produce an adequate response to it. Having experienced this failure we usually relax and return shamefaced, irritated, or perhaps even relieved, to the human dimensions of our psychic life commensurable with our everyday surroundings. Such a return, however pleasant it may be subjectively, is of course sheer suicide from the objective point of view. For there is nothing and there can be nothing that increases the danger more than our failure to realize it intellectually and emotionally, and our resigned acceptance of this failure. In fact, the helplessness with which contemporary mankind reacts—or rather fails to react—to the existence of the superbomb bespeaks a lack of freedom the like of which has never before existed in history—and surely history cannot be said to have been poor in varieties of unfreedom.

We have indeed reached the freezing point of human freedom.

The Stoic, robbed of the autonomy of action, was certainly unfree; but how free the Stoic still was, since he could think and feel as he pleased!

Later there was the even more impoverished type of man, who could think only what others had thought for him, who indeed could not feel anything except what he was supposed to feel; but how free even this type of man was, since he still could speak, think, and feel what he was supposed to speak, think, and feel!

Truly unfree, divested of all dignity, definitively the most deprived of men are those confronted with situations and things with which they cannot cope by definition, to which they are unequal linguistically, intellectually, and emotionally—ourselves.

7. The crucial task—the development of the moral imagination

If all is not to be lost we must first and foremost develop our moral imagination: this is the crucial task facing us. We must strive to increase the capacity and elasticity of our intellectual and emotional faculties, to match the incalculable increase of our productive and destructive powers. Only where these two aspects of man's nature are properly balanced can there be responsibility, and moral action and counter-action.

Whether we can achieve such a balance, is an open question. Our emotional capacity may turn out to be limited a priori; perhaps it cannot be extended at will and *ad infinitum*. If this were so, and if we were to resign ourselves to such a state of affairs, we would have to give up all hope. But the moralist cannot do so in any case: even if he believed in the theoretical impossibility of transcending those limits, he would still have to demand that they be transcended in practice. Academic discussions are pointless here: the question can be decided only by an actual attempt, or, more accurately, by repeated attempts, i.e., spiritual exercises. It is immaterial whether such exercises aim at a merely quantitative extension of our ordinary imagination and emotional performance, or at a sensational, "impossible" transcending of our *proportio humana,* whose boundaries are supposedly fixed once and for all. The philosophical significance of such exercises can be worried about later. What matters at present is only that an attempt at violent self-transformation be made, and that it be successful. For we cannot continue as we are.

In our emotional responses we remain at the rudimentary stage of small artisans: we are barely able to repent an individual murder; whereas in our capacity for killing, for producing corpses, we have already entered the proud stage of industrial mass production. Indeed, the performances of our heart—our inhibitions, fears, worries, regrets—are in inverse ratio to the dimensions of our deeds, i.e., the former grow smaller as the latter increase. This gulf between our emotional capacity and our destructive powers, aside from representing a physical threat to our lives, makes us the most divided, the most disproportionate, the most inhuman beings that have ever existed. As against this modern cleavage, all older spiritual conflicts, for instance, the conflict between mind and body or duty and inclination, were relatively harmless. However violently the struggle may have raged within us, it remained human; the contending principles were attuned to each other, they were in actual contact, neither of them lost sight of the other, and each of them was essentially human. At least on the battlefield of the contending principles man preserved his existence unchallenged: man was still there.

Not so today. Even this minimum of man's identity with himself is gone. For the horror of man's present condition consists precisely in this, that the conflicting forces within him are no longer inter-related: they are so far removed from each other, each has become so completely independent, that they no longer even come to grips.* They can no longer confront each other in battle, the conflict can no longer be fought out. In short, man *as* producer, and man *as* a being capable of emotions, have lost sight of each other. Reality now seems attributable only to each of the specialized fragments designated by an "as." What made us shudder ten years ago—the fact that one and the same man could be guard in an extermination camp and good father and husband, that *as* the former he could be so radically

---

* Strikingly enough, the very phrase "inner conflict," which only a generation ago was taken for granted, even among the young, today sounds stale, pompous, and implausible.

different from himself *as* the latter, and that the two parts he played or the two fragments he was did not in the least stand in each other's way because they no longer knew each other—this horrifying example of guilelessness in horror has not remained an isolated phenomenon. Each of us, like this schizophrenic in the truest sense of the term, is split into two separate beings; each of us is like a worm artificially or spontaneously divided into two halves, which are unconcerned with each other and move in different directions.

True, the split has not been entirely consummated; despite everything the two halves of our being are still connected by the thinnest of threads, and the producer half, by far the stronger, drags the emotional half behind it. The unity is not organic, it is that of two different beings meaninglessly grown together. But the existence of this minimal connection is no comfort. On the contrary, the fact that we are split in two, and that there is no internal principle integrating these halves, defines the misery and disgrace of our condition.

ISAIAH BERLIN
1909-

SIR ISAIAH BERLIN IS a literary critic, historian, and social and political philosopher. He received his education in Corpus Christi College, Oxford University, where he excelled in literature, philosophy, politics, and economics. He has taught in New College and All Souls, Oxford, and was a visiting lecturer at Harvard University, Bryn Mawr College, and the University of Chicago. He has been Chichele Professor of Social and Political Theory at Oxford since 1957. Among his books are *Karl Marx, His Life and Environment* (1939), *The Hedgehog and the Fox* (1953), *The Inevitability of History* (1954), *The Age of Enlightenment* (1956), and *Two Concepts of Liberty* (1959).

[45]   *Political Ideas in the Twentieth Century*

"Anyone desiring a quiet life has done badly to be born in the twentieth century."   —L. Trotsky

*   *   *

The central point which I wish to make is this: during all the centuries of recorded history the course of intellectual endeavor, the purpose of education, the substance of controversies about the truth or value of ideas, presupposed the existence of certain crucial questions, the answers to which were of paramount importance. How valid, it was asked, were the various claims to the best methods of discovering absolute knowledge and truth made by such great and famous disciplines as metaphysics, ethics, theology, and the sciences of nature and of man? What was the right life for men to lead, and how was it discovered? Did God exist, and could His purposes be known or even guessed at? Did the universe, and in particular human life, have a purpose? If so, whose purpose did it fulfil? How did one set about answering such questions? Were they or were they not analogous to the kind of questions to which the sciences or common sense provided satisfactory, generally accepted, replies? If not, did it make sense to ask them?

And as in metaphysics and ethics, so in politics too. The political problem was concerned with asking why any individual or individuals should obey other individuals or associations of individuals. All the classical doctrines which deal with the familiar topics of liberty and authority, sovereignty and natural rights, the ends of the state and the ends of the individual, the General Will and the rights of minorities, secularism and theocracy, functionalism and centralization—all these are but various ways of attempting to formulate methods in terms of which this fundamental question can be answered in a manner compatible with the other beliefs and the general outlook of the inquirer and his generation. Great and sometimes mortal conflicts have arisen over the proper techniques for the answering of such questions. Some sought answers in sacred books, others in direct

From *Foreign Affairs,* **XXVIII** (April, 1950), 369–72, 375–85. Reprinted by special permission from *Foreign Affairs,* April, 1950. Copyright by Council on Foreign Relations, New York.

personal revelation, some in metaphysical insight, others in the pronouncements of infallible sages or in speculative systems or in laborious empirical
investigations. The questions were of vital importance for the conduct of
life. There were, of course, skeptics in every generation who suggested that
there were, perhaps, no final answers, that solutions hitherto provided depended on highly variable factors such as the climate in which the theorist's
life was lived, or his social or economic or political condition, or those of his
fellows, or his or their emotional disposition, or the kinds of intellectual interests which absorbed him or them. But such skeptics were usually treated
as either frivolous and so not important, or else unduly disturbing and even
dangerous; so that in times of instability they were liable to persecution.
But even they—even Sextus Empiricus or Montaigne or Hume—did not
actually doubt the importance of the questions themselves. What they
doubted was the possibility of obtaining final and absolute solutions.

It was left to the twentieth century to do something more drastic than
this. For the first time it was now asserted that the way to answer questions,
particularly those recurrent issues which had perplexed and often tormented
original and honest minds in every generation, was not by employing the
tools of reason, still less those of the more mysterious capacities called "insight" and "intuition," but by obliterating the questions themselves. And this
method consists not in removing them by rational means—by proving, for
example, that they are founded on intellectual confusion or verbal muddles
or ignorance of the facts—for to prove this would in its turn presuppose the
need for rational methods of logical or psychological argument. Rather it
consists in so treating the questioner that problems which appeared at once
overwhelmingly important and utterly insoluble vanish from the questioner's
consciousness like evil dreams and trouble him no more. It consists, not in
developing the logical implications and elucidating the meaning, the context,
or the relevance and origin of a specific problem—in seeing what it
"amounts to"—but in altering the outlook which gave rise to it in the first
place. Questions for whose solution no ready-made technique could easily
be produced are all too easily classified as obsessions from which the patient must be cured. Thus if a man is haunted by the suspicion that, for
example, full individual liberty is not compatible with coercion by the
majority in a democratic state, and yet continues to hanker after both
democracy and individual liberty, it may be possible by appropriate treatment to rid him of his *idée fixe,* so that it will disappear to return no more.
The worried questioner of political institutions is thereby relieved of his
burden and freed to pursue socially useful tasks, unhampered by disturb-

ing and distracting reflections which have been eliminated by the eradication of their cause.

The method has the bold simplicity of genius: it secures agreement on matters of political principle by removing the psychological possibility of alternatives, which itself depends, or is held to depend, on the older form of social organization, rendered obsolete by the revolution and the new social order. And this is how Communist and Fascist states—and all other quasi- and semi-totalitarian societies and secular and religious creeds— have in fact proceeded in the task of imposing political and ideological conformity.

For this the works of Karl Marx are not more directly to blame than the other tendencies of our time. Marx was a typical nineteenth century social theorist, in the same sense as Mill or Comte or Buckle. A policy of deliberate psychological conditioning was as alien to him as to them. He believed that many of the questions of his predecessors were quite genuine, and thought that he had solved them. He supported his solutions with arguments which he honestly supposed to conform to the best scientific and philosophical canons of his time. Whether his outlook was in fact as scientific as he claimed, or his solutions as plausible, is another question. What matters is that he recognized the genuineness of the questions he was attempting to answer and offered a theory with a claim to being scientific in the accepted sense of the term; and thereby poured much light (and darkness) on many vexed problems, and led to much fruitful (and sterile) revaluation and reinterpretation.

But the practice of Communist states and, more logically of Fascist states (since they openly deny and denounce the value of the question-and-answer method), is not at all the training of the critical, or solution-finding, powers of their citizens, nor yet the development in them of any capacity for special insights or intuitions regarded as likely to reveal the truth. It consists in something which any nineteenth century thinker with respect for the sciences would have regarded with genuine horror—the training of individuals incapable of being troubled by questions which, when raised and discussed, endanger the stability of the system; the building and elaboration of a strong framework of institutions, "myths," habits of life and thought intended to preserve it from sudden shocks or slow decay. This is the intellectual outlook which attends the rise of totalitarian ideologies— the substance of the hair-raising satires of George Orwell and Aldous Huxley—the state of mind in which troublesome questions appear as a form of mental perturbation, noxious to the mental health of individuals and, when too widely discussed, to the health of societies. This is an attitude which looks on all inner conflict as an evil, or at best as a form of futile self-frustration; which considers the kind of friction, the moral or emotional or intellectual collisions, the particular kind of acute spiritual discomfort which rises to a condition of agony from which great works of the human intellect and imagination, inventions, philosophies, works of art, have sprung, as being no better than purely destructive diseases—neuroses, psychoses, mental derangements, genuinely requiring psychiatric aid; above all as being dangerous deviations from that line to which individuals and societies must adhere if they are to continue in a state of well-ordered, painless, contented, self-perpetuating equilibrium.

* * *

The new attitude, resting as it does upon the policy of diminishing strife and misery by the atrophy of the faculties capable of causing them, is naturally hostile to, or at least suspicious of, disinterested curiosity (which might end anywhere), and looks upon the practice of all arts not obviously useful to society as being at best forms of social frivolity. Such occupations, when they are not a positive menace, are, in this view, an irritating and wasteful irrelevance, a trivial fiddling, a dissipation or diversion of energy which is difficult enough to accumulate at all and should therefore be directed wholeheartedly and unceasingly to the task of building and maintaining the well-adjusted—sometimes called the "well-integrated"—social whole. In this state of mind it is only natural that such terms as truth or honor or obligation or beauty become transformed into purely offensive or defensive weapons, used by a state or a party in the struggle to create a community impervious to influences beyond its own direct control. The result can be achieved either by rigid censorship and insulation from the rest of the world—a world which remains free at least in the sense that its inhabitants continue to say what they wish, in which words are relatively unorganized, with all the "dangerous" consequences thereby brought about; or else it can be achieved by extending the area of strict control until it stretches over all possible sources of anarchy, i.e. the whole of mankind. Only by one of these two expedients can a state of affairs be achieved in which human behavior can be manipulated with relative ease of technically qualified specialists—adjusters of conflicts and promoters of peace both of body and of mind, engineers and other scientific experts, psychologists, sociologists, economic and social planners and so on. Clearly this is not an intellectual climate which favors originality of judgment, moral independence or uncommon powers of insight. The entire trend of such an order is to reduce all issues to technical problems of lesser or greater complexity, in particular the problem of how to survive, get rid of maladjustments, achieve a condition in which the individual's psychological or economic capacities are harnessed to producing the maximum of unclouded social contentment; and this in its turn depends upon the suppression of whatever in him might raise doubt or assert itself against the single all-embracing, all-clarifying, all-satisfying plan.

The tendency has taken acute forms in, for example, the Soviet Union. There subordination to the central plan, and the elimination of disturbing factors, whether by education or repression, has been enacted with that capacity for believing in the literal inspiration of ideologies—in the ability and duty of human beings to translate ideas into practice fully, rigorously and immediately—to which Russian thinkers of all schools seem singularly addicted. The Soviet pattern is clear, simple and correctly deduced from "scientifically demonstrated" premises. The task of realizing it must be entrusted to technically trained believers who look on the human beings at their disposal as material which is infinitely malleable within the confines revealed by the sciences. Stalin's remark that creative artists are "engineers of human souls" is a very precise expression of this spirit. The presence of it in the various Fascist societies destroyed by the recent war, with intuition or instinct substituted for science, and cynicism for hypocrisy, are equally clear for all to see. In Western Europe this tendency has taken the milder form of a shift of emphasis away from disagreement about political principles (and from party struggles which sprang from genuine differences of moral and spiritual outlook) towards disagreements, ultimately technical, about methods—about the best ways of achieving that degree of minimum economic or social stability without which arguments concerned with fundamental principles and the ends of life are felt to be "abstract," "academic" and unrelated to the urgent needs of the hour. Hence that noticeably growing lack of interest in long-term political issues—as opposed to current day-to-day economic or social problems—on the part of the populations of the Western European continent which is occasionally deplored by shocked American and British observers who falsely ascribe it to the growth of cynicism and disenchantment with ideals.

No doubt all abandonment of old values for new must appear to the surviving adherents of the former as conscienceless disregard for morality as such. But this is a great delusion. There is all too little disbelief, whether conscienceless or apathetic, of the new values. On the contrary, they are clung to with unreasoning faith and that blind intolerance towards skepticism which springs, as often as not, from a profound inner bankruptcy, the hope against hope that here is a safe haven at least, narrow, dark, cut off, but secure. Growing numbers of human beings are prepared to purchase this sense of security even at the cost of allowing vast tracts of life to be controlled by persons who, whether consciously or not, act systematically to narrow the horizon of human activity to manageable proportions, to train human beings into more easily combinable parts—interchangeable, almost prefabricated—of a total pattern. In the face of such a strong desire to stabilize, if need be, at the lowest level—upon the floor from which you cannot fall, which cannot betray you, "let you down"—all the ancient political principles begin to vanish, feeble symbols of creeds no longer relevant to the new realities.

This process does not move at a uniform pace everywhere. In the United States perhaps, for obvious economic reasons, the nineteenth century survives far more powerfully than anywhere else. The political issues and conflicts, the topics of discussion, and the idealized personalities of democratic leaders are far more reminiscent of Victorian Europe than anything to be found on that continent now.

Woodrow Wilson was a nineteenth century liberal in a very full and unqualified sense. The New Deal and the personality of President Roosevelt excited political passions far more like those of the battles which raged round Gladstone or Lloyd George, or the anti-clerical governments at the turn of the century in France, than anything actually contemporary with it in Europe; and this great liberal enterprise, certainly the most constructive compromise between individual liberty and economic security which our own time has witnessed, corresponds more closely to the political and economic ideals of John Stuart Mill in his last, humanitarian-Socialist phase than to left-wing thought in Europe in the thirties. The controversy about international organization, about the United Nations and its subsidiaries, as well as the other postwar international institutions, like the controversies which in the years after 1918 surrounded the League of Nations, are fully intelligible in terms of nineteenth century political ideals, and therefore occupied far more attention and meant much more in America than in Europe. The United States may have disavowed President Wilson, but it continued to live in a moral atmosphere not very different from that of Wilson's time —the easily recognizable black-and-white moral world of the Victorian values. The events of 1918 preyed on the American conscience for 25 years, whereas in Europe the *exalté* atmosphere of 1918–1919 disappeared without a trace—a brief moment of illumination which in restrospect seems more American than European, the last manifestation in Europe of a great but dying tradition in a world already living, and fully conscious of living, in a new medium, too well aware of its differences from, and resentful of, its past. The break was not sudden and total, a dramatic *coup de théâtre*. Many of the seeds planted in the eighteenth or nineteenth centuries have flowered only in the twentieth: the political and ethical climate in which trade unions were founded in Germany, or England, or France did of course contain as elements the old, familiar doctrines of human rights and duties which were the common property, avowed or not, of almost all parties and views in the liberal, humanitarian, expansionist hundred years of peaceful progress.

The main current of the nineteenth century does, of course, survive into the present, and especially in America and the British Dominions; but it is not what is most characteristic of our time. . . . What is genuinely typical of our time is a new concept of the society, the values of which derive not from the desires or the moral sense of this or that individual's view of his ultimate ends but from some factual hypothesis or metaphysical dogma about history, or race, or national character in terms of which the answers to the question what is good, right, required, desirable, fitting, can be "scientifically" deduced, or intuited, or expressed in this or that kind of behavior. There is one and only one direction in which a given aggregate of individuals is conceived to be travelling, driven thither by quasi-occult impersonal forces, such as their class structure, or their unconscious selves, or their racial origin, or the "real" social or physical roots of this or that "popular" or "group" "mythology." The direction is alterable only by tampering with the hidden cause of behavior—those who wish to tamper being, according to this view, free to determine their own direction and that of others by having an understanding of the machinery of social behavior and skill in manipulating it.

In this sinister fashion have the words of St. Simon's prophecy finally come true—words which once seemed so brave and optimistic: "The government of man will be replaced by the administration of things." The cosmic forces are conceived as omnipotent and indestructible. Hopes, fears, prayers cannot wish them out of existence; but the élite of experts can canalize them and control them to some extent. The task of these experts is to adjust human beings to these forces and to develop in them an unshakable faith in the new order, and unquestioning loyalty to it, which will anchor it securely and forever. Consequently the technical disciplines which direct natural forces and adjust men to the new order must take primacy over humane pursuits—philosophical, historical, artistic. Such pursuits, at most, will serve only to prop up and embellish the new establishment. Turgenev's naïve materialist, the hero of his novel "Fathers and Sons," the nihilist Bazarov, has finally come into his own, as St. Simon and his more pedestrian follower Comte always felt sure that he would, but for reasons very different from those which seemed plausible a century ago. Bazarov's faith rested on the claim that the dissection of frogs was more important than poetry because it led to the truth, whereas the poetry of Pushkin did not.

The reason given today is more devastating: anatomy is superior to art because it generates no independent ends of life, provides no experiences which act as independent criteria of good or evil, truth or falsehood, and which are therefore liable to clash with the orthodoxy which we have created as the only bulwark strong enough to preserve us from doubts and despairs and all the horrors of maladjustment. To be torn this way and that emotionally or intellectually is a form of *malaise*. Against it nothing will work but the elimination of alternatives so nearly in equal balance that choice between them is—or even appears—possible.

This is, of course, what the Grand Inquisitor in Dostoevsky's "Brothers Karamazov" maintained with deadly eloquence: that what men dreaded most was freedom of choice, to be left alone to grope their way in the dark; and the Church by lifting the responsibility from their shoulders made them willing, grateful and happy slaves. The Grand Inquisitor stood for the dogmatic organization of the life of the spirit: Bazarov for its theoretical opposite—free scientific inquiry, the facing of the "hard" facts, the acceptance of the truth however brutal. But by an irony of history (not unforeseen by Dostoevsky) they have formed a pact, they are allies, and today are almost indistinguishable. Buridan's ass, we are told, unable to choose between two equi-distant bundles of hay, starved to death. Against this fate the only remedy is blind obedience and faith. Whether the refuge is a dogmatic religion or a dogmatic natural science matters relatively little: for without such obedience and faith there is no confidence and no hope, no optimistic, "constructive," "positive" form of life.

At this point it might be said that the situation I have described is not altogether new. Has not every authoritarian institution, every irrationalist movement, been engaged upon something of this kind—the artificial stilling of doubts, the attempt either to discredit uncomfortable questions or to educate men not to ask them? Was this not the practice of the great organized churches, indeed of every institution from the national state to small sectarian establishments? Was this not the attitude of the enemies of reason from the earliest mystery cults to the romanticism, anarchistic nihilism or surrealism of the last century and a half? Why should our age be specially accused of addiction to the particular tendency which formed the central theme of the social doctrines of Plato, or of the sect of the mediaeval Assassins, or of much Eastern thought and mysticism?

But there are two great differences which separate the political characteristics of our age from their origins in the past. In the first place, the reactionaries or romantics of previous periods, however much they might have advocated the superior wisdom of institutional authority or the revealed word over that of individual reason, did not in their moments of wildest unreason minimize the importance of the questions to be answered. On the contrary they maintained that so crucial was it to obtain the correct answer that only hallowed institutions, or inspired leaders, or mystical revelation, or divine grace could vouchsafe a solution of sufficient depth and universality. No doubt a hierarchy of the relative importance of questions underlies any established social system—a hierarchy the authority of which is itself not intended to be open to question. Moreover, the obscurity of some among the answers offered has in every age concealed their lack of truth or their irrelevance to the questions which they purported to solve. And perhaps much hypocrisy has traditionally been necessary to secure their success. But hypocrisy is very different from cynicism or blindness. Even the censors of opinion and the enemies of the truth felt compelled to pay formal homage to the vital importance of obtaining true answers to the great problems by the best available means. If their practice belied this, at least there was something to be belied: traitors and heretics often keep alive the memory—and the authority—of the beliefs which they are intent on betraying.

The second difference consists in the fact that in the past such attempts to becloud the nature of the issues were associated specifically with the avowed enemies of reason and individual freedom. The alignment of forces has been clear at any rate since the Renaissance; progress and reaction, however much these words have been abused, are not empty concepts. On one side stood the supporters of authority, unreasoning faith, suspicious of, or openly opposed to, the uncontrolled pursuit of truth or the free realization of individual ideals. On the other, whatever their differences, were those supporters of free inquiry and self-expression who looked upon Voltaire and Lessing, Mill and Darwin and Ibsen as their prophets. Their

common quality—perhaps their only common quality—was some degree
of devotion to the ideals of the Renaissance and a hatred of all that was
associated, whether justly or not, with the Middle Ages—darkness, suppression, the stifling of all heterodoxy, the hatred of the flesh and of gaiety
and of the love of natural beauty. There were of course many who cannot
be classified so simply or so crudely; but until our own day the lines were
drawn sharply enough to determine clearly the position of the men who
most deeply influenced their age. A combination of devotion to scientific
principles with "obscurantist" social theory seemed altogether unthinkable.
Today the tendency to circumscribe and confine and limit, to determine
the range of what may be asked and what may not, to what may be believed
and what may not, is no longer a distinguishing mark of the "reactionaries."
On the contrary, it comes as powerfully from the heirs of the radicals, the
rationalists, the "progressives," of the nineteenth century as from the
descendants of their enemies. There is a persecution not only of science,
but by science and in its name; and this is a nightmare scarcely foreseen by
the most Cassandra-like prophets of either camp.

We are often told that the present is an age of cynicism and despair, of
crumbling values and the dissolution of the fixed standards and landmarks
of our civilization. But this is neither true nor even plausible. So far from
showing the loose texture of a collapsing order, the world is today stiff
with rigid rules and codes and ardent, irrational religions. So far from
evincing the toleration which springs from cynical disregard of the ancient
sanctions, it treats heterodoxy as the supreme danger.

Whether in the East or West, the danger has not been greater since the
ages of faith. Conformities are called for much more eagerly today than
yesterday; loyalties are tested far more severely; skeptics and liberals and
individuals with a taste for private life and their own inner standards of
behavior, if they do not take care to identify themselves with an organized
faith, are objects of fear or derision and targets of persecution for either
side, execrated or despised by all the embattled parties in the great ideological wars of our time. And although this is less acute in societies traditionally averse to extremes—Great Britain, say, or Switzerland—this makes
little difference to the general pattern. In the world today individual stupidity
and wickedness are forgiven more easily than failure to be identified with a
recognized party or attitude, to achieve an approved political or economic
or intellectual status. In earlier periods, when more than one authority
ruled human life, a man might escape the pressure of the state by taking
refuge in the fortress of the opposition—of an organized church or a dis-

sident feudal establishment. The mere fact of conflict between authorities allowed room for a narrow and shifting, but still never entirely non-existent, no-man's-land, where private lives might still precariously be lived, because neither side dared to go too far for fear of too greatly strengthening the other. Today the very virtues of the paternalistic state, its genuine anxiety to reduce destitution and disease and inequality; to penetrate all the neglected nooks and crannies of life which may stand in need of its justice and its bounty—its very success in those beneficent activities—has narrowed the area within which the individual may commit blunders, has curtailed his liberties in the interest (the very real interest) of his welfare or of his sanity, his health, his security, his freedom from want and fear. His area of choice has grown smaller not in the name of some opposing principle— as in the Dark Ages or during the rise of the nationalities—but in order to create a situation in which the very possibility of opposed principles, with all their unlimited capacity to cause mental stress and danger and destructive collisions, is eliminated in favor of a simpler and better regulated life, a robust faith in an efficiently working order, untroubled by agonizing moral conflict.

Yet this is not a gratuitous development: the social and economic situation in which we are placed, the failure to harmonize the effects of technical progress with the forces of political and economic organization inherited from an earlier phase, do call for a greater measure of social control to prevent chaos and destitution, no less fatal to the development of human faculties than blind conformity. And certainly it is morally unthinkable that we give up our social gains and meditate for an instant the possibility of a return to ancient injustice and inequality and hopeless misery. The progress of technological skill makes it rational and indeed imperative to plan, and anxiety for the success of a particular planned society naturally inclines the planners to seek insulation from dangerous, because incalculable, forces which may jeopardize the plan. And this is a powerful incentive to "autarky" and "Socialism in one country" whether imposed by conservatives, or New Dealers, or isolationists, or Social Democrats, or indeed imperialists. And this in its turn generates artificial barriers and increasingly restricts the planners' own resources. In extreme cases it leads to repression of the discontented and a perpetual tightening of discipline, until it absorbs more and more of the time and ingenuity of those who originally conceived it only as a means to a minimum of efficiency. Presently it grows to be a hideous end in itself, since its realization spells ruin to the system now caught in a vicious circle of repression in order to survive and of survival mainly to repress. So the remedy grows to be worse than the disease, and takes the form of those orthodoxies which rest on the simple puritanical faith of individuals who never knew or have forgotten what *douceur de vivre,* free self-expression, the infinite variety of persons and of the relationships between them, and the right of free choice, difficult to endure but more intolerable to surrender, can ever have been like.

The dilemma is logically insoluble: we cannot sacrifice either freedom or a minimum standard of welfare. The way out must therefore lie in some logically untidy, flexible, and even ambiguous compromise: every situation calls for its own specific policy, since out of the crooked timber of humanity, as Kant once remarked, no straight thing was ever made. What the age calls for is not (as we are so often told) more faith or stronger leadership or more rational organization. Rather is it the opposite—less Messianic ardor, more enlightened skepticism, more toleration of idiosyncrasies, more frequent *ad hoc* and ephemeral arrangements, more room for the attainment of their personal ends by individuals and by minorities whose tastes and beliefs find (whether rightly or wrongly must not matter) little response among the majority. What is required is a less mechanical, less fervent application of general principles, however rational or righteous, a more cautious and less self-confident application of accepted, scientifically tested, general solutions in unexamined individual cases. We must not submit to authority because it is infallible but only for strictly and openly utilitarian reasons, as a necessary evil. Since no solution can be guaranteed against error, no disposition is final. And therefore a loose texture and a measure of inefficiency and even muddle, even a degree of indulgence in idle talk, idle curiosity, aimless pursuit of this or that without authorization—"conspicuous waste" itself—may allow more spontaneous, individual variation (for which the individual must in the end assume full responsibility), and will always be worth far more than the neatest and most delicately fashioned imposed pattern. Above all, it must be realized that the kinds of problems which this or that method of education or system of scientific or religious or social organization of life is guaranteed to solve are *eo facto* not the central questions of human life. They are not, and never have been, the fundamental issues which embody the changing outlook and the most intense preoccupation of their time and generation. It is from absorbed preoccupation with these fundamental issues and these alone, unplanned and at times without technical equipment, more often than not without conscious hope of success, still less of the approbation of the official auditor, that the best moments come in the lives of individuals and peoples.

IX

Civilization and
the political imagination

IN THE OPENING CHAPTERS we discussed the twilight of
modernism, explaining how political events and intellectual
changes darkened the vision of the common life that nineteenth-century
thinkers had beheld so clearly. New realities impugned the idea of civilization by dramatically contradicting the conceptions of reason, freedom, and
progress which had defined that idea. Consequently, the familiar explanations of social and political behavior, which had depended on the idea of
civilization, and even the categories through which behavior was understood could no longer be taken for granted. If the old assumptions were
not false, they were at least ambiguous.

In the twilight of modernism, many writers believed that the forces of
history were producing a society the very opposite of the modern ideal.
The evidence was formidable: instead of reason, the spread of ideologies;
instead of civilization, mass society; instead of freedom, increasing regulation. Yet at this time they believed that society *could* be reconstructed.
Obviously, historical forces were not creating civilization by impersonal
momentum; by their own design and effort, men might still create a good
society. Full of blueprints and programs, the interbellum was an era of
experimentalism and reconstruction, inspired by a mood of guarded opti-

mism. Many men who were skeptical about "truths" of nature or history placed their faith in effort and in the *efficacy* of ideals, even if they regarded ideals as fictions. In the postmodern era, political events and intellectual changes have combined to unsettle the will to action.

THOUGHT AND ACTION

In a society regulated by traditional rules, the idea of how things ought to be tends to correspond to the sense of how things really are. In Western civilization before the modern period, particular traditions in every realm of thought and action competed with one another; yet tradition, which in practice meant the dominant tradition, was accepted as the major source— sometimes the only source—of norms. In the modern period, tradition steadily lost authority and became only one source of norms in a world of competing normative orders.

Political action in the modern world was formed by the tension between the normative order and the picture of social reality, even that of the most contented and optimistic mid-Victorians, who despite their positive outlook emphasized the difference between the imperfect present and the putatively perfect future. Norm and reality directed each political stance. Some conservatives looked back to a lost order for their norms, shaping their effort in the form of *restoration*. Other conservatives, looking to the future, opposed the designs of the liberals and socialists, but acted in their own way according to laissez-faire ideals, proposing vigorous resistance to increasing government regulation. The framework of the liberals was *reform*. The wide distance between norm and reality in the minds of many radicals shaped their action in the form of *revolution*.

The growing confusion in the normative order and the clouding picture of social reality, which we have discussed, tend to either diminish or to exaggerate effort. The pragmatic notion of ideals as useful fictions supported political thinking and political movements during the interbellum, but such a notion is difficult to sustain over a long period of time. If ideals are fictions, then any ideal or norm may be substituted for another as long as it appears useful; but the alternation of ideals and norms consequent to this notion necessarily makes the normative order lose its clarity and stability, weakening effort.

However, just as apathy seems to be widespread in the present age, the same may be said of the other extreme, the exaggerated effort espoused by mass movements. In the structure of fanatic action, the unbearable tension between the picture of an undesirable reality, full of danger, conspiracy, and chimeric obstacles designed by evil men, and the norm, a compelling, desirable state to be achieved *at all costs,* induces an explosive form of effort.

THE REACTION TO TOTALITARIANISM

The structure of moral action in premodern times was shaped not only by the tension between norm and reality, but also by the opposition between norm and antinorm, expressed theologically by the warfare between heaven and hell. In postmodern thought, the most paralyzing blow to political action has come from the reaction to totalitarianism, the image of which has become a secular version of hell.

In premodern thinking, of course, hell was the destination of the wicked as well as the headquarters of the Permanent Enemy, who sent his agents to subvert the moral foundations of Christendom, to conspire with the wicked, and to seize the unwary. Men reached hell through negligence, willfully evil acts, or dangerous beliefs. The kinetic effect of the idea of hell was to place men on guard, to direct their energies toward warding off evil, and to fix the limits of moral action. Postmodern thinkers have regained the notion of hell in the realm of political action, but they have lost the idea of heaven.

In theology, moral theory, and ordinary behavior, the symbols of heaven and hell were incorporated in principles of movement and action. As moral agents, men tended to move by attraction and repulsion—desiring salvation and dreading damnation, seeking to reach heaven and to avoid hell. Particular acts were justified as attempts to cooperate with grace or to ward off evil. Orthodoxy always insisted, however, that the positive principle prevailed over the negative: that ultimately the diabolic principle would be turned, against its will, to serve heavenly power, and that grace was sufficient to conquer evil. Despite their profound concern with the problem of evil, orthodox thinkers remained optimistic; Christians were heartened by the words of Christ in the Gospel: "Be of good cheer; I have overcome the world."

Early-modern thinkers, it has been shown many times, abolished hell, but dismantled heaven and reconstructed it on earthly foundations. Now the heavenly city was located in the future, but it was still a loadstone. As Carl Becker observed:

> The new heaven had to be located somewhere within the confines of the earthly life, since it was an article of philosophical faith that the end of life is life itself, the perfected temporal life of man; and in the future, since the temporal life was not yet perfected. But if the celestial heaven was to be dismantled in order to be rebuilt on earth, it seemed that the salvation of mankind must be attained, not by some outside, miraculous, catastrophic agency (God or the philosopher-king), but by man himself, by the progressive improvement made by the efforts of successive generations of men. . . .[1]

This secular version of heaven—the good society imagined by the *philosophes*—was more than fantasy. It entered history, directing the energies of men and shaping their actions. Throughout the modern period, the loadstone remained in the future, and modern man was drawn forward by the principle of attraction. We emphasize this characteristic because it so clearly demonstrates the modern style of thought and action. Ancient man, in contrast, tended to look backward, his consciousness directed not ahead but behind. As Thomas Mann stated it, this kind of life depended on "reanimation" from the past; it was a life in myth.[2] The man of antiquity relied on tradition and ancestral ways, searching the past for a pattern to inform him and protect him in his moment of action. Ortega y Gasset expressed it another way by saying that the man of antiquity, before he did anything, stepped backward—like the bullfighter who leaps back to deliver the thrust.

Postmodern man lacks a positive principle of action; he is attracted neither to the future nor to the past. However, he has recovered a negative principle. Totalitarianism (or, on a more popular level, the cold-war enemy) performs for political life the function that the religious idea of hell had performed for moral life: it places men on guard against "dangerous" forms of political action, organizes their energies to ward off evil, and fixes the limits of action. The fear of totalitarianism is partly responsible for truncating the range of political alternatives. Forms of action falling outside the official policy or the limits of political orthodoxy are marked as dangerous instead of being ignored or merely permitted to exist. If they are

[1] Carl L. Becker, *The Heavenly City of the Eighteenth-Century Philosophers* (New Haven: Yale University Press, 1932), p. 129.
[2] Thomas Mann, *Essays of Three Decades,* trans. H. T. Lowe-Porter (New York: Alfred A. Knopf, Inc., 1948), p. 424.

not proscribed outright, they are constantly watched for signs of affinity with the Permanent Enemy.

In such an atmosphere political action is charged with a sense of danger. The source of danger is not only intentional subversion but also the unguarded or deluded actions of well-meaning men. Postmodern theorists are suspicious and wary of the "unanticipated consequences" of political movements, which is a secular way of saying that the road to hell is paved with good intentions.

The general effect is to guard against many forms of action. Just as the titans of the late-modern period and the writers of the interbellum convinced men of the limits of reason, postmodern writers insist on the limits of effort. The range of ideals is narrowed and the political imagination constricted.

ALIENATION

The crisis of action in the postmodern period, many writers insist, is related to alienation, "the crisis of values," and the growing sense of estrangement. Political action loses vitality because it is involved, they argue, in the general deterioration of all forms of meaning in Western culture. Judith Shklar observes, "Politics has induced an estrangement from the entire social world and with it a mixture of hatred for, and anxiety about, the future of European culture as a whole." [3] The themes of alienation, absurdity, and estrangement are conveyed dramatically in, one is tempted to say, almost all of contemporary literature, and explored in existentialist philosophy.[4] Some writers suggest that nihilism emerges inevitably from the human condition in the twentieth century. The characteristic inhabitant of the century, it is said, is "the stranger," out of touch with a world not his own; the thought that this world may be destroyed evokes in him no moral revulsion or emotional reaction.

The loss of meaning in the present age, Glenn Tinder argues, is the result of "mass disintegration," producing what the French existentialist writer Gabriel Marcel has called the broken world. The process of cultural disintegration, Tinder explains, is well known:

[3] Judith N. Shklar, *After Utopia: The Decline of Political Faith* (Princeton: Princeton University Press, 1957), p. 269.

[4] The political significance of these themes is examined in the eloquent essays of Glenn Tinder. See "Encounter with Chaos," *Yale Review*, L (1961), 357–69, and the work cited in footnote 5.

. . . almost every contact which human beings desire and value has been weakened or broken. The enjoyment of nature is difficult and occasional; one's roots in a place are taken up or not allowed to form; possessions stand in a largely outward and merely instrumental relationship to the personality; the past is obscure and the future almost totally darkened; the more deep and satisfying contacts among persons, always difficult, have become more fragile. These circumstances of course vary greatly in their impact on persons, vocations, and peoples; but relatively few in the West can altogether escape them.[5]

The beginnings of this corrosive process, as we showed in Chapter I, were recognized by some of the titans in late-modern times. Kierkegaard wrote a century ago of a "reflective and passionless" revolution that "leaves everything standing but cunningly empties it of significance." Likewise, Durkheim spoke of *anomie,* and Weber of "the disenchantment of the world." Yet later on, when the men of the interbellum discussed the "crisis of civilization" in spiritual terms, they were not confronted with the emptiness that disturbs writers today. They believed that men were being moved by wrong or dangerous meanings—only a few detected the dissolution of meaning. When Dean Inge lamented that Western civilization had abandoned transcendental principles to lust after gratification of desires, he still believed that the principle of sensuality, though less than human, still contained a meaning, though a false meaning, which had the power to motivate men. Present writers claim that although men continue to satisfy their appetites, even sensuality has lost its "meaning." Moreover, when Valéry wrote about the disintegration of Western culture, he pointed to the loss of an integrating principle and to the whirl and fragmentation of many principles; he saw a chaos full of conflicting meanings, not an empty void.

Although the picture of estrangement expresses an important truth about certain trends in Western civilization, we would contend that it is often overdrawn and grotesque. The reality is not so extreme—not crowds of "strangers," but societies of men who often feel strange.

Whereas the stranger cares nothing about the future, living men care a great deal. In contrast to the olympian optimism of the past, the sense of the future has changed from hope to dread.

Fear of technology has contributed to this feeling of dread. Yet we wish to make it clear that although crisis and foreboding are prominent at the present time, late-modern points of view, far from disappearing, are important survivals. The fear of technology has expressed itself, as we shall

----

[5] Glenn Tinder, "Human Estrangement and the Failure of Political Imagination," *Review of Politics,* XXI (1959), 624–25.

show, in the literary genre of the inverted utopia. Yet some writers continue to look at the future hopefully, placing their trust in science and technology, expressing a qualified faith in progress. In this vein, Franz Borkenau has argued against prophecies of doom:

> Let me say at once that I do not deny the dangers of technology, which are tremendous. But what strikes one constantly about . . . lamentations over the evils of technology is their minimization of its unique achievements in modern times, achievements by no means limited to the sphere of the "practical. . . ."
>
> In dismissing as an incidental matter the knowledge we have finally won of the basic structure of the material world, the critics of technology for the most part overlook the fact that these very insights have given us a glimpse into the basic structure of all existence, spiritual as well as material. Are these insights tragic in their refutation of cherished illusions?—well, all culture is tragic, all culture is paid for by the surrender of primitive consolations of the human soul. . . .
>
> Let us try for a more balanced perspective of this whole popular question of "the threatened disappearance of civilization. . . ."
>
> Very possibly [the truths of science and technology] can be lost sight of in chaotic transitional periods, but is it conceivable that they should vanish as if they had never existed? Or isn't it far more likely that, after having been purged in the fires of a great cultural change, they should first really begin to shine forth? [6]

POSTMODERN UTOPIAS

The olympian idea of civilizing forces controlling history had implied increasing and ultimate harmony. It conjured an image of the future diametrically contrary to typical postmodern expectations. Utopian literature is valuable because it records each generation's sense of the prospects for mankind.

Some utopias are located nowhere—that is, out of time altogether—but most are placed somewhere in the future. Within the utopian genre one may find several kinds of intention: some writers satirize their own age; others imagine concretely the good or perfect society; still others project into the future the forces they detect in the present. The positive utopias of the modern period were dominated by the expectation of—or at least the wish for—a better world. As Lewis Mumford said, "The sort of thinking that

[6] Franz Borkenau, "Will Technology Destroy Civilization? Why the Prophets of Doom Are Wrong," *Commentary*, XI (1951), 20–26.

has created our utopias has placed desire above reality; and so their chief fulfillment has been in the realm of fantasy." [7] Herbert Marcuse observes:

As a fundamental, independent mental process, phantasy has a truth value of its own, which corresponds to an experience of its own—namely, the surmounting of the antagonistic human reality. Imagination envisions the reconciliation of the individual with the whole, of desire with realization, of happiness with reason. While this harmony has been removed into utopia by the established reality principle, phantasy insists that it must and can become real, that behind the illusion lies *knowledge*. The truths of imagination are first realized when phantasy itself takes form, and when it creates a universe of perception and comprehension—a subjective and at the same time objective universe. [8]

Just as Marcuse argues that utopian literature reflects a deep nonrational truth—the struggle of the pleasure principle with the reality principle—Ernst Cassirer declares that utopianism has carried out an extremely important rational task. The great ethical philosophers, Cassirer claims, never thought exclusively in terms of actuality; their ideas always enlarged and transcended the limits of the actual world:

Possessed of great intellectual and moral power, the ethical teachers of mankind were endowed too with a profound imagination. Their imaginative insight permeates and animates all their assertions. . . .
The ethical world is never given; it is forever in the making. . . . The great political and social reformers are indeed constantly under the necessity of treating the impossible as though it were possible. [9]

Unless men know what is possible, they are doomed to accept what they are given. The realm of possibilities, the ideal world, is the special province of utopias. To conceive of possibilities is the rational task of utopian thinking.

It is nothing new for utopianism to be attacked from the right. Edmund Burke set the argument for this attack, and the reader may find it reflected in this volume in the writings of Lippman, Röpke, Kirk, and others. They fear the enforcement of a rational plan for the entire society. As Karl Popper asserts, utopianism leads to violence because it insists that rational political action be based

[7] Lewis Mumford, *The Story of Utopias* (New York: Boni and Liveright, 1922), p. 267.
[8] Herbert Marcuse, *Eros and Civilization* (Boston: Beacon Press, 1955), pp. 143–44.
[9] Ernst Cassirer, *An Essay on Man* (New York: Doubleday Anchor Books, 1953), pp. 84–86.

. . . upon a more or less clear and detailed description or blueprint of our ideal state, and also upon a plan or blueprint of the path that leads in the right direction—in the direction toward this aim. . . .

But . . . differences of opinion concerning what the ideal state should be cannot be smoothed out by the method of argument. They will have the character of religious differences. But there can be no tolerance between these different Utopian religions. The Utopian aims are designed in order to serve as a basis for rational political action, and such action appears to be possible only if the aim is definitely decided upon. Thus the only possibility for a Utopianist is to win over, or otherwise to crush, the Utopianist competitors, that is, those who do not share his own Utopian aims, or in other words, those who do not profess his own Utopianist religion.

But he has to do more. He has to be very thorough in eliminating and stamping out all heretical competing views. For the way to the Utopian goal is a long way. Thus the rationality of his political action demands that you assure the constancy of aims for a long time ahead; and this can be achieved only if he not only crushes competing Utopian religions, but stamps out, as far as possible, all memory of them.[10]

Similarly, J. L. Talmon argues that utopias can only be realized by force. Indeed, Talmon insists that respect for tradition is the only escape from brute force, for people will follow the prescription of traditional institutions—even when they bring privation—whereas they will resist other forms of command.[11]

In the postmodern period, however, one finds utopianism also under attack from the left.[12] The reason is that some of the great utopian wishes of the past, including the desire for extensive control over nature and over human behavior, have been realized, and the result is far from the liking of writers who cherish freedom and spontaneity.[13] Critics of social planning point out that a planned society loses liveliness. Moreover, it is said, utopias are static societies, frozen in ideal patterns in which every problem is solved and all conflicts eliminated, and in which there is no set of tensions or forces making for change.[14]

[10] Karl Popper, "Utopia and Violence," *Hibbert Journal*, XLVI (1948), 112–13. See Popper's book *The Open Society and Its Enemies* (Princeton: Princeton University Press, 1950).

[11] J. L. Talmon, *Utopianism and Politics* (London: Conservative Political Centre, 1958). See Talmon's book *Political Messianism: The Romantic Phase* (London: Secker and Warburg, Ltd, 1960).

[12] The reader should be aware that in the last century the "utopian socialists" were attacked by Marx and Engels—but for different reasons.

[13] George Woodcock, "Utopias in Negative," *Sewanee Review*, LXIV (1956), 81–82; Eugen Weber, "The Anti-Utopia of the Twentieth Century," *South Atlantic Quarterly*, LVIII (1959), 441–42.

[14] See Ralf Dahrendorf, "Out of Utopia: Towards a Reorientation of Sociological Analysis," *American Journal of Sociology*, LXIV (1958), 115–27.

Lewis Mumford, classifying utopias in 1922, made the distinction between utopias of escape and utopias of reconstruction; now, in response to postmodern conditions, a new genre has come into being: the negative utopia, or the utopia of warning.[15]

Kenneth Keniston explains:

If we define a utopia as any attempt to make the possibilities of the future imaginatively concrete, utopias have not in our day ceased to exist; they merely have been transvalued. The contrast between nineteenth- and twentieth-century utopias is drastic. Our visions of the future have shifted from images of hope to vistas of despair . . . negative visions, extensions of the most pernicious trends of the present. They are deterrents, cautionary tales: utopia has become counter-utopia.[16]

Of all the counterutopian literature, the books *1984* by George Orwell and *Brave New World* by Aldous Huxley have made the greatest impact on postmodern thinking. Both of them were deeply influenced by an earlier book—perhaps the first of the genre—entitled *We,* written by the Russian Eugeny Zamiatin in 1924 and banned by the Communists. All three writers implicitly condemn the present and the trends leading to the future, which they fear. At the same time they detect the signs of a new social order forming around them as they write. The value of the antiutopian literature is not only its warning, but also its acceptance of the break with the late-modern past and its attempt to find concepts, language, and emotions to fit the contours of the social reality emerging from the present.

PROSPECTS

In ages of dislocation and turmoil in the past, some writers have offered the temptation of Epicurean withdrawal from collective agony to the realm of private sensibility. In this century, however, it is less possible to shut out the political world, there are fewer secluded gardens, and in some societies there is no place to hide.

As Karl Jaspers declares, to refrain from participating in the course of events is to assume the guilt of the evil that takes place. And to surrender to the powers that be is to lose hope of controlling one's destiny.[17] To re-

[15] We suggest that the reader decide whether B. F. Skinner's *Walden Two* (New York: The Macmillan Co., 1948) is a positive or a negative utopia.

[16] Kenneth Keniston, "Alienation and the Decline of Utopia," *American Scholar,* XXIX (1960), 182.

[17] Karl Jaspers, *Man in the Modern Age,* trans. Eden and Cedar Paul (New York: Doubleday Anchor Books, 1957), pp. 95 ff.

nounce political action, no matter how great the forces opposing one's effort, is to renounce one's humanity.

The notion of mass society has become a cliché rather than a useful conception; it conveys an impression of certain tendencies which are well known, but it has become the expression of a kind of phobic and romantic reaction to technology and social change rather than an accurate description of reality or theory of society. Yet critics of the mass society conception should not be blind to its value. To discard the idea of mass society entirely, as several writers suggest, would be to invite the danger of returning to obsolete conceptions of much less value.

Karl Jaspers, who has done as much as any writer to circulate the notion of mass society, has recently protested against the oversimplified image of the paralyzed individual absorbed by the overwhelming mass:

It is not true that the individual has disappeared. It is not true that it is necessary for him to be completely lost amidst the most frightful, extreme conditions. We have learned how even in the totalitarian world the individual may put on armor, may prepare himself, even under the most extreme circumstances, from falling prey to delusions, may judge in secret and refuse to place faith in the false gods.[18]

Individualism in the future will find new kinds of expression.[19] In his profound and moving book *The Rebel,* Albert Camus used the phrase "We are" to express the solidarity and the new form of individualism contained in the act of rebellion. He explained:

. . . the "We are" paradoxically defines a new form of individualism. "We are" in terms of history, and history must reckon with this "We are," which must in its turn keep its place in history. I have need of others who have need of me and of each other. Every collective action, every form of society, supposes a discipline, and the individual, without this discipline, is only a stranger, bowed down under the weight of an inimical collectivity. But society and discipline lose their direction if they deny the "We are." I alone, in one sense, support the common dignity that I cannot allow either myself or others to debase.[20]

[18] Karl Jaspers, "The Individual and Mass Society," trans H O I Brown, in Walter Leibrecht, ed., *Religion and Culture: Essays in Honor of Paul Tillich* (New York: Harper & Brothers, 1959), p. 43. Italics in the original.

[19] The challenge of "evolving a personal style within a mass society" is explored perceptively in Maurice R. Stein, Arthur J. Vidich, and David M. White, eds., *Identity and Anxiety: Survival of the Person in Mass Society* (Glencoe: The Free Press, 1960).

[20] Albert Camus, *The Rebel,* trans. Anthony Bower (New York: Vintage Books, 1956), p. 297.

In the near future, conditions of thought and action will give rise to new tensions between the individual and society and will demand new kinds of forbearance on the part of both the individual and the group. And new conflicts will give rise to new forms of heroism.

New forms of action and political expression depend on a liberation of the understanding. Such liberation in turn depends not only on our ability to work free of the stereotypes of the cold war, as we have said, but also on our success in clearing away the intellectual debris of the nineteenth century which obscures vision and stifles imagination. Even though the content of the olympian system has been abandoned, its structure remains with us. It is difficult to discard because structures of thought survive in unexpected ways. The vision that haunts postmodern thinkers—the configuration of irrationality, oppression, deterioration, and mass society—is the inversion of the olympian structure—reason, freedom, progress, and civilization—which had tumbled down. It fits the contours of reality no better upside down than it does right side up.

Still, clearing the debris of modernism does not mean that we can ignore the work of the modern theorists or of their predecessors. On the contrary, we must learn, better than they did, the realities that faced them and the artful ways in which they set about comprehending and mastering those realities. If we seek to build new structures of theory according to new designs with new materials on a new terrain, we must know, and know well, the builder's art.

INDEX

Index*

* Numbers in italics under an author's name indicate pages on which a selection in this volume appears.

politics (*cont.*)
  of mass behavior, 26–28
  primacy of, 10
  Schmitt on meaning of, 190–98
Politics, Economics, and Welfare (Dahl and Lindblom), 30 fn., 404 fn.
Polybius, 1
Poor White (Anderson), 72
Popper, Karl, 449, 568
populism, 26–27
  democratic, 107
Poskrebyshev (Stalin's secretary), 299
postmodern period, 3, 285 ff.
Pound, Roscoe, 107
power
  relation between civilization and, 2
  Ricoeur on control of, 434–41
  systems of, 2, 3
Power Elite, The (Mills), 352 fn.
pragmatism, 98–100, 107
Present Age, The (Kierkegaard), 17 fn.
primitivism, 11, 12
Principles of Communism (Engels), 299 fn.
progress, 17, 37, 287
  concept of, 7, 9–15, 19, 21, 22–23
  essay by Dewey on, 53–59
  peace and, 19–20, 21
progressive movement, 27, 107
progressivism, 106–08
Prokofiev, Serge, 296
Prometheus Unbound (Shelley), 8
propaganda, Hitler on, 281–83
Protestant Ethic and the Spirit of Capitalism, The (Weber), 29, 85 fn.
Protestantism, 110
Proudhon, Pierre, 97
Psychic Factors of Civilization, The (Ward), 100 fn.
Pure Sociology (Ward), 100
Puritanism, 29
Pushkin, Alexander, 556

R.U.R. (Capek), 28
race, Hitler on, 267–70
Radcliffe-Brown, A. R., 11
Radek, Karl, 210
radicalism
  recusant, 412–13
  Woodcock on, 491–98
Radin, Paul, 11

radio, Lederer on influence of, 65
rationalization, 11, 17, 19, 28, 307–09
realism, 25, 72
  political, 24
reason, 17
  abstract, 25, 26
  concept of, 7, 9–15, 19, 287
  flight from, 26
  historical, 25
Reason and Revolution: Hegel and the Rise of Social Theory (Marcuse), 219 fn., 343
Rebel, The (Camus), 571
Reflections on Government (Barker), 26 fn.
Reflections on the End of an Era (Niebuhr), 111
reform, moral necessity for, 104–05
religion, 109–15, 413–15
  olympians and, 17
Renaissance, 557
Renaudel, 250
Revolt of the Masses, The (Ortega y Gasset), 26
Ricoeur, Paul, 405
  biographical sketch, 433–34
  on the control of power, *434–41*
Rienzo, Cola di, 227
Riesman, David, 403
Rimbaud, 31, 36
Ritvo, Herbert, 300 fn.
Road to Serfdom, The (Hayek), 411 fn.
Robespierre, Maximilien, 227
Röhm, Ernst, 214
Rommen, Heinrich, 414
Roosevelt, Franklin D., 123, 554
Röpke, Wilhelm, 409, 411, 568
  biographical sketch, 475
  on collectivism, *475–90*
Rosenberg, Alfred, 207, 220
Rosenzweig, Franz, 455
Rostow, W. W., 306
Rousseau, Jean Jacques, 12, 39, 332, 364–65, 369, 370, 376, 380, 384, 466, 469, 472, 473, 521
Rozenblum, 293
Russell, Bertrand, 77, 423, 427, 445
Russia, *see* Soviet Union
Russia in Transition (Deutscher), 308 fn.
Russian Purge and the Extraction of Confession (Beck and Godin), 293 fn.